ALLIANCE
TO CONFERENCE

1979-2004
THE FIRST 25 YEARS

COMPILED BY
JOHN HARMAN
THE OFFICIAL
CONFERENCE STATISTICIAN

ISBN 1869833-52-X

Published by Tony Williams Publications Ltd
Printed by Latimer Trend & Company Ltd
Typesetting & design by George Brown & Mike Williams
All distribution queries to Pat Vaughan
Tel: 01458 241592 or 01823 490080

Front Cover design by:
Bob Bickerton
Front Cover Caption: Portraits on left: Noel Ashford (top), Mark Carter and John Davison,
central action Clive Walker and Ken McKenna and action on left, Paul Davies (top) Eddie
Stein and Colin Cowperthwaite.

FOREWARD

It was 25 years ago before many of the players now competing in it were born that The Alliance Premier Football League, now known as The Nationwide Conference, was formed from the top clubs of The Southern Football League and The Northern Premier League. They were later joined by clubs from The Isthmian League as a single National competition, from which a successful club could be promoted by right to The Football League. At the same time the Conference accepted its responsibility to provide an environment of quality in which those relegated Football League clubs could maintain their standards and aspire to return to their previous status.

How successful it has been in achieving these aims can be judged from John Harman's marvellous statistical record of those momentous years which are illustrated superbly by the work of many dedicated photographers. It is not too much of an exaggeration to say that The Conference has changed the face of a significant section of our national game. To appreciate this, one only has to trace through John's meticulous statistics to see the fortunes of those original founder clubs and to look at the names of the ex Conference clubs now

Jim Thompson (left) on an historic day for the Conference.

competing as worthy members of those higher echelons. Importantly those Football League clubs which having been relegated to The Conference and whose supporters have enjoyed the glory of winning silverware are now playing once more with renewed confidence in The Football League.

However, not only has The Conference provided an environment of playing excellence, but it has also actively ensured the improvement and development of its member clubs' facilities as is shown by such splendid stadiums at Rushden, Wycombe and Yeovil which now grace The Football League. At the same time by setting standards for entry and providing counselling and support to candidate clubs, it has ensured that the quality of their stadiums has been enhanced and this book provides a wonderful record of these achievements.

Now backed by 25 years of successful achievement, The Conference has expanded to encompass the top 66 clubs outside The Football League. They now speak with one voice on behalf of this powerful grouping and we can look forward to them exerting a greater influence within the overall governing structure of the game on behalf of the grass roots in the coming years. Those 25 years have seen some wonderful achievements and also some heartaches, and this book, truly a labour of love by its author, is a worthy tribute to those years, for which The Conference through both its past and present members and indeed the whole of the Pyramid of football owes a debt of gratitude to John Harman and to Tony Williams its publisher.

Jim Thompson
President
The Nationwide Football Conference

PUBLISHER'S INTRODUCTION

The introduction of the Football Alliance came in 1979 and proved to be a very important milestone in the development of the game outside the Football League.

The fact that well known regional competitions such as the Cheshire County League and the Lancashire Combination had recently agreed to lose their identity had helped create the Northern Premier League, and now that collection of all the powerful northern clubs were being asked to lose their top half to a national competition.

In the South, the ex-amateur world of the Isthmian League and its feeders remained independent from the semi-professional Southern League 'family,' but the new national competition had been given the go ahead and its constitution was equally shared between the Northern and Southern Premier Leagues.

This exciting development gave all the clubs a genuine opportunity to work their way through the regional leagues into the national competition, and if crowned champions, they would be accepted as the only serious contender for membership of the Football League.

Within three years, the top Isthmian clubs Dagenham and Enfield had been accepted into the Alliance and the Isthmian family were able to feed the national competition on an annual basis.

After much appreciated financial backing by the private kit manufacturing company 'Gola', the league turned to the massive Vauxhall Motors for sponsorship and they introduced the term Conference to the competition. With the name proving a winner and the standard of the club's facilities and attendances forever improving, it wasn't surprising that the Football League agreed to a one up and one down link between the Fourth Division and the Vauxhall Football Conference.

Lincoln City and Scarborough duly swapped places at the end of the 1986-87 season and at last non-league football had its automatic promotion. The excitement and pride that was associated with long term non-league clubs who won the Conference championship and the right to be promoted was emotional for all involved. They had dreamed about this day for years and now it had come true and they were about to move into 'the promised land'!

Three clubs; Kidderminster Harriers, Macclesfield Town and Stevenage Borough were prevented from accepting promotion for 'ground irregularities' but this very unsatisfactory situation has not been repeated and at least two of the three eventually reached their goal. They, along with Scarborough, Maidstone United, Barnet, Wycombe Wanderers, Cheltenham Town, Rushden & Diamonds, Boston United and Yeovil Town have all taken advantage of the system and brought Football League competition to their towns. Nothing can have been so thrilling for their supporters as clinching that magic promotion.

Sadly, it is a very different situation for the ex Football League clubs being relegated to the Conference. They don't want to be there and their supporters are disappointed and often take quite some time before learning to enjoy and appreciate the friendliness and spirit of the game outside the Football League. Their officials, players and supporters often have difficulty showing any enthusiasm for non-league England International games or indeed the FA.Challenge Trophy.

If the truth be known, most of the League clubs who have bounced back, such as Lincoln City, Darlington,Colchester United, Halifax Town, Chester City, Doncaster Rovers and Shrewsbury Town have benefited greatly from the break, and although some have taken longer than others to 'steady the ship' most have appreciated the recuperation and used it successfully.

Most ex Alliance/Conference club players will remember with pleasure their games with member clubs but will they remember or have recorded the results, their goals or even their colleagues or opponents in those special days? The book has been compiled by the official Conference statistician John Harman and to illustrate the statistics we have had a lot of fun sorting out our old photos originally collected for past Non-League Club Directories and Team Talk magazine.

This book features the first twenty five years of the single division in which Northwich Victoria and Telford United are ever presents despite their desperate recent experiences. Many wonderful memories will be aroused by John Harman's detailed statistics and hopefully the photos will bring back memories of many great players and special games.

The Football Conference is now a completely different organisation from the first version in 1979. It has three divisions and many full time clubs but its members are all ambitious and standards on and off the field are improving by the season.

It's been a pleasure working with John Harman whose love of football and knowledge of the Conference is second to none, while the sponsorship from Victor Gladwish Land Sales has been a tremendous help. Victor's overall service to non-League football can not be measured but is greatly appreciated by the game in general.

We hope you enjoy the book and let's hope the next twenty five years for the Conference are just as progressive and exciting. Congratulations to those who had the idea, made it happen and have looked after the competition during its steady development.

TONY WILLIAMS (Tony Williams Publications Ltd)

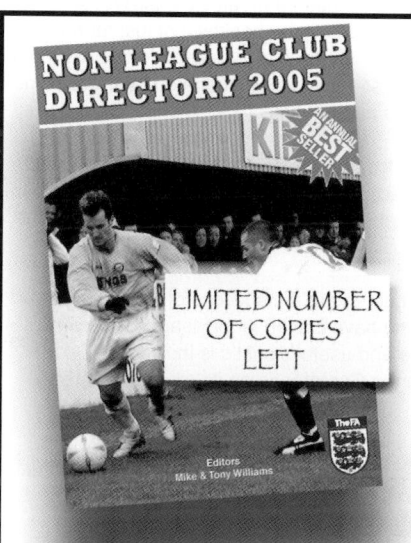
5

25 YEARS OF THE CONFERENCE

This book is a must for all lovers of football commemorating 25 years of the Conference from its days as the Alliance through its evolution to the present day and its link between the apex of the pyramid of professional football and the base of that pyramid. It provides a valuable training ground for many players who have gone on to achieve great success at a higher level and at the same time accommodating the hopes of those players who wish to make a contribution to football as a professional, and is, of course, a league where top players can end their careers passing on the benefit of their experience to younger colleagues.

I was delighted to be involved in discussions in the 80's with the restructuring of the Football League and to be part of the Committee which proposed automatic promotion and relegation from the Conference into the Football League, as I believe that this could only be healthy, not just for the Football League, but for the Conference. Since that time the number has increased to two which has given more encouragement to the hopes and aspirations of so many clubs illustrated by the full-time status of at least half the members of the Conference at the present time.

Perhaps one of the finest examples of the regeneration process provided by the Conference would be one of the founder members of the Football League – Accrington Stanley – who nearly half a century after their demise from the Football League have a chance to take their place once again in the League.

The contribution of Conference clubs to the Football League and to the success of the FA Cup has been immense and this book details the 70 or so clubs who have played in this league, everyone who has participated, every goal scorer, every attendance and useful statistic is included - it is a must for football fans everywhere and may I congratulate the Conference on its silver anniversary and offer my best wishes for the next 25 years!

Gordon Taylor
Chief Executive, PFA

A WORD FROM THE EDITOR

A lifelong West Bromwich Albion fan since wartime, I was persuaded in 1987 by a good friend to go and watch some non-league football. Little did I realise as I stood on the Willenhall Town terraces on the evening of 22 September 1987 what my friend had started (and he a Villa fan too!)

The crunch day was 6 May 1989 when I chose to watch Atherstone United play Rushden Town instead of Albion v Sunderland, something I never imagined I would ever contemplate, let alone do.

Anyway, 'The Adders' won and secured promotion to the Beezer Homes League Premier Division. For the next six seasons I never missed an Atherstone game, home or away, and helped out by running the Club Shop, operating the daily telephone 'Newsline', writing for the local newspapers, helping with the programme, being the PA announcer, and doing some of the 101 jobs necessary in helping a non-league Club. It's a fair bet that a lot of you reading this have "been there and done it"?

Having kept detailed statistics on anything to do with WBA for many years, I thought that I would try and start keeping statistics on aspects of the non-league game. I chose the Conference as it seemed all nice and neat, one division, only ten seasons in existence, and so, in 1989, I began.

Over the ensuing years, I have gathered details from a whole host of people I have met over the country, and some, sad to say, who I have still never met. Some have gone on to be friends for many years, and simply put, without them, all of this would not have been possible.
They know who they are, and to mention just some of them by name would be wrong. To you all "Thank you".

I have details of every date, result, attendance, line up, goalscorer and substitution of every game ever played in league, F A Cup, F A Trophy, and League Cup since the league's inception in 1979, both on detailed handwritten sheets and also on the computer.

Actually, the above paragraph is not quite true! There are still about twenty 'gaps' with missing attendances and goalscorers for FAC and FAT games played in the early years by the likes of Redditch United, AP Leamington and Frickley Athletic, but I keep on hoping . . . .

I was made "Official Conference Statistician" by Chief Executive John Moules in the summer of 2003 after several seasons when I was 'unofficial'. I get calls and emails weekly from the League itself, from newspapers, from the Clubs, and even from Sky and Channel 4 television, asking for various information on the Conference, and I am usually able to help them, and this always pleases me.

Although this position is a purely Honorary one, and everything has to be done in my spare time, I can honestly say that everything I do regarding the Conference is totally enjoyable to me. The enlargement into 66 clubs for the 2004/05 season has simply meant trying to find even more 'friends' and even less sleep!

I started badgering Tony Williams about getting something published in the early 1990's and we have kept in constant touch ever since. After several 'false starts' this is the result, and I sincerely hope that this book will be the first of at least three which will cover every aspect of my records. Match results, line-ups, scorers and attendances will follow, and then possibly a detailed book of every player who has ever appeared in a Conference game will follow that. As I say, hopefully . . . . .

I have visited a lot of the Conference grounds, but there are some I have never been to, a situation which, hopefully, will gradually be resolved. On my travels, I have seen most of the players who have appeared in the Conference. The best side I ever saw must be the Altrincham team of season 1990/91, when, surely only fatigue from playing so many games in so few days at the end of the season prevented them from joining the Football League.

My 'best' team of players would be (in 4-4-2 formation):-

Paul Hyde
(Wycombe Wanderers)

Ian Atkins
(Colchester United)

Chris Brindley
(Kidderminster Harriers)

Jim Rodwell
(Rushden & Diamonds)

Paul Webb
(Kidderminster Harriers)

Gary Butterworth
(Rushden & Diamonds)

Steve McGavin
(Colchester United)

Michael McElhatton
(Rushden & Diamonds)

Paul Showler
(Altrincham)

John Brady
(Altrincham)

Ken McKenna
(Altrincham)

But I am sure that you will all have your own ideas on that.

This book has been many years in compilation. It is the work of a self-confessed 'anorak', but I hope that it will be both of interest and useful perhaps to not only Conference and non-league fans, but also to all football fans in general

JOHN HARMAN (October 2004)

JOHN HARMAN

Born in West Bromwich in 1943, John Harman's earliest football recollection was of West Bromwich Albion beating Bradford PA 5-1, and he can still recall Jackie Vernon leaving the field to have a cut eye attended to and of Bradford scoring whilst he was absent. This was in 1947.

John was educated at West Bromwich Grammar School, then at Trent Park Training College in North London. A three year stint as a teacher at Joseph Edward Cox School in Wednesbury followed, before a year as Assistant Commercial manager at his beloved West Bromwich Albion FC.

Eleven years as Commercial manager at a Tipton structural steelworks firm ensued, before being made redundant. Six years as a Residential Social Worker at a local Children's Home followed before ill health brought that to an end. Since then he has worked as a freelance football statistician and part time gardener.

John was captain of the West Bromwich Dartmouth sports quiz team which reached the quarter final of the Sunday People Inn Quiz (quite an achievement in a national competition with a televised final), and twice appeared on BBC Radio's "Brain Of Sport" competition which was chaired by the late Peter Jones.

He also worked part time for BBC Local Radio (Birmingham and WM) for many years, running sports quizzes, reading both football and horse racing results, and, in fact, was on Nick Owen's very last programme as a Radio Birmingham presenter.

Never having been good enough to play the game at any serious level, John's flair for statistics and record keeping have meant that he has compensated off the field for what he might have missed on it.

ABOUT OUR SPONSOR

Victor Gladwish was born 1944 during the blitz in the City of Westminster, London and although his parents came as free fighting Belgians (and his grandparents includes French and Dutch blood) the surname is in fact a Sussex one stemming from Glydwishe near Burwash and it means 'from the watered meadow where the Kite flies' - a kite being a bird of prey.

A self made man of a poor background Victor had his first success as a statistician at the age of 13 winning a prize in the Ice Hockey World. Leaving school at the age of 15 he then firstly worked as an accountant and then into telephone sales before doing seven years in the Royal Engineers.

On returning to England in 1970 he found himself homeless with a family of 4 (two in nappies) with all his possessions in a car. He managed to get a job as a pig farm labourer which gave him tied accommodation and then he got a franchise with Mothers Pride in Taunton, Somerset which he did until 1974 and it was his first taste of being self employed and indeed he has been ever since.

In 1974 he moved to Cambridgeshire to take up a job in printing the Country Life magazine which an army friend had started but upon arriving in Cambridgeshire his friend sold the magazine to someone else and Victor found himself out of work and two mortgages to pay as he had not sold his house in Somerset prior to moving. He then turned a boyhood hobby of collecting matchbox labels into a job by writing and producing his own publications entitled 'The Gladwish Encyclopedia of English written matchbox labels' and this sold worldwide and consisted of over 200 separate books produced between 1974 and 1981 and beating the world record number of books written by anyone which was previously held by the Swedish botanist Carl von Linne who gave latin names to flowers.

After he was awarded a silver medal for literature at the 'Moscow Exhibition' in Poland in 1981 he was also made a professor of phillumeny and famously started a match factory when he said to his first wife that 'the match industry in England do not know how to make matchbox labels anymore' and she had told him to start his own match company. 'What with, I only have £30' he replied and she said 'No, £10 as I need £20 for shopping'

Between 1981 and 1983 he supplied over 20,000 different shops, football clubs and pubs with personalised matchboxes and indeed when a third of the pubs in the UK were buying his matches he appeared in the 'Man on the top series' in 1983 where it explained how he started the business in a garden shed and eventually bought the village school to use as a factory.

Between 1983 and 1985 the match business was moved to Norfolk and he simultaneously started writing about Sussex Social History when he studied his family tree with the Sussex Family History Group and needless to say he published his stories, which are now free and available by email.

By 1986 his business was so big that he had half a per cent of the UK trade and he was given an offer he could not refuse for his business and he retired and moved into East Sussex where he bought 46 acres of land to 'potter about on' and got some animals and made walks for school children to visit. He found that local poachers were stealing his ducks, geese etc, so he moved unto the land to protect his animals but he did so without planning permission and after three years of arguing with the Council his first wife left him and he had to sell the land so that they both could buy somewhere to live. As no farmers were coming into the industry and subsidies had stopped he had to devise a method whereby he could sell land in small plots and also handle the surveying, conveyancing and selling himself to save on professional fees. In this respect all his previous jobs had taught him varied skills that now became useful. The business therefore started by necessity.

Having moved to Steyning in 1989 (into his second wife's flat) selling the farm and the business started with a typewriter on her window sill. They then moved into Horsham in 1990. That from the land he sold that 90 families moved onto the land that had been his home was big television news in the early 1990's and Tina (his second wife) suggested a policy of telling people the plain truth that the land was not sold with planning permission but what they did after they bought the land was up to them.

By 1993 he had sold all his farm and the family moved for a short while to France but found that they could not live happily there so they returned in 1994 and decided to buy land for the purpose of reselling. Not so easy, as a law was passed in Parliament in 1993 that specifically mentioned his name and within 6 days of buying land at Kirdford he received a High Court injunction that lasted nearly two years and the family went from owning two big houses to selling one in France to pay the Inland Revenue and the other one sold to pay for huge barristers fees so that eventually they had used all their savings and landed up living in a small terraced house in Bewbush, Crawley. Needless to say Victor was by this time broke and on the dole saving £1 a week to buy a Sunday joint every third week.

Eventually in 1996 the injunction was lifted on the Court steps when it was agreed that he would go away with no counter claim for loss of earnings. So, the land business started again but this time it started in a broom cupboard underneath the stairs.

From 1996 to 2001 Victor worked a seventeen hour day, 7 days a week and did everything himself until he got his first staff in 2001, with a move of offices to London Road in 2002 and a second office in 2003.

The rest (as they say) is now history with Victor and Tina being directors of several companies and having land in over 100 places in over 30 counties of England.

Although recently he has been on two television documentaries about his business and he is often on the news the past is not forgotten by Victor and he is still an 'ordinary straight talking Joe' who helps single parent families in paying for sports fees for their children and he also sponsors many football teams as a thank you to the public (or God) who helped him to be what he is today.

TEAM STRIPS
15 PLUS GOALIE

Green on White
Red on Yellow
Red on White
Yellow on Blue
Black on White

only £350.00
(inc. vat & delivery)

Blue on Yellow
White on Green
White on Blue
Blue on Sky Blue
White on Red

£60 EXTRA WITH SPONSORS NAME ON ALL 16 SHIRTS
£60 EXTRA FOR CLUB BADGE ON ALL 16 SHIRTS

ACCRINGTON STANLEY

PROMOTED FROM: The Northern Premier League 2002-03
2004-2005 SEASON: The Conference

Back row ,left to right: Steve Hacker, Gordon Armstrong, Steve Flitcroft, Paul Cook, Jamie Speare, Jonathon Smith, Paul Howarth, Robbie Williams, Steve Hollis and Andy Proctor. Front row: Andy Gouck, Brian Welch, Andy Waine, Lutel James, Peter Cavanagh, Darren Connell, Dean Calcutt and Rory Prendegast

	HOME							AWAY						
	P	W	D	L	F	A	Pts	P	W	D	L	F	A	Pts	Position
	21	13	3	5	46	31	42	21	2	10	9	22	30	16	10

SEASON 2003-04

HIGHEST ATTENDANCE
3143 v Shrewsbury T. 16.8.03

LOWEST ATTENDANCE
1058 v Forest Green R. 10.4.04

SEASON GOALSCORER
Paul Mullin 20

SEASON APPEARANCES
Paul Mullin 41

APPEARANCES

	03-04
ARMSTRONG Gordon	4+9
BRANNAN Ged	19+1
CALCUTT Dean	6+14
CAVANAGH Peter	35+1
COOK Paul	28+6
DURNIN John	4+12
FITZGERALD Jerome	7
FLITCROFT Steve	13+11
GOUCK Andy	20+6
HALFORD Steve	24+2

APPEARANCES cont.

	03-04
HINDLE Damien	1
HOLLIS Steve	27+2
HOWARTH Paul	15+2
JACKSON Justin	0+2
JAMES Lutel	40+1
KEMPSON Darren	9+2
KENNEDY Jon	32+1
MADIN Lee	0+2
McEVILLY Lee	3+3
MULLIN Paul	41
PRENDERGAST Rory	36+2
PROCTOR Andy	36+3
SMITH Jonathan	18+4
SPEARE Jamie	10+1
WAINE Andrew	0+1
WELCH Brian	1+1
WILLIAMS Robbie	33

GOALSCORERS

	03-04
BRANNAN Ged	1
CALCUTT Dean	1
CAVANAGH Peter	2
COOK Paul	1
DURNIN John	4
FLITCROFT Steve	2
GOUCK Andy	5
HOLLIS Steve	1
HOWARTH Paul	2
JAMES Lutel	17(4p)
KEMPSON Darren	1
McEVILLY Lee	2
MULLIN Paul	20
PRENDERGAST Rory	6
PROCTOR Andy	2

ACCRINGTON STANLEY

	Aldershot Town		Barnet		Burton Albion		Chester City		Dagenham & Redbridge		Exeter City		Farnborough Town	
	H	A	H	A	H	A	H	A	H	A	H	A	H	A
02-03														
03-04	4-1	1-2	2-0	0-0	3-1	1-1	0-2	3-3	2-3	1-0	1-2	2-3	3-1	1-1

	Forest Green Rovers		Gravesend & N'fleet		Halifax Town		Hereford United		Leigh RMI		Margate		Morecambe	
	H	A	H	A	H	A	H	A	H	A	H	A	H	A
02-03														
03-04	4-1	1-2	3-3	0-0	2-1	1-1	2-0	0-1	4-1	2-1	3-2	1-3	1-0	0-1

	Northwich Victoria		Scarborough		Shrewsbury Town		Stevenage Borough		Tamworth		Telford United		Woking	
	H	A	H	A	H	A	H	A	H	A	H	A	H	A
02-03														
03-04	2-2	3-3	1-0	1-2	0-1	0-0	2-1	1-2	3-0	1-1	1-5	0-1	3-3	2-2

	HOME						AWAY					
	P	W	D	L	F	A	P	W	D	L	F	A
ALDERSHOT T	1	1	0	0	4	2	1	0	0	1	1	2
BARNET	1	1	0	0	2	0	1	0	1	0	0	0
BURTON A	1	1	0	0	3	1	1	0	1	0	1	1
CHESTER C	1	0	0	1	0	2	1	0	1	0	3	3
DAGENHAM & R	1	0	0	1	2	3	1	1	0	0	1	0
EXETER C	1	0	0	1	1	2	1	0	0	1	2	3
FARNBOROUGH T	1	1	0	0	3	1	1	0	1	0	1	1
FOREST GREEN R	1	1	0	0	4	1	1	0	0	1	1	2
GRAVESEND & N	1	0	1	0	3	3	1	0	1	0	0	0
HALIFAX T	1	1	0	0	2	1	1	0	1	0	1	1
HEREFORD U	1	1	0	0	2	0	1	0	0	1	0	1
LEIGH R M I	1	1	0	0	4	1	1	1	0	0	2	1
MARGATE	1	1	0	0	3	2	1	0	0	1	1	3
MORECAMBE	1	1	0	0	1	0	1	0	0	1	0	1
NORTHWICH V	1	0	1	0	2	2	1	0	1	0	3	3
SCARBOROUGH	1	1	0	0	1	0	1	0	0	1	1	2
SHREWSBURY T	1	0	0	1	0	1	1	0	1	0	0	0
STEVENAGE B	1	1	0	0	2	1	1	0	0	1	1	2
TAMWORTH	1	1	0	0	3	0	1	0	1	0	1	1
TELFORD U	1	0	0	1	1	5	1	0	0	1	0	1
WOKING	1	0	1	0	3	3	1	0	1	0	2	2
TOTAL	21	13	3	5	46	31	21	2	10	9	22	30

ALDERSHOT TOWN

PROMOTED FROM: The Isthmian League 2002-03
2004-2005 SEASON: The Conference

Back row, left to right:Lee Charles, John Notter, Tim Sills, Mark Kleboe, Richard Barnard, Ben Lauder-Dyke, Anthony Charles, Ray Warburton, Dominic Sterling and Jason Chewins. MIddle row: Simon Pullen(Res.Youth Man), Martin Kuhl, Dean Hooper, Jamie Taylor, Stuart Tanfield, Roscoe D'Sane, Nick Roddis, Aaron McLean, Michael Harper, Luke Gedling,Jon Challinor, Paul Priddy (GK Coach) and Alan McCreeney (Physio). Front row: Luke Walker ,Brett Cooper Lee Champion, Terry Brown (Manager), Stuart Cash (Asst Man.),Tyrone Smith, Rob Westall and Steve Valanda. Photo: Eric Marsh.

SEASON 2003-04

HIGHEST ATTENDANCE
4637 v Woking 23.8.03

LOWEST ATTENDANCE
2398 v Forest Green 1.11.03

SEASON GOALSCORER
Roscoe D'Sane 21 (8p)

SEASON APPEARANCES
Roscoe D'Sane 39+1

HOME							AWAY							
P	W	D	L	F	A	Pts	P	W	D	L	F	A	Pts	Position
21	12	6	3	40	24	42	21	8	4	9	40	43	28	5

APPEARANCES cont.

03-04

JOHNSON Brett	1+5
LOVETT Jay	1
MANUELLA Fiston	8
McLEAN Aaron	24+13
MILLER Adam	23+1
MUMFORD Andrew	4
NUTTER John	10+11
REES Matt	7
RODDIS Nick	9+1
RODWELL Jim	11+2
SHIELDS Tony	12+1
SILLS Tom	39
SMITH Tyrone	2+1
STERLING Dominic	33+5
TANFIELD Stuart	1+5
TAYLOR Jamie	0+3
THOMAS Bradley	5
WARBURTON Ray	40
WESTELL Rob	0+1

APPEARANCES

03-04

ANTWI Will	13
BARNARD Richard	18+3
BULL Nikki	24
CHALLINOR John	26
CHARLES Lee	20+10
CHEWINS Jason	26+9
DOWNER Simon	8
D'SANE Roscoe	39+1
GEDLING Luke	1+6
GILES Chris	4+1
GOSLING Jamie	7+1
HAMMOND Dean	7
HARPER Michael	0+13
HOOPER Dean	29

GOALSCORERS

03-04

CHALLINOR John	12
CHARLES Lee	7
CHEWINS Jason	1
D'SANE Roscoe	21(8p)
GOSLING Jamie	1
MANUELLA Fiston	1
McLEAN Aaron	6
MILLER Adam	5
MUMFORD Andrew	1
SILLS Tom	18
TAYLOR Jamie	1
THOMAS Bradley	1
WARBURTON Ray	2

ALDERSHOT TOWN

	Accrington Stanley		Barnet		Burton Albion		Chester City		Dagenham & Redbridge		Exeter City		Farnborough Town	
	H	A	H	A	H	A	H	A	H	A	H	A	H	A
02-03														
03-04	2-1	2-4	1-1	1-2	3-1	4-1	1-1	2-4	2-1	3-2	2-1	1-2	2-0	0-4

	Forest Green Rovers		Gravesend & N'fleet		Halifax Town		Hereford United		Leigh RMI		Margate		Morecambe	
	H	A	H	A	H	A	H	A	H	A	H	A	H	A
02-03														
03-04	3-0	1-3	2-2	3-1	3-1	2-1	1-2	3-4	2-0	2-2	0-2	2-1	2-2	0-2

	Northwich Victoria		Scarborough		Shrewsbury Town		Stevenage Borough		Tamworth		Telford United		Woking	
	H	A	H	A	H	A	H	A	H	A	H	A	H	A
02-03														
03-04	4-3	1-1	1-2	0-1	1-1	2-1	2-0	1-0	1-1	3-3	3-1	5-2	2-1	2-2

	HOME						AWAY					
	P	W	D	L	F	A	P	W	D	L	F	A
ACCRINGTON S	1	1	0	0	2	1	1	0	0	1	2	4
BARNET	1	0	1	0	1	1	1	0	0	1	1	2
BURTON A	1	1	0	0	3	1	1	1	0	0	4	1
CHESTER C	1	0	1	0	1	1	1	0	0	1	2	4
DAGENHAM & R	1	1	0	0	2	1	1	1	0	0	3	2
EXETER C	1	1	0	0	2	1	1	0	0	1	1	2
FARNBOROUGH T	1	1	0	0	2	0	1	0	0	1	0	4
FOREST GREEN R	1	1	0	0	3	0	1	0	0	1	1	3
GRAVESEND & N	1	0	1	0	2	2	1	1	0	0	3	1
HALIFAX T	1	1	0	0	3	1	1	1	0	0	2	1
HEREFORD U	1	0	0	1	1	2	1	0	0	1	3	4
LEIGH R M I	1	1	0	0	2	0	1	0	1	0	2	2
MARGATE	1	0	0	1	0	2	1	1	0	0	2	1
MORECAMBE	1	0	1	0	2	2	1	0	0	1	0	2
NORTHWICH V	1	1	0	0	4	3	1	0	1	0	1	1
SCARBOROUGH	1	0	0	1	1	2	1	0	0	1	0	1
SHREWSBURY T	1	0	1	0	1	1	1	1	0	0	2	1
STEVENAGE B	1	1	0	0	2	0	1	1	0	0	1	0
TAMWORTH	1	0	1	0	1	1	1	0	1	0	3	3
TELFORD U	1	1	0	0	3	1	1	1	0	0	5	2
WOKING	1	1	0	0	2	1	1	0	1	0	2	2
TOTAL	21	12	6	3	40	24	21	8	4	9	40	43

ALTRINCHAM

PROMOTED FROM: Northern Premier League 1979, 1999
RELEGATED TO: Northern Premier League 1997, 2000
2004-2005 SEASON: Conference North

1982 Squad.
Back Row (L-R):
John Owens,
Jeff Johnson,
John Davidson,
Mal Bailey,
John Connaughton,
Derek Goulding,
Barry Whitbread,
Phil Gardiner,
John Evans (Physio).
Front Row:
John Rogers,
John Cavanah,
Barry Howard,
Tony Sanders (Manager),
John King (Captain),
Ivan Crossley,
Graham Heathcote,
Stan Allan.
Photo: John Rooney.

SEASONS
19

TOTAL POINTS
601 + 475 = 1076

HIGHEST POSITION
1 (79/80) (80/81)

LOWEST POSITION
22 (96/97)

HIGHEST ATTENDANCE
2864 Yeovil T (4-5-81)

LOWEST ATTENDANCE
332 Sutton U (5-4-89)

SEASON GOALSCORER
Ken McKenna 22 (90/91)

CAREER GOALSCORER
Graham Bennett 62

CAREER APPEARANCES
John Davison 270+3

	HOME							AWAY							Position
	P	W	D	L	F	A	Pts	P	W	D	L	F	A	Pts	
79-80	19	16	3	0	45	9	35	19	8	5	6	34	26	21	1
80-81	19	14	2	3	40	21	30	19	9	6	4	32	20	24	1
81-82	21	10	6	5	39	22	36	21	4	7	10	27	34	19	11
82-83	21	13	5	3	40	17	44	21	2	5	14	22	39	11	12
83-84	21	13	3	5	40	20	29	21	10	6	5	24	19	36	3
84-85	21	13	2	6	39	21	28	21	8	4	9	24	26	28	5
85-86	21	14	3	4	42	27	31	21	8	8	5	28	22	32	4
86-87	21	11	7	3	35	18	40	21	7	8	6	31	35	29	5
87-88	21	11	5	5	41	21	38	21	3	5	13	18	38	14	14
88-89	20	6	8	6	24	23	26	20	7	2	11	27	38	23	14
89-90	21	8	5	8	31	20	29	21	4	8	9	18	28	20	16
90-91	21	12	6	3	48	22	42	21	11	7	3	39	24	40	3
91-92	21	5	8	8	33	39	23	21	6	4	11	28	43	22	18
92-93	21	7	7	7	21	25	28	21	8	6	7	28	27	30	10
93-94	21	8	5	8	23	22	29	21	8	4	9	18	20	28	10
94-95	21	10	3	8	34	27	33	21	10	5	6	43	33	35	4
95-96	21	9	6	6	33	29	33	21	6	7	8	26	35	25	12
96-97	21	6	3	12	25	34	21	21	3	9	9	24	39	18	22
1997-1999															
99-00	21	6	8	7	31	26	26	21	3	11	7	20	34	20	21
Total	394	192	95	107	664	443	601	394	125	117	152	511	580	475	

	Home						Away					
	P	W	D	L	F	A	P	W	D	L	F	A
A P LEAMINGTON	3	2	0	1	9	4	3	3	0	0	9	3
AYLESBURY U	1	1	0	0	1	0	1	1	0	0	2	1
BANGOR C	4	4	0	0	11	1	4	2	1	1	9	7
BARNET	12	9	2	1	23	8	12	1	3	8	8	19
BARROW	9	3	6	0	15	9	9	5	2	2	15	6
BATH C	16	9	3	4	24	11	16	7	5	4	21	17
BOSTON U	14	6	6	2	30	16	14	5	5	4	29	26
BROMSGROVE R	5	2	2	1	11	7	5	2	1	2	6	9
CHELTENHAM T	7	5	1	1	17	4	7	2	2	3	8	7
CHORLEY	2	1	0	1	2	2	2	0	0	2	1	3
COLCHESTER U	2	0	1	1	3	4	2	0	2	0	4	4
DAGENHAM	7	5	1	1	19	5	7	2	2	3	10	11
DAGENHAM & R	5	2	0	3	5	7	5	2	1	2	7	6
DARLINGTON	1	0	0	1	0	1	1	0	0	1	0	2
DARTFORD	3	2	1	0	4	1	3	1	0	2	3	4
DONCASTER R	1	0	0	1	1	2	1	1	0	0	1	0
DOVER A	5	3	1	1	11	4	5	2	2	1	11	7
ENFIELD	9	4	2	3	16	13	9	2	4	3	12	12
FARNBOROUGH T	6	1	3	2	9	11	6	2	3	1	10	9
FISHER A	4	0	3	1	4	5	4	0	2	2	3	7
FOREST GREEN R	1	0	1	0	1	1	1	0	1	0	1	1
FRICKLEY A	7	3	3	1	11	8	7	1	3	3	7	11
GATESHEAD	10	3	3	4	15	12	10	5	1	4	13	13
GRAVESEND & N	3	3	0	0	9	3	3	2	1	0	5	1
HALIFAX T	4	3	1	0	8	4	4	0	4	0	3	3
HAYES	2	0	0	2	1	4	2	0	1	1	2	4
HEDNESFORD T	3	1	1	1	3	3	3	0	1	2	3	9
HEREFORD U	1	1	0	0	2	1	1	0	1	0	2	2
KETTERING T	19	8	8	3	38	28	19	5	7	7	26	35
KIDDERMINSTER H	15	6	4	5	20	16	15	8	4	3	20	16
KINGSTONIAN	1	0	0	1	1	3	1	0	1	0	2	2
LEEK T												
LINCOLN C	1	0	1	0	0	0	1	0	0	1	0	5
MACCLESFIELD T	10	3	0	7	12	19	10	2	3	5	9	13
MAIDSTONE U	10	6	1	3	12	6	10	2	3	5	12	23
MERTHYR T	6	4	1	1	18	5	6	2	3	1	10	7
MORECAMBE	3	1	1	1	5	3	3	0	1	2	4	12
NORTHWICH V	19	4	7	8	23	27	19	6	6	7	25	28
NUNEATON B	8	3	2	3	16	15	8	1	3	4	6	14
REDDITCH U	1	1	0	0	2	0	1	1	0	0	1	0
RUNCORN	15	5	5	5	20	21	15	4	5	6	17	22
RUSHDEN & D	2	1	0	1	5	5	2	0	0	2	2	4
SCARBOROUGH	9	9	0	0	20	5	9	1	3	5	9	13
SLOUGH T	6	2	1	3	9	10	6	5	1	0	15	7
SOUTHPORT	5	2	2	1	6	3	5	3	0	2	10	8
STAFFORD R	14	9	2	3	30	15	14	8	2	4	20	18
STALYBRIDGE C	5	3	2	0	3	0	5	1	0	4	4	6
STEVENAGE B	4	0	0	4	2	7	4	0	2	2	5	8
SUTTON U	6	4	1	1	10	3	6	2	0	4	9	13
TELFORD U	19	9	3	7	25	23	19	7	2	10	26	30
TROWBRIDGE T	3	2	0	1	7	2	3	1	1	1	4	3
WEALDSTONE	8	5	0	3	9	6	8	3	3	2	12	9
WELLING U	12	6	3	3	17	8	12	2	7	3	11	13
WEYMOUTH	10	8	1	1	19	8	10	2	4	4	7	9
WITTON A	3	1	1	1	5	6	3	1	1	1	2	3
WOKING	6	2	2	2	6	6	6	2	1	3	5	14
WORCESTER C	6	4	1	1	16	9	6	1	2	3	7	9
WYCOMBE W	7	3	1	3	12	15	7	2	1	4	7	11
YEOVIL T	14	8	4	2	31	18	14	5	3	6	19	21
Newport C												
TOTALS	394	192	95	107	664	443	394	125	117	152	511	580

	A P Leamington		Aylesbury United		Bangor City		Barnet		Barrow		Bath City		Boston United		Bromsgrove Rovers		Cheltenham Town	
	H	A	H	A	H	A	H	A	H	A	H	A	H	A	H	A	H	A
79-80	3-0	4-1			5-0	1-1	1-0	0-2	3-1	3-1	4-0	1-1	3-0	5-2				
80-81	4-1	4-2			2-0	5-4	2-0	2-3	2-2	4-0	3-1	1-0	2-0	1-1				
81-82	2-3	1-0			2-0	0-1	2-0	0-0	1-1	0-1	1-0	1-1	1-1	1-1				
82-83					2-1	3-1	3-0	1-2	2-2	2-2	0-0	2-0	2-2	0-3				
83-84							3-2	2-1			2-0	0-0	3-0	2-2				
84-85							0-2	0-1	2-0	2-0	0-0	0-1	7-2	0-0				
85-86							2-0	2-2	2-0	1-0	1-2	2-0	1-3	3-1			4-1	0-2
86-87							2-0	0-1			1-1	1-1	3-1	2-4			2-0	1-1
87-88							1-1	1-3			2-0	0-2	4-1	2-2			1-1	0-1
88-89			1-0	2-1			1-1	0-3					0-0	1-3			0-1	1-2
89-90							2-1	0-1	1-1	1-1			0-0	3-2			5-0	0-0
90-91							4-1	0-0	1-1	0-1	2-0	3-2	1-1	6-2			3-0	4-1
91-92									1-1	2-0	4-0	2-3	2-4	1-2			2-1	2-0
92-93											1-0	0-3	1-1	2-1	2-2	1-4		
93-94											0-2	1-0			2-3	2-1		
94-95											1-0	3-0			1-1	3-0		
95-96											1-2	2-2			3-0	0-0		
96-97											1-3	2-1			3-1	0-4		
97-98																		
98-99																		
99-00																		

	Chorley		Colchester United		Dagenham		Dagenham & Redbridge		Darlington		Dartford		Doncaster Rovers		Dover Athletic		Enfield	
	H	A	H	A	H	A	H	A	H	A	H	A	H	A	H	A	H	A
79-80																		
80-81																		
81-82					1-1	0-2					2-0	1-0					1-0	1-1
82-83					2-0	1-1											2-2	1-2
83-84					4-0	2-0											1-3	1-0
84-85					3-1	1-1					2-1	0-1					3-2	3-3
85-86					3-1	3-1					0-0	2-3					1-4	1-1
86-87					0-2	1-3											0-1	2-0
87-88					6-0	2-3											5-1	1-1
88-89	1-2	0-1															0-0	1-2
89-90	1-0	1-2							0-1	0-2							3-0	1-2
90-91			2-2	1-1														
91-92			1-2	3-3					0-3	1-0								
92-93									1-0	2-2								
93-94									1-2	0-3					2-0	0-1		
94-95									0-1	4-0					3-0	3-1		
95-96									3-1	0-1					2-2	4-1		
96-97															1-2	2-2		
97-98																		
98-99																		
99-00													1-2	1-0	3-0	2-2		

Above: Barry Whitbread.
scores agreat goal against
A.P. Leamington

Left: Charlie Bradshaw out jumps the
Kidderminster Harriers defence

Right: Paul Rowlands and Gary Anderson
attack the Kettering Town defence at a
corner

Below: John Davison in 'full flight'
against Cheltenham Town

First table

	Farnborough Town		Fisher Athletic		Forest Green Rovers		Frickley Athletic		Gateshead		Gravesend & Northfleet		Halifax Town		Hayes		Hednesford Town	
	H	A	H	A	H	A	H	A	H	A	H	A	H	A	H	A	H	A
79-80											4-1	2-0						
80-81							2-0	2-0			2-1	2-0						
81-82							1-1	1-1			3-1	1-1						
82-83							2-2	0-3										
83-84							1-0	1-3	5-0	1-0								
84-85							3-4	1-2	2-0	1-0								
85-86							1-0	0-0										
86-87							1-1	2-2	1-1	3-1								
87-88			2-3	2-3														
88-89			1-1	1-1														
89-90	2-3	0-0	1-1	0-3														
90-91			0-0	0-0					4-1	3-0								
91-92	1-1	0-3							1-1	0-4								
92-93	2-2	5-2							0-1	0-2								
93-94									0-3	1-2			0-0	0-0				
94-95	2-0	3-2							1-3	0-1			3-1	1-1				
95-96	2-2	1-1							1-1	3-2			3-2	1-1			2-1	1-2
96-97	0-3	1-1							0-1	1-1			2-1	1-1	0-2	1-3	1-1	2-2
97-98																		
98-99																		
99-00					1-1	1-1									1-2	1-1	0-1	0-5

Second table

	Hereford United		Kettering Town		Kidderminster Harriers		Kingstonian		Lincoln City		Macclesfield Town		Maidstone United		Merthyr Tydfil		Morecambe	
	H	A	H	A	H	A	H	A	H	A	H	A	H	A	H	A	H	A
79-80			0-0	2-1									1-0	2-2				
80-81			4-1	1-1									2-1	2-1				
81-82			2-1	4-5									1-2	0-0				
82-83			3-1	2-3									0-2	2-3				
83-84			1-1	1-1	0-1	2-0							1-0	0-1				
84-85			2-1	2-1	2-1	2-0							2-0	0-3				
85-86			2-2	2-2	2-1	2-0							1-0	2-1				
86-87			4-1	2-0	3-1	0-3							4-0	0-3				
87-88			2-2	2-1	2-3	1-4			0-0	0-5	1-3	0-1	0-0	2-2				
88-89			1-2	1-0	3-1	3-2					1-3	0-1	0-1	2-7				
89-90			1-1	0-3	0-1	2-1					0-1	0-1			4-1	0-0		
90-91			3-2	1-1	1-2	1-0					5-3	1-0			9-2	2-0		
91-92			1-1	0-5	1-1	0-1					3-1	1-1			1-1	1-3		
92-93			3-0	1-1	2-2	1-0					1-0	1-1			0-1	2-2		
93-94			1-1	0-1	1-0	1-0					0-1	0-1			3-0	0-0		
94-95			2-4	2-2	2-0	2-2					1-2	2-4			1-0	5-2		
95-96			1-3	2-4	1-1	1-1					0-4	3-2					3-0	0-7
96-97			4-3	1-3	0-1	1-1					0-1	1-1					0-1	1-2
97-98																	2-2	3-3
98-99																		
99-00	2-1	2-2	1-1	0-0	0-0	1-1	1-3	2-2										

	Northwich Victoria		Nuneaton Borough		Redditch United		Runcorn		Rushden & Diamonds		Scarborough		Slough Town		Southport		Stafford Rangers	
	H	A	H	A	H	A	H	A	H	A	H	A	H	A	H	A	H	A
79-80	0-0	0-1	3-1	0-2	2-0	1-0					2-0	1-1					3-1	2-1
80-81	1-1	0-1	0-3	0-0							4-3	0-1					4-2	3-1
81-82	0-2	0-2					2-2	4-5			2-0	3-1					0-1	0-2
82-83	3-0	1-2	1-2	1-3			2-1	0-1			2-1	1-1					4-0	3-2
83-84	1-1	1-1	0-1	1-0			1-3	0-0			2-0	1-3						
84-85	1-2	2-1	1-0	1-4			0-1	2-1			3-0	1-2						
85-86	2-1	2-1	7-4	0-0			1-1	1-2			2-0	0-1					1-3	1-1
86-87	1-1	1-1	2-2	2-2			0-0	1-1			1-0	2-2					2-0	3-2
87-88	2-0	2-1					2-0	1-1									2-0	0-3
88-89	2-2	3-4					1-2	0-3									2-1	2-0
89-90	0-2	3-2					1-2	0-0									3-1	1-3
90-91	0-2	1-1					1-0	3-1					3-0	3-3			0-0	1-2
91-92	0-1	2-1					2-2	2-2					3-7	3-2			3-0	2-1
92-93	0-0	2-1					0-2	1-0					1-1	4-1			1-5	0-0
93-94	2-2	0-2					2-1	1-2					2-0	2-0	1-2	1-3	0-0	1-0
94-95	1-3	1-1					3-2	0-3							0-0	4-1	5-1	1-0
95-96	3-4	1-2					2-2	1-0					0-1	2-1	1-1	2-1		
96-97	2-3	2-2							4-3	2-3			0-1	1-0	1-0	3-1		
97-98																		
98-99																		
99-00	2-0	1-1	2-2	1-3					1-2	0-1	2-1	0-1			3-0	0-2		

	Stalybridge Celtic		Stevenage Borough		Sutton United		Telford United		Trowbridge Town		Wealdstone		Welling United		Weymouth		Witton Albion	
	H	A	H	A	H	A	H	A	H	A	H	A	H	A	H	A	H	A
79-80							2-0	2-3			2-1	4-1			3-2	0-0		
80-81							0-2	2-3			2-0	2-1			1-2	0-0		
81-82							3-0	3-4	1-2	2-0					0-0	0-1		
82-83							1-0	1-1	2-0	2-3	0-1	1-1			1-0	0-2		
83-84							1-1	1-2	4-0	0-0	1-0	1-3			2-1	1-0		
84-85							0-1	2-0			1-2	0-1			2-0	1-2		
85-86							1-0	1-2			1-0	2-2			3-1	0-0		
86-87					2-1	3-2	2-1	0-4			1-2	2-0	1-1	1-0	2-1	2-2		
87-88					0-1	1-2	0-3	0-1			1-0	0-0	1-0	1-0	3-0	0-1		
88-89					1-0	2-3	0-0	1-0					3-1	0-0	2-1	3-1		
89-90					0-0	1-2	0-1	3-1					4-0	1-1				
90-91					4-1	2-1	2-1	2-1					0-1	2-2				
91-92							2-3	1-2					1-2	2-2			2-2	0-2
92-93	0-0	0-1					0-3	1-2					2-0	0-2			2-1	1-1
93-94	0-0	3-1					2-0	2-0					2-0	1-2			1-3	1-0
94-95	1-0	1-2	1-2	2-4			3-1	3-2					1-1	0-0				
95-96	1-0	0-1	0-2	1-1			1-0	0-2					1-0	1-1				
96-97	1-0	0-1	1-2	1-2			2-3	0-0					1-1	0-1				
97-98																		
98-99																		
99-00			0-1	1-1	3-0	0-3	3-3	1-0					0-1	2-2				

	Woking		Worcester City		Wycombe Wanderers		Yeovil Town	
	H	A	H	A	H	A	H	A
79-80			3-1	2-3			1-1	2-3
80-81			1-0	0-0			2-1	1-1
81-82			6-3	3-4			7-1	1-2
82-83			2-0	0-1			4-1	1-2
83-84			3-4	1-0			2-1	2-1
84-85			1-1	1-1			2-0	2-1
85-86					4-3	1-0		
86-87								
87-88					4-2	0-1		
88-89					2-2	1-2	2-2	3-2
89-90					1-2	1-1	2-1	0-0
90-91					1-0	0-3	2-2	3-2
91-92					0-4	2-4	2-1	1-2
92-93	1-0	2-0			0-2	2-0	1-2	0-1
93-94	0-2	1-1					1-0	0-0
94-95	1-2	0-4					1-3	3-1
95-96	2-0	0-2						
96-97	1-1	1-7						
97-98								
98-99								
99-00	1-1	1-0					2-2	0-3

LEADING APPEARANCES

John DAVISON	270+3	(273)
Paul CUDDY	238+17	(255)
Jeff JOHNSON	230+12	(242)
Ronnie ELLIS	219+10	(229)
Jeff WEALANDS	202	(202)
Paul FRANCE	193+3	(196)
Darren HEESOM	184+7	(191)
Andy REID	183+8	(191)
Phil GARDNER	170+21	(191)
Gary ANDERSON	165+6	(171)
Barry HOWARD	158+2	(160)
Graham HEATHCOTE	142+18	(160)
Mick CARMODY	153+6	(159)
Mike FARRELLY	151+8	(159)
Nigel SHAW	134+12	(146)
Stuart TERRY	141+2	(143)
Nicky DAWS	130+10	(140)
Ricky HARRIS	130+7	(137)
Stan ALLAN	127+2	(129)
Graham BENNETT	102+17	(119)
Steve CROSS	113	(113)
John ROGERS	109	(109)
Paul ROWLANDS	103+4	(107)
David CONSTANTINE	104+2	(106)
Malcolm BAILEY	101+5	(106)

Jason Gallagher.
Photo: Colin Stevens.

John Timmons scores
against Boston United
Photo: John Rooney.

LEADING GOALSCORERS

BENNETT Graham	62
ELLIS Ronnie	59(4p)
JOHNSON Jeff	46
ROGERS John	45
HEATHCOTE Graham	45(9p)
TERRY Stuart	44(13p)
HOWARD Barry	41
McKENNA Ken	41
ANDERSON Gary	37(1p)
DAVISON John	34(10p)
WHITBREAD Barry	33
SHAW Nigel	33(5p)

ALTRINCHAM APPEARANCES	79-80	80-81	81-82	82-83	83-84	84-85	85-86	86-87	87-88	88-89	89-90	90-91	91-92	92-93	93-94	94-95	95-96	96-97	97-98	98-99	99-00	TOTAL
ADAMS Brian									2+2													2+2
ADAMS Danny																					41	41
AINSCOW Andy								7+2														7+2
ALCIDE Colin														2+1								2+1
ALLAN Andy																	3+5					3+5
ALLAN Stan	37	38	32	20+1	0+1																	127+2
ALMAN Steve			0+1																			0+1
ANDERSON Gary			1	15+2		32+2	35	25+2				26	31									165+6
ANDERSON Lee																	7+2					7+2
ARMSTRONG Darren																	0+3					0+3
ASPINALL John							5+2															5+2
AYORINDE Sam																		6				6
BAILEY Malcolm	32	25+2	17+1	25+1	2+1																	101+5
BAKER Ian												1										1
BAKER Martin										25+1	41											67+1
BAKER Wayne														2	2							4
BANNER Nick			4																			4
BARROW Graham	23+1	38																				61+1
BECKFORD Jason																		3				3
BELL Willie															6							6
BENNETT Graham				26+5	28+8	33+3	15+1															102+17
BERRYMAN Steve			3																			3
BILLINGTON Ian													11									11
BIRCH Jimmy									17+2													17+2
BISHOP Eddie								15+6	14+2													29+8
BOLLAND Phil																0+1	3+3					3+4
BRADSHAW Charlie														9+6								9+6
BRADY John					8	2+2						30+2	18+3									58+7
BROOKE Mickey	2+1																					2+1
BROWN Andrew																		10+1				10+1
BROWN Richard																		7				7
BURKE Brendan																					18+4	18+4
BURNS Paul													8+4									8+4
BURTON Simon															2							2
BUTCHER John									34	9												43

ALTRINCHAM APPEARANCES	79-80	80-81	81-82	82-83	83-84	84-85	85-86	86-87	87-88	88-89	89-90	90-91	91-92	92-93	93-94	94-95	95-96	96-97	97-98	98-99	99-00	TOTAL
BUTLER Barry															1	25+7	31+2	9				66+9
BUXTON Steve							4+4															4+4
BYRNE Chris									2+2	6+4												8+6
BYRNE Peter											9+14	4+5						5				18+19
CAIN Peter																		2+10				2+10
CANTELLO Len				4																		4
CARMODY Mick														32+2	38	36	27+2	20+2				153+6
CARRODUS Frank								0+2														0+2
CARROLL Steve																		3+14				3+14
CARTER Mike													2+1									2+1
CAVANAH John			10+5	2+1																		12+6
CHALLENDER Greg																	4+1					4+1
CHAMBERS Leroy																					20+6	20+6
CHAPMAN Campbell									1													1
CHESTERS Colin						21	13+2															34+2
CHILTON Tony													4									4
CLANCY Mark																	2					2
CLARKE Tim															12							12
COBURN Stuart																					9	9
COCKRAM Dave															3+5	2+4	1+1					6+10
COLLINGS Paul															26	42	25					93
COLLINS Jimmy									2+1													2+1
CONNAUGHTON John	15	38	34																			87
CONNING Peter					0+2	27+1	31+4															58+7
CONSTABLE Shaun																5+15						5+15
CONSTANTINE David				31+1	36	37+1																104+2
CONWAY Chris			1																			1
COOK Chris											5											5
COOK Neil										14+3												14+3
COX Paul																0+2						0+2
COY Bobby									2													2
CRAVEN Steve					2																	2
CRERAND Danny										3+1												3+1
CREWE John									0+4													0+4
CROFT Brian																		1				1

ALTRINCHAM APPEARANCES	79-80	80-81	81-82	82-83	83-84	84-85	85-86	86-87	87-88	88-89	89-90	90-91	91-92	92-93	93-94	94-95	95-96	96-97	97-98	98-99	99-00	TOTAL
CROMPTON Jonathan											8+7											8+7
CROSS Steve															29	42	42					113
CROSSLEY Ivan	3+2	3+4	18+1																			24+7
CROWE Barry																					0+2	0+2
CRUICKSHANK Paul					21																	21
CUDDY Paul			13	28+1	32+2	31+3	29	29+10	39+1	37												238+17
DANCE Trevor					29	42	2															73
DARCY Colin	6																					6
DAUGHTRY Paul																	2+1					2+1
DAVIES Mark													4									4
DAVIES Steve											1+1											1+1
DAVISON John	36	38	35	41	40	42	33+1	5+2														270+3
DAWS Nicky									4	18+5	27+3	42	39+2									130+10
DAWS Tony																		6				6
DEMPSEY Mark															12+1							12+1
DENNIS Ray														7								7
DENSMORE Peter							18	34					34+2									86+2
DERBYSHIRE Phil					28+3																	28+3
DIAMOND Barry											7+1											7+1
DICKINS Matt																		42				42
DOHERTY Martin																					0+3	0+3
DOHERTY Mick															9							9
DOHERTY Neil																	15+1	39				54+1
DOHERTY Tommy										2												2
DONNACHIE Danny															0+1							0+1
DONNELLEY John					11+1																	11+1
DUNN Joey										4+3												4+3
DUNNE Tony							0+1															0+1
DYKE Colin							1+1															1+1
DYSON Carl									6	1+4				16+5								23+9
EASTER Graham											3											3
EDWARDS Elfyn						38	20															58
EDWARDS Levi							4+2															4+2
EDWARDS Paul								35+2	21													56+2
EDWARDS Terry													36+1									36+1

ALTRINCHAM APPEARANCES	79-80	80-81	81-82	82-83	83-84	84-85	85-86	86-87	87-88	88-89	89-90	90-91	91-92	92-93	93-94	94-95	95-96	96-97	97-98	98-99	99-00	TOTAL
ELLENDER Paul																					11	11
ELLIS Ronnie				9	38+1	25+1	29+3	38+1	38+1	33	9+3											219+10
ELLISON Kevin																					36+1	36+1
EMMETT Darren														4								4
ENTWISTLE Wayne											12											12
ESDAILLE Dave															4+1							4+1
ESSER David					9+3																	9+3
FAGAN Mick						37	6+1															43+1
FARRAR Mick														16								16
FARRELL Terry										15+2												15+2
FARRELLY Mike							33+2	41	32+2	37	8+4											151+8
FRANCE Paul														39	41	41	41+1	31+2				193+3
FRASER Bobby								37	41+1	6												84+1
FREEMAN Clive														26+6								26+6
GALLAGHER Jason																					36+1	36+1
GAMBLE David											9+4	8										17+4
GARDNER Dave																						1
GARDNER Phil			23	33+5	29+3	42	35+1	8+12														170+21
GLASSAR Tony			1																			1
GOODWIN Shaun																					11+2	11+2
GORTON Andy														9	2							11
GOULDING Derek			23																			23
GREEN Andy										14+2					15	35+1	14+1					78+4
GREEN Russell														13+1	18+9							31+10
GREENHOUGH Ricky											6											6
GRESTY Simon													0+1	0+1								0+2
GREYGOOSE Dean																					18+1	18+1
HALL Derek																	3+1					3+1
HAMILL Stewart								14+5														14+5
HANCHARD Martin								2	7+3	4												13+3
HARDMAN Mick						7																7
HARDY Niell																	26+7	30+3				56+10
HARRIS Ricky										2+2				34+3	37+1	16	10+1	31				130+7
HARRIS Sam																		1+1				1+1
HATTON Ben																0+3						0+3

Above: Graham Heathcote takes a free-kick with Jeff Johnson making a dummy run
Photo: John Rooney

Left: Nigel Shaw and Andy Reid. defend against Kettering Town
Photo: Mick Cheney.

Right: Jeff Wealands clears a Farnborough Town attack.

Below: Anderson, Bennett and Reid in attack against Wealdstone.
Photo: John Rooney

ALTRINCHAM APPEARANCES	79-80	80-81	81-82	82-83	83-84	84-85	85-86	86-87	87-88	88-89	89-90	90-91	91-92	92-93	93-94	94-95	95-96	96-97	97-98	98-99	99-00	TOTAL
HAW Steve		4									11+1											15+1
HAWKINS Kevan										9+1												9+1
HAWSE Steve																					25+3	25+3
HAYDE Mike													9+3	20+9	22							51+12
HEATHCOTE Graham	22+4	30+3	31+2	27+5	20+1	11+3																142+18
HEESOM Darren									7	31+3	14+2				18	41	37+2	36				184+7
HEMMINGS Tony																					0+2	0+2
HENSHAW Mark										6+1												6+1
HIGGINBOTTOM Paul								0+2	1+1													1+3
HILDITCH Mark								1+1														1+1
HODGERT Carl									3+2					3								6+2
HODSON Simeon																					33+1	33+1
HOOLEY Gary					3																	3
HORRIGAN Ian																	2+2	19+6				21+8
HOWARD Barry	36+1	38	35	40	9+1																	158+2
HOYLAND Jamie																					0+1	0+1
HUGHES John				6+1																		6+1
HUGHES Mark											26	12+13	8+13		3+2		6+4					55+32
HULMES Gary		4+1																				4+1
IMRIE John									2+2													2+2
IRO Lawrence			8+2						15+3	5												29+5
JACKSON Phil							6	1	8													15
JARDINE Jamie																		3				3
JOHN Jerome																	16+1					16+1
JOHNSON David																		5				5
JOHNSON Dick				21																		21
JOHNSON Ian								0+5	25+3	18												43+3
JOHNSON Jeff	37	37	34	39	28+2	27+2	28+2	0+1														230+12
JOHNSON Paul					14																	14
JOHNSON Steve									0+2													0+2
JONES Graham								30+3														30+3
JONES Martin																	1					1
JONES Paul														0+4								0+4
KELLY Neil												0+6										0+6
KELLY Tony																	9					9

ALTRINCHAM APPEARANCES	79-80	80-81	81-82	82-83	83-84	84-85	85-86	86-87	87-88	88-89	89-90	90-91	91-92	92-93	93-94	94-95	95-96	96-97	97-98	98-99	99-00	TOTAL
KENYON Roger																						41
KEY Lance																					15	15
KIELTY Ged																					8+3	8+3
KILNER Andy									9+2	9+6												18+8
KILSHAW Brian													3+4									3+4
KING Jeff					7																	7
KING John	34	32+1	24																			90+1
KNOWLES Barry										15	12											27
LANDON Richard																					14+22	14+22
LEAROYD Steve														3								3
LEE Andy								32+1					30+1									62+2
LEES Terry																	1					1
LEITCH Grant				8																		8
LEWIS Martin											6	9+5	23+2									38+7
LIMBERT Marc																		14				14
LLOYD David														1								1
LOOKER Damian							4															4
LOVELOCK Andy																					4+27	4+27
LUNT Ian								0+1														0+1
MACFADZEAN John															1							1
MADDOX Mark																		23			17+1	40+1
MANN Adrian									2													2
MARTINDALE Dave																2						2
MAY Leroy															2+1							2+1
McCARRICK Mark												12										12
McDONALD Alan													10+4									10+4
McGOONA Danny																		15+3				15+3
McGREAL Phil			11+1	4																		15+1
McKENNA Ken												39	35									74
McMAHON John							13+3				28+5											41+8
McMULLEN Gary							1															1
MELLISH Stewart											3+2				1							4+2
MILLER Tommy												25	1									26
MOORE Mike																		0+9				0+9
MORAN D									1													1

ALTRINCHAM APPEARANCES	79-80	80-81	81-82	82-83	83-84	84-85	85-86	86-87	87-88	88-89	89-90	90-91	91-92	92-93	93-94	94-95	95-96	96-97	97-98	98-99	99-00	TOTAL
MORGAN Alan																		3				3
MORLEY Andy			3+1																			3+1
MORRELL Mike																					8+4	8+4
MORRIS Andrew				8																		8
MORTON Neil																27+1						27+1
MOUNTFORD Keith										12												12
MURRAY Eddie											16+6											16+6
MYCOCK Dave											0+2											0+2
NESBITT Walter												3+1										3+1
NEWELL Andy														6								6
NEWTON Doug							22+1															22+1
NIEMAN Albie				2																		2
OGLEY Mark														32+1	17							49+1
OLIVER Darren																	10+5					10+5
O'NEILL Steve																18+7	1+1					19+8
OWENS John	38	31+1	21+3																			90+4
PAGE Don				3+1	8+12	1+1					4											16+14
PALADINO Joe														13								13
PARKER Jeff									6+1													6+1
PARRY Bill										5+3												5+3
PARSLEY Neil								1														1
PENNINGTON Steve															4+1							4+1
PHILIPS Steve										1+1												1+1
PICKERING Ally																					5	5
POLLITT Mike														5								5
POWELL Gary															9+2							9+2
POWER Phil																					17+7	17+7
PRICE Gavin																					6+2	6+2
PRITCHARD Dean																	10	9+2				19+2
PYBUS Darren																		1+3				1+3
QUINN Stuart																					1	1
RAFFERTY Nick										0+1												0+1
RAMOON Lee																0+3						0+3
RAYMOND Steve														2+2	1+2							3+4
REID Andy											35+2	29+2	34	25		34+1	26	0+3				183+8

ALTRINCHAM APPEARANCES	79-80	80-81	81-82	82-83	83-84	84-85	85-86	86-87	87-88	88-89	89-90	90-91	91-92	92-93	93-94	94-95	95-96	96-97	97-98	98-99	99-00	TOTAL
REID Paul							41	21+3														62+3
RICHARDS Alan														0+2	6+2							6+4
RIMMER Neil																		5				5
ROBERTS Steve										2	1	4	6									13
ROGERS John	35	30	32	12																		109
ROONEY Andy											19	16+1										35+1
ROSS Trevor									5													5
ROUND Paul			12+1	2																		14+1
ROWLANDS Paul											39	39	22+1		3+3							103+4
ROYLE Darren																	4+11	0+1				4+12
RUDGE Simon													20+5	6+1								26+6
RUSSELL Keith																					29	29
RUTTER Tim				2																		2
RYAN Tim																		5				5
SAUNDERS Steve														33+1	5							38+1
SENIOR Ian					2																	2
SERELLA Dave					7	1																8
SHARPE Phil														2+3								2+3
SHARRATT Chris															10	39	21	11+3				81+3
SHAW Nigel										19	33+3	40	29+4			13+5						134+12
SHEPHERD George																		20+1				20+1
SHOWLER Paul												41										41
SIDDERLEY Ray														38								38
SIMPSON Gary											22+1	2										24+1
SKEETE Leo					30																	30
SKELTON Craig																					1+3	1+3
SMITH Andy															1+1							1+1
SMITH Gareth				21	11																	32
SMITH John														21+3	13+1							34+4
SMITH Ossie									37+2	6												43+2
SMITH Richard									1													1
SMITH Tommy						6+4																6+4
STAMPER Graham										0+1												0+1
STAUNTON Chris												2+2										2+2
STEPNEY Alex	17		1																			18

ALTRINCHAM APPEARANCES	79-80	80-81	81-82	82-83	83-84	84-85	85-86	86-87	87-88	88-89	89-90	90-91	91-92	92-93	93-94	94-95	95-96	96-97	97-98	98-99	99-00	TOTAL
STEWART Gary								14	21+7	25+2	5											65+9
STRANGE Andrew															6+1							6+1
STRANGE Steve															1+3							1+3
TALBOT Gary																					38	38
TERRY Stuart															27+2	34	40	40				141+2
THOMPSON Ian														5								6
TIMMONS John								31+1	32+1	19												82+2
TIMONS Chris																					34+1	34+1
TOBIN Graham	5	3+1																				8+1
TODD Allan			2																			2
TREES Robert																					2	2
TUNNACLIFFE Ian														21	9							30
VINCE James										0+1												0+1
WALKER Phil									2													2
WALKER Stuart																					0+1	0+1
WALLACE Ray																					1	1
WEALANDS Jeff							34	41		28	41	38	20									202
WHALLEY Neil																10	19					29
WHITBREAD Barry	29	33+1	29+2																			91+3
WIGGINS Harry												40	24+3									64+3
WILLIAMS Colin									5+5													5+5
WILLIAMS Mark																		2+1				2+1
WILLIAMS Paul																		5+2				5+2
WILSON Phil	11+3																					11+3
WILSON Robert														6+2								6+2
WILSON Scott																					3+2	3+2
WOOD Nicky											2											2
WOODHEAD Simon														36+4	18+3							54+7
WORRALL Garry									18													18
WORRALL Steve													1+1									1+1
WRIGHT Mark															3							3
YOUNG Neil												0+3										0+3
ZUMRUTEL Soner																	3+1					3+1

Shaun Constable. Photo: Colin Stevens.

Nicky Daws.

Paul France & Charlie Bradshaw. Photo: C.Roberts.

Andy Reid. Photo: Dave West.

,Alty's England caps in 1982 : John Davison and Barry Howard (standing) with Jeff Johnson and John Rogers.   Photo: Bob Thomas

Paul Showler. Photo: Dave West.

ALTRINCHAM GOALSCORERS	79-80	80-81	81-82	82-83	83-84	84-85	85-86	86-87	87-88	88-89	89-90	90-91	91-92	92-93	93-94	94-95	95-96	96-97	97-98	98-99	99-00	TOTAL
AINSCOW Andy								1														1
ALLAN Andy																	1					1
ALLAN Stan	2																					2
ANDERSON Gary				1		5	7	9				5	10(1p)									37(1p)
ASPINALL John							2															2
AYORINDE Sam																		2				2
BAILEY Malcolm	1	2	1	3																		7
BAKER Martin										1	4											5
BARROW Graham	2	8																				10
BELL Willie															2							2
BENNETT Graham				15	17	20	10															62
BIRCH Jimmy									1													1
BISHOP Eddie								8	5													13
BOLLAND Phil																	1					1
BRADSHAW Charlie														5								5
BRADY John					1							14	4(1p)									19(1p)
BURKE Brendan																					2(1p)	2(1p)
BURNS Paul													2									2
BUTLER Barry																1	2					3
BUXTON Steve							1															1
BYRNE Chris										1												1
BYRNE Peter											2(1p)											2(1p)
CAIN Paul																		1				1
CARMODY Mick														2			1					3
CHAMBERS Leroy																					1	1
CHESTERS Colin						5	6															11
COCKRAM Dave															1	1						2
CONNING Peter						6	7															13
CONSTABLE Shaun																3						3
CRAVEN Steve					1																	1
CROSS Steve															2	2						4
CRUICKSHANK Paul					1																	1
CUDDY Paul									1													1
DAVISON John	5(1p)	5(3p)		8	8(5p)	4(1p)																34(10p)
DAWS Nicky									1	1	1	6	4									13
DENSMORE Peter								1														1
DERBYSHIRE Phil					1																	1
DIAMOND Barry											2											2
DOHERTY Mick															1(1p)							1(1p)

John Rogers scores with support from John Owens Photo: John Rooney.

Clive Freeman. Photo: E. Joy Griffiths.

Gary Anderson. Photo: Colin Stevens.

Ronnie Ellis scores with this twenty-yard effort against Enfield. Photo: John Rooney.

ALTRINCHAM GOALSCORERS	79-80	80-81	81-82	82-83	83-84	84-85	85-86	86-87	87-88	88-89	89-90	90-91	91-92	92-93	93-94	94-95	95-96	96-97	97-98	98-99	99-00	TOTAL
DOHERTY Neil																						10
DONNELLEY John																						1
DUNN Joey										1												1
DYSON Carl									5													6
EASTER Graham											3											3
EDWARDS Eifyn						1	2															3
EDWARDS Paul								3														3
EDWARDS Tony													2									2
ELLIS Ronnie				4	5	7	5	8	10	17(4p)	3											59(4p)
ELLISON Kevin																					14	14
EMMETT Darren														1								1
ENTWISTLE Wayne											2											2
FAGAN Mick						3																3
FARRELL Terry										1												1
FARRELLY Mike							2	7(5p)	4	2(1p)												15(6p)
FRANCE Paul														7	3	6	4	2				22
FRASER Bobby								2	1													3
FREEMAN Clive														8(2p)								8(2p)
GALLAGHER Jason																					2	2
GARDNER Phil			1	1	2	2																7
GOULDING Derek			2																			2
GREEN Andy										1					5	19	3					28
GREEN Russell														3	2							5
GREENHOUGH Ricky								1			2(1p)											2(1p)
HAMILL Stewart									1													1
HANCHARD Martin																						1
HARDY Neill																	10	14				24
HARRIS Ricky										1				4	7	5	2	3				22
HAW Steve			1								4			1								5
HAYDE Mike			1																			1
HEATHCOTE Graham	7(1p)	17(4p)	12(1p)	4	2(1p)	3(2p)																45(9p)
HEESOM Darren																1	1					2
HENSHAW Mark										1												1
HODGERT Carl									1													1
HOOLEY Gary					1																	1
HOWARD Barry	12	9	10	10																		41
HUGHES Mark											8	8	2									18
JOHNSON David																		2				2
JOHNSON Ian									3													3

37

ALTRINCHAM GOALSCORERS	79-80	80-81	81-82	82-83	83-84	84-85	85-86	86-87	87-88	88-89	89-90	90-91	91-92	92-93	93-94	94-95	95-96	96-97	97-98	98-99	99-00	TOTAL
JOHNSON Jeff	6	7	9	11	9	3	1															46
KELLY Tony																	1					1
KENYON Roger																					1	1
KIELTY Ged			1																			1
KILNER Andy										1												1
KING Jeff					1(1p)																	1(1p)
KING John	3	2	3																			8
KNOWLES Barry										1	1(1p)											2(1p)
LANDON Richard																					11(2p)	11(2p)
LEE Andy								3														3
LEWIS Martin													2									2
LIMBERT Marc																		1				1
LOOKER Damien							1															1
LOVELOCK Andy												2										2
McCARRICK Mark																					2	2
McDONALD Alan													2									2
McGOONA Danny																		3				3
McGREAL Phil			6	2																		8
McKENNA Ken												22	19									41
McMAHON John											5(1p)											5(1p)
MORRELL Mike																					1	1
MORTON Neil																10(1p)						10(1p)
MOUNTFORD Keith										2												2
MURRAY Eddie											3											3
NEWTON Doug							8															8
OGLEY Mark														1	2							3
OLIVER Darren																	1					1
ONEILL Steve																4						4
PAGE Don				1	3																	4
PARKER Jeff									2													2
PENNINGTON Steve															1							1
POWELL Gary															1							1
POWER Phil																					3	3
PRICE Gavin																					2	2
PRITCHARD Dean																	3	1				4
PYBUS Darren																		1				1
RAMOON Lee																1						1
RAYMOND Steve														2								2
REID Andy												1				3						5

ALTRINCHAM GOALSCORERS	79-80	80-81	81-82	82-83	83-84	84-85	85-86	86-87	87-88	88-89	89-90	90-91	91-92	92-93	93-94	94-95	95-96	96-97	97-98	98-99	99-00	TOTAL
REID Paul							11	4														15
RICHARDS Alan															2							2
ROGERS John	19	16	9	1																		45
ROONEY Andy												1										1
ROUND Paul			1																			1
ROWLANDS Paul											3	5	1									9
ROYLE Darren																	1					1
RUDGE Simon													1									1
RUSSELL Keith																					4	4
SAUNDERS Steve														2(1p)								2(1p)
SERELLA Dave					1																	1
SHARRATT Chris															3	6	6	1				16
SHAW Nigel									4		4	12(1p)	10(3p)			3(1p)						33(5p)
SHOWLER Paul												7										7
SKEETE Leo					8																	8
SMITH John														3								3
SMITH Ossie									7	1												8
SMITH Tommy						2																2
STEWART Gary								2	7(1p)	8(1p)												17(2p)
STRANGE Andrew															2							2
TALBOT Gary																					5	5
TERRY Stuart															5(1p)	12(3p)	15(7p)	12(2p)				44(13p)
THOMPSON Ian														1								1
TIMMONS John								16	8	4												28
TIMONS Chris																					2	2
TOBIN Graham	1																					1
TUNNACLIFF Ian														5								5
WHALLEY Neil																	1					1
WHITBREAD Barry	16	7	10																			33
WIGGINS Harry												1										1
WILSON Phil	1																					1
WOOD Nicky											1											1
WOODHEAD Simon									1													1
WORRALL Garry														3								3
YOUNG Neil												1										1

Ronnie Ellis directs a header towards the Macclesfield Town goal in what was to prove to be a disappointing 'derby' result for Altrincham, Macclesfield coming out on top by 3-1 with Burr scoring a hat-trick.

Photo: John Rooney.

Stan Allan.

John Brady vollies Altrincham into a 2-0 lead over Kettering Town.
Photo: John Rooney.

A.P. LEAMINGTON

FOUNDER MEMBER
elected from Southern League
RELEGATED TO: Southern League 1982
Disbanded 1985, Reformed as Leamington F.C. 2000
2004-2005 SEASON: Midland Combination

1981-82 Squad.
Back Row (L-R): Jack Chapman, Paul cooper, Alan Jones, Sean Hemming, Malcolm Kavanagh, Gordon Livesy, Cliff Campbell, Ian Britton, Graham Alner.
Front Row: Trevor Smith, Kim Casey, Graham McKenzie, Alan Ollis, Phil Griffin, Roy Morton.

	SEASONS
	3

SEASONS
3

TOTAL POINTS
44 + 34 = 78

HIGHEST POSITION
16 (80-81)

LOWEST POSITION
22 (81-82)

HIGHEST ATTENDANCE
818 v Worcester C (8-12-79)

LOWEST ATTENDANCE
197 v Stafford R (9-3-82)

SEASON GOALSCORER
Doug Hickton 12 (80/81)

CAREER GOALSCORER
Duncan Gardner 21

CAREER APPEARANCES
Alan Jones 104+1

	HOME						AWAY						
	P	W	D	L	F	A	Pts	P	W	D	L	F	A	Pts	Position
79-80	19	5	5	9	16	27	15	19	2	6	11	16	36	10	18
80-81	19	6	7	6	29	26	19	19	4	4	11	18	40	12	16
81-82	21	1	7	13	20	44	10	21	3	3	15	20	61	12	22
Total	59	12	19	28	65	97	44	59	9	13	37	54	137	34	

	Altrincham		Bangor City		Barnet		Barrow		Bath City		Boston United		Dagenham		Dartford		Enfield	
	H	A	H	A	H	A	H	A	H	A	H	A	H	A	H	A	H	A
79-80	1-4	0-3	1-1	2-3	2-1	0-1	0-1	2-6	1-2	0-0	2-0	0-2						
80-81	2-4	1-4	1-0	0-1	0-1	0-1	2-2	2-0	0-4	0-5	0-0	3-2						
81-82	0-1	3-2			0-1	0-0	1-1	2-4	0-1	0-7	2-2	0-2	0-4	0-0	0-2	2-2	2-3	1-6

	Frickley Athletic		Gravesend & Northfleet		Kettering Town		Maidstone United		Northwich Victoria		Nuneaton Borough		Redditch United		Runcorn		Scarborough	
	H	A	H	A	H	A	H	A	H	A	H	A	H	A	H	A	H	A
79-80			0-1	2-3	1-3	1-1	0-2	0-0	2-2	1-2	0-0	1-1	0-2	1-3			1-1	0-5
80-81	2-2	0-0	4-1	0-4	3-3	0-3	2-3	1-2	1-1	0-2	0-1	0-3					2-0	0-0
81-82	1-0	1-4	3-3	1-4	3-3	2-1	1-1	0-4	0-2	0-3					1-1	0-3	1-2	1-6

	Stafford Rangers		Telford United		Trowbridge Town		Wealdstone		Weymouth		Worcester City		Yeovil Town	
	H	A	H	A	H	A	H	A	H	A	H	A	H	A
79-80	2-0	1-1	2-1	1-0			0-0	2-2	0-2	1-2	1-0	1-1	0-4	0-1
80-81	1-1	1-1	5-0	3-2			1-1	2-1	0-1	2-3	2-1	3-3	1-0	0-3
81-82	1-5	1-3	0-2	0-2	0-1	1-2			2-2	2-1	0-1	1-2	2-5	2-3

(Left) Alan Dulleston kept goal for the club in 1979-80, the first ever APL season. (Centre) Full-back Paul Cooper was a regular fixture throughout Brakes' three-season tenure in the APL. (Right) Non league legend Kim Casey joined Brakes mid-way through what proved to be their final APL campaign. The striker helped them to the Southern League Premier Division title a year later before jumping ship to Kidderminster Harriers with manager Graham Allner and several team-mates. Photos: Courtesy of Leamington Courier.

		HOME						AWAY				
	P	W	D	L	F	A	P	W	D	L	F	A
ALTRINCHAM	3	0	0	3	3	9	3	1	0	2	4	9
BANGOR C	2	1	1	0	2	1	2	0	0	2	2	4
BARNET	3	1	0	2	2	4	3	0	1	2	0	2
BARROW	3	0	2	1	3	4	3	1	0	2	6	10
BATH C	3	0	0	3	1	7	3	0	1	2	0	12
BOSTON U	3	1	2	0	4	2	3	1	0	2	3	6
DAGENHAM	1	0	0	1	0	4	1	0	1	0	0	0
DARTFORD	1	0	0	1	0	2	1	0	1	0	2	2
ENFIELD	1	0	0	1	2	3	1	0	0	1	1	6
FRICKLEY A	2	1	1	0	3	2	2	0	1	1	1	4
GRAVESEND & N	3	1	1	1	7	5	3	0	0	3	3	11
KETTERING T	3	0	2	1	7	9	3	1	1	1	3	5
MAIDSTONE U	3	0	1	2	3	6	3	0	1	2	1	6
NORTHWICH V	3	0	2	1	3	5	3	0	0	3	1	7
NUNEATON B	2	0	1	1	0	1	2	0	1	1	1	4
REDDITCH U	1	0	0	1	0	2	1	0	0	1	1	3
RUNCORN	1	0	1	0	1	1	1	0	0	1	0	3
SCARBOROUGH	3	1	1	1	4	3	3	0	1	2	1	11
STAFFORD R	3	1	1	1	4	6	3	0	2	1	3	5
TELFORD U	3	2	0	1	7	3	3	2	0	1	4	4
TROWBRIDGE T	1	0	0	1	0	1	1	0	0	1	1	2
WEALDSTONE	2	0	2	0	1	1	2	2	0	0	4	2
WEYMOUTH	3	0	1	2	2	5	3	1	0	2	5	6
WORCESTER C	3	2	0	1	3	2	3	0	2	1	5	6
YEOVIL T	3	1	0	2	3	9	3	0	0	3	2	7
TOTALS	59	12	19	28	65	97	59	9	13	37	54	137

GOALSCORERS

	79/80	80/81	81/82	TOTAL
ASHENDEN Russell		1	3	4
BAIN Roger	1			1
BRISCOE Steve	5			5
BROWN Gary		4	2	6
CAMPBELL Cliff			2	2
CASEY Kim			11	11
COOPER Paul	1		1	2
DERBY Lennie	1			1
FARRINGTON John		3		3
GARDNER Duncan	12	9	1	22
GORMAN Tommy	3	5	5(1p)	13(1p)
GRIFFIN Phil			1	1
HICKTON Doug		12		12
JENNINGS Kirk			1	1
JONES Alan		2(1p)	1	3(1p)
KAVANAGH Gary			1	1
KELLY Errington		2		2
KILKELLY Tom	4(2p)	1	1(1p)	6(3p)
LEWIS Nick			2	2
McNULTY J	2			2
MEE Paul		1		1
MONTGOMERY Paul		1	2	3
OLLIS Alan			4	4
RIGBY Steve			1	1
SMITH Trevor			1	1
TAYLOR Micky		5		5

APPEARANCES

	79/80	80/81	81/82	TOTAL
ASHENDEN Russell		21+1	33+4	54+5
BAIN Roger	17+4			17+4
BRISCOE Steve	34			34
BROWN Gary	26+1	35	21	82+1
CAMPBELL Cliff			11	11
CASEY Kim			26	26
COOPER Paul	27	31	38	96
DERBY Lennie	7+1			7+1
DIGHT Chris	13			13
DULLESTON Alan	38	27		65
FARRINGTON John		37	7	44
GARDNER Duncan	37	36	13	86
GARNER Tim			1	1
GORMAN Tommy	26+1	31+1	31+1	88+3
GRIFFIN Phil			16+4	16+4
HALL Ken			15	15
HEMMINGS Sean			2	2
HICKTON Doug		29		29
HOUSTON Frank	2			2
JAYES Carl		11		11
JENNINGS Kirk			6+4	6+4
JOHNSON Howard		1		1
JONES Alan	32+1	37	35	**104+1**
KAVANAGH Gary			3+2	3+2
KAVANAGH Malcolm			19	19
KELLY Errington		4+2		4+2
KILKELLY Tom	34+1	19+2	9	62+3
KNIGHT Bob			1	1
LEWIS Nick			7+1	7+1
LIVSEY Gordon			23	23
McNULTY J	16+1			16+1
MEE Paul		7+3		7+3
MONTGOMERY Paul	28	31	31	90
MONTGOMERY Steve			0+1	0+1
MORTON Roy	14+1		2+1	16+2
MUIR Maurice		0+1	5+1	5+2
OLLIS Alan			16+1	16+1
RAINBOW Mal	4			4
RANKIN Brian			8	8
RIGBY Steve			30+1	30+1
SLAUGHTER Steve			4	4
SMITH Trevor			21	21
STARKEY Tom	1			1
TAYLOR Dennis	37	24+2		61+2
TAYLOR Micky	8	37+1	28+3	73+4
VINCENT Bobby	15+2			15+2
WOODHOUSE John	2			2

AYLESBURY UNITED

PROMOTED FROM: Southern League 1988
RELEGATED TO: Isthmian League 1989
2004-2005 SEASON: Southern Premier League

1988-89 Squad. Back (L-R): Colin Barker, Cliff Hercules, Nick Taylor, Tim Garner, Petter Hutter, Peter Robinson, Rowan Dodds, Bob Coy, Paul Saunders, Pat Smith (Physio). Front: Gary Harthill, Kevin James, Derek Duggan, David Botterill, Trevor Gould (Manager), Adrian Mann, Adrian O'Dowd, Brendon Phillips, Paul Hackett.

SEASON 1988-89
HIGHEST ATTENDANCE 2406 v Wycombe W 26.12.88
LOWEST ATTENDANCE 742 v Welling U 4.4.89
SEASON GOALSCORER Cliff Hercules 11 (88/89)
SEASON APPEARANCES Peter Hutter 40

	HOME						AWAY						
P	W	D	L	F	A	Pts	P	W	D	L	F	A	Pts	Position
20	7	4	9	27	30	25	20	2	5	13	16	41	11	20

APPEARANCES cont.

	88-89
HARTHILL Gary	25+4
HERCULES Cliff	32+1
HUTTER Peter	**40**
JAMES Kevin	12+3
KING Andy	2
LAWRENCE Les	18+1
LISSAMAN Jeff	27
MANN Adrian	12+3
O'DOWD Adrian	16
PHILLIPS Brendan	14+5
POOLE Gary	2
PREECE Andy	4
ROBINSON Peter	2+2
SAUNDERS Paul	11
SEASMAN John	15
SMITH Herbie	2+1
TAYLOR Nick	4
TURNER Paul	1
WILSON Junior	33

APPEARANCES

	88-89
ALTENOR Albert	5+3
ANGOL Ivor	13
BOTTERILL Dave	7
BOYLAND Mark	19+1
COY Bobby	25
DAY Kevin	9
DODDS Rowan	6
DUGGAN Derek	4
ESSEX Steve	32
FRIAR Paul	2
GARNER Tim	36
HACKETT Paul	10+6

GOALSCORERS

	88-89
ALTENOR Albert	1
BOTTERILL Dave	2(1p)
BOYLAND Mark	4
DODDS Rowan	1
DUGGAN Derek	1
ESSEX Steve	2
HACKETT Paul	1
HERCULES Cliff	**11**
HUTTER Peter	6
LAWRENCE Les	1
LISSAMAN Jeff	6(4p)
MANN Adrian	2
O'DOWD Adrian	2
PREECE Andy	1
SMITH Herbie	1

AYLESBURY UNITED

	Altrincham		Barnet		Boston United		Cheltenham Town		Chorley		Enfield		Fisher Athletic		Kettering Town	
	H	A	H	A	H	A	H	A	H	A	H	A	H	A	H	A
88-89	1-2	0-1	1-3	0-1	1-2	0-2	0-0	0-0	4-3	1-1	2-1	1-2	1-1	2-0	0-1	2-5

	Kidderminster H.		Macclesfield Town		Maidstone United		Northwich Victoria		Runcorn		Stafford Rangers		Sutton United		Telford United	
	H	A	H	A	H	A	H	A	H	A	H	A	H	A	H	A
88-89	1-5	3-4	1-2	1-3	1-2	1-1	2-0	1-1	1-2	0-5	1-1	1-3	1-0	2-5	2-0	1-0

	Welling United		Weymouth		Wycombe Wanderers		Yeovil Town	
	H	A	H	A	H	A	H	A
88-89	0-0	0-5	4-1	0-0	0-2	0-1	3-2	0-1

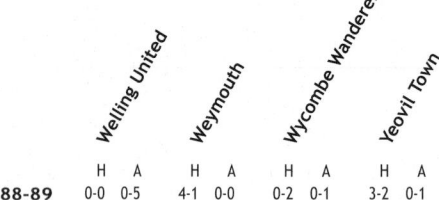

Cliff Hercules.
A local hero and top scorer for the
club for many years.
Photo: Dave West.

Tim Garner bravely smothers
a close range shot.
Photo: Paul Dennis.

BANGOR CITY

FOUNDER MEMBER
ELECTED FROM: Northern Premier League 1979, 1982 (PROMOTED)
RELEGATED TO: Northern Premier League 1981, 1984
2004-2005 SEASON: Welsh Premier League

Back row, left to right: Derek Goulding, L.Davies (Trainer), Paul Whelan, Bernard Purdie, Gareth Hughes, Phil Lunn, Graham Murphy, G.Jones, Mark Gray, Dave Elliott (Manager). Front Row: Mark Carter, Bruce Urquhart, Chris Roberts, Jon Cavanagh, Ian Howat, Andy Lee and Gwynfor Owen.

SEASONS
4

TOTAL POINTS
91 + 59 = 150

HIGHEST POSITION
9th (79-80)

LOWEST POSITION
21st (83-84)

HIGHEST ATTENDANCE
1500 v Altrincham (28-8-79)

LOWEST ATTENDANCE
154 v Maidstone U (25-4-81)

SEASON GOALSCORER
Mark Carter 17(4p) (83/84)

CAREER GOALSCORER
Mark Carter 27(4p)

CAREER APPEARANCES
Phil Lunn 119+2

	HOME							AWAY							
	P	W	D	L	F	A	Pts	P	W	D	L	F	A	Pts	Position
79-80	19	9	6	4	21	18	24	19	5	8	6	20	28	18	9
80-81	19	5	6	8	25	34	16	19	1	6	12	10	34	8	20
81-82															
82-83	21	8	9	4	33	29	33	21	6	4	11	38	48	22	13
83-84	21	7	4	10	35	32	18	21	3	2	16	19	50	11	21
Total	80	29	25	26	114	113	91	80	15	20	45	87	160	59	

	Altrincham		A P Leamington		Barnet		Barrow		Bath City		Boston United		Dagenham		Enfield		Frickley Athletic	
	H	A	H	A	H	A	H	A	H	A	H	A	H	A	H	A	H	A
79-80	1-1	0-5	3-2	1-1	1-1	1-1	1-1	1-1	2-1	1-2	2-0	1-3						
80-81	4-5	0-2	1-0	0-1	4-2	1-0	2-6	0-3	0-1	0-0	1-1	1-1					4-3	0-4
81-82																		
82-83	1-0	0-2			1-0	3-1	2-2	5-1	0-0	2-1	0-1	3-4	1-1	1-1	0-0	2-6	1-0	3-3
83-84	1-3	1-2			0-1	1-3			1-0	1-5	0-0	2-3	2-4	1-3	2-1	1-3	4-1	0-2

	Gateshead		Gravesend & Northfleet		Kettering Town		Kidderminster Harriers		Maidstone United		Northwich Victoria		Nuneaton Borough		Redditch United		Runcorn	
	H	A	H	A	H	A	H	A	H	A	H	A	H	A	H	A	H	A
79-80			1-2	1-1	1-1	1-0			1-0	1-0	0-3	0-4	1-0	2-2	1-0	5-1		
80-81			1-1	0-1	0-1	1-3					1-1	0-1	2-5	2-3				
81-82																		
82-83					4-2	4-3			2-2	1-6	1-1	4-1	5-2	1-2			1-2	2-1
83-84	3-3	1-2			3-1	3-1	1-2	1-2	0-2	0-2	0-1	1-2	1-2	0-3			2-3	2-0

	Home						Away					
	P	W	D	L	F	A	P	W	D	L	F	A
ALTRINCHAM	4	1	1	2	7	9	4	0	0	4	1	11
A P LEAMINGTON	2	2	0	0	4	2	2	0	1	1	1	2
BARNET	4	2	1	1	6	4	4	2	1	1	6	5
BARROW	3	0	2	1	5	9	3	1	1	1	6	5
BATH C	4	2	1	1	3	2	4	1	1	2	4	8
BOSTON U	4	1	2	1	3	2	4	0	1	3	7	11
DAGENHAM	2	0	1	1	3	5	2	0	1	1	2	4
ENFIELD	2	1	1	0	2	1	2	0	0	2	3	9
FRICKLEY A	3	3	0	0	9	4	3	0	1	2	3	9
GATESHEAD	1	0	1	0	3	3	1	0	0	1	1	2
GRAVESEND & N	2	0	1	1	2	3	2	0	1	1	1	2
KETTERING T	4	2	1	1	8	5	4	3	0	1	9	7
KIDDERMINSTER H	1	0	0	1	1	2	1	0	0	1	1	2
MAIDSTONE U	4	1	2	1	4	5	4	1	0	3	2	9
NORTHWICH V	4	0	2	2	1	5	4	1	0	3	6	9
NUNEATON B	4	2	0	2	9	9	4	0	1	3	5	10
REDDITCH U	1	1	0	0	1	0	1	1	0	0	5	1
RUNCORN	2	0	0	2	3	5	2	2	0	0	4	1
SCARBOROUGH	4	1	1	2	2	7	4	0	2	2	1	6
STAFFORD R	3	1	2	0	2	1	3	1	1	1	2	5
TELFORD U	4	2	2	0	8	2	4	0	1	3	2	7
TROWBRIDGE T	2	2	0	0	8	3	2	1	0	1	4	4
WEALDSTONE	4	1	2	1	3	4	4	0	2	2	1	8
WEYMOUTH	4	2	0	2	8	8	4	0	0	4	3	15
WORCESTER C	4	0	1	3	3	9	4	0	4	0	2	2
YEOVIL T	4	2	1	1	6	4	4	1	1	2	5	6
TOTALS	80	29	25	26	114	113	80	15	20	45	87	160

	Scarborough		Stafford Rangers		Telford United		Trowbridge Town		Wealdstone		Weymouth		Worcester City		Yeovil Town	
	H	A	H	A	H	A	H	A	H	A	H	A	H	A	H	A
79-80	1-0	0-0	1-1	1-0	1-1	0-2			1-0	0-0	1-2	2-4	0-2	0-0	1-0	2-1
80-81	0-3	1-1	0-0	0-4	2-0	1-1			0-2	1-1	2-0	0-4	1-1	1-1	0-2	0-1
81-82																
82-83	0-3	0-2	1-0	1-1	1-1	0-2	4-3	2-3	2-2	0-2	4-3	1-2	0-2	1-1	2-2	2-3
83-84	1-1	0-3			4-0	1-2	4-0	2-1	0-0	0-5	1-3	0-5	2-4	0-0	3-0	1-1

BANGOR CITY

APPEARANCES

	79-80	80-81	81-82	82-83	83-84	TOTAL
ATHERTON Dewi	16+1	15+2				31+3
BANKS Jerry					30	30
BANNER Nicky		28				28
BARNES Keith	6+2					6+2
BARNETT Dave	37					37
BENNETT Graham		20				20
BROADHEAD Tony	13+4	4			1	18+4
CARTER Mark				35+4	35	70+4
CAVANAGH Jon				8	37	45
CHARLTON Kevin	27					27
CLAGUE Ian		9				9
COFFEY Dave	15+1					15+1
CRAVEN Steve					11+5	11+5
EDWARDS Gary	2+1	14				16+1
ELLIOTT Dave					0+2	0+2
EVANS Peter					1	1
FEAR Keith				11		11
GOULDING Derek				22	3+1	25+1
GRAY Mark				38+1	29	67+1
GUNN Tony					1+1	1+1
HART Brian		36			3	39
HOLLIS Derek		0+1				0+1
HOWAT Ian				41	24+4	65+4
HUGHES Derek		30+2				30+2
HUGHES Gareth				22	7	29
HUGHES John	25+2	19+2			0+1	44+5
HUGHES M.				1+1		1+1
JONES Brinley					5	5
JONES Clive	5+2					5+2
JONES D.					1	1
JONES Frankie				10+4		10+4

Bruce Urquhart shoots for goal during Bangor's 1983/84 FA Cup tie against Blackpool.

Ian Howat.

Gareth Hughes.

1982-83 Squad - Back Row (L-R): Graham Bennett, Keith Fear, Peter Williams, Phil Tottey, Mark Gray, Meilir Owen, Gwyn Peris Jones. Front Row: Len Davies, Ritchie Gendall, Bruce Urquhart, Dave Elliott, Phil Lunn, Chris Roberts, Andy Lee.

BANGOR CITY   APPEARANCES

	79-80	80-81	81-82	82-83	83-84	TOTAL
JONES Mel				1		1
JONES Selwyn				2		2
JONES Wayne					0+1	0+1
KASPEREK Peter		1+2				1+2
KEEN Mike	6					6
KENWORTHY Steve					4	4
KILNER John				20		20
KING Alan	28	28+1				56+1
LEE Andy				30	0+1	30+1
LETHEREN Glan					32	32
LEWIS Paul	5	4			1	10
LUNN Phil	32	37		18+1	32+1	**119+2**
MATHER Dave	13					13
MOONEY Kevin	12+2					12+2
MORRIS Alan					23+5	23+5
MURPHY Graham				9+3	15+8	24+11
MURPHY Tony	30					30
OLNEY Pat	19+1					19+1
OWEN Dave				1+1		1+1
OWEN Gwynfor				4	13	17
OWEN Mark	2	4				6
OWEN Meilir	31+2	36				67+2
PEEL Bobby					16	16
PERIS-JONES Gwyn	6	21+3		27	10	64+3
PUDDLE Andy					13+7	13+7
PURDIE Bernard				13+1	4	17+1
PYE Tom					1	1
RICKETTS Alan				0+3		0+3
ROBERTS Andy				2+2		2+2
ROBERTS Chris				32+2	1	33+2
ROBERTS Gareth				2+1		2+1
ROBERTS Ian		5+1				5+1
ROBERTS Mike		31				31
RYLANDS Dave	13					13
SARGEANT Jim		34				34
SIMPSON Gary					5+1	5+1
SMITH Jim	38				13+1	51+1
SUTCLIFFE Peter				37	10+3	47+3
TOTTEY Phil	5	10			3	18
URQUHART Bruce				40	25+2	65+2
WALKER Alan	27					27
WESTWOOD Kevin					33+1	33+1
WHELAN Paul				36	19+3	55+3
WILLIAMS Hugh	4	1+5				5+5
WILLIAMS Vivian					1	1
WRIGHT Billy		31				31
YOUNG Tony	1					1

BANGOR CITY GOALSCORERS

	79-80	80-81	81-82	82-83	83-84	TOTAL
BANKS Jerry					1	1
BARNES Keith	1(1p)					1(1p)
BARNETT Dave	3					3
BENNETT Graham		5				5
BROADHEAD Tony	3					3
CARTER Mark				10	17(4p)	27(4p)
COFFEY Mike	2					2
FEAR Keith				5(3p)		5(3p)
GOULDING Derek				2		2
GRAY Mark				3	2	5
HART Brian		3				3
HOWAT Ian				21	3	24
HUGHES Derek		5				5
HUGHES John	3	2				5
JONES Frankie				1		1
KING Alan		1				1
LEWIS Paul	1					1
LUNN Phil		2(2p)				2(2p)
MATHER Dave	6					6
MOONEY Kevin	1					1
MORRIS Alan					3(1p)	3(1p)
MURPHY Graham				3	3	6
MURPHY Tony	3					3
OWEN Meilir	5	9				14
PEEL Bobby					3	3
PERIS-JONES Gwyn				1		1
PUDDLE Alan					2	2
RICKETTS Alan				1		1
ROBERTS Andy				1		1
ROBERTS Mike		4				4
RYLANDS Dave	1					1
SARGEANT Jim		3				3
SIMPSON Gary					1	1
SMITH Jim	10(1p)				2	12(1p)
SUTCLIFFE Peter				7(4p)		7(4p)
URQUHART Bruce				11	9(1p)	20(1p)
WALKER Alan	1					1
WESTWOOD Kevin					5	5
WHELAN Paul				5	2	7

BARNET
FOUNDER MEMBER
ELECTED FROM: Southern League 1979
PROMOTED TO: The Football League 1990-91
RELEGATED FROM: The Football League 2000-01
2004-2005 SEASON: The Conference

1990-91 Squad. Back Row (L-R): Paul Loman (Physio), Herbie Smith, Nicky Ironton, Richard Nugent, Darren Angell, Andy Lomas, Mark Flashman, Frank Murphy, George Reilly, Geoff Cooper, Dave Regis, Gordon Ogboure (Kit man). Front Row: Andy Clarke, David Gipp, Hakan Hayrettin, Phil Stacey, Edwin Stein, Barry Fry (Manager), Wayne Turner, Derek Payne, Gary Bull, Paul Wilson, Alan Crosby.

	HOME							AWAY							Position
	P	W	D	L	F	A	Pts	P	W	D	L	F	A	Pts	
79-80	19	7	6	6	18	18	20	19	3	4	12	14	30	10	17
80-81	19	8	5	6	27	26	21	19	4	2	13	12	38	10	17
81-82	21	5	8	8	17	20	23	21	4	6	11	19	32	18	18
82-83	21	9	3	9	37	39	30	21	7	0	14	18	39	21	15
83-84	21	9	3	9	27	28	21	21	7	7	7	28	30	28	9
84-85	21	9	7	5	36	20	25	21	6	4	11	23	32	22	15
85-86	21	9	4	8	32	23	22	21	4	7	10	24	37	19	14
86-87	21	13	4	4	47	22	43	21	12	6	3	39	17	42	2
87-88	21	15	4	2	57	23	49	21	8	7	6	36	22	31	2
88-89	20	11	2	7	36	30	35	20	7	5	8	28	39	26	8
89-90	21	15	4	2	46	14	49	21	11	3	7	35	27	36	2
90-91	21	13	4	4	50	23	43	21	13	5	3	53	29	44	1
					1991 to 2001										
01-02	21	10	4	7	30	19	34	21	9	6	6	34	29	33	5
02-03	21	9	4	8	32	28	31	21	4	10	7	33	40	22	11
03-04	21	11	6	4	30	17	39	21	8	8	5	30	29	32	4
Total	310	153	68	89	522	350	485	310	107	80	123	426	470	394	

SEASONS
15

TOTAL POINTS
879

HIGHEST POSITION
1st 1990-91

LOWEST POSITION
18th 1981-82

HIGHEST ATTENDANCE
5880 v Darlington 31.3.90

LOWEST ATTENDANCE
410 v Northwich V 24.1.83

SEASON GOALSCORER
Gary Bull 30(8p) (90/91)

CAREER GOALSCORER
Nicky Evans 99(1p)

CAREER APPEARANCES
Edwin Stein 329+15

	Accrington Stanley		Aldershot Town		Altrincham		A P Leamington		Aylesbury United		Bangor City		Barrow		Bath City		Boston United	
	H	A	H	A	H	A	H	A	H	A	H	A	H	A	H	A	H	A
79-80					2-0	0-1	1-0	1-2			1-1	1-1	1-1	1-3	1-0	2-1	0-0	1-1
80-81					3-2	0-2	1-0	1-0			0-1	2-4	0-0	1-1	1-5	0-1	2-2	0-3
81-82					0-0	0-2	0-0	2-0					1-2	1-2	0-1	1-2	0-0	1-1
82-83					2-1	0-3					1-3	0-1	2-1	1-0	2-1	2-0	1-4	0-1
83-84					1-2	2-3					3-1	1-0			1-2	1-0	1-2	0-0
84-85					1-0	2-0							4-0	0-1	2-1	1-2	1-0	1-2
85-86					2-2	0-2							4-1	1-0	1-0	1-1	3-0	2-1
86-87					1-0	0-2									2-1	1-0	5-1	3-0
87-88					3-1	1-1									4-0	1-0	1-0	1-2
88-89					3-0	1-1			1-0	3-1							0-0	0-5
89-90					1-0	1-2							1-0	1-1			1-2	2-1
90-91					0-0	1-4							3-1	2-4	2-0	4-1	5-0	3-1
1991																		
2001																		
01-02																		
02-03																		
03-04	0-0	0-2	2-1	1-1														

	Burton Albion		Cheltenham Town		Chester City		Chorley		Colchester United		Dagenham		Dagenham & Redbridge		Darlington		Dartford	
	H	A	H	A	H	A	H	A	H	A	H	A	H	A	H	A	H	A
79-80																		
80-81																		
81-82											1-2	1-1					2-0	1-2
82-83											2-2	2-1						
83-84											3-1	1-3						
84-85											0-0	0-0					0-1	0-2
85-86			2-2	1-2							4-1	1-2					2-0	3-5
86-87			0-1	2-1							1-0	3-1						
87-88			1-1	2-0							3-2	0-0						
88-89			3-1	2-1			2-4	3-2										
89-90			4-0	0-2			5-0	4-1							0-2	2-1		
90-91			2-1	4-1					1-3	0-0								
1991																		
2001																		
01-02					3-1	0-1							4-0	1-1				
02-03	2-2	3-0			0-3	1-1							2-1	1-5				
03-04	2-1	3-2			0-0	0-1							2-4	2-5				

BARNET

	Doncaster Rovers		Dover Athletic		Enfield		Exeter City		Farnborough Town		Fisher Athletic		Forest Green Rovers		Frickley Athletic		Gateshead	
	H	A	H	A	H	A	H	A	H	A	H	A	H	A	H	A	H	A
79-80																		
80-81															2-0	0-3		
81-82					4-1	0-0									0-0	1-0		
82-83					1-3	0-5									4-1	1-0		
83-84					2-1	1-0									3-2	1-3	0-1	3-2
84-85					3-2	3-3									1-2	1-3	1-1	2-0
85-86					0-1	0-1									1-2	3-3		
86-87					1-0	3-0									3-0	3-0	3-1	5-1
87-88					3-0	0-2					2-0	2-2						
88-89					2-1	0-4					2-3	2-1						
89-90					2-0	3-1			4-1	1-0	4-1	2-1						
90-91											8-1	4-2					1-1	3-1
1991																		
2001																		
01-02	2-0	3-2	2-0	2-2					0-3	1-2			0-1	2-2				
02-03	1-2	1-2							1-2	2-2			2-0	4-4				
03-04							2-3	1-1	0-2	1-1			5-0	1-1				

	Gravesend & N'fleet		Halifax Town		Hayes		Hereford United		Kettering Town		Kidderminster H.		Leigh RMI		Lincoln City		Macclesfield Town	
	H	A	H	A	H	A	H	A	H	A	H	A	H	A	H	A	H	A
79-80	3-0	0-1							0-2	0-1								
80-81	1-1	2-0							0-1	1-2								
81-82	2-0	3-2							2-1	2-5								
82-83									2-3	1-3								
83-84									0-3	1-0	0-2	4-4						
84-85									4-2	0-4	2-4	4-1						
85-86									3-0	1-1	0-1	2-0						
86-87									1-2	1-1	5-2	3-0						
87-88									4-0	1-1	1-1	1-1			4-2	1-2	2-1	2-2
88-89									3-2	1-3	0-2	0-1					1-4	1-1
89-90									4-1	2-3	2-1	1-0					0-0	1-0
90-91									0-1	3-1	2-3	3-0					3-1	3-3
1991																		
2001																		
01-02					3-1	2-0	2-0	1-2					1-1	3-3				
02-03	1-4	2-2	0-0	4-2			2-1	0-4	0-2	2-1			4-0	2-4				
03-04	1-0	1-1	4-1	2-1			1-1	0-2					2-1	4-1				

	Maidstone United		Margate		Merthyr Tydfil		Morecambe		Northwich Victoria		Nuneaton Borough		Redditch United		Runcorn		Scarborough	
	H	A	H	A	H	A	H	A	H	A	H	A	H	A	H	A	H	A
79-80	0-1	0-2							0-2	0-2	2-1	1-2	0-0	0-1			0-0	0-0
80-81	4-1	1-4							1-0	1-4	1-0	1-0					1-2	0-3
81-82	1-1	0-0							0-1	1-1					1-3	0-1	1-1	0-1
82-83	1-3	0-2							4-2	0-1	1-0	0-1			2-0	0-2	2-3	2-0
83-84	0-4	1-1							2-1	0-0	1-2	2-2			2-0	0-2	0-1	0-1
84-85	0-0	0-1							1-1	0-2	1-1	1-1			1-1	2-1	1-2	1-1
85-86	3-3	2-2							1-0	1-0	0-1	1-4			1-2	0-0	1-0	1-3
86-87	3-1	0-1							4-0	2-1	4-1	3-1			3-0	1-1	2-2	0-0
87-88	2-0	1-2							4-1	1-2					1-2	1-0		
88-89	2-1	2-3							2-0	1-1					3-2	0-3		
89-90					4-0	1-2			1-0	2-0					2-2	2-2		
90-91					2-3	1-1			1-1	2-0					2-0	2-3		
1991																		
2001																		
01-02			4-1	1-0			1-0	0-1	1-0	3-0	0-1	3-2					1-1	0-3
02-03			0-1	2-2			1-1	1-1	3-4	1-1	2-1	2-3					3-0	1-1
03-04			3-1	1-0			2-1	3-1	1-0	1-1							0-0	2-2

	Shrewsbury Town		Slough Town		Southport		Stafford Rangers		Stalybridge Celtic		Stevenage Borough		Sutton United		Tamworth		Telford United	
	H	A	H	A	H	A	H	A	H	A	H	A	H	A	H	A	H	A
79-80							2-1	2-1									4-1	2-1
80-81							1-1	0-1									2-1	0-0
81-82							0-2	0-1									1-0	0-3
82-83							1-0	0-1									0-2	0-3
83-84																	0-0	0-0
84-85																	0-1	0-2
85-86							0-2	0-0									1-2	2-2
86-87							1-2	3-0					1-2	1-3			2-2	1-0
87-88							2-2	1-1					6-2	1-0			0-2	4-2
88-89							1-2	2-1					1-1	1-5			1-3	3-0
89-90							1-1	1-1					4-1	3-1			2-1	3-1
90-91			6-1	3-1			2-0	2-2					1-0	1-0			0-0	1-1
1991																		
2001																		
01-02					0-0	1-0			1-2	1-1	0-3	2-3					0-0	2-1
02-03					3-1	1-2					0-2	2-1					3-0	1-2
03-04	0-1	1-0									0-0	2-1			1-0	0-2	2-0	2-1

BARNET

	Trowbridge Town H	A	Wealdstone H	A	Welling United H	A	Weymouth H	A	Woking H	A	Worcester City H	A	Wycombe Wanderers H	A	Yeovil Town H	A
79-80			1-3	1-2			0-2	1-1			0-0	1-2			0-3	0-5
80-81			3-0	0-2			0-3	0-3			0-2	0-4			4-4	2-1
81-82	0-0	1-1					0-3	2-0			1-2	1-3			0-0	1-4
82-83	1-3	2-0	0-0	0-6			1-2	3-1			3-1	2-4			4-4	2-4
83-84	2-1	4-0	1-1	0-3			1-1	2-2			2-0	0-2			2-0	4-2
84-85			7-0	2-1			0-0	0-3			2-0	2-1			4-1	1-2
85-86			1-0	0-2			2-2	2-4					0-1	0-2		
86-87			2-1	0-0	1-1	1-1	2-2	3-3								
87-88			5-1	6-0	5-2	2-0	3-2	0-2					1-1	7-0		
88-89					2-3	1-1	4-1	1-1					1-0	3-2	2-0	1-2
89-90					1-1	1-3							2-0	0-1	1-0	2-3
90-91					3-2	4-1							3-2	3-1	3-2	4-1
1991																
2001																
01-02									3-0	3-1					2-3	2-1
02-03									0-0	0-0					2-1	0-0
03-04									0-0	2-2						

Barry Fry. Photo: Eric Marsh

Andy Clarke.

	Home						Away					
	P	W	D	L	F	A	P	W	D	L	F	A
ACCRINGTON S	1	0	1	0	0	0	1	0	0	1	0	2
ALDERSHOT T	1	1	0	0	2	1	1	0	1	0	1	1
ALTRINCHAM	12	8	3	1	19	8	12	1	2	9	8	23
A P LEAMINGTON	3	2	1	0	2	0	3	2	0	1	4	2
AYLESBURY U	1	1	0	0	1	0	1	1	0	0	3	1
BANGOR C	4	1	1	2	5	6	4	1	1	2	4	6
BARROW	8	5	2	1	16	6	8	2	2	4	8	12
BATH C	10	7	0	3	16	11	10	6	1	3	14	8
BOSTON U	13	5	4	4	20	12	13	4	4	5	15	19
BURTON A	2	1	1	0	4	3	2	2	0	0	6	2
CHELTENHAM T	6	3	2	1	12	6	6	4	0	2	11	7
CHESTER C	3	1	1	1	3	4	3	0	1	2	1	3
CHORLEY	2	1	0	1	7	4	2	2	0	0	7	3
COLCHESTER U	1	0	0	1	1	3	1	0	1	0	0	0
DAGENHAM	7	4	2	1	14	8	7	2	3	2	8	8
DAGENHAM & R	3	2	0	1	8	5	3	0	1	2	4	11
DARLINGTON	1	0	0	1	0	2	1	1	0	0	2	1
DARTFORD	3	2	0	1	4	1	3	0	0	3	4	9
DONCASTER R	2	1	0	1	3	2	2	1	0	1	4	4
DOVER A	1	1	0	0	2	0	1	0	1	0	2	2
ENFIELD	9	7	0	2	18	9	9	3	2	4	10	16
EXETER C	1	0	0	1	2	3	1	0	1	0	1	1
FARNBOROUGH T	4	1	0	3	5	8	4	1	2	1	5	5
FISHER A	4	3	0	1	16	5	4	3	1	0	10	6
FOREST GREEN R	3	2	0	1	7	1	3	0	3	0	7	7
FRICKLEY A	7	4	1	2	14	7	7	3	1	3	10	12
GATESHEAD	4	1	2	1	5	4	4	4	0	0	13	4
GRAVESEND & N	5	3	1	1	8	5	5	2	2	1	8	6
HALIFAX T	2	1	1	0	4	1	2	2	0	0	6	3
HAYES	1	1	0	0	3	1	1	1	0	0	2	0
HEREFORD U	3	2	1	0	5	2	3	0	0	3	1	8
KETTERING T	13	6	0	7	23	20	13	3	3	7	16	26
KIDDERMINSTER H	8	2	1	5	12	16	8	5	2	1	18	7
LEIGH RMI	3	2	1	0	7	2	3	1	1	1	9	8
LINCOLN C	1	1	0	0	4	2	1	0	0	1	1	2
MACCLESFIELD T	4	2	1	1	6	6	4	1	3	0	7	6
MAIDSTONE U	10	4	3	3	16	15	10	0	3	7	7	18
MARGATE	3	2	0	1	7	3	3	2	1	0	4	2
MERTHYR T	2	1	0	1	6	3	2	0	1	1	2	3
MORECAMBE	3	2	1	0	4	2	3	1	1	1	4	3
NORTHWICH V	15	10	2	3	26	13	15	5	5	5	16	16
NUNEATON B	9	5	1	3	12	8	9	3	2	4	14	16
REDDITCH U	1	0	1	0	0	0	1	0	0	1	0	1
RUNCORN	10	5	2	3	18	12	10	2	3	5	8	15
SCARBOROUGH	11	2	5	4	12	12	11	1	5	5	7	15
SHREWSBURY T	1	0	0	1	0	1	1	1	0	0	1	0
SLOUGH T	1	1	0	0	6	1	1	1	0	0	3	1
SOUTHPORT	2	1	1	0	3	1	2	1	0	1	2	2
STAFFORD R	10	3	3	4	11	13	10	3	4	3	11	9
STALYBRIDGE C	1	0	0	1	1	2	1	0	1	0	1	1
STEVENAGE B	3	0	1	2	0	5	3	2	0	1	6	5
SUTTON U	5	3	1	1	13	6	5	3	0	2	7	9
TAMWORTH	1	1	0	0	1	0	1	0	0	1	0	2
TELFORD U	15	6	4	5	18	15	15	7	4	4	21	18
TROWBRIDGE T	3	1	1	1	3	4	3	2	1	0	7	1
WEALDSTONE	8	5	2	1	20	6	8	2	1	5	9	16
WELLING U	5	2	2	1	12	9	5	2	2	1	9	6
WEYMOUTH	10	2	4	4	13	18	10	2	4	4	14	20
WOKING	3	1	2	0	3	0	3	1	2	0	5	3
WORCESTER C	6	3	1	2	8	5	6	1	0	5	6	16
WYCOMBE W	5	3	1	1	7	4	5	3	0	2	13	6
YEOVIL T	11	6	3	2	24	18	11	4	1	6	19	25
TOTAL	310	153	68	89	522	350	310	107	80	123	426	470

Mark Carter . Photo: Keith Gillard.

Richard Nugent. Photo: Keith Gillard.

Wayne Purser. Photo: Peter Barnes.

Eddie Stein and Phil Gridelet threaten the Altrincham defence.

Photo: P.D.Shepherd

BARNET LEADING APPEARANCES

BARNET LEADING APPEARANCES

	79-80	80-81	81-82	82-83	83-84	84-85	85-86	86-87	87-88	88-89	89-90	90-91	91-01	01-02	02-03	03-04	TOTAL
Edwin STEIN	34											24+3					329+15
Kevin MILLETT		38	25	21	26+3	25			32	5	38+2						246+3
Peter BROWN			41	16	39	36	36	39	39+2	5+2							210+4
Gary PHILLIPS		11			42	19			2	2	24	42					213
Nicky EVANS					24	32+2	31+1	41	32+2	18+3		15					193+8
John MARGERRISON				41	36+1	31+1	25+2	35	6+2	6+1							139+7
Mike PITTAWAY			34+2	41	24+2	38+1											137+5
Dave SANSOM					35+3		35+3	23+6	35	22+5							115+14
Steve MAHONEY			10+2	9+6		29+3	3+1	12+16									98+31
Glyn CREASER						14	35	28	42	2+2							121+2
Steve HUMPHRIES						15	41	37	15	3							111
Robert CODNER							29+5	20+6	39+2	6							94+13
Steve ROBINSON	33	37	33	2													105
Stuart ATKINS			11	40	34	16+2											101+2
Colin BARNES		19+1	40	40+1													99+2
Paul WILSON										20+5	41+1	29+4					90+10
Bill BALDRY					40	38+1	18+2	1									97+3

BARNET APPEARANCES

	79-80	80-81	81-82	82-83	83-84	84-85	85-86	86-87	87-88	88-89	89-90	90-91	91-01	01-02	02-03	03-04	TOTAL
ABBOTT Gary	1+2																27+9
ADAMS Lou																	1+2
ADAMS Steve			1														1
AGOGO Junior															36+4		36+4
ALEXANDER Keith								39+1	28+5								67+6
ANGELL Darren										20							20
ANGOL Ivor								1+1									1+1
ANSCOMB D.				1+1													1+1
ARBER Mark														37+1	12		49+1
ARMSTRONG Gary				2+1													2+1
ASHFORD Noel									37								37

60

BARNET APPEARANCES

BARNET APPEARANCES	79-80	80-81	81-82	82-83	83-84	84-85	85-86	86-87	87-88	88-89	89-90	90-91	91-01	01-02	02-03	03-04	TOTAL
ASHWORTH Lawrence																	9
ATKINS Stuart			11	40	34	16+2											101+2
AWARITEFE Francis									5								5
BAILEY Kingsley			1+1														1+1
BAILEY R.			1														1
BALDRY Bill					40	38+1	18+2	1									97+3
BANKOLE Ademola																8	8
BARNES Colin		19+1	40	40+1													99+2
BEADLE Peter																10+3	10+3
BEATTIE Andy								14			29+1						43+1
BEATTIE Kevin							1										1
BELL Leon														23+6	3+7		26+13
BENNETT Tony				13+5	0+1												13+6
BERKLEY Austin														10+3			10+3
BISSETT Nicky									11+1	4							15+1
BLACKWELL Kevin	25							5									30
BLACKWELL Noel	4	1+1															5+1
BODLEY Mick											7	32					39
BOLTON Ian	7																7
BOOKER Bob						7											7
BOWEN Keith									2+2								2+2
BRINKMAN Steve	34	34	10+1	2		6+4											86+5
BROWN Danny														20+5	12+2		32+7
BROWN Peter				16	39	36	36	39	39+2	5+2							210+4
BULL Gary										10	40	30+3					80+3
BUTTERS Guy															7		7
CAMPBELL Alan		10	39														49
CAMPBELL G.							0+1										0+1
CAMPION Adam																0+1	0+1
CARR Everton									1+5								1+5
CARTER Mark												7+4					7+4
CASHMAN Chris															0+2		0+2
CHIVERS Martin				7													7

L-R) Noel Ashford & Keith Alexander. Photo: John Vass.

Colin Barnes.

Kevin Blackwell.

Mick Bodley powers in a header. Photo: Colin Stevens.

Gary Bull. Photo: John Vass.

Nicky Evans in full flight. Photo: John Vass.

BARNET APPEARANCES

	79-80	80-81	81-82	82-83	83-84	84-85	85-86	86-87	87-88	88-89	89-90	90-91	91-01	01-02	02-03	03-04	TOTAL
CLARKE Andy										1	35+1	26					62+1
CLAYTON Roy		24+4															24+4
CLIST Simon																13+2	13+2
CODNER Robert							29+5	20+6	39+2	6							94+13
CONQUEST Martin	2+2																2+2
COOPER Geoff											31+5	24+1					55+6
COSBY Alan											0+1						0+1
COX Steve							4+1	22+2	11+3	28							65+6
CRAIG Geoff					2+2												2+2
CREASER Glyn						14	35	28	42	2+2							121+2
CULPIN Paul												3+1					3+1
DAISH Liam										12							12
DARCY Ross														1+1			1+1
DAVIES Donny							1										1
DLOMO Blessing		0+1															0+1
DOCKER John					34+1					22+1							73+2
DOOLAN John														16+3	31		47+3
DUBLIN Dion										0+1							0+1
DURHAM Kevin												29+2					29+2
ESSANDOH Roy														3+3			3+3
EVANS Nicky					24	32+2	31+1	41	32+2	18+3		15					193+8
FEAREY Dave						0+1											0+1
FERGUSSON Ian					15	22+4			3+4	1+2							41+10
FINLAY Rodney			1														1
FLASHMAN Mark										1							1
FLYNN Lee														34+4	23+1		57+5
FOODY Steve		28	24+2														66+2
FORDE Clevere										1							1
FORDE David																7	7
FRENCH Gary	20+5	18+3	5+5														44+13
FRY Barry	1		0+1		0+1												1+2
GALLAGHER Alan				5+5													5+5
GAMBLE Joe															40		40

63

Mark Gower.

Phil Gridelet. Photo: Eric Marsh.

Paul Harding.

Greg Heald.

Steve Humphreys. Photo: Bob Thomas.

Kenny Lowe. Photo: Dave West.

BARNET APPEARANCES

	79-80	80-81	81-82	82-83	83-84	84-85	85-86	86-87	87-88	88-89	89-90	90-91	91-01	01-02	02-03	03-04	TOTAL
GARNER Alan	17																17
GIPP David											0+12	1					1+12
GITTINGS Martin								1+2									1+2
GLEDHILL Lee														36+1	10+2		46+3
GOODCHILD Andy						10+3	9+3										19+6
GOODHIND Warren														7			7
GORE Shane																19	19
GORMLEY Eddie										2+1							2+1
GOWER Mark														34+1			34+1
GRAZIOLI Guiliano																38	38
GRIDELET Phil											37+2						37+2
GUTHRIE Peter											18						18
HALSEY Mark						1											1
HARDING Paul											12+2	10					22+2
HARDMAN Colin	18	10+1		1	3+6												32+7
HARDY Duncan						19+3											19+3
HARRIOTT Les			13+1	11+2	5+1												29+4
HARRISON Lee														36	14		50
HATCH Liam																17+6	17+6
HAYES Austin							3										3
HAYRETTIN Hakan											4+2	3+6					7+8
HEALD Greg														38	23		61
HENDON Ian															4	37+1	41+1
HENDRICK Jimmy		24	12+1														36+1
HENRY Solomon																0+4	0+4
HILLIER David															6		6
HODDLE Carl								2+7									2+7
HOGG Lewis																11+5	11+5
HOLMES Billy			9														9
HORTON Duncan												2+3					2+3
HOWELL Dave												19+2					19+2
HOWELL Ronnie				14+1													14+1
HUGHES Gary	11+2																11+2

BARNET APPEARANCES

	79-80	80-81	81-82	82-83	83-84	84-85	85-86	86-87	87-88	88-89	89-90	90-91	91-01	01-02	02-03	03-04	TOTAL
HULLETT Chris	38																38
HUMPHRIES Steve						15	41	37	15	3							111
IANNONE Aniello										1+1							1+1
IRONTON Nicky									2+5	6+1	2+1						10+7
JOHNSON Nigel							9	4+9									13+9
JOHNSON Peter			15														15
JONES Davy										2+1							2+1
KETTERIDGE Steve										7+1							7+1
KING Simon																33+2	33+2
KINNEAR Chris			4		30+1												34+1
KRUSE Pat				28													28
LACY John							6										6
LANGSTON Matt															3+2		3+2
LAWRENSON Mark										2							2
LAWSON David	2+1																2+1
LEADBITTER Chris										12							12
LETTE JALLOW Bai Mass															0+7		0+7
LEWIN Gary				10													10
LITTLE Barry							36+3	27+6									63+9
LOMAS Andy									26	34							60
LOPEZ Guy															4+1	15+10	19+11
LOWE Kenny												18					18
LYNCH Tony												3+11					3+11
MADDIX Danny			10+2	9+6	35+3	29+3	3+1	12+16									98+31
MAHONEY Steve			0+1														0+1
MANCINI Mark																32	32
MANN Adrian										3+2							3+2
MARGERRISON John					36+1	31+1	25+2	35	6+2	6+1							139+7
MARTIN Tony				1													1
McALLISTER Don						8+1	4										12+1
McCORMACK Les	2+1																2+1
McNAMEE Anthony																2+3	2+3
MEASHAM Ian										1							1

BARNET APPEARANCES

	79-80	80-81	81-82	82-83	83-84	84-85	85-86	86-87	87-88	88-89	89-90	90-91	91-01	01-02	02-03	03-04	TOTAL
MEHMET Dave											2						2
MIDGLEY Neil														30+9	30+6		60+15
MILLARD Ricky															2+1	1	3+1
MILLETT Kevin	34	38	25	21	26+3	25		40	32	5							246+3
MORRIS John					1+2												1+2
MURPHY Frank										27+3	14+16	3+7					44+26
NAISBITT Danny														6+1	26	7	39+1
NEAL John							3+5										3+5
NIVEN Stuart														25+9	0+1		25+10
NUGENT Richard										14+9		33					47+9
O'HARE Tony	13+2	1+1															14+3
OLAYINKA Ade														1			1
OLIVER Steve	37																37
O'NEILL Steve							13										13
OSHITOLA Toby														0+9	3+20		3+29
PARKER Trevor					1	14+7	10+9										25+16
PARRATT D.			0+1														0+1
PARSONS Steve									5+6								5+6
PAYNE Derek										15	25+7	3+2					43+9
PAYNE Lee									1+1	1+2							2+3
PEARCE David						13	5+2										18+2
PEARCE Graham	30	31	14														75
PEARSON Greg																2+8	2+8
PHILLIPS Gary		11	41	32	42	19				2	24	42					213
PITCHER Geoff																5	5
PITTAWAY Bob				13	3+1												16+1
PITTAWAY Mike			34+2	41	24+2	38+1											137+5
PLUCK Lee														5+3	36+2	0+1	41+6
PLUMMER Chris																34	34
POOLE Gary										11	28+1	31+2					70+3
POPE Craig														5+1	22+5		27+6
POWLING Richie			3														3
PRICE Michael															4		4

Neil Midgley. Photo: Alan Coomes.

Frank Murphy. Photo: Mick Cheney.

Gary Phillips. Photo: M.Close.

Gary Poole. Photo: Dennis Nicholson.

Dave Regis. Photo: K. Gillard.

George Reilly. Photo: M.Close.

BARNET APPEARANCES

	79-80	80-81	81-82	82-83	83-84	84-85	85-86	86-87	87-88	88-89	89-90	90-91	91-01	01-02	02-03	03-04	TOTAL
PURCHES John														0+1			0+1
PURSER Wayne														26+3	20+6		46+9
RAGAN Steve			13+1	30+2	24+5	7+3	1+3										75+14
REDMILE Matt																12	12
REGIS Dave										2+5	21+6	6+3					29+14
REILLY George										10	16+2						26+2
RICHARDSON Paul												21+4					21+4
ROACH Lee																0+1	0+1
ROBERTS Elwyn	18+1	21+2															39+3
ROBERTS Gary								8+7									8+7
ROBINSON Peter				2+1													2+1
ROBINSON Steve	33	37	33	2													105
ROFFEY Bill										1							1
ROONEY Mark																23+6	23+6
ROWLAND Keith															6+2		6+2
RYAN Laurie											0+1						0+1
SANDERCOCK Phil				15													15
SANSOM Dave							35+3	23+6	35	22+5							115+14
SARGEANT Gary		19	36+1	18													73+1
SAUNDERS Neil																0+1	0+1
SAWYERS Rob														23+6			23+6
SCHIAVI Mark								2									2
SCULLY Tony																1	1
SEARLE Steve														2+3			2+3
SHARRATT Peter			5														5
SHINNERS Paul										5+2							5+2
SIANI Brian	11+6	7+2															18+8
SILK Gary																1	1
SLACK Trevor										2							2
SMITH Chris	11+9	3+2															14+11
SMITH Gordon							17										17
SMITH Herbie									1+13	2+6							3+19
SOLOMAN Jason															18+3		18+3

Ben Strevens. Photo: Alan Coomes.

John Watson. Photo: Bob Thomas.

Roger Willis heads for goal against Northwich Vic toria.

Photo: Keith Gillard.

BARNET APPEARANCES

	79-80	80-81	81-82	82-83	83-84	84-85	85-86	86-87	87-88	88-89	89-90	90-91	91-01	01-02	02-03	03-04	TOTAL
SPERRIN Martin	20+3	3															23+3
STACEY Phil									6	18+1	31+3						55+4
STEEL Gary	13	27	1														41
STEIN Edwin				41	39+1	32+3	35+2	42	41+1	37+3	38+2	24+3					329+15
STEPHENS Kirk									22+6								22+6
STREVENS Ben														24	21+2	35+4	80+6
SUGRUE Paul												0+1					0+1
SYLLA Norman																0+4	0+4
TAGGART Tony																8+14	8+14
TAYLOR K.							0+1										0+1
TAYLOR Mark														0+5			0+5
THOMAS Kevin							4+2	1									5+2
TOMLINSON David												7+3					7+3
TOMS Fraser														17+10	16+8		33+18
TOWNSEND Russell	6	26+1	23+1														55+2
TUFFS Bobby			13	1													14
TURNER Steve						6+2				26+1		11+3					48+2
TURNER Wayne											1						38+4
VOYCE Terry		1+2	1+3			0+2											2+7
WALLER Steve						7	1										8
WATSON John			5														5
WEBSTER Simon				3													3
WELSH Steve											6+3	3+3					9+6
WESTLEY Graham									1+2								1+2
WESTWOOD Danny			19	18+6													37+6
WHITWORTH Steve							39	18+1		1							58+1
WILLIAMS Darren									1								1
WILLIAMS Mark																19+15	19+15
WILLIS Roger												27+10					27+10
WILSON Paul										20+5	41+1	29+4					90+10
WIMBLETON Paul							8										8
WIPER Ben															0+1		0+1
YAKUBU Ismail														3+1	29+7	32+7	64+15

BARNET LEADING GOALSCORERS

BARNET LEADING GOALSCORERS

	79-80	80-81	81-82	82-83	83-84	84-85	85-86	86-87	87-88	88-89	89-90	90-91	91-01	01-02	02-03	03-04	TOTAL
Nicky EVANS					7	13	20(1p)	22	22	5	10						99(1p)
Steve MAHONEY			1	3	19	19		12									54
Gary BULL										6(1p)	17(5p)	30(8p)					53(14p)
Dave SANSOM							13	11(1p)	19(5p)	6(1p)							49(7p)
Stuart ATKINS			3	12	13	4											32
Colin BARNES		2	12(2p)	17(2p)													31(4p)
Andy CLARKE										1	17	12					30

BARNET GOALSCORERS

	79-80	80-81	81-82	82-83	83-84	84-85	85-86	86-87	87-88	88-89	89-90	90-91	91-01	01-02	02-03	03-04	TOTAL
ABBOTT Gary									7	5							12
AGOGO Junior															20(3p)		20(3p)
ALEXANDER Keith								9	12								21
ANGELL Darren										1							1
ARBER Mark														7(3p)	1		8(3p)
ARMSTRONG Gary				1													1
ASHFORD Noel									5								5
ATKINS Stuart			3	12	13	4											32
AWARITIFE Francis									1								1
BALDRY Bill						1(1p)	2										3(1p)
BARNES Colin		2	12(2p)	17(2p)													31(4p)
BEADLE Peter																3	3
BEATTIE Andy											1						1
BELL Leon														2			2
BERKLEY Austin														2			2
BODLEY Mick												6					6
BOOKER Bob	1																1

BARNET GOALSCORERS

	79-80	80-81	81-82	82-83	83-84	84-85	85-86	86-87	87-88	88-89	89-90	90-91	91-01	01-02	02-03	03-04	TOTAL
BRINKMAN Steve	2(1p)																7(1p)
BROWN Danny															2		5
BROWN Peter				4										3			11
BULL Gary										6(1p)	17(5p)	30(8p)					53(14p)
CAMPBELL Alan			1														1
CARTER Mark												1					1
CLARKE Andy										1	17	12					30
CLAYTON Roy		4															4
CLIST Simon																1	1
CODNER Robert							6	1	11(1p)								18(1p)
CONQUEST Martin	2																2
COOPER Geoff																	5
COX Steve								3	1	1							5
CREASER Glyn							2	2	3								7
CULPIN Paul											2						2
DOCKER John					2					5							7
DOOLAN John														2(1p)	3		5(1p)
DURHAM Kevin												2					2
ESSANDOH Roy														1			1
EVANS Nicky					7	13	20(1p)	22	22	5		10					99(1p)
FERGUSSON Ian					1(1p)	2			1								4(1p)
FLYNN Lee														3			3
FOODY Steve		2	1														3
FRENCH Gary	2(1p)	3(2p)	2														7(3p)
GAMBLE Joe																1	1
GIPP David											3						3
GOWER Mark														5	9		14
GRAZIOLI Guiliano																24(2p)	24(2p)
GRIDELET Phil											5						5
HARDING Paul											3	2					5
HARDY Duncan						4											4
HATCH Liam																4	4
HAYES Austin							2										2
HEALD Greg														2	3		5

BARNET GOALSCORERS

BARNET GOALSCORERS	79-80	80-81	81-82	82-83	83-84	84-85	85-86	86-87	87-88	88-89	89-90	90-91	91-01	01-02	02-03	03-04	TOTAL
HENDON Ian															1	7(4p)	8(4p)
HOGG Lewis																1	1
HOLMES Billy			1														1
HOWELL David												1					1
HULLETT Chris	3																3
IRONTON Nicky									1								1
JOHNSON Nigel							2	1									3
JOHNSON Peter			1														1
KINNEAR Chris					2												2
KRUSE Pat				1													1
LITTLE Barry							4(1p)	4(2p)									8(3p)
LOWE Kenny												2					2
LYNCH Tony												7					7
MAHONEY Steve			1	3	19	19		12									54
MARGERRISON John					3	2		10									16
MIDGLEY Neil														9	5		14
MILLETT Kevin				1			1		1								3
MURPHY Frank										14(2p)	9	4(1p)					27(3p)
NEAL John							1										1
NIVEN Stuart														1			1
NUGENT Richard										2		2					4
O'HARE Tony	1																1
OLIVER Steve	2																2
OSHITOLA Toby														2	2		4
PARKER Trevor						4	1										5
PARSONS Steve									2								2
PAYNE Derek											2						2
PEARCE David						3	1										4
PEARCE Graham	2	2															4
PEARSON Greg																1	
PITCHER Geoff																1	
PLUMMER Chris																3	
POOLE Gary										1	3	2(2p)					6(2p)
POPE Craig															1		1

74

BARNET GOALSCORERS

BARNET GOALSCORERS	79-80	80-81	81-82	82-83	83-84	84-85	85-86	86-87	87-88	88-89	89-90	90-91	91-01	01-02	02-03	03-04	TOTAL
PURSER Wayne														8(1p)	4		12(1p)
RAGAN Steve			2	5	3	2											12
REDMILE Matt																1	1
REGIS Dave										1	9	5					15
REILLY George										2	3						5
RICHARDSON Paul												2					2
ROBERTS Elwyn	3	6															9
ROBERTS Gary								3									3
ROBINSON Steve	4	4	3														11
SANSOM Dave							13	11(1p)	19(5p)	6(1p)							49(7p)
SARGENT Gary		3	1														4
SAWYERS Rob														2			2
SHINNERS Paul										3							3
SIANI Brian		1															1
SMITH Chris	2																2
SMITH Herbie									2								2
SOLOMAN Jason															2		2
STACEY Phil											2						2
STEIN Edwin				8	2	1	1	6	1	4	2	1					26
STEPHENS Kirk									2								2
STREVENS Ben														9	9(1p)	9	27(1p)
TAGGART Tony																1	1
TOMS Fraser														5	1		6
TOWNSEND Russell			2														2
TUFFS Bobby			1														1
TURNER Steve	7(2p)	6(4p)															13(6p)
TURNER Wayne										3							3
WATSON John			2														2
WESTLEY Graham									1								1
WESTWOOD Danny			3	3													6
WILLIS Roger												10					10
WILSON Paul										3							3
WIPER Ben															1		1
YAKUBU Ismael															1	2	3

Season 1982-1983. Back row, left to right: Alan Campbell, Terry Voyce, John Watson, Kevin Millett, Danny Westwood, Gary Phillips, Steve Foody, Steve Robinson, Bobby Tuffs and Les Harriott. Front row: Colin Meldrum (Coach), Mike Pittaway, Gary Sargent, Barry Fry (Manager), Colin Barnes, Russell Townsend and Derek French (Physio).

Mark Carter beats Merthyr 'keeper Gary Wager with this diving header but sees his effort come back off the post. Photo: Keith Gillard.

1989-90 Squad. Back Row (L-R): Gordon Ogbourne (Kit Manager), Paul Harding, Phil Gridelet, David Regis, Richard Nugent, Mark Flashman, Gary Phillips, Mick Bodley, Wayne Turner, Geoff Cooper, Gary Poole, John Green (Physio). Front Row: Derek Payne, David Gipp, Phil Stacey, Gary Bull, Edwin Stein, Barry Fry (Manager), Andrew Clarke, Paul Wilson, Frank Murphy, Jonathan Hunt, Alan Cosby.

BARROW

FOUNDER MEMBER
ELECTED FROM: Northern Premier League 1979
PROMOTED FROM: Northern Premier 1984, 1989, 1998
RELEGATED TO: Northern Premier League 1983, 1986, 1992, 1999
2004-2005 SEASON: Conference North

Barrow FC 1990-91

L-R - **Back Row:** Keith Nelson (Football Secretary), Billy Gilmour, Lee Copeland, Garry Messenger, Kenny Lowe, Ken Gordon, Mick Cloudsdale (Physio), Peter McDonnell, Kevin Proctor, Jimmy Capstick, Malcolm Jackson, Glen Skivington, Terry Rhodes (Trainer). **Front Row:** Steve Higgins, Neil McDonald (Asst. Man.), Stuart Todhunter, Peter Farrell, Neil Doherty, Ray Wilkie (manager), Colin Cowperthwaite, Paul Ferris, Ian Burgess, Tony Chilton.

SEASONS
10

TOTAL POINTS
334 + 255 = 589

HIGHEST POSITION
8 (81/82)

LOWEST POSITION
22 (85/86, 91/92)

HIGHEST ATTENDANCE
4244 Darlington (1-1-90)

LOWEST ATTENDANCE
298 Yeovil T (4-5-85)

SEASON GOALSCORER
Colin Cowperthwaite
18 (90/91)

CAREER GOALSCORER
Colin Cowperthwaite 116(9p)

CAREER APPEARANCES
Colin Cowperthwaite 287+6

| | HOME | | | | | | | AWAY | | | | | | | |
	P	W	D	L	F	A	Pts	P	W	D	L	F	A	Pts	Position
79/80	19	10	3	6	27	18	23	19	4	3	12	20	37	11	14
80/81	19	10	3	6	25	18	23	19	5	5	9	25	31	15	9
81/82	21	15	4	2	45	17	49	21	3	7	11	14	33	16	8
82/83	21	7	4	10	26	35	25	21	1	8	12	20	39	11	21
83/84															
84/85	21	6	9	6	25	22	21	21	5	7	9	22	35	22	18
85/86	21	5	6	10	26	34	16	21	2	2	17	15	52	8	22
86 - 89															
89/90	21	11	8	2	33	25	41	21	1	8	12	18	42	11	14
90/91	21	10	8	3	34	24	38	21	5	4	12	25	41	19	10
91/92	21	5	8	8	29	23	23	21	3	6	12	23	49	15	22
92 - 98															
98/99	21	7	5	9	17	23	26	21	4	5	12	23	40	17	19
Total	206	86	58	62	287	239	285	206	33	55	118	205	399	145	

	Altrincham		A P Leamington		Bangor City		Barnet		Bath City		Boston United		Cheltenham Town		Chorley		Colchester United	
	H	A	H	A	H	A	H	A	H	A	H	A	H	A	H	A	H	A
79-80	1-3	1-3	6-2	1-0	1-1	1-1	3-1	1-1	2-1	0-1	0-1	0-3						
80-81	0-4	2-2	0-2	2-2	3-0	6-2	1-1	0-0	0-0	1-2	0-2	2-0						
81-82	1-0	1-1	4-2	1-1			2-1	2-1	0-1	0-0	1-0	1-2						
82-83	2-2	2-2			1-5	2-2	0-1	1-2	0-1	1-4	1-1	1-2						
83-84																		
84-85	0-2	0-2					1-0	0-4	0-1	2-1	1-1	3-1						
85-86	0-1	0-2					0-1	1-4	1-1	0-6	2-1	1-2	2-2	0-2				
86-87																		
87-88																		
88-89																		
89-90	1-1	1-1					1-1	0-1	1-1	1-1	2-1	1-2	2-1	0-1	3-1	1-0		
90-91	1-0	1-1					4-2	1-3	2-0	1-2	1-1	2-0	0-0	1-3			2-2	0-1
91-92	0-2	1-1									2-2	1-4	0-0	0-0			1-1	0-5
92-93																		
93-94																		
94-95																		
95-96																		
96-97																		
97-98																		
98-99													1-1	1-4				

	Dagenham		(Dagenham &) Redbridge F.		Darlington		Dartford		Doncaster Rovers		Dover Athletic		Enfield		Farnborough Town		Fisher Athletic	
	H	A	H	A	H	A	H	A	H	A	H	A	H	A	H	A	H	A
79-80																		
80-81																		
81-82	2-2	0-1					2-0	2-0					0-2	2-7				
82-83	1-2	0-0											0-3	0-2				
83-84																		
84-85	3-1	1-1					0-0	0-2					1-1	0-0				
85-86	1-0	0-3					1-2	2-3					1-2	0-4				
86-87																		
87-88																		
88-89																		
89-90					1-1	0-0							2-2	0-3	3-1	0-3	1-1	0-4
90-91																	3-1	2-1
91-92			0-1	2-2											0-1	0-5		
92-93																		
93-94																		
94-95																		
95-96																		
96-97																		
97-98																		
98-99									2-2	1-2	1-0	1-1			1-0	2-2		

	Forest Green Rovers		Frickley Athletic		Gateshead		Gravesend & Northfleet		Hayes		Hednesford Town		Hereford United		Kettering Town		Kidderminster Harriers	
	H	A	H	A	H	A	H	A	H	A	H	A	H	A	H	A	H	A
79-80							1-1	1-5							1-2	4-0		
80-81			0-0	0-5			3-1	2-0							2-1	1-0		
81-82			2-0	1-2			3-1	1-3							7-2	2-0		
82-83			2-0	1-1											2-0	1-3		
83-84																		
84-85			6-0	2-2	0-1	2-1									0-1	0-0	1-3	1-0
85-86			2-2	0-2											1-0	2-4	3-4	1-2
86-87																		
87-88																		
88-89																		
89-90															1-0	0-2	2-1	2-2
90-91					3-1	1-5									0-1	0-2	1-3	1-3
91-92					1-1	1-1									0-0	2-3	5-1	2-1
92-93																		
93-94																		
94-95																		
95-96																		
96-97																		
97-98																		
98-99	2-1	1-1							0-1	0-1	0-2	0-1	0-1	0-3	0-0	0-2	0-4	2-1

	Kingstonian		Leek Town		Macclesfield Town		Maidstone United		Merthyr Tydfil		Morecambe		Northwich Victoria		Nuneaton Borough		Redditch United	
	H	A	H	A	H	A	H	A	H	A	H	A	H	A	H	A	H	A
79-80							0-2	0-2					1-0	3-6	1-0	0-3	2-0	3-1
80-81							4-1	0-1					2-1	0-0	1-0	1-3		
81-82							2-0	0-1					6-1	0-2				
82-83							0-3	0-2					0-0	0-1	2-2	1-1		
83-84																		
84-85							0-2	0-2					0-0	0-1	0-0	2-5		
85-86							1-1	0-0					1-2	1-0	2-0	1-0		
86-87																		
87-88																		
88-89																		
89-90					1-1	1-2			1-5	3-3			1-0	0-1				
90-91					1-1	0-3			0-2	2-0			2-2	2-2				
91-92					2-0	1-0			2-2	1-2			0-2	1-6				
92-93																		
93-94																		
94-95																		
95-96																		
96-97																		
97-98																		
98-99	0-1	1-5	2-1	1-3							2-1	2-3	0-1	0-1				

Top Left:	**Danny Wheatley**	Photo: Ged Rule
Middle Left:	**Paul Doolan**	Photo: Ged Rule
Botton Left:	**Tony Chilton**	
Top Right:	**John Brady**	Photo: Ged Rule
Above Right:	**Peter McDonnell**	

	Runcorn		Rushden & Diamonds		Scarborough		Slough Town		Southport		Stafford Rangers		Stevenage Borough		Sutton United		Telford United	
	H	A	H	A	H	A	H	A	H	A	H	A	H	A	H	A	H	A
79-80					0-0	0-2					2-1	1-1					2-0	2-3
80-81					0-1	0-0					5-1	0-1					0-1	2-5
81-82	1-1	0-0			3-2	0-2					1-1	1-1					2-0	0-0
82-83	1-2	1-2			1-2	1-1					2-1	0-2					0-5	3-1
83-84																		
84-85	1-1	0-0			1-1	1-1											2-1	1-3
85-86	0-4	1-3			2-4	1-3					0-1	0-1					1-0	1-3
86-87																		
87-88																		
88-89																		
89-90	2-2	3-4									2-1	1-1			1-0	3-3	3-0	0-3
90-91	2-1	1-3					2-1	0-3			2-0	2-2			3-1	1-2	2-1	1-0
91-92	2-3	2-2					3-4	0-1			0-0	0-0					3-0	2-4
92-93																		
93-94																		
94-95																		
95-96																		
96-97																		
97-98																		
98-99			0-2	0-4					0-0	4-0			0-1	2-1			1-1	1-1

	Trowbridge Town		Wealdstone		Welling United		Weymouth		Witton Albion		Woking		Worcester City		Wycombe Wanderers		Yeovil Town	
	H	A	H	A	H	A	H	A	H	A	H	A	H	A	H	A	H	A
79-80			1-0	1-2			0-1	0-1					1-2	0-2			2-0	1-0
80-81			1-0	0-2			0-1	1-2					1-0	4-2			2-1	1-2
81-82	1-0	0-2					2-0	0-3					0-0	0-4			3-1	0-0
82-83	3-2	1-2	0-2	0-4			3-0	1-1					2-0	1-2			3-1	2-2
83-84			2-1	2-2														
84-85			1-1	0-4			3-3	1-3					1-0	2-3			2-2	2-1
85-86							3-4	2-3							1-1	1-1		
86-87																		
87-88																		
88-89																		
89-90					1-1	0-0									0-3	0-4	2-1	2-2
90-91					1-1	2-4									2-2	1-2	1-0	3-0
91-92					6-1	3-5			0-1	1-0					0-1	2-3	0-0	0-2
92-93																		
93-94																		
94-95																		
95-96																		
96-97																		
97-98																		
98-99					2-1	1-1					1-2	3-2					2-0	0-1

Above:
Paul Rowlands scored with this powerful header.
Photo: Ged Rule

Left:
Kevin Proctor (with a bit of help from Colin Cowperthwaite) gets above the defence.

Below:
Ken Gordon about to shoot.

	Home						Away					
	P	W	D	L	F	A	P	W	D	L	F	A
ALTRINCHAM	9	2	2	5	6	15	9	0	6	3	9	15
A P LEAMINGTON	3	2	0	1	10	6	3	1	2	0	4	3
BANGOR C	3	1	1	1	5	6	3	1	2	0	9	5
BARNET	8	4	2	2	12	8	8	1	2	5	6	16
BATH C	8	2	3	3	6	6	8	1	2	5	6	17
BOSTON U	9	3	4	2	10	10	9	3	0	6	12	16
CHELTENHAM T	5	1	4	0	5	4	5	0	1	4	2	10
CHORLEY	1	1	0	0	3	1	1	1	0	0	1	0
COLCHESTER U	2	0	2	0	3	3	2	0	0	2	0	6
DAGENHAM	4	2	1	1	7	5	4	0	2	2	1	5
DAGENHAM & R	1	0	0	1	0	1	1	0	1	0	2	2
DARLINGTON	1	0	1	0	1	1	1	0	1	0	0	0
DARTFORD	3	1	1	1	3	2	3	1	0	2	4	5
DONCASTER R	1	0	1	0	2	2	1	0	0	1	1	2
DOVER A	1	1	0	0	1	0	1	0	1	0	1	1
ENFIELD	5	0	2	3	4	10	5	0	1	4	2	16
FARNBOROUGH T	3	2	0	1	4	2	3	0	1	2	2	10
FISHER A	2	1	1	0	4	2	2	1	0	1	2	5
FOREST GREEN R	1	1	0	0	2	1	1	0	1	0	1	1
FRICKLEY A	5	3	2	0	12	2	5	0	2	3	4	12
GATESHEAD	3	1	1	1	4	3	3	1	1	1	4	7
GRAVESEND & N	3	2	1	0	7	3	3	1	0	2	4	8
HAYES	1	0	0	1	0	1	1	0	0	1	0	1
HEDNESFORD T	1	0	0	1	0	2	1	0	0	1	0	1
HEREFORD U	1	0	0	1	0	1	1	0	0	1	0	3
KETTERING T	10	5	2	3	14	7	10	3	1	6	12	16
KIDDERMINSTER H	6	2	0	4	12	16	6	3	1	2	9	9
KINGSTONIAN	1	0	0	1	0	1	1	0	0	1	1	5
LEEK T	1	1	0	0	2	1	1	0	0	1	1	3
MACCLESFIELD T	3	1	2	0	4	2	3	1	0	2	2	5
MAIDSTONE U	6	2	1	3	7	9	6	0	1	5	0	8
MERTHYR T	3	0	1	2	3	9	3	1	1	1	6	5
MORECAMBE	1	1	0	0	2	1	1	0	0	1	2	3
NORTHWICH V	10	4	3	3	13	9	10	1	2	7	7	20
NUNEATON B	5	3	2	0	6	2	5	1	1	3	5	12
REDDITCH U	1	1	0	0	2	0	1	1	0	0	3	1
RUNCORN	7	1	3	3	9	14	7	0	3	4	8	14
RUSHDEN & D	1	0	0	1	0	2	1	0	0	1	0	4
SCARBOROUGH	6	1	2	3	7	10	6	0	3	3	3	9
SLOUGH T	2	1	0	1	5	5	2	0	0	2	0	4
SOUTHPORT	1	0	1	0	0	0	1	1	0	0	4	0
STAFFORD R	8	5	2	1	14	6	8	0	5	3	5	9
STEVENAGE B	1	0	0	1	0	1	1	1	0	0	2	1
SUTTON U	2	2	0	0	4	1	2	0	1	1	4	5
TELFORD U	10	7	1	2	16	9	10	2	2	6	13	23
TROWBRIDGE T	2	2	0	0	4	2	2	0	0	2	1	4
WEALDSTONE	5	3	1	1	5	4	5	0	1	4	3	14
WELLING U	4	2	2	0	10	4	4	0	2	2	6	10
WEYMOUTH	6	2	1	3	11	9	6	0	1	5	5	13
WITTON A	1	0	0	1	0	1	1	1	0	0	1	0
WOKING	1	0	0	1	1	2	1	1	0	0	3	2
WORCESTER C	5	3	1	1	5	2	5	1	0	4	7	13
WYCOMBE W	4	0	2	2	3	7	4	0	1	3	4	10
YEOVIL T	9	7	2	0	17	6	9	3	3	3	11	10
TOTAL	206	86	58	62	287	239	206	33	55	118	205	399

BARROW — LEADING APPEARANCES

	79/80	80/81	81/82	82/83	83/84	84/85	85/86	86/87	89/90	90/91	91/92	92/98	98/99	TOTAL
Colin COWPERTHWAITE	34+1	30+2	42	34+2		36	29		34	33	15+1			287+6
GORDON Kenny	11	22	42	38		40			36+1					189+1
TAYLOR Royston	38	36+1	42	36+1		20+2	7+2							179+6
SKIVINGTON Glen	23+3					23+3	34		31	34	32			177+6
McDONNELL Peter						32			40	41	42			155
THOMAS Kevin	35	37	42	31										145
DOHERTY Neil									41+1	42	41		3+2	127+3
BROOKES Steve		30+1	40	31+1		24+1								125+3
JACKSON Phil	15	23+2	32+1	33										103+3
PROCTOR Kevin							27		19	31+1	21+2			98+3

BARROW — APPEARANCES

	79/80	80/81	81/82	82/83	83/84	84/85	85/86	86/87	89/90	90/91	91/92	92/98	98/99	TOTAL
ARMES George						13+3	15+1							28+4
ASPINALL Wayne						7+1	6+1							13+2
ATKINSON Paddy											19+11			19+11
BAK Johnny							6							6
BALLANTYNE Mike											9			9
BALM Jon						9+3								9+3
BARRETT Colin							0+1							0+1
BAURESS Gary													25	25
BELL Jimmy				9+1										9+1
BOWLES Paul							4+1							4+1
BRADFORD Dave						6								6
BRADY John											15			15
BRAMHALL Neil							7+2							7+2
BRISSETT Trevor						5								5
BROCKBANK Kevin	3	1		11		10	18							43
BROOKES Steve		30+1	40	31+1		24+1								125+3
BROWN Mike										4+1	9+7			13+8
BURGESS Dave											4+8			4+8
BURGESS Ian									24+7	4+5				28+12
BUSBY Dave	10													10
BUTLER Charlie										13				13
BUTLER John						7								7
BYRON Paul				4+2		12								16+2
CAIN Gary		0+1												0+1
CALE Andy		0+1	17+8	4		1								22+9
CAMPBELL Paul											0+5			0+5
CAPSTICK Jimmy							29+2		14+1	17+1				60+4
CARROLL Joe	2+8													2+8

84

BARROW APPEARANCES

	79/80	80/81	81/82	82/83	83/84	84/85	85/86	86/87	89/90	90/91	91/92	92/98	98/99	TOTAL
CAVANAGH John						4								4
CHALLENDER Greg													12	12
CHILTON Tony									31	36+2	21			88+2
CLELLAND Bruce				9+5										9+5
COATES Marc													15+6	15+6
COATHUP Lee													4+2	4+2
CONLIN Dave							11+6							11+6
COOK Alan	7+1													7+1
COPELAND Lee							24		2	1				27
COWPERTHWAITE Colin	34+1	30+2	42	34+2		36	29		34	33	15+1			287+6
DALY Matt													1	1
DAVIS Craig													12	12
DAWSON Brian													12+2	12+2
DAWSON Paul							1							1
DIAMOND Barry	3			12			5							20
DOBIE Mark													5+1	5+1
DOHERTY Neil									41+1	42	41		3+2	127+3
DOOLAN Paul											22+1			22+1
DOWELL Wayne													5+1	5+1
EATOUGH Martin	32+1	18+6												50+7
EDWARDS Brian							13+1							13+1
EDWARDS Levi				2										2
ELLIOTT Andy						10+6								10+6
FARRELL Peter									32+2	12+8				44+10
FENSOME Andy													26+2	26+2
FERRIS Paul									21					21
FORBES Andy				4		3+3	21+1							28+4
FOSTER Ian													15+15	15+15
FRANKLAND Jamie							13+2							13+2
GAMBLE Frank				26+1		17								43+1
GERRARD John	13+2	9+2												22+4
GILMOUR Billy									31+3	29+1	2+5			62+9
GOODLASS Ronnie						16	23+2							39+2
GORDON Kenny	11	22	42	38		40			36+1					189+1
GORMAN Kenny						20								20
GRAHAM Don			32+1											32+1
HADDOW Paul													10+3	10+3
HAMPSON Peter									0+3					0+3
HARDMAN John	2													2
HARRISON Wayne						12+2								12+2
HAYTON Kyle													0+1	0+1
HAYWARD Andy													13+1	13+1
HETHERINGTON Mark							2+1							2+1
HIGGINS Dave													36+1	36+1
HIGGINS Steve									34					34
HILL Andy													8+3	8+3
HUBBOLD Mark	14+6	0+2												14+8
HULME Ken						1								1
JACKSON Malcolm									6+3					6+3
JACKSON Phil	15	23+2	32+1	33										103+3
JOHNSON David							20+1							20+1

BARROW — APPEARANCES

	79/80	80/81	81/82	82/83	83/84	84/85	85/86	86/87	89/90	90/91	91/92	92/98	98/99	TOTAL
JOHNSON Eddie													30+2	30+2
JONES Paul													30	30
KEELAN Kevan						21								21
KEEN Nigel			27+1	26+3		10								63+4
KELLY Neil											21			21
KENNEDY Eddie							12+1						13+2	25+3
KENNEDY Keith						34								34
KETTLE Brian							13							13
KIDD Brian						1+2								1+2
KIELTY Ged													8+8	8+8
KING Peter										16				16
KNOWLES Barry		8+2	21+2	30		5								64+4
KNOX Steve											13+5			13+5
LARGE Dave	2	5+1	17+2	24+2										48+5
LEWIS Gary													4+2	4+2
LODGE Paul							14							14
LOWE Kenny									38	24				62
MACAULEY Carl													24	24
MADDOX Mark													3+1	3+1
MAHON Kevin				6+4										6+4
MARGINSON Karl													2+11	2+11
MARSH Darren										18+1				18+1
MARSH Mike													16+1	16+1
MASON Stuart									2+6					2+6
McCULLOUGH Steve							5+2							5+2
McDONALD Neil	37	33+2	3+1				19+1							92+4
McDONALD Rod													1	1
McDONNELL Peter						32			40	41	42			155
McHUGH Shaun											7			7
McINTYRE Kevin													5	5
McMANUS Brian	2+1													2+1
McNALL Keith											18			18
McPHILLIPS Terry											5			5
MESSENGER Gary									6+6	34+3	32			72+9
MILLIGAN John	4													4
MOORE Colin			3+3				1+1							4+4
MOORE Micky		33+1	32+3	12+1										77+5
MOORE Tony						1								1
MORAN Brian	9													9
MORTON Neil													18+2	18+2
MULGROVE Keith		11												11
MUTCH Andy													21+3	21+3
NAYLOR Roy													4	4
NESBITT Walter							18+1							18+1
NICHOLSON Graham		2												2
NICHOLSON Peter							5							5
NOLAN Dave											7+3			7+3
NUTTALL Martin						17+1								17+1
O'KEEFE Lee													20+3	20+3
ORR Chris													0+1	0+1
O'TOOLE John													5	5

BARROW APPEARANCES

	79/80	80/81	81/82	82/83	83/84	84/85	85/86	86/87	89/90	90/91	91/92	92/98	98/99	TOTAL
PALMER Tony							1+2							1+2
PARK Terry							8+1							8+1
PARKER Stuart							15							15
PARKS Tony													20	20
PEARSON Jim	10	26	10											46
PHILLIPS Benny						16								16
PHILLIPS Ron		2+1												2+1
PHIZACKLEA Dave							10							10
POWER Phil										17+1				17+1
PRIOR LEE												2+2		2+2
PROCTOR Kevin							27		19	31+1	21+2			98+3
REEVES Kevin							3							3
REYNOLDS Andy						1								1
RICHMOND Micky	38	32	33	36+1			2							141+1
ROBERTSON Paul												5		5
ROBINSON Matthew										2+1				2+1
ROGERS John				19+1										19+1
ROUND Paul				3+2										3+2
ROWLANDS Paul											15			15
RUTTER Mark											5+7			5+7
SANDWITH Kevin												10+2		10+2
SEAGRAVES Mark												13		13
SHAUGHNESSY Steve							3							3
SKIVINGTON Glen	23+3					23+3	34		31	34	32			177+6
SLATER Paul										6	36+1			42+1
SMITH Dave			4+4	10+5										14+9
SMITH Mike												4+1		4+1
SMITH Steve						7+2								7+2
SNOOKES Eric							8							8
SOUTHWORTH Brian												1		1
STIMPSON Barrie										13+6				13+6
TAYLOR Mike	3+1													3+1
TAYLOR Royston	38	36+1	42	36+1		20+2	7+2							179+6
THOMAS Kevin	35	37	42	31										145
THOMAS Rob	19+2													19+2
TODHUNTER Stuart									20+9	27+5	16			63+14
TONG David							3							3
TOWERS Frank		2+4												2+4
TULLEY Kevin			12											12
VAUGHAN Dave						1								1
VINCENT Robbie										1+5				1+5
WHARTON Andy						16								16
WHEATLEY Danny										24	18			42
WHITTLE Maurice	13	31	11+4				3+1							58+5
WOOD Greg										0+3				0+3
WOODS Andy												1		1
WORSWICK Micky	31	27+2		0+1										58+3
WRIGHT Andy						2	4							6
WRIGHT Anthony												0+3		0+3
WRIGHT Jeff				14+2										14+2
WYNN Mark	8+1													8+1

Above:
Peter McDonnell
Photo: M Close

Left:
Glen Skivington

Right:
Peter Farrell

BARROW GOALSCORERS

	79/80	80/81	81/82	82/83	83/84	84/85	85/86	86/87	89/90	90/91	91/92	92/98	98/99	TOTAL
ARMES George				2										2
ASPINALL Wayne						1	2							3
ATKINSON Paddy										3				3
BALLANTYNE Mike										2				2
BALM Jon						1								1
BELL Jimmy				1										1
BRADY John											11(1p)			11(1p)
BRAMHALL Neil							2							2
BROOKS Steve			3	2										5
BROWN Mike										3				3
BURGESS Ian									3					3
BUSBY Dave	2													2
BUTLER Charlie										3				3
CALE Andy			3			1								4
CAPSTICK Jimmy							4		3	2				9
CARROLL Joe	1													1
CLELLAND Bruce				1										1
COATES Marc													5	5
CONLIN Dave							1							1
COOK Alan	1													1
COWPERTHWAITE Colin	12	15	16	12(1p)		13(2p)	15(4p)		12(1p)	18	3(1p)			116(9p)
DAWSON Brian												2		2
DIAMOND Barry				1										1
DOHERTY Neil									5	12	7			24
EATOUGH Martin	4(2p)													4(2p)
EDWARDS Brian							2							2
ELLIOTT Andy						2								2
FARRELL Peter									8(3p)					8(3p)
FERRIS Paul									1					1
FOSTER Ian												7		7
GAMBLE Frank			8(4p)			3								11(4p)
GERRARD John	2													2
GILMOUR Billy									8	8	1			17
GOODLASS Ronnie						2	2(1p)							4(1p)
GORDON Kenny		1	4						3					8
GORMAN Kevin						1								1
GRAHAM Don			4(3p)											4(3p)
HARRISON Wayne						1								1
HAYWARD Andy												3		3
HIGGINS Steve									1					1
HUBBOLD Mark	1													1
JACKSON Phil	1(1p)	4(2p)	8(4p)											13(7p)
JOHNSON David							3(1p)							3(1p)
JOHNSON Eddie											3(1p)			3(1p)
JONES Paul												1		1

89

Colin Cowperthwaite - one of the
All Time Conference Greats

BARROW   GOALSCORERS

	79/80	80/81	81/82	82/83	83/84	84/85	85/86	86/87	89/90	90/91	91/92	92/98	98/99	TOTAL
KEELAN Kevin						5								5
KEEN Nigel			4	4		2								10
KENNEDY Eddie							2							2
KETTLE Brian							1							1
KIDD Brian						1								1
KING Peter										1				1
LOWE Kenny									2					2
MACAULEY Carl													2	2
MAHON Kevin				2										2
MARGINSON Karl													2(1p)	2(1p)
McDONALD Neil	3													3
McDONALD Neil							1							1
McNALL Keith											5			5
MESSENGER Gary									2	5	3			10
MOORE Micky		5	6	1										12
MORTON Neil													4	4
MUTCH Andy													8	8
NESBITT Walter							2							2
NICHOLSON Graham		3(1p)												3(1p)
NUTTALL Martin						8								8
O'KEEFE Lee													1	1
PEARSON Jim	3	9	2											14
POWER Phil										1				1
PROCTOR Kevin							1		3	3	2			9
RICHMOND Micky	1	1	1											3
ROGERS John				6										6
ROWLANDS Paul											3			3
SEAGRAVES Mark													1	1
SLATER Paul											2			2
SMITH Dave			1	3										4
STIMPSON Barrie										1(1p)				1(1p)
TAYLOR Royston	5	5	5	3		2(1p)								20(1p)
THOMAS Kevin			1(1p)											1(1p)
THOMAS Rob	4													4
TODHUNTER Stuart										1				1
TOWERS Frank		1												1
WHARTON Andy						2								2
WHEATLEY Danny										5	4			9
WHITTLE Maurice	1	1												2
WORSWICK Micky	4	5												9
WRIGHT Jeff				1(1p)										1(1p)

Billy Gilmour

Neil Doherty

L-R - Kevin Proctor. Peter McDonnell, Billy Gilmour, Paul Ferris, Jimmy Capstick, Neil Doherty, Stuart Todhunter, Ian Burgess, Kenny Gordon, Ken Lowe, Gary Messenger.

BATH CITY

FOUNDER MEMBER
ELECTED FROM: Southern League 1979, 1990 (PROMOTED)
RELEGATED TO: Southern League 1988, 1997
2004-2005 SEASON: Southern League Premier Division

Photographed in 1984-85 the season Bath achieved their highest ever Conference position.
Back Row: Mike Lyons (Asst. Manager), David Palmer, Garry Smith, David Mogg, Tony Ricketts, Dave Singleton, Richard Crowley, Ricky Chandler, Bobby Jones (Manager). Front Row: Phil Barton, Peter Aitken, Peter Hayes, David Payne, Jeff Sherwood, Mike Adams. This team group between them, made a total of 2398 appearances for Bath and Keith Brown was missing from this photo.

SEASONS
16

TOTAL POINTS
811

HIGHEST POSITION
4th 1984-85

LOWEST POSITION
20th 87-88, 90-91, 96-97

HIGHEST ATTENDANCE
2015 v Trowbridge T (1-1-82)

LOWEST ATTENDANCE
277 v Telford U (27-4-87))

SEASON GOALSCORER
Dave Singleton 19 (82/83)
Paul Randall
19 (90/91) 19(1p) (91/92)

CAREER GOALSCORER
Graham Withey 69

CAREER APPEARANCES
David Mogg 395

	HOME							AWAY							
	P	W	D	L	F	A	Pts	P	W	D	L	F	A	Pts	Position
79-80	19	7	9	3	26	21	23	19	3	3	13	17	48	9	16
80-81	19	9	6	4	23	8	24	19	7	4	8	28	24	18	6
81-82	21	7	7	7	30	26	28	21	8	3	10	20	31	27	12
82-83	21	12	3	6	41	25	39	21	5	6	10	17	30	21	10
83-84	21	10	7	4	33	17	27	21	7	5	9	27	31	26	6
84-85	21	15	1	5	30	22	31	21	6	8	7	22	27	26	4
85-86	21	5	8	8	28	25	18	21	8	3	10	25	29	27	12
86-87	21	9	5	7	35	31	32	21	8	7	6	28	31	31	10
87-88	21	7	5	9	27	32	26	21	2	5	14	21	44	11	20
88-89															
89-90															
90-91	21	9	4	8	39	27	31	21	1	8	12	16	34	11	20
91-92	21	8	6	7	27	22	30	21	8	6	7	27	29	30	9
92-93	21	9	8	4	29	23	35	21	6	6	9	24	23	24	7
93-94	21	6	8	7	28	21	26	21	7	9	5	19	17	30	12
94-95	21	10	6	5	35	26	36	21	5	6	10	20	30	21	12
95-96	21	9	4	8	29	31	31	21	4	3	14	16	35	15	18
96-97	21	9	5	7	27	28	32	21	3	6	12	26	52	15	20
Total	332	141	92	99	487	385	469	332	88	88	156	353	515	342	

Bath City	Home						Away					
	P	W	D	L	F	A	P	W	D	L	F	A
ALTRINCHAM	16	4	5	7	17	21	16	4	3	9	11	24
A P LEAMINGTON	3	2	1	0	12	0	3	3	0	0	7	1
BANGOR C	4	2	1	1	8	4	4	1	1	2	2	3
BARNET	10	3	1	6	8	14	10	3	0	7	11	16
BARROW	8	5	2	1	17	6	8	3	3	2	6	6
BOSTON U	12	10	0	2	25	12	12	3	3	6	13	23
BROMSGROVE R	5	1	1	3	2	6	5	1	2	2	5	8
CHELTENHAM T	5	2	3	0	9	3	5	2	3	0	8	6
COLCHESTER U	2	0	1	1	1	2	2	0	0	2	0	7
DAGENHAM	7	4	1	2	12	8	7	4	2	1	7	5
DAGENHAM & R	5	2	2	1	5	3	5	1	0	4	3	9
DARTFORD	3	2	1	0	4	1	3	2	1	0	6	3
DOVER A	4	2	2	0	4	2	4	1	1	2	5	6
ENFIELD	7	2	1	4	7	11	7	1	1	5	6	16
FARNBOROUGH T	5	3	1	1	11	6	5	1	2	2	4	7
FISHER A	2	0	0	2	1	4	2	1	0	1	3	2
FRICKLEY A	7	5	0	2	17	10	7	2	1	4	10	12
GATESHEAD	10	2	4	4	12	11	10	4	1	5	11	16
GRAVESEND & N	3	3	0	0	4	0	3	1	0	2	3	4
HALIFAX T	4	1	3	0	4	3	4	1	1	2	8	11
HAYES	1	1	0	0	3	1	1	1	0	0	1	0
HEDNESFORD T	2	2	0	0	3	1	2	0	0	2	1	4
KETTERING T	16	6	6	4	23	23	16	5	6	5	17	21
KIDDERMINSTER H	12	5	2	5	25	23	12	3	3	6	16	24
LINCOLN C	1	1	0	0	2	1	1	0	0	1	0	3
MACCLESFIELD T	8	2	3	3	11	12	8	2	3	3	6	7
MAIDSTONE U	9	2	4	3	7	9	9	1	2	6	5	18
MERTHYR T	5	1	2	2	2	6	5	0	4	1	3	5
MORECAMBE	2	2	0	0	5	3	2	0	1	1	1	2
NORTHWICH V	16	5	8	3	18	18	16	2	3	11	18	37
NUNEATON B	7	2	2	3	7	7	7	1	3	3	6	14
REDDITCH U	1	0	1	0	1	1	1	0	1	0	1	1
RUNCORN	13	5	3	5	21	15	13	3	4	6	11	16
RUSHDEN & D	1	1	0	0	3	2	1	0	0	1	1	4
SCARBOROUGH	8	4	1	3	11	9	8	1	3	4	5	13
SLOUGH T	6	4	1	1	12	3	6	0	4	2	6	11
SOUTHPORT	4	2	0	2	7	5	4	0	1	3	4	9
STAFFORD R	12	4	3	5	19	18	12	3	1	8	9	18
STALYBRIDGE C	5	0	2	3	4	11	5	2	2	1	7	5
STEVENAGE B	3	1	1	1	3	3	3	0	0	3	1	7
SUTTON U	3	0	1	2	3	9	3	0	1	2	4	11
TELFORD U	16	5	4	7	23	20	16	2	4	10	16	30
TROWBRIDGE T	3	2	1	0	5	2	3	1	2	0	4	3
WEALDSTONE	8	4	3	1	16	10	8	5	3	0	11	4
WELLING U	9	3	5	1	10	8	9	3	2	4	17	10
WEYMOUTH	9	6	1	2	18	12	9	3	3	3	9	11
WITTON A	3	0	2	1	1	3	3	1	2	0	5	2
WOKING	5	2	1	2	5	5	5	1	2	2	6	10
WORCESTER C	6	2	2	2	8	8	6	4	0	2	13	8
WYCOMBE W	5	3	1	1	9	5	5	1	2	2	6	6
YEOVIL T	11	9	2	0	22	5	11	4	1	6	14	16
TOTAL	332	141	92	99	487	385	332	88	88	156	353	515

	Altrincham		A P Leamington		Bangor City		Barnet		Barrow		Boston United		Bromsgrove Rovers		Cheltenham Town		Colchester United	
	H	A	H	A	H	A	H	A	H	A	H	A	H	A	H	A	H	A
79-80	1-1	0-4	0-0	2-1	2-1	1-2	1-2	0-1	1-0	1-2	0-1	2-3						
80-81	0-1	1-3	5-0	4-0	0-0	1-0	1-0	5-1	2-1	0-0	2-0	2-4						
81-82	1-1	0-1	7-0	1-0			2-1	1-0	0-0	1-0	1-2	0-4						
82-83	0-2	0-0			1-2	0-0	0-2	1-2	4-1	1-0	3-2	2-2						
83-84	0-0	0-2			5-1	0-1	0-1	2-1			4-2	0-0						
84-85	1-0	0-0					2-1	1-2	1-2	1-0	2-1	2-1						
85-86	0-2	2-1					1-1	0-1	6-0	1-1	2-0	1-1			1-1	2-1		
86-87	1-1	1-1					0-1	1-2			4-2	2-1			0-0	1-1		
87-88	2-0	0-2					0-1	0-4			2-1	0-2			1-1	3-3		
88-89																		
89-90																		
90-91	2-3	0-2					1-4	0-2	1-1	1-1	1-0	0-3			2-0	0-0	1-2	0-2
91-92	3-2	0-4							2-1	0-2	2-0	0-1			5-1	2-1	0-0	0-5
92-93	3-0	0-1									2-1	2-1	0-3	1-1				
93-94	0-1	2-0											0-1	1-0				
94-95	0-3	0-1											1-1	1-1				
95-96													0-1	1-4				
96-97													1-0	1-2				

	Dagenham		Dagenham & Redbridge		Dartford		Dover Athletic		Enfield		Farnborough Town		Fisher Athletic		Frickley Athletic		Gateshead	
	H	A	H	A	H	A	H	A	H	A	H	A	H	A	H	A	H	A
79-80																		
80-81															3-0	1-2		
81-82	0-3	1-0			1-1	1-1			0-1	1-5					1-3	3-1		
82-83	3-1	1-0							2-2	0-3					4-3	1-2		
83-84	0-1	1-3							3-2	0-2					1-0	2-1	1-1	1-3
84-85	2-0	0-0			1-0	3-1			1-0	1-1					3-0	0-2	1-1	1-1
85-86	1-1	1-0			2-0	2-1			0-2	1-3					1-2	1-2		
86-87	2-0	2-1							1-3	0-1					4-2	2-2	1-1	2-1
87-88	4-2	1-1							0-1	3-1			1-3	0-2				
88-89																		
89-90																		
90-91													0-1	3-0			3-0	0-2
91-92			0-0	1-3							1-2	2-1					0-1	1-0
92-93			2-1	1-2							5-2	1-2					1-1	4-0
93-94			0-0	0-3			0-0	3-0									2-3	0-1
94-95			3-0	0-1			0-0	0-3			2-0	0-0					0-2	1-0
95-96			0-2	1-0			2-1	0-1			2-1	0-0					0-1	1-3
96-97							2-1	2-2			1-1	1-4					3-0	0-5

Season	Gravesend & Northfleet		Halifax Town		Hayes		Hednesford Town		Kettering Town		Kidderminster Harriers		Lincoln City		Macclesfield Town		Maidstone United	
	H	A	H	A	H	A	H	A	H	A	H	A	H	A	H	A	H	A
79-80	2-0	0-2							3-0	2-1							1-1	0-6
80-81	1-0	1-2							0-0	2-2							0-0	1-2
81-82	1-0	2-0							3-2	3-1							1-1	0-1
82-83									2-1	2-4							0-1	1-0
83-84									1-1	0-0	3-0	1-1					1-2	1-1
84-85									1-6	2-1	0-2	2-2					1-0	0-2
85-86									1-1	0-2	2-4	1-3					1-1	2-3
86-87									1-2	0-2	3-2	4-2					1-0	0-0
87-88									2-0	1-1	3-3	2-3	2-1	0-3	3-4	2-0	1-3	0-3
88-89															0-2	1-3		
89-90															1-1	0-0		
90-91									3-3	1-1	4-1	2-3			0-0	0-1		
91-92									1-1	2-2	0-1	1-0			5-1	0-0		
92-93									0-0	1-0	2-1	0-1			1-0	0-1		
93-94			2-2	0-0					0-3	1-0	4-0	0-0			1-1	1-0		
94-95			0-0	2-4					2-0	0-0	3-5	1-2			0-3	2-2		
95-96			2-1	1-3			1-0	1-2	3-1	0-3	1-1	2-1						
96-97			0-0	5-4	3-1	1-0	2-1	0-2	0-2	0-1	0-3	0-6						

Season	Merthyr Tydfil		Morecambe		Northwich Victoria		Nuneaton Borough		Reddoitch United		Runcorn		Rushden & Diamonds		Scarborough		Slough Town	
	H	A	H	A	H	A	H	A	H	A	H	A	H	A	H	A	H	A
79-80					0-0	1-6	1-1	1-1	1-1	1-1					1-0	1-6		
80-81					0-0	1-3	0-0	0-0							0-1	0-1		
81-82					1-1	1-2					0-2	1-5			2-0	1-1		
82-83					3-0	0-3	3-0	0-5			2-1	0-1			2-3	1-0		
83-84					2-0	2-3	0-1	2-5			1-1	1-2			4-1	0-0		
84-85					0-3	1-3	1-0	0-0			0-1	0-0			2-1	0-2		
85-86					0-0	2-1	0-2	3-2			0-1	0-2			0-0	1-2		
86-87					1-1	1-1	2-3	0-1			1-2	1-0			0-3	1-1		
87-88					0-0	1-2					0-1	1-2						
88-89																		
89-90																		
90-91	0-0	0-0			4-1	0-2					6-1	1-1					4-0	0-2
91-92	0-0	1-1			2-0	3-1					3-1	2-0					2-1	2-2
92-93	1-3	1-1			0-5	1-3					1-1	3-1					0-1	1-1
93-94	0-3	1-1			0-0	1-3					0-0	0-0					3-0	0-0
94-95	1-0	0-2			2-2	1-1					4-3	1-1						
95-96			3-2	0-1	0-3	2-2					3-0	0-1					3-1	1-1
96-97			2-1	1-1	3-2	0-1							3-2	1-4			0-0	2-5

	Southport		Stafford Rangers		Stalybridge Celtic		Stevenage Borough		Sutton United		Telford United		Trowbridge Town		Wealdstone	
	H	A	H	A	H	A	H	A	H	A	H	A	H	A	H	A
79-80			2-1	0-4							1-1	1-3			4-4	1-1
80-81			0-0	2-0							0-1	1-2			2-0	1-0
81-82			1-1	0-2							1-2	2-0	1-1	1-1	3-2	1-1
82-83			5-1	1-1							0-0	0-2	2-0	1-1	0-0	3-0
83-84											1-1	2-3	2-1	2-1	3-1	1-0
84-85											2-1	1-3			2-3	1-0
85-86			0-1	0-1							3-0	0-1			2-0	2-1
86-87			4-2	1-0					1-3	2-7	3-1	2-4			0-0	1-1
87-88			0-3	0-1					0-4	1-3	1-2	1-3				
88-89									2-2	1-1						
89-90																
90-91			0-1	1-2							0-1	2-2				
91-92			0-1	0-2							1-2	2-0				
92-93			2-1	2-3	1-1	1-1					4-1	0-0				
93-94	2-1	1-1	2-3	0-2	1-1	3-1					3-0	0-0				
94-95	1-2	1-3	3-3	2-0	2-3	1-0	2-1	0-3			1-1	0-3				
95-96	4-0	1-2			0-4	0-1	1-2	0-2			0-3	1-3				
96-97					0-2	2-2	0-0	1-2			2-3	1-1				

	Welling United		Weymouth		Witton Albion		Woking		Worcester City		Wycombe Wanderers		Yeovil Town	
	H	A	H	A	H	A	H	A	H	A	H	A	H	A
79-80			4-2	2-1					0-4	1-2			1-1	0-1
80-81			2-3	1-1					3-0	2-0			2-1	2-1
81-82			2-1	0-2					2-3	0-2			2-0	0-2
82-83			0-1	0-1					0-0	4-1			2-0	0-1
83-84			1-0	1-0					0-0	4-2			3-1	2-0
84-85			2-1	2-2					3-1	2-1			1-0	2-3
85-86			2-2	0-0							3-1	4-1		
86-87	1-1	1-1	2-1	2-1										
87-88	0-0	1-2	3-1	1-3							2-1	2-2		
88-89														
89-90														
90-91	2-1	1-2									1-2	0-0	2-1	2-3
91-92	0-3	5-0			0-2	2-2					1-1	0-1	3-1	1-1
92-93	1-1	3-0			0-0	0-0	2-0	1-0			2-0	0-2	0-0	1-2
93-94	0-0	0-0			1-1	3-0	0-1	1-4					3-0	2-1
94-95	2-0	5-1							2-0	2-2			3-0	2-1
95-96	1-1	1-2							0-3	0-2				
96-97	3-1	0-2					1-1	2-2						

LEADING APPEARANCES

Dave MOGG	395 (395)	David PAYNE	199+16 (215)
Tony RICKETTS	274+28 (302)	Graham WITHEY	192+14 (206)
Dave SINGLETON	212+49 (261)	Jeff SHERWOOD	186+4 (190)
David PALMER	254+6 (260)	Ian HEDGES	180 (180)
Keith BROWN	225+9 (234)	Grantley DICKS	175+1 (176)
Richard CROWLEY	213+6 (219)	Peter HAYES	161+13 (174)
Rob COUSINS	209+9 (218)	Jeremy GILL	154+10 (164)

Chris BANKS	154 (154)
Adie MINGS	106+43 (149)
Gary SMART	121+16 (137)
Ricky CHANDLER	126+3 (129)
Mike ADAMS	114+14 (128)
Paul RANDALL	93+18 (111)
Paul BODIN	106 (106)
Peter AITKEN	98+5 (103)

LEFT:
Chris Smith showing great determination.

BELOW: Dave Singleton

Photo: Paul Dennis

BELOW
Keith Brown steps in to clear the danger
with Tony Ricketts on the ground.

Bath City APPEARANCES

	79-80	80-81	81-82	82-83	83-84	84-85	85-86	86-87	87-88	88-89	89-90	90-91	91-92	92-93	93-94	94-95	95-96	96-97	TOTAL
ADAMS Mike					3	33+4	32+3	21+3	25+4										114+14
ADCOCK Paul															38+2	22+4	23+7	3	86+13
ADEKOLA David																5+2			5+2
AITKEN Peter				24	32+2	33+2			9+1										98+5
BAILEY Peter														1					1
BAKER Mike		4+1																	4+1
BALDWIN Danny																3+2			3+2
BANKS Chris												39	41	41	33				154
BARNES Neil						3+4													3+4
BARTON Phil				15+1	14+5	26	18	12											85+6
BATTERS Mark									1										1
BATTY Paul															21+10				21+10
BAVERSTOCK Ray														2					2
BELL Andy					7+1														7+1
BELL Gordon			4						2										6
BENNETT Martin	35																		35
BIRKBY Dean																35+2	17+4		52+6
BIRKS Steve																21+1			21+1
BODIN Paul							40	42	24										106
BOND Len									27										27
BOOK Kim	3																		3
BOYLE Martin													32+7	26+5	21+6				79+18
BRAKE Phil		3+1	24+1	2															29+2
BRAY Wayne						3													3
BROOKS Mike																		11+5	11+5
BROOKS Nicky															21+1	25	15+1	21	82+2
BROOM Glyn	1																		1
BROWN Bobby	34	15+1																	49+1
BROWN Keith		18	11+2	40	36+1	34	31+2					29	26+2						225+9
BROWN Richard								0+4						0+2					0+4
BRYANT Derek	7																		7
BYRNE Gerry				32															32
CAINS Andy			3																3
CANN Darren																		1+1	1+1
CARR Everton									6										6
CASEY Mike							0+2												0+2

Bath City APPEARANCES

	79-80	80-81	81-82	82-83	83-84	84-85	85-86	86-87	87-88	88-89	89-90	90-91	91-92	92-93	93-94	94-95	95-96	96-97	TOTAL
CHALLENDER Greg																	5+1		5+1
CHANDLER Ricky				12	38+2	30+1	34		12										126+3
CHENOWETH Paul															37+2	28+6	12+1		77+9
CHIVERTON Eston																26+4			26+4
CHURCH Mark								0+2											0+2
CHURCHWARD Alan												33	31						64
CLARK Billy												2							2
CLARKE Gary			4+2																4+2
CLEMENTS Steve																0+1			0+1
CLEVERLEY Jay																		5	5
COLBOURNE Graham																		13	13
COUSINS Rob												24+6	32	37+1	42	36+1	38+1		209+9
CRAIG Dave									23+1										23+1
CRAWFORD Alan								20+9											20+9
CRAWLEY Gerry								5+1											5+1
CROCKER Marcus																3			3
CROFT Brian																	1		1
CROSS Steve																		7	7
CROWLEY Richard												31	31+3	40	31	14	7+2	11	213+6
CUNNINGHAM Mark									3+2										3+2
DAVEY Joe																		16+1	16+1
DAVIS Mike																		33+7	33+7
DAY Graham	13				28+1														41+1
DEAN Steve		16+1	11+2																27+3
DICKS Grantley													22	33+1	31	26	42	21	175+1
DOWLING John			7+1																7+1
DUNN Russell	1																		1
DURBIN Brian	31+1																		31+1
ELLIOTT Dean														0+5					0+5
ENGLAND Mike			10	28+1	12+2			25											75+3
FINNIGAN Trevor						10													10
FORBES Donald																14+2			14+2
FRANKLAND Tony														1					1
FREEGARD John									17+1			22+1							39+2
FRENCH Jon																		10	10
FULBROOK Gary							25	37	23										85

BATH CITY

Bath City APPEARANCES

	79-80	80-81	81-82	82-83	83-84	84-85	85-86	86-87	87-88	88-89	89-90	90-91	91-92	92-93	93-94	94-95	95-96	96-97	TOTAL
GAMBLE David												1							1
GEORGE Ricky							0+1												0+1
GILL Jeremy												5	10+8	39	35+2	40	25		154+10
GILL Tony																		1+2	1+2
GOCAN Peter												0+4							0+4
GOUGH Jimmy					1														1
GOVER Paul	25	2																	27
GRAHAM Ben																	4+2		4+2
GRAPES Steve					23+2														23+2
GRIFFIN Kevin		14+1																	15+1
GRIMSHAW Martyn							9+3	38	10+8										57+11
GUEST Brendan		4																	4
HALLIDAY Bruce									30+1										30+1
HANCOCK Paul			9																9
HARRINGTON Mark																		36+4	36+4
HARRISON Gerry															3				3
HARRISON Mike	22	5																	27
HARTE Stuart																		1+3	1+3
HARVEY Ian																		2+8	2+8
HAYES Peter	21+2	35	36+1	30+3	31+2	8+5													161+13
HAZLEHURST Danny																		0+11	0+11
HEDGES Ian												7	40	21	22	32	30	28	180
HENDY Nicky									7+1										7+1
HERVIN Mark																4	0+2	27	31+2
HEWLETT Matthew																3			3
HIRONS Paul												1+4	0+2					7+2	8+8
HIRST Martin				18															18
HONOR Christian																		10	10
HUGHES Wayne				40	10+1														50+1
JACKSON Darren																8			8
JAMES Lea																2+1			2+1
JAMES Stuart																	18+8	33+4	51+12
JASPER Steve	1																		1
JENKINS Jimmy	30+4	16	12	24+5															82+9
JOHNS Mark	12+3	4+1																	16+4
JONES Vaughan														6+1		7			13+1

101

Bath City 1990-91

Back Row (L-R)
Dave Singleton
Richard Crowley
Tony Ricketts
Jim Preston
John Freegard
Paul Randall
Chris Banks

Middle:
Graham Jemmott
Paul Hirons
Ian Weston
Dave Palmer
Rob Cousins
Dave Payne
Keith Brown

Front:
George Rooney (Manager)
Chris Smith
Paul Stevens
Philip Underhill
Peter Gocan
David Monks (Physio)

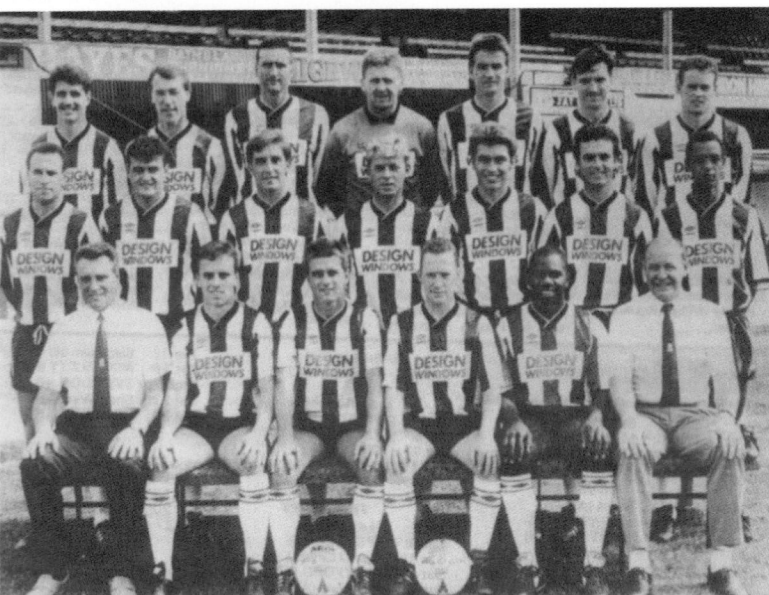

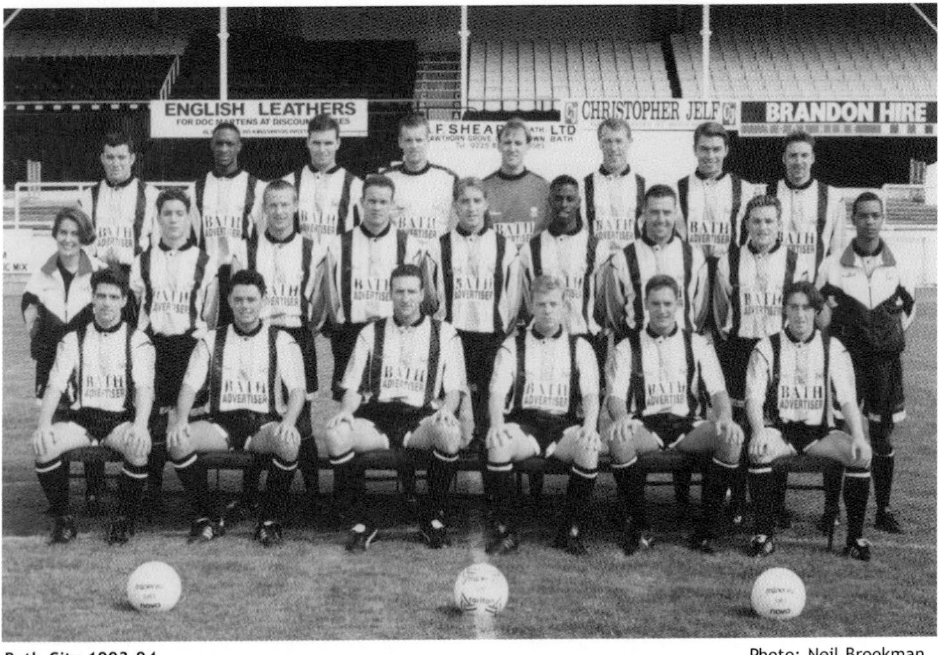

Bath City 1993-94 Photo: Neil Brookman

Back Row (L-R): Grantley Dicks, Kevin Thaws, Martin Boyle, Steve Book, Dave Mogg, Richard Crowley, Rob Cousins, Gary Smart. **Middle Row:** Rachel Jackson (Physio), Steve Slocombe, Colston Gwyther, Chris Banks, Ian Weston, Deion Vernon, Wayne Noble, Paul Chenoweth, Keith Brown (Res. Manager). **Front:** Paul Batty, Jerry Gill, Tony Ricketts (Manager), Dave Palmer (Asst. Manager), Ian Hedges, Paul Adcock.

Bath City APPEARANCES

Player	79-80	80-81	81-82	82-83	83-84	84-85	85-86	86-87	87-88	88-89	89-90	90-91	91-92	92-93	93-94	94-95	95-96	96-97	TOTAL
KEAN Steve													9+1						9+1
LAIGHT Ellis																		4	4
LEITCH Andy	4+3																		4+3
LEWIS Rob									0+1										0+1
LILYGREEN Chris								6+9	20+7										26+16
LOSS Colin																5			5
LOWE Tiv												8							8
LUCAS Jay															2+3	1+3	5+6	1+7	9+19
LUNDON Sean		24+1										22+1							34+6
MACKAY Bob			28+1	3									12+5						55+2
MADDISON Lee														4					4
MADGE Mark																		9	9
MALPAS Mike	21+1																		21+1
MANN Adrian									4										4
McKELVANEY Peter	1																		1
McLOUGHLIN Paul																14			14
McNEILL Brian				1															1
MEACHAM Jeff						4+2													4+2
MEHEW Dave									2+1			3							5+1
MELLON Micky																		10	10
MERRICK Geoff				5															5
MICCICHE Marco																	6+1		6+1
MILES Andy							1												1
MILES Kevin						4+1													4+1
MILLE Sean									8+2										8+2
MINGS Adie												17+9	21+4	17+5	18+8	17+5	16+12		106+43
MOGG Dave				42	42	42	41	42	12					42	37	38	42	15	395
MORRELL Paul	12+1	30																	42+1
MURPHY Ricky			6+1	2															8+1
MURRAY Eddie																		1	1
NICHOLL Jimmy																		1	1
NOBLE Wayne															9+3				9+3
O'DONNELL Brian							13	32+3											45+3
OGDEN Chris		38	38																76
PAINTER Steve													0+1						1+1
PALMER Dave		5+1	38	23	25+4	39	16	36	31+1			23		18					254+6

Bath City APPEARANCES

	79-80	80-81	81-82	82-83	83-84	84-85	85-86	86-87	87-88	88-89	89-90	90-91	91-92	92-93	93-94	94-95	95-96	96-97	TOTAL
PAUL Martin																		9+6	9+6
PAYNE David					26+2	38+2	34+4	36+2	41+1			23+4	1+1						199+16
PEARSON Gerry				2+2															2+2
PENNY Shaun				28+4	4+3													16+6	48+13
PLATT David						12													12
PLAYER Keith								0+1											0+1
POWELL Wayne	16+7	5+4																	21+11
PRATT Mike							22+4	16+2	25+3										63+9
PRESTON Jim												9	11						20
PRUE Kevin			8	0+1															8+1
RADFORD Dean												0+3	4+1						4+4
RANDALL Paul												38+4	39+3	16+11					93+18
RICKETTS Tony	29+2	31	36+1	42	42	40	13					16+1	22+3	1+2	0+5	2+10	0+4		274+28
RISDALE Steve			2																2
ROBERTS Dave					2+1														2+1
ROLLO Jim																		4	4
RUDGLEY Simon															2				2
RYAN Nigel	9																		9
SANDERS Alan				0+1															0+1
SAUNDERS Neil																	18+5		18+5
SCOTT Andy																	10	12	22
SHAW Chris								27+3	3										30+3
SHAW Martin		29+4	25																54+4
SHERWOOD Jeff			38		30+1	32+2	35+1	37									14		186+4
SINGLETON Dave			24	40	24+2	3+4	25+5	9+3	18+12			31+3	17+12	21+8					212+49
SMART Gary														31+4	29+7	30	31+5		121+16
SMITH Chris												10+6							10+6
SMITH Gary				1+1	29+2	32+2	1+1												63+6
SOWTER Mark							1												1
SPENCER Mickey																3+4	7+5		10+9
STANTON Chris								1+1											1+1
STEVENS Paul							27+4	16	28			6							77+4
STROUD Ken							1												1
SUGAR Chris																	15+1		15+1
SUMMERS Steve	17+2	1																	18+2
TANNER Micky									12			5+1							17+1

Bath City APPEARANCES

	79-80	80-81	81-82	82-83	83-84	84-85	85-86	86-87	87-88	88-89	89-90	90-91	91-92	92-93	93-94	94-95	95-96	96-97	TOTAL
TAVENER Colin	30+2																		33+2
TAYLOR Craig																12+1			12+1
TAYLOR Mark						0+3	1+1												1+4
TAYLOR Stuart		36+1	21+2																57+3
THAWS Kevin															5+3				5+3
THEOBALD Alan													0+1						0+1
THOMAS Rod				2															2
THOMPSON Mike					1														1
THOMSON Barry		15	4	7+1	0+1														26+2
TILLEY Darren							0+1									1+2			1+3
TORRES Raphael															3				3
TOVEY Paul																		12+1	12+1
TOWLER Colin																		18	18
TOWNSEND Chris												7+8							7+8
UNDERHILL Phil												25+2							25+2
VERNON Deion														12+14	10+14	6+12	9+11		37+51
WADE Brian		3+2	13+2																17+5
WALKER Matthew																		6+6	6+6
WALSH Alan																5+3	3+2		8+5
WARD Dave									2										2
WEBBER Mike	1+1		5+3																6+4
WESTON Ian												11+1	27	23+4	2				63+5
WHEELER Martin	31+1	29+3	9+1				12+3												81+8
WHITEHOUSE Mark												2							2
WIFFILL Dave	12								18										30
WIGLEY Russell																	2+1		2+1
WILLIAMS Gary															10+3				10+3
WILLIAMS Keith									4										4
WILLIAMS Paul									10+6										10+6
WILLMOTT Martin				0+1	0+1	1+1													1+3
WITHEY Graham		32	34+1				14	4	5			11	34+4	30+2			21	7+7	192+14
WRIGHT Mark						1+8	3+5												4+13
WYATT Mike																		40	40

LEFT: Paul Batty "kissing" the boot that put Bath through to the 3rd Round of the Cup in 1993. Photo: Paul Dennis
BELOW: Paul Randall, hair flying, scores with this strike against Kettering.   Photo: Alan Casse.

RIGHT: Paul Paul Chenoweth gets his cross in despite the challenge.
Photo: Keith Clayton

BELOW: Gary Smart   Photo: Paul Dennis

Bath City GOALSCORERS

	79-80	80-81	81-82	82-83	83-84	84-85	85-86	86-87	87-88	88-89	89-90	90-91	91-92	92-93	93-94	94-95	95-96	96-97	TOTAL
ADAMS Mike					1	7	4	4											16
ADCOCK Paul															17	10(1p)	4(1p)	1	32(2p)
ADEKOLA David																2			2
AITKEN Peter				3	4(3p)	1(1p)													8(4p)
BANKS Chris													2						2
BARNES Neil						2													2
BARTON Phil				1	1	1	1												4
BATTY Paul															3				3
BELL Andy					2														2
BIRKBY Dean																16(1p)	3		19(1p)
BIRKS Steve																1			1
BODIN Paul							7	16	9(2p)										32(2p)
BOYLE Martin													10	7	3				20
BRAKE Phil			6																6
BROOKS Nicky															1	4		1	6
BROWN Bobby	3(1p)		1																4(1p)
BROWN Keith	2	2	7	7	2	4													24
BROWN Richard							1												1
BRYANT Derek	2																		2
CHANDLER Ricky				2	6	4	2		1										15
CHENOWETH Paul															4	3(1p)			7(1p)
CHIVERTON Eston																	4		4
COLBOURNE Graham																		6	6
COUSINS Rob												1	3	4	5	1	2		16
CRAIG Dave									2										2
CRAWFORD Alan								5											5
CROCKER Marcus																2			2
CROSS Steve																		1	1
CROWLEY Richard												3	1	11	4	1			20
DAVIS Mike																		14(1p)	14(1p)
DAY Graham	1																		1
DICKS Grantley																1			1
DOWLING John			1																1
DURBIN Brian	2(1p)																		2(1p)
ENGLAND Mike		2			1			2											5

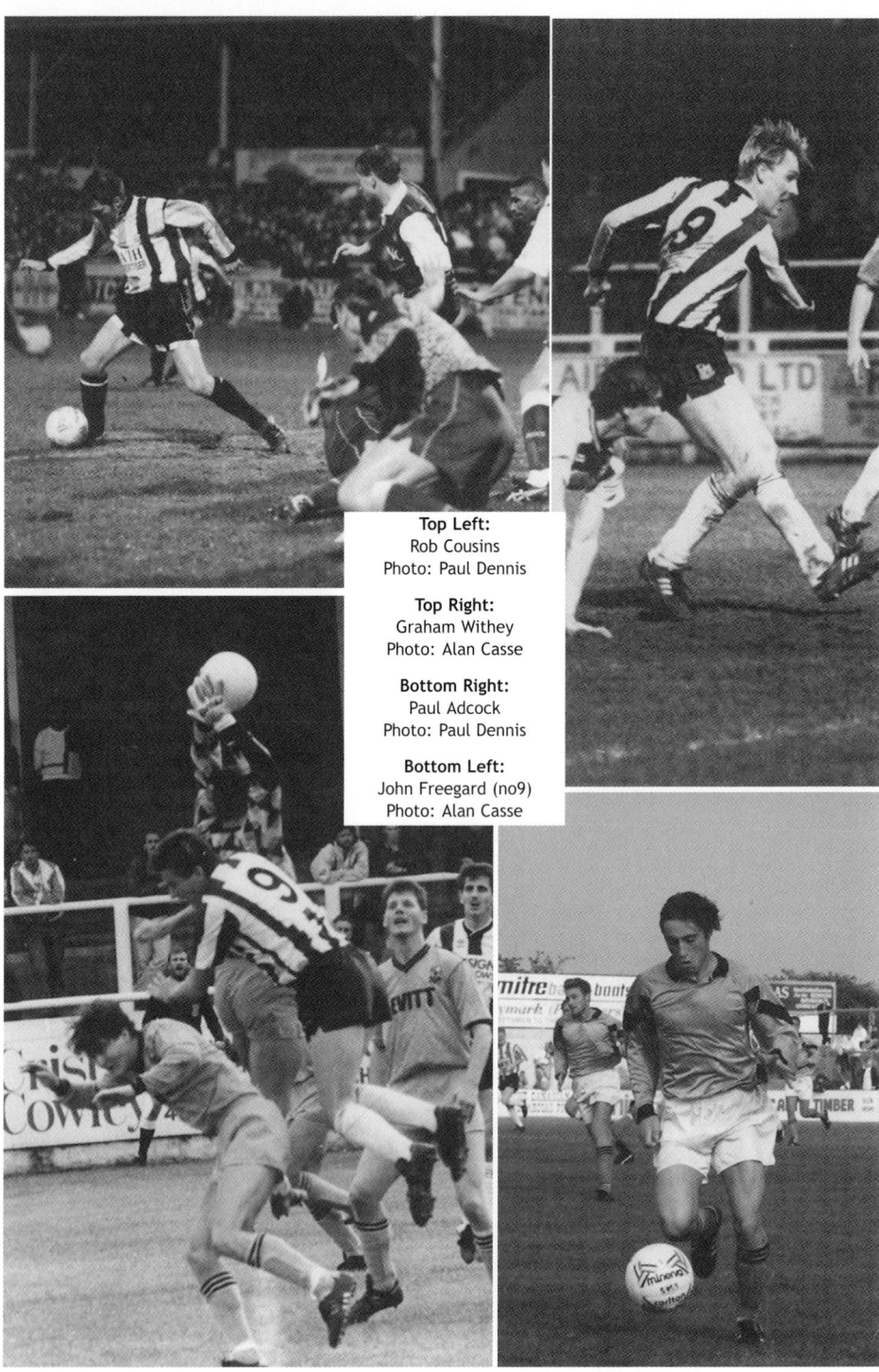

Top Left:
Rob Cousins
Photo: Paul Dennis

Top Right:
Graham Withey
Photo: Alan Casse

Bottom Right:
Paul Adcock
Photo: Paul Dennis

Bottom Left:
John Freegard (no9)
Photo: Alan Casse

Bath City GOALSCORERS

	79-80	80-81	81-82	82-83	83-84	84-85	85-86	86-87	87-88	88-89	89-90	90-91	91-92	92-93	93-94	94-95	95-96	96-97	TOTAL
FINNIGAN Trevor												4							4
FREEGARD John									5			7							12
FULBROOK Gary								2	1										3
GILL Jeremy													1	6	2				9
GRAPES Steve					2														2
GRIFFIN Kevin		5																	5
GRIMSHAW Martyn							3	8											11
HARRINGTON Mark																		3	3
HAYES Peter	1	2	5(1p)	1	3	2													14(1p)
HEDGES Ian													3					1	4
HIRONS Paul																		2	2
HIRST Martin				1															1
HUGHES Wayne				2(1p)	1														3(1p)
JAMES Stuart																	1	1	2
JENKINS Jimmy	10	4	2	10															26
JOHNS Mark		1																	1
KEAN Steve													1						1
LAIGHT Ellis																		1	1
LEITCH Andy	1																		1
LILYGREEN Chris								2	8(2p)										10(2p)
LOWE Tiv												2							2
LUNDON Sean												4							4
MACKAY Bob		2	2																4
MALPAS Mike	1																		1
McLOUGHLIN Paul																2			2
MEACHAM Jeff						1													1
MEHEW David																		3	3
MERRICK Geoff				1															1
MILLS Sean									1										1
MINGS Adie												4	2	5	2	3	7		23
NOBLE Wayne															1(1p)				1(1p)
PALMER Dave				1	1	4	2	5				1							14
PAUL Martin																		3	3
PAYNE Dave					5	8	2	14	9										38
PEARSON Gerry					2														2

Bath City GOALSCORERS

	79-80	80-81	81-82	82-83	83-84	84-85	85-86	86-87	87-88	88-89	89-90	90-91	91-92	92-93	93-94	94-95	95-96	96-97	TOTAL
PENNY Shaun				7	1													5	13
PLATT David						2													2
POWELL Wayne	4	1																	5
PRATT Mike									1										1
PRUE Kevin			1																1
RANDALL Paul												19	19(1p)	1					39(1p)
RICKETTS Tony												1							9
RISDALE Steve			1																1
SCOTT Andy																	2		2
SHAW Chris								3											3
SHAW Martin		2	1																3
SHERWOOD Jeff			4																4
SINGLETON Dave			5	19	10		14		4										54
SMART Garry														5(1p)	4(2p)	7(2p)	5(2p)		21(7p)
SMITH Chris												2							2
SMITH Gary					14	8													22
SPENCER Micky																	1		1
STEVENS Paul							1		2(1p)										3(1p)
SUGAR Chris																	1		1
SUMMERS Steve	2																		2
TAVENER Colin	1																		1
TAYLOR Stuart			1																1
THOMSON Barry		1																	1
TOWLER Colin																		2	2
TOWNSEND Chris												4							4
VERNON Deion														7		1	4		12
WADE Brian		1	2																3
WALKER Matthew																		1	1
WESTON Ian													1						1
WHEELER Martin	13	11(5p)					2												26(5p)
WIFFILL Dave								1	2										3
WITHEY Graham		16	16				7		2			3	7	5			10	2	69
WRIGHT Mark						2	1												3
WYATT Mike																		5	5

BOSTON UNITED

FOUNDER MEMBER
ELECTED FROM: Northern Premier 1979
PROMOTED FROM: Northern Premier League 1993 Southern League 2000
RELEGATED TO: Northern Premier 1993   PROMOTED TO: Football League 2002
2004-2005 SEASON: Football League Division 2

Boston United 2001-02 L-R **Back Row:** Daryl Clare, Nick Conroy, Paul Bastock, Simon Weatherstone, James Gould. **Middle Row:** Dan Wormham, Mark Clifford, Peter Costeloe, Ross Weatherstone, Jamie Cook, Mickey Brown, Anthony Elding, Mark Monington, Gez Murphy, Paul Taylor. **Front Row:** Gerry Evans (Touth Team Coach), Simon Rusk, David Town, Steve Evans (Manager), Michael Sneddon, Mark Angel, Alan Lewer (Asst. Manager)

	HOME							AWAY							
	P	W	D	L	F	A	Pts	P	W	D	L	F	A	Pts	Position
79-80	19	11	7	1	40	20	29	19	5	6	8	12	23	16	4
80-81	19	10	4	5	39	30	24	19	6	5	8	24	28	17	8
81-82	21	14	4	3	46	23	46	21	3	7	11	15	34	16	10
82-83	21	14	5	2	46	25	47	21	6	7	8	31	32	25	5
83-84	21	10	6	5	39	30	26	21	3	6	12	27	50	15	17
84-85	21	10	5	6	43	32	25	21	5	5	11	26	37	20	17
85-86	21	11	5	5	41	26	27	21	5	2	14	25	50	17	13
86-87	21	11	4	6	40	28	37	21	10	2	9	42	46	32	6
87-88	21	9	5	7	33	25	32	21	5	2	14	27	50	17	16
88-89	20	12	3	5	36	28	39	20	10	5	5	25	23	35	3
89-90	21	10	3	8	36	30	33	21	3	5	13	12	37	14	18
90-91	21	9	4	8	40	31	31	21	3	7	11	15	38	16	18
91-92	21	10	4	7	40	35	34	21	8	5	8	31	31	29	8
92-93	21	5	6	10	23	31	21	21	4	7	10	27	38	19	22
1993-2000															
00-01	21	10	7	4	43	28	37	21	3	10	8	31	35	19	12
01-02	21	12	5	4	53	24	41	21	13	4	4	31	18	43	1
Total	331	168	77	86	638	446	529	331	92	85	154	401	570	350	

SEASONS
16

TOTAL POINTS
879

HIGHEST POSITION
1st (01-02)

LOWEST POSITION
22nd (92-93)

HIGHEST ATTENDANCE
5822 v Lincoln C (26-12-87))

LOWEST ATTENDANCE
502 v Altrincham (28-4-93)

SEASON GOALSCORER
Jim Lumby 27(1p) (82/83)
Gary Jones 27 (91/92)

CAREER GOALSCORER
Chris Cook 93

CAREER APPEARANCES
Paul Casey 268+11

111

Table 1

	Altrincham		A P Leamington		Aylesbury United		Bangor City		Barnet		Barrow		Bath City		Bromsgrove Rovers		Cheltenham Town	
	H	A	H	A	H	A	H	A	H	A	H	A	H	A	H	A	H	A
79-80	2-5	0-3	2-0	0-2			3-1	0-2	1-1	0-0	3-0	1-0	3-2	1-0				
80-81	1-1	0-2	2-3	0-0			1-1	1-1	3-0	2-2	0-2	2-0	4-2	0-2				
81-82	1-1	1-1	2-0	2-2					1-1	0-0	2-1	0-1	4-0	2-1				
82-83	3-0	2-2					4-3	1-0	1-0	4-1	2-1	1-1	2-2	2-3				
83-84	2-2	0-3					3-2	0-0	0-0	2-1			0-0	2-4				
84-85	0-0	2-7							2-1	0-1	1-3	1-1	1-2	1-2				
85-86	1-3	3-1							1-2	0-3	2-1	1-2	1-1	0-2			1-2	1-2
86-87	4-2	1-3							0-3	1-5			1-2	2-4			1-1	3-1
87-88	2-2	1-4							2-1	0-1			2-0	1-2			4-1	5-1
88-89	3-1	0-0			2-0	2-1			5-0	0-0							1-1	1-3
89-90	2-3	0-0							1-2	2-1							2-1	0-0
90-91	2-6	1-1							1-3	0-5	0-2	1-1	3-0	0-1			2-1	0-5
91-92	2-1	4-2									4-1	2-2	1-0	0-2			3-3	1-1
92-93	1-2	1-1											1-2	1-2	1-2	1-2		
93-94																		
94-95																		
95-96																		
96-97																		
97-98																		
98-99																		
99-00																		
00-01																		
01-02									1-1	1-0								
02-03																		

Table 2

	Chester City		Chorley		Colchester United		Dagenham		Dagenham & Redbridge		Darlington		Dartford		Doncaster Rovers		Dover Athletic	
	H	A	H	A	H	A	H	A	H	A	H	A	H	A	H	A	H	A
79-80																		
80-81																		
81-82							3-4	0-2					3-2	1-2				
82-83							3-3	1-1										
83-84							3-0	0-2										
84-85							4-1	2-1					2-0	1-1				
85-86							3-0	2-2					3-0	1-0				
86-87							1-0	2-3										
87-88							1-0	2-4										
88-89			2-0	1-0														
89-90			0-1	0-0							1-3	1-6						
90-91					1-3	1-3												
91-92					0-4	0-1			2-1	4-1								
92-93									3-1	0-1								
93-94																		
94-95																		
95-96																		
96-97																		
97-98																		
98-99																		
99-00																		
00-01	0-0	2-2							5-1	1-2					3-1	2-4	1-2	0-0
01-02	0-1	2-1							1-2	0-1					2-2	1-0	4-2	2-3
02-03																		

	Enfield		Farnborough Town		Fisher Athletic		Forest Green Rovers		Frickley Athletic		Gateshead		Gravesend & Northfleet		Hayes		Hednesford Town	
	H	A	H	A	H	A	H	A	H	A	H	A	H	A	H	A	H	A
79-80													4-0	0-0				
80-81									1-2	1-0			2-1	2-1				
81-82	1-0	0-4							3-1	1-4			2-2	1-3				
82-83	0-2	2-4							2-1	0-2								
83-84	3-2	0-1							2-2	1-7	0-4	5-5						
84-85	3-2	1-1							2-1	1-2	1-1	2-1						
85-86	1-2	0-3							0-3	1-5								
86-87	5-1	3-2							2-2	1-0	6-0	3-1						
87-88	2-3	2-3			2-1	0-0												
88-89	3-2	2-1			2-4	3-1												
89-90	1-0	1-0	2-2	0-1	2-0	0-1												
90-91					4-1	2-1					5-1	1-0						
91-92			0-1	0-5							4-0	1-2						
92-93			0-0	0-4							0-2	2-2						
93-94																		
94-95																		
95-96																		
96-97																		
97-98																		
98-99																		
99-00																		
00-01							0-0	3-0							0-1	1-1	3-4	4-2
01-02			4-0	2-0			6-1	3-0							4-1	2-0		
02-03																		

	Hereford United		Kettering Town		Kidderminster Harriers		Kingstonian		Leigh RMI		Lincoln City		Macclesfield Town		Maidstone United		Margate	
	H	A	H	A	H	A	H	A	H	A	H	A	H	A	H	A	H	A
79-80			1-0	1-3											1-1	0-1		
80-81			2-1	0-0											1-1	2-2		
81-82			4-2	1-1											6-0	2-0		
82-83			2-1	0-2											1-0	0-2		
83-84			3-3	1-2	2-3	1-1									1-0	2-2		
84-85			3-1	1-2	2-3	0-2									1-0	2-2		
85-86			4-1	1-3	2-1	2-3									2-2	2-1		
86-87			2-1	2-1	2-1	2-1									0-3	2-2		
87-88			0-2	0-3	1-0	0-1					1-2	1-5	0-2	1-2	3-3	2-1		
88-89			1-1	2-1	0-2	2-0							3-2	1-0	1-4	0-3		
89-90			1-2	0-5	2-3	3-1							3-0	0-0				
90-91			1-2	1-1	3-1	3-3							1-1	0-2				
91-92			1-1	3-1	1-2	3-1							1-5	1-0				
92-93			0-1	3-3	0-3	2-0							3-1	1-2				
93-94																		
94-95																		
95-96																		
96-97																		
97-98																		
98-99																		
99-00																		
00-01	5-3	1-1	4-3	2-2			2-1	0-0	0-1	2-2								
01-02	3-4	1-0							2-1	2-1							0-1	1-1
02-03																		

	Merthyr Tydfil		Morecambe		Northwich Victoria		Nuneaton Borough		Redditch United		Runcorn		Rushden & Diamonds		Scarborough		Slough Town	
	H	A	H	A	H	A	H	A	H	A	H	A	H	A	H	A	H	A
79-80					2-0	1-0	2-2	0-2	2-0	2-0					2-2	4-2		
80-81					2-3	1-3	3-1	2-0							0-3	2-3		
81-82					2-0	0-1					0-1	0-4			2-1	1-1		
82-83					1-0	1-1	1-1	2-1			2-4	2-3			1-0	0-0		
83-84					3-1	1-3	3-0	0-4			1-2	1-3			1-1	0-2		
84-85					3-4	0-1	2-3	2-4			2-0	2-1			3-3	0-1		
85-86					3-0	4-3	3-2	1-0			2-1	0-3			2-1	1-2		
86-87					0-1	0-4	2-1	5-1			2-0	1-3			1-3	0-0		
87-88					0-1	0-6					2-2	0-3						
88-89					2-1	1-0					0-6	2-1						
89-90	2-2	0-1			1-3	0-1					3-2	1-3						
90-91	3-0	0-2			4-1	1-3					2-2	1-2					0-1	0-2
91-92	2-0	0-2			0-2	1-1					2-1	2-2					3-1	1-3
92-93	2-0	3-0			3-5	3-3					0-0	2-1					0-0	0-3
93-94																		
94-95																		
95-96																		
96-97																		
97-98																		
98-99																		
99-00																		
00-01			2-1	0-2	1-1	3-0	4-1	1-3					1-1	0-0	2-2	2-2		
01-02			2-1	0-0	3-2	2-1	4-1	1-1							2-2	0-2		
02-03																		

	Southport		Stafford Rangers		Stalybridge Celtic		Stevenage Borough		Sutton United		Telford United		Trowbridge Town		Wealdstone		Welling United	
	H	A	H	A	H	A	H	A	H	A	H	A	H	A	H	A	H	A
79-80			3-2	0-0							3-1	1-4			0-0	1-1		
80-81			2-2	3-2							5-3	0-2			2-1	0-3		
81-82			2-1	0-0							4-2	1-4	1-0	0-1				
82-83			1-1	2-0							4-0	2-3	3-0	2-1	0-0	0-0		
83-84											2-3	2-3	2-0	2-0	1-1	1-1		
84-85											1-3	1-1			1-1	1-0		
85-86	1-1	1-2									2-2	1-2			1-0	2-7		
86-87	2-0	1-0							0-0	1-3	2-3	2-5			2-0	4-0	4-3	2-4
87-88	4-1	4-3							0-0	2-1	1-1	1-2			0-1	1-1	1-2	1-3
88-89	2-1	1-4							3-1	0-0	1-0	1-0					2-0	2-3
89-90	2-0	0-0							3-1	0-2	2-2	2-4					2-1	0-6
90-91	0-2	2-1							2-2	0-0	2-1	0-1					0-0	0-0
91-92	2-2	1-0									1-2	2-0					5-1	3-1
92-93	0-1	0-0			1-1	1-2					2-2	1-0					2-1	2-2
93-94																		
94-95																		
95-96																		
96-97																		
97-98																		
98-99																		
99-00																		
00-01	1-0	1-3					3-3	2-3			2-1	2-3						
01-02	0-0	3-2			4-1	1-2	0-0	2-1			3-1	2-2						
02-03																		

Boston United FC 1988-89   Photo: Bob Whitaker

	Weymouth		Witton Albion		Woking		Worcester City		Wycombe Wanderers		Yeovil Town	
	H	A	H	A	H	A	H	A	H	A	H	A
79-80	2-2	0-3					1-1	0-0			3-0	0-0
80-81	2-1	1-2					3-1	4-1			3-1	1-2
81-82	0-2	1-2					3-2	0-0			0-0	1-0
82-83	3-2	2-4					4-1	1-1			6-3	4-0
83-84	4-3	2-0					0-1	2-2			3-2	2-4
84-85	2-2	1-2					4-1	1-2			3-0	4-2
85-86	5-0	0-0							1-1	1-4		
86-87	1-1	4-3										
87-88	1-0	1-3							4-0	2-1		
88-89	2-0	2-2							0-1	1-2	1-1	1-1
89-90									2-0	0-1	0-1	1-2
90-91									0-1	0-3	4-0	1-1
91-92			3-2	0-1					2-2	1-2	1-3	1-1
92-93			2-2	0-2	1-2	0-3			0-3	3-3	1-0	1-2
93-94												
94-95												
95-96												
96-97												
97-98												
98-99												
99-00												
00-01					0-0	1-1					4-1	1-2
01-02					4-0	2-0					4-0	1-0
02-03												

Left to Right

Back Row:
Ted Goddard (Physio)
Alex Coupland
Lee Hurford
Gary Baines
Glenn Beech
Don Robisnon (Trainer)

Middle Row:
Martin King
David Vaughan
Martin Hardy
John McKenna
David Cusack
Billy Millar
Allen Crombie
Warren Ward
Gerald Creane

Front Row:
Paul Shirtliff
Chris Cook
Gary Simpson
George Kerr (Manager)
Ronnie Reid (Team Manager)
Paul Wilson
David Beavon
Stewart Hamill

115

Middle LEFT:
(L-R) Andrew Stanhope,
Paul Bastock & Tim Wooding
Photo: Peter Barnes

Middle RIGHT:
Jim Rodwell heads just over.
Photo: Peter Barnes

BOTTOM:
Richard Dawson & Gerald
Creane covering Lincoln's
John McGinlay in front of
5,822 fans.
Photo: David Dales.

LEADING APPEARANCES		LEADING GOALSCORERS	
Paul CASEY	268+11	Chris COOK	93
Chris COOK	228+46	Jim LUMBY	44(6p)
Gary MALLENDER	225+4	Gary JONES	43
Kevin BLACKWELL	227	Paul WILSON	31
John McKENNA	196	Bob LEE	30
Gary SIMPSON	186+7	Bobby BROWN	28
Martin HARDY	177+3	David GILBERT	27(10p)
Gerard CREANE	156+4	Warren WARD	25
Paul SHIRTLIFF	151	Daryl CLARE	24(7p)
Paul BASTOCK	125	Paul CAVELL	23
Derek NUTTELL	100+25	Ken CHARLERY	21(3p)
David VAUGHAN	107+5	John McGINLEY	20(1p)
Dave ADAMSON	105+1	Gary MALLENDER	20

Boston U	Home						Away					
	P	W	D	L	F	A	P	W	D	L	F	A
ALTRINCHAM	14	4	5	5	26	29	14	2	6	6	16	30
A P LEAMINGTON	3	2	0	1	6	3	3	0	2	1	2	4
AYLESBURY U	1	1	0	0	2	0	1	1	0	0	2	1
BANGOR C	4	3	1	0	11	7	4	1	2	1	2	3
BARNET	13	5	4	4	19	15	13	4	4	5	12	20
BARROW	9	6	0	3	16	12	9	2	4	3	10	10
BATH C	12	6	3	3	23	13	12	2	0	10	12	25
BROMSGROVE R	1	0	0	1	1	2	1	0	0	1	1	2
CHELTENHAM T	7	3	3	1	14	10	7	2	2	3	11	13
CHESTER CITY	2	0	1	1	0	1	2	1	1	0	4	3
CHORLEY	2	1	0	1	2	1	2	1	1	0	1	0
COLCHESTER U	2	0	0	2	1	7	2	0	0	2	1	4
DAGENHAM	7	5	1	1	18	8	7	1	2	4	9	15
DAGENHAM & R	4	3	0	1	11	5	4	1	0	3	5	5
DARLINGTON	1	0	0	1	1	3	1	0	0	1	1	6
DARTFORD	3	3	0	0	8	2	3	1	1	1	3	3
DONCASTER R	2	1	1	0	5	3	2	1	0	1	3	4
DOVER A	2	1	0	1	5	4	2	0	1	1	2	3
ENFIELD	9	6	0	3	19	14	9	3	1	5	11	19
FARNBOROUGH T	4	1	2	1	6	3	4	1	0	3	2	10
FISHER A	4	3	0	1	10	6	4	2	1	1	5	3
FOREST GREEN R	2	1	1	0	6	1	2	2	0	0	6	0
FRICKLEY A	7	3	2	2	12	12	7	2	0	5	6	20
GATESHEAD	6	3	1	2	16	8	6	3	2	1	14	11
GRAVESEND & N	3	2	1	0	8	3	3	1	1	1	3	4
HAYES	2	1	0	1	4	2	2	1	1	0	3	1
HEDNESFORD T	1	0	0	1	3	4	1	1	0	0	4	2
HEREFORD U	2	1	0	1	8	7	2	1	1	0	2	1
KETTERING T	15	9	2	4	29	20	15	3	5	7	18	30
KIDDERMINSTER H	10	4	0	6	15	19	10	5	2	3	18	13
KINGSTONIAN	1	1	0	0	2	1	1	0	1	0	0	0
LEIGH RMI	2	1	0	1	2	2	2	1	1	0	4	3
LINCOLN C	1	0	0	1	1	2	1	0	0	1	1	5
MACCLESFIELD T	6	3	1	2	11	11	6	2	1	3	4	6
MAIDSTONE U	10	4	4	2	17	14	10	3	4	3	14	16
MARGATE	1	0	0	1	0	1	1	0	1	0	1	1
MERTHYR T	4	3	1	0	9	2	4	1	0	3	3	5
MORECAMBE	2	2	0	0	4	2	2	0	1	1	0	2
NORTHWICH V	16	8	1	7	30	25	16	5	3	8	19	31
NUNEATON B	9	6	2	1	24	12	9	4	1	4	14	16
REDDITCH U	1	1	0	0	2	0	1	1	0	0	2	0
RUNCORN	12	5	3	4	18	21	12	3	1	8	14	29
RUSHDEN & D	1	0	1	0	1	1	1	0	1	0	0	0
SCARBOROUGH	10	3	5	2	16	18	10	1	4	5	10	15
SLOUGH T	3	1	1	1	3	2	3	0	0	3	1	8
SOUTHPORT	2	1	1	0	1	0	2	1	0	1	4	5
STAFFORD R	12	6	4	2	21	14	12	6	4	2	15	12
STALYBRIDGE C	2	1	1	0	5	2	2	0	0	2	2	4
STEVENAGE B	2	0	2	0	3	3	2	1	0	1	4	4
SUTTON U	5	2	3	0	8	4	5	1	2	2	3	6
TELFORD U	16	8	4	4	37	27	16	3	2	11	21	36
TROWBRIDGE T	3	3	0	0	6	0	3	2	0	1	4	2
WEALDSTONE	8	3	4	1	7	4	8	2	4	2	10	13
WELLING U	7	5	1	1	16	8	7	1	2	4	10	19
WEYMOUTH	10	6	3	1	22	13	10	2	2	6	14	21
WITTON A	2	1	1	0	5	4	2	0	0	2	0	3
WOKING	3	1	1	1	5	2	3	1	1	1	3	4
WORCESTER C	6	4	1	1	15	7	6	1	4	1	8	6
WYCOMBE W	7	2	2	3	9	8	7	1	1	5	8	16
YEOVIL T	13	9	2	2	33	12	13	4	4	5	19	17
TOTAL	331	168	77	86	638	446	331	92	85	154	401	570

Boston United

	79-80	80-81	81-82	82-83	83-84	84-85	85-86	86-87	87-88	88-89	89-90	90-91	91-92	92-93	1993 - 2000	00-01	01-02	TOTAL
ADAMS Steve	36											13						48+3
ADAMSON Dave		32	37+1										35+3					105+1
ALEXANDER Keith		4+4																4+4
ALLEN Russ			38	26+3														64+3
ALLPRESS Tim														4				4
ANGEL Mark																	26+8	26+8
ANNABLE Phil		35	19															54
ASH Mark									11									11
BAINES G									1+3									1+3
BARTLETT Paul		11+3	32+5	4+6														47+14
BASTOCK Paul														42		42	41	125
BEATTIE Andy										2								2
BEAVON David								32+1	34+1	4								70+2
BEECH Glenn										20		33+3	0+1					53+4
BEESLEY Darren																	3+3	3+3
BELL Charlie					5													5
BELL Derek							8	1+7										9+7
BENNETT Desmond												0+1						0+1
BIRD Kevin					24+1													24+1
BLACKWELL Kevin	38	38	36	37	40	34	42											227
BRABIN Gary																	1	1
BROGAN Mark											2							2
BROLLY Mike									9+3									9+3
BROWN Bobby	33	22+1																55+1
BROWN Graham				5														5
BROWN Mick																	21+5	21+5
BROWN Richard									15+1									15+1
BUCKLEY Steve										20+1	25+6	1+1						46+8
BUTLER Lee								2										2
CALLERY Neil	37	36	5															78
CAMPBELL Winston											19	31+2						50+2
CARR Peter									14+4									14+4
CASEY Paul				31+4	39+2	37	35	40	26+3				34+2	26				268+11
CAVELL Paul												31	11					42
CHAMBERS Steve														37+3				37+3

Boston United	79-80	80-81	81-82	82-83	83-84	84-85	85-86	86-87	87-88	88-89	89-90	90-91	91-92	92-93	1993 - 2000	00-01	01-02	TOTAL
CHARLERY Ken																30+1	12	42+1
CLARE Daryl																	39+1	39+1
CLIFFORD Mark																11	40	51
COLLIER Graham		11	19+1															30+1
COLLINS Steve													38+1					38+1
CONROY Nicky																0+2	0+1	0+3
COOK Chris	0+2	3+1	7+6	14+2	33+4	21+11	39+1	38+1	18+5	31+4	14+7	10+2						228+46
COOK Jamie																11+2	11+20	22+22
COOK Mark											19	9+1						28+1
CORDER Peter								3										3
CORK David														6				6
COSTELLO Peter																14+6	17+8	31+14
COUPLAND A									0+1									0+1
COVERDALE Drew														7+6				7+6
COX Mark			25+4	13+1														38+5
CRAMMAN Kenny																1		1
CREANE Gerard					9+3	32	40	33+1	36	6								156+4
CROMBIE Allen									7	14+7	11							32+7
CURTIS Andy														8+2				8+2
CURTIS Hamish														13				13
CURTIS Lennie																4		4
CURTIS Robbie														21+2				21+2
CUSACK David										24+8	27+1	29+2						80+11
CZUCZMAN Mick						21+1	24											45+1
DALTON Tim								3				1						3
DANZEY Michael											3+1							4+1
DAVIS Darren														9				9
DAWSON Richard								7+2	21									28+2
DE SOUZA Miquel																7+2		7+2
DEANE Tony											4+3	10+2						14+5
DENYER Peter							4	6										10
DIAF Farid																3+2		3+2
DICK Jim																27+1		27+1
DUGGAN Derek										5+8								5+8
DULSON Gary			29															29

Boston United	79-80	80-81	81-82	82-83	83-84	84-85	85-86	86-87	87-88	88-89	89-90	90-91	91-92	92-93	1993 - 2000	00-01	01-02	TOTAL
ELDING Anthony																1+10	12+6	13+16
ELLENDER PAUL																	36	36
ENDERBY Phil		8+1																8+1
EVANS Gary													0+1					0+1
EVANS James																	1	1
FEE Greg								27										27
FEWINGS Paul																15+11		15+11
FLETCHER Mark													0+1					0+1
FOSTER Barry				14														14
FOX Kevin	4																	4
FOXCROFT D								1										1
FRASER Steven												2						2
FRENCH Daniel																2+4		2+4
FROGGATT John	28+1																	28+1
FUTCHER Ron														2				2
GALLAGHER Jackie											14+5							14+5
GAMBLE Willie											18+5							18+5
GARWOOD Colin				18														18
GAVIN Pat														1				1
GENOVESE Domenico						18+5	2+3											20+8
GILBERT David				28	31+5	30+1	39+1											128+7
GILDING Simon						1												1
GILL Martyn								41	17+1									58+1
GILLIVER Andy												0+2						0+2
GORDON Jimmy			6															6
GOULD James																	26+6	26+6
GOWSHALL Joby																35+2		35+2
GRAHAM Jon														26+12				26+12
GRANT Dave										6+3	19+6							25+9
GRAY Phil																	3	3
GRAYSON Neil														36+2				36+2
GROCOCK Chris											11							11
HALLAM Mark														6+8				6+8
HAMILL Stewart										32+3	34+4	1						67+7
HARDY Martin										35+1	39+1	32	34+1	37				177+3

BOSTON UNITED

Boston United	79-80	80-81	81-82	82-83	83-84	84-85	85-86	86-87	87-88	88-89	89-90	90-91	91-92	92-93	1993 - 2000	00-01	01-02	TOTAL
HARRISON Andy	12+3																	12+3
HARTFORD Asa												15						15
HAWKEY Shaun											1+1							1+1
HEARMON Richard				2+2	3	3+1												8+3
HIBBERD Stuart				5+5														5+5
HILL Andy								2+1										2+1
HIMSWORTH Bobby					2+1													2+1
HIRST Stephen					6+6													6+6
HOLLAND Wayne					1													1
HOOKS Paul							28+3	23+2										51+5
HOUGH J	1																	1
HOWARTH Lee													10	7		30		47
HOYLE Colin																26+3		26+3
HUBBARD Phil	22	21+1	7+6															50+7
JONES Gary													41+1	34+1				75+2
JONES Phil				33	20+3													53+3
KABIA Jim	18+5	24+1						7+2	3+8									52+16
KNIGHT Ian														10+1				10+1
KOWALSKI Andy									11+1									11+1
LADD Ian						32	28+1	17+1										77+2
LAMONT Lee													1					1
LANCASTER Kevan		12																12
LAVERICK Mick				5+1	26	12	16+1											59+2
LEE Bob					28	38	11+3											77+3
LEE Gary														25				25
LEIGH Dennis	30	29																59
LISSAMAN Jeff								29+3	23+2									52+5
LISTER Steve														7				7
LIVETT Simon																2+4		2+4
LODGE Andy																17+5	19+3	36+8
LUCAS Richard																29+4		29+4
LUMBY Jim				39	25+3	7+4												71+7
LYON Mick			4	16+2	4	7+4	1+1											32+7
MALLENDER Gary	37	37	40	38+1	39+2	34+1												225+4
MANN Arthur	37			42	23	3+2	5+1											73+3

Boston United	79-80	80-81	81-82	82-83	83-84	84-85	85-86	86-87	87-88	88-89	89-90	90-91	91-92	92-93	1993 - 2000	00-01	01-02	TOTAL
MARKHAM Dave	10																	10
MARSH Mike																	7	7
MARSHALL Gary											1							1
McEWAN Stan											14+2							14+2
McGARRY Steve																	2+4	2+4
McGINLEY John											17	20+3	12+7					49+10
McJANNET Les														5				5
McKENNA John									33	40	40	42	41					196
McKENZIE Roger														1				1
McLAUGHLIN Steve										2+7	10+6							12+13
McMANUS Eric								9										9
McPHERSON John					1	7		9										17
McVAY David			17															17
MELL Stewart										4								4
MILLAR Billy								10	9+1									19+1
MILLER Jason														3+1				3+1
MILLS Gary																5+3		5+3
MINETT Jason																4+5		4+5
MITCHELL Barry									11+2									11+2
MONINGTON Mark																	25	25
MOORE Andy													20+7					20+7
MOORE David											1+1							1+1
MORRIS Colin											9							9
MORRIS Wayne												1+6						1+6
MOSS David														17				17
MOSSMAN Dave										26+3	2+1	6+7						34+11
MOYES John	7+7																	7+7
MUNTON Darren														5+14				5+14
MURPHY Gez																	4+14	4+14
MYLES Steve													3+1					3+1
NESBITT Mick												13+2	12+4					25+6
NEWTON Doug								7	20									27
NORRIS David																5		5
NORTH Marc													1					1
NUTTELL Derek					10+3	25+3	30+5	15+10	20+4									100+25

Boston United	79-80	80-81	81-82	82-83	83-84	84-85	85-86	86-87	87-88	88-89	89-90	90-91	91-92	92-93	1993-2000	00-01	01-02	TOTAL
NUTTELL Micky													23			12+7		35+7
OAKES Keith														1				1
O'BRIEN Derek	11																	11
O'BRIEN Ray						33	2+1											35+1
OTTEWLL Gavin							9+3	31+4	25+12									65+19
PARR Trevor			27+1	26+1	20													73+2
PEACOCK John		29																29
PHELAN Albert	19	1																20
PHILLIPS Brendan		8+2	34+1	6														48+3
POPLAR Dave	35	28+1																63+1
RAFFELL Stephen												25+5	22+2					47+7
RAWCLIFFE Peter										15+2	4+3							19+5
RAWLE Mark																13+14		13+14
RAYNOR Paul																31+1		31+1
REDDIN Dave													0+1					0+1
RENNIE David																3		3
RETALLICK Graham													7+7					7+7
RICHARDS Pedro								17										17
RICHARDSON Mark					5+3													5+3
RICHARDSON Paul												4	9					13
RODWELL Jim																	16	16
RUSK Simon																6+2	23+4	29+6
SCOTT Dion																	7	7
SCOTT Keith												2						2
SCRUPPS Ian								0+1										0+1
SCRUPPS K						0+1												0+1
SEARCHWELL Neville											0+2							0+2
SHIRTLIFF Paul										39	39	36	37					151
SIMMONITE Gordon	30	3																33
SIMPSON Gary		25+1	39	12+2	33+1	39	5+3			28	5							186+7
SLACK Trevor														10				10
SMITH Alan													0+1					0+1
SORRELL Tony														1				1
STANHOPE Andy																17+5		17+5
STENSON David							29											29

Above: James Gould

Photos: Peter Barnes

Below: Jim Rodwell

RIGHT:

Top:
David Adamson
Photo: D J Gregory

Middle:
Gordon Simmonite
Photo: D J Gregory

Bottom:
Mark Angel
Photo: Peter Barnes

Boston United	79-80	80-81	81-82	82-83	83-84	84-85	85-86	86-87	87-88	88-89	89-90	90-91	91-92	92-93	1993-2000	00-01	01-02	TOTAL
STEPHENSON Geoff												16+1						16+1
STEWART Gary	33																	33
STOUTT Steve											7		34+3	23+8				64+11
SWAILES Chris													28+2					28+2
TARRANT Neil																	4+6	4+6
THOMPSON Neil																	4	4
THOMPSON Steve	26																	26
THOMSON Brian						27+1	38+3	13+3										78+7
TILER Kenny			39	32+1														71+1
TOMLINSON David												16+1						16+1
TOONE Richard												15+3	9+9	2+1				26+13
TOWLE S	1																	1
TOWN David																6+1	5+18	11+19
TOWNSEND Chris							11											11
TROTT Dean														9+5				9+5
TURNER Andy																4		4
VAUGHAN David									25+3	34+1	28	20+1						107+5
WAITT Mick											2							2
WARBURTON Ray																	5+1	5+1
WARD Warren								25+3	35+3	14+7								74+13
WEATHERSTONE Ross																6+1	19+5	25+6
WEATHERSTONE Simon																13	33+1	46+1
WEST Gary														9				9
WHARTON David											13	28+1						41+1
WHITE Chris														10				10
WHITE Devon							4+3	9+3										13+6
WHITEHOUSE Carl								5										5
WILKINSON Alan														2				2
WILLIS Roger											10							10
WILSON Paul									38+1	39+1								77+2
WILSON Paul																18		18
WOOD Ian				19	29													48
WOODING Tim																12		12
WORTHINGTON Clive					1+2	1+1												2+3
WORTHINGTON Dave		1	2+1	2														5+1

Left:
John McKenna
Photo: Mick Cheney

Right:
Paul Cavell
A & K Markham Photographers

Below Left:
Daryl Clare
Photo: Peter Barnes

Below Right:
John McGinlay
A & K Markham Photographers

Boston United	79-80	80-81	81-82	82-83	83-84	84-85	85-86	86-87	87-88	88-89	89-90	90-91	91-92	92-93	1993 - 2000	00-01	01-02	TOTAL
ADAMS Steve												2(1p)	1					3(1p)
ADAMSON Dave	6(3p)	2	10(8p)															18(11p)
ALLEN Russ			4	4														8
ANGEL Mark																	4	4
ANNABLE Phil		2																2
BAINES G									1									1
BARTLETT Paul		4	5															9
BEECH Glenn										3		2(1p)						5(1p)
BELL Charlie					3													3
BELL Derek							5											5
BIRD Kevin					2													2
BROWN Bobby	19	9																28
BROWN Mick																	3	3
CALLERY Neil	2																	2
CAMPBELL Winston											1		1	1				3
CASEY Paul				3	2	3		3				2						13
CAVELL Paul												16	7					23
CHARLERY Ken																13(3p)	8	21(3p)
CLARE Daryl																	24(7p)	24(7p)
COLLIER Graham		8	8															16
COOK Chris		1		6	15	8	13	23	6	15	3	3						93
COOK Jamie																2	4	6
COOK Mark												1						1
COSTELLO Peter												7(4p)					1	8(4p)
COVERDALE Drew														1				1
COX Mark			13	6														19
CREANE Gerard					1	4	2	7(4p)	4(3p)									18(7p)
CROMBIE Allan									2(1p)									2(1p)
CURTIS Andy														1				1
CUSACK David						1												1
CZUCZMAN Mick							3			1								4
DE SOUZA Miguel																1		1
DEANE Tony											3	4						7

Left: Paul Ellender   Photo: Bill Wheatcroft

Above: Chris Cook and then Chairman Pat Mallinson.   Photo: T Houch

Below: An acrobatic John McKenna

BOSTON UNITED

Boston United	79-80	80-81	81-82	82-83	83-84	84-85	85-86	86-87	87-88	88-89	89-90	90-91	91-92	92-93	1993 - 2000	00-01	01-02	TOTAL
DENYER Peter								1										1
DIAF Farid																1		1
DICK Jim																1		1
ELDING Anthony																	6	6
ELLENDER Paul																	2	2
FEE Greg								7										7
FEWINGS Paul																4		4
FLETCHER Mark													1					1
FROGGATT John	4																	4
GAMBLE Willie											2							2
GARWOOD Colin				10														10
GENOVESE Domenico						11(1p)												11(1p)
GILBERT David				3	4	4(3p)	16(7p)											27(10p)
GILL Martyn								6	1									7
GOULD James																	3	3
GRAHAM Jon														7				7
GRANT Dave										1	1							2
GRAYSON Neil														4				4
GROCOCK Chris											2							2
HAMILL Stewart										12(10p)	6(1p)							18(11p)
HARDY Martin										1	3	5	4	2				15
HEARMON Richard					1													1
HIRST Stephen					1													1
HOOKS Paul							6	4										10
HOWARTH Lee														1		3		4
HOYLE Colin																1		1
HUBBARD Phil		11	4															15
JONES Gary													27	16				43
JONES Phil				1	3													4
KABIA Jim	5	11																19
LADD Ian						1	1											2
LAVERICK Mick				2	5	3	3(1p)											13(1p)
LEE Bob					10	19	1											30

Above: Martin Hardy
Photo: Mick Cheney

Right: Paul Casey
Photo: Tim Hoff

Below: John McGinlay scoring.
Photo: A & JK Markham Photographers

BOSTON UNITED

Boston United	79-80	80-81	81-82	82-83	83-84	84-85	85-86	86-87	87-88	88-89	89-90	90-91	91-92	92-93	1993 - 2000	00-01	01-02	TOTAL
LEIGH Dennis		1(1p)																1(1p)
LISSAMAN Jeff								5(1p)	1									6(1p)
LUMBY Jim				27(1p)	13(4p)	4(1p)												44(6p)
LYON Mick				2														2
MALLENDER Gary	2	3	5	3	4	3												20
MANN Arthur				1	1													2
MARSH Mike																	1	1
McEWAN Stan											2							2
McGINLEY John											10(1p)	5	5					20(1p)
McLAUGHLIN Steve										1	2							3
MELL Stewart										1								1
MILLER Jason														1				1
MINETT Jason																1(1p)		1(1p)
MOORE Andy													1					1
MORRIS Colin											3(2p)							3(2p)
MOSS David														10				10
MOSSMAN Dave										4		1						5
MUNTON Darren														1				1
MURPHY Gez																	2	2
NESBITT Mick												2	3					5
NEWTON Doug								4	6(1p)									10(1p)
NORRIS David																4		4
NORTH Marc													1					1
NUTTELL Derek							5	2										7
NUTTELL Micky													9(2p)					9(2p)
O'BRIEN Ray						1												1
OTTEWELL Gavin								3	4									7
PARR Trevor			3	3														6
PHILLIPS Brendan			5	1														6
POPLAR Dave	9	7																16
RAWCLIFFE Peter										1	1							2
RAWLE Mark																10		10
RAYNOR Paul																3		3

BOSTON UNITED — GOALSCORERS

Boston United	79-80	80-81	81-82	82-83	83-84	84-85	85-86	86-87	87-88	88-89	89-90	90-91	91-92	92-93	1993 - 2000	00-01	01-02	TOTAL
RODWELL Jim																	2	2
RUSK Simon																2	2	4
SCOTT Dion																	1	1
SCOTT Keith												2						2
SHIRTLIFF Paul										1								1
SIMMONITE Gordon	1																	1
SIMPSON Gary		3	2	2		1				1								9
STANHOPE Andy																2		2
STOUTT Steve											3		7	1				11
SWAILES Chris													1					1
TARRANT Neil																	1	1
THOMPSON Steve	2																	2
THOMSON Brian						6	2	2										10
TILER Kenny				1														1
TOMLINSON Dave												4(1p)						4(1p)
TOONE Richard													2					2
TOWN David																3	4	7
TOWNSEND Chris							5											5
TROTT Dean														4				4
VAUGHAN David												2						2
WARBURTON Ray																	1	1
WARD Warren								9	13	3								25
WEATHERSTONE Ross																	1	1
WEATHERSTONE Simon																5	12	17
WHARTON David												4						4
WHITE Devon							2	2										4
WILLIS Roger											5							5
WILSON Paul									16	15								31
WILSON Paul																7(5p)		7(5p)
WOOD Ian				1	1													2

BROMSGROVE ROVERS

PROMOTED FROM: Southern League 1992
RELEGATED TO: Southern League 1997
2004-2005 SEASON: Southern League, Div. 1 West

Bromsgrove Rovers 1991-92 with Southern League Championship.
L-R **Back Row:** J Hanks, S Pinfield, L Taiton, S Cooper, C Hanks, M Crisp, P Wardle, S Cooksey, R Moran, P Masefield, S Stott, P Sunners, D Griffiths, B Hewings.
Front Row: T Daly, M O'Connor, P Webb, S Brighton, K Richardson, B Hope, S Burgher, J Skelding, S O'Meara, M Whitehouse.

SEASONS
5

TOTAL POINTS
274

HIGHEST POSITION
2nd (92-93)

LOWEST POSITION
21st (96-97)

HIGHEST ATTENDANCE
4398 v Kidderminster H
(26-12-95)

LOWEST ATTENDANCE
557 v Hayes (22-3-97)

SEASON GOALSCORER
Mark Whitehouse
23(1p) (92/93)

CAREER GOALSCORER
Recky Carter 44(3p)

CAREER APPEARANCES
Jimmy Skelding 189

	HOME						AWAY						
	P	W	D	L	F	A	Pts	P	W	D	L	F	A	Pts	Position
92-93	21	9	7	5	35	22	34	21	9	7	5	32	27	34	2
93-94	21	5	8	8	26	32	23	21	7	7	7	28	34	28	18
94-95	21	9	7	5	42	35	34	21	5	6	10	24	34	21	13
95-96	21	11	6	4	33	20	39	21	4	8	9	26	37	20	11
96-97	21	8	4	9	29	30	28	21	4	1	16	12	37	13	21
Total	105	42	32	31	165	139	158	105	29	29	47	122	169	116	

	Altrincham		Bath City		Boston United		Dagenham & Redbridge		Dover Athletic		Farnborough Town		Gateshead		Halifax Town		Hayes		Hednesford Town	
	H	A	H	A	H	A	H	A	H	A	H	A	H	A	H	A	H	A	H	A
92-93	4-1	2-2	1-1	3-0	2-1	2-1	1-2	1-1			2-2	1-1	3-0	0-0						
93-94	1-2	3-2	0-1	1-1			2-0	2-4	1-2	3-4			3-0	1-0	1-0	0-3				
94-95	0-3	1-1	1-1	1-1			2-2	0-2	2-0	2-0	2-2	3-0	2-2	1-2	0-1	2-4				
95-96	0-0	0-3	4-1	1-0			2-0	2-2	3-0	2-0	1-2	0-1	3-1	0-1	0-1	1-1			1-4	2-4
96-97	4-0	1-3	2-1	0-1					3-1	0-2	1-1	1-2	2-2	0-1	3-0	0-1	2-2	0-1	1-0	0-3

	Kettering Town		Kidderminster Harriers		Macclesfield Town		Merthyr Tydfil		Morecambe		Northwich Victoria		Runcorn		Rushden & Diamonds		Slough Town		Southport	
	H	A	H	A	H	A	H	A	H	A	H	A	H	A	H	A	H	A	H	A
92-93	1-1	2-3	2-2	0-1	3-0	2-0	1-2	1-1			1-2	1-0	0-0	1-2			0-1	3-1		
93-94	0-4	1-0	0-3	1-1	3-0	3-4	3-3	1-2			0-0	1-1	0-0	1-4			0-1	1-1	2-2	2-1
94-95	2-4	1-0	4-3	1-0	2-2	2-2	2-0	1-2			1-4	1-3	1-0	1-3					1-1	1-2
95-96	3-2	2-2	2-1	0-1	1-0	1-2			1-0	1-4	1-1	2-1	2-0	0-0			0-0	3-2	4-1	2-1
96-97	1-2	0-2	0-1	2-1	0-3	0-4			2-3	0-1	0-5	0-1			0-1	2-1	4-1	0-2	0-1	0-0

	Stafford Rangers		Stalybridge Celtic		Stevenage Borough		Telford United		Welling United		Witton Albion		Woking		Wycombe Wanderers		Yeovil Town	
	H	A	H	A	H	A	H	A	H	A	H	A	H	A	H	A	H	A
92-93	2-3	4-3	4-0	1-0			0-0	1-0	2-2	2-4	3-2	1-1	1-0	2-0	1-0	0-4	1-0	2-2
93-94	3-3	0-0	2-0	2-0			0-5	0-0	1-1	1-1	3-3	1-4	0-0	0-0			1-2	3-2
94-95	2-1	1-1	2-1	1-1	2-1	0-1	0-1	2-2	4-1	2-1			5-5	0-4			5-0	0-2
95-96			1-1	1-2	1-1	3-3	0-2	0-0	1-1	2-5			2-1	1-1				
96-97			0-1	0-3	1-1	0-3	2-1	1-3	1-0	2-1			0-3	3-1				

LEADING

	92/93	93/94	94/95	95/96	96/97	TOTAL
APPEARANCES						
Jimmy SKELDING	36	42	38	37	36	189
Mark CRISP	28+3	32+1		39	38+1	137+5
Kevin RICHARDSON	34	35	27	36	5	137
Steve STOTT	32+1	37	39			108+1
GOALSCORERS						
Recky CARTER		13	18(1p)	13(2p)		44(3p)
Mark CRISP	7	5		13	7	32
Mark WHITEHOUSE	23(1p)					23(1p)
Steve STOTT	2	10	9			21

	Home						Away					
	P	W	D	L	F	A	P	W	D	L	F	A
ALTRINCHAM	5	2	1	2	9	6	5	1	2	2	7	11
BATH C	5	2	2	1	8	5	5	3	1	1	6	2
BOSTON U	1	1	0	0	2	1	1	1	0	0	2	1
DAGENHAM & R	4	2	1	1	7	4	4	0	2	2	5	9
DOVER A	4	3	0	1	9	3	4	2	0	2	7	6
FARNBOROUGH T	4	0	3	1	6	7	4	1	1	2	5	4
GATESHEAD	5	3	2	0	13	5	5	1	1	3	2	4
HALIFAX T	4	2	0	2	4	2	4	0	1	3	3	9
HAYES	1	0	1	0	2	2	1	0	0	1	0	1
HEDNESFORD T	2	1	0	1	2	4	2	0	0	2	2	7
KETTERING T	5	1	1	3	7	13	5	2	1	2	6	7
KIDDERMINSTER H	5	2	1	2	8	10	5	2	1	2	4	4
MACCLESFIELD T	5	3	1	1	9	5	5	1	1	3	8	12
MERTHYR T	3	1	1	1	6	5	3	0	1	2	3	5
MORECAMBE	2	1	0	1	3	3	2	0	0	2	1	5
NORTHWICH V	5	0	2	3	3	12	5	1	2	2	5	7
RUNCORN	4	2	2	0	3	0	4	0	1	3	3	9
RUSHDEN & D	1	0	0	1	0	1	1	1	0	0	2	1
SLOUGH T	4	1	1	2	4	3	4	2	1	1	7	6
SOUTHPORT	4	1	2	1	7	5	4	2	1	1	5	4
STAFFORD R	3	1	1	1	7	7	3	1	2	0	5	4
STALYBRIDGE C	5	3	1	1	9	3	5	2	1	2	5	6
STEVENAGE B	3	1	2	0	4	3	3	0	1	2	3	7
TELFORD U	5	1	1	3	2	9	5	1	3	1	4	5
WELLING U	5	2	3	0	9	5	5	2	1	2	9	12
WITTON A	2	1	1	0	6	5	2	0	1	1	2	5
WOKING	5	2	2	1	8	9	5	2	2	1	6	6
WYCOMBE W	1	1	0	0	1	0	1	0	0	1	0	4
YEOVIL T	3	2	0	1	7	2	3	1	1	1	5	6
TOTAL	105	42	32	31	165	139	105	29	29	47	122	169

Adie Smith

Photo: Eric Marsh

LEFT: Scott Cooksey

BELOW: Chris Pearce
Photo: Paul Dennis

BOTTOM RIGHT: Colin Radburn
Photo: Dennis Nichoslon

BOTTOM LEFT: Mark Crisp
Photo: Paul Dennis

BROMSGROVE ROVERS APPEARANCES

	91-92	92-93	93-94	94-95	95-96	96-97	97-98	TOTAL
AMOS Nick					18+1	24+1		42+2
BOSTON Kevin				1+1				1+1
BRAIN Simon		1		1+1	3+5			5+6
BRIGHTON Stewart		35	34	11+2	18+3	26+1		124+6
BURGHER Symon		11	13	11	5	3		43
CARTER Recky			26+1	33	22+1			81+2
CARTY Paul		6	7+4					13+4
CLARKE Nicky			5	34	35+1	22+1		96+2
CLARKE Stuart						1+1		1+1
COOKSEY Scott		25	17					42
COOPER Steve		9+4						9+4
CRANE Scott				0+1				0+1
CRISP Mark		28+3	32+1		39	38+1		137+5
DALE Andy					20+5			20+5
DALY Tommy		23+7		0+2				23+9
DAVIS Mark		3						3
DEVERY Brendan			4+5	17+4				21+9
DOWLING Fergus					2+10			2+10
DUNPHY Nick						9+4		9+4
EADES Gary					2			2
ELMES Robin						3		3
GARDNER Richard					2+4	22+7		24+11
GAUNT Craig			12	41	33			86
GLASSER Nick				17+2	6+3			23+5
GRAY Brian		29+3	11+7	18+6				58+16
GRAY Michael			0+1	12+2				12+3
GREALISH Tony		13+2		3				16+2
GREEN Ron		13	25	21+1				59+1
GREENMAN Chris				2				2
GROCUTT Darren					29+1	27		56+1
HANKS Chris		5+4	8+3					13+7
HODGES Dave			1					1
HOLMES Stephen			9					9
HUMPHREY Paul				4+1				4+1
HUNT John					24+2	23+1		47+3
JUDGE Alan				21+1				21+1
KNIGHT Richard						12+2		12+2
LEWIS Colin						6		6
MAINWARING Andy						26+5		26+5
MARLOWE Andy				10+4	4+6	3+7		17+17
MASEFIELD Paul			6+3					6+3
McKEEVER Scott			1					1
MEYRICK Dean						0+2		0+2
NESBITT Jon						0+5		0+5
OAKES Michael		4						4
OLDEN Neil					2			2
O'MEARA Shaun		16+6	13+1					29+7
PEARCE Chris			6+11	7+4				13+15
PETERS Mark						14+11		14+11
PETTY Jamie						0+1		0+1
PITCHER Steve			0+1					0+1

BROMSGROVE ROVERS   APPEARANCES

	91-92	92-93	93-94	94-95	95-96	96-97	97-98	TOTAL
POWELL Marcus					0+1			0+1
POWELL Robert						0+2		0+2
POWER Andy				29	15+5			44+5
RADBURN Colin			21+3	1	7+5			29+8
RANDALL Stuart					18			18
RICHARDSON Kevin	34	35	27	36	5			137
ROSS Jason	2							2
SCANDRETT Mark	1+1	2						3+1
SHILVOCK Rob	25+5	17+3	12+3					54+11
SIMPSON Barry						0+2		0+2
SKELDING Jimmy	36	42	38	37	36			189
SMITH Adie				16+4	38	38		92+4
SMITH Chris						17+2		17+2
STOTT Steve	32+1	37	39					108+1
SUTTON Peter						0+1		0+1
TALBOT Nolan						2		2
TAYLOR Chris					40	39		79
TAYLOR Steve		14+2	30+1			20		64+3
TROWMAN Ward					1+2	0+3		1+5
WALKER Richard				0+2				0+2
WARDLE Paul	27+1	23+2				28		78+3
WARNER Ashley				4				4
WEBB Paul	42	38						80
WHITE Chris					2	5+1		7+1
WHITEHEAD Matt						3		3
WHITEHEAD Stuart				0+1	1+1			1+2
WHITEHOUSE Adam					1			1
WHITEHOUSE Mark		37+2						37+2
WILLGRASS Alex						10		10
WILLIAMS Lee	5+1							5+1
YOUNG Lee			3+1	2+3	2+3			7+7

Stewart Brighton
Photo: Eric Marsh

Shaun O'Meara clears with an anxious Steve Stott looking on.
Photo: Paul Dennis

Left: Steve Stott

Photo: Dave West.

Above: Kevin Richardson & Paul Webb

Below: Recky Carter

Botton Left: Jimmy Skelding

Photo: Dennis Nicholson

BROMSGROVE ROVERS   GOALSCORERS

	91-92	92-93	93-94	94-95	95-96	96-97	97-98	TOTAL
AMOS Nick					3	1		4
BRAIN Simon		1		1				2
BRIGHTON Stewart		1	1	1	2(2p)	1		6(2p)
BURGHER Symon		2	1			3		6
CARTER Recky			13	18(1p)	13(2p)			**44(3p)**
CARTY Paul		1						1
CLARKE Nicky			1	1	1	1		4
COOPER Steve		2						2
CRISP Mark		7	5		13	7		32
DALE Andy					3			3
DALY Tommy		4						4
DEVERY Brendan			1	2				3
DUNPHY Nick						2		2
GARDNER Richie						3		3
GAUNT Craig				2	5			7
GRAY Brian		7	1	6				14
GRAY Michael				1				1
GROCUTT Darren					2	1		3
HANKS Chris		1	3					4
HUNT John					5	2		7
MAINWARING Andy						9		9
MARLOWE Andy				1	1			2
O'MEARA Shaun		1	1					2
PEARCE Chris				4				4
POWER Andy				1				1
RADBURN Colin			4		1			5
RICHARDSON Kevin		1	1					2
SHILVOVK Rob		5	2	1				8
SKELDING Jimmy			2(2p)	6(5p)	5(5p)	2(2p)		15(14p)
SMITH Adie				1	4	1		6
SMITH Chris						1		1
STOTT Steve		2	10	9				21
TAYLOR Steve			2	9		5		16
WARDLE Paul		1	1			1		3
WARNER Ashley				1				1
WEBB Paul		8(4p)	5(3p)					13(7p)
WHITEHOUSE Mark		23(1p)						23(1p)
YOUNG Lee				1				1

140

BURTON ALBION

PROMOTED FROM: The Northern Premier League 2002
2004-2005 SEASON: The Conference

2003-04 Squad - Back Row (L-R): Ray Hudson, Matt Brown, Glenn Kirkwood, Darren Stride, Colin Hoyle, Aaron Webster, Dan Robinson, Matt Duke, Barry Williams, Ian Wright, Lee Colkin, Ryan Sugden, Steve Booth, Andy Garner.
Front Row: Dale Anderson, Andy Sinton, Robbie Talbot, Andy Ducros, Nigel Clough (Player/Manager), Gary Crosby (Assistant Manager), Christian Moore, Terry Henshaw, Darren Wassall, Jon Howard.

SEASONS		HOME						AWAY						
		P	W	D	L	F	A	Pts	P	W	D	L	F	A	Pts	Position

SEASONS			P	W	D	L	F	A	Pts	P	W	D	L	F	A	Pts	Position
2	**02-03**		21	6	6	9	25	31	24	21	7	4	10	27	46	25	16
TOTAL POINTS 101	**03-04**		21	7	4	10	30	29	25	21	8	3	10	27	30	27	14
HIGHEST POSITION 14th 2003-04	**Total**		42	13	10	19	55	60	49	42	15	7	20	54	76	52	

NB 1pt deducted 2003-04

HIGHEST POSITION
14th 2003-04

LOWEST POSITION
16th 2002-03

HIGHEST ATTENDANCE
3203 v Shrewsbury T. 12.8.03

LOWEST ATTENDANCE
1240 v Margate 27.3.04

SEASON GOALSCORER
Christian Moore 16 (02/03)

CAREER GOALSCORER
Christian Moore 19

CAREER APPEARANCES
Matt Duke 78

	Accrington Stanley		Aldershot Town		Barnet		Chester City		Dagenham & Redbridge		Doncaster Rovers		Exeter City		Farnborough Town		Forest Green Rovers	
	H	A	H	A	H	A	H	A	H	A	H	A	H	A	H	A	H	A
02-03					0-3	2-2	2-0	1-2	0-0	2-1	1-2	0-1			2-0	1-5	2-3	0-2
03-04	1-1	1-3	1-4	1-3	2-3	1-2	1-1	1-3	0-1	2-0			3-4	0-2	1-0	1-2	2-3	1-1

	Gravesend & N'fleet		Halifax Town		Hereford United		Kettering Town		Leigh RMI		Margate		Morecambe		Northwich Victoria		Nuneaton Borough	
	H	A	H	A	H	A	H	A	H	A	H	A	H	A	H	A	H	A
02-03	1-1	2-3	2-2	1-0	2-0	0-4	2-0	2-1	0-1	2-4	0-1	0-0	1-4	0-5	1-1	3-1	1-0	2-1
03-04	3-0	2-1	2-2	4-1	4-1	2-1			3-2	1-0	0-1	2-1	0-1	1-2	0-1	2-1		

	Scarborough		Shrewsbury Town		Southport		Stevenage Borough		Tamworth		Telford United		Woking		Yeovil Town	
	H	A	H	A	H	A	H	A	H	A	H	A	H	A	H	A
02-03	1-1	1-4			1-0	2-2	1-2	1-0			4-7	2-0	0-2	2-2	1-1	1-6
03-04	2-0	2-1	0-1	0-1			1-1	0-1	0-1	1-1	2-1	2-2	2-0	0-1		

Dale Anderson. Photo: Peter Barnes.

Steve Chettle.

	P	W	D	L	F	A	P	W	D	L	F	A
	Home						**Away**					
ACCRINGTON S	1	0	1	0	1	1	1	0	0	1	1	3
ALDERSHOT T	1	0	0	1	1	4	1	0	0	1	1	3
BARNET	2	0	0	2	2	6	2	0	1	1	3	4
CHESTER C	2	1	1	0	3	1	2	0	0	2	2	5
DAGENHAM & R	2	0	1	1	0	1	2	2	0	0	4	1
DONCASTER R	1	0	0	1	1	2	1	0	0	1	0	1
EXETER C	1	0	0	1	3	4	1	0	0	1	0	2
FARNBOROUGH T	2	2	0	0	3	0	2	0	0	2	2	7
FOREST GREEN R	2	0	0	2	4	6	2	0	1	1	1	3
GRAVESEND & N	2	1	1	0	4	1	2	1	0	1	4	4
HALIFAX T	2	0	2	0	4	4	2	2	0	0	5	1
HEREFORD U	2	2	0	0	6	1	2	1	0	1	2	5
KETTERING T	1	1	0	0	2	0	1	1	0	0	2	1
LEIGH R M I	2	1	0	1	3	3	2	1	0	1	3	4
MARGATE	2	0	0	2	0	2	2	1	1	0	2	1
MORECAMBE	2	0	0	2	1	5	2	0	0	2	1	7
NORTHWICH V	2	0	1	1	1	2	2	2	0	0	5	2
NUNEATON B	1	1	0	0	1	0	1	1	0	0	2	1
SCARBOROUGH	2	1	1	0	3	1	2	1	0	1	3	5
SHREWSBURY T	1	0	0	1	0	1	1	0	0	1	0	1
SOUTHPORT	1	1	0	0	1	0	1	0	1	0	2	2
STEVENAGE B	2	0	1	1	2	3	2	1	0	1	1	1
TAMWORTH	1	0	0	1	0	1	1	0	1	0	1	1
TELFORD U	2	1	0	1	6	8	2	1	1	0	4	2
WOKING	2	1	0	1	2	2	2	0	1	1	2	3
YEOVIL T	1	0	1	0	1	1	1	0	0	1	1	6
TOTAL	42	13	10	19	55	60	42	15	7	20	54	76

APPEARANCES

	02-03	03-04	Total		02-03	03-04	Total
ANDERSON Dale	12+14	26+11	38+25	KAVANAGH Jason	13+3		13+3
BLOUNT Mark	19+2		19+2	KIRKWOOD Glenn	20+5	19+6	39+11
BURNS John	7+1		7+1	McMAHON Sam		12+3	12+3
CAMP Lee	5		5	MOORE Christian	34+2	8+3	42+5
CHETTLE Steve		22+2	22+2	MURRAY Adam		2	2
CLOUGH Nigel	27+7	15+12	42+19	O'HALLORAN Matthew	5+1		5+1
COLKIN Lee		12+2	12+2	PETTY Ben	3+6		3+6
CORBETT Andy		10+15	10+15	REDDINGTON Stuart	25		25
CROSBY Gary		0+2	0+2	ROBINSON Dan	1		1
DUCROS Andy	10+1	20+6	30+7	SHILTON Sam		15	15
DUDLEY Craig	24+6	23+3	47+9	SINTON Andy	27+6	2+3	29+9
DUKE Matt	36	42	78	STRIDE Darren	29+4	28+2	57+6
EVANS Steve	6+5		6+5	SUGDEN Ryan		2+2	2+2
FARRELL Steve	1+12		1+12	SWINSLOE Craig	0+1		0+1
GILL Robert		4+1	4+1	TALBOT Paul	21+10		21+10
GLASSER Neil	19+1		19+1	TALBOT Robbie		28+9	28+9
GLOVER Lee	6+3		6+3	TWIGG Gary		3+1	3+1
GOUGH Steve	0+4		0+4	WASSALL Darren	7	27+3	34+3
GUMMER Sean	1+2	0+1	1+3	WEBSTER Aaron	34+6	31+3	65+9
HENSHAW Terry	33+3	29+2	62+5	WHITE Andy		3	3
HOWARD Jon	8	30+6	38+6	WILLIAMS Barry		13+5	13+5
HOYLE Colin	28+2	12+4	40+6	WILLIS Adam		6	6
JOHN -BAPTISTE Alex		3	3	WRAITH Paul	1+1		1+1
JOHNSON Aaron	0+1		0+1	WRIGHT Ian		15+4	15+4

GOALSCORERS

	02-03	03-04	Total
ANDERSON Dale	5(1p)	8	13(1p)
CHETTLE Steve		1	1
CLOUGH Nigel	1		1
COLKIN Lee		1	1
CORBETT Andy		1	1
DUCROS Andy	1	2	3
DUDLEY Craig	1(1p)		1(1p)
EVANS Steve	2		2
FARRELL Steve	1		1
GILL Robert		1	1
GLOVER Lee	2		2
GUMMER Sean	1		1
HENSHAW Terry		1	1
HOWARD Jon	2	4	6
KAVANAGH Jason	3(3p)		3(3p)
KIRKWOOD Glen	2	4	6
McMAHON Sam		1	1
MOORE Christian	16	2	18
O'HALLORAN Matthew	1		1
REDDINGTON Stuart	3		3
SINTON Andy	1	1	2
STRIDE Darren	5	5	10
TALBOT Paul	1		1
TALBOT Robbie		12	12
TWIGG Gary		1	1
WEBSTER Aaron	4	6(5p)	10(5p)
WHITE Andy		1	1
WILLIAMS Barry		3	3
WRIGHT Ian		2	2

Nigel Clough. Photo: Peter Barnes.

Darren Stride. Photo: Peter Barnes.

Aaron Webster.

CHELTENHAM TOWN

PROMOTED FROM: Southern League 1985, 1997
RELEGATED TO: Southern League 1992   PROMOTED TO: Football League 1999
2004-2005 SEASON: Football League Division 2

SEASONS
9

TOTAL POINTS
516

HIGHEST POSITION
1st (98-99)

LOWEST POSITION
21st (91-92)

HIGHEST ATTENDANCE
6150 v Yeovil T (22-4-99)

LOWEST ATTENDANCE
450 Runcorn (2-11-91)

SEASON GOALSCORER
Chris Townsend 22 (86/87)

CAREER GOALSCORER
Mark Boyland 47(2p)

CAREER APPEARANCES
Kevin Willetts 242+9

	HOME						AWAY						
	P	W	D	L	F	A	Pts	P	W	D	L	F	A	Pts	Position
85-86	21	13	4	4	47	27	30	21	3	7	11	22	42	16	11
86-87	21	11	4	6	43	25	37	21	5	9	7	21	25	24	11
87-88	21	6	11	4	36	32	29	21	5	9	7	28	35	24	13
88-89	20	7	7	6	32	29	28	20	5	5	10	23	29	20	15
89-90	21	9	6	6	30	22	33	21	7	5	9	28	38	26	11
90-91	21	8	6	7	29	25	30	21	4	6	11	25	47	18	16
91-92	21	8	5	8	28	35	29	21	2	8	11	28	47	14	21
1992-1997														
97-98	21	15	4	2	39	15	49	21	8	5	8	24	28	29	2
98-99	21	11	9	1	35	14	42	21	11	5	5	36	22	38	1
Total	**188**	**88**	**56**	**44**	**319**	**224**	**307**	**188**	**50**	**59**	**79**	**235**	**313**	**209**

	Home						Away					
	P	W	D	L	F	A	P	W	D	L	F	A
ALTRINCHAM	7	3	2	2	7	8	7	1	1	5	4	17
AYLESBURY U	1	0	1	0	0	0	1	0	1	0	0	0
BARNET	6	2	0	4	7	11	6	1	2	3	6	12
BARROW	5	4	1	0	10	2	5	0	4	1	4	5
BATH C	5	0	3	2	6	8	5	0	3	2	3	9
BOSTON U	7	3	2	2	13	11	7	1	3	3	10	14
CHORLEY	2	1	1	0	4	2	2	2	0	0	6	1
COLCHESTER U	2	0	1	1	2	3	2	0	0	2	1	7
DAGENHAM	3	2	1	0	13	4	3	2	1	0	7	3
DAGENHAM & R	1	0	0	1	0	7	1	1	0	0	2	1
DARLINGTON	1	0	0	1	0	1	1	0	0	1	1	5
DARTFORD	1	1	0	0	3	1	1	0	1	0	3	3
DONCASTER R	1	1	0	0	2	1	1	0	1	0	2	2
DOVER A	2	1	1	0	4	2	2	0	1	1	0	3
ENFIELD	5	4	1	0	11	4	5	2	1	2	9	10
FARNBOROUGH T	4	3	1	0	9	3	4	2	1	1	7	8
FISHER A	4	1	3	0	4	2	4	1	1	2	6	6
FOREST GREEN R	1	0	1	0	1	1	1	1	0	0	2	1
FRICKLEY A	2	1	1	0	3	1	2	1	0	1	3	2
GATESHEAD	4	4	0	0	10	4	4	0	3	1	5	6
HALIFAX T	1	1	0	0	4	0	1	0	1	0	1	1
HAYES	2	1	1	0	5	4	2	0	1	1	3	4
HEDNESFORD T	2	1	1	0	1	0	2	1	0	1	3	3
HEREFORD U	2	0	1	1	3	4	2	1	0	1	4	3
KETTERING T	9	5	2	2	19	11	9	2	2	5	6	14
KIDDERMINSTER H	9	3	2	4	13	15	9	3	0	6	12	22
KINGSTONIAN	1	1	0	0	1	0	1	1	0	0	2	1
LEEK T	2	0	2	0	1	1	2	1	1	0	2	0
LINCOLN C	1	0	1	0	3	3	1	0	0	1	1	5
MACCLESFIELD T	5	2	1	2	9	7	5	0	2	3	4	12
MAIDSTONE U	4	2	1	1	6	7	4	0	2	2	3	6
MERTHYR T	3	0	0	3	1	5	3	0	1	2	2	7
MORECAMBE	2	2	0	0	6	2	2	1	0	1	2	1
NORTHWICH V	9	4	3	2	17	12	9	0	2	7	5	16
NUNEATON B	2	1	1	0	6	4	2	1	1	0	1	0
RUNCORN	7	2	4	1	11	9	7	1	2	4	10	16
RUSHDEN & D	2	2	0	0	3	0	2	1	0	1	3	5
SCARBOROUGH	2	1	0	1	7	4	2	1	0	1	3	2
SLOUGH T	3	2	1	0	4	1	3	3	0	0	8	2
SOUTHPORT	2	2	0	0	5	0	2	2	0	0	4	1
STAFFORD R	7	2	1	4	9	11	7	2	4	1	9	9
STALYBRIDGE C	1	1	0	0	2	0	1	1	0	0	4	1
STEVENAGE B	2	1	1	0	4	1	2	1	1	0	4	3
SUTTON U	5	2	1	2	9	8	5	2	2	1	6	6
TELFORD U	9	5	1	3	15	8	9	3	2	4	8	11
WEALDSTONE	3	0	1	2	2	4	3	1	1	1	4	2
WELLING U	8	4	4	0	15	8	8	3	3	2	10	7
WEYMOUTH	4	2	1	1	5	3	4	0	2	2	6	8
WITTON A	1	0	0	1	0	1	1	0	0	1	2	4
WOKING	2	1	1	0	4	3	2	0	0	2	0	3
WYCOMBE W	6	3	2	1	10	7	6	2	2	2	14	11
YEOVIL T	6	4	2	0	10	5	6	1	3	2	8	12
TOTAL	188	88	56	44	319	224	188	50	59	79	235	313

	Altrincham		Aylesbury United		Barnet		Barrow		Bath City		Boston United		Chorley		Colchester United		Dagenham	
	H	A	H	A	H	A	H	A	H	A	H	A	H	A	H	A	H	A
85-86	2-0	1-4			2-1	2-2	2-0	2-2	1-2	1-1	2-1	2-1					2-2	3-1
86-87	1-1	0-2			1-2	1-0			1-1	0-0	1-3	1-1					6-1	1-1
87-88	1-0	1-1			0-2	1-1			3-3	1-1	1-5	1-4					5-1	3-1
88-89	2-1	1-0	0-0	0-0	1-2	1-3					3-1	1-1			2-2	4-1		
89-90	0-0	0-5			2-0	0-4	1-0	1-2			0-0	1-2	2-0	2-0				
90-91	1-4	0-3			1-4	1-2	3-1	0-0	0-0	0-2	5-0	1-2			1-2	1-3		
91-92	0-2	1-2					0-0	0-0	1-2	1-5	1-1	3-3			1-1	0-4		
92-93																		
93-94																		
94-95																		
95-96																		
96-97																		
97-98																		
98-99							4-1	1-1										

	(Dagenham &) Redbridge F.		Darlington		Dartford		Doncaster Rovers		Dover Athletic		Enfield		Farnborough Town		Fisher Athletic		Forest Green Rovers	
	H	A	H	A	H	A	H	A	H	A	H	A	H	A	H	A	H	A
85-86					3-1	3-3					2-0	0-1						
86-87											2-0	2-2						
87-88											1-1	1-0			2-0	0-1		
88-89											3-2	4-3			2-2	0-2		
89-90			0-1	1-5							3-1	2-4	4-0	0-4	0-0	5-2		
90-91															0-0	1-1		
91-92	0-7	2-1											4-3	1-1				
92-93																		
93-94																		
94-95																		
95-96																		
96-97																		
97-98									3-1	0-3			1-0	2-1				
98-99							2-1	2-2	1-1	0-0			0-0	4-2			1-1	2-1

Above: Steve Book in action.   Photo: Peter Barnes

Bottom Left: Clive Walker   Photo: Colin Stevens
Bottom Right: Andy Gray   Photo: Malc Tompkins

	Frickley Athletic		Gateshead		Halifax Town		Hayes		Hednesford Town		Hereford United		Kettering Town		Kidderminster Harriers		Kingstonian	
	H	A	H	A	H	A	H	A	H	A	H	A	H	A	H	A	H	A
85-86	1-1	1-2											5-1	1-2	2-6	1-5		
86-87	2-0	2-0	4-2	1-1									3-1	0-0	1-2	1-5		
87-88													1-2	1-1	2-2	2-3		
88-89													2-1	0-2	4-1	2-3		
89-90													1-1	0-1	2-1	2-1		
90-91			1-0	3-3									2-2	1-5	0-0	0-2		
91-92			3-2	1-2									0-3	0-3	1-2	1-2		
92-93																		
93-94																		
94-95																		
95-96																		
96-97																		
97-98			2-0	0-0	4-0	1-1	2-1	1-1	1-0	1-0	1-2	2-3	2-0	1-0	0-1	2-1		
98-99							3-3	2-3	0-0	2-3	2-2	2-0	3-0	2-0	1-0	1-0	1-0	2-1

	Leek Town		Lincoln City		Macclesfield Town		Maidstone United		Merthyr Tydfil		Morecambe		Northwich Victoria		Nuneaton Borough		Runcorn	
	H	A	H	A	H	A	H	A	H	A	H	A	H	A	H	A	H	A
85-86							2-1	0-1					2-0	1-3	5-3	1-0	1-1	0-5
86-87							2-0	1-1					5-2	0-1	1-1	0-0	1-1	0-1
87-88			3-3	1-5	1-0	0-1	2-2	2-2					1-1	0-0			0-0	2-2
88-89					3-0	0-0	0-4	0-2					2-2	0-1			2-1	1-2
89-90					1-2	0-3			0-2	1-1			2-3	0-0			2-2	4-2
90-91					2-2	1-5			0-1	0-3			1-1	2-5			1-3	2-2
91-92					2-3	3-3			1-2	1-3			1-0	1-3			4-1	1-2
92-93																		
93-94																		
94-95																		
95-96																		
96-97																		
97-98	1-1	0-0									2-1	0-1	3-2	1-2				
98-99	0-0	2-0									4-1	2-0	0-1	0-1				

149

	Rushden & Diamonds		Scarborough		Slough Town		Southport		Stafford Rangers		Stalybridge Celtic		Stevenage Borough		Sutton United		Telford United	
	H	A	H	A	H	A	H	A	H	A	H	A	H	A	H	A	H	A
85-86			5-1	0-1					2-0	0-2							1-1	0-3
86-87			2-3	3-1					2-1	1-0					1-2	0-0	3-1	1-3
87-88									2-3	2-2					1-1	0-3	3-0	1-0
88-89									1-2	1-1					2-3	1-1	0-1	0-2
89-90									1-3	1-0					2-0	2-0	1-2	0-0
90-91					2-0	3-0			1-2	2-2					3-2	3-2	0-1	2-1
91-92					1-0	3-1			0-0	2-2							2-1	1-2
92-93																		
93-94																		
94-95																		
95-96																		
96-97																		
97-98	2-0	1-4			1-1	2-1	2-0	2-1			2-0	4-1	1-1	2-1			3-1	0-0
98-99	1-0	2-1					3-0	2-0					3-0	2-2			2-0	3-0

	Wealdstone		Welling United		Weymouth		Witton Albion		Woking		Wycombe Wanderers		Yeovil Town	
	H	A	H	A	H	A	H	A	H	A	H	A	H	A
85-86	1-2	0-0			0-1	0-0					4-2	3-3		
86-87	0-1	0-1	2-0	3-1	2-0	3-4								
87-88	1-1	4-1	2-2	1-0	2-1	1-1					2-2	3-5		
88-89			1-1	2-0	1-1	2-3					0-1	0-1	1-1	3-1
89-90			3-2	1-1							1-1	4-0	2-1	1-1
90-91			3-0	0-0							1-0	2-0	1-0	0-4
91-92			3-2	1-1			0-1	2-4			2-1	2-2	1-1	1-1
92-93														
93-94														
94-95														
95-96														
96-97														
97-98			1-1	1-2					3-2	0-2			2-0	1-3
98-99			0-0	1-2					1-1	0-1			3-2	2-2

CHELTENHAM TOWN APPEARANCES

	85-86	86-87	87-88	88-89	89-90	90-91	91-92	1992-	1997	97-98	98-99	TOTAL
ABBLEY Steve	41	19+2	17+1									77+3
ADAMS Mark						0+1						0+1
AIZLEWOOD Steve	4											4
ANGELL Brett			25									25
ANGELL Darren			11									11
BADDELEY Kevin	26	1										27
BAILEY Dennis											7+1	7+1
BANKS Chris										39+1	34+1	73+2
BARRETT Mike						31	11					42
BARRON Paul						5						5
BARTRAM Vince						4						4
BAVERSTOCK Ray	39	34+1	36+1	28+1	24+3							161+6
BAYLIFFE Tim	7											7
BAYLISS Karl		0+1	0+1									0+2
BEACOCK Gary		4+4										4+4
BEASLEY Andy					7							7
BENTON Steve										5+6		5+6
BLACKLER Martin	22+1											22+1
BLOOMER Bob										32	15+13	47+13
BLOOMFIELD Paul						26+2	13+12					39+14
BOOK Steve										42	42	84
BOXALL Clive	16											16
BOYLAND Mark	42	38	14	11	17+9							122+9
BRAIN Simon					13+5	12+1						25+6
BROGAN Paul						41	22+1					63+1
BROOKS Steve	40	38	33+1	28	36	22+3	35					232+4
BROUGH John											34+6	34+6
BROWN Jeremy	0+2											0+2
BROWN Keith		40+1	24+4	3+1								67+6
BROWN Richard						4						4
BUCKLAND Mark		3+1	34+3	40	41	35+2	29+2					182+8
BURNS Chris				29+4	19+6	20+4						68+14
BURTON Chris						16+3						16+3
BUTLER David							10					10
CALLINAN Tommy			0+2									0+2
CAMDEN Chris						12+3						12+3
CASEY Kim						31+2	23					54+2
CASEY Ross										1+2		1+2
CHURCHWARD Alan		1	29	12	26							68
CLARK Billy										6		6
CLARK Richard						9						9
COATES Marc						6						6
COLLICUTT Paul	12+2	25										37+2
COLLINS Rod				0+1								0+1
CORNES Stuart	31											31
COTTERILL Steve		4+5										4+5
CRAIG David				12+3	6							18+3
CRISP Mark										6+15		6+15

151

5 Proud 'Robins'

Left to Right, Standing: Lee Howells, Jamie Victory & Chris Banks. Kneeling: Dale Watkins & Neil Grayson

CHELTENHAM TOWN   APPEARANCES

	85-86	86-87	87-88	88-89	89-90	90-91	91-92	1992-	1997	97-98	98-99	TOTAL
CROUCH Steve				2+2	10+5	19+4						31+11
CROWLEY Richard		15	42	32+1	35+3							124+4
DAVIES Mark							6					6
DOUGHERTY Paul					0+1							0+1
DUFF Mike										41	41	82
EATON Jason										28+6	27+7	55+13
ELLIOTT Russell		0+2										0+2
EVANS Paul							3+1					3+1
FINCH Paul			0+1									0+1
FOX Matthew							4					4
FREEMAN Mark										28	36+1	64+1
FRY Chris				0+2								0+2
FRY David							3					3
GANSAL Martin							0+2					0+2
GAYLE Mark							3					3
GAZZARD Nick	3+5											3+5
GENNARD Mark					10+2							10+2
GORDON Russell			6+2									6+2
GRAY Andy					20							20
GRAYSON Neil										13+2	39+2	52+4
HANCOX Richard					2							2
HARDS Neil	41	39										80
HENRY Charlie							5+2					5+2
HEWLETT Gary				2+3								2+3
HORLICK Andy							0+2					0+2
HOULT Russell							3					3
HOWARTH Frank					0+1							0+1
HOWARTH Neil											5+4	5+4
HOWELLS Gareth		1	1									2
HOWELLS Lee							26			31	37+1	94+1
HUGHES Brian	42	41	40+1									123+1
JACKSON Michael										4+2	0+1	4+3
JENKINS Steve				20+1								20+1
JORDAN Nick	24+16	32+8	26+7	36+2	29+5	32+6	8					187+44
KNIGHT Keith			2+2	5		3				26+8	10+13	46+23
LANGE Tony							6					6
LISSAMAN Jeff					2+3							2+3
LIVINGSTONE Glen							3					3
LYNCH Tony						3						3
MARDENBOROUGH Steve					9+3							9+3
MASEFIELD Paul							7					7
MATTHEWS Wayne							5					5
MILTON Russell										21+4	6+11	27+15
MOGG Dave		13	28	9								50
MORTIMORE Paul							0+2					0+2
MULVANEY Paul			4+7									4+7
NICHOLLS Alan							11					11
NORTON David											35+1	35+1

Photos: Peter Barnes

Bottom Left: Russell Milton
Bottom Right: John Brough

Right: Steve Cotterill

Below: Keith Knight

CHELTENHAM TOWN APPEARANCES

	85-86	86-87	87-88	88-89	89-90	90-91	91-92	1992-	1997	97-98	98-99	TOTAL
NUTTELL Micky				13	22+5	7+1						42+6
OLSON Matthew							2					2
OWEN Steve							24					24
PAYNE Derek					23							23
PAYNE Mark		0+1										0+1
PERRETT Darren							11+6					11+6
PHILLIPS Stewart							1					1
POUNTAIN Alan			2+3	1+8								3+11
POWELL Barry							0+1					0+1
POWELL John	18+1	8+9										26+10
PURDIE Jon					5+4		26					31+4
RECK Sean							9+3					9+3
SANDERSON Paul					4+8							4+8
SHEARER Peter				19								19
SISSONS Jon						1+3						1+3
SMART Gary		11										11
SMITH Jimmy							15			20+7	2+5	37+12
SMITH Neil							17+1					17+1
SMITH Nigel	14											14
STOBART Loy							16+1					16+1
STUART Tony						7						7
TANNER Micky				14+1								14+1
TEAGUE Simon										0+1		0+1
TEGGART Darren							6+3					6+3
TESTER Paul							5+1					5+1
THORP Michael										2		2
TOWNSEND Chris	16+7	39+2	13+12	8+2								76+23
TUCKER Lloyd						0+1						0+1
TUOHY Micky						3+5						3+5
TURNBULL Peter							0+3					0+3
UPSHALL Jason						3	0+1					3+1
VICTORY Jamie										42	42	84
VIRCAVS Anton		37	34	28+2	31	27	34					191+2
WALKER Clive										23+3	17+7	40+10
WALKER Richard											14+2	14+2
WALSH Ian				3								3
WARREN Christer							1+3					1+3
WATKINS Dale										35+5	9+10	44+15
WEAVER Steve					2							2
WEST David		3+1	2+1									5+2
WHELAN Sean		2	0+2	25	26+1							53+3
WHITE Les	1	2										3
WILLETTS Kevin	23+3	36+4	33	35+1	34	42	40					243+8
WILLIAMS Phil				6	37	19+6						62+6
WITHEY Graham			10									10
WRIGHT Darren										17+6		17+6
WRING Jimmy						4+4						4+4
YATES Mark											10	10

Top Left:	Nick Jordan	Photo: Mike Floate
Top Right:	Jon Purdie	Photo: Mike Floate
Above:	Kim Casey	Photo: Elaine Sarjeant
Right:	Brett Angell	Photo: Gloucestershire Echo

CHELTENHAM TOWN LEADING APPEARANCES

	85-86	86-87	87-88	88-89	89-90	90-91	91-92	92-99	TOTAL
Kevin WILLETTS	23+3	36+4	33	35+1	34	42	40		243+8
Steve BROOKS	40	38	33+1	28	36	22+3	35		232+4
Nick JORDAN	24+16	32+8	26+7	36+2	29+5	32+6	8		187+44
Anton VIRCAVS		37	34	28+2	31	27	34		191+2
Mark BUCKLAND		3+1	34+3	40	41	35+2	29+2		182+8
Ray BAVERSTOCK	39	34+1	36+1	28+1	24+3				161+6
Mark BOYLAND	42	38	14	11	17+9				122+9
Richard CROWLEY		15	42	32+1	35+3				124+4
Brian HUGHES	42	41	40+1						123+1

CHELTENHAM TOWN GOALSCORERS

	85-86	86-87	87-88	88-89	89-90	90-91	91-92	1992-	1997	97-98	98-99	TOTAL
ABBLEY Steve	6	1	1									8
ANGELL Brett			15									15
ANGELL Darren			1									1
BAILEY Dennis											2	2
BANKS Chris											1	1
BAVERSTOCK Ray	1	2	1(1p)	1(1p)								5(2p)
BAYLIFFE Tim	1											1
BLOOMER Bob										1		1
BOYLAND Mark	16	15	5	8(2p)	3							47(2p)
BRAIN Simon					4	4						8
BROGAN Paul						2						2
BROOKS Steve	10	5	7	4	5	3	5					39
BROUGH John											4	4
BROWN Keith		3	3									6
BUCKLAND Mark		1	3	9	11	6	7					37
BURNS Chris					1	4						5
BURTON Chris						8						8
CASEY Kim						14	4					18
CLARK Richard							1					1
COATES Marc							1					1
CORNES Stuart	4											4
COTTERILL Steve		1										1
CRAIG David				1	1							2
CROUCH Steve				1								1
CROWLEY Richard			1	5	3							9
DUFF Mike										1	3	4
EATON Jason										16	10	26
EVANS Paul						1						1
FREEMAN Mark										1	5	6
GAZZARD Nick	1											1
GRAY Andy					5							5
GRAYSON Neil										6	18(1p)	24(1p)
HOWELLS Lee						2				3	6	11
HUGHES Brian	6	8	2(2p)									16(2p)
JENKINS Steve				4								4

CHELTENHAM TOWN — GOALSCORERS

	85-86	86-87	87-88	88-89	89-90	90-91	91-92	1992-	1997	97-98	98-99	TOTAL
JORDAN Nick	1	3	6	6	7	2	1					26
KNIGHT Keith										2	3	5
MARDENBOROUGH Steve					2							2
MULVANEY Paul			3									3
NORTON David											3	3
NUTTELL Micky				1	5							6
OWEN Steve							2					2
PAYNE Derek						4						4
PERRETT Darren							3					3
POWELL John	5	1										6
PURDIE Jon							7					7
SHEARER Peter				4								4
SMART Garry			1									1
SMITH Jimmy							6			5(1p)	1(1p)	12(2p)
SMITH Neil							1					1
SMITH Nigel	2											2
STOBART Loy							1					1
TANNER Micky				3								3
TOWNSEND Chris	14	22	3	3								42
TURNBULL Pete							1					1
VICTORY Jamie										5	4	9
VIRCAVS Anton		1	5	3	1	2	3					15
WALKER Clive										4	4	8
WATKINS Dale										17(4p)	5(2p)	22(6p)
WHELAN Sean		1										1
WILLETTS Kevin	2		2	1	6	4(3p)	9(7p)					24(10p)
WILLIAMS Phil					2							2
WITHEY Graham			5									5

Dale Watkins and Jason Eaton

Photo: Peter Barnes

CHESTER CITY

RELEGATED FROM: The Football League 2000
PROMOTED TO: The Football League 2004
2004-2005 SEASON: The Football LeagueDivison 2

SEASONS
4

TOTAL POINTS
283

HIGHEST POSITION
1st 2003-04

LOWEST POSITION
14th 2001-02

HIGHEST ATTENDANCE
5987 v Scarborough 17.4.04

LOWEST ATTENDANCE
605 v Telford U. 4.9.01 &
605 v Stalybridge C. 11.9.01

SEASON GOALSCORER
Daryl Clare 29(6p) (03/4)

CAREER GOALSCORER
Daryl Clare 46(8p)

CAREER APPEARANCES
Wayne Brown 115

2000-2001 Back row,left to right: Neil Fisher, David Kerr, Martyn Lancaster, Dean Greygoose, Mattie Woods, Wayne Brown, Paul Beesley, Paul Carden and Neil Fitzhenry.
Middle row: Gordon Hill (Youth Coach), Mark Beesley, Andy Shelton, Dean Spink, Scott Roscoe, Nick Richardson, Darren Moss, Chris Blackburn, Craig Gaunt, Graham Vile (Director of Centre of Excellence).
Front row: Darren Wright, Paul Berry, Terry Smith (Chairman), Graham Barrow (Manager), Joe HInnegan (Physio), Matt Doughty and Steve Finney.

	HOME							AWAY							
	P	W	D	L	F	A	Pts	P	W	D	L	F	A	Pts	Position
00-01	21	9	8	4	29	19	35	21	7	6	8	20	24	27	8
01-02	21	7	7	7	26	23	28	21	8	2	11	28	28	26	14
02-03	21	10	6	5	36	21	36	21	11	6	4	23	10	39	4
03-04	21	16	4	1	45	18	52	21	11	7	3	40	16	40	1
Total	84	42	25	17	136	81	151	84	37	21	26	111	78	132	

CHESTER CITY

	Accrington Stanley		Aldershot Town		Barnet		Boston United		Burton Albion		Dagenham & Redbridge		Doncaster Rovers		Dover Athletic		Exeter City	
	H	A	H	A	H	A	H	A	H	A	H	A	H	A	H	A	H	A
00-01							2-2	0-0			1-1	1-1	3-0	0-1	1-0	1-1		
01-02					1-0	1-3	1-2	1-0			0-1	0-3	1-1	0-2	3-0	0-1		
02-03					1-1	3-0			2-1	0-2	5-2	0-1	1-0	0-0				
03-04	3-3	2-0	4-2	1-1	1-0	0-0			3-1	1-1	2-1	0-0					3-2	1-2

	Farnborough Town		Forest Green Rovers		Gravesend & N'fleet		Halifax Town		Hayes		Hednesford Town		Hereford United		Kettering Town	
	H	A	H	A	H	A	H	A	H	A	H	A	H	A	H	A
00-01			0-1	1-1					0-0	3-1	0-1	0-0	2-1	0-2	2-1	0-4
01-02	1-0	1-1	2-3	2-0					3-1	3-1			2-0	0-1		
02-03	0-2	2-1	0-1	2-0	1-1	1-0	2-0	0-0					0-1	0-0	0-0	1-0
03-04	3-2	2-1	1-0	1-2	2-2	4-0	2-0	3-0					0-0	1-2		

	Kingstonian		Leigh RMI		Margate		Morecambe		Northwich Victoria		Nuneaton Borough		Rushden & Diamonds		Scarborough	
	H	A	H	A	H	A	H	A	H	A	H	A	H	A	H	A
00-01	0-0	3-1	1-1	1-0			1-0	2-0	1-1	1-1	4-0	2-1	1-2	0-2	3-2	2-0
01-02			1-1	0-3	0-3	0-0	1-1	3-0	1-2	1-3	1-0	3-1			0-0	1-2
02-03			2-1	4-0	5-0	1-0	2-1	1-1	2-3	1-1	1-2	0-1			0-0	1-0
03-04			5-0	6-2	3-0	2-1	2-1	1-0	4-0	4-0					1-0	2-2

	Shrewsbury Town		Southport		Stalybridge Celtic		Stevenage Borough		Tamworth		Telford United		Woking		Yeovil Town	
	H	A	H	A	H	A	H	A	H	A	H	A	H	A	H	A
00-01			0-1	0-1			1-1	2-1			1-0	0-3	3-3	0-1	2-1	1-2
01-02			0-2	2-3	0-0	4-0	5-1	1-2			2-2	3-0	0-2	1-2	1-1	1-0
02-03			2-0	3-1			2-0	1-0			4-1	1-0	2-2	0-1	2-2	1-1
03-04	2-1	0-0					1-2	0-0	1-0	5-1	0-0	2-0	2-1	2-1		

	Home						Away					
	P	W	D	L	F	A	P	W	D	L	F	A
ACCRINGTON S	1	0	1	0	3	3	1	1	0	0	2	0
ALDERSHOT T	1	1	0	0	4	2	1	0	1	0	1	1
BARNET	3	2	1	0	3	1	3	1	1	1	4	3
BOSTON U	2	0	1	1	3	4	2	1	1	0	1	0
BURTON A	2	2	0	0	5	2	2	0	1	1	1	3
DAGENHAM & R	4	2	1	1	8	5	4	0	2	2	1	5
DONCASTER R	3	2	1	0	5	1	3	0	1	2	0	3
DOVER A	2	2	0	0	4	0	2	0	1	1	1	2
EXETER C	1	1	0	0	3	2	1	0	0	1	1	2
FARNBOROUGH T	3	2	0	1	4	4	3	2	1	0	5	3
FOREST GREEN R	4	1	0	3	3	5	4	2	1	1	6	3
GRAVESEND & N	2	0	2	0	3	3	2	2	0	0	5	0
HALIFAX T	2	2	0	0	4	0	2	1	1	0	3	0
HAYES	2	1	1	0	3	1	2	2	0	0	6	2
HEDNESFORD T	1	0	0	1	0	1	1	0	1	0	0	0
HEREFORD U	4	2	1	1	4	2	4	0	1	3	1	5
KETTERING T	2	1	1	0	2	1	2	1	0	1	1	4
KINGSTONIAN	1	0	1	0	0	0	1	1	0	0	3	1
LEIGH R M I	4	2	2	0	9	3	4	3	0	1	11	5
MARGATE	3	2	0	1	8	3	3	2	1	0	3	1
MORECAMBE	4	3	1	0	6	3	4	3	1	0	7	1
NORTHWICH V	4	1	1	2	8	6	4	1	2	1	7	5
NUNEATON B	3	2	0	1	6	2	3	2	0	1	5	3
RUSHDEN & D	1	0	0	1	1	2	1	0	0	1	0	2
SCARBOROUGH	4	2	2	0	4	2	4	2	1	1	6	4
SHREWSBURY T	1	1	0	0	2	1	1	0	1	0	0	0
SOUTHPORT	3	1	0	2	2	3	3	1	0	2	5	5
STALYBRIDGE C	1	0	1	0	0	0	1	1	0	0	4	0
STEVENAGE B	4	2	1	1	9	4	4	2	1	1	4	3
TAMWORTH	1	1	0	0	1	0	1	1	0	0	5	1
TELFORD U	4	2	2	0	7	3	4	3	0	1	6	3
WOKING	4	1	2	1	7	8	4	1	0	3	3	5
YEOVIL T	3	1	2	0	5	4	3	1	1	1	3	3
TOTAL	84	42	25	17	136	81	84	37	21	26	111	78

Ben Davies on the ball against Stevenage. Photo: Peter Barnes.

CHESTER CITY

	00-01	01-02	02-03	03-04	Total
BAXTER Brett		1+1			1+1
BEESLEY Mark	36+4	34	10+9	0+3	80+16
BEESLEY Paul	32				32
BERRY Paul	0+1				0+1
BLACKBURN Chris	33	22+8	15+4		70+12
BOLLAND Phil		14	30	30+5	74+5
BRABIN Gary		16			1
BRADY Jon			15+4	15	30+4
BRODIE Steve			3+1	0+2	3+3
BROWN David		11+2			11+2
BROWN Micky		6+17			6+17
BROWN Wayne	34	42	39	16	**131**
CAMERON David		7+8			7+8
CARDEN Paul	36	13+2	31	33+2	**113+4**
CAREY Shaun		11	15	21+1	47+1
CLARE Daryl			23	27+3	50+3
CLIFFORD Mark			1		1
COLLINS Danny		3+4	10	41	54+4
DAVIES Ben			24+5	26+9	50+14
DOUGHTY Matt	35+5				35+5
ELAM Lee				1+3	1+3
EVANS Andy	5+3				5+3
FINNEY Steve	4+5				4+5
FISHER Neil	31+5				31+5
FOSTER Ian				10+10	10+10
GAUNT Craig	21+4				21+4
GILL Robert				3+1	3+1
GREYGOOSE Dean	3				3
GRIFFIN Adam		0+1			0+1
GUYETT Scott			32	24+3	56+3
HAARHOFF Jimmy	5+8	7+17			12+25
HALFORD Steve		10			10
HARKNESS Steve			10		10
HARRIS Andy				10+6	10+6
HATSWELL Wayne			27+2	8	35+2
HEARD Jamie				24+1	24+1
HIGGINS Alex		0+1			0+1
HILL Sam		13			13
HOPWOOD Chris		0+4			0+4
JENKINS Iain		5+1			5+1
JOY Ian			3		3
KELLY Jimmy			29+3		29+3
KERR David	4+5	9+2			13+7
KILGANNON Wesley		8+4			8+4
LANCASTER Martyn	37+2	35	2+1		74+3
LANE Chris				1+3	1+3
LINIGHAN Andy		3			3
LOPEZ Carlos		0+2			0+2
MALKIN Chris		5+4			5+4
McCALDON Ian			2	13	15

APPEARANCES

	00-01	01-02	02-03	03-04	Total
McELHATTON Michael		8			8
McGORRY Brian		14			14
McINTYRE Kevin			39+1	40	79+1
McNIVEN David		3			3
MOSS Darren	16+4				16+4
O'BRIEN Chris		9			9
O'BRIEN Mike		8+2			8+2
PEACOCK Richard		6			6
PORTER Andy	10+2	25+2			35+4
PRIESTLEY Phil	5+1				5+1
QUAYLE Mark			6+3		6+3
RAPLEY Kevin				9+17	9+17
REGAN Carl				4	4
RICHARDSON Nick	1+4				1+4
ROBERTS Paul		1+5			1+5
ROSE Michael		33+1			33+1
ROSE Steve		8+3			8+3
RUFFER Carl	16+4	16+2	24+7	23+1	79+14
RUSCOE Scott	19+7	17+5			36+12
SHELTON Andy	0+3				0+3
SMITH Alex				20	20
SPINK Dean		19+2			19+2
STAMP Darryn				35+3	35+3
SUGDEN Ryan			26+7		26+7
TATE Chris		4	0+2		4+2
TURNER Iain				12	12
TWISS Michael			21+16	10+20	31+36
WHITEHALL Steve	26+3				26+3
WHITTAKER Stuart		6+1			6+1
WILLIAMS Danny				5	5
WILLIAMS Gary		6+5			6+5
WOODS Andy				1	1
WOODS Matthew	33+3				33+3
WOODYATT Lee	7+7	14+5	11+2		32+14
WORSNOP John			1		1
WRIGHT Darren	13+16	3+8			16+24

Steve Whitehall against Hednesford Town.

CHESTER CITY

	00-01	01-02	02-03	03-04	Total
BEESLEY Mark	12(1p)	16	6(1p)		34(2p)
BLACKBURN Chris	2	4			6
BOLLAND Phil			1	4	5
BRABIN Gary		3			3
BRADY Jon			1	1	2
BROWN David		2			2
CAMERON David			2(1p)		2(1p)
CARDEN Paul	1		2	1	4
CAREY Shaun			1		1
CLARE Daryl			17(2p)	29(6p)	**46(8p)**
COLLINS Danny				3	3
DAVIES Ben			2	5	7
DOUGHTY MATT	1				1
EVANS Andy	2				3
FISHER Neil	4				4
FOSTER Ian				2(1p)	2(1p)
GAUNT Craig	1				1
GUYETT Scott			2	2	4
HAARHOFF Jimmy	1	1			2
HATSWELL Wayne			1	1	2
HILL Sam		1			1

GOALSCORERS

	00-01	01-02	02-03	03-04	Total
KELLY Jimmy			1(1p)		1(1p)
LANCASTER Martyn	1	1			2
McELHATTON Michael		2			2
McINTYRE Kevin			1	1	2
O'BRIEN Mike		2			2
PORTER Andy	2(1p)	2(1p)			4(2p)
QUAYLE Mark			1		1
RAPLEY Kevin				2	2
ROSE Michael		4			4
RUFFER Carl		2	2	2	6
RUSCOE Scott	1	4			5
SMITH Alex				4	4
SPINK Dean		2			2
STAMP Darryn				20	20
SUGDEN Ryan			12		12
TATE Chris		1			1
TWISS Michael			6	7	13
WHITEHALL Steve	9(1p)				9(1p)
WHITTAKER Stuart		4			4
WOODS Matthew	5(1p)				5(1p)
WRIGHT Darren	4(1p)	1			5(1p)

Chris Blackburn.

Wayne Brown. Photo: Andrew Chitty.

David Kerr (11) supports his colleagues in stopping Diamonds striker Justin Jackson. Photo: Peter Barnes.

Paul Carden.

Paul Beesley.   Photo: Andrew Chitty.

Jimmy Haarhoff.

CHORLEY

PROMOTED FROM: Northern Premier League 1988
RELEGATED TO: Northern Premier League 1990
2004-2005 SEASON: Northern Premier League, Division One

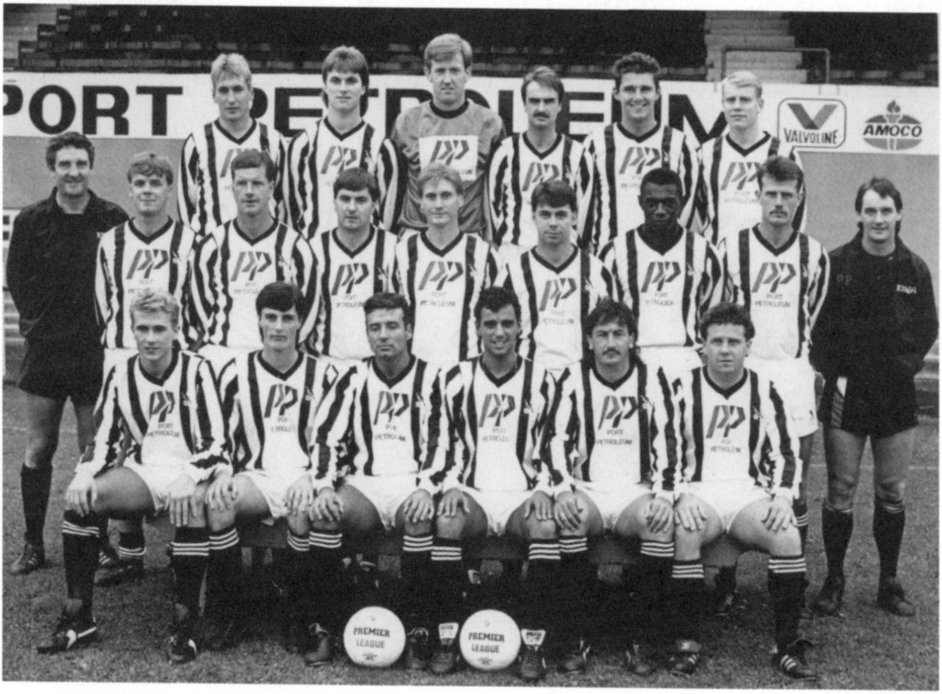

Chorley 1988-89

Left to Right
Back Row: Paul Moss, Brian Ross, Joe Neenan, Colin Jackson, Shaun Allen, K Allcock.
Middle Row: Ken Wright (Manager), Neil Peters, Craig Wardle, Kevin Glendon, Mike Lester, Geoff Lomax, D Hanson, Graham Jones, P Parry (Coach).
Front Row: Paul Griffin, Charlie Cooper, John Brady, Phil Power, Peter Sayer, K Budd

	HOME							AWAY							
	P	W	D	L	F	A	Pts	P	W	D	L	F	A	Pts	Position
88-89	20	6	4	10	26	32	22	20	7	2	11	31	39	23	17
89-90	21	9	5	7	26	26	32	21	4	1	16	16	41	13	20
Total	41	15	9	17	52	58	54	41	11	3	27	47	80	36	

	Altrincham		Aylesbury United		Barnet		Barrow		Boston United		Cheltenham Town		Darlington		Enfield		Farnborough Town	
	H	A	H	A	H	A	H	A	H	A	H	A	H	A	H	A	H	A
88-89	1-0	2-1	1-1	3-4	2-3	4-2			0-1	0-2	1-4	2-2	0-3	0-3	1-2	2-1		
89-90	2-1	0-1			1-4	0-5	0-1	1-3	0-0	1-0	0-2	0-2			2-2	0-2	1-0	3-1
90-91																		

	Fisher Athletic		Kettering Town		Kidderminster H.		Macclesfield Town		Maidstone United		Merthyr Tydfil		Northwich Victoria		Runcorn		Stafford Rangers	
	H	A	H	A	H	A	H	A	H	A	H	A	H	A	H	A	H	A
88-89	1-1	0-4	0-1	0-3	1-3	2-0	0-1	2-3	1-3	0-2			3-1	4-0	1-3	0-3	3-1	2-3
89-90	2-0	0-2	2-2	1-2	1-0	1-3	0-0	0-0			1-0	0-1	1-2	1-0	0-2	2-3	1-1	0-1
90-91																		

	Sutton United		Telford United		Welling United		Weymouth		Wycombe Wanderers		Yeovil Town	
	H	A	H	A	H	A	H	A	H	A	H	A
88-89	2-1	2-1	2-0	1-2	1-1	0-1	0-0	3-2	3-2	1-1	2-3	1-2
89-90	3-2	0-3	1-2	4-0	4-0	1-3			1-0	0-4	3-2	1-2
90-91												

	HOME						AWAY					
	P	W	D	L	F	A	P	W	D	L	F	A
ALTRINCHAM	2	2	0	0	3	1	2	1	0	1	2	2
AYLESBURY U	1	0	1	0	1	1	1	0	0	1	3	4
BARNET	2	0	0	2	3	7	2	1	0	1	4	7
BARROW	1	0	0	1	0	1	1	0	0	1	1	3
BOSTON U	2	0	1	1	0	1	2	1	0	1	1	2
CHELTENHAM T	2	0	0	2	1	6	2	0	1	1	2	4
DARLINGTON	1	0	0	1	0	3	1	0	0	1	0	3
ENFIELD	2	0	1	1	3	4	2	1	0	1	2	3
FARNBOROUGH T	1	1	0	0	1	0	1	1	0	0	3	1
FISHER A	2	1	1	0	3	1	2	0	0	2	0	6
KETTERING T	2	0	1	1	2	3	2	0	0	2	1	5
KIDDERMINSTER H	2	1	0	1	2	3	2	1	0	1	3	3
MACCLESFIELD T	2	0	1	1	0	1	2	0	1	1	2	3
MAIDSTONE U	1	0	0	1	1	3	1	0	0	1	0	2
MERTHYR T	1	1	0	0	1	0	1	0	0	1	0	1
NORTHWICH V	2	1	0	1	4	3	2	2	0	0	5	0
RUNCORN	2	0	0	2	1	5	2	0	0	2	2	6
STAFFORD R	2	1	1	0	4	2	2	0	0	2	2	4
SUTTON U	2	2	0	0	5	3	2	1	0	1	2	4
TELFORD U	2	1	0	1	3	2	2	1	0	1	5	2
WELLING U	2	1	1	0	5	1	2	0	0	2	1	4
WEYMOUTH	1	0	1	0	0	0	1	1	0	0	3	2
WYCOMBE W	2	2	0	0	4	2	2	0	1	1	1	5
YEOVIL T	2	1	0	1	5	5	2	0	0	2	2	4
TOTALS	41	15	9	17	52	58	41	11	3	27	47	80

ABOVE
Chorley's first ever goal in the Conference scored by Shaul Allen.
Photo courtesy of the Lancashire Evening Post

RIGHT
Brian Ross
Photo: Colin Stephens

CHORLEY APPEARANCES

	88/89	89/90	TOTAL
ALLEN Shaun	32	33+1	65+1
BRADY John	39	41	80
BRANAGAN Jim	13		13
BUCKLEY Gary	10		10
CALDWELL Tony		18+1	18+1
CLEGG Tony	6	1+1	7+1
COLLINS Jimmy	7+4		7+4
COOPER Charlie		35+1	35+1
DAWSON Richard		17	17
DIAMOND Barry		7	7
EDEY Cec		10	10
GLENDON Kevin	9+1	23+2	32+3
GOULDING Derek	4		4
GRIFFIN Paul	2+5	11+5	13+10
HENSHAW Mark	1+1		1+1
HUGHES John	23	3	26
JACKSON Colin		38	38
JONES Graham	5+5	8	13+5
KEELEY Glyn		21	21
LESTER Mike	10	14	24
LLOYD Ian	16+6		16+6
LOMAX Geoff		7+3	7+3
MADRICK Carl	7+2		7+2
MELLOR Peter		1+1	1+1
MOSS Paul	37	23+6	60+6
NEENAN Joe		42	42
NICHOLL Joe	3		3
PAWSEY Charlie	14		14
PETERS Neil	38	26+1	64+1
PHILLIPS Steve	7		7
POWER Phil	29+1	20+5	49+6
REDSHAW Ray	2+6		2+6
RIDLER Colin	40		40
ROSS Brian	14+6	16+10	30+16
RUSSELL Mark	8+8		8+8
SAYER Peter		2+1	2+1
SMITH Barry		9+3	9+3
STEPHENS Glyn	27+1		27+1
STIMPSON Barrie		4	4
THOMAS David	0+1		0+1
WALKER Gary		2+1	2+1
WARDLE Craig	33+1	26	59+1
WOODS Ray	1		1
WORTHINGTON Frank	3		3
WRIGHT Neil		3+2	3+2
YATES Steve		1	1

GOALSCORERS

	88/89	89/90	TOTAL
ALLEN Shaun	2		2
BRADY John	10	4	14
BUCKLEY Gary	1		1
CALDWELL Tony		5(2p)	5(2p)
CLEGG Tony	1		1
COOPER Charlie		2	2
DAWSON Richard		3	3
DIAMOND Barry		3(1p)	3(1p)
GLENDON Kevin		2	2
GRIFFIN Paul	2	1	3
HUGHES John	1		1
KEELEY Glyn		2	2
MADRICK Carl	1		1
MOSS Paul	9	4	13
PAWSEY Charlie	1		1
POWER Phil	16	11(3p)	27(3p)
ROSS Brian	8	3	11
RUSSELL Mark	1		1
SMITH Barry		1	1
WARDLE Craig	2	1	3

Goalkeeper Colin Ridler punches clear under extreme pressure.   Photo: John B Vass

COLCHESTER UNITED

RELEGATED FROM: The Football League 1990
PROMOTED TO: The Football League 1992
2004-2005 SEASON: The Football League Division 1

The 1991-92 Colchester Squad. L-R - Back Row: Steve Foley (coach), Ian Phillips (player-coach), Martin Grainger, Scott Daniels, Paul Gothard, Scott Barrett, Mario Walsh, Tony English, Stuart Bevis (physio), Roy McDonough (player-manager). Front Row: Steve McGavin, Mark Kinsella, Nicky Smith, Warren Donald, Steve Restarick, Gary Bennett, Shaun Elliott, Eamonn Collins.

Below: The 3 Wembley goalscorers (L-R) Nicky Smith, Steve McGavin & Mike Masters.   **Photo**: Alan Coomes

SEASONS
2

TOTAL POINTS
179

HIGHEST POSITION
1st 1991-92

LOWEST POSITION
2nd (90-91)

HIGHEST ATTENDANCE
7193 v Barrow (2-5-92)

LOWEST ATTENDANCE
1966 v Northwich V (1-9-90)

SEASON GOALSCORER
Roy McDonough 26(2p) 91-92

CAREER GOALSCORER
Roy McDonough 34(2p)

CAREER APPEARANCES
Scott Barrett 84
(Ever present)

| | HOME | | | | | | AWAY | | | | | | | |
	P	W	D	L	F	A	Pts	P	W	D	L	F	A	Pts	Position
90-91	21	16	4	1	41	13	52	21	9	6	6	27	22	33	2
91-92	21	19	1	1	57	11	58	21	9	9	3	41	29	36	1
Total	42	35	5	2	98	24	110	42	18	15	9	68	51	69	

ABOVE: Mike Masters
Photo: John Robinson

RIGHT: Steve McGavin 'congratulates' Roy McDonough.
Photo: John Robinson

BELOW: Eamonn Collins
Photo: Mike Floate

COLCHESTER UNITED

	Altrincham		Barnet		Barrow		Bath City		Boston United		Cheltenham Town		Farnborough Town		Fisher Athletic		Gateshead	
	H	A	H	A	H	A	H	A	H	A	H	A	H	A	H	A	H	A
89-90	1-1	2-2	0-0	3-1	1-0	2-2	2-0	2-1	3-1	3-1	3-1	2-1			2-1	0-0	3-0	2-1
90-91	3-3	2-1			5-0	1-1	5-0	0-0	1-0	4-0	4-0	1-1	2-3	2-0			2-0	2-0
91-92																		

	Kettering Town		Kidderminster H.		Macclesfield Town		Merthyr Tydfil		Northwich Victoria		Redbridge Forest		Runcorn		Slough Town		Stafford Rangers	
	H	A	H	A	H	A	H	A	H	A	H	A	H	A	H	A	H	A
89-90	3-1	0-1	2-0	0-0	1-0	0-1	3-1	0-3	4-0	2-2			2-2	3-0	2-1	2-0	2-0	2-0
90-91	3-1	2-2	3-0	2-2	2-0	4-4	2-0	0-2	1-0	1-1	1-0	1-2	2-1	3-1	4-0	4-2	2-0	3-3
91-92																		

	Sutton United		Telford United		Welling United		Witton Albion		Wycombe Wanderers		Yeovil Town	
	H	A	H	A	H	A	H	A	H	A	H	A
89-90	1-0	1-0	2-0	0-2	2-1	1-1			2-2	0-1	0-1	0-2
90-91			2-0	3-0	3-1	1-4	3-2	2-2	3-0	2-1	4-0	1-0
91-92												

Roy McDonough

	HOME						AWAY					
	P	W	D	L	F	A	P	W	D	L	F	A
ALTRINCHAM	2	0	2	0	4	4	2	1	1	0	4	3
BARNET	1	0	1	0	0	0	1	1	0	0	3	1
BARROW	2	2	0	0	6	0	2	0	2	0	3	3
BATH C	2	2	0	0	7	0	2	1	1	0	2	1
BOSTON U	2	2	0	0	4	1	2	2	0	0	7	1
CHELTENHAM T	2	2	0	0	7	1	2	1	1	0	3	2
DAGENHAM & R	1	1	0	0	1	0	1	0	0	1	1	2
FARNBOROUGH T	1	0	0	1	2	3	1	1	0	0	2	0
FISHER A	1	1	0	0	2	1	1	0	1	0	0	0
GATESHEAD	2	2	0	0	5	0	2	2	0	0	4	1
KETTERING T	2	2	0	0	6	2	2	0	1	1	2	3
KIDDERMINSTER H	2	2	0	0	5	0	2	0	2	0	2	2
MACCLESFIELD T	2	2	0	0	3	0	2	0	1	1	4	5
MERTHYR T	2	2	0	0	5	1	2	0	0	2	0	5
NORTHWICH V	2	2	0	0	5	0	2	0	2	0	3	3
RUNCORN	2	1	1	0	4	3	2	2	0	0	6	1
SLOUGH T	2	2	0	0	6	1	2	2	0	0	6	2
STAFFORD R	2	2	0	0	4	0	2	1	1	0	5	3
SUTTON U	1	1	0	0	1	0	1	1	0	0	1	0
TELFORD U	2	2	0	0	4	0	2	1	0	1	3	2
WELLING U	2	2	0	0	5	2	2	0	1	1	2	5
WITTON A	1	1	0	0	3	2	1	0	1	0	2	2
WYCOMBE W	2	1	1	0	5	2	2	1	0	1	2	2
YEOVIL T	2	1	0	1	4	1	2	1	0	1	1	2
TOTALS	42	35	5	2	98	24	42	18	15	9	68	51

APPEARANCES

	90/91	91/92	TOTAL
ABRAHAMS Paul		0+3	0+3
ATKINS Ian	40		40
BARRETT Scott	42	42	84
BENNETT Gary	34+2	31+8	65+10
BRUCE Marcelle	2+2		2+2
COLLINS Eammon	36	29+3	65+3
COOK Jason		27+3	27+3
DANIELS Scott	40		40
DONALD Warren	33+5	38+3	71+8
ELLIOTT Shaun	14+5	33+5	47+10
ENGLISH Tony	39+1	37+1	76+2
GOODWIN Jamie		0+3	0+3
GRAINGER Martin	3+2	9+2	12+4
GRAY Simon		1+1	1+1
HEDMAN Rudi	10		10
KINSELLA Mark	6+5	37+4	43+9
LEWORTHY David	9		9
MARMON Neale	36+1		36+1
MARTIN David		8+1	8+1
MASTERS Mike	2+9	7+8	9+17
McDONOUGH Roy	17+7	40	57+7
McGAVIN Steve	2+6	39	41+6
OSBOURNE Gary	5+1		5+1
PHILLIPS Ian		1+2	1+2
RADFORD Mark	1+3		1+3
REES Mark	0+1		0+1
RESTARICK Steve		1+6	1+6
ROBERTS Paul		34	34
RYAN Laurie	3+10		3+10
SCOTT Morrys	1+3		1+3
SMITH Nicky	34	42	76
STEWART Ian		6+4	6+4
WALSH Mario	31+1	0+1	31+2
YATES Mark	22+3		22+3

GOALSCORERS

	90/91	91/92	TOTAL
ATKINS Ian	7		7
BARRETT Scott		1	1
BENNETT Gary	9	16	25
COLLINS Eamonn	2	2	4
COOK Jason		2	2
DANIELS Scott	1		1
DONALD Warren	1		1
ELLIOTT Shaun		1	1
ENGLISH Tony	7	6	13
KINSELLA Mark		3	3
LEWORTHY David	4		4
MARMON Neil	2		2
MASTERS Mick	1	7	8
McDONOUGH Roy	8	26(2p)	34(2p)
McGAVIN Steve		20	20
ROBERTS Paul		1	1
RYAN Laurie	3		3
SMITH Nicky		8	8
STEWART Ian		2	2
WALSH Mario	17		17
YATES Mark	6		6

ABOVE: Mark Kinsella
Photo: John Robinson

LEFT: Steve McGavin
Photo: Mike Floate

DAGENHAM

PROMOTED FROM: Isthmian League 1981
RELEGATED TO: Isthmian League 1988
2004-2005 SEASON: Merged with Redbridge Forest in 1992 to form Dagenham & Redbridge.

Dagenham Squad 1983-84

Left to Right - **Back Row:** George Ashton (Kit Man), Alan Campbell, Ron Duke (Coach), Bill Fenlon (Coach), Terry Scales, Peter Burton, Dave Hubbick, John Dear, Ron Francis, Terry Moore, Jon Sille, Ernie Jones (Physio), Ted Hardy (Manager), Ian Huttley.
Front Row: Roger Wade, Jeff Bryant, Joe Dunwell, John Knapman, Chris Maycock, Paul Lazarus

SEASONS
7

TOTAL POINTS
173 + 134 = 307

HIGHEST POSITION
5th (81-82)

LOWEST POSITION
22nd (87-88)

HIGHEST ATTENDANCE
1317 v Barnet (7-9-81))

LOWEST ATTENDANCE
368 v Kidderminster (28-3-87)

SEASON GOALSCORER
Peter Burton 13 (81/82)
Les Whitton 13 (84/85)

CAREER GOALSCORER
Joe Dunwell 28

CAREER APPEARANCES
Joe Dunwell 171+19

	HOME							AWAY							
	P	W	D	L	F	A	Pts	P	W	D	L	F	A	Pts	Position
81-82	21	10	6	5	32	23	36	21	9	6	6	37	28	33	5
82-83	21	5	9	7	30	26	24	21	7	6	8	30	39	27	14
83-84	21	10	3	8	34	26	23	21	4	5	12	23	43	17	18
84-85	21	8	6	7	28	27	22	21	5	4	12	19	40	19	19
85-86	21	6	7	8	23	29	19	21	4	5	12	25	37	17	19
86-87	21	10	4	7	32	29	34	21	4	3	14	24	43	15	15
87-88	21	4	3	14	20	46	15	21	1	3	17	17	58	6	22
Total	147	53	38	56	199	206	173	147	34	32	81	175	288	134	

DAGENHAM

	Altrincham		A P Leamington		Bangor City		Barnet		Barrow		Bath City		Boston United		Cheltenham Town		Dartford	
	H	A	H	A	H	A	H	A	H	A	H	A	H	A	H	A	H	A
81-82	2-0	1-1	0-0	4-0			1-1	2-1	1-0	2-2	0-1	3-0	2-0	4-3			2-1	3-0
82-83	1-1	0-2			1-1	1-1	1-2	2-2	0-0	2-1	0-1	1-3	1-1	3-3				
83-84	0-2	0-4			3-1	4-2	3-1	1-3			3-1	1-0	2-0	0-3				
84-85	1-1	1-3					0-0	0-0	1-1	1-3	0-0	0-2	1-2	1-4			0-1	0-3
85-86	1-3	1-3					2-1	1-4	3-0	0-1	0-1	1-1	2-2	0-3	1-3	2-2	2-1	1-1
86-87	3-1	2-0					1-3	0-1			1-2	0-2	3-2	0-1	1-1	1-6		
87-88	3-2	0-6					0-0	2-3			1-1	2-4	4-2	0-1	1-3	1-5		

	Enfield		Fisher Athletic		Frickley Athletic		Gateshead		Gravesend & N'fleet		Kettering Town		Kidderminster H.		Lincoln City		Macclesfield Town	
	H	A	H	A	H	A	H	A	H	A	H	A	H	A	H	A	H	A
81-82	2-4	2-3			2-0	1-3			1-1	2-1	2-1	1-3						
82-83	1-0	1-2			4-1	2-1					2-3	2-1						
83-84	1-4	0-3			1-1	0-4	1-2	1-1			2-0	2-2			0-0	2-4		
84-85	0-3	2-3			4-1	2-0	0-2	1-2			2-1	1-0			2-2	1-5		
85-86	0-2	1-3			0-0	2-3					1-0	2-0			0-1	0-2		
86-87	0-3	0-1			0-1	3-1	0-0	2-3			1-2	1-3	3-1	2-4				
87-88	1-2	2-2	1-5	1-5							0-5	0-3	1-2	1-1	0-3	0-3	0-0	1-3

	Maidstone United		Northwich Victoria		Nuneaton Borough		Runcorn		Scarborough		Stafford Rangers		Sutton United		Telford United		Trowbridge Town	
	H	A	H	A	H	A	H	A	H	A	H	A	H	A	H	A	H	A
81-82	1-1	2-2	2-1	0-3			0-1	0-1	2-2	1-1	2-2	0-0			3-2	2-0	1-2	1-0
82-83	0-1	3-1	3-1	0-3	0-0	1-1	3-1	1-5	1-1	1-1	3-3	2-1			1-1	0-3	0-1	2-2
83-84	0-1	0-2	3-1	1-3	4-2	1-1	0-2	0-1	1-1	0-0					1-2	1-3	6-2	4-1
84-85	4-1	1-0	2-1	1-0	2-1	2-2	2-1	0-3	0-2	0-5					1-0	1-1		
85-86	0-0	1-2	1-0	1-0	3-2	2-1	2-3	1-1	0-0	1-2	1-1	1-3			1-4	1-2		
86-87	0-2	1-2	3-3	3-2	3-1	3-3	3-2	0-4	0-2	1-2	1-0	1-1	2-1	0-1	3-1	2-0		
87-88	0-3	0-2	1-0	0-1			1-4	1-2			2-4	0-4	0-1	1-1	0-1	0-1		

DAGENHAM

	Wealdstone H	A	Welling United H	A	Weymouth H	A	Worcester City H	A	Wycombe Wanderers H	A	Yeovil Town H	A
81-82					2-1	1-1	1-2	1-2			3-0	4-1
82-83	1-2	1-3			1-2	1-0	3-3	4-1			3-0	0-2
83-84	1-0	0-1			1-2	1-3	0-1	2-2			1-0	2-0
84-85	1-2	0-0			2-2	0-1	1-3	3-1			2-0	1-2
85-86	0-2	4-0			2-2	1-2			1-1	1-1		
86-87	1-0	2-2	1-1	0-1	2-0	0-3						
87-88	1-2	3-2	1-2	1-6	0-3	0-1			2-1	1-2		

	Home						Away					
	P	W	D	L	F	A	P	W	D	L	F	A
ALTRINCHAM	7	3	2	2	11	10	7	1	1	5	5	19
A P LEAMINGTON	1	0	1	0	0	0	1	1	0	0	4	0
BANGOR C	2	1	1	0	4	2	2	1	1	0	5	3
BARNET	7	2	3	2	8	8	7	1	2	4	8	14
BARROW	4	2	2	0	5	1	4	1	1	2	5	7
BATH C	7	1	2	4	5	7	7	2	1	4	8	12
BOSTON U	7	4	2	1	15	9	7	1	1	5	8	18
CHELTENHAM T	3	0	1	2	3	7	3	0	1	2	4	13
DARTFORD	3	2	0	1	4	3	3	1	1	1	4	4
ENFIELD	7	1	0	6	5	18	7	0	1	6	8	17
FISHER A	1	0	0	1	1	5	1	0	0	1	1	5
FRICKLEY A	6	3	2	1	11	4	6	3	0	3	10	12
GATESHEAD	3	0	1	2	1	4	3	0	1	2	4	6
GRAVESEND & N	1	0	1	0	1	1	1	1	0	0	2	1
KETTERING T	7	4	0	3	10	12	7	3	1	3	9	12
KIDDERMINSTER H	5	1	2	2	6	6	5	0	1	4	6	16
LINCOLN C	1	0	0	1	0	3	1	0	0	1	0	3
MACCLESFIELD T	1	0	1	0	0	0	1	0	0	1	1	3
MAIDSTONE U	7	1	2	4	5	9	7	2	1	4	8	11
NORTHWICH V	7	6	1	0	15	7	7	3	0	4	6	12
NUNEATON B	5	4	1	0	12	6	5	1	4	0	9	8
RUNCORN	7	3	0	4	11	14	7	0	1	6	3	17
SCARBOROUGH	6	0	4	2	4	8	6	0	3	3	4	11
STAFFORD R	5	1	3	1	9	10	5	1	2	2	4	9
SUTTON U	2	1	0	1	2	2	2	0	1	1	1	2
TELFORD U	7	3	1	3	10	11	7	2	1	4	7	10
TROWBRIDGE T	3	1	0	2	7	5	3	2	1	0	7	3
WEALDSTONE	6	2	0	4	5	8	6	2	2	2	10	8
WELLING U	2	0	1	1	2	3	2	0	0	2	1	7
WEYMOUTH	7	2	2	3	10	12	7	1	1	5	4	11
WORCESTER C	4	0	1	3	5	9	4	2	1	1	10	6
WYCOMBE W	2	1	1	0	3	2	2	0	1	1	2	3
YEOVIL T	4	4	0	0	9	0	4	2	0	2	7	5
TOTALS	147	53	38	56	199	206	147	34	32	81	175	288

DAGENHAM
LEADING APPEARANCES

	81/82	82/83	83/84	84/85	85/86	86/87	87/88	TOTAL
Joe DUNWELL	37	23	42	26+10	32+4	5+1	6+4	171+19
Steve SCOTT			32+1	42	39+2	37+2		150+5
Tommy HORAN	31+2			20+1	36+1	7	18	112+4
Roger WADE	22	21	30+1	40				113+1
Frank COLES				10+1	38+1	38+2	19+2	105+6
Alan CAMPBELL		33	33	37	6+1			109+1

LEADING GOALSCORERS

	81/82	82/83	83/84	84/85	85/86	86/87	87/88	TOTAL
Joe DUNWELL	9	3	8	6	1	1		28
Les WHITTON			2	13	4			19
John McCOMBE			11	6	1			18
Steve SCOTT			5	5	3	4		17
Peter BURTON	13	3						16

DAGENHAM — APPEARANCES

	81/82	82/83	83/84	84/85	85/86	86/87	87/88	TOTAL
ALLEN Greg							13+1	13+1
ARBER Bobby		12+1						12+1
ARMSTRONG Gary		5						5
AYRTON Neil				5+1				5+1
BAILEY Danny			1+2					1+2
BANFIELD Neil					9			9
BASS Tony		0+3	0+1					0+4
BAXTER Paul					17+1	13+1		30+2
BICKLES Glen						3+4		3+4
BISSETT Nicky						39	32	71
BOLLE Jon			2+2				18	20+2
BOND Ricky							6	6
BOYCE Phil		16	1					17
BROWN Steve	24+1	8						32+1
BROWNE Bryan					0+1			0+1
BRYANT Jeff		24						24
BURTON Peter	38	6						44
CAMPBELL Alan		33	33	37	6+1			109+1
CAMPBELL John						15+2		15+2
CAVANAGH Steve		2						2
CLARKE Peter							2+2	2+2
CODNER Robert				25+6				25+6
COLES Frank				10+1	38+1	38+2	19+2	105+6
COLLINS Gary		6						6
COX Steve					21+1			21+1
CRAMPTON Gary				28+1				28+1
CRIBB Paul					0+1			0+1
CRUMPTON Dean						11+1		11+1
DALORTO George						28+4	6+6	34+10
DANIEL Errol				3+2				3+2
DANSON Dave	26							26
DAY Alan					14		10	24
DAY Clive					35+1			35+1

DAGENHAM   APPEARANCES

	81/82	82/83	83/84	84/85	85/86	86/87	87/88	TOTAL
DEADMAN Peter	11							11
DEAR John		9	1					10
DENNEHY Mark		3						3
DENNIS Darren	4+3							4+3
DENNIS Desmond			3+1					3+1
DOCKER John							20+4	20+4
DUNWELL Joe	37	23	42	26+10	32+4	5+1	6+4	171+19
EDKINS Steve		4+5						4+5
ELLEY Keith	37							37
FIELD Tony		0+1						0+1
FITT John							24	24
FLETCHER Spencer						6+2		6+2
FLYNN Tony				4+1			7+1	11+2
FRANCIS Ron	17+2	22+1						39+3
GAYLE Devon					17	17+4		34+4
GIBSON Tony	38+1	15	14					67+1
GILES Graham					0+3			0+3
GOYETTE Paul						38+2	7	45+2
GREAVES Danny			1+1					1+1
GREENAWAY Brian							2+2	2+2
HALLYBONE Jimmy			9+1					9+1
HARDWICK Glen				0+2				0+2
HARRIS Steve						0+4	0+2	0+6
HEAD Richard					8+4			8+4
HOLMES Lee						21+1	16+3	37+4
HORAN Tommy	31+2			20+1	36+1	7	18	112+4
HOWELL Ron	25+1							25+1
HUBBICK Dave		19+1						19+1
HUNT Paul							0+2	0+2
HUTTLEY Ian	16	16						32
JACOBS Allen						18+1	14+1	32+2
JACOBS John					34	3		37
JENNINGS Billy		3						3
KEAN Russell		5						5
KEYES Robert							15+2	15+2
KIDD Ricky	23+3							23+3
KINNEAR Chris				27				27
KITCHEN Peter				5				5
KNAPMAN John		32+4	33					65+4
KNOCK Bob				1				1
La RONDE Everald							8+1	8+1
LANSDOWNE Bill				10		13	3+1	26+1
LAWRENCE Mark							7	7
LAZARUS Paul		9						9
LEVY Neil		0+1						0+1
LITTLE Barry				37+2				37+2
MAKIN Bob		11						11
MANDERSON Lincoln			10+4	11+2	13+4			34+10
MARTIN Eddie							21	21
MAYCOCK Chris	17+8	22+12	19+6					58+26
McCOMBE John			23+3	13	8+4			44+7

DAGENHAM   APPEARANCES

	81/82	82/83	83/84	84/85	85/86	86/87	87/88	TOTAL
MOORE Terry		20	25					45
MURCOTT Lee							10+1	10+1
NELSON Rupert							18	18
OLALEYE Samson							18	18
OLIVER Steve			22+3	26			1+2	49+5
PAGE Steve			11+4	3		3+1		17+5
PARRATT Dean							3	3
PEARCE Dave					14	24+3		38+3
POWELL Paul					10+2			10+2
PURLL Lee							0+3	0+3
RAGAN Steve	8+1							8+1
REEVES John		10+1			2	23+2		35+3
RHODEN Delroy			19+2					19+2
RISK Alan					26	27+2		53+2
ROAST Jesse	9							9
ROLPH Gary		1						1
SCALES Terry	34	31	23					88
SCOTT Craig						0+1		0+1
SCOTT Lloyd			17	40			17	74
SCOTT Steve			32+1	42	39+2	37+2		150+5
SHERINGHAM Jim		7	1					8
SILLE Jon		12	29+1					41+1
SILMAN Dave			2					2
SIMPSON Mark			6					6
SIMS Micky							2+4	2+4
SMITH Peter			12+6					12+6
STACEY Phil							28+1	28+1
STEIN Eddie	20+2							20+2
STEWART Malcolm	25+1	29						54+1
SULLIVAN Terry					27+2	7+5		34+7
SUTTON Richard				9+2				9+2
TAPPIN Bobby		9						9
TAYLOR Paul					33+1	35+2	6+2	74+5
THRIFT Paul						1+1	0+1	1+2
TONE John			11					11
TONGE Keith						6+2		6+2
TURNPENNY Paul					3+8			3+8
TYDEMAN Richard				4+2				4+2
WADE Roger	22	21	30+1	40				113+1
WAITE Dave							3+3	3+3
WALLACE Gary							6+1	6+1
WATSON John				12				12
WEEKES Brian							10+5	10+5
WELLS Derek			15					15
WHITTON Les			15+1	23+2	12+1			50+4
WIGGINS Steve							17	17
WILLIAMS Darren				1	8	39	25	73
WILSON Richard		8						8
WOODRUFF Melvin							7+1	7+1
WRIGHT Mark		9						9

DAGENHAM GOALSCORERS

	81/82	82/83	83/84	84/85	85/86	86/87	87/88	TOTAL
ALLEN Greg							2	2
ARBER Bobby		1						1
AYRTON Neil				1				1
BISSETT Nicky							2	2
BOLLE Jon			1				7	8
BOND Ricky							1	1
BROWN Steve	11(5p)	2(1p)						13(6p)
BRYANT Jeff		6						6
BURTON Peter	13	3						16
CAMPBELL Alan			1	1				2
CAMPBELL John							1	1
CODNER Robert				4(2p)				4(2p)
COLES Frank					2	1	1	4
COX Steve					9(1p)			9(1p)
CRAMPTON Gary				1				1
DALORTO George						5		5
DAY Alan					1		1	2
DOCKER John							1	1
DUNWELL Joe	9	3	8	6	1	1		28
EDKINS Steve		2						2
FITT John							2	2
FRANCIS Ron	2	6						8
GAYLE Devon					7(2p)	5		12(2p)
GIBSON Tony	4		1					5
GOYETTE Paul						10(3p)	1	11(3p)
HALLYBONE Jimmy			1					1
HEAD Richard					1			1
HOLMES Lee						6		6
HOWELL Ron	5(2p)							5(2p)
HUBBICK Dave		5(1p)						5(1p)
JACOBS John					1			1
KIDD Ricky	5							5
KINNEAR Chris				1				1
KNAPMAN John		3	1					4
La RONDE Everald						1		1
LANSDOWNE Billy				2		3		5
LAZARUS Paul		4						4
LITTLE Barry				3				3
MAKIN Bob		1						1
MANDERSON Lincoln			1	1	3			5
MAYCOCK Chris	3	2	5					10
McCOMBE John			11	6	1			18
OLALEYE Samson							6	6
OLIVER Steve			1	2				3
PAGE Steve		1(1p)				1		2(1p)
PEARCE Dave					1	9		10

DAGENHAM GOALSCORERS

	81/82	82/83	83/84	84/85	85/86	86/87	87/88	TOTAL
POWELL Paul					3			3
RAGAN Steve	4							4
REEVES John		1						1
RHODEN Delroy			3					3
RISK Alan						1		1
SCALES Terry	2							2
SCOTT Steve			5	5	3	4		17
SHERINGHAM Jim		3						3
SILLE Jon		3	7(1p)					10(1p)
SILMAN Dave			1					1
SIMS Micky							1	1
SMITH Peter			4					4
STACEY Phil							1	1
STEIN Edwin	2							2
STEWART Malcolm	3	3						6
SULLIVAN Terry					1	2		3
TAPPIN Barry		3						3
TAYLOR Paul					9	3		12
THRIFT Paul						1		1
TONGE Keith						2		2
WADE Roger	1		2					3
WALLACE Gary							1	1
WEEKES Brian							3	3
WHITTON Les			2	13	4			19
WIGGINS Steve							2	2
WILSON Richard		4						4
WOODRUFF Melvin							3	3
WRIGHT Mark		1						1

Dagenham 1982-83. Back row, left to right:- Bill Fenton, Ted Hardy, Eddie Stein, Chris Maycock, Joe Dunwell, Peter Burton, Ian Hutley, Ricky Kidd, Ronnie Francis, Terry Scales and Dennis Moore. Front row: Ronnie Hales, Tommy Horan Roger Wade, Keith Elley, Darren Dennis, Steve Brown and Malcolm Stewart.

DAGENHAM & REDBRIDGE

including 1991-92 as **REDBRIDGE FOREST**

PROMOTED FROM: The Isthmian League 1990-91, 1999-2000
RELEGATED TO: The Isthmian League 1995-96
2004-2005 SEASON: The Conference

Dagenham & Redbridge 2001-2002 Back row,left to right:Steve Perkins, Ollie Berquez, Steve West,Tony Roberts, Paul Gothard, Ashley Vickers, Mark Rooney and Paul Bruce. Middle Row: Ross Johnson, Danny Shipp, Mark Smith, Lee Matthews , Steve Heffer, Danny Hilll and Mark Stein. Front Row:John Keeling, Steve McGavin, Mark Janney, Paul Terry, Lee Goodwin, Danny Hayzelden, Junior McDougald and Steve Vaughan.

		HOME							AWAY						
SEASONS		P	W	D	L	F	A	Pts	P	W	D	L	F	A	Pts	Position

		HOME							AWAY							
SEASONS 9		**P**	**W**	**D**	**L**	**F**	**A**	**Pts**	**P**	**W**	**D**	**L**	**F**	**A**	**Pts**	**Position**
TOTAL POINTS 526 - 1pt deducted 92-93	**91-92**	21	12	4	5	42	27	40 (as Redbridge Forest)	21	6	5	10	27	29	23	7
HIGHEST POSITION 2nd 2001-02	**92-93**	21	10	5	6	48	29	35	21	9	6	6	27	18	33	3
	93-94	21	12	5	4	41	23	41	21	3	9	9	21	31	18	6
LOWEST POSITION 22nd 1995-96	**94-95**	21	8	5	8	28	32	29	21	5	8	8	28	37	23	15
HIGHEST ATTENDANCE 3939 v Chester C. 28.4.02	**95-96**	21	5	7	9	31	34	22	21	2	5	14	12	39	11	22
	96-00															
LOWEST ATTENDANCE 332 v Barrow 19.10.92	**00-01**	21	13	4	4	39	19	43	21	10	4	7	32	35	34	3
SEASON GOALSCORER Mark Stein 24(1p) (01/02)	**01-02**	21	13	6	2	35	20	45	21	11	6	4	35	27	39	2
	02-03	21	12	5	4	38	23	41	21	9	4	8	33	36	31	5
CAREER GOALSCORER Paul Cavell 53	**03-04**	21	8	3	10	30	34	27	21	7	6	8	29	30	27	13
CAREER APPEARANCES Jason Broom 169+26	**Total**	189	93	44	52	332	241	323	189	62	53	74	244	282	239	

	Accrington Stanley		Aldershot Town		Altrincham		Barnet		Barrow		Bath City		Boston United		Bromsgrove Rovers		Burton Albion		Cheltenham Town	
	H	A	H	A	H	A	H	A	H	A	H	A	H	A	H	A	H	A	H	A
91-92					0-1	3-0			2-2	1-0	3-1	0-0	1-4	1-2					1-2	7-0
92-93					2-2	0-1					2-1	1-2	1-0	1-3	1-1	2-1				
93-94					3-0	2-1					3-0	0-0			4-2	0-2				
94-95					0-4	1-0					1-0	0-3			2-0	2-2				
95-96					1-0	1-3					0-1	2-0			2-2	0-2				
96-00																				
00-01															2-1	1-5				
01-02							1-1	0-4							1-0	2-1				
02-03							5-1	1-2									1-2	0-0		
03-04	0-1	3-2	2-3	1-2			5-2	4-2									0-2	1-0		

	Chester City		Colchester United		Doncaster Rovers		Dover Athletic		Exeter City		Farnborough Town		Forest Green Rovers		Gateshead		Gravesend & N'fleet		Halifax Town	
	H	A	H	A	H	A	H	A	H	A	H	A	H	A	H	A	H	A	H	A
91-92			2-1	0-1							2-0	0-1			2-1	1-0				
92-93											5-1	4-1			3-1	1-1				
93-94							2-1	1-1							1-1	1-3			3-0	1-0
94-95							2-0	1-1			0-1	3-1			0-0	1-2			1-4	1-1
95-96							3-0	1-0			2-2	0-2			0-4	0-2			1-1	0-3
96-00																				
00-01	1-1	1-1			2-1	0-1	1-1	1-3					3-1	4-4						
01-02	3-0	1-0			1-0	0-0	1-0	1-0			2-1	2-1	1-1	4-2						
02-03	1-0	2-5			3-3	1-5					1-0	0-1	3-1	2-5			4-0	2-1	0-0	3-3
03-04	0-0	1-2							0-2	1-1	2-2	1-0	5-2	3-1			0-4	2-1	0-1	0-3

	Hayes		Hednesford Town		Hereford United		Kettering Town		Kidderminster H.		Kingstonian		Leigh RMI		Macclesfield Town		Margate		Merthyr Tydfil	
	H	A	H	A	H	A	H	A	H	A	H	A	H	A	H	A	H	A	H	A
91-92							4-0	2-3	5-0	1-5					0-0	0-0			1-1	2-2
92-93							1-2	0-0	3-2	1-0					1-2	1-1			6-1	2-0
93-94							2-3	1-1	1-1	1-2					1-1	0-3			0-1	0-0
94-95							2-1	2-2	1-2	1-1					0-4	0-2			2-1	0-2
95-96			1-2	0-0			1-2	0-2	4-2	1-5					3-0	1-3				
96-00																				
00-01	2-0	1-4	6-1	2-0			2-1	1-0	5-1	0-0	1-2	3-2	2-1	2-1						
01-02	1-1	4-2					1-0	0-1					0-1	0-2			4-1	1-1		
02-03							1-0	1-2					3-1	3-1			3-0	1-0		
03-04							0-9	1-1					1-2	1-2			4-0	3-3		

DAGENHAM & REDBRIDGE includes 91-92 as Redbridge Forest

	Morecambe		Northwich Victoria		Nuneaton Borough		Runcorn		Rushden & Diamonds		Scarborough		Shrewsbury Town		Slough Town		Southport		Stafford Rangers	
	H	A	H	A	H	A	H	A	H	A	H	A	H	A	H	A	H	A	H	A
91-92			4-3	2-0			1-2	0-1							4-0	0-4			4-3	1-2
92-93			4-1	1-1			5-1	0-1							4-4	0-2			0-1	1-0
93-94			1-1	2-2			2-1	1-2							1-0	1-3	3-3	0-0	1-0	0-2
94-95			1-2	0-5			3-2	0-0									5-1	1-1	3-3	2-1
95-96	2-2	2-2	0-3	0-1			2-3	0-2							1-3	0-5	1-2	1-2		
96-00																				
00-01	3-2	3-2	1-0	0-3	1-1	0-2			0-2	1-2	1-0	1-0					0-1	1-0		
01-02	3-2	1-1	1-1	2-1	2-0	0-2					4-2	0-0					1-1	2-2		
02-03	1-1	1-2	2-0	2-0	1-2	3-1							1-0	1-0			0-3	3-2		
03-04	1-3	2-3	1-0	2-0							1-0	0-0	5-0	1-2						

	Stalybridge Celtic		Stevenage Borough		Tamworth		Telford United		Welling United		Witton Albion		Woking		Wycombe Wanderers		Yeovil Town	
	H	A	H	A	H	A	H	A	H	A	H	A	H	A	H	A	H	A
91-92							1-0	3-3	2-0	2-2	3-1	0-2			0-5	0-1	0-0	1-0
92-93	1-2	3-0					0-2	1-0	1-0	2-0	1-1	2-2	5-1	1-1	1-2	0-1	1-1	3-0
93-94	0-1	0-5					4-1	0-0	2-0	0-0	2-1	1-1	3-4	8-1			2-1	1-2
94-95	2-2	0-1	0-1	1-3			3-2	4-0	0-0	1-4			0-2	5-3			0-0	2-2
95-96	4-1	1-2	1-2	0-1			1-1	0-0	1-1	0-0			0-0	2-2				
96-00																		
00-01			3-0	2-0			0-0	1-0					1-2	4-4			2-0	3-1
01-02	2-1	3-2	1-0	3-1			1-5	4-1					3-1	2-0			1-1	3-3
02-03			3-2	0-2			1-1	2-1					1-1	0-0			0-4	2-2
03-04			2-0	1-2	0-0	0-2	0-1	1-1					0-0	1-0				

Redbridge Forest 1991-92. Back row, left to right: Jim Payne (Physio), K.Davidson, R.Garvey, K.Foster, T.Pamphlett, M.Cawston , K.Barrett, S.Connor, A Dafforn. Front row: M.Gurney, T.Williams, L.Fulling, T.Sullivan, D.Jacques, J.Simmonds M.Stewart, J, Brfoom and P.Watts

	Home						Away					
	P	W	D	L	F	A	P	W	D	L	F	A
ACCRINGTON S	1	0	0	1	0	1	1	1	0	0	3	2
ALDERSHOT T	1	0	0	1	2	3	1	0	0	1	1	2
ALTRINCHAM	5	2	1	2	6	7	5	3	0	2	7	5
BARNET	3	2	1	0	11	4	3	1	0	2	5	8
BARROW	1	0	1	0	2	2	1	1	0	0	1	0
BATH C	5	4	0	1	9	3	5	1	2	2	3	5
BOSTON U	4	3	0	1	5	5	4	1	0	3	5	11
BROMSGROVE R	4	2	2	0	9	5	4	1	1	2	4	7
BURTON A	2	0	0	2	1	4	2	1	1	0	1	0
CHELTENHAM T	1	0	0	1	1	2	1	1	0	0	7	0
CHESTER C	4	2	2	0	5	1	4	1	1	2	5	8
COLCHESTER U	1	1	0	0	2	1	1	0	0	1	0	1
DONCASTER R	3	2	1	0	6	4	3	0	1	2	1	6
DOVER A	5	4	1	0	9	2	5	2	2	1	5	5
EXETER C	1	0	0	1	0	2	1	0	1	0	1	1
FARNBOROUGH T	7	5	1	1	13	5	7	3	1	3	11	9
FOREST GREEN R	4	3	1	0	12	5	4	2	1	1	13	12
GATESHEAD	5	2	2	1	6	7	5	1	1	3	4	8
GRAVESEND & N	2	1	0	1	4	4	2	2	0	0	4	2
HALIFAX T	5	1	2	2	5	6	5	1	2	2	5	10
HAYES	2	1	1	0	3	1	2	1	0	1	5	6
HEDNESFORD T	2	1	0	1	7	3	2	1	1	0	2	0
HEREFORD U	4	3	0	1	4	10	4	1	1	2	3	4
KETTERING T	7	4	0	3	18	10	7	1	4	2	8	9
KIDDERMINSTER H	5	3	1	1	14	7	5	1	1	3	5	13
KINGSTONIAN	1	0	0	1	1	2	1	1	0	0	3	2
LEIGH RMI	4	2	0	2	6	5	4	2	0	2	6	6
MACCLESFIELD T	5	1	2	2	5	7	5	0	2	3	2	9
MARGATE	3	3	0	0	11	1	3	1	2	0	5	4
MERTHYR T	4	2	1	1	9	4	4	1	2	1	4	4
MORECAMBE	5	2	2	1	10	10	5	1	2	2	9	10
NORTHWICH V	9	5	2	2	16	11	9	4	2	3	10	13
NUNEATON B	3	1	1	1	4	3	3	1	0	2	3	5
RUNCORN	5	3	0	2	13	9	5	0	1	4	1	6
RUSHDEN & D	1	0	0	1	0	2	1	0	0	1	1	2
SCARBOROUGH	4	4	0	0	7	2	4	2	2	0	2	0
SHREWSBURY T	1	1	0	0	5	0	1	0	0	1	1	2
SLOUGH T	4	2	1	1	10	7	4	0	0	4	1	14
SOUTHPORT	6	1	2	3	10	11	6	2	3	1	8	7
STAFFORD R	4	2	1	1	8	7	4	2	0	2	4	5
STALYBRIDGE C	5	2	1	2	9	7	5	2	0	3	7	10
STEVENAGE B	6	3	0	3	9	7	6	3	0	3	8	7
TAMWORTH	1	0	1	0	0	0	1	0	0	1	0	2
TELFORD U	9	3	4	2	12	13	9	5	3	1	15	6
WELLING U	5	3	2	0	6	1	5	1	3	1	5	6
WITTON A	3	2	1	0	6	3	3	0	2	1	3	5
WOKING	8	3	2	3	14	11	8	3	5	0	22	11
WYCOMBE W	2	0	0	2	1	7	2	0	0	2	0	2
YEOVIL T	7	2	4	1	6	7	7	3	3	1	15	10
TOTALS	189	93	44	52	332	241	189	62	53	74	244	282

DAGENHAM & REDBRIDGE — LEADING APPEARANCES

	91-92	92-93	93-94	94-95	95-96	96-00	00-01	01-02	02-03	03-04	TOTAL
Jason BROOM	19+7	36+2	16	31	28+2		25+2	11+9	3+4		169+26
Danny SHIPP				9	7+1		21+10	32+5	32+9	29+6	130+31
Steve CONNER	42	38	36	26+1	17+1						159+2
Paul WATTS	40	40	41	33							154
Gary STEBBING		22+3	42	41	34						139+3
Tony ROBERTS							40	36	37	26	139
Mark JANNEY							28+5	30+5	14+11	22+15	94+36
Ashley VICKERS							28+1	26+1	29+4	30+1	113+7
Paul TERRY							35+3	36+3	32+2	2	105+8
Paul CAVELL	28	37	27	14+3							106+3
Steve HEFFER							35+2	34+2	28+3		97+7

DAGENHAM & REDBRIDGE — APPEARANCES

	91-92	92-93	93-94	94-95	95-96	96-00	00-01	01-02	02-03	03-04	TOTAL
ALDRIDGE Martin					3						3
ALEXANDER Tim					2+1						2+1
ALLEN Greg		1+2									1+2
ASHFORD Noel	9+3										9+3
AYRES James							1				1
BACON Paul			3								3
BARRETT Keith	10+1										10+1
BECKWITH Dean										4	4
BENNETT Gary				9	3+3						12+3
BENNETT Ian	18										18
BENTLEY Mark									23+2		23+2
BLACKFORD Gary	21+1	34+2	33+2								88+5
BOLDER Bob				29	2						31
BOYLE Gary				2							2
BRAITHWAITE Leon										20+14	20+14
BRENNAN Mark							17+7	8+8			25+15
BROOM Jason	19+7	36+2	16	31	28+2		25+2	11+9	3+4		169+26
BROUGHTON Drewe							8+1				8+1
BROWNE Stafford							0+3				0+3
BRUCE Paul									13+1	30+6	43+7
BUTTERWORTH Gary		38+3	42								80+3
CAVELL Paul	28	37	27	14+3							106+3
CAWSTON Mervyn	2										2
CHARLERY Ken								19+4			19+4
CHERRY Richard	6+3										6+3
COBB Paul							10+18				10+18
COLE Michael	1+3										1+3
COLE Tim							35	2+2	10+4	29	76+6
COLLINS Darren					1+3						1+3
CONNER Steve	42	38	36	26+1	17+1						159+2
COOK Jason				19	3+1						22+1

Garry Butterworth.   Photo: Paul Dennis

David Culverhouse.

Paul Cavell.   Photo: Dave West.

Jason Broom   Photo: Dennis Nicholson.

David Crown.   Photo: V J Robertson.

Gary Kimble.   Photo: Dave West.

186

DAGENHAM & REDBRIDGE   APPEARANCES

	91-92	92-93	93-94	94-95	95-96	96-00	00-01	01-02	02-03	03-04	TOTAL
COOPER William				0+1							0+1
CREASER Glyn					15						15
CROOKES Dominic					28						28
CROWN David			19+14								19+14
CULVERHOUSE David				23+3	29						52+3
DAVIDSON Jon					5+1						5+1
DAVIDSON Kurt	7+3										7+3
DE SOUZA Juan Mequel		3	17+1								20+1
DERRY Dave					9+4						9+4
DEVEREUX Jay				6+4	1+2						7+6
DOCKER Ian	6+3										6+3
DOUBLE Lee					0+1						0+1
DUNPHY Nick				6							6
DYER Kenny					12+8						12+8
EATON Ben									0+2		0+2
EBDON Marcus	22										22
FILSON Martin			5								5
FLETCHER Gary								7+1			7+1
FORBES Rodney				7+3							7+3
FORBES Steve							8+4	0+3			8+7
FOSTER Kevin	9		1								10
FOWLER Lee			8+1	5+1							13+2
FULLING Lee	1+1										1+1
GALLAGHER Keiran							3+3				3+3
GAMMONS Robbie				3+9	6+3						9+12
GARVEY Robbie	11+3										11+3
GEORGIOU George		3+2									3+2
GILL Robert										5	5
GOODWIN Lee							27+1	28+1	12+2	15+5	82+9
GOTHARD Paul				4	18+2			6+1	5+2		33+5
GRAHAM Deiniol					7						7
GREAVES Steve			6+1								6+1

Dagenham's Steve Connor gets in a powerful header above Woking's Clive Walker. Photo: Alan Coomes.

Lee Matthews leads his team out against Charlton, followed by Mark Janney and Tony Roberts.
Photo: Alan Coomes.

Roy McDonough.
Photo: Paul Dennis.

Stafford Browne and Lee Goodwin.
Photo: Peter Singh.

DAGENHAM & REDBRIDGE APPEARANCES

	91-92	92-93	93-94	94-95	95-96	96-00	00-01	01-02	02-03	03-04	TOTAL
GREENE Dennis			17+2	33+6	8+2						58+10
GRICE Neil	4										4
GROVES Perry				6							6
HAAG Kelly				12+1	12						24+1
HAGUE Paul					6						6
HAMSHER John							4				4
HAWORTH Rob							3+5				3+5
HAYRETTIN Hakan	5										5
HAYZELDEN Danny							6+3	12+14	2+3		20+20
HEALER Tony				0+2							0+2
HEFFER Steve							35+2	34+2	28+3		97+7
HENRY Liburd					1+1						1+1
HESSENTHALER Andy	3										3
HEWES Nigel					3+7						3+7
HILL Danny								12+7	20+12	16+8	48+27
HONEY Danny							2				2
HOOPER Dean								14			14
HOPPING Andy	1										1
HOYLE Colin										1	1
HUCKER Peter	6										6
JACKMAN Pat	8										8
JACKSON Jimmy									17+2		17+2
JACKSON Kirk									4		4
JACQUES David	33+1										33+1
JANNEY Mark							28+5	30+5	14+11	22+15	94+36
JOHNSON Dean					0+1						0+1
JOHNSON Ross									7		7
JONES David				6+1							6+1
JONES Gary			5								5
JONES Matt							32+6	25+4			57+10
KALOGERACOS Vasili				1							1
KEELING John									2		2
KEEN Mark							7+15				7+15
KIMBLE Alan										19+3	19+3
KIMBLE Gary		10+15		2+3							12+18
LIVETT Simon			12	6	6+1						24+1
LOCK Tony							6+1	5+8			11+9
MARQUIS Paul		5									5
MARTIN Dean				3+4							3+4
MARTIN Eddie			2+2								2+2
MATTHEWS Lee							35		32	15+1	82+1
MATTHEWS Neil					3						3
MAYES Bobby	30+4	7+2									37+6
MAYO Paul									2+1		2+1
McDONOUGH Roy				22	1+1						23+1
McDOUGALD Junior							34+3	14+12	27+9		75+24
McGAVIN Steve								9+17	4+3		13+20
McGOWEN Tom										0+4	0+4
McGRATH John								21+1			21+1
McKENNA John		40+1	41								81+1
McPARLAND Ian					1						1

DAGENHAM & REDBRIDGE APPEARANCES

	91-92	92-93	93-94	94-95	95-96	96-00	00-01	01-02	02-03	03-04	TOTAL
McPHERSON Malcolm				4+1							4+1
MEECHAN Alex										6+10	6+10
METTIOUI Ahmed			1+1								1+1
MOORE Chris				10							10
MOORE Chris										19+1	19+1
MOORE Matthew				0+1							0+1
MUSTAFA Tarkan									13+3	35+1	48+4
NAISBITT Danny										7	7
NAYLOR Dominic							1				1
NUTTELL Micky		30+2									30+2
OLIVER Steve				2							2
OPARA Kelechi							1+4		0+1		1+5
O'SULLIVAN John				0+1							0+1
OWERS Adrian	7+2	32+1	10+3								49+6
PACQUETTE Richard										3	3
PAMPHLETT Tony	39	27									66
PAPE Andy		1									1
PARRATT Dean			5+1								5+1
PAYNE Chris			3+3								3+3
PAYNE Derek							2+4				2+4
PEARSON Ricky		1									1
PERFECT Tony										1+4	1+4
PERKINS Steve									10+3		10+3
PETTINGER Paul				7							7
PHILP Richard				1							1
PIPER Chris										29+4	29+4
PIPER Lenny										6+9	6+9
PITCHER Geoff									1		1
PORTER Steve		1									1
POTTS Steve									19+2		19+2
PRINDIVILLE Steve					22						22
PULLEN James										9	9

Paul Terry. Photo: Andrew Chitty.

Paul Richardson (centre) Photo: Mike Float.

DAGENHAM & REDBRIDGE APPEARANCES

	91-92	92-93	93-94	94-95	95-96	96-00	00-01	01-02	02-03	03-04	TOTAL
RAMAGE Andy			1								1
REED Graham					15						15
REED Peter			10								10
REES Matt										1	1
RICHARDSON Ian		8+2	37	36							81+2
RICHARDSON Paul	27+1	10+4									37+5
RILEY David	7										7
RISLEY Mark				2+2							2+2
ROBERTS Barry				7+5							7+5
ROBERTS Tony							40	36	37	26	139
RODWELL Jim								1			1
ROONEY Mark							6	17+4	9+11		32+15
SCOTT Lloyd	3										3
SCULLY Tony										13	13
SHIPP Danny			9		7+1		21+10	32+5	32+9	29+6	130+31
SHIRTLIFF Paul		30+2									30+2
SHOEMAKE Kevin	3										3
SINCLAIR Robert				0+1							0+1
SMART Lee		1+1									1+1
SMITH Mark								40+1	15+3	5	60+4
SORRELL Tony			14	15+1							29+1
SOUTHON Jamie					6						6
SOWERBY Colin	8+1										8+1
STEBBING Gary		22+3	42	41	34						139+3
STEIN Mark								33+1	28+3	6	67+4
STIMSON John			0+1								0+1
STRINGFELLOW Ian					20						20
SULLIVAN Terry	0+2										0+2
TAYLOR Peter	1+1										1+1
TAYLOR Robin					32						32
TERRY Paul							35+3	36+3	32+2	2	105+8
THOMPSON Simon					13+1						13+1
TOMLINSON David		2		1							3
TRIPP Danny					6						6
VAUGHAN Steve								0+2	0+1		0+3
VENUS Mark										5	5
VICKERS Ashley							28+1	26+1	29+4	30+1	113+7
WALLACE Andy				9+1							10+1
WALSH Mario	25+4	5+7	4								34+11
WARNER John		1+1									1+1
WATTS Paul	40	40	41	33							154
WATTS Steve									5+1	7+7	12+8
WELLS Mark					2						2
WEST Steve								12+1	23+15		35+16
WHITMAN Tristram										3+1	3+1
WIGNALL Jack							2+3				2+3
WILLIAMS Darren					22						22
WILSON Lee					31						31
WORDSWORTH Dean			3+5	10							13+5
WORTHINGTON Gary					21						21

DAGENHAM & REDBRIDGE   GOALSCORERS

	91-92	92-93	93-94	94-95	95-96	96-00	00-01	01-02	02-03	03-04	TOTAL
ALDRIDGE Martin					1						1
BECKWITH Dean									1		1
BENNETT Gary			3	2							5
BENTLEY Mark										6	6
BLACKFORD Gary	2	10	2								14
BRAITHWAITE Leon										5	5
BRENNAN Mark							2	1			3
BROOM Jason	2	6	4	3	1		3				19
BROUGHTON Drewe							5(1p)				5(1p)
BROWNE Stafford							1				1
BRUCE Paul									1	2	3
BUTTERWORTH Gary		6(2p)	2								8(2p)
CAVELL Paul	22	20	7	3							**52**
CHARLERY Ken								9(1p)			9(1p)
CHERRY Richard	1										1
COBB Paul							7(1p)				7(1p)
COLE Tim							4	1		5	10
CONNER Steve	3	3	4	2	1						13
COOK Jason				1							1
COOPER William				1							1
CROOKES Dominic					1						1
CROWN David			9								9
DE SOUZA Jean Mequel		1	7								8
DERRY Dave					3						3
DYER Kenny					1						1
EBDON Marcus	7(1p)										7(1p)
FLETCHER Gary									1		1
GALLAGHER Keiran							1				1
GARVEY Robbie	2										2
GOODWIN Lee							7	2		2	11
GREENE Dennis			8	5	1						14
GRICE Neil	1										1
HAAG Kelly				6	3(1p)						9(1p)
HAWORTH Rob							2				2
HAYRATTIN Hakan	1										1
HAYZELDEN Danny							2	1			3
HEFFER Steve							1	1			2
HESSENTHALER Andy	1										1
HEWES Nigel					1						1
HILL Danny								3	3	1	7
JACKSON Jimmy										1	1
JACKSON Kirk										1	1
JANNEY Mark							2	1	2	2	7
JONES David				1							1
JONES Gary			1								1

DAGENHAM & REDBRIDGE GOALSCORERS

	91-92	92-93	93-94	94-95	95-96	96-00	00-01	01-02	02-03	03-04	TOTAL
ALDRIDGE Martin					1						1
BECKWITH Dean										1	1
BENNETT Gary				3	2						5
BENTLEY Mark										6	6
BLACKFORD Gary	2	10	2								14
BRAITHWAITE Leon										5	5
BRENNAN Mark							2	1			3
BROOM Jason	2	6	4	3	1		3				19
BROUGHTON Drewe							5(1p)				5(1p)
BROWNE Stafford							1				1
BRUCE Paul								1	2		3
BUTTERWORTH Gary		6(2p)	2								8(2p)
CAVELL Paul	22	20	7	3							52
CHARLERY Ken								9(1p)			9(1p)
CHERRY Richard	1										1
COBB Paul							7(1p)				7(1p)
COLE Tim							4	1		5	10
CONNER Steve	3	3	4	2	1						13
COOK Jason				1							1
COOPER William				1							1
CROOKES Dominic					1						1
CROWN David			9								9
DE SOUZA Jean Mequel		1	7								8
DERRY Dave					3						3
DYER Kenny					1						1
EBDON Marcus	7(1p)										7(1p)
FLETCHER Gary								1			1
GALLAGHER Keiran							1				1
GARVEY Robbie	2										2
GOODWIN Lee							7	2		2	11
GREENE Dennis		8		5	1						14
GRICE Neil	1										1
HAAG Kelly				6	3(1p)						9(1p)
HAWORTH Rob							2				2
HAYRATTIN Hakan	1										1
HAYZELDEN Danny							2	1			3
HEFFER Steve							1	1			2
HESSENTHALER Andy	1										1
HEWES Nigel					1						1
HILL Danny								3	3	1	7
JACKSON Jimmy									1		1
JACKSON Kirk									1		1
JANNEY Mark							2	1	2	2	7
JONES David				1							1
JONES Gary			1								1

Danny Shipp.
Photo: Roger Turner.

Steve Conner.
Photo: Gavin Ellis.

Junior McDougald.

Photo: Peter Singh.

194

DARLINGTON

RELEGATED FROM: The Football League 1988-89
PROMOTED TO: The Football League 1989-90
2004-2005 SEASON: The Football League, Division 2

L-R - Back Row:
Mark Hine
David Corner
Keith Granger
Nigel Batch
Mark Prudhoe
Kevan Smith
Gary Coatsworth.
Middle Row:
Archie Stephens
Paul Emson
Paul Willlis
Drew Coverdale
Jim Wills
John Borthwick
Gary Hyde.
Front Row:
Neil Robinson
Andy Toman
Frank Gray (Player/Coach)
Brian Little (Manager)
Tony McAndrew (Youth Coach)
David Cork
Les McJannet.

SEASON 1989-90

HIGHEST ATTENDANCE
5525 v Cheltenham T. 28.4.90

LOWEST ATTENDANCE
2616 v Kidderminster H. 26.8.89

SEASON GOALSCORER
John Borthwick 18

SEASON APPEARANCES
John Borthwick 41+1

HOME							AWAY							Position
P	W	D	L	F	A	Pts	P	W	D	L	F	A	Pts	
21	13	6	2	43	12	45	21	13	3	5	33	3	42	1

APPEARANCES   03-04

ANDERSON Dave	1+2
BATCH Nigel	8
BORTHWICK John	41+1
COATSWORTH Gary	3
CORK David	41
CORNER David	41
COVERDALE Drew	12+7
EMSON Paul	28+6
GEDDIS David	9

APPEARANCES cont.   03-04

GILL Garry	6+2
GRAY Frank	36
HINE Mark	21
HYDE Gary	1+7
KASULE Victor	2
LINACRE Phil	1+1
MARDENBOROUGH Steve	9+8
McJANNET Les	40
PRUDHOE Mark	34
ROBINSON Neil	8
SMITH Kevan	39
STEPHENS Archie	4+19
TOMAN Andy	39+1
WILLIS Jim	38
WILLIS Paul	0+3

GOALSCORERS   03-04

BORTHWICK John	18
COATSWORTH Gary	1
CORK David	14
CORNER David	9(2p)
COVERDALE Drew	1
EMSON Paul	7
GEDDIS David	3
GRAY Frank	1(1p)
HINE Mark	6
KASULE Victor	1
MARDENBOROUGH Steve	1
McJANNET Les	1
SMITH Kevan	3
STEPHENS Archie	2
TOMAN Andy	7
WILLIS Jim	1

DARLINGTON

	Altrincham		Barnet		Barrow		Boston United		Cheltenham Town		Chorley		Enfield	
	H	A	H	A	H	A	H	A	H	A	H	A	H	A
88-89														
89-90	2-0	1-0	1-2	2-0	0-0	1-1	6-1	3-1	5-1	1-0	3-0	3-0	2-1	3-0

	Farnborough Town		Fisher Athletic		Kettering Town		Kidderminster H.		Macclesfield Town		Merthyr Tydfil		Northwich Victoria	
	H	A	H	A	H	A	H	A	H	A	H	A	H	A
88-89														
89-90	1-1	0-1	5-0	2-0	2-1	3-1	3-0	2-3	1-1	0-0	0-0	1-1	4-0	0-1

	Runcorn		Stafford Rangers		Sutton United		Telford United		Welling United		Wycombe Wanderers		Yeovil Town	
	H	A	H	A	H	A	H	A	H	A	H	A	H	A
88-89														
89-90	1-1	1-2	2-1	4-0	2-0	1-2	1-1	1-0	1-0	1-0	0-1	1-0	1-0	2-0

	HOME						AWAY					
	P	W	D	L	F	A	P	W	D	L	F	A
ALTRINCHAM	1	1	0	0	2	0	1	1	0	0	1	0
BARNET	1	0	0	1	1	2	1	1	0	0	2	0
BARROW	1	0	1	0	0	0	1	0	1	0	1	1
BOSTON U	1	1	0	0	6	1	1	1	0	0	3	1
CHELTENHAM T	1	1	0	0	5	1	1	1	0	0	1	0
CHORLEY	1	1	0	0	3	0	1	1	0	0	3	0
ENFIELD	1	1	0	0	2	1	1	1	0	0	3	0
FARNBOROUGH T	1	0	1	0	1	1	1	0	0	1	0	1
FISHER A	1	1	0	0	5	0	1	1	0	0	2	0
KETTERING T	1	1	0	0	2	1	1	1	0	0	3	1
KIDDERMINSTER H	1	1	0	0	3	0	1	0	0	1	2	3
MACCLESFIELD T	1	0	1	0	1	1	1	0	1	0	0	0
MERTHYR T	1	0	1	0	0	0	1	0	1	0	1	1
NORTHWICH V	1	1	0	0	4	0	1	0	0	1	0	1
RUNCORN	1	0	1	0	1	1	1	0	0	1	1	2
STAFFORD R	1	1	0	0	2	1	1	1	0	0	4	0
SUTTON U	1	1	0	0	2	0	1	0	0	1	1	2
TELFORD U	1	0	1	0	1	1	1	1	0	0	1	0
WELLING U	1	1	0	0	1	0	1	1	0	0	1	0
WYCOMBE W	1	0	0	1	0	1	1	1	0	0	1	0
YEOVIL T	1	1	0	0	1	0	1	1	0	0	2	0
TOTAL	**21**	**13**	**6**	**2**	**43**	**12**	**21**	**13**	**3**	**5**	**33**	**13**

Left: John Borthwick   Photo: N.R.G. photography
Bottom Left: Mark Prudhoe at full stretch.
Below: Frank Gray (with Barnet's Phil Gridelet)
                                        Photo: Simon Jacobs, Barnet Press
Opposite Page:
John Borthwick scoring Darlington's first goal in the Conference against
Northwich Victoria.   Photo: Alex White

LEFT: David Geddis   Photo: Dennis Nicholson
MIDDLE: Andy Toman   Photo: N.R.G. Photography
RIGHT: Gary Gill   Photo: Dennis Nicholson

BELOW: Gary Coatsworth (11) scores Darlington's last & Title winning goal.
Photo: A R Turner

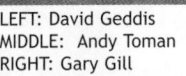

DARTFORD

PROMOTED FROM: Southern League 1981, 1984
RELEGATED TO: Southern League 1982, 1986
2004-2005 SEASON: Southern League Division 1 East

1981-82 Squad - Back Row (L-R): Glen Coupland, Leon Mitchell, Tony Pamphlett, Roger Keen, Aidan O'Sullivan, Steve Robinson, Ray Tunbridge, Brian Gregory.
Front Row: Tom Burman, Willie O'Sullivan, Mascot, Richard Wilson, Alan Budden, Carl Larraman.

		HOME						AWAY						
	P	W	D	L	F	A	Pts	P	W	D	L	F	A	Pts	Position
81-82	21	7	5	9	23	25	26	21	3	4	14	24	44	13	21
82-83															
83-84															
84-85	21	7	7	7	28	25	21	21	10	6	5	29	23	36	3
85-86	21	7	6	8	36	33	20	21	1	3	17	15	49	6	21
Total	63	21	18	24	87	83	67	63	14	13	36	68	116	55	

SEASONS
3

TOTAL POINTS
67 + 55 = 122

HIGHEST POSITION
3rd 84-85

LOWEST POSITION
21st (81-82, 85-86)

HIGHEST ATTENDANCE
1182 v Gravesend & N 22-9-81

LOWEST ATTENDANCE
349 v Barrow (16-3-86)

SEASON GOALSCORER
Tony Burman 14 (85/86)

CAREER GOALSCORER
Tony Burman (34)

CAREER APPEARANCES
Tony Burman 122

DARTFORD

	Altrincham		A P Leamington		Barnet		Barrow		Bath City		Boston United		Cheltenham Town		Dagenham		Enfield	
	H	A	H	A	H	A	H	A	H	A	H	A	H	A	H	A	H	A
80-81																		
81-82	0-1	0-2	2-2	2-0	2-1	0-2	0-2	0-2	1-1	1-1	2-1	2-3			0-3	1-2	0-2	1-1
82-83																		
83-84																		
84-85	1-0	1-2			2-0	1-0	2-0	0-0	1-3	0-1	1-1	0-2			3-0	1-0	1-2	1-0
85-86	3-2	0-0			5-3	0-2	3-2	2-1	1-2	0-2	0-1	0-3	3-3	1-3	1-1	1-2	2-3	0-1
86-87																		

	Frickley Athletic		Gateshead		Gravesend & N'fleet		Kettering Town		Kidderminster H.		Maidstone United		Northwich Victoria		Nuneaton Borough		Runcorn	
	H	A	H	A	H	A	H	A	H	A	H	A	H	A	H	A	H	A
80-81																		
81-82	1-0	0-3			0-1	0-1	2-2	4-4			2-1	1-5	0-1	4-3			1-2	2-4
82-83																		
83-84																		
84-85	0-2	4-2	1-2	0-0			0-1	2-0	2-1	1-1	1-1	1-2	1-0	1-0	2-2	1-5	1-1	1-1
85-86	1-2	0-1					0-2	2-2	5-1	1-4	1-1	0-3	2-0	0-2	0-1	1-3	0-1	0-5
86-87																		

	Scarborough		Stafford Rangers		Telford United		Trowbridge Town		Wealdstone		Weymouth		Worcester City		Wycombe Wanderers		Yeovil Town	
	H	A	H	A	H	A	H	A	H	A	H	A	H	A	H	A	H	A
80-81																		
81-82	0-1	0-2	2-2	3-0	2-0	0-2	1-0	1-2			0-0	1-2	0-2	0-2			5-0	1-1
82-83																		
83-84																		
84-85	3-1	3-1			0-0	2-1			2-3	0-0	1-1	2-1	2-3	5-2			1-1	2-2
85-86	1-1	1-1	3-3	1-5	2-1	1-2			1-2	1-2	1-1	1-2			1-0	2-3		
86-87																		

	Home						Away					
	P	W	D	L	F	A	P	W	D	L	F	A
ALTRINCHAM	3	2	0	1	4	3	3	0	1	2	1	4
A P LEAMINGTON	1	0	1	0	2	2	1	1	0	0	2	0
BARNET	3	3	0	0	9	4	3	1	0	2	1	4
BARROW	3	2	0	1	5	4	3	1	1	1	2	3
BATH C	3	0	1	2	3	6	3	0	1	2	1	4
BOSTON U	3	1	1	1	3	3	3	0	0	3	2	8
CHELTENHAM T	1	0	1	0	3	3	1	0	0	1	1	3
DAGENHAM	3	1	1	1	4	4	3	1	0	2	3	4
ENFIELD	3	0	0	3	3	7	3	1	1	1	2	2
FRICKLEY A	3	1	0	2	2	4	3	1	0	2	4	6
GATESHEAD	1	0	0	1	1	2	1	0	1	0	0	0
GRAVESEND & N	1	0	0	1	0	1	1	0	0	1	0	1
KETTERING T	3	0	1	2	2	5	3	1	2	0	8	6
KIDDERMINSTER H	2	2	0	0	7	2	2	0	1	1	2	5
MAIDSTONE U	3	1	2	0	4	3	3	0	0	3	2	10
NORTHWICH V	3	2	0	1	3	1	3	2	0	1	5	5
NUNEATON B	2	0	1	1	2	3	2	0	0	2	2	8
RUNCORN	3	0	1	2	2	4	3	0	1	2	3	10
SCARBOROUGH	3	1	1	1	4	3	3	1	1	1	4	4
STAFFORD R	2	0	2	0	5	5	2	1	0	1	4	5
TELFORD U	3	2	1	0	4	1	3	1	0	2	3	5
TROWBRIDGE T	1	1	0	0	1	0	1	0	0	1	1	2
WEALDSTONE	2	0	0	2	3	5	2	0	1	1	1	2
WEYMOUTH	3	0	3	0	2	2	3	1	0	2	4	5
WORCESTER C	2	0	0	2	2	5	2	1	0	1	5	4
WYCOMBE W	1	1	0	0	1	0	1	0	0	1	2	3
YEOVIL T	2	1	1	0	6	1	2	0	2	0	3	3
TOTALS	63	21	18	24	87	83	63	14	13	36	68	116

DARTFORD   APPEARANCES   GOALS

	81-82	82-84	84-85	85-86	Total	81-82	82-84	84-85	85-86	Total
AITKEN Glenn	17				17	2				2
BLADE Paul				8+1	8+1					
BORG George			37	10	47			2(2p)		2(2p)
BROWN Derek	10+2			8+2	18+4				3	3
BUDDEN Alan	29+1				29+1					
BURKE Trevor	1				1					
BURMAN Tom	41		41	40	122	8		12	14	34
CAMPBELL Gary				9	9				1	1
CLARK David			0+1	7+5	7+6					
CLARK Dickie	6				6					
COATES Martin			1+3		1+3					
COUPLAND Glen	35+1				35+1					
COWLEY Francis			42	32+2	74+2			2	2	4
CROWN Nicky			25+3	12+6	37+9			10	3	13
DINGWALL Micky			19+2	22	41+2			7	8	15
DIXSON Steve	11				11					
DUDLEY Tony				2	2					
FULLER J				1	1					
GERBALDI Mark				3+4	3+4					

DARTFORD

	APPEARANCES					GOALS				
	81-82	82-84	84-85	85-86	Total	81-82	82-84	84-85	85-86	Total
GIBSON Tony			33+1	22+1	55+2			1	1	2
GLYNN Terry			12+2		12+2			4		4
GREGORY Brian	17+3				17+3	8				8
GRIFFITHS Owen			0+3		0+3					
HALLEYBONE Jimmy			2		2					
HARDWICK Glen				2+3	2+3					
HORGAN Seamus	1+1				1+1					
ISAACS Tony				14	14					
JACQUES David			39	41	80			1		1
JESSOP Terry				2	2					
JULIANS Gary	9				9	2				2
KEEN Roger	42				42					
KEEPING Phil	2				2					
LARRAMAN Carl	1				1					
LEAHY Steve	8				8	3				3
LEE Terry				12+1	12+1				1	1
MACE Colin	10			1	11	1				1
MAKIN Bob			15+2		15+2					
MALLETT Dave			42	27	69					
McCAYNA Martin			40	17	57			6(1p)	2(1p)	8(2p)
MITCHELL Leon	1+1				1+1					
NEWBY Tim	16+2				16+2	3				3
O'SULLIVAN Aiden	30				30	5				5
O'SULLIVAN Willie	26+5				26+5	3				3
PAMPHLETT Tony	34		38	33	**105**	4		3	4	11
POOLEY Charlie	1				1					
POULTNEY Mark				8	8					
POWELL Paul			0+3	3+3	3+6				1	1
REEVES John				29	29				2	2
ROBINSON Steve	25+4		36+2	26+2	87+8			5	2	7
ROGERS Tony				12+5	12+5				2	2
SATCHELL Neil			1		1					
SCOTT Lloyd				5	5					
SILLE Jon				17	17				3(1p)	3(1p)
SMITH David			1+1		1+1					
STARKEY Ian	2				2					
STEWART Malcolm				23+3	23+3					
SULLIVAN Terry			38		38			4		4
SULMAN Mark	1				1					
SWEETZER Jimmy	11+2				11+2	1				1
TIMMS Trevor	16				16	1				1
TUMBRIDGE Ray	33				33	3(1p)				3(1p)
WADHAMS Dave				12+2	12+2					
WHITTON Les				2+2	2+2				1	1
WILSON Richard	22+2				22+2	2				2
YOUNG David	4				4					

DONCASTER ROVERS

RELEGATED FROM: The Football League 1998
PROMOTED TO: The Football League (Div.3) 2003
2004-2005 SEASON: The Football League Division 1

Doncaster Rovers 2002-03

L-R - Back row: Paul Green, Andy Watson, Francis Tierney, Dave Morley, Ricky Ravenhill, Kevin Sandwith, Paul Barnes.
Middle: Justin Jackson, Robert Gill, Mark Albrighton, Andy Warrington, Stuart Nelson, Barry Miller, Tim Ryan, Ross Thompson.
Front: Mickey Walker (assistant manager), Alan Morgan, Jamie Price, Tristram Whitman, Dean Barrick, Gareth Owen, Jamie Paterson, Simon Marples, Dave Penney (manager)

SEASONS
5

TOTAL POINTS
305

HIGHEST POSITION
3rd (02/03)

LOWEST POSITION
16 (98/99)

HIGHEST ATTENDANCE
5344 v Yeovil T (12-4-03)
NB 7160 v Farnborough T.
(ECT Final) (3-5-99)

LOWEST ATTENDANCE
1489 v Northwich V 19-3-02

SEASON GOALSCORER
Paul Barnes 25(4p) (02/03)

CAREER GOALSCORER
Jamie Paterson 32(10p)

CAREER APPEARANCES
Andy Warrington 107

| | HOME | | | | | | | AWAY | | | | | | | |
	P	W	D	L	F	A	Pts	P	W	D	L	F	A	Pts	Position
97-98															
98-99	21	7	5	9	26	26	26	21	5	7	9	25	29	22	16
99-00	21	7	5	9	19	21	26	21	8	4	9	27	27	28	12
00-01	21	11	5	5	28	17	38	21	4	8	9	19	26	20	9
01-02	21	11	6	4	41	23	39	21	7	7	7	27	23	28	4
02-03	21	11	6	4	28	17	39	21	11	6	4	45	30	39	3
03-04															
TOTAL	105	47	27	31	142	104	168	105	35	32	38	143	135	137	

DONCASTER ROVERS

	Altrincham		Barnet		Barrow		Boston United		Burton Albion		Cheltenham Town		Chester City		Dagenham & Redbridge		Dover Athletic	
	H	A	H	A	H	A	H	A	H	A	H	A	H	A	H	A	H	A
97-98																		
98-99					2-1	2-2					2-2	1-2					5-4	0-1
99-00	0-1	2-1															0-1	3-1
00-01							4-2	1-3					1-0	0-3	1-0	1-2	1-1	1-1
01-02			2-3	0-2			0-1	2-2					2-0	1-1	0-0	0-1	2-1	1-0
02-03			2-1	2-1					1-0	2-1			0-0	0-1	5-1	3-3		
03-04																		

	Farnborough Town		Forest Green Rovers		Gravesend & N'fleet		Halifax Town		Hayes		Hednesford Town		Hereford United		Kettering Town		Kidderminster H.	
	H	A	H	A	H	A	H	A	H	A	H	A	H	A	H	A	H	A
97-98																		
98-99	1-2	0-1	0-1	0-0					0-1	0-2	0-1	1-1	3-1	0-1	1-1	1-0	1-0	3-3
99-00			3-2	0-1					0-0	4-3	3-1	1-2	2-2	3-5	2-1	2-2	1-2	0-1
00-01			3-0	2-2					0-0	3-0	3-1	4-2	2-1	1-0	0-0	0-0		
01-02	1-1	1-0	5-1	2-0					5-2	5-1			4-0	0-0				
02-03	1-0	0-0	1-0	2-1	4-1	2-2	0-0	1-2					2-0	4-2	1-0	2-0		
03-04																		

	Kingstonian		Leek Town		Leigh RMI		Margate		Morecambe		Northwich Victoria		Nuneaton Borough		Rushden & Diamonds		Scarborough	
	H	A	H	A	H	A	H	A	H	A	H	A	H	A	H	A	H	A
97-98																		
98-99	0-1	1-2	0-1	1-1					2-1	2-1	2-2	3-1			1-1	3-1		
99-00	1-0	1-0							0-1	1-2	2-0	1-2	0-1	0-0	0-1	0-0	0-1	0-0
00-01	0-2	1-1			4-0	1-0			1-0	1-2	0-2	1-1	1-1	0-1	3-2	0-0	0-2	1-3
01-02					2-0	4-1	1-0	1-1	3-3	1-2	2-2	3-2	2-2	3-2			4-3	0-1
02-03					1-0	2-0	3-1	1-2	1-1	0-3	1-2	2-1	1-1	3-0			0-1	5-2
03-04																		

DONCASTER ROVERS

	Southport		Stalybridge Celtic		Stevenage Borough		Sutton United		Telford United		Welling United		Woking		Yeovil Town	
	H	A	H	A	H	A	H	A	H	A	H	A	H	A	H	A
97-98																
98-99	0-1	2-3			0-0	0-2			2-1	2-0	4-1	1-1	0-1	0-2	0-2	2-2
99-00	1-1	0-1			1-2	0-3	1-0	0-1	2-0	2-0	1-1	1-0	0-0	3-1	0-3	3-1
00-01	1-0	0-1			0-0	0-0			1-2	0-1			0-1	1-1	2-0	0-2
01-02	1-0	0-1	0-1	0-1	2-0	0-0			1-0	1-1			1-1	1-3	1-2	1-1
02-03	0-0	4-0			0-0	3-2			1-3	4-4			3-1	2-2	0-4	1-1
03-04																

	Home						Away					
	P	W	D	L	F	A	P	W	D	L	F	A
ALTRINCHAM	1	0	0	1	0	1	1	1	0	0	2	1
BARNET	2	1	0	1	4	4	2	1	0	1	2	3
BARROW	1	1	0	0	2	1	1	0	1	0	2	2
BOSTON U	2	1	0	1	4	3	2	0	1	1	3	5
BURTON A	1	1	0	0	2	1	1	1	0	0	2	1
CHELTENHAM T	1	0	1	0	2	2	1	0	0	1	1	2
CHESTER CITY	3	2	1	0	3	0	3	0	1	2	1	5
DAGENHAM & R	3	2	1	0	6	1	3	0	1	2	4	6
DOVER A	4	2	1	1	8	7	4	2	1	1	5	3
FARNBOROUGH T	3	1	1	1	3	3	3	1	1	1	1	1
FOREST GREEN R	5	4	0	1	12	4	5	2	2	1	6	4
GRAVESEND & N	1	1	0	0	4	1	1	0	1	0	2	2
HALIFAX T	1	0	1	0	0	0	1	0	0	1	1	2
HAYES	4	1	2	1	5	3	4	3	0	1	12	6
HEDNESFORD T	3	2	0	1	5	3	3	1	1	1	6	5
HEREFORD U	5	4	1	0	13	4	5	2	1	2	8	8
KETTERING T	4	2	2	0	4	2	4	2	2	0	5	2
KIDDERMINSTER H	2	1	0	1	2	2	2	0	1	1	3	4
KINGSTONIAN	3	1	0	2	1	3	3	1	1	1	3	3
LEEK T	1	0	0	1	0	1	1	0	1	0	1	1
LEIGH RMI	3	3	0	0	7	0	3	3	0	0	7	1
MARGATE	2	2	0	0	4	1	2	0	1	1	2	3
MORECAMBE	5	2	2	1	7	6	5	1	0	4	5	10
NORTHWICH V	5	1	2	2	7	8	5	3	1	1	10	7
NUNEATON B	4	0	3	1	4	5	4	2	1	1	6	3
RUSHDEN & D	3	1	1	1	4	4	3	1	2	0	3	1
SCARBOROUGH	4	1	0	3	4	7	4	1	1	2	6	6
SOUTHPORT	5	2	2	1	3	2	5	1	0	4	6	6
STALYBRIDGE C	1	0	0	1	0	1	1	0	0	1	0	1
STEVENAGE B	5	1	3	1	3	2	5	1	2	2	3	7
SUTTON U	1	1	0	0	1	0	1	0	0	1	0	1
TELFORD U	5	3	0	2	7	6	5	2	2	1	9	6
WELLING U	2	1	1	0	5	2	2	1	1	0	2	1
WOKING	5	1	2	2	4	4	5	1	2	2	7	9
YEOVIL T	5	1	0	4	3	11	5	1	3	1	7	7
TOTALS	105	47	27	31	142	104	105	35	32	38	143	135

Doncaster Rovers Squad 2001-02

Back Row (L-R): Barry Miller, Robert Gill, Neil Campbell, Barry Richardson, Andy Warrington, Mark Sale, Francis Tierney, Paul Barnes.

Middle Row: Paul Carden, Andy Watson, Tim Ryan, Kevin Sandwith, Colin Hawkins, Jamie Price, Kevin McIntyre, Gareth Owen.

Front Row: Jimmy Kelly, Mattie Caudwell, Tristram Whitman, Steve Wignall (Manager), Dave Penney (Asst. Manager), Paul Green, Simon Marples, Dean Barrick, Jamie Paterson.

Left:
Mark Atkins
Photo: Peter Barnes

Below:
Jamie Paterson

DONCASTER ROVERS   APPEARANCES

	98-99	99-00	00-01	01-02	02-03	TOTAL
ALBRIGHTON Mark					22+3	22+3
ALFORD Carl			12+6			12+6
ARTUN Erdem					1+1	1+1
ATKINS Mark		24	20+2			44+2
BARNARD Mark		35+2	14			49+2
BARNES Paul				19+4	41	60+4
BARNWELL-EDINBORO Jamie	7+4					7+4
BARRICK Dean			11	20+3	28	59+3
BECKETT Duane	3+8					3+8
BEECH Chris					17	17
BLUNDELL Gregg					0+1	0+1
BLUNT Jason					12+1	12+1
BRADLEY Mark	1					1
BROOKES Darren	0+3					0+3
BUBALOVIC Mirsad		0+1				0+1
BURTON Steve					1	1
BUTLER Lee				8+1		8+1
CAMPBELL Neil		9+2	27+5	23+8		59+15
CARDEN Paul				10+6		10+6
CAUDWELL Matt	6+6	17+6	17+9	16+6		56+27
CUNNINGHAM Harvey	0+1					0+1
DOOLAN John					7	7
DUERDEN Ian	24+2	18+3	0+7			42+12
FOSTER Martin	4+1	21+7	2			27+8
FOSTER Steve					19+2	19+2
FOY Keith					1	1
FUTCHER Andy		5				5
FUTCHER Ben				2		2
GEORGE Danny	3+10					3+10
GILL Robert				13+10	21+9	34+19
GOODMAN Don					2+4	2+4
GOODWIN Shaun	21+4	8+2				29+6
GREEN Paul				5+3	16+14	21+17
HALLIDAY Steve			8+4			8+4
HAWKINS Colin			22+5	10+1		32+6
HAYWARD Andy	3					3
HUDSON Danny					9	9
HUME Mark	17+9	2+7				19+16
ILLMAN Neil		0+1				0+1
JACKSON Justin				14+2	16+7	30+9
JONES David	0+1					0+1
KELLY Jimmy			23+6	35		58+6
KIRKWOOD Glenn	24+12	10+10				34+22
MAAMRIA Noureddine	18+9	20+15				38+24
MARPLES Simon		22	29+3	23+2	29+3	103+8
MAXFIELD Scott	27+7	18+3				45+10
McCARTHY Jon					1	1

Above: Colin Sutherland   Photo: Roger Turner

Top Left: Paul Barnes   Photo: Peter Barnes

Bottom Left: Steve Nicol   Photo: Peter Barnes

Below: Mike Newall   Photo: Eric Marsh

DONCASTER ROVERS — APPEARANCES

	98-99	99-00	00-01	01-02	02-03	TOTAL
McINTYRE Kevin	29	29+1	37+1			95+2
MILLER Barry			29+1	38+1		67+2
MINETT Jason	20+5	33+4				53+9
MORGAN Alan					2+1	2+1
MORLEY David					25	25
MUIRHEAD Ben					3+3	3+3
MUSTAFA Tarkan					5	5
NELSON Stuart					2	2
NEWELL Mike		18+1				18+1
NICOL Steve	25					25
OWEN Gareth				33	20+3	53+3
PATERSON Jamie			30+5	30+6	20+1	80+12
PENNEY David	30+1	29+6	23+4	1		83+11
PEYTON Warren					4+2	4+2
PRICE Jamie				13+4	2+2	15+6
QUAILEY Brian					0+2	0+2
RAVENHILL Ricky				6+4	16+10	22+14
RICHARDSON Barry			30	21		51
RIMMER Steve	2					2
RYAN John				0+1		0+1
RYAN Tim		27	28+1	37+1		92+2
SALE Mark				6+9		6+9
SANDWITH Kevin				5+5	1+1	6+6
SHAW Simon	35	8	26+3			69+3
SHERIDAN John	8					8
SHIELDS Dene					1+3	1+3
SMITH Peter			1			1
SNODIN Glynn	0+1					0+1
SNODIN Ian	10+1	1+1				11+2
SOUTHALL Neville	9					9
SQUIRES Jamie				29+1		29+1
STONE Michael			2			2
SUTHERLAND Colin	34	7+2				41+2
THOMPSON Tyrone					1	1
TIERNEY Francis			7+2	17+4	15+3	39+9
TURNER Mike			17+7			17+7
WALLING Dean		39+1	5			44+1
WARREN Lee	38+2	27+5				65+7
WARRINGTON Andy		42	12	13	40	107
WATSON Andy	3+1	13+11	6+17	10+7	22+4	54+40
WHITMAN Tristram		0+1	19+5	14+10	3+18	36+34
WILLIAMS Danny			6			6
WILLIAMS Gary		3+9				3+9
WOODS Andy	33					33
WRIGHT Tommy	24	4+4				28+4
YBARRA Ignacio	4+2					4+2

DONCASTER ROVERS

APPEARANCES

	98-99	99-00	00-01	01-02	02-03	TOTAL
ALBRIGHTON Mark					1	1
ATKINS Mark		3	1			4
BARNARD Mark		1	3			4
BARNES Paul				6(1p)	25(4p)	31(5p)
BARRICK Dean			1		1	2
BLUNDELL Gregg					1	1
BLUNT Jason					3	3
BURTON Steve					1	1
CAMPBELL Neil		1	7	8		16
CARDEN Paul				1		1
CAUDWELL Matt	1	1	4	2		8
DUERDEN Ian	13	4				17
FOSTER Martin		1				1
FOSTER Steve					1	1
GILL Robert				3	8	11
GOODWIN Shaun	5(2p)					5(2p)
GREEN Paul				2	4	6
HAWKINS Colin			1			1
HUDSON Danny					1	1
HUME Mark	7	2				9
JACKSON Justin				3	2	5
KELLY Jimmy			2	3(1p)		5(1p)
KIRKWOOD Glenn	8	3				11
MAAMRIA Noureddine	3	10				13
MAXFIELD Scott	1					1
McINTYRE Kevin		5	1			6
MILLER Barry				2		2
MINETT Jason	1	3(2p)				4(2p)
MORLEY David					5	5
NEWELL Mike		2				2
OWEN Gareth				6(1p)	1	7(1p)
PATERSON Jamie			12(7p)	13(2p)	7(1p)	32(10p)
PENNEY David	6(1p)	6	2			14(1p)
SALE Mark				3		3
SHAW Simon			1			1
SQUIRES Jamie				2		2
SUTHERLAND Colin	2					2
TIERNEY Francis			2	1	4	7
TURNER Mike			4			4
WARREN Lee		1				1
WATSON Andy	1			4	4	9
WHITMAN Tristram			5	8	2	15
WILLIAMS Gary		1				1
WRIGHT Tommy	1					1

DOVER ATHLETIC

PROMOTED FROM: Southern League 1993
RELEGATED TO: Southern League 2002
2004-2005 SEASON: Isthmian League Premier Division

Dover Athletic 1999-2000
L-R - Back Row: Per Christensen, Neil Le Bihan, Tony Browne, Anthony Hogg, Marc Coates, Jake LeBerl, Simon Wormull, James Virgo, Joe Dunne.
Middle Row: Frank Brooks (Physio), Dave Clarke, Paul Hyde, Simon Beard, Joff Vansittart, Charlie Mitten, Scott Daniels, Robin Hastie (Kit Manager).
Front Row: Roy Godden, Steve Norman, Mark Hynes, Bill Williams, (Manager), Stuart Munday, Clive Walker (Asst. Man.), Lee Shearer, Mark Clarke, Paul Manning

	SEASONS
	9

TOTAL POINTS 468

HIGHEST POSITION 6th (99-00)

LOWEST POSITION 22nd (01-02)

HIGHEST ATTENDANCE 2904 v Rushden & D (12-2-00)

LOWEST ATTENDANCE 619 v Slough (26-9-95)

SEASON GOALSCORER David Leworthy 20(3p) (95/96)

CAREER GOALSCORER David Leworthy 61(6p)

CAREER APPEARANCES Jimmy Strouts 191+21

	HOME							AWAY							
	P	W	D	L	F	A	Pts	P	W	D	L	F	A	Pts	Position
93/94	21	9	3	9	28	24	30	21	8	4	9	20	25	28	8
94/95	21	6	10	5	28	25	28	21	5	6	10	20	30	21	16
95/96	21	8	1	12	29	38	25	21	3	6	12	22	36	15	20
96/97	21	7	9	5	32	30	30	21	5	5	11	25	38	20	17
97/98	21	10	4	7	34	29	34	21	5	6	10	26	41	21	13
98/99	21	7	9	5	27	21	30	21	8	4	9	27	27	28	11
99/00	21	10	7	4	43	26	37	21	8	5	8	22	30	29	6
00/01	21	9	6	6	32	22	33	21	5	5	11	22	34	20	15
01/02	21	6	5	10	20	25	23	21	5	1	15	21	40	16	22
Total	189	72	54	63	273	240	270	189	52	42	95	205	301	198	

	Altrincham		Barnet		Barrow		Bath City		Boston United		Bromsgrove Rovers		Cheltenham Town		Chester City		Dagenham & Redbridge	
	H	A	H	A	H	A	H	A	H	A	H	A	H	A	H	A	H	A
93-94	1-0	0-2					0-3	0-0			4-3	2-1					1-1	1-2
94-95	1-3	0-3					3-0	0-0			0-2	0-2					1-1	0-2
95-96	1-4	2-2					1-0	1-2			0-2	0-3					0-1	0-3
96-97	2-2	2-1					2-2	1-2			2-0	1-3						
97-98													3-0	1-3				
98-99					1-1	0-1									0-0	1-1		
99-00	2-2	0-3																
00-01									0-0	2-1					1-1	0-1	3-1	1-1
01-02			2-2	0-2					3-2	2-4					1-0	0-3	0-1	0-1

	Doncaster Rovers		Farnborough Town		Forest Green Rovers		Gateshead		Halifax Town		Hayes		Hednesford Town		Hereford United		Kettering Town	
	H	A	H	A	H	A	H	A	H	A	H	A	H	A	H	A	H	A
93-94							3-1	2-1	1-2	1-0							0-1	0-1
94-95			1-1	0-1			2-2	0-1	1-1	0-4							0-2	0-1
95-96			1-3	2-3			1-1	1-1	3-2	0-1			1-3	2-2			2-1	2-2
96-97			0-0	3-2			0-1	3-1	2-2	3-1	1-0	0-2	2-2	1-1			0-1	1-1
97-98			2-2	0-1			0-1	2-1	0-1	1-1	1-0	0-0	1-3	0-1	1-1	1-0	0-0	1-2
98-99	1-0	4-5	2-1	2-1	1-1	1-0					0-0	2-1	0-0	2-1	3-1	0-2	0-1	2-0
99-00	1-3	1-0			4-0	1-3					2-2	2-1	4-1	0-1	2-0	0-2	1-1	2-1
00-01	1-1	1-1			1-2	1-2					4-1	2-3	4-0	0-0	1-0	2-4	1-0	2-0
01-02	0-1	1-2	2-1	0-1	1-2	1-2					3-2	1-2			0-1	0-3		

	Kidderminster H.		Kingstonian		Leek Town		Leigh RMI		Macclesfield Town		Margate		Merthyr Tydfil		Morecambe		Northwich Victoria	
	H	A	H	A	H	A	H	A	H	A	H	A	H	A	H	A	H	A
93-94	3-1	0-3							1-2	2-0			1-0	0-0			2-0	1-0
94-95	1-0	0-0							0-0	0-3			2-2	3-2			3-1	3-1
95-96	2-1	1-1							2-3	1-0					2-3	1-3	0-1	2-1
96-97	0-5	1-4							2-1	0-1					3-0	1-3	2-2	0-2
97-98	0-4	3-3			2-1	1-5									2-3	3-3	4-0	1-2
98-99	0-1	0-1	5-1	0-1	2-1	0-2									2-3	4-0	0-0	0-2
99-00	0-1	2-1	0-1	1-4											3-1	0-2	4-1	1-1
00-01			1-3	0-0			1-2	1-2							2-2	2-1	3-0	0-2
01-02							0-0	2-1			0-0	1-0			1-1	1-2	2-1	1-2

	Nuneaton Borough		Runcorn		Rushden & Diamonds		Scarborough		Slough Town		Southport		Stafford Rangers		Stalybridge Celtic		Stevenage Borough	
	H	A	H	A	H	A	H	A	H	A	H	A	H	A	H	A	H	A
93-94			2-3	1-2					0-0	0-1	0-2	2-3	2-0	2-2	1-1	0-0		
94-95			1-1	3-3							1-2	2-2	3-2	0-1	0-0	1-2	2-0	3-0
95-96			4-2	3-1					0-1	2-3	0-1	0-0			1-3	0-2	1-2	2-3
96-97					1-1	1-1			0-0	2-2	0-1	1-0			2-1	2-4	3-3	1-4
97-98					0-3	1-4			2-1	4-2	3-1	1-0			3-1	0-1	1-1	2-2
98-99					1-1	2-2					2-1	0-3					1-1	0-1
99-00	3-1	2-0			0-4	1-1	1-1	2-1			1-1	2-1					4-2	1-3
00-01	2-1	2-1			4-1	1-2	0-2	0-2			0-1	1-2					1-0	1-1
01-02	1-2	0-3					0-2	1-1			0-1	2-0			1-0	2-0	0-1	3-1

Dover Athletic 1993-94

L-R - Back Row:
Bob Jennings (Physio),
Eddie Avery (Reserve Team Manager),
Joe Jackson, Jason Bartlett,
Tony Dixon, Maurice Munden,
Iain O'Connell, Corey Browne,
Steve Cuggy, Tony MacDonald,
Kevin Raines (Asst. Manager),
T Terry (Asst. Physio).

Front Row:
Nicky Dent, Richard Donkor,
Russell Milton, Steve Warner,
Nigel Donn, Chris Kinnear
(Manager), Barry Little,
Tim Dixon, Colin Blewden,
Dave Walker, Mark Harrop.
Photo: S Harris

	Sutton United		Telford United		Welling United		Witton Albion		Woking		Yeovil Town	
	H	A	H	A	H	A	H	A	H	A	H	A
93-94			0-1	1-0	0-1	0-2	1-0	2-1	5-0	0-3	0-2	3-1
94-95			2-0	1-1	1-1	1-0			2-3	0-0	1-1	3-1
95-96			1-0	0-1	2-1	0-1			4-3	0-1		
96-97			1-4	0-1	2-1	0-1			5-1	1-1		
97-98			6-3	1-0	2-1	2-2			0-2	0-4	1-0	1-4
98-99			1-1	1-1	1-2	3-0			3-2	2-1	1-2	1-1
99-00	1-1	1-0	3-0	1-1	2-1	1-1			2-2	0-2	3-0	1-1
00-01			1-3	2-0					0-0	1-4	1-1	0-4
01-02			0-1	3-4					2-2	0-4	1-2	0-2

Above: Dave Clarke   Photo: Roger Turner

Above: Jemaine Darlington   Photo: V J Robertson

Below: Simon Wormull   Photo: Roger Turner

Below: Tony Dixon   Photo: Dave West

	Home						Away					
	P	W	D	L	F	A	P	W	D	L	F	A
ALTRINCHAM	5	1	2	2	7	11	5	1	1	3	4	11
BARNET	1	0	1	0	2	2	1	0	0	1	0	2
BARROW	1	0	1	0	1	1	1	0	0	1	0	1
BATH C	4	2	1	1	6	5	4	0	2	2	2	4
BOSTON U	2	1	1	0	3	2	2	1	0	1	4	5
BROMSGROVE R	4	2	0	2	6	7	4	1	0	3	3	9
CHELTENHAM T	2	1	1	0	3	0	2	0	1	1	2	4
CHESTER CITY	2	1	1	0	2	1	2	0	0	2	0	4
DAGENHAM & R	5	1	2	2	5	5	5	0	1	4	2	9
DONCASTER R	4	1	1	2	3	5	4	1	1	2	7	8
FARNBOROUGH T	6	2	3	1	8	8	6	2	0	4	7	9
FOREST GREEN R	4	1	1	2	7	5	4	1	0	3	4	7
GATESHEAD	5	1	2	2	6	6	5	3	1	1	8	5
HALIFAX T	5	1	2	2	7	8	5	2	1	2	5	7
HAYES	6	4	2	0	11	5	6	2	1	3	7	9
HEDNESFORD T	6	2	2	2	12	9	6	1	3	2	5	6
HEREFORD U	5	3	1	1	7	3	5	1	0	4	3	11
KETTERING T	8	2	2	4	4	7	8	3	2	3	10	8
KIDDERMINSTER H	7	3	0	4	6	13	7	1	3	3	7	13
KINGSTONIAN	3	1	0	2	6	5	3	0	1	2	1	5
LEEK T	2	2	0	0	4	2	2	0	0	2	1	7
LEIGH RMI	2	0	1	1	1	2	2	1	0	1	3	3
MACCLESFIELD T	4	1	1	2	5	6	4	2	0	2	3	4
MARGATE	1	0	1	0	0	0	1	1	0	0	1	0
MERTHYR T	2	1	1	0	3	2	2	1	1	0	3	2
MORECAMBE	7	2	2	3	15	13	7	2	1	4	12	14
NORTHWICH V	9	6	2	1	20	6	9	3	1	5	9	13
NUNEATON B	3	2	0	1	6	4	3	2	0	1	4	4
RUNCORN	3	1	1	1	7	6	3	1	1	1	7	6
RUSHDEN & D	5	1	2	2	6	10	5	0	3	2	6	10
SCARBOROUGH	3	0	1	2	1	5	3	1	1	1	3	4
SLOUGH T	4	1	2	1	2	2	4	1	1	2	8	8
SOUTHPORT	9	2	1	6	7	11	9	4	2	3	11	11
STAFFORD R	2	2	0	0	5	2	2	0	1	1	2	3
STALYBRIDGE C	6	3	2	1	8	6	6	1	1	4	5	9
STEVENAGE B	8	3	3	2	13	10	8	2	2	4	13	15
SUTTON U	1	0	1	0	1	1	1	1	0	0	1	0
TELFORD U	9	4	1	4	15	13	9	3	3	3	10	9
WELLING U	7	4	1	2	10	8	7	2	2	3	7	7
WITTON A	1	1	0	0	1	0	1	1	0	0	2	1
WOKING	9	4	3	2	23	15	9	1	2	6	4	20
YEOVIL T	7	2	2	3	8	8	7	2	2	3	9	14
TOTAL	189	72	54	63	273	240	189	52	42	95	205	301

Top left: Gerald Dobbs Photo: Andrew Chitty

Top right: John Budden Photo: Keith Gillard

Bottom left: Simon Beard Photo: Paul Dennis

Below: Sam Ayorinde Photo: Martin Wray

DOVER ATHLETIC LEADING APPEARANCES

	93-94	94-95	95-96	96-97	97-98	98-99	99-00	00-01	01-02	TOTAL
Jimmy STROUTS		5+1	27+3	35+3	34+1	18+1	8+7	34+3	30+2	191+21
John BUDDEN		38	38	28+4	37	35+1				176+5
Lee SHEARER					25	26+1	40	41	28+3	160+4
Jake LEBERL					19+4	31	37+1	26+1	42	155+6
Neil LE BIHAN					30+2	37	21+2	30+1	25+2	143+7
Stuart MUNDAY				29+1	28	20+2	25	30		132+3
Russell MILTON	34+3	31	25+4	30+2						120+9
David LEWORTHY	39	35+2	30	21						125+2
Steve NORMAN						1+5	35+3	41	39	116+8
Matt CARRUTHERS		0+7	0+5			14+2	13+11	32+8	21+4	80+37
Paul HYDE							40	42	30	112

DOVER ATHLETIC APPEARANCES

	93-94	94-95	95-96	96-97	97-98	98-99	99-00	00-01	01-02	TOTAL
ADAMS Darren				12+1	25+8	9+3				46+12
ADAMS Keiron						4+1				4+1
AGGREY Jimmy									8	8
ALFORD Carl					15					15
ALLEN Chris									12+6	12+6
AYORINDE Sam					18+1					18+1
BARBER Phil				26+6	12+1					38+7
BARTLETT Jason	40+1	7								47+1
BATHGATE David								0+2		0+2
BEALL Matthew							3+1			3+1
BEARD Simon						11+1	32+2	32+2		75+5
BLEWDEN Colin	28+3	18+7								46+10
BOLT Danny							4+1			4+1
BOND Kevin		7	1							8
BRADY Matthew						5+1				5+1
BRIGGS Ryan							1+1			1+1
BROWN Steve				3		6	30+3	18+10		57+13
BROWNE Corey	29	26+2	7							62+2
BROWNE Tony							30+4	17+5	11+1	58+10
BUDDEN John		38	38	28+4	37	35+1				176+5
CAMPBELL Corey			26+3							26+3
CARR Darren								1+1		1+1
CARRUTHERS Matt		0+7	0+5			14+2	13+11	32+8	21+4	80+37
CARTER Ian		17								17
CHAMBERS Paul		5+6	4+2							9+8
CHAPMAN Danny							24			24
CHIVERS Steve	4									4
CLARKE Dave					12+2	31+1	31	0+1		74+4
CLARKE Mark							0+3			0+3
CLOKE Craig									0+1	0+1
COATES Danny							6+1			6+1
CODNER Robert									1	1

DOVER ATHLETIC   APPEARANCES

	93-94	94-95	95-96	96-97	97-98	98-99	99-00	00-01	01-02	TOTAL
COSTELLO Peter		3+1								3+1
DALLI Jean			2							2
DANIELS Scott			36	33	15	4	1+2			89+2
DARCY Ross								5		5
DARLINGTON Jermaine	3+5	9+6	21+6							33+17
DAVIES Darren									15+3	15+3
DAVIES Martin					28					28
DAY Jamie									18+8	18+8
DEMPSEY Mark					5					5
DIXON Tim	7+7		0+1							7+8
DIXON Tony	37	35								72
DOBBS Gerald				29+4	12+10					41+14
DONN Nigel	18+5	26+5	19+7							63+17
DORRIAN Chris								14		14
DUNNE Joe						11+1				11+1
EBBLI Effrem		13	37							50
EELES Tony		10+1								10+1
ELLIOTT John								10+4		10+4
ELLIOTT Simon						1+2				1+2
EMBERY John		0+2								0+2
FEARON Ron				15	12					27
FERNEY Martin			5							5
FOOT Danny			10							10
FRENCH Jay					0+1					0+1
FROST Dean								0+1		0+1
GLOVER Simon								0+1		0+1
GODDEN Roy					1+6	2+9	3+3	0+1		6+19
HAAG Kelly			2							2
HALL Mark		10								10
HAMBLEY Tim	0+4									0+4
HANLON Ritchie				6						6
HANSON Dave					4					4
HARRIS Jason			13+1							13+1
HARRISON Ashley						1				1
HAYES Martin			14							14
HENRY Liburd					29+6	7+3				36+9
HICKMAN Tom								0+3		0+3
HOCKTON Danny							12+4	0+1		12+5
HOGG Anthony					1+1		2+1	3+7		6+9
HORNE Brian				27						27
HUDSON Kevin						1				1
HYDE Paul							40	42	30	112
HYNES Mark					16+8	12+20				28+28
INMAN Niall								5+1		5+1
IORFA Dominic					1+2					1+2
JACKSON Joe	36									36
JAMES Kristian								9+4		9+4
JONES Steve			0+6	0+5	2+3					2+14
KELLY Leon								13		13
LAWRENCE Steve			2+3							2+3

DOVER ATHLETIC   APPEARANCES

	93-94	94-95	95-96	96-97	97-98	98-99	99-00	00-01	01-02	TOTAL
LE BIHAN Neil					30+2	37	21+2	30+1	25+2	143+7
LEBERL Jake					19+4	31	37+1	26+1	42	155+6
LEWIS Junior	23	30+3	22+4							75+7
LEWORTHY David	39	35+2	30	21						125+2
LILLIS Jason		4								4
LINDSEY Scott			24+2	23+9						47+11
LIVETT Simon		4					0+1			4+1
MANNING Paul							0+3			0+3
McCABE Ryan				3+2	0+1					3+3
McROBERT Lee					6+3			15+19	1+4	22+26
MILTON Russell	34+3	31	25+4	30+2						120+9
MITTEN Charlie		5+1			2	41	1			49+1
MOORE Jason						9+7		0+4		9+11
MORRISH Luke				7+1						7+1
MORRISON Dave							9+2			9+2
MOSELY Steve			8+1							8+1
MUNDAY Stuart				29+1	28	20+2	25	30		132+3
MUNDEN Maurice	38	6								44
NORMAN Steve						1+5	35+3	41	39	116+8
O'BRIEN Paul	7+5	13+5	12+13							32+23
O'CONNELL Iain	40	15+2		26+4						81+6
OKAFAR Sam								3+1		3+1
OMEGBEHIN Colin		1+2								1+2
ONWERE Udo				0+3						0+3
OVARD John									0+6	0+6
PALMER Lee				14	38+1	29+4				81+5
PARSONS David									1	1
PILKINGTON Paul			22+3	3+1						25+4
PINNOCK James								7+6		7+6
PLUCK Colin								8+3		8+3
RAMSAY Scott									11+2	11+2
REINA Ricky				28	5	23+3				56+3
RESTARICK Steve		9+1	13+3							22+4
RISBRIDGER Gareth									3	3
ROGERS Tony			16+2							16+2
ROGET Leo		4								4
SCOTT David	33+4	26								59+4
SCOTT Keith								40		40
SEABURY Kevin								15		15
SHEARER Lee					25	26+1	40	41	28+3	160+4
SHEPHERD Iain			0+4							0+4
SMITH Phil									12+1	12+1
SOUTHON Jamie		0+1								0+1
SOWERBY Colin			7+5	4+4						11+9
STANT Phil									1+3	1+3
STEBBING Gary				41	35+2					76+2
STROUTS Jimmy		5+1	27+3	35+3	34+1	18+1	8+7	34+3	30+2	191+21
THEODOSIOU Andy			4+5	17+4						21+9
TYNE Tommy									18+6	18+6
ULLATHORNE Simon									0+1	0+1

Top left:
Charlie Mitten Photo: Peter Barnes
Top right:
John Budden Photo: Andrew Chitty
Middle left:
Joff Vansittart Photo: Garry Letts
Middle right:
David Leworthy Photo: V J Robertson

Opposite:
Brian Horne Photo: Keith Gillard

DOVER ATHLETIC APPEARANCES

	93-94	94-95	95-96	96-97	97-98	98-99	99-00	00-01	01-02	TOTAL
VANSITTART Joff						18+6	33	36+2		87+8
VIRGO James						33+4	14+6			47+10
VOWDEN Coiln									23+1	23+1
WALKER David	42	36+3	8+1							86+4
WALSH Mario	4									4
WHITE Ben								2+1	5	7+1
WILLIAMS Darren		23								23
WILSON Paul				0+3	12+4					12+7
WORMULL Simon						29+1	23+1			52+2

DOVER ATHLETIC GOALSCORERS

	93-94	94-95	95-96	96-97	97-98	98-99	99-00	00-01	01-02	TOTAL
ADAMS Darren				5	7	3				15
AGGREY Jimmy									1	1
ALFORD Carl					7					7
ALLEN Chris								2		2
AYORINDE Sam					5					5
BARBER Phil					3					3
BARTLETT Jason	2									2
BATHGATE David								1		1
BEARD Simon							2			2
BLEWDEN Colin	4	3								7
BRADY Matthew						1				1
BROWN Steve				2		1	7	4(1p)		14(1p)
BROWNE Corey	11	2								13
BUDDEN John		2(2p)		1	4(2p)	4(3p)				11(7p)
CARRUTHERS Matt		1	1			7	3	4	2	18
CARTER Ian		1								1
CHAMBERS Paul		4	1							5
CLARKE Dave						1	2			3
COATES Marc						1				1
COSTELLO Peter		1(1p)								1(1p)
DANIELS Scott			1			1				2
DARLINGTON Jermaine		2	2							4
DAY Jamie									1	1
DIXON Tim	1									1
DOBBS Gerald				5	1					6
DONN Nigel	1									1
DUNNE Joe							2			2
EELES Tony		2								2
ELLIOTT John								2		2
GODDEN Roy					1					1

Top:
David Leworthy scores
against Kidderminster
Harriers
Photo: Dave Webb

Middle:
Stuart Munday clears
off the line despite the
challenge of Welling
United's Mike
Rutherford.
Photo: Keith Gillard

Bottom:
Paul Wilson scores
against Stevenage
Borough
Photo: Alan Coomes

DOVER ATHLETIC   GOALSCORERS

	93-94	94-95	95-96	96-97	97-98	98-99	99-00	00-01	01-02	TOTAL
HAAG Kelly				1						1
HALL Mark		2								2
HANLON Ritchie				2						2
HANSON Dave					1					1
HARRIS Jason			5							5
HAYES Martin			2(1p)							2(1p)
HENRY Liburd					4	2				6
HOCKTON Danny								9(3p)		9(3p)
HYNES Mark						10	7			17
IORFA Dominic						1				1
JACKSON Joe	1									1
KELLY Leon									3	3
LE BIHAN Neil					3	3	2	3	2	13
LEBERL Jake						1	5	1	2	9
LEWIS Junior	2	5	2							9
LEWORTHY David	15(3p)	18	20(3p)	8						**61(6p)**
LILLIS Jason		1								1
LINDSEY Scott			1	1(1p)						2(1p)
McROBERT Lee					3(1p)			3		6(1p)
MILTON Russell	5		3	4						12
MORRISON Dave							3			3
MUNDAY Stuart				2(2p)	1					3(2p)
NORMAN Steve							4			4
O'CONNELL Iain	3			1						4
PILKINGTON David			2							2
PINNOCK James								2		2
REINA Ricky				7	2	4				13
RESTARICK Steve		2	2							4
RISBRIDGER Gareth									1	1
SCOTT David	1	1								2
SCOTT Keith								14(2p)		14(2p)
SEABURY Kevin									2(1p)	2(1p)
SHEARER Lee					1	2(1p)	9(5p)	7(2p)		19(8p)
SOWERBY Colin			4							4
STEBBING Gary			2							2
STROUTS Jimmy			2	11	13			4	5	35
THEODOSIOU Andy			1	4						5
TYNE Tommy									3	3
VANSITTART Joff						5	15	12		32
VIRGO James						4				4
WALKER David	1									1
WALSH Mario	1									1
WILSON Paul				1	2					3
WORMULL Simon						2	3			5

Top:
Ricky Reina
Photo: Roger Turner

Middle:
Liburd Henry (No.10)
Photo: Martin Wray

Bottom:
Ian Carter (No.3)
scores the winner at
Welling.
Photo: V J Robertson

ENFIELD

PROMOTED FROM: Isthmian League 1981
RELEGATED TO: Isthmian League 1990
2004-2005 SEASON: Isthmian League Division 2

Enfield Squad 1985   Photo: Sports-Press Photography

Left to Right: Dermot Drummy, Harry Hill, Keith Hayzelden, Dave Hatchett, Paul Haverson, Terry Graves, Dave Flint, Trevor Savage, Jeff Wood, Steve Waller, Carl Richards, Keith Barrett, Steve Cox, John Cooper, Neil Satchell, Nicky Ironton, Paul Taylor, Martin Buglione.
Front: Dave Jones (Trainer), Eddie McCluskey (Manager)

SEASONS
9

TOTAL POINTS
553

HIGHEST POSITION
1st (82-83 & 85-86)

LOWEST POSITION
22nd (89-90)

HIGHEST ATTENDANCE
2240 v Barnet (26-12-88)

LOWEST ATTENDANCE
335 v Yeovil (24-3-84)

SEASON GOALSCORER
Carl Richards 27 (85/86)

CAREER GOALSCORER
Noel Ashford 73(1p)

CAREER APPEARANCES
Steve King 242 +16

			HOME							AWAY					
	P	W	D	L	F	A	Pts	P	W	D	L	F	A	Pts	Position
79-80															
80-81															
81-82	21	14	4	3	55	22	46	21	12	4	5	35	24	40	2
82-83	21	16	3	2	57	21	51	21	9	6	6	38	27	33	1
83-84	21	8	3	10	27	27	19	21	6	6	9	34	31	24	14
84-85	21	11	7	3	48	27	29	21	6	6	9	36	34	24	7
85-86	21	15	4	2	48	20	34	21	12	6	3	46	27	42	1
86-87	21	9	5	7	32	21	32	21	12	2	7	34	26	38	4
87-88	21	8	5	8	35	34	29	21	7	5	9	33	44	26	12
88-89	20	7	4	9	33	32	25	20	7	4	9	29	35	25	13
89-90	21	9	3	9	36	34	30	21	1	3	17	16	55	6	22
Total	188	97	38	53	371	238	295	188	72	42	74	301	303	258	

Top: Andy Pape & David Howell   Photo: John Rooney

Left: Nicky Ironton   Photo: Roger Price

Above: Paul Furlong   Photo: John Vass

80-81

Season	Altrincham H	A	A P Leamington H	A	Aylesbury United H	A	Bangor City H	A	Barnet H	A	Barrow H	A	Bath City H	A	Boston United H	A	Cheltenham Town H	A	Chorley H	A
80-81																				
81-82	1-1	0-1	6-1	3-2					0-0	1-4	7-2	2-0	5-1	1-0	4-0	0-1				
82-83	2-1	2-2					6-2	0-0	5-0	3-1	2-0	3-0	3-0	2-2	4-2	2-0				
83-84	0-1	3-1					3-1	1-2	0-1	1-2			2-0	2-3	1-0	2-3				
84-85	3-3	2-3							3-3	2-3	0-0	1-1	1-1	0-1	1-1	2-3				
85-86	1-1	4-1							1-0	1-0	4-0	2-1	3-1	2-0	3-0	2-1	1-0	0-2		
86-87	0-2	1-0							0-3	0-1			1-0	3-1	2-3	1-5	2-2	0-2		
87-88	1-1	1-5							2-0	0-3			1-3	1-0	3-2	3-2	0-1	1-1		
88-89	2-1	0-0			2-1	1-2			4-0	1-2					1-2	2-3	3-4	2-3	1-2	2-1
89-90	2-1	0-3							1-3	0-2	3-0	2-2			0-1	0-1	4-2	1-3	2-0	2-2

80-81

Season	Dagenham H	A	Darlington H	A	Dartford H	A	Farnborough Town H	A	Fisher Athletic H	A	Frickley Athletic H	A	Gateshead H	A	Gravesend & N'fleet H	A	Kettering Town H	A	Kidderminster H. H	A
80-81																				
81-82	3-2	4-2			1-1	2-0					3-0	1-1			4-0	2-1	1-1	1-0		
82-83	2-1	0-1									2-2	2-5					5-2	2-0		
83-84	3-0	4-1									3-3	1-1	0-3	1-1			2-2	0-1	0-1	1-1
84-85	3-2	3-0			0-1	2-1					1-0	0-1	3-1	5-0			5-3	3-4	5-2	3-1
85-86	3-1	2-0			1-0	3-2					3-1	4-1					1-1	1-2	2-2	2-1
86-87	1-0	3-0									0-0	4-1	1-1	2-1			0-0	0-2	3-0	4-3
87-88	2-2	2-1							0-0	3-2							2-0	1-2	5-2	0-4
88-89									2-1	2-1							1-1	1-0	1-3	3-1
89-90			0-3	1-2			0-0	3-2	1-2	2-3							0-3	2-3	2-1	0-2

80-81

Season	Lincoln City H	A	Macclesfield Town H	A	Maidstone United H	A	Merthyr Tydfil H	A	Northwich Victoria H	A	Nuneaton Borough H	A	Runcorn H	A	Scarborough H	A	Stafford Rangers H	A	Sutton United H	A
80-81																				
81-82					3-2	4-1			1-0	1-2			2-0	0-2	1-4	4-1	2-0	1-0		
82-83					1-0	1-1			2-1	1-3	1-1	2-0	0-0	2-2	5-3	2-0	0-1	3-0		
83-84					0-3	1-1			1-2	1-3	0-1	0-4	0-1	0-0	2-1	4-0				
84-85					1-2	2-2			3-2	1-1	1-0	2-2	1-1	1-1	3-4	3-2				
85-86					1-3	3-3			1-0	2-2	3-2	5-1	2-0	1-1	4-0	3-1	3-1	1-1		
86-87					0-1	2-0			1-2	0-2	3-1	0-2	5-0	1-1	0-1	1-1	2-0	3-0	0-0	1-0
87-88	0-0	0-4	1-2	3-0	2-4	2-3			0-1	1-1			1-3	2-2			0-0	1-3	2-3	3-3
88-89			2-1	1-1	1-1	1-3			1-2	2-2			0-3	2-1			4-2	1-3	1-1	1-3
89-90			1-1	0-4			2-0	1-5	2-0	0-1			3-2	0-9			4-1	0-1	2-3	0-2

ENFIELD

80-81	Telford United H	A	Trowbridge Town H	A	Wealdstone H	A	Welling United H	A	Weymouth H	A	Worcester City H	A	Wycombe Wanderers H	A	Yeovil Town H	A
81-82	3-4	0-0	2-1	2-2					3-0	2-2	1-2	2-1			2-0	2-1
82-83	6-2	3-4	2-0	1-2	0-1	3-1			2-1	0-1	4-0	1-1			3-1	3-1
83-84	3-1	3-0	2-1	0-0	0-2	1-2			0-1	3-1	2-2	3-1			3-0	2-3
84-85	0-0	0-2			2-0	2-1			2-1	2-4	6-0	0-1			4-0	0-0
85-86	4-0	2-2			1-0	4-2			4-4	2-2			2-3	0-1		
86-87	3-1	1-2			4-2	3-0	0-2	3-2	4-0	1-0						
87-88	1-4	0-4			5-2	0-1	1-0	1-1	3-2	3-1			3-2	5-1		
88-89	0-1	0-3					0-1	0-0	3-0	3-2			3-4	2-3	1-1	2-1
89-90	1-2	1-1					2-3	0-3					3-5	0-1	1-1	1-3

	Home						Away					
	P	W	D	L	F	A	P	W	D	L	F	A
ALTRINCHAM	9	3	4	2	12	12	9	3	2	4	13	16
A P LEAMINGTON	1	1	0	0	6	1	1	1	0	0	3	2
AYLESBURY U	1	1	0	0	2	1	1	0	0	1	1	2
BANGOR C	2	2	0	0	9	3	2	0	1	1	1	2
BARNET	9	4	2	3	16	10	9	2	0	7	9	18
BARROW	5	4	1	0	16	2	5	3	2	0	10	4
BATH C	7	5	1	1	16	6	7	4	1	2	11	7
BOSTON U	9	5	1	3	19	11	9	3	0	6	14	19
CHELTENHAM T	5	2	1	2	10	9	5	0	1	4	4	11
CHORLEY	2	1	0	1	3	2	2	1	1	0	4	3
DAGENHAM	7	6	1	0	17	8	7	6	0	1	18	5
DARLINGTON	1	0	0	1	0	3	1	0	0	1	1	2
DARTFORD	3	1	1	1	2	2	3	3	0	0	7	3
FARNBOROUGH T	1	0	1	0	0	0	1	1	0	0	3	2
FISHER A	3	1	1	1	3	3	3	2	0	1	7	6
FRICKLEY A	6	3	3	0	12	6	6	2	2	2	12	10
GATESHEAD	3	1	1	1	4	5	3	2	1	0	8	2
GRAVESEND & N	1	1	0	0	4	0	1	1	0	0	2	1
KETTERING T	9	3	5	1	17	13	9	3	0	6	11	14
KIDDERMINSTER H	7	4	1	2	18	11	7	4	1	2	13	13
LINCOLN C	1	0	1	0	0	0	1	0	0	1	0	4
MACCLESFIELD T	3	1	1	1	4	4	3	1	1	1	4	5
MAIDSTONE U	8	2	1	5	9	16	8	2	4	2	16	14
MERTHYR T	1	1	0	0	2	0	1	0	0	1	1	5
NORTHWICH V	9	5	0	4	12	10	9	0	4	5	9	17
NUNEATON B	5	3	1	1	8	5	5	2	1	2	9	9
RUNCORN	9	4	2	3	14	10	9	1	6	2	9	19
SCARBOROUGH	6	3	0	3	15	13	6	5	1	0	17	5
STAFFORD R	7	5	1	1	15	5	7	3	1	3	10	8
SUTTON U	4	0	2	2	5	7	4	1	1	2	5	8
TELFORD U	9	4	1	4	21	15	9	1	3	5	10	18
TROWBRIDGE T	3	3	0	0	6	2	3	0	2	1	3	4
WEALDSTONE	6	4	0	2	12	7	6	4	0	2	13	7
WELLING U	4	1	0	3	3	6	4	1	2	1	4	6
WEYMOUTH	8	6	1	1	21	9	8	4	2	2	16	13
WORCESTER C	4	2	1	1	13	4	4	2	1	1	6	4
WYCOMBE W	4	1	0	3	11	14	4	1	0	3	7	6
YEOVIL T	6	4	2	0	14	3	6	3	1	2	10	9
TOTALS	188	97	38	53	371	238	188	72	42	74	301	303

ENFIELD LEADING APPEARANCES

	81/82	82/83	83/84	84/85	85/86	86/87	87/88	88/89	89/90	TOTAL
Steve KING	35+3	37+3	36+2	31	41+1	31+3	28+3	3+1		242+16
Nicky IRONTON	41	35+1	27	27+2	29+1	25+5	2+1		19+1	205+11
Andy PAPE					42	42	40	40	39	203
Dave HOWELL				40	27+1	36	34	38	25	200+1
Dave FLINT	17+11	15+19	22+16	32+7	13+11	21+7				120+71
Noel ASHFORD	37	41+1	35	36	33+1					182+2
John COOPER			22	24+1	30+1	27+3	29+2	24+8	7+5	163+20
Keith BARRETT	34+1	37	37+1	31	38+1					177+3
Keith HAYZELDEN			22	31+1	30+1	30+1	16	7+7	7	143+10
Paul TAYLOR	41	37	30	30+3						138+3
Nicky FRANCIS						29+4	36	31	22+2	118+6
Martin DUFFIELD					38	39	30+3			107+3
Paul HARDING						29+1	23+3	25	22	99+4
Paul FURLONG							22+3	36+3	36+1	94+7
Lee HOLMES	37+2	37+2	21+1							95+5

ENFIELD APPEARANCES

	81/82	82/83	83/84	84/85	85/86	86/87	87/88	88/89	89/90	TOTAL
ABBOTT Gary								12	20+6	32+6
ASHFORD Noel	37	41+1	35	36	33+1					182+2
ATKIN Paul									2	2
ATKINS Stewart				5+4						5+4
BARRETT Keith	34+1	37	37+1	31	38+1					177+3
BATE Frank								3		3
BAXTER Paul					1					1
BENSTOCK Danny								3+13	10+6	13+19
BOULTER Dave			5							5
BRACHER Tony							2			2
BUGLIONE Martin			0+2	0+1	1	0+2				1+5
CAMPBELL Alan									8+1	8+1
CANNOVILLE Paul								6+3		6+3
COLES Frank									4+5	4+5
COOPER John			22	24+1	30+1	27+3	29+2	24+8	7+5	163+20
COPE Andy			7+2							7+2
COTTER Paul		14	11							25
COTTINGTON Brian							8+1	23	14+2	45+3
COX Steve			19+3	10+5						29+8
DALORTO George									3+4	3+4
DAVEY Mark		8								8
DIONISIOU Dean						0+1		1+1		1+2
DOCKER John				20+3	24+1	23+5			2	69+9
DONNELLAN Gary									8	8
DRUMMY Dermot				36+2	29+2	1				66+4
DUFFIELD Martin					38	39	30+3			107+3
EDMONDS Andy						17+5	22+6	4	17+4	60+15
EDWARDS Chris						3+1				3+1
FERGUSSON Ian									4	4
FLINT Dave	17+11	15+19	22+16	32+7	13+11	21+7				120+71

Above: Robin Lewis   Photo: Thomas Scott   Above: Andy Pape   Photo: John B Vass

Below: Andy Edwards   Photo: Thomas Scott   Below: Steve King   Photo: Thomas Scott

ENFIELD

APPEARANCES

	81/82	82/83	83/84	84/85	85/86	86/87	87/88	88/89	89/90	TOTAL
FRANCIS Carlos				1+2						1+2
FRANCIS Nicky						29+4	36	31	22+2	118+6
FRIAR Paul								10+6		10+6
FURLONG Paul							22+3	36+3	36+1	94+7
FURNEAUX Mark				11	5+1	10+3				26+4
GALLAGHER John								0+1		0+1
GRAY Nigel					23+4	33+1				56+5
GRIFFITHS Des		1								1
HAGAN Kevin	7+2									7+2
HARDING Paul						29+1	23+3	25	22	99+4
HATCHETT Dave			15+4							15+4
HAVERSON Paul		8+1	17+3							25+4
HAYRETTIN Hakan									7+2	7+2
HAYZELDEN Keith			22	31+1	30+1	30+1	16	7+7	7	143+10
HILL Harry			6+3							6+3
HINDS Peter				8	13+5					21+5
HOLLINGSWORTH Eric		0+1	0+1							0+2
HOLMES Lee	37+2	37+2	21+1							95+5
HOLSGROVE Paul									1+2	1+2
HOWELL Dave				40	27+1	36	34	38	25	200+1
HOWELLS Gareth									2	2
HUGHTON Henry								1	8+2	9+2
IRONTON Nicky	41	35+1	27	27+2	29+1	25+5	2+1		19+1	205+11
JACOBS John	41	24	33							98
JACQUES David							10+2			10+2
JENNINGS Tony	39									39
JOHNSON Robbie								3		3
KEEN Nigel						24+4	26+2	10	19	79+6
KELLY Omele							0+3			0+3
KELLY Tony								2		2
KEMPLEN Clive	1	4							1	6
KENNEDY Alan									2	2
KING Steve	35+3	37+3	36+2	31	41+1	31+3	28+3	3+1		242+16
KINSELLA Tony							21+1			21+1
LANE Graham							3			3
LEWIS Robin							30+3	17+9		47+12
LOMAS Mark			2+4							2+4
LUFF Neil							2			2
MALLETT Dave			31							31
MARTIN David					0+1					0+1
McCLURE Doug							31+2			31+2
MEHMET Dave									4	4
MOUAT Neil			12+4	0+4						12+8
MUDD Kevin									20+3	20+3
NEIGHBOUR Jimmy			3							3
OLIVER Steve	39	41								80
PAPE Andy					42	42	40	40	39	203
PARKYN Roy							4+2	18	22	44+2
POULTNEY Mark			3							3
QUINN Jimmy									12	12
QUINNELL Robert						0+1				0+1

231

Left:
Carl Richards

Bottom Left:
Nicky Francis
Photo: John B Vass

Below:
Paul Furlong
Photo: Thomas Scott

ENFIELD   APPEARANCES

	81/82	82/83	83/84	84/85	85/86	86/87	87/88	88/89	89/90	TOTAL
RADOVIC Zoran					1+3					1+3
REEVES John								16		16
RICHARDS Carl				35+6	39+2					74+8
SATCHELL Neil				1+2						1+2
SAVAGE Trevor		18	26+3	10+3						54+6
SCHIAVI Mark							6+3	10+6		16+9
SCOTT Steve							23+9	0+2		23+11
SIANI Brian	2+3	0+1								2+4
SIM Peter									0+1	0+1
SMART Erskine									22	22
SMART Steve									1	1
SMITH Gary								31	9+5	40+5
SMITH Peter								6		6
SPARROW Brian							11	34+2	10+1	55+3
STACEY Phil					5+3	21+1				26+4
STONE Peter									0+1	0+1
TAPLEY Steve							17+1			17+1
TAYLOR Paul	41	37	30	30+3						138+3
TOMBS Brian	1									1
TONE John	27	29	21+1							77+1
TURNER Paul									16	16
TURNER Steve	23+7	34+2								57+9
TURPIN Robert		2	15+1							17+1
WAITE Dave	32	29	15					6	9	91
WALLER Steve				6						6
WARBURTON Mark	8	11+1	5+1	1+1						25+3
WARMINGTON Curtis									11	11
WILKINSON Trevor							6	20	17+1	43+1
WOOD Andy			0+1							0+1
WOODHURST Darren							1+4			1+4

ENFIELD   GOALSCORERS

	81/82	82/83	83/84	84/85	85/86	86/87	87/88	88/89	89/90	TOTAL
ABBOTT Gary								8	9	17
ASHFORD Noel	18	20(1p)	14	8	13					73(1p)
ATKINS Stewart				1						1
BARRETT Keith	7	4	1	1						13
BATE Frank								1		1
BENSTOCK Danny								3	3	6
BUGLIONE Martin					1					1
CANOVILLE Paul								2		2
COOPER John						1	1	2		4
COPE Andy			2							2
COTTINGTON Brian									1	1
COX Steve			6(3p)	4(4p)						10(7p)
DOCKER John				3	2				1	6
DONNELLAN Gary									1	1
DRUMMY Dermot				5	4					9

Left:
Noel Ashford
Photo:
Bob Thomas Sports Photography

Below:
Noel Ashford in action against Harrow.
Photo: Tom Scott

ENFIELD GOALSCORERS

	81/82	82/83	83/84	84/85	85/86	86/87	87/88	88/89	89/90	TOTAL
DUFFIELD Martin					9(4p)	9	3			21(4p)
EDMONDS Andy						2	2			4
FERGUSSON Ian								1		1
FLINT Dave	10	10	6	19	4	4				53
FRANCIS Nicky						10	21	10	5	46
FRIAR Paul							1			1
FURLONG Paul							6	11	17	34
FURNEAUX Mark						1				1
GRAY Nigel						2				2
HARDING Paul						6	4	5	4	19
HAVERSON Paul		1	1							2
HAYZELDEN Keith				2(1p)	1(1p)					3(2p)
HINDS Peter				3	6					9
HOLMES Lee	6	7	6							19
HOWELL Dave				6	6	4	2	4	1	23
IRONTON Nicky	15	12	5	5	7	6				50
JACOBS John	1(1p)			1(1p)						2(2p)
JENNINGS Tony	1									1
KEEN Nigel						6		1	1	8
KING Steve	9(4p)	14(2p)	7	10	10	8	7			65(6p)
KINSELLA Tony						4				4
LANE Graham							1			1
LEWIS Robin							6	6		12
LOMAS Mark			1							1
McCLURE Doug							1			1
MEHMET Dave								1		1
MOUAT Neil			1							1
NEIGHBOUR Jimmy			1							1
OLIVER Steve	7(1p)	3								10(1p)
REEVES John								3		3
RICHARDS Carl				12	27					39
SATCHELL Neil				1						1
SAVAGE Trevor			3	1						4
SCHIAVI Mark							7	1		8
SCOTT Steve							2			2
SIANI Brian	2									2
SMART Erskine								1		1
SPARROW Brian							1			1
STACEY Phil					1	2				3
TAPLEY Steve							1			1
TAYLOR Paul	4	5	3	2						14
TONE John	1	1	1							3
TURNER Paul									2	2
TURNER Steve	4(2p)	13(5p)								17(7p)
WAITE Dave	3	3	2							8
WARBURTON Mark		1								1
WILKINSON Trevor							3	3	3	9

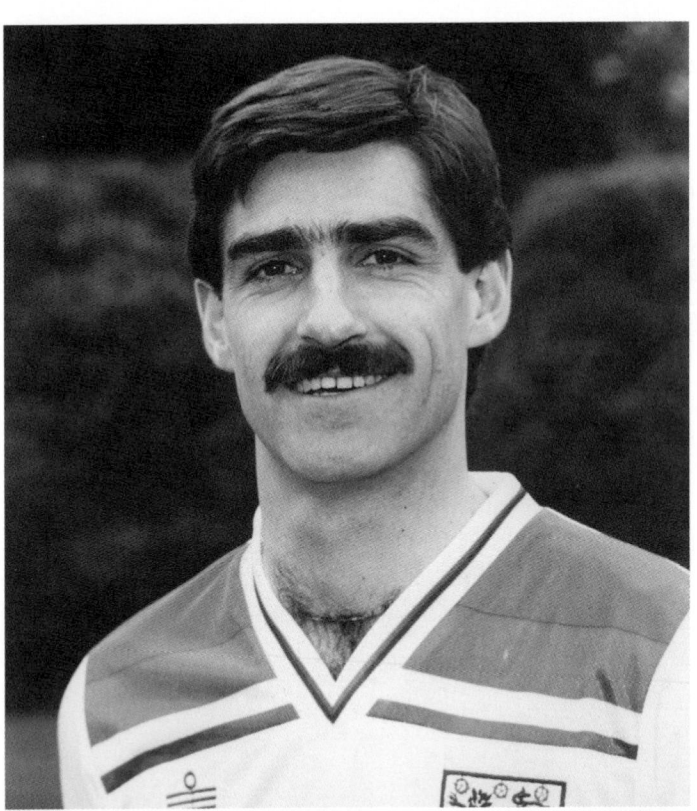

Left:
Keith Barrett
Photo: Roger Price

Below:
John Cooper (left)
and Nicky Francis
Photo: John B Vass

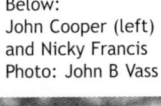

EXETER CITY

RELEGATED FROM: The Football League 2002-03
2004-2005 SEASON: The Conference

Back Row (L-R): Dixie Dean (Physio), Gareth Sheldon, Alex Stanley, Alex Jeannin, Barry McConnell, Olivier Brassart, Lewis Reed, Leslie Afful, Judith Ansell (Physio). Middle Row: John Wills (Fitness adviser) Reinier Moor, Sean Canham, Steve Flack, James Bittner, Chris Todd, Martin Rice, Santos Gaia, Kwame Ampadu, Martin Thomas, Dick Bedford (Matchday staff). Front Row: Tiv Lowe (Centre of excellence manager), Sean Devine, Julian Tagg (Director), Scott Hiley (player-coach), Eamonn Dolan (manager), Steve Perryman (Director of Football), Glenn Cronin, Ian Huxham (Director), James Coppinger, Mike Redford (Youth Development).

SEASON 2003-04

HIGHEST ATTENDANCE
5345 v Accrington S. 24.4.04

LOWEST ATTENDANCE
2672 v Farnborough T. 20.8.03

SEASON GOALSCORER
Sean Devine 20 (2p)

SEASON APPEARANCES
Scott Hiley 42

	HOME							AWAY						
	P	W	D	L	F	A	Pts	P	W	D	L	F	A	Pts	Position
	21	10	7	4	33	24	37	21	9	5	7	38	33	32	6

GOALSCORERS 03-04

AFFUL Leslie	2
CANHAM Sean	5
COPPINGER James	7(2p)
CRONIN Glen	5
DEVINE Sean	20(2p)
FLACK Steve	6
GAIA Santos	4
JEANNIN Alex	2
LEE Dwayne	3
McCONNELL Barry	2(1p)
MOOR Reiner	2
MOXEY Dean	2
SHELDON Gareth	8
THOMAS Martin	1
TODD Chris	1

APPEARANCES

	03-04			03-04
AFFUL Leslie	17+13	LEE Dwayne	18+3
AMPADU Kwame	29+10	McCONNELL Barry	13+7
BITTNER James	37	MOOR Reiner	7+5
CANHAM Sean	10+11	MOXEY Dean	9+8
CHEESEMAN Graham	0+2	REED Lewis	0+1
COPPINGER James	36+3	RICE Martin	5+2
CRONIN Glen	40	SHELDON Gareth	30+4
DEVINE Sean	24+8	TAYLOR Andy	0+7
FLACK Steve	24+13	THOMAS Martin	5+6
GAIA Santos	39	TODD Chris	38+1
HILEY Scott	42		
JEANNIN Alex	39		

EXETER CITY

	Accrington Stanley		Aldershot Town		Barnet		Burton Albion		Chester City		Dagenham & Redbridge		Farnborough Town	
	H	A	H	A	H	A	H	A	H	A	H	A	H	A
02-03														
03-04	3-2	2-1	2-1	1-2	1-1	3-2	2-0	4-3	2-1	2-3	1-1	2-0	1-1	2-1

	Forest Green Rovers		Gravesend & N'fleet		Halifax Town		Hereford United		Leigh RMI		Margate		Morecambe	
	H	A	H	A	H	A	H	A	H	A	H	A	H	A
02-03														
03-04	2-2	5-2	0-1	2-3	1-1	0-2	0-1	1-1	3-2	1-1	1-1	1-0	4-0	3-0

	Northwich Victoria		Scarborough		Shrewsbury Town		Stevenage Borough		Tamworth		Telford United		Woking	
	H	A	H	A	H	A	H	A	H	A	H	A	H	A
02-03														
03-04	2-0	1-1	0-0	3-2	3-2	2-2	1-0	2-2	3-2	1-2	0-3	0-2	1-2	0-1

Front Programme
Cover photos:

Left: Steve Flack

Right: Gareth Sheldon

FARNBOROUGH TOWN

PROMOTED FROM: Isthmian League 1989; Southern League 1991,
Southern League 1994, Isthmian Lge.2001
RELEGATED TO: Southern League 1990; Southern League 1993; Isthmian Lge. 1999
2004-2005 SEASON: The Conference

Season 1991-92.Back row.left to right; Paul Coombs, Andy Bye, Paul Thompson, John Power, Jim Wigmore, and Jamie Horton.Middle row: Ron Manville, Graham Johnson, David Hawtin, Gary Stevens, Alan Coles, Keith Baker, Mick Doherty, Keith Rowland, David Morris, Julian Hickman and Alan Morris. Front row: Ken Ballard, Simon Read, Andy Rogers, Ted Pearce (Manager), Colin Fielder, Brian Broome and Alan Taylor

| | HOME | | | | | | | AWAY | | | | | | | |
	P	W	D	L	F	A	Pts	P	W	D	L	F	A	Pts	Position
89-90	21	7	5	9	33	30	26	21	3	7	11	27	43	16	21
90-91															
91-92	21	8	7	6	36	27	31	21	10	5	6	32	26	35	5
92-93	21	8	5	8	34	36	29	21	4	6	11	34	51	18	21
93-94															
94-95	21	8	5	8	23	31	29	21	7	5	9	22	33	26	14
95-96	21	8	6	7	29	23	30	21	7	8	6	34	35	29	10
96-97	21	9	6	6	35	29	33	21	7	7	7	23	24	28	7
97-98	21	10	3	8	37	27	33	21	2	5	14	19	43	11	18
98-99	21	6	5	10	29	48	23	21	1	6	14	12	41	9	22
99-00															
00-01															
01-02	21	11	3	7	38	23	36	21	7	4	10	28	31	25	7
02-03	21	8	6	7	37	29	30	21	5	6	10	20	27	21	13
03-04	21	7	6	8	31	34	27	21	3	3	15	22	40	12	20
TOTAL	231	90	57	84	362	337	327	231	56	62	113	273	394	230	

SEASONS
11

TOTAL POINTS
557

HIGHEST POSITION
5th 1991-92

LOWEST POSITION
22nd 1998-99

HIGHEST ATTENDANCE
3233 v Aldershot T. 24.1.04

LOWEST ATTENDANCE
416 v Dover A. 19.3.96

SEASON GOALSCORER
David Leworthy 33(2p) (92/93)

CAREER GOALSCORER
Simon Read 52(1p)

CAREER APPEARANCES
Steve Baker 213+3

FARNBOROUGH TOWN

	Accrington Stanley		Aldershot Town		Altrincham		Barnet		Barrow		Bath City		Boston United		Bromsgrove Rovers		Burton Albion		Cheltenham Town	
	H	A	H	A	H	A	H	A	H	A	H	A	H	A	H	A	H	A	H	A
89-90					0-0	3-2	0-1	1-4	3-0	1-3			1-0	2-2					4-0	0-4
90-91	-		-				-		-		-		-		-		-		-	
91-92					3-0	1-1			5-0	1-0	1-2	2-1	5-0	1-0					1-1	3-4
92-93					2-5	2-2					2-1	2-5	4-0	0-0	1-1	2-2				
93-94	-		-		-		-		-				-		-				-	
94-95					2-3	0-2					0-0	0-2			0-3	2-2				
95-96					1-1	2-2					0-0	1-2			1-0	2-1				
96-97					1-1	3-0					4-1	1-1			2-1	1-1				
97-98																			1-2	0-1
98-99									2-2	0-1									2-4	0-0
99-00	-		-		-		-		-		-		-		-		-		-	
00-01	-		-		-		-		-		-		-		-		-		-	
01-02							2-1	3-0					0-2	0-4						
02-03							2-2	2-1									5-1	0-2		
03-04	1-1	1-3	4-0	0-2			1-1	2-0									2-1	0-1		

	Chester City		Chorley		Colchester United		Dagenham & Redbridge		Darlington		Doncaster Rovers		Dover Athletic		Enfield		Exeter City	
	H	A	H	A	H	A	H	A	H	A	H	A	H	A	H	A	H	A
89-90			1-3	0-1					1-0	1-1					2-3	0-0		
90-91			-		-		-		-		-		-		-		-	
91-92					0-2	3-2	1-0	0-2										
92-93							1-4	1-5										
93-94	-				-		-		-		-		-		-		-	
94-95							1-3	1-0					1-0	1-1				
95-96							2-0	2-2					3-2	3-1				
96-97													2-3	0-0				
97-98													1-0	2-2				
98-99											1-0	2-1	1-2	1-2				
99-00			-		-		-		-		-		-		-		-	
00-01			-		-		-		-		-		-		-		-	
01-02	1-1	0-1					1-2	1-2			0-1	1-1	1-0	1-2				
02-03	1-2	2-0					1-0	0-1			0-0	0-1						
03-04	1-2	2-3					2-2	0-1									1-2	1-1

240

	Fisher Athletic		Forest Green Rovers		Gateshead		Gravesend & N'fleet		Halifax Town		Hayes		Hednesford Town		Hereford United		Kettering Town	
	H	A	H	A	H	A	H	A	H	A	H	A	H	A	H	A	H	A
89-90	1-1	2-4															1-1	1-1
90-91			-		-		-		-		-		-		-			
91-92					3-1	2-0											1-3	2-1
92-93					6-1	0-1											3-2	1-2
93-94			-				-		-		-		-		-			
94-95					3-1	0-2			2-0	1-0							0-0	1-4
95-96					2-3	1-1			0-0	0-0			1-3	1-4			1-1	2-0
96-97					1-2	0-1			3-0	0-3	1-1	0-0	1-0	1-0			0-2	1-3
97-98					4-0	0-3			1-2	0-1	0-2	1-3	1-3	0-1	0-2	1-2	3-2	1-2
98-99			2-2	0-0							1-5	0-1	0-1	0-0	0-4	0-2	1-3	1-4
99-00			-				-		-		-		-		-		-	
00-01			-				-		-		-		-		-		-	
01-02			3-0	0-1							1-2	3-0			4-2	2-4		
02-03			0-3	1-3			1-1	0-0	3-0	0-1					2-2	1-2	0-1	4-1
03-04			1-3	1-1			1-2	0-2	1-0	0-2					0-5	0-2		

	Kidderminster H.		Kingstonian		Leek Town		Leigh RMI		Macclesfield Town		Margate		Merthyr Tydfil		Morecambe		Northwich Victoria	
	H	A	H	A	H	A	H	A	H	A	H	A	H	A	H	A	H	A
89-90	0-1	1-3							1-2	0-0			0-1	1-1			0-1	2-0
90-91			-		-		-				-		-		-		-	
91-92	2-1	1-1							4-2	2-1			0-0	0-1			2-4	1-1
92-93	2-2	5-1							0-0	2-1			2-1	3-1			0-3	0-3
93-94			-		-		-				-		-		-		-	
94-95	1-0	1-0							1-0	1-4			2-1	1-1			2-1	2-1
95-96	3-1	3-3							6-1	0-1					3-1	3-2	0-1	3-1
96-97	2-1	3-2							0-1	0-3					2-2	1-1	2-2	1-1
97-98	3-3	0-2			2-0	1-3									0-2	1-1	2-3	3-3
98-99	2-4	0-2	4-2	1-1	2-1	0-4									1-6	0-1	1-6	0-3
99-00			-		-		-		-		-		-		-		-	
00-01			-		-		-		-		-		-		-		-	
01-02							3-0	0-3			0-0	1-2			2-1	1-1	4-1	2-1
02-03							1-0	2-3			4-1	0-0			2-3	1-1	3-2	2-2
03-04							1-1	2-0			1-1	0-3			2-4	2-3	2-0	1-1

Left - Right: Jamie Horton, David Coleman, Dean Coney and David Leworthy celebrate a goal.

Farnborough Town Season 1995-96. Back row, left to right: Keith Baker, Wayne Stamp, Bradley Pratt, Andy Rowe, Stuart Mackenzie, Ian Juryeff and Gordon McEvoy. Middle row: Mike Savage (Trainer), Mike Critchell (Trainer), Mark Turkington, Darren Rodson, Trevor Senior, Keith Day, Ron Manville (Groundsmani/c Kit) and Alan Morris (Physio). Front Row: Jamie Horton, Ricky Denny, Ken Ballard (Assistant Manager), Dean Coney, David Harlow, Alan Taylor (Manager), Chris Boothe and Steve Baker.

FARNBOROUGH TOWN

	Nuneaton Borough		Runcorn		Rushden & Diamonds		Scarborough		Shrewsbury Town		Slough Town		Southport		Stafford Rangers		Stalybridge Celtic	
	H	A	H	A	H	A	H	A	H	A	H	A	H	A	H	A	H	A
89-90			6-3	2-3											3-3	2-3		
90-91			-		-		-		-		-		-		-		-	
91-92			0-2	1-1							2-1	5-0			1-1	1-0		
92-93			2-3	4-1							1-0	1-3			1-1	2-2	1-2	0-2
93-94			-		-		-		-		-		-		-		-	
94-95			0-4	0-1									1-4	1-0	0-0	1-1	0-0	1-4
95-96			0-1	3-0							0-1	1-1	1-0	1-7			1-1	2-2
96-97					2-2	2-0					2-1	1-1	3-3	3-0			1-0	0-2
97-98					2-0	5-5					1-0	0-1	3-2	1-3			6-0	1-1
98-99					1-2	0-1							1-1	2-2				
99-00			-		-		-		-		-		-		-		-	
00-01			-		-		-		-		-		-		-		-	
01-02	2-1	1-1					4-2	0-1					0-1	5-2			2-0	1-1
02-03	0-2	2-0					1-1	0-1					2-1	0-0				
03-04							1-2	1-2	1-3	0-3								

	Stevenage Borough		Sutton United		Tamworth		Telford United		Welling United		Witton Albion		Woking		Wycombe Wanderers		Yeovil Town	
	H	A	H	A	H	A	H	A	H	A	H	A	H	A	H	A	H	A
89-90			1-3	3-2			2-1	2-4	3-1	3-4					1-1	0-1	2-4	0-0
90-91			-		-		-		-		-		-		-		-	
91-92							2-2	2-1	1-1	0-1	1-1	1-4			1-3	1-2	0-0	2-2
92-93							0-1	3-6	3-2	1-3	1-1	1-1	0-3	1-4	0-2	1-1	2-1	2-5
93-94			-		-		-		-		-		-		-		-	
94-95	1-1	1-3					5-3	1-1	1-2	3-1			0-2	2-3			0-3	1-0
95-96	2-2	0-0					2-1	2-3	0-1	1-0			0-2	1-2				
96-97	3-1	1-3					0-2	0-2	2-1	2-0			1-2	2-0				
97-98	1-2	0-5					1-0	1-0	0-0	0-1			3-0	0-3			2-2	1-0
98-99	1-0	1-3					3-1	1-3	1-1	0-0			2-1	0-4			0-0	3-6
99-00			-		-		-		-		-		-		-		-	
00-01			-		-		-		-		-		-		-		-	
01-02	6-1	2-1					1-1	1-0					0-1	2-3			1-3	1-0
02-03	0-1	0-5					2-2	2-0					5-0	1-1			2-4	0-2
03-04	2-0	2-3			3-3	1-2	2-1	4-2					1-0	2-3				

243

Chris Boothe

Roddy Braithwaite.

Dean Coney.

Paul Coombes.   Photo: N. Jackson

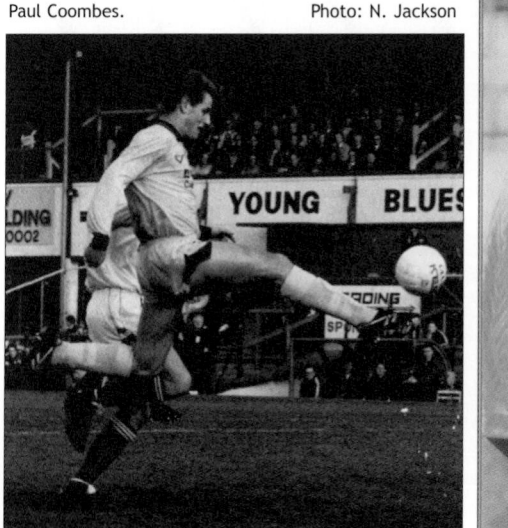

	Home						Away					
	P	W	D	L	F	A	P	W	D	L	F	A
ACCRINGTON S	1	0	1	0	1	1	1	0	0	1	1	3
ALDERSHOT T	1	1	0	0	4	0	1	0	0	1	0	2
ALTRINCHAM	6	1	3	2	9	10	6	2	3	1	11	9
BARNET	4	1	2	1	5	5	4	3	0	1	8	5
BARROW	3	2	1	0	10	2	3	1	0	2	2	4
BATH C	5	2	2	1	7	4	5	1	1	3	6	11
BOSTON U	4	3	0	1	10	2	4	1	2	1	3	6
BROMSGROVE R	4	2	1	1	4	5	4	1	3	0	7	6
BURTON A	2	2	0	0	7	2	2	0	0	2	0	3
CHELTENHAM T	4	1	1	2	8	7	4	0	1	3	3	9
CHESTER C	3	0	1	2	3	5	3	1	0	2	4	4
CHORLEY	1	0	0	1	1	3	1	0	0	1	0	1
COLCHESTER U	1	0	0	1	0	2	1	1	0	0	3	2
DAGENHAM & R	7	3	1	3	9	11	7	1	1	5	5	13
DARLINGTON	1	1	0	0	1	0	1	0	1	0	1	1
DONCASTER R	3	1	1	1	1	1	3	1	1	1	3	3
DOVER A	6	4	0	2	9	7	6	1	3	2	8	8
ENFIELD	1	0	0	1	2	3	1	0	1	0	0	0
EXETER C	1	0	0	1	1	2	1	0	1	0	1	1
FISHER A	1	0	1	0	1	1	1	0	0	1	2	4
FOREST GREEN R	4	1	1	2	6	8	4	0	2	2	2	5
GATESHEAD	6	4	0	2	19	8	6	1	1	4	3	8
GRAVESEND & N	2	0	1	1	2	3	2	0	1	1	0	2
HALIFAX T	6	4	1	1	10	2	6	1	1	4	1	7
HAYES	4	0	1	3	3	10	4	1	1	2	4	4
HEDNESFORD T	4	1	0	3	3	7	4	1	1	2	2	5
HEREFORD U	5	1	1	3	6	15	5	0	0	5	4	12
KETTERING T	9	2	3	4	10	15	9	3	1	5	14	18
KIDDERMINSTER H	8	4	2	2	15	13	8	3	2	3	14	14
KINGSTONIAN	1	1	0	0	4	2	1	0	1	0	1	1
LEEK T	2	2	0	0	4	1	2	0	0	2	1	7
LEIGH RMI	3	2	1	0	5	1	3	1	0	2	4	6
MACCLESFIELD T	6	3	1	2	12	6	6	2	1	3	5	10
MARGATE	3	1	2	0	5	2	3	0	1	2	1	5
MERTHYR T	4	2	1	1	4	3	4	1	2	1	5	4
MORECAMBE	7	2	1	4	12	19	7	1	4	2	9	10
NORTHWICH V	11	4	1	6	18	24	11	4	5	2	17	17
NUNEATON B	2	1	0	1	2	3	2	1	1	0	3	1
RUNCORN	5	1	0	4	8	13	5	2	1	2	10	6
RUSHDEN & D	3	1	1	1	5	4	3	1	1	1	7	6
SCARBOROUGH	3	1	1	1	6	5	3	0	0	3	1	4
SHREWSBURY T	1	0	0	1	1	3	1	0	0	1	0	3
SLOUGH T	5	4	0	1	6	3	5	1	2	2	8	6
SOUTHPORT	7	3	2	2	11	12	7	3	2	2	13	14
STAFFORD R	4	0	4	0	5	5	4	1	2	1	6	6
STALYBRIDGE C	6	3	2	1	11	3	6	0	3	3	5	12
STEVENAGE B	8	4	2	2	16	8	8	1	1	6	7	23
SUTTON U	1	0	0	1	1	3	1	1	0	0	3	2
TAMWORTH	1	0	1	0	3	3	1	0	0	1	1	2
TELFORD U	11	6	3	2	20	15	11	5	1	5	19	22
WELLING U	8	3	3	2	11	9	8	3	1	4	10	10
WITTON A	2	0	2	0	2	2	2	0	1	1	2	5
WOKING	9	4	0	5	12	11	9	1	1	7	11	23
WYCOMBE W	3	0	1	2	2	6	3	0	1	2	2	4
YEOVIL T	8	1	3	4	9	17	8	3	2	3	10	15
TOTAL	231	90	57	84	362	337	231	56	62	113	273	394

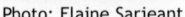

Goalkeeper Peter Hucker.   Photo: Elaine Sarjeant.

Mick Doherty.   Photo: Francis Short.    David Harlow.   Photo: Mark Sandom.

FARNBOROUGH TOWN · LEADING APPEARANCES

	89-90	90-91	91-92	92-93	93-94	94-95	95-96	96-97	97-98	98-99	99-00	00-01	01-02	02-03	03-04	TOTAL
Steve BAKER			16	30		37	37	32+2	37	24+3						213+5
Wayne STEMP			17			30	39	40	42	26+1						194+1
Darren ROBSON							41	36+1	26+10	37+2						140+13
David HARLOW				20			42	42	37+3	4+1						145+4
Stuart MACKENZIE							37	42	29	36						144
Chris BOOTHE						39	42	37+2	8+2	9						135+4
Jamie HORTON	27+2		28+10	42		16+4	9									122+16
Jon UNDERWOOD						11+5	18+1	37+1	31+5	22+5						119+17
Phil WINGFIELD							23	38	36+1	28+1						125+2
Andy BYE	40		37	36												113
Simon READ	40		34+2	10+8	11+3											95+13
Dean CONEY			20	23		30	12	21								106

FARNBOROUGH TOWN · APPEARANCES

	89-90	90-91	91-92	92-93	93-94	94-95	95-96	96-97	97-98	98-99	99-00	00-01	01-02	02-03	03-04	TOTAL
ALLEN-PAGE Danny														3+1		3+1
ANNON Darren													30+5	27+4		57+9
ASHWOOD Jon														1		1
AYRES Mark													0+1			0+1
BAILEY Dennis										30						30
BAKER Keith			35+2			10	24+2									69+4
BAKER Neil								13	27+8	23+9						63+17
BAKER Steve			16	30		37	37	32+2	37	24+3						213+5
BANKS Neil	0+2															0+2
BAPTISTE Rocky													9+6	26+3		35+9
BASS David									2							2
BATEY Peter			9	18+2												27+2
BATTY Laurence	4															4
BEALL Billy														31+3		31+3
BELGRAVE Barrington														12+13		12+13
BELL Philip				3+5												3+5
BENNETTS Scott								0+3					0+1			0+4
BENSTEAD Graham													4+1			4+1
BONFIELD Darren													9			9
BOOTHE Chris						39	42	37+2	8+2	9						135+4
BRAITHWAITE Roddy	33+6															33+6
BROOME Brian			35+1	7+2												42+3
BUNCE Nathan													15+3	13		28+3
BURTON Nick															30	30
BUTTERWORTH Gary														25+2		25+2
BYE Andy	40		37	36												113
CALDICOTT Mark	0+1															0+1
CALVERT Tony	0+3															0+3
CARROLL Danny														13+5		13+5
CHABAAN Ali															18+5	18+5
CHARLERY Ken														30+7	12+10	42+17

FARNBOROUGH TOWN   APPEARANCES

	89-90	90-91	91-92	92-93	93-94	94-95	95-96	96-97	97-98	98-99	99-00	00-01	01-02	02-03	03-04	TOTAL
CHARLES Anthony														16		16
CHARLES Julian											4					4
CHEESMAN Kevin								0+1								0+1
CHRISTOU Alex														1+2		1+2
CLARKE Dwayne														6+3		6+3
COCKRAM Allan			3+1													3+1
COLEMAN David			10	29+3												39+3
COLES Alan			2+2	1+1												3+3
COLES David							3	1								4
COLLINS Eammon				11+2												11+2
COMFORT Alan			6+1													6+1
CONEY Dean			20	23		30	12	21								106
COOMBS Paul			8+3													8+3
COOPER Geoff			4													4
CRAWSHAW Gary											6+14					6+14
DALTON Tim			9													9
DANZEY Michael				1												1
DARLINGTON Steve											0+7					0+7
DAVIS Neil								4+2								4+2
DAY Justin								1+5								1+5
DAY Keith						34+1	34	21+3								89+4
DE SOUZA Miguel											8+4					8+4
DEACONS James														2+1		2+1
DENNY Ricky						12+8	18+7	9+5								39+20
DOBSON Richard						3+1		0+1	0+2							3+4
DOHERTY Mick			17+3													17+3
DONNELLAN Leo	10															10
DONOVAN James														7		7
DOUDOU Ebeli														5+3		5+3
DUBLIN Keith											4+4					4+4
FARRELLY Steve											17					17
FASHANU Andre														7+6		7+6
FIELDER Colin	34+2															34+2
FLANAGAN Tony	12+6															12+6
FLEMING Mark			16+7													16+7
FORINTON Howard														21+4		21+4
FRAMPTON Mark	9+2															9+2
GAVIN Pat							26	30+7								56+7
GOODSELL Bruce				1												1
GRAY Julian	23															23
GREEN Dean											14+10	17+11	1+1			32+22
GREGORY Justin											16+2	20				36+2
GRIFFITHS Leroy													1+4	5		6+4
GUTHRIE Peter	14															14
GWILLEM Gareth											0+1					0+1
HARFORD Paul							20+1	30+1	7							57+2
HARKNESS Paul														6+3	15+13	21+16
HARLOW David						20	42	42	37+3	4+1						145+4
HARPER Mark											15					15
HARTE Stuart							2+4	25+1								27+5
HAYES Adie														27+7		27+7

FARNBOROUGH TOWN　　　APPEARANCES

	89-90	90-91	91-92	92-93	93-94	94-95	95-96	96-97	97-98	98-99	99-00	00-01	01-02	02-03	03-04	TOTAL
HAYWARD Danny					0+1	0+1	0+3		6+5							6+10
HENRIKSEN Tony								3								3
HICKS Jim	3+1															3+1
HICKS Mark													0+3			0+3
HOBSON Gordon			3													3
HODGES Danny													0+1			0+1
HODGSON Richard														32+1		32+1
HOLLAND Matthew				21												21
HOLLOWAY Gary													12+3	20+5		32+8
HOLMES Danny			37+3	16												53+3
HOLSGROVE Paul	14+6															14+6
HOOPER Nick							2+2	8+6								10+8
HORNE Brian							9									9
HORNER Richard									10							10
HORTON Jamie	27+2		28+10	42	16+4	9										122+16
HOWELL Simieon														2+2		2+2
HOWELLS Gareth				9												9
HUCKER Peter			11													11
HUGHES Doug	12+3															12+3
HUTCHINGS Carl													20			20
HUTT Martin									1							1
IFURA Mupepele														5+1		5+1
JANSEN Nick							2+2		1+1							3+3
JONES Danny													3+6			3+6
JONES Mark			7+2	26												33+2
JONES Murray				17+2												17+2
JURYEFF Ian				3	2+2											5+2
KELLY Mark							1									1
KEMP Steve							1+1									1+1
KERRINS Wayne	1+1															1+1
LAIDLAW Jamie							13+9									13+9
LAKE Stuart									2+2							2+2
LAKER Barry													36	18+1		54+1
LAVIN Gerard														1		1
LEE Christian													14+3	16+7		30+10
LEWORTHY David			19	42												61
LINK Declan	5															5
LOVELL Matthew			3+5													3+5
LOVETT Jay														3+6		3+6
LOW Josh								4+1								4+1
MACKENZIE Stuart						37	42	29	36							144
MANNING Paul				14												14
MANUELLA Fiston														9+4		9+4
MARTIN Ben														2+2		2+2
MARTIN John														1		1
MASON Tommy	42															42
McAVOY Gordon					20+3	0+3										20+6
McDONALD Ian	15+2															15+2
McKIMM Steve									15							15
MEHEW Dave							32									32
MENDONCA Bruno														0+1		0+1

FARNBOROUGH TOWN   APPEARANCES

	89-90	90-91	91-92	92-93	93-94	94-95	95-96	96-97	97-98	98-99	99-00	00-01	01-02	02-03	03-04	TOTAL
MILLER Barry								25+7	27							52+7
MINTRAM Spencer						3	26+4	20+1								49+5
MORRIS David	2+1		3													5+1
MOUSSALI Michael														1+1		1+1
MULHERN John														6		6
NEILL Tom														5		5
NEWBERRY Richard				11+7												11+7
OLI Dennis														4		4
OPINEL Sasha														35		35
OSBORN Mark												2	1+2	39		42+2
OSGOOD Dave	1+1															1+1
O'SHEA Tim											22+1	3+1				25+2
PACKHAM Will														2		2
PARDESAI Dalvinder														0+1		0+1
PARSONS Frank	1															1
PATTERSON Gary											24	13+3				37+3
PATTISON Matt													8+10			8+10
PENNOCK Tony											10	41				51
PETERS Mark													2+1			2+1
PIPER Chris											36+5	30+6				66+11
PIPER Lenny											31+11	35+4				66+15
PITCHER Geoff												10	3			13
POTTER Danny												1+7				1+7
POWELL Darren	13															13
POWER John		21	26													47
PRATT Bradley			8+3	36	2											46+3
RADFORD Joe									1							1
READ Simon	40	34+2	10+8	11+3												95+13
REDKNAPP Mark	5															5
REECE Dominic													1+1			1+1
REEKS Stuart												5				5
ROBSON Darren						41	36+1	26+10	37+2							140+13
RODWELL Jim												18+1				18+1
ROGERS Andy	42	17+4	11+2													70+6
ROSE Chris											0+1					0+1
ROWE Andy				6	5+1	0+1	1									12+2
ROWE David				1+1												1+1
ROWLANDS Keith						3+2	12+14	13+9								28+25
ROWLANDS Martin							29+5									29+5
SAPPLETON Pat														7		7
SAVAGE Ian			12+8		3+5											15+13
SEMPLE Ryan														9		9
SENIOR Trevor						13										13
SIMPSON Colin								1+4								1+4
SIMPSON Phil								4								4
SMITH Darren	1+1															1+1
SOMBILI Jalo														3+8		3+8
STANLEY Alex														0+1		0+1
STEADMAN Chris					2	0+2	1+2									3+4
STEMP Wayne		17		30	39	40	42	26+1								194+1
STEVENS Gary		1+2		1+2												2+4

FARNBOROUGH TOWN — APPEARANCES

	89-90	90-91	91-92	92-93	93-94	94-95	95-96	96-97	97-98	98-99	99-00	00-01	01-02	02-03	03-04	TOTAL
TAGGART Tony													16+9	27+9		43+18
TAYLOR Andy							17+5									17+5
TAYLOR Maik			6	36												42
TERRY Peter					26+5											26+5
THEO Adam															3+2	3+2
THOMPSON Mark															16+5	16+5
THOMPSON Nigel					11+2											11+2
THOMPSON Paul			1													1
TOMS Fraser															4	4
TURKINGTON Mark	31+1	7+1	5+3	29+1	0+1											72+7
TURNER Paul	13															13
UNDERWOOD Jon					11+5	18+1	37+1	31+5	22+5							119+17
VANSITTART Joff											29+5	10+11				39+16
WALTERS Derek					12+1											12+1
WARNER Michael											40	21				61
WATSON Steve											36	15+1				51+1
WEATHERSTONE Ross														19+2		19+2a
WEST Mark								33+7								33+7
WHITE Chris									9+1	13+1						22+2
WIGMORE Jim	15	36+2	41													92+2
WILLIAMS Richard						15+2	12+2									27+4
WILLIAMSON Barry			4													4
WILSON Robert			14+2													14+2
WINGFIELD Phil							23	38	36+1	28+1						125+2
WYE Lloyd										24						24

Bruno Mendonca · Photo: Mark Sandom.

David Leworthy · Photo: Paul Dennis.

Left - Right: Andy Bye, Jim Wigmore, Mick Doherty and Paul Coombes. Photo: Eric Marsh.

A superb header from ace goalscorerSimon Read (10) against Telford United

	89-90	90-91	91-92	92-93	93-94	94-95	95-96	96-97	97-98	98-99	99-00	00-01	01-02	02-03	03-04	TOTAL
BAILEY Dennis										13(2p)						13(2p)
BAKER Neil								1	2							3
BAKER Steve				1		1	4	2	1							9
BAPTISTE Rocky													4	11		15
BATEY Peter				1												1
BEALL Billy															1	1
BELGRAVE Barrington															2	2
BOOTHE Chris						14(1p)	21	13	2	1(1p)						51(2p)
BRAITHWAITE Roddy	5															5
BROOME Brian			5													5
BUNCE Nathan													3			3
BURTON Nick															8	8
BUTTERWORTH Gary														1		1
BYE ANDY	5		3	2												10
CARROLL Danny														2		2
CHABAAN Ali															4	4
CHARLERY Ken														12	3	15
CHARLES Anthony														1		1
CHARLES Julian													1			1
COCKRAM Allan			1													1
COLEMAN David				3(1p)												3(1p)
COLLINS Eamonn				2												2
COMFORT Alan			1													1
CONEY Dean			6	6			1	2								15
COOMBS Paul			4													4
COOPER Geoff			1													1
CRAWSHAW Gary													2			2
DAY Keith						1	1									2
DE SOUZA Miguel													1			1
DENNY Ricky						9	2									11
DOHERTY Mick			5													5
DOUDOU Ebeli														1		1
FASHANU Andre														5(1p)		5(1p)
FIELDER COLIN	1															1
FORINTON Howard														3(1p)		3(1p)
FRAMPTON Mark	3															3
GAVIN Pat							9	8								17
GREEN Dean													3	3		6
GRIFFITHS Leroy														1(1p)		1(1p)
HARFORD Paul								1	1							2
HARKNESS Paul														1	4	5
HARLOW David						3(1p)	4	5(1p)	2							14(2p)
HARTE Stuart										1						1
HAYES Adie														2		2
HODGSON Richard														9(2p)		9(2p)
HOLLOWAY Gary													3	1		4
HOLMES Danny			4													4
HOLSGROVE Paul	3															3
HORNER Richard										1						1

FARNBOROUGH TOWN   GOALSCORERS

	89-90	90-91	91-92	92-93	93-94	94-95	95-96	96-97	97-98	98-99	99-00	00-01	01-02	02-03	03-04	TOTAL
HORTON Jamie	6		3	8	1	2										20
HUGHES Doug	1															1
JANSEN Nic							1									1
JONES Murray				2												2
KERRINS Wayne	1															1
LAIDLAW Jamie								5								5
LAKER Barry													1	1		2
LEE Christian													7	1		8
LEWORTHY David			12(1p)	33(2p)												45(3p)
LINK Declan	2															2
LOW Josh									2							2
MANUELLA Fiston														1		1
MASON Tommy	1															1
McAVOY Gordon						1										1
McDONALD Ian	1															1
MEHEW Dave								15								15
MILLER Barry								1	2							3
MINTRAM Spencer							2									2
MULHERN John														1		1
NEWBERY Richard				1												1
O'SHEA Tim													1			1
PATTERSON Gary													1	1		2
PIPER Chris													5	1		6
PIPER Lenny													15(1p)	10(1p)		25(2p)
PITCHER Geoff														4		4
PRATT Bradley					1											1
READ Simon	23(1p)		21	3	5											52(1p)
ROBSON Darren						6	5	4	2							17
RODWELL Jim														1		1
ROGERS Andy	3		1	1												5
ROWLANDS Keith								8	2							10
ROWLANDS Martin								6(1p)								6(1p)
SEMPLE Ryan															2	2
SENIOR Trevor						5										5
SIMPSON Colin									1							1
SOMBILI Jalo														1		1
TAGGART Tony													5	1		6
TERRY Peter					1											1
THOMPSON Nigel					1											1
TURKINGTON Mark	2(1p)				5											7(1p)
UNDERWOOD Jon						2	4	1	1							8
VANSITTART Joff													12	5		17
WATSON Steve														1		1
WEATHERSTONE Ross															2	2
WEST Mark									8(1p)							8(1p)
WIGMORE Jim			1	3(1p)												4(1p)
WILLIAMS Richard							1									1
WILSON Robert				4												4
WINGFIELD Phil						5	13	9	2							29
WYE Lloyd									1							1

FISHER ATHLETIC

PROMOTED FROM: Southern League 1987
RELEGATED TO: Southern League 1991
2004-2005 SEASON: Southern League Division 1 East

Fisher Athletic 1988-89   Photo: Francis Short

Back Row (L-R): Steve Bowtell, Paul Collins, Andy Massey, Pat Cunningham (Physio), Dean Neal, Micky Nutton, Ray Shinners, Mark Harmsworth, David Fry, Mark Dorrington (Coach), Ossie Bayram.
Front Row: Tony Field, Micky Stead, Leroy Ambrose, Barry Little (Captain), Paul Gorman, Tony Towner.

SEASONS
4

TOTAL POINTS
99 + 70 = 169

HIGHEST POSITION
15th 87-88

LOWEST POSITION
22nd 90-91

HIGHEST ATTENDANCE
4283 v Barnet (4-5-91)

LOWEST ATTENDANCE
175 v Boston U (15-12-90)

SEASON GOALSCORER
Ken Charlery 17 (88/89)
Paul Gorman 17(1p) (89/90)

CAREER GOALSCORER
Paul Gorman 31(2p)

CAREER APPEARANCES
Barry Little 145 + 2

	HOME							AWAY							Position
	P	W	D	L	F	A	Pts	P	W	D	L	F	A	Pts	
87-88	21	8	7	6	28	23	31	21	5	6	10	30	38	21	15
88-89	20	6	4	10	31	32	22	20	4	7	9	24	33	19	18
89-90	21	9	1	11	34	34	28	21	4	6	11	21	44	18	19
90-91	21	3	9	9	22	30	18	21	2	6	13	16	49	12	22
Total	83	26	21	36	115	119	99	83	15	25	43	91	164	70	

FISHER ATHLETIC

	Altrincham		Aylesbury United		Barnet		Barrow		Bath City		Boston United		Cheltenham Town		Chorley		Colchester United	
	H	A	H	A	H	A	H	A	H	A	H	A	H	A	H	A	H	A
86-87																		
87-88	3-2	3-2			2-2	0-2			2-0	3-1	0-0	1-2	1-0	0-2				
88-89	1-1	1-1	0-2	1-1	1-2	3-2					1-3	4-2	2-0	2-2	4-0	1-1		
90-91	3-0	1-1			1-2	1-4	4-0	1-1			1-0	0-2	2-5	0-0	2-0	0-2		
91-92	0-0	0-0			2-4	1-8	1-2	1-3	0-3	1-0	1-2	1-4	1-1	0-0			0-0	1-2
92-93																		

	Dagenham		Darlington		Enfield		Farnborough Town		Gateshead		Kettering Town		Kidderminster H.		Lincoln City		Macclesfield Town	
	H	A	H	A	H	A	H	A	H	A	H	A	H	A	H	A	H	A
86-87																		
87-88	5-1	5-1			2-3	0-0					1-1	1-2	3-1	1-1	1-1	0-3	1-2	4-2
88-89					1-2	1-2					3-0	1-2	2-0	1-2			2-2	2-2
90-91			0-2	0-5	3-2	2-1	4-2	1-1			3-1	0-3	1-1	1-1			1-3	1-0
91-92									0-2	0-1	0-0	2-3	1-1	3-3			1-2	1-1
92-93																		

	Maidstone United		Merthyr Tydfil		Northwich Victoria		Runcorn		Slough Town		Stafford Rangers		Sutton United		Telford United		Wealdstone	
	H	A	H	A	H	A	H	A	H	A	H	A	H	A	H	A	H	A
86-87																		
87-88	0-3	2-2			0-0	2-1	0-2	1-5			1-2	2-3	1-1	0-2	0-1	1-2	3-1	1-2
88-89	0-2	0-1			2-4	0-3	0-1	1-1			0-1	1-0	1-1	1-2	0-1	1-1		
90-91			1-2	4-1	1-0	1-2	0-1	0-4			0-2	3-1	1-2	1-2	1-3	1-3		
91-92			0-0	0-7	5-2	0-0	0-1	1-5	1-1	0-1	1-3	0-2	1-1	1-3	2-0	1-3		
92-93																		

	Welling United		Weymouth		Wycombe Wanderers		Yeovil Town	
	H	A	H	A	H	A	H	A
86-87								
87-88	1-0	1-1	1-0	1-1	0-0	1-1		
88-89	1-3	1-3	3-2	0-1	3-3	0-3	4-2	2-1
90-91	1-3	0-2			3-1	1-6	1-2	2-2
91-92	1-1	1-1			2-3	0-2	2-1	1-0
92-93								

	Home						Away					
	P	W	D	L	F	A	P	W	D	L	F	A
ALTRINCHAM	4	2	2	0	7	3	4	1	3	0	5	4
AYLESBURY U	1	0	0	1	0	2	1	0	1	0	1	1
BARNET	4	0	1	3	6	10	4	1	0	3	5	16
BARROW	2	1	0	1	5	2	2	0	1	1	2	4
BATH C	2	1	0	1	2	3	2	2	0	0	4	1
BOSTON U	4	1	1	2	3	5	4	1	0	3	6	10
CHELTENHAM T	4	2	1	1	6	6	4	0	3	1	2	4
CHORLEY	2	2	0	0	6	0	2	0	1	1	1	3
COLCHESTER U	1	0	1	0	0	0	1	0	0	1	1	2
DAGENHAM	1	1	0	0	5	1	1	1	0	0	5	1
DARLINGTON	1	0	0	1	0	2	1	0	0	1	0	5
ENFIELD	3	1	0	2	6	7	3	1	1	1	3	3
FARNBOROUGH T	1	1	0	0	4	2	1	0	1	0	1	1
GATESHEAD	1	0	0	1	0	2	1	0	0	1	0	1
KETTERING T	4	2	2	0	7	2	4	0	0	4	4	10
KIDDERMINSTER H	4	2	2	0	7	3	4	0	3	1	6	7
LINCOLN C	1	0	1	0	1	1	1	0	0	1	0	3
MACCLESFIELD T	4	0	1	3	5	9	4	2	2	0	8	5
MAIDSTONE U	2	0	0	2	0	5	2	0	1	1	2	3
MERTHYR T	2	0	1	1	1	2	2	1	0	1	4	8
NORTHWICH V	4	2	1	1	8	6	4	1	1	2	3	6
RUNCORN	4	0	0	4	0	5	4	0	1	3	3	15
SLOUGH T	1	0	1	0	1	1	1	0	0	1	0	1
STAFFORD R	4	0	0	4	2	8	4	2	0	2	6	6
SUTTON U	4	0	3	1	4	5	4	0	0	4	3	9
TELFORD U	4	1	0	3	3	5	4	0	1	3	4	9
WEALDSTONE	1	1	0	0	3	1	1	0	0	1	1	2
WELLING U	4	1	1	2	4	7	4	0	2	2	3	7
WEYMOUTH	2	2	0	0	4	2	2	0	1	1	1	2
WYCOMBE W	4	1	2	1	8	7	4	0	1	3	2	12
YEOVIL T	3	2	0	1	7	5	3	2	1	0	5	3
TOTALS	83	26	21	36	115	119	83	15	25	43	91	164

Above: My ball Paul! Paul Collins (8) in action against Kettering Town with support from Paul Gorman and Paul Roberts.
Photo: Mick Cheney

Below: Boxing Day (1989) action against Welling United
Photo: Mike Floate

FISHER ATHLETIC

	APPEARANCES					GOALS				
	87-88	88-89	89-90	90-91	TOTAL	87-88	88-89	89-90	90-91	TOTAL
AMBROSE Leroy	21+4	15+18	15+6		51+28	4	3	2		9
ANGELL Darren			2		2					
BARTON Stewart				3	3					
BASTOCK Paul				28	28					
BAYRAM Ossie	2+1	1+1			3+2	1				1
BILEY Alan				3	3				1	1
BLACKFORD Gary			22+1	24+3	46+4			2	2	4
BOYS Steve			0+1		0+1					
BRIGHT Tony				4	4					
BUTLER Gavin			3+6		3+6					
CAREY Neil			1+2		1+2					
CHARLERY Ken	10+3	24			34+3	6	17			23
CLARK Frank			10+2		10+2					
COLLINS Paul	26+1	35	31	33	125+1					
COOPER Gary	30+2	12+4			42+6	2	1			3
CORMACK Lee			0+1		0+1					
CUNNINGHAM Tommy	18				18					
DARK Trevor	14+5				14+5	4				4
DAVIS Burt	9+2				9+2					
DOCKER John			25+1	15+2	40+3			3		3
DODDS Arron			0+1		0+1					
DONNELLY Jamie			3+2		3+2					
DRYDEN Mark				3+1	3+1					
EDWARDS Billy			5	11+6	16+6					
ENGLAND Sean			1+2		1+2					
FIELD Tony		9+5			9+5		1			1
FOLEY Paul			0+1		0+1				1	1
FORDE Clevere			3+2		3+2			1		1
FRIAR Paul			25+1	18	43+1					
FRY David	41	23			64					
GIPP David			2		2			1		1
GORMAN Paul		10+1	37+4	30	77+5		2	17(1p)	12(1p)	**31(2p)**
HAMILL Stewart				1	1					
HAMMOND Paul			1		1					
HARMSWORTH Lee	1	7+6			8+6		1			1
HAYRETTIN Hakan			1		1					
HISCOCK Chris	10+3	4+1	3+2		17+6					
HODGESON Pat	0+5				0+5					
HUNTLEY Jason	3				3					
JACOBS Godfrey				3+1	3+1				1	1
JOLLY Simon				11	11					
KELLEHER John				1+3	1+3					
KENNEDY Michael			7+3		7+3					
KEYS Robert			0+1		0+1					
LATIGO John				8+2	8+2					
LAZARUS Paul	16+1				16+1	5				5
LEE Jason		7			7			3		3
LESLIE John	32+2				32+2	10				10

259

Left: Dean Neal saves against Kettering Town.
Photo: Mick Cheney

Below: Boxing Day (1989) action against Welling United
Photo: Mike Floate

FISHER ATHLETIC

	APPEARANCES					GOALS				
	87-88	88-89	89-90	90-91	TOTAL	87-88	88-89	89-90	90-91	TOTAL
LEWINGTON Colin	20+2				20+2	2				2
LITTLE Barry	29+2	38	37	41	**145+2**	2	2	4	4(1p)	12(1p)
MALCOLM Paul	2+4		1		3+4	2		1		3
MANN Hughie			12	13+4	25+4			9	2	11
MARKS Michael			6	3+2	9+2			1		1
MARSTON Andy	3+9	0+1			3+10	3				3
MARTIN Dean			1+2	29+7	30+9				5	5
MASSEY Andy	18+6	22+11	38		78+17	3	2	3		8
McCLURE Doug		29+2			29+2					
MEHMET Dave	17	18	24	21	80	3(1p)	2	4	4	13(1p)
MITCHELL Jimmy			0+1	7+4	7+5				1	1
MOUNTFORD Peter	7+4				7+4					
MUMMERY Jason				2+2	2+2					
MURPHY Gerry				6	6					
MURRAY Simon			2		2					
NEAL Dean		36	7		43		15	1		16
NORMAN Neil	34+1	23	11	3	71+1	5	2	1		8
NUGENT Kevin			7		7			1		1
NUNES Steve		6+6	4+2	2	12+8		1			1
NUTTON Micky	18	12	6		36		1			1
O'BRIEN Tony				2+2	2+2					
PALMER Lee			3		3					
PARRY John				2+1	2+1					
PAYNE Derek				1	1					
PEARSON Ricky				16	16				1	1
POLLARD John				5	5					
QUINN Jimmy				27	27				1(1p)	1(1p)
RESTARICK Steve				11	11				1	1
RICHARDSON Derek		17			17					
RILEY Ron				1	1				1	1
ROBERTS Paul				24	24					
ROCADAS George			5		5			1		1
ROLES John			15+4		15+4					
SCOTTING Alan			2		2					
SHINNERS Ray	39	27	1		67			1		1
SMART Marcus				17+1	17+1					
SMITH Herbie	8+4				8+4	3				3
SMITH Phil	13+2				13+2	1				1
STEAD Micky		34+1	37+2		71+3					
SWEALES Paul				1	1					
TAGOE Gavin				5+1	5+1					
TIVEY Mark			2		2					
TOWNER Tony	18+2	38			56+2	2	3			5
VICTOR Roy				11	11					
VOGT Martin			1		1					
WARD Dave				16	16					
WEBB Terry	3				3					
WELCH Robert			0+1		0+1					
WELLS Peter			36		36					

Fisher Athletic 'keeper Paul Bastock prevents Barnet's Gary Bull from scoring in the last game of season 1990-91 when Barnet eventually secured three points to win the championship and promotion. Photo: David Watson.

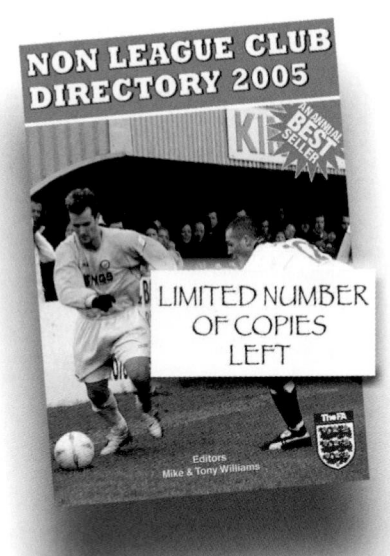

FOREST GREEN ROVERS

PROMOTED FROM: The Southern League 1998
2004-2005 SEASON: The Conference

Season 1998-99. Back row, left to right: Dave Tyrell (Physio), Alan McDougall (Scout), Mark Hallam, Chris Honor, Rob Cook, Justin Shuflewood, Martin Woodhouse, Don Forbes, Martin Boyle, Tim Banks, Tommy Callinan and Mike Kilgour (Coach). Front Row: Tom Jones, Paul Hunt, Grantley Dicks, Paul McLoughlin, Frank Gregan (Manager), Gary Smart (Captain), Alex Sykes, Matthew Coupe, Toby Jackson and Steve Winter.

			HOME						AWAY						
		P	W	D	L	F	A	Pts	P	W	D	L	F	A	Pts	Position
98-99	21	9	5	7	28	22	32	21	6	8	7	27	28	26	12
99-00	21	11	2	8	35	23	35	21	2	6	13	19	40	12	19
00-01	21	6	9	6	28	28	27	21	5	6	10	15	26	21	16
01-02	21	7	7	7	28	32	28	21	5	8	8	26	44	23	18
02-03	21	12	3	6	41	29	39	21	5	5	11	20	33	20	9
03-04	21	6	8	7	32	36	26	21	6	4	11	26	44	22	18
Total	126	51	34	41	192	170	187	126	29	37	60	133	215	124	

SEASONS
6

TOTAL POINTS
311

HIGHEST POSITION
9th 2002-03

LOWEST POSITION
19th 1999-00

HIGHEST ATTENDANCE
1909 v Cheltenham T. 26.8.98

LOWEST ATTENDANCE
404 v Barrow 14.4.99

SEASON GOALSCORER
Mark Cooper 17(7p) (01/02)

CAREER GOALSCORER
Alex Meechan 39(4p)

CAREER APPEARANCES
Steve Perrin 138+2

	Accrington Stanley		Aldershot Town		Altrincham		Barnet		Barrow		Boston United		Burton Albion		Cheltenham Town	
	H	A	H	A	H	A	H	A	H	A	H	A	H	A	H	A
97-98																
98-99									1-1	1-2					1-2	1-1
99-00					1-1	1-1										
00-01											0-3	0-0				
01-02							2-2	1-0			0-3	1-6				
02-03							4-4	0-2					2-0	3-2		
03-04	2-1	1-4	3-1	0-3			1-1	0-5					1-1	3-2		

	Chester City		Dagenham & Redbridge		Doncaster Rovers		Dover Athletic		Exeter City		Farnborough Town		Gravesend & N'fleet		Halifax Town	
	H	A	H	A	H	A	H	A	H	A	H	A	H	A	H	A
97-98																
98-99					0-0	1-0	0-1	1-1			0-0	2-2				
99-00					1-0	2-3	3-1	0-4								
00-01	1-1	1-0	4-4	1-3	2-2	0-3	2-1	2-1								
01-02	0-2	3-2	2-4	1-1	0-2	1-5	2-1	2-1			1-0	0-3				
02-03	0-2	1-0	5-2	1-3	1-2	0-1					3-1	3-0	2-1	1-1	0-2	1-1
03-04	2-1	0-1	1-3	2-5					2-5	2-2	1-1	3-1	1-2	1-1	1-2	1-0

	Hayes		Hednesford Town		Hereford United		Kettering Town		Kidderminster H.		Kingstonian		Leek Town		Leigh RMI	
	H	A	H	A	H	A	H	A	H	A	H	A	H	A	H	A
97-98																
98-99	1-2	3-0	1-0	1-1	2-1	0-4	1-0	1-2	5-0	2-2	1-0	1-0	3-1	2-0		
99-00	0-1	0-3	3-0	0-1	0-1	0-1	2-0	0-1	3-2	3-3	0-3	1-0				
00-01	1-2	0-1	0-2	1-1	1-1	1-3	3-2	3-1			3-1	1-0			3-1	1-1
01-02	2-1	1-1			1-1	0-0									1-2	2-1
02-03					1-3	1-1	1-0	3-2							4-1	0-1
03-04					1-7	1-5									2-2	2-1

264

FOREST GREEN ROVERS

	Margate		Morecambe		Northwich Victoria		Nuneaton Borough		Rushden & Diamonds		Scarborough		Shrewsbury Town		Southport	
	H	A	H	A	H	A	H	A	H	A	H	A	H	A	H	A
97-98																
98-99			2-2	1-3	3-1	0-1			0-2	0-4					1-0	1-1
99-00			1-2	1-1	5-1	0-0	1-2	3-2	1-0	2-3	0-1	0-5			1-0	1-2
00-01			0-0	2-0	1-0	0-0	0-0	0-2	0-0	0-0	2-3	0-1			2-0	1-1
01-02	3-3	1-1	3-1	0-2	2-0	2-2	1-2	1-2			2-2	1-1			2-1	1-5
02-03	4-1	0-3	1-0	0-4	1-0	1-2	6-1	2-3			0-0	0-3			0-2	2-2
03-04	1-2	0-2	1-2	0-4	0-0	4-0					4-0	2-2	1-1	0-2		

	Stalybridge Celtic		Stevenage Borough		Sutton United		Tamworth		Telford United		Welling United		Woking		Yeovil Town	
	H	A	H	A	H	A	H	A	H	A	H	A	H	A	H	A
97-98																
98-99			1-2	1-1					1-1	1-2	3-2	2-0	0-2	1-1	1-2	4-0
99-00			3-2	1-1	1-2	2-3			5-2	0-2	1-2	1-1	0-0	1-2	3-0	0-1
00-01			2-3	1-3					1-1	0-1			0-0	0-2	0-1	0-2
01-02	0-2	1-2	0-0	1-4					1-1	0-0			2-1	4-3	1-1	2-2
02-03			0-3	0-0					1-1	1-0			3-2	0-1	2-1	0-1
03-04			3-1	1-2			2-1	0-1	0-0	2-0			2-2	1-1		

Adrian Foster   Rob Cousins   Tony Daley.   Stuart Slater.

	Home						Away					
	P	W	D	L	F	A	P	W	D	L	F	A
ACCRINGTON S	1	1	0	0	2	1	1	0	0	1	1	4
ALDERSHOT T	1	1	0	0	3	1	1	0	0	1	0	3
ALTRINCHAM	1	0	1	0	1	1	1	0	1	0	1	1
BARNET	3	0	3	0	7	7	3	1	0	2	1	7
BARROW	1	0	1	0	1	1	1	0	0	1	1	2
BOSTON U	2	0	0	2	0	6	2	0	1	1	1	6
BURTON A	2	1	1	0	3	1	2	2	0	0	6	4
CHELTENHAM T	1	0	0	1	1	2	1	0	1	0	1	1
CHESTER C	4	1	1	2	3	6	4	3	0	1	5	3
DAGENHAM & R	4	1	1	2	12	13	4	0	1	3	5	12
DONCASTER R	5	1	2	2	4	6	5	1	0	4	4	12
DOVER A	4	3	0	1	7	4	4	2	1	1	5	7
EXETER C	1	0	0	1	2	5	1	0	1	0	2	2
FARNBOROUGH T	4	2	2	0	5	2	4	2	1	1	8	6
GRAVESEND & N	2	1	0	1	3	3	2	0	2	0	2	2
HALIFAX T	2	0	0	2	1	4	2	1	1	0	2	1
HAYES	4	1	0	3	4	6	4	1	1	2	4	5
HEDNESFORD T	3	2	0	1	4	2	3	0	2	1	2	3
HEREFORD U	6	1	2	3	6	14	6	0	2	4	3	14
KETTERING T	4	4	0	0	7	2	4	2	0	2	7	6
KIDDERMINSTER H	2	2	0	0	8	2	2	0	2	0	5	5
KINGSTONIAN	3	2	0	1	4	4	3	3	0	0	3	0
LEEK T	1	1	0	0	3	1	1	1	0	0	2	0
LEIGH RMI	4	2	1	1	10	6	4	2	1	1	5	4
MARGATE	3	1	1	1	8	6	3	0	1	2	1	6
MORECAMBE	6	2	2	2	8	7	6	1	1	4	4	14
NORTHWICH V	6	5	1	0	12	2	6	1	3	2	7	5
NUNEATON B	4	1	1	2	8	5	4	1	0	3	6	9
RUSHDEN & D	3	1	1	1	1	2	3	0	1	2	2	7
SCARBOROUGH	5	1	2	2	8	6	5	0	2	3	3	12
SHREWSBURY T	1	0	1	0	1	1	1	0	0	1	0	2
SOUTHPORT	5	4	0	1	6	3	5	0	3	2	6	11
STALYBRIDGE C	1	0	0	1	0	2	1	0	0	1	1	2
STEVENAGE B	6	2	1	3	9	11	6	0	3	3	5	11
SUTTON U	1	0	0	1	1	2	1	0	0	1	2	3
TAMWORTH	1	1	0	0	2	1	1	0	0	1	0	1
TELFORD U	6	1	5	0	9	6	6	2	1	3	4	5
WELLING U	2	1	0	1	4	4	2	1	1	0	3	1
WOKING	6	2	3	1	7	7	6	1	2	3	7	10
YEOVIL T	5	2	1	2	7	5	5	1	1	3	6	6
TOTAL	126	51	34	41	192	170	126	29	37	60	133	215

Jason Drysdale.   Paul Hunt.   Marc McGregor.   Alex Sykes.

FOREST GREEN ROVERS   LEADING APPEARANCES

	98-99	99-00	00-01	01-02	02-03	03-04	TOTAL
Steve PERRIN	7	26+1	26	39+1	40	42	180+2
Alex SYKES	36+5	30+9	7+1	11+1	31+2	16+8	131+26
Martyn FOSTER			15+1	38	38	42	133+1
Alex MEECHAN			31	40+2	27+8	22	120+10

FOREST GREEN ROVERS   APPEARANCES

	98-99	99-00	00-01	01-02	02-03	03-04	TOTAL
ADAMS Adie				2+7	1+5	0+4	3+16
ALLEN Danny				9+6	6+6		15+12
AUBREY Matt					2+6		2+6
BAILEY Danny	27+2		6+1				33+3
BAILEY Dennis		34+5	9+12				43+17
BARNETT Dave		3					3
BENNETT Frankie		9	10+8				19+8
BIRKBY Dean	8+5		0+3				8+8
BOWEN Sam					2		2
BRODIE Steve					7		7
BURNS Chris		33	32				65
CALLINAN Tommy	1						1
CAMPBELL Steve			1+5				1+5
CANT John					4+7		4+7
CATLEY Andrew	2+2	0+2					2+4
CHAPPLE Shaun	8+6	2+1					10+7
CLARK Billy		36+1	38				74+1
CLEVERLEY Ben					6+2		6+2
COOK Rob	28+9	13+4		3+16	0+1		44+30
COOPER Mark			11	37			48
CORT Leon			12				12
COUPE Matthew	17+9			9+2	18+1		44+12
COUSINS Rob			40+1	31+2			71+3
COWE Steve					9+8	21+13	30+21
DALEY Tony		26	23+7	6+6			55+13
DOBSON Tony			0+2				0+2
DRYSDALE Jason	28+1	32+1	30				90+2
EATON Jason			11+1				11+1
EVANS Richard	0+1						1
FITZPATRICK Ian					4+1		4+1
FORBES Don	39	18+8					57+8
FOSTER Adrian			27+5				27+5
FOSTER Martyn			15+1	38	38	42	133+1
FREESTONE Chris				0+1			0+1
FUTCHER Simon				18+9	2+6		20+15
GHENT Matthew			2				2
GILROY Dave					2+3		2+3
GLASSUP Ellis				0+1			0+1
GRAYSON Neil					30+8	24+1	54+9

Dennis Bailey. Photo: Martin Wray.

Rob Cook. Photo: Peter Barnes.

Below: Chris Burns & Billy Clark.
Photo: Peter Barnes.

Mark Hallam (9). Photo: Peter Barnes.

FOREST GREEN ROVERS   APPEARANCES

	98-99	99-00	00-01	01-02	02-03	03-04	TOTAL
GREEN Michael						5	5
HALLAM Mark	13+3						13+3
HATSWELL Wayne		30+4	19				49+4
HEDGES Ian	32+1	41	14+9				87+10
HEGGS Carl				28+2	4+5		32+7
HODSON Ben	3+1						3+1
HONOR Christian	29	12+1					41+1
HOPKINS Gareth				6+2			6+2
HOWEY Lee				15			15
HUNT Paul	23	10+18	0+2				33+20
IMPEY James				30+1	3		33+1
INGRAM Denny					32		32
JACKSON Toby	0+3						0+3
JENKINS Steve			36	36+1	10+1		82+2
JONES Darren					27	10	37
JONES Jimmi Lee					3+2		3+2
JONES Luke				0+1	0+1	0+9	0+11
JONES Steve					11		11
JORDAN Tom					5		5
KENNEDY Richard					11+2		11+2
KILGOUR Mike	25	12+3	1+1				38+4
LANGAN Kevin				24+1	28+3	11+5	63+9
LEE David				3+3			3+3
LIGHTBODY Nathan		9+8	3+8				12+16
LOCKWOOD Adam			10				10
McAULEY Hugh					6+7		6+7
McGREGOR Mark	19+9	25+3					44+12
McLOUGHLIN Alan				10+1			10+1
MEECHAN Alex			31	40+2	27+8	22	120+10
MEHEW Dave	15+1	8+13					23+14
MIDDLETON Darren			4+3				4+3
MIDDLETON Luke				0+7			0+7
MINGS Adie		8+12					8+12
MOORE Paul					4+2		4+2
MORALEE Jamie					6+4		6+4
MORGAN Scott					7		7
NICHOLSON Kevin			1				1
NORTON Dave		18	25				43
ODEJAYI Kayode				5+1	37+1		42+2
OLNEY Ian			0+2				0+2
OWERS Gary					35+1	14	49+1
PEARCEY Jason				3			3
PERRIN Steve	7	26+1	26	39+1	40	42	180+2
PHILLIPS Lee					19+2		19+2
PRINCE Luke			4+3				4+3
PRITCHARD Lee				0+1			0+1
RANDALL Adie		9+2					9+2
RICHARDSON Jon					34+1	33	67+1
ROGERS Scott						27+12	27+12
ROLLO Jim	7+9						7+9
RUSSELL Lee					14		14

Ian Hedges. Photo: Martin Wray.

Nathan Wigg. Photo: Peter Barnes.

Mike Kilgour wins the header with Chris Burns in attendance.

FOREST GREEN ROVERS   APPEARANCES

	98-99	99-00	00-01	01-02	02-03	03-04	TOTAL
RUSSELL Matthew					20	3+1	23+1
SEARLE Damon						31	31
SHAW Mark			5+1	21+4			26+5
SHUTTLEWOOD Justin	34	16			2		52
SIMPSON Sekani						2+1	2+1
SLATER Stuart			20+1				20+1
SMALL Bryan				5			5
SMART Gary	16+13						16+13
SMITH Chris	3+7	0+2					3+9
SPINK Nigel			14				14
STOKER Gareth						24	24
SULLIVAN Martyn			3+1				3+1
SYKES Alex	36+5	30+9	7+1	11+1	31+2	16+8	131+26
TEARNEY Trevor				7+6	1+3		8+9
THOMAS Bradley		8+7	2+7				10+14
TRAVIS Simon				31+4			31+4
TWEDDLE Steve					0+3		0+3
WARD Chris				5			5
WESTLAKE Tristan	1						1
WIGG Nathan	25+5						25+5
WINTER Steve	16+5	3+3					19+8

Neil Grayson. Photo: Peter Barnes.

Alex Sykes. Photo: Alan Coomes.

FOREST GREEN ROVERS   GOALSCORERS

	98-99	99-00	00-01	01-02	02-03	03-04	TOTAL
ALLEN Danny				1			1
BAILEY Dennis		9					9
BENNETT Frankie		1	1				2
BOWEN Sam					3		3
BRODIE Steve					3		3
BURNS Chris		5					5
CANT John					1		1
CLARK Billy		3	3				6

FOREST GREEN ROVERS   GOALSCORERS

	98-99	99-00	00-01	01-02	02-03	03-04	TOTAL
COOK Rob	5	1			1		7
COOPER Mark			1	17(7p)			18(7p)
COUPE Matthew	2						2
COUSINS Rob				1			1
COWE Steve					3	6	9
DALEY Tony		4	2(1p)				6(1p)
DRYSDALE Jason	3	2(1p)					5(1p)
EATON Jason			2				2
FOSTER Adrian			8				8
FOSTER Martyn			1		1	3	5
GRAYSON Neil				15(4p)	9(1p)		24(5p)
HALLAM Mark	4						4
HATSWELL Wayne		2	5				7
HEDGES Ian	3	1					4
HEGGS Carl				10(2p)	1		11(2p)
HOWEY Lee				2			2
HUNT Paul	7(2p)	4					11(2p)
INGRAM Denny					2(1p)		2(1p)
JENKINS Steve				2			2
JONES Darren					2		2
KENNEDY Richard						1	1
KILGOUR Mike	1						1
LANGAN Kevin				1		1	2
LEE David				1			1
LIGHTBODY Nathan			1	3			4
LOCKWOOD Adam			1				1
McGREGOR Mark	11	12(1p)					23(1p)
MEECHAN Alex			13(1p)	8(2p)	12(1p)	6	**39(4p)**
MEHEW Dave	5						5
MOORE Paul					1		1
MORALEE Jamie					2		2
NORTON Dave		1	1				2
ODEJAYI Kayode				1	13		14
OWERS Gary					1		1
PHILLIPS Lee					2		2
RANDALL Adie		1					1
RICHARDSON Jon					4		4
ROGERS Scott					9		9
SEARLE Damon					4(3p)		4(3p)
SHAW Mark				1			1
SLATER Stuart			1				1
SMART Gary	2						2
SULLIVAN Martyn			1				1
SYKES Alex	8	7	1	1	5	3	25
THOMAS Bradley		1					1
TRAVIS Simon				3			3
TWEDDLE Steve				1			1
WARD Chris				1			1
WINTER Steve	3						3

FRICKLEY ATHLETIC

PROMOTED FROM: Northern Premier League 1980
RELEGATED TO: Northern Premier League 1987
2004-2005 SEASON: Northern Premier League, Premier Division

Frickley Athletic 1985-86
L-R - **Back Row:** Paul Wilson, Stevie Daniels, Wayne Noteman, Tommy Meehan, Mally Wright, Sean Marshall, Alan Semley.
Front Row: Gary Hatto, Paul Shirtliff, Peter Howey, Colin Bishop, Gary Mallender
Photo: John Womack

SEASONS																
7		HOME							AWAY							
		P	W	D	L	F	A	Pts	P	W	D	L	F	A	Pts	Position
TOTAL POINTS	79-80															
337																
HIGHEST POSITION	80-81	19	10	4	5	36	22	24	19	5	4	10	25	40	14	10
2nd 85-86	81-82	21	11	4	6	35	23	37	21	3	6	12	12	37	15	15
LOWEST POSITION	82-83	21	11	6	4	41	25	39	21	1	7	13	25	52	10	16
21st 86-87	83-84	21	13	3	5	49	25	29	21	4	7	10	19	31	19	12
HIGHEST ATTENDANCE	84-85	21	12	3	6	38	25	27	21	6	4	11	27	46	22	11
988 Altrincham (22-2-85)	85-86	21	16	4	1	46	21	36	21	9	6	6	32	29	33	2
LOWEST ATTENDANCE	86-87	21	5	7	9	28	37	22	21	2	4	15	19	45	10	21
201 Barrow (4-3-83)	Total	145	78	31	36	273	178	214	145	30	38	77	159	280	123	

SEASON GOALSCORER
Gary Hooley 29(2p) (84/85)

CAREER GOALSCORER
Gary Hooley 75(4p)

CAREER APPEARANCES
Barry Gill 257

	Altrincham		A P Leamington		Bangor City		Barnet		Barrow		Bath City		Boston United		Cheltenham Town		Dagenham		Dartford	
	H	A	H	A	H	A	H	A	H	A	H	A	H	A	H	A	H	A	H	A
80-81	0-2	0-2	0-0	2-2	4-0	3-4	3-0	0-2	5-0	0-0	2-1	0-3	0-1	2-1						
81-82	1-1	1-1	4-1	0-1			0-1	0-0	2-1	0-2	1-3	3-1	4-1	1-3			3-1	0-2	3-0	0-1
82-83	3-0	2-2			3-3	0-1	0-1	1-4	1-1	0-2	2-1	3-4	2-0	1-2			1-2	1-4		
83-84	3-1	0-1			2-0	1-4	3-1	2-3			1-2	0-1	7-1	2-2			4-0	1-1		
84-85	2-1	4-3					3-1	2-1	2-2	0-6	2-0	0-3	2-1	1-2			0-2	1-4	2-4	2-0
85-86	0-0	0-1					3-3	2-1	2-0	2-2	2-1	2-1	5-1	3-0	2-1	1-1	3-2	0-0	1-0	2-1
86-87	2-2	1-1					0-3	0-3			2-2	2-4	0-1	2-2	0-2	0-2	1-3	1-0		

	Enfield		Gateshead		Gravesend & N'fleet		Kettering Town		Kidderminster H.		Maidstone United		Northwich Victoria		Nuneaton Borough		Runcorn		Scarborough	
	H	A	H	A	H	A	H	A	H	A	H	A	H	A	H	A	H	A	H	A
80-81			2-4	1-3			1-1	1-6			2-1	1-1	0-1	3-1	4-3	1-0			1-0	1-2
81-82	1-1	0-3					1-1	1-4			0-3	0-0	1-0	0-0			2-0	0-1	2-3	1-0
82-83	5-2	2-2					3-2	1-4			2-1	0-4	0-0	1-2	2-1	1-5	0-2	3-3	2-1	2-1
83-84	1-1	3-3			4-1	0-2	1-1	1-0	0-2	1-1	2-0	1-3	4-1	1-1	1-3	0-1	2-1	1-2	2-1	1-3
84-85	1-0	0-1			1-0	2-3	3-0	0-5	3-0	4-2	1-3	1-1	4-0	0-3	1-1	0-0	1-1	0-0	2-3	2-1
85-86	1-4	1-3					3-0	0-2	3-1	1-1	2-0	2-3	1-0	3-2	2-2	1-0	3-1	2-2	2-1	3-2
86-87	1-4	0-0			3-1	0-2	2-2	2-1	0-1	1-4	0-2	0-1	1-1	1-1	1-1	1-2	0-2	0-1	0-2	2-4

	Stafford Rangers		Sutton United		Telford United		Trowbridge Town		Wealdstone		Welling United		Weymouth		Worcester City		Wycombe Wanderers		Yeovil Town	
	H	A	H	A	H	A	H	A	H	A	H	A	H	A	H	A	H	A	H	A
80-81	3-2	3-3			4-1	0-1			1-1	2-0			1-2	2-1	1-1	0-3			2-1	3-5
81-82	2-0	0-0			0-0	1-7	2-0	0-2					0-1	0-5	1-2	2-3			2-1	2-1
82-83	3-0	1-1			2-2	1-1	2-2	0-2	2-2	0-2			1-2	0-0	2-0	4-4			3-0	1-2
83-84					1-1	1-0	2-0	1-0	2-5	0-0			1-2	2-0	3-1	0-0			3-0	0-3
84-85					1-2	3-5			0-2	1-1			2-0	1-2	2-1	1-2			3-1	2-1
85-86	3-0	0-0			3-1	1-2			2-1	0-2			1-0	3-2			2-2	3-1		
86-87	2-1	0-2	1-1	0-3	4-2	1-4			3-1	1-2	3-1	2-3	2-2	2-3						

	Home						Away					
	P	W	D	L	F	A	P	W	D	L	F	A
ALTRINCHAM	7	3	3	1	11	7	7	1	3	3	8	11
A P LEAMINGTON	2	1	1	0	4	1	2	0	1	1	2	3
BANGOR C	3	2	1	0	9	3	3	0	0	3	4	9
BARNET	7	3	1	3	12	10	7	2	1	4	7	14
BARROW	5	3	2	0	12	4	5	0	2	3	2	12
BATH C	7	4	1	2	12	10	7	2	0	5	10	17
BOSTON U	7	5	0	2	20	6	7	2	2	3	12	12
CHELTENHAM T	2	1	0	1	2	3	2	0	1	1	1	3
DAGENHAM	6	3	0	3	12	10	6	1	2	3	4	11
DARTFORD	3	2	0	1	6	4	3	2	0	1	4	2
ENFIELD	6	2	2	2	10	12	6	0	3	3	6	12
GATESHEAD	3	3	0	0	8	2	3	0	0	3	2	7
GRAVESEND & N	2	0	1	1	3	5	2	0	0	2	2	7
KETTERING T	7	4	3	0	16	8	7	2	1	4	5	18
KIDDERMINSTER H	4	2	0	2	6	4	4	1	2	1	7	8
MAIDSTONE U	7	4	0	3	9	10	7	0	3	4	5	13
NORTHWICH V	7	4	2	1	11	3	7	2	3	2	9	10
NUNEATON B	6	2	3	1	11	11	6	2	1	3	4	8
RUNCORN	6	3	1	2	8	7	6	0	3	3	6	9
SCARBOROUGH	7	4	0	3	11	11	7	4	0	3	12	13
STAFFORD R	5	5	0	0	13	3	5	0	4	1	4	6
SUTTON U	1	0	1	0	1	1	1	0	0	1	0	3
TELFORD U	7	3	3	1	15	9	7	1	1	5	8	20
TROWBRIDGE T	3	2	1	0	6	2	3	1	0	2	1	4
WEALDSTONE	6	2	2	2	10	12	6	1	2	3	4	7
WELLING U	1	1	0	0	3	1	1	0	0	1	2	3
WEYMOUTH	7	2	1	4	8	9	7	3	1	3	10	13
WORCESTER C	5	3	1	1	9	5	5	0	2	3	7	12
WYCOMBE W	1	0	1	0	2	2	1	1	0	0	3	1
YEOVIL T	5	5	0	0	13	3	5	2	0	3	8	12
TOTALS	145	78	31	36	273	178	145	30	38	77	159	280

FRICKLEY ATHLETIC LEADING APPEARANCES

	79/80	80/81	81/82	82/83	83/84	84/85	85/86	86/87	87/88	TOTAL
Barry GILL		38	34	41	40	40	33	31		257
Peter HOWEY		24		22	29+1	31+2	42	40		188+3
Stevie DANIELS			40+1	40	37	14	30+1	27		188+2
Graham REED		31+2	40	38	35	36+1				180+3
Tommy MEEHAN		31	12	35	22	27+1	18	22		167+1
Mally WRIGHT				32	35	41	28	30		166
Gary HOOLEY				31	31+4	39+1	26	15+2		142+7
Paul WILSON				14	34+1	30+3	34+1	15+1		127+6
Russ WILCOX				17	36	34+2	40			127+2
Keith WHITELEY		37	42	33+1	7+2					119+3
Sean MARSHALL			16	20	11	21	18+2	13+3		99+5

Above: Mally Wright

Right: Paul Wilson

Photos: SE Sports Extra

Above Right:
Russ Wilcox
and Supporters' Club
Chairman Frank Lawley.
Photo: Paul Taxon

FRICKLEY ATHLETIC   APPEARANCES

	79/80	80/81	81/82	82/83	83/84	84/85	85/86	86/87	87/88	TOTAL
ABBESHAW A								1		1
ADAMS Tim							1			1
BEAGLEHOLE Steve			1							1
BENNETT Des			10+7							10+7
BENTHAM John			0+2							0+2
BISHOP Colin						31+5	30+2	22+8		83+15
BRADSHAW P	2									2
BROWN Kenny	17+5									17+5
BURGIN Ian	25+6	18+4								43+10
CALLERY Neil		17								17
CAMPBELL Phil		1+1	20+5	10+13	9+7		8+11			48+37
CLARK Martin						3+3				3+3
COCHRANE Jim		15								15
CORKE David		1								1
CORKE Steve		1+1								1+1
COTTON Jeff		1								1
CROSSLEY B			1+1							1+1
DANIELS Stevie		40+1	40	37	14	30+1	27			188+2
DAVIES A		1								1
DAWSON Richard							13			13
DUNN Harry				42	12					54
ELLIOTT Don					1+1					1+1
FAULKNER Steve		29+1	8+1							37+2
FERGUSON Seamus		4+1								4+1
FIELD G		1								1
FLANAGAN Shaun		35	2							37
FOLEY Will						4+2	7+2			11+4
FOWLER Sean							7+3			7+3
FOX C		0+4								0+4
GILL Barry	38	34	41	40	40	33	31			257
GILL Martyn	29+2	36	17							82+2
HALL David	9+8									9+8
HALL Howard	3									3
HARRIS Graham	11									11
HARVEY Lennie					1					1
HATTO Gary						12+14	6+4			18+18
HILL Martin							20			20
HINCHCLIFFE Stuart	7			20						27
HOOLEY Gary			31	31+4	39+1	26	15+2			142+7
HOTTE Tim						1+1	14+2			15+3
HOWEY Peter	24		22	29+1	31+2	42	40			188+3
HOYLAND Dave						10+2				10+2
JOICEY Brian	3									3
JONES Alan		0+2								0+2
LADLEY Ian						1				1

277

FRICKLEY ATHLETIC   APPEARANCES

	79/80	80/81	81/82	82/83	83/84	84/85	85/86	86/87	87/88	TOTAL
LONG Nigel		27+3								27+3
MALLENDER Gary							37+1	39		76+1
MARSHALL P				2+2						2+2
MARSHALL Sean			16	20	11	21	18+2	13+3		99+5
MAXTED Paul						14	24			38
McDONNELL Dave					0+1					0+1
McSHANE Stuart				7						7
MEEHAN Tommy		31	12	35	22	27+1	18	22		167+1
MELLOR R		1								1
MOORE Tony				2						2
MOUNTAIN Bob								6+2		6+2
MYLES Steve					7+8	32+1	2+3	31+1		72+13
NOTEMAN Wayne							27+1	16+3		43+4
OLNEY Kevin	15		2							17
OVERTON John				24	15+4			4		43+4
PEACOCK John						1+1				1+1
PROBERT Eric			3+1							3+1
REED Graham		31+2	40	38	35	36+1				180+3
ROSE Nigel						6				6
ROWLANDS S			1+1							1+1
SEMLEY Alan							2+2	28+4		30+6
SHIPLEY Mark			30							30
SHIRTLIFF Paul							40	38		78
SLEIGHT Geoff	0+1									0+1
SMITH Dave	37	27								64
SMITH Ian				27	16+3	25+5				68+8
SMITH Malcolm					33+1					33+1
SPURR C			4							4
THOMPSON Dave	5	9+1								14+1
TODD D			2	2						4
VAUGHAN A			2							2
WADSWORTH Mick	37	29	10							76
WAKEFIELD Paul						16+6				16+6
WALSH Jimmy			13							13
WARD G								1		1
WEBSTER Ian								4		4
WHITELEY Keith		37	42	33+1	7+2					119+3
WIGGAN Trenton								2		2
WILCOX Russ				17	36	34+2	40			127+2
WILKES Glyn								2+2		2+2
WILSON Paul				14	34+1	30+3	34+1	15+1		127+6
WOODALL John		29+2								29+2
WORSFOLD Steve			0+3	4+3						4+6
WRIGHT Mally				32	35	41	28	30		166

FRICKLEY ATHLETIC GOALSCORERS

	79/80	80/81	81/82	82/83	83/84	84/85	85/86	86/87	87/88	TOTAL
BENNETT Des				2						2
BISHOP Colin						2	1	1		4
BROWN Kenny	3									3
BURGIN Ian	1									1
CAMPBELL Phil				1	1	3		1		6
CLARK Martin							1			1
COCHRANE Jim		1(1p)								1(1p)
DANIELS Stevie				1				1		2
DUNN Harry					1					1
FAULKNER Steve			3							3
FERGUSON Seamus				1						1
FLANAGAN Shaun			4							4
FOLEY Will							4	1		5
FOWLER Sean								1		1
GILL Barry	5	3	3	4	3	1		3		22
GILL Martyn	4	4	3							11
HALL David	2									2
HATTO Gary							5(3p)	2		7(3p)
HOOLEY Gary			10	16	29(2p)	13		7(2p)		**75(4p)**
HOTTE Tim								2(2p)		2(2p)
HOWEY Peter	2			2		1	6	2		13
HOYLAND Dave							4			4
LONG Nigel	3									3
MALLENDER Gary							2	3		5
MARSHALL Sean				1				1		2
MYLES Steve					2	1		3		6
NOTEMAN Wayne							6	3		9
OVERTON John				2	2			1		5
REED Graham	8	7	12(6p)	17(4p)	6					50(10p)
ROSE Nigel						1				1
SEMLEY Alan								6		6
SHIRTLIFF Paul							1			1
SMITH Dave	9	8								17
SMITH Ian				14	4	1				19
THOMPSON Dave	1									1
WADSWORTH Mick	11	7	3							21
WAKEFIELD Paul					3					3
WALSH Jimmy			1(1p)							1(1p)
WHITELEY Keith	1	9	1							11
WILCOX Russ					6	1	12			19
WILSON Paul				7	14	12	18	5		56
WOODALL John		11								11
WRIGHT Mally				1		2	2	1		6

Frickley Athletic 1982-83. Back row, left to right: Geoff Slight (manager), Barry Gill, Gary Hooley, Mally Wright, Tommy Meehan, Graham Reed, Sean Marshall and Martyn Gill. Front row: Steve Daniels, John Overton, Des Bennett, Phil Campbell and Ian Smith.

GATESHEAD

PROMOTED FROM: Northern Premier League 1983, 1986, 1990
RELEGATED TO: Northern Premier League 1985, 1987, 1998
2004-2005 SEASON: Northern Premier League, Premier Division

Gateshead FC 1994

Back Row: Simon Smith, Phil Sharpe, Steve Higgins, Keith Nobbs, Michael Farrey, John Tinkler, George Cook (Coach). **Middle Row:** Billy Thompson (Physio), Paul Shirtliff, Paul Sweeney, Paul Proudlock, Paul Dobson, Mark Hine, Brian Rowe, Gary Nicholson, Ian Bruce (Kit Man). **Front Row:** David Corner, Ged Parkinson, Clive Thirkell (Vice Chairman), John Gibson (Chairman), Colin Richardson (Manager), Peter Robinson (Director), Jeff Bowron (Press Officer), Alan Lamb, Jeff Wrightson

SEASONS
11

TOTAL POINTS
536

HIGHEST POSITION
5th (95/96)

LOWEST POSITION
22nd (86/87)

HIGHEST ATTENDANCE
1276 Kidderminster (3-5-97)
NB 2734 Yeovil (3-9-94)
(at St James Park)

LOWEST ATTENDANCE
121 Trowbridge (10-12-83)

SEASON GOALSCORER
Paul Dobson 25(5p) (93/94)
Paul Dobson 25(3p) (94/95)

CAREER GOALSCORER
Paul Dobson 61(12p)

CAREER APPEARANCES
Simon Smith 211

| | HOME | | | | | | | AWAY | | | | | | | |
	P	W	D	L	F	A	Pts	P	W	D	L	F	A	Pts	Position
83-84	21	7	9	5	35	30	23	21	5	4	12	24	43	19	16
84-85	21	5	6	10	27	42	16	21	4	6	11	24	40	18	21
85-86															
86-87	21	3	7	11	26	45	16	21	3	6	12	22	50	15	22
87-90															
90-91	21	10	3	8	32	38	33	21	4	3	14	20	54	15	17
91-92	21	8	5	8	22	22	29	21	4	7	10	27	35	19	14
92-93	21	9	6	6	27	19	33	21	5	4	12	26	37	19	14
93-94	21	10	6	5	23	18	36	21	5	6	10	22	35	21	11
94-95	21	12	4	5	28	13	40	21	7	6	8	33	40	27	7
95-96	21	9	7	5	32	24	34	21	9	6	6	26	22	33	5
96-97	21	8	6	7	32	27	30	21	7	5	9	27	36	26	10
97-98	21	7	6	8	32	35	27	21	1	5	15	19	52	8	21
Total	231	88	65	78	316	313	317	231	54	58	119	270	444	220	

Gateshead FC 1991

Back Row: Ronnie Sills (Asst. Manager), Jeff Bowron (Press Officer), George Ramshaw (Match Secretray), Paul Sharkey, Andy Gowers, Simon Smith, Tony Hall, Tom Statham, Terry Ainsley (Physio), Ian Bruce (Kit Man), Billy Horner (Coach).

Front Row: Keith McNall, Michael Farrey, Tony Robinson, Andy Dixon, Tony Lee (Manager), Derek Bell (Captain), Sean O'Brien, Steve Plaskett, John Trewick

Gateshead FC 1983-84
Photo: Gateshead Post

Back Row (L-R): E G Hill (Chairman), Lance Jobling, David Parnaby, Kenny Dodds, Jim Pearson, Steve Higgins, Gordon Hindson, George Ramshaw (Asst. Manager).   **Front Row:** Tony Robinson, Bob Topping, Terry Hibbitt, Ray Wilkie (Manager), Kevin Pugh, Martin Henderson, Paul Grigg.

GATESHEAD

	Altrincham		Bangor City		Barnet		Barrow		Bath City		Boston United		Bromsgrove Rovers		Cheltenham Town		Colchester United	
	H	A	H	A	H	A	H	A	H	A	H	A	H	A	H	A	H	A
79-83																		
83-84	0-1	0-5	2-1	3-3	2-3	1-0			3-1	1-1	5-5	4-0						
84-85	0-1	0-2			0-2	1-1	1-2	1-0	1-1	1-1	1-2	1-1						
85-86																		
86-87	1-3	1-1			1-5	1-3			1-2	1-1	1-3	0-6			1-1	2-4		
87-88																		
88-89																		
89-90																		
90-91	0-3	1-4			1-3	1-1	5-1	1-3	2-0	0-3	0-1	1-5			3-3	0-1	1-2	0-3
91-92	4-0	1-1					1-1	1-1	0-1	1-0	2-1	0-4			2-1	2-3	0-2	0-2
92-93	2-0	1-0							0-4	1-1	2-2	2-0	0-0	0-3				
93-94	2-1	3-0							1-0	3-2			0-1	0-3				
94-95	1-0	3-1							0-1	2-0			2-1	2-2				
95-96	2-3	1-1							3-1	1-0			1-0	1-3				
96-97	1-1	1-0							5-0	0-3			1-0	2-2				
97-98															0-0	0-2		
98-04																		

	Dagenham		Dagenham & Redbridge		Dartford		Dover Athletic		Enfield		Farnborough Town		Fisher Athletic		Frickley Athletic	
	H	A	H	A	H	A	H	A	H	A	H	A	H	A	H	A
79-83																
83-84	1-1	2-1							1-1	3-0					2-0	1-4
84-85	2-1	2-0			0-0	2-1			0-5	1-3					3-2	0-1
85-86																
86-87	3-2	0-0							1-2	1-1					2-0	1-3
87-88																
88-89																
89-90																
90-91													1-0	2-0		
91-92			0-1	1-2							0-2	1-3				
92-93			1-1	1-3							1-0	1-6				
93-94			3-1	1-1			1-2	1-3								
94-95			2-1	0-0			1-0	2-2			2-0	1-3				
95-96			2-0	4-0			1-1	1-1			1-1	3-2				
96-97							1-3	1-0			1-0	2-1				
97-98							1-2	1-0			3-0	0-4				
98-04																

	Halifax Town		Hayes		Hednesford Town		Hereford United		Kettering Town		Kidderminster H.		Leek Town		Macclesfield Town	
	H	A	H	A	H	A	H	A	H	A	H	A	H	A	H	A
79-83																
83-84									1-2	0-3	1-0	0-1				
84-85									1-4	1-1	4-1	0-3				
85-86																
86-87									1-1	1-5	2-4	1-3				
87-88																
88-89																
89-90																
90-91									1-2	0-1	2-1	3-2			1-1	0-4
91-92									0-0	1-1	0-3	3-5			2-0	0-1
92-93									1-1	0-2	1-0	3-3			1-0	0-1
93-94	2-1	1-3							0-0	0-0	0-2	1-1			1-0	1-6
94-95	1-2	2-3							0-0	4-2	1-0	3-2			2-1	1-2
95-96	3-2	0-2			0-3	1-0			1-1	0-1	4-1	1-1			0-1	0-1
96-97	0-1	0-2	1-1	0-0	0-1	0-0			1-1	1-4	3-1	2-3			0-0	0-3
97-98	2-2	0-2	1-1	0-1	2-5	0-3	1-1	0-1	2-0	0-3	2-0	1-1	0-2	2-2		
98-04																

	Maidstone United		Merthyr Tydfil		Morecambe		Northwich Victoria		Nuneaton Borough		Runcorn		Rushden & Diamonds		Scarborough	
	H	A	H	A	H	A	H	A	H	A	H	A	H	A	H	A
79-83																
83-84	0-2	0-1					1-3	1-3	1-1	2-3	1-1	2-4			1-1	1-1
84-85	2-1	0-1					2-6	0-2	0-2	0-3	0-3	1-1			3-1	1-5
85-86																
86-87	1-4	0-3					1-1	2-1	3-2	1-1	1-3	0-4			0-1	2-3
87-88																
88-89																
89-90																
90-91			1-0	1-3			0-4	2-3			3-1	0-2				
91-92			0-1	4-1			2-0	1-1			1-1	1-1				
92-93			4-0	1-1			0-2	0-0			4-1	2-4				
93-94			0-0	0-3			1-0	2-1			2-2	1-1				
94-95			2-0	2-1			4-0	1-1			4-0	2-3				
95-96					3-0	3-2	1-1	2-1								
96-97					0-3	0-4	5-1	2-4					1-0	4-0		
97-98					1-4	0-2	2-2	1-1					2-1	2-3		
98-04																

GATESHEAD

	Slough Town		Southport		Stafford Rangers		Stalybridge Celtic		Stevenage Borough		Sutton United		Telford United		Trowbridge Town	
	H	A	H	A	H	A	H	A	H	A	H	A	H	A	H	A
79-83																
83-84													2-1	0-4	2-2	2-0
84-85													1-1	1-1		
85-86																
86-87					2-2	0-1					1-1	0-3	0-2	1-2		
87-88																
88-89																
89-90																
90-91	1-0	1-1			2-1	1-0					0-9	3-3	5-1	2-1		
91-92	2-1	0-2			0-0	3-1							0-2	1-1		
92-93	1-0	0-1			0-1	1-2	0-0	1-2					0-1	0-1		
93-94	0-0	1-2	1-3	1-1	0-0	1-3	2-1	1-2					0-2	0-0		
94-95			0-1	0-5	1-1	1-3	0-0	1-0	1-2	3-2			0-0	1-3		
95-96	2-1	2-1	2-2	0-1			1-0	2-0	2-2	1-1			1-2	0-0		
96-97	2-1	1-0	2-2	1-1			0-2	5-2	2-2	1-4			2-3	3-0		
97-98	5-1	0-1	0-2	1-3			3-3	2-2	2-1	1-6			0-2	4-4		
98-04																

	Wealdstone		Welling United		Weymouth		Witton Albion		Woking		Worcester City		Wycombe Wanderers		Yeovil Town	
	H	A	H	A	H	A	H	A	H	A	H	A	H	A	H	A
79-83																
83-84	1-1	0-4			3-0	0-2					1-1	1-3			4-2	0-0
84-85	1-2	2-4			2-2	4-5					2-2	1-4			1-1	4-0
85-86																
86-87	1-1	2-2	1-1	4-3			1-4	1-0								
87-88																
88-89																
89-90																
90-91			0-3	0-6									2-1	0-4	1-1	1-4
91-92			1-1	2-2			2-1	3-0					2-3	1-2	1-0	0-1
92-93			1-2	1-2			3-1	3-1	1-1	4-1			0-1	1-2	4-1	3-1
93-94			1-0	2-1			3-0	0-1	1-1	0-1					2-1	2-0
94-95			2-0	0-3					2-0	1-1					0-3	1-1
95-96			1-1	2-1					0-1	0-2						
96-97			1-2	0-2					3-2	1-1						
97-98			2-1	0-2					1-2	1-3					0-3	3-6
98-04																

Simon
Smith

GATESHEAD

	Home						Away					
	P	W	D	L	F	A	P	W	D	L	F	A
ALTRINCHAM	10	4	1	5	13	13	10	4	3	3	12	15
BANGOR C	1	1	0	0	2	1	1	0	1	0	3	3
BARNET	4	0	0	4	4	13	4	1	2	1	4	5
BARROW	3	1	1	1	7	4	3	1	1	1	3	4
BATH C	10	5	1	4	16	11	10	4	4	2	11	12
BOSTON U	6	1	2	3	11	14	6	2	1	3	8	16
BROMSGROVE R	5	3	1	1	4	2	5	0	2	3	5	13
CHELTENHAM T	4	1	3	0	6	5	4	0	0	4	4	10
COLCHESTER U	2	0	0	2	1	4	2	0	0	2	0	5
DAGENHAM	3	2	1	0	6	4	3	2	1	0	4	1
DAGENHAM & R	5	3	1	1	8	4	5	1	2	2	7	6
DARTFORD	1	0	1	0	0	0	1	1	0	0	2	1
DOVER A	5	1	1	3	5	8	5	2	2	1	6	6
ENFIELD	3	0	1	2	2	8	3	1	1	1	5	4
FARNBOROUGH T	6	4	1	1	8	3	6	2	0	4	8	19
FISHER A	1	1	0	0	1	0	1	1	0	0	2	0
FRICKLEY A	3	3	0	0	7	2	3	0	0	3	2	8
HALIFAX T	5	2	1	2	8	8	5	0	0	5	3	12
HAYES	2	0	2	0	2	2	2	0	1	1	0	1
HEDNESFORD T	3	0	0	3	2	9	3	1	1	1	1	3
HEREFORD U	1	0	1	0	1	1	1	0	0	1	0	1
KETTERING T	11	1	7	3	9	12	11	1	3	7	8	23
KIDDERMINSTER H	11	8	0	3	20	13	11	2	4	5	18	25
LEEK T	1	0	0	1	0	2	1	0	1	0	2	2
MACCLESFIELD T	7	4	2	1	7	3	7	0	0	7	2	18
MAIDSTONE U	3	1	0	2	3	7	3	0	0	3	0	5
MERTHYR T	5	3	1	1	7	1	5	2	1	2	8	9
MORECAMBE	3	1	0	2	4	7	3	1	0	2	3	8
NORTHWICH V	11	4	3	4	19	20	11	3	4	4	14	18
NUNEATON B	3	1	1	1	4	5	3	0	1	2	3	7
RUNCORN	9	4	3	2	17	12	9	0	4	5	10	21
RUSHDEN & D	2	2	0	0	3	1	2	1	0	1	6	3
SCARBOROUGH	3	1	1	1	4	3	3	0	1	2	4	9
SLOUGH T	7	6	1	0	13	4	7	2	1	4	5	8
SOUTHPORT	5	0	2	3	5	10	5	0	2	3	3	11
STAFFORD R	6	1	4	1	5	5	6	2	0	4	7	10
STALYBRIDGE C	6	2	3	1	6	6	6	3	1	2	12	8
STEVENAGE B	4	1	2	1	7	7	4	1	1	2	6	13
SUTTON U	2	0	1	1	1	10	2	0	1	1	3	6
TELFORD U	11	2	2	7	11	17	11	2	5	4	13	17
TROWBRIDGE T	1	1	0	0	2	2	1	1	0	0	2	0
WEALDSTONE	3	0	2	1	3	4	3	0	1	2	4	10
WELLING U	9	3	3	3	10	11	9	3	1	5	11	22
WEYMOUTH	3	1	1	1	6	6	3	1	0	2	5	7
WITTON A	3	3	0	0	8	2	3	2	0	1	6	2
WOKING	6	2	2	2	8	7	6	1	2	3	7	9
WORCESTER C	2	0	2	0	3	3	2	0	0	2	2	7
WYCOMBE W	3	1	0	2	4	5	3	0	0	3	2	8
YEOVIL T	8	4	2	2	13	12	8	3	2	3	14	13
TOTALS	231	88	65	78	316	313	231	54	58	119	270	444

GATESHEAD — LEADING APPEARANCES

	83-84	84-85	85-86	86-87	87-90	90-91	91-92	92-93	93-94	94-95	95-96	96-97	97-98	TOTAL
Simon SMITH	1	8		42		42	42	42	33	1				211
Jeff WRIGHTSON								38+1	35	40+2	41	26+1		180+4
Paul PROUDLOCK									30+10	22+11	35+6	22+4	27+6	136+37
Michael FARREY						16+7	31+3	35+2	17+2	31+3	10+9			140+26
Justin ROBSON	35	41		38								19+9	15+3	148+12
Brian ROWE									25+2	32+3	40	35	15+4	147+9
Steve HIGGINS	40	19		23		13	25+1	25+1						145+2
Derek BELL		7+2		21+1		40	40+1	32						140+4
Alan LAMB							26	40	29+6	12+18				107+24
John WATSON									18	31+3	33+3	34+4		116+10
Sam KITCHEN											38+2	40	35	113+2
Paul DOBSON								18	38+2	39	3+9			98+11
Mark HINE									32	35+1	32+7			99+8
Keith McNALL	12	35+2		36+1		12+8								95+11
Derek ORD											36+3	34+2	26+4	96+9

GATESHEAD — APPEARANCES

	83-84	84-85	85-86	86-87	87-90	90-91	91-92	92-93	93-94	94-95	95-96	96-97	97-98	TOTAL
ADAMS Steve									1+1					1+1
ALLEN Richie						21+1								21+1
ARMSTRONG Steve								1						1
ARNOTT Kevin						0+1								0+1
ASKEW Billy							4	26+12	2					32+12
ATKINSON Paddy						11+4								11+4
ATKINSON Paul						3+2								3+2
BAXTER Steve						8								8
BELL Derek		7+2		21+1		40	40+1	32						140+4
BOCHENSKI Simon												2		2
BOND Richie							2							2
BORTHWICK John									3+3					3+3
BOS Gijsbert											10			10
BOWEY Steve											8	40+1		48+1
BRABIN Gary						10	0+2							10+2
BRADY Ian											7+2			7+2
BRYSON Paul				5										5
BUTLER Charlie						26	21+13							47+13
BYRNE Wes											5+2	8+1		13+3
CAMPBELL Ian		18+1												18+1
CARTER Graeme						2								2
CARTER Mark													9	9
CAVELL Paul										16+3				16+3
CHAMBERS Steve						10								10
CHARLTON Paul											0+1			0+1

GATESHEAD APPEARANCES

	83-84	84-85	85-86	86-87	87-90	90-91	91-92	92-93	93-94	94-95	95-96	96-97	97-98	TOTAL
ADAMS Steve									1+1					1+1
ALLEN Richie				21+1										21+1
ARMSTRONG Steve								1						1
ARNOTT Kevin						0+1								0+1
ASKEW Billy							4	26+12	2					32+12
ATKINSON Paddy						11+4								11+4
ATKINSON Paul						3+2								3+2
BAXTER Steve						8								8
BELL Derek		7+2	21+1	40		40+1	32							140+4
BOCHENSKI Simon												2		2
BOND Richie							2							2
BORTHWICK John									3+3					3+3
BOS Gijsbert											10			10
BOWEY Steve											8	40+1		48+1
BRABIN Gary						10	0+2							10+2
BRADY Ian											7+2			7+2
BRYSON Paul			5											5
BUTLER Charlie				26			21+13							47+13
BYRNE Wes											5+2	8+1		13+3
CAMPBELL Ian		18+1												18+1
CARTER Graeme				2										2
CARTER Mark													9	9
CAVELL Paul									16+3					16+3
CHAMBERS Steve							10							10
CHARLTON Paul										0+1				0+1
CHILTON Tony								8+1						8+1
CLYDE Darren													4	4
COLE Anth									8+1					8+1
CONLON Paul											4			4
CONNOLLY John	6													6
CONNOLLY Stuart											1+3			1+3
CONNOR Paul													5	5
COOKE John								31+2						31+2
COPELAND Lee										2				2
CORNER David							35	26	26+6	5+1				92+7
CRAMMAN Kenny										38+2	31+1			69+3
CUGGY Steve											2+3			2+3
CULLEN Tony								1+1						1+1
CURRIE David												2+1		2+1
CUTHBERT Steve							10+2							10+2
DALZIEL Ian									7+3					7+3
DAVIES Kenny							2+1							2+1
DAVIES Peter	31+3	20+1	15+7	0+4										66+15
DAVISON George		6												6
DAVISON Wayne								5+1						5+1
DIA Aly											5+3			5+3

289

Above: Alan Lamb

Above: Derek Bell

Below: Shaun Elliott

Below: Bruce Halliday   Photo: Alan Watson

GATESHEAD   APPEARANCES

	83-84	84-85	85-86	86-87	87-90	90-91	91-92	92-93	93-94	94-95	95-96	96-97	97-98	TOTAL
DIXON Andy						24+7	5					5+1		34+8
DIXON Colin	10+1													10+1
DIXON Kevin							9+8							9+8
DOBSON Paul								18	38+2	39	3+9			98+11
DODDS Kenny	36	34												70
DONALDSON Ian	17+6	31		21+9										69+15
DOOLAN Paul		33+1		36+2	4+2									73+5
DOWSON Alan										37	11+7	7+3		55+10
EDGCUMBE Wayne												3+1	4+4	7+5
ELLIOTT Andy								2+15						2+15
ELLIOTT Shaun								28+4						28+4
EMMERSON Neil						0+2								0+2
EMSON Paul							2+2							2+2
FAGAN Mick		17		19+1										36+1
FARNABY Craig								20+8						20+8
FARREY Michael						16+7	31+3	35+2	17+2	31+3	10+9			140+26
FELL Gavin										0+2				0+2
FOREMAN Darren												7+2		7+2
FORREST Gerry							31+2							31+2
GIBSON Tony									3+1					3+1
GOURLAY Archie							2							2
GOWENS Andy						25+1								25+1
GRADY John	9+4													9+4
GRAHAM Arthur						0+2								0+2
GRANYCOME Neil						26	22+2							48+2
GRAYSON Neil							14							14
GREWCOCK Glen				7+2										7+2
GUTHRIE Peter									8					8
GUTHRIE Simon							4	21+5						25+5
HAGUE Paul											13+6			13+6
HALL Tony						30+2							12+2	42+4
HALLIDAY Bruce						20	28	33						81
HAMPSON Peter				12+3										12+3
HARKUS Steve										25+1	6+6	10+12		41+19
HARPER Steve											12			12
HARRISON Peter						15								15
HARVEY Lee									3+2					3+2
HEALEY Brian							14							14
HENDERSON Martin	19+2	26+6		37+2										82+10
HERON Chris												0+1		0+1
HEWSON Kevin	1+1													1+1
HIBBITT Terry	19+3	6		3+1										28+4
HIGGINS Steve	40	19		23				13	25+1	25+1				145+2
HINDSON Gordon	11													11
HINE Mark									32	35+1	32+7			99+8
HOLDEN Robbie		1+1												1+1

APPEARANCES

	83-84	84-85	85-86	86-87	87-90	90-91	91-92	92-93	93-94	94-95	95-96	96-97	97-98	TOTAL
HOPKINSON Marc						0+1								0+1
HOUSTON John												0+6		0+6
HOWARTH Andy												2+4		2+4
HOWEY Colin	2+6													2+6
HULSE Bob				13		9+1								22+1
HUNTER David													2	2
HURST Bobby		5+4												5+4
HUTCHINSON Steve													3+4	3+4
INNES Gary												8	10+17	18+17
JOBLIN Lance	4													4
JOHNSON Billy							6+4							6+4
JOHNSON Frank												8	2	10
JOHNSON Ian						7+1								7+1
JOHNSON Kevin		13+1												13+1
JOHNSON Paul				3+3										3+3
KETTER Delano											3+2			3+2
KEY Danny												4+4		4+4
KITCHEN Sam											38+2	40	35	113+2
LACEY Neil										9				9
LAGAVILLE Tony												0+1		0+1
LAMB Alan						26	40	29+6	12+18					107+24
LANGLEY Geoff	8+4													8+4
LEISHMAN Graham						5								5
LEONARD Gary						8+2								8+2
LINACRE Phil						11+6								11+6
LOWE Kenny				23							17+1	23+7	21	84+8
LOWERY Tony							8+2	3+3						11+5
MARQUIS Paul											6	25+1		31+1
MASON Phil							1							1
McDONALD Gary								0+3						0+3
McGARGLE Steve													0+7	0+7
McINERNEY Ian						2								2
McLEOD Bob	4+1													4+1
McNALL Keith	12	35+2		36+1		12+8								95+11
MITCHELL Kenny				7										7
MITCHINSON Dave	30	37												67
MOORE Rick													10	10
MUSGRAVE Sean										9	12+1			21+1
NICHOLLS Darren									4+7					4+7
NICHOLSON Gary								2	3					5
NICHOLSON Paul						10+9								10+9
NOBBS Keith									38+1	28+5				66+6
O'BRIEN Sean						31	11+2							42+2
O'DONNELL Paddy		17+7		9+4										26+11
O'HAGAN Paul				15										15
ORD Derek											36+3	34+2	26+4	96+9

GATESHEAD APPEARANCES

	83-84	84-85	85-86	86-87	87-90	90-91	91-92	92-93	93-94	94-95	95-96	96-97	97-98	TOTAL
ORTON Robbie	5													5
PARKINSON Ged									27	39	1+2			67+2
PARNABY Dave	31	19+3		19										69+3
PATTERSON Mark												1+4		1+4
PAYNE Lee								1						1
PEARSON Gary											18+12	4		22+12
PEARSON Jim		6												6
PEARSON Laurie	22+3													22+3
PEGG Ray		0+3												0+3
PENFOLD Brian	11	16+3												27+3
PEVERELL Nicky							2+2					14+2		16+4
PLASKETT Steve				7+4										7+4
PLATT David												6		6
PROUDLOCK Paul									30+10	22+11	35+6	22+4	27+6	136+37
PUGH Kevin	34+2													34+2
PYLE Steve								0+2						0+2
REACH Paul		13												13
ROBINSON David										6+13				6+13
ROBINSON Graham												20+3		20+3
ROBINSON Tony	15			7	3+4									25+4
ROBSON Gary										9	27+2	31		67+2
ROBSON Justin	35	41		38								19+9	15+3	148+12
ROCHE David								4						4
ROSE Colin												4+1		4+1
ROWE Brian							25+2	32+3	40	35		15+4		147+9
ROWNTREE Paul									0+1					0+1
SADDINGTON Nigel						17								17
SCAIFE Nicky										2+1				2+1
SCOPE David						2								2
SCOTT Keith				3										3
SCOTT Mark												23+6		23+6
SHARKEY Paul				20+6										20+6
SHARPE Phil								10+4						10+4
SHERWOOD Steve										30	22			52
SHIRTLIFF Paul								15						15
SKEDD Tony												5+5	0+1	5+6
SMITH George				1										1
SMITH Michael											1			1
SMITH Simon	1	8		42	42	42	42	33	1					211
STATHAM Tom					10+1									10+1
STEEL Ian				8+9										8+9
STEPHENSON Geoff							1							1
STEPHENSON Neil										0+2				0+2
STOKES Wayne					7									7
SUNDERLAND Jon												2+3		2+3
SWEENEY Paul								12+1	0+4					12+5

Top left: Paul Dobson

Top right: Kenny Lowe   Photo: Andrew Chitty

Left: Paul Proudlock   Photo: Graham Cotterill

Below: David Corner   Photo: Peter Lirettoc

GATESHEAD   GOALSCORERS

	83-84	84-85	85-86	86-87	87-90	90-91	91-92	92-93	93-94	94-95	95-96	96-97	97-98	TOTAL
ALLEN Richie						10								10
ASKEW Billy							3							3
ATKINSON Paddy				1										1
BELL Derek			1			4	1							6
BOS Gijsbert											8(1p)			8(1p)
BOWEY Steve												12(3p)		12(3p)
BRYSON Paul			1											1
BUTLER Charlie						12	4							16
CARTER Mark												1		1
CAVELL Paul									3					3
CHAMBERS Steve							2							2
CONLON Paul											2			2
CONNOLLY John	1													1
CONNOR Paul													3	3
COOKE John								5						5
CORNER David							4	3(2p)	1					8(2p)
CRAMMAN Kenny									6	6				12
CUGGY Steve											1			1
CUTHBERT Steve							4							4
DAVIES Peter	10	4	3											17
DIA Aly											2			2
DIXON Andy						1								1
DIXON Keith							3							3
DOBSON Paul								10(3p)	25(5p)	25(3p)	1(1p)			**61(12p)**
DONALDSON Ian	6	17	9											32
DOOLAN Paul			3											3
DOWSON Alan									2					2
EDGCUMBE Wayne											1			1
ELLIOTT Andy								1						1
EMSON Paul							1							1
FAGAN Mick		2	1											3
FARNABY Craig								4						4
FARREY Michael								7	3	2				12
FOREMAN Darren											2			2
FORREST Gerry							1							1
GOURLAY Archie							1							1
GOWENS Andy						1								1
GRANYCOME Neil						5	1							6
GRAYSON Neil							3							3
GUTHRIE Simon							1	2						3
HALL Tony						1							1	2
HALLIDAY Bruce						1	1							2
HARKUS Steve										19(2p)	5	5		29(2p)
HARRISON Peter						1								1
HEALEY Brian							2							2
HENDERSON Martin	5	5	7											17
HIBBITT Terry	3													3
HIGGINS Steve	1	1						2						4
HINDSON Gordon	1													1

GATESHEAD   GOALSCORERS

	83-84	84-85	85-86	86-87	87-90	90-91	91-92	92-93	93-94	94-95	95-96	96-97	97-98	TOTAL
HINE Mark									2	5	1			8
HOLDEN Robbie		1												1
HUTCHINSON Steve												1		1
INNES Gary											1	4		5
JOHNSON Kevin		1												1
KITCHEN Sam												1		1
LACEY Neil										1				1
LAMB Alan						14	15(1p)	4	6					39(1p)
LANGLEY Geoff	1													1
LINACRE Phil						4								4
LOWE Kenny				2							1	1		4
MARQUIS Paul											1		3	4
McNALL Keith	7	11		10	2									30
MITCHINSON Dave	3													3
NICHOLSON Paul					2									2
NOBBS Keith									1					1
O'BRIEN Sean				1										1
O'DONNELL Paddy		1												1
ORD Derek											5	2		7
PARKINSON Ged									1					1
PARNABY Dave	1	2		1										4
PEARSON Gary											2	1		3
PEARSON Jim		1												1
PENFOLD Brian		1												1
PEVERELL Nicky													3	3
PROUDLOCK Paul									3	4	7	7	7	28
PUGH Kevin	5													5
ROBINSON David										2				2
ROBINSON Graham													7	7
ROBINSON Tony				1										1
ROBSON Gary											1	1		2
ROBSON Justin		3		1							2			6
ROWE Brian									3					3
SCOTT Keith					4									4
SHARKEY Paul					4									4
SHARPE Phil									2					2
SKEDD Tony											1			1
STATHAM Tom					3									3
STEEL Ian				1										1
THOMPSON Paul											8(1p)	15(5p)		23(6p)
TOPPING Bob	13													13
TROTT Dean											8			8
TWEEDY John	2	1												3
VEART Craig							1							1
WARDROBE Barry				6										6
WATSON John										1	1	3		5
WHITMARSH Paul									1					1
WRIGHTSON Jeff												1		1

GRAVESEND & NORTHFLEET

FOUNDER MEMBER elected from The Southern League
PROMOTED FROM: The Isthmian League 2001-02
RELEGATED TO: The Southern League 1981-82
2004-2005 SEASON: The Conference

Season 2003-2004 Back row, left to right: Anthony Hogg, Andrew Drury, Kevin Budge, Lee Shearer, Jimmy Strouts, Robin Trott and Louie Evans. Middle Row: Neil Withington, James Bent, Rob Owen, Jake Slade, Perry Spackman, Terry Penfold, Robbie Grace, Eddie McClements and Ron Hilyard. Front row: Dave Lawson, Matt Lee, Justin Skinner, Steve McKimm, Andy Ford, Patrick Gradley, James Pinnock and Gary Farr.

		HOME						AWAY						
		P	W	D	L	F	A	Pts	P	W	D	L	F	A	Pts	Position
SEASONS 5	**79-80**	19	12	4	3	36	18	28	19	5	6	8	13	26	16	5
TOTAL POINTS 223	**80-81**	19	8	4	7	26	21	20	19	5	4	10	22	34	14	15
HIGHEST POSITION 5th 1979-80	**81-82**	21	7	6	8	34	31	27	21	3	4	14	17	38	13	20
LOWEST POSITION 20th 1981-82						1982 - 2002										
HIGHEST ATTENDANCE 2051 v Dartford 18.8.82	**02-03**	21	8	5	8	37	35	29	21	4	7	10	25	38	19	17
LOWEST ATTENDANCE 552 v Bangor C. 2.5.81	**03-04**	21	7	6	8	34	35	27	21	7	9	5	35	31	30	11
SEASON GOALSCORER Phil Stonebridge 15 (79/80)	**Total**	101	42	25	34	167	140	131	101	24	30	47	112	167	92	
CAREER GOALSCORER Phil Stonebridge 26																
CAREER APPEARANCES Geoff Idle 107																

	Accrington Stanley		Aldershot Town		Altrincham		A P Leamington		Bangor City		Barnet		Barrow		Bath City		Boston United	
	H	A	H	A	H	A	H	A	H	A	H	A	H	A	H	A	H	A
79-80					0-2	1-4	3-2	1-0	1-1	2-1	1-0	0-3	5-1	1-1	2-0	0-2	0-0	0-4
80-81					0-2	1-2	4-0	1-4	1-0	1-1	0-2	1-1	0-2	1-3	2-1	0-1	1-2	1-2
81-82					1-1	1-3	4-1	3-3			2-3	0-2	3-1	1-3	0-2	0-1	3-1	2-2
1982 to 2002																		
02-03											2-2	4-1						
03-04	0-0	3-3	1-3	2-2							1-1	0-1						

	Burton Albion		Chester City		Dagenham		Dagenham & Redbridge		Dartford		Doncaster Rovers		Enfield		Exeter City		Farnborough Town	
	H	A	H	A	H	A	H	A	H	A	H	A	H	A	H	A	H	A
79-80																		
80-81																		
81-82					1-2	1-1			1-0	1-0			1-2	0-4				
1982 to 2002																		
02-03	3-2	1-1	0-1	1-1			1-2	0-4			2-2	1-4					0-0	1-1
03-04	1-2	0-3	0-4	2-2			1-2	4-0							3-2	1-0	2-0	2-1

	Forest Green Rovers		Frickley Athletic		Halifax Town		Hereford United		Kettering Town		Leigh RMI		Maidstone United		Margate		Morecambe	
	H	A	H	A	H	A	H	A	H	A	H	A	H	A	H	A	H	A
79-80									2-2	0-0			1-0	0-3				
80-81			3-1	4-2					1-0	0-2			1-2	1-1				
81-82			4-1	1-1					1-3	1-2			2-2	1-0				
1982 to 2002																		
02-03	1-1	1-2			1-0	1-2	3-0	0-3	0-2	1-1	1-3	0-0			1-2	2-4	3-2	0-2
03-04	1-1	2-1			1-0	0-1	2-5	3-3			3-1	2-1			2-1	3-1	6-0	2-2

GRAVESEND & NORTHFLEET

	Northwich Victoria		Nuneaton Borough		Redditch United		Runcorn		Scarborough		Shrewsbury Town		Southport		Stafford Rangers		Stevenage Borough	
	H	A	H	A	H	A	H	A	H	A	H	A	H	A	H	A	H	A
79-80	2-1	0-0	2-2	1-3	1-0	2-0			3-0	1-1					2-0	1-0		
80-81	0-1	0-4	4-0	2-1					1-1	0-1					1-1	3-2		
81-82	0-1	0-1					2-4	0-1	3-0	0-5					1-1	0-1		
1982 to 2002																		
02-03	1-1	2-1	4-1	1-0					5-2	2-3			1-3	1-1			2-1	0-1
03-04	2-2	0-0							1-1	0-2	0-3	1-1					2-3	2-2

	Tamworth		Telford United		Trowbridge Town		Wealdstone		Weymouth		Woking		Worcester City		Yeovil Town	
	H	A	H	A	H	A	H	A	H	A	H	A	H	A	H	A
79-80			1-2	2-1			3-0	0-0	2-3	0-1			3-2	0-1	2-0	1-1
80-81			2-2	0-0			0-1	1-3	1-0	1-0			2-1	1-3	2-2	3-1
81-82			0-2	0-1	1-1	1-2			2-1	2-1			1-1	1-2	1-1	1-2
1982 to 2002																
02-03			0-2	1-2							4-2	3-2			2-4	2-2
03-04	2-0	3-1	1-2	1-1							2-2	2-3				

Season 2002-2003 with trophies won in 2001-2002. Back row, left to right: Ron Hillyard (goalkeeping coach), Jimmy Strouts, Lew Watts, Mark Bentley, Robert Owen, Jamie Turner, Paul Wilkerson, Craig Wilkins, Liam Hatch, Danny Lye, Paul Booth, Aaron Barnett and Neil Witherton (Fitness Coach). Front row: Martin Allen (physio), Lewis Phillip, Adolph Amoko, Steve McKimm, Justin Skinner, Phil Handford (Asst. Man.), Andy Ford (Manager), Jimmy Jackson (captain), Darren Smith, Austin Berkley, Matt Lee and Eliot Martin (Reserve Team Coach)

	Home						Away					
	P	W	D	L	F	A	P	W	D	L	F	A
ACCRINGTON S	1	0	1	0	0	0	1	0	1	0	3	3
ALDERSHOT T	1	0	0	1	1	3	1	0	1	0	2	2
ALTRINCHAM	3	0	1	2	1	5	3	0	0	3	3	9
A P LEAMINGTON	3	3	0	0	11	3	3	1	1	1	5	7
BANGOR C	2	1	1	0	2	1	2	1	1	0	3	2
BARNET	5	1	2	2	6	8	5	1	1	3	5	8
BARROW	3	2	0	1	8	4	3	0	1	2	3	7
BATH C	3	2	0	1	4	3	3	0	0	3	0	4
BOSTON U	3	1	1	1	4	3	3	0	1	2	3	8
BURTON A	2	1	0	1	4	4	2	0	1	1	1	4
CHESTER C	2	0	0	2	0	5	2	0	2	0	3	3
DAGENHAM	1	0	0	1	1	2	1	0	1	0	1	1
DAGENHAM & R	2	0	0	2	2	4	2	1	0	1	4	4
DARTFORD	1	1	0	0	1	0	1	1	0	0	1	0
DONCASTER R	1	0	1	0	2	2	1	0	0	1	1	4
ENFIELD	1	0	0	1	1	2	1	0	0	1	0	4
EXETER C	1	1	0	0	3	2	1	1	0	0	1	0
FARNBOROUGH T	2	1	1	0	2	0	2	1	1	0	3	2
FOREST GREEN R	2	0	2	0	2	2	2	1	0	1	3	3
FRICKLEY A	2	2	0	0	7	2	2	1	1	0	5	3
HALIFAX T	2	2	0	0	2	0	2	0	0	2	1	3
HEREFORD U	2	1	0	1	5	5	2	0	1	1	3	6
KETTERING T	4	1	1	2	4	7	4	0	2	2	2	5
LEIGH RMI	2	1	0	1	4	4	2	1	1	0	2	1
MAIDSTONE U	3	1	1	1	4	4	3	1	1	1	2	4
MARGATE	2	1	0	1	3	3	2	1	0	1	5	5
MORECAMBE	2	2	0	0	9	2	2	0	1	1	2	4
NORTHWICH V	5	1	2	2	5	6	5	1	2	2	2	6
NUNEATON B	3	2	1	0	10	3	3	2	0	1	4	4
REDDITCH U	1	1	0	0	1	0	1	1	0	0	2	0
RUNCORN	1	0	0	1	2	4	1	0	0	1	0	1
SCARBOROUGH	5	3	2	0	13	4	5	0	1	4	3	12
SHREWSBURY T	1	0	0	1	0	3	1	0	1	0	1	1
SOUTHPORT	1	0	0	1	1	3	1	0	1	0	1	1
STAFFORD R	3	1	2	0	4	2	3	2	0	1	4	3
STEVENAGE B	2	1	0	1	4	4	2	0	1	1	2	3
TAMWORTH	1	1	0	0	2	0	1	1	0	0	3	1
TELFORD U	5	0	1	4	4	10	5	1	2	2	4	5
TROWBRIDGE T	1	0	1	0	1	1	1	0	0	1	1	2
WEALDSTONE	2	1	0	1	3	1	2	0	1	1	1	3
WEYMOUTH	3	2	0	1	5	4	3	2	0	1	3	2
WOKING	2	1	1	0	6	4	2	1	0	1	5	5
WORCESTER C	3	2	1	0	6	4	3	0	0	3	2	6
YEOVIL T	4	1	2	1	7	7	4	1	2	1	7	6
TOTAL	101	42	25	34	167	140	101	24	30	47	112	167

Mass defence at Gravesend, left to right:
Jimmy Strouts, Liam Hatch (hidden), Darren Smith (21), Justin Skinner and Matt Lee (2)
Photo: Alan Coomes.

GRAVESEND & NORTHFLEET   APPEARANCES

	79-80	80-81	81-82	1982	to	2002	02-03	03-04	TOTAL
ABBEY Ben								11+12	11+12
ABBOTT Gary							4		4
ALDOUS Gary		12+7							12+7
ARMSTRONG Gary			4						4
BARNETT Aaron							10+3		10+3
BARR Hamid							6		6
BATTERSBY Tony								0+1	0+1
BENTLEY Mark							27		27
BERKELEY Austin							0+3		0+3
BOOTH Paul							7+6		7+6
BROWN Steve	20+4	9							29+4
BRYANT Jeff	9+1	36+1	40						85+2
BUDGE Kevin							7+3		7+3
BURRETT Ken	22+1	31	33						86+1
BURTON Nick							29+1		29+1
BUSBY Dave	14+1	10+2							24+3
CARTER Jamie							0+2		0+2
COLE Tim							5		5
COYLE Jamie							3+1		3+1
DALY Wes								0+1	0+1
DAUBNEY John			7						7
DOUST Tommy			4						4
DRURY Andy								25+6	25+6
DUDMAN Bob	36+2	35	32+2						**103+4**
DUKU Francis							7	17+2	24+2
DYER Paul		18+2	15						33+2
ESSANDOH Roy								14	14
EVANS Louie							7+8	1+6	8+14
FINN Anthony								0+1	0+1
FRANKLIN Graham	2+1								2+1
GALVIN Dave	7+1	9							16+1
GEDLING Luke							0+1		0+1
GIBBS Paul								2	2
GILES Chris							11		11
GLEDHILL Lee								12+1	12+1
GOODWIN Scott								0+2	0+2
GRACE Robbie							0+4		0+4
GRADLEY Pat								12+1	12+1
GREGORY Brian	17+4	8+2							25+6
GREGORY Dave			15						15
HARDING Paul	3	13+1	21						37+1
HART Alan	30	31+1	34+1						95+2
HATCH Liam							17+6		17+6
HAWORTH Rob								21+1	21+1
HUBBICK Dave			25						25
HUGGINS Leroy								2	2
IDLE Geoff	34	35	38						**107**
JACKS George	29+2	27							56+2
JACKSON Jimmy							41		41
KEIRS John	26								26

301

Aaron Barnett clashes with Yeovil Town's Andy Lindegard   Photo: Alan Coomes.

Jimmy Jackson. Photo: Darren C Thomas.

Robert Owen. Photo: Darren C Thomas.

GRAVESEND & NORTHFLEET   APPEARANCES

	79-80	80-81	81-82	1982	to	2002	02-03	03-04	TOTAL
KNIGHTS P			1						1
KWASHI Tostao							18+16	1+1	19+17
LEE Matt							23	25+4	48+4
LEWINGTON Colin		30	36						66
LOVETT Jay							5		5
LYE Danny							5		5
MARRINER Graham			9						9
McCLEMENTS Eddie								12+1	12+1
McKIMM Steve							22+2	36+2	58+4
McVEIGH Jimmy			5						5
MILLER Adam								4	4
MITTEN Charlie								5	5
MOORE Chris								33	33
NUTTER John							3+1		3+1
OLI Dennis								5	5
OMOYINMI Manny								4+3	4+3
O'REILLY Alex								10+1	10+1
OSBORNE Peter	22+1								22+1
OWEN Robert							15+6	30+3	45+9
PAIN Vic	1+3								1+3
PARKER Simon							2+7		2+7
PENN Nicky		8	6						14
PENNOCK Adrian							10	4	14
PERKINS Steve								30+7	30+7
PINNOCK Jamie								22+8	22+8
PLUMMER Dwayne							0+1		0+1
POOLEY Charlie		20							20
PROTHEROE Lee								10	10
PUGH Gary			20+2						20+2
REYNOLDS Kenny		2							2
RICHARDSON Damien			25+1						25+1
RISK Alan			6+1						6+1
ROUSE Matthew								1+1	1+1
SHEARER Lee								26+3	26+3
SIDIBE Moussa								5+7	5+7
SKINNER Justin							23+1		23+1
SKINNER Justin								26	26
SMELT Lee	38								38
SMELT Marc		1+1							1+1
SMITH Steve	1+2								1+2
SMITH Trevor		24+1	29+6						53+7
SODJE Akpo							4+3		4+3
STADHART Che							29+5		29+5
STONEBRIDGE Phil	34	32+3	6+4						72+7
STREETER Malcolm	36		1						37
STROUTS Jimmy							31+3	4+7	35+10
STURGESS Paul							8		8
SUREY Ben								7+1	7+1
TODD Kenny			8						8
TOPPIN Carl		4+3	10+2						14+5
TROTT Robin								1+1	1+1

GRAVESEND & NORTHFLEET — APPEARANCES

	79-80	80-81	81-82	1982	to	2002	02-03	03-04	TOTAL
TURNER Jamie							2		2
WALLIS Kevin	12+2								12+2
WALSHE Ben								17+6	17+6
WARD Jamie			5+4						5+4
WATTS Len							13+2		13+2
WHITE Ben							9		9
WILKERSON Paul							40	27+1	67+1
WILKINS Craig							19+6		19+6
WILLIAMS Gary		19+1	20+4						39+5
WILLIAMS John	25	4							29
WOTHERSPOON Keith			7+2						7+2

Craig Wilkins gets in a challenge against Yeovil Town
Photo: Alan Coomes.

Paul Wilkerson punches clear.
Photo: Alan Coomes.

GRAVESEND & NORTHFLEET — GOALSCORERS

	79-80	80-81	81-82	1982	to	2002	02-03	03-04	TOTAL
ABBEY Ben								6	6
ALDOUS Gary		5							5
BARNETT Aaron							1		1
BENTLEY Mark							7		7
BOOTH Paul							2(1p)		2(1p)
BROWN Steve	8	2(1p)							10(1p)
BRYANT Jeff	2	5	9						16
BUDGE Kevin							1		1
BURRETT Ken			2						2
BURTON Nick							3		3

GRAVESEND & NORTHFLEET GOALSCORERS

	79-80	80-81	81-82	1982 to 2002	02-03	03-04	TOTAL
BUSBY Dave	4	3					7
COLE Tim					1		1
DAUBNEY John			1				1
DOUST Timmy			1				1
DRURY Andy						9(3p)	9(3p)
DUDMAN Bob	1	6(1p)	3(3p)				10(4p)
DUKU Francis					2	1	3
DYER Paul		1					1
ESSANDOH Roy						10	10
EVANS Louie					1	1	2
GALVIN Dave	1						1
GILES Chris					2		2
GRADLEY Pat						2	2
GREGORY Brian	2	2					4
HART Alan	1	3	4				8
HATCH Liam					7		7
HAWORTH Rob						6	6
HUBBICK Dave			6				6
IDLE Geoff	2		1				3
JACKS George	3						3
JACKSON Jimmy					7		7
KWASHI Tostao					5		5
LEE Matt						1	1
LYE Danny					1		1
MARRINER Graham			1				1
McKIMM Steve					1	1	2
MILLER Adam						1	1
MOORE Chris						7	7
OMOYINMI Manny						2	2
OSBORNE Peter	5						5
OWEN Robert						2	2
PAIN Vic	1						1
PERKINS Steve						6	6
PINNOCK Jamie						9	9
POOLEY Charlie		4					4
PUGH Gary			8				8
RICHARDSON Damien			5				5
SHEARER Lee						1	1
SIDIBE Moussa						1	1
SMITH Trevor		6	6				12
SODJE Akpo					2		2
STADHART Che					12(2p)		12(2p)
STONEBRIDGE Phil	15	10	1				26
STREETER Malcolm	1						1
STROUTS Jimmy					3	1	4
TODD Kenny			1				1
WALLIS Kevin	2						2
WALSHE Ben						2	2
WILKINS Craig					2		2
WILLIAMS Gary			1				1

Invest in land – make 60% profit and your football club will get 4% commission.

Ring **01403 262646**

or email
michelle@gladwish.com
to order

or visit: **www.GLSfootball.com**

HALIFAX TOWN

RELEGATED FROM: The Football League 1992-93, 2001-02
PROMOTED TO: The Football League 1997-98
2004-2005 SEASON: The Conference

Season 1997-98. Back row, left to right: Paul Hand, Darren Lyons, Peter Jackson, Lee Williams, Paul Stoneman, Noel Horner, Geoff Horsfield, Ady Thackeray and Mark Bradshaw. Middle Row: Alan Russell-Cox(Physio), Martin Ayscough, Chris Newton, Gareth Hamlet, Paul Trudgill, Michael Rosser, Karl Cochrne, Phil McDonald, Ryan Gonsalves, Billy Callaghan and David Worthington (Reserve Team Manager) Front row: Damian Place, Willie Griffiths, Kieron O'Regan (Player/Coach), George Mulhall (Manager), Jamie Paterson, Jon Brown, Gary Brook and Kevin Hulme.

			HOME							AWAY					
		P	W	D	L	F	A	Pts	P	W	D	L	F	A	Pts	Position
93-94		21	7	9	5	28	18	30	21	6	7	8	27	31	25	13
94-95		21	11	6	4	46	20	39	21	6	6	9	22	34	24	8
95-96		21	8	7	6	30	25	31	21	5	6	10	19	38	21	15
96-97		21	9	5	7	39	37	32	21	3	7	11	16	37	16	19
97-98		21	17	4	0	51	15	55	21	8	8	5	23	28	32	1
						1998-2002										
02-03		21	11	5	5	34	28	38	21	7	5	9	16	23	26	8
03-04		21	9	4	8	28	26	31	21	3	4	14	15	39	13	19
Total		147	72	40	35	256	169	256	147	38	43	66	138	230	157	

SEASONS
7

TOTAL POINTS
413

HIGHEST POSITION
1st 1997-98

LOWEST POSITION
19th 1996-97, 2003-04

HIGHEST ATTENDANCE
6357 v Cheltenham T. 25.4.98

LOWEST ATTENDANCE
509 v Stalybridge C. 5.3.96

SEASON GOALSCORER
Geoff Horsfield 30 (97/8)

CAREER GOALSCORER
Geoff Horsfield 39

CAREER APPEARANCES
Paul Stoneman 118+2

	Accrington Stanley		Aldershot Town		Altrincham		Barnet		Bath City		Bromsgrove Rovers		Burton Albion		Cheltenham Town		Chester City	
	H	A	H	A	H	A	H	A	H	A	H	A	H	A	H	A	H	A
93-94					0-0	0-0			0-0	2-2	3-0	0-1						
94-95					1-1	1-3			4-2	0-0	4-2	1-0						
95-96					1-1	2-3			3-1	1-2	1-1	1-0						
96-97					1-1	1-2			4-5	0-0	1-0	0-3						
97-98															1-1	0-4		
98-02	-		-		-		-		-		-		-		-		-	
02-03							2-4	0-0					0-1	2-2			0-0	0-2
03-04	1-1	1-2	1-2	1-3			1-2	1-4					1-4	2-2			0-3	0-2

	Dagenham & Redbridge		Doncaster Rovers		Dover Athletic		Exeter City		Farnborough Town		Forest Green Rovers		Gateshead		Gravesend & N'fleet		Hayes	
	H	A	H	A	H	A	H	A	H	A	H	A	H	A	H	A	H	A
93-94	0-1	0-3			0-1	2-1							3-1	1-2				
94-95	1-1	4-1			4-0	1-1			0-1	0-2			3-2	2-1				
95-96	3-0	1-1			1-0	2-3			0-0	0-0			2-0	2-3				
96-97					1-3	2-2			3-0	0-3			2-0	1-0			2-2	0-0
97-98					1-1	1-0			1-0	2-1			2-0	2-2			1-1	2-1
98-02	-		-		-		-		-		-		-		-		-	
02-03	3-3	0-0	2-1	0-0					1-0	0-3	1-1	2-0			2-1	0-1		
03-04	3-0	1-0					2-0	1-1	2-0	0-1	0-1	2-1			1-0	0-1		

	Hednesford Town		Hereford United		Kettering Town		Kidderminster H.		Leek Town		Leigh RMI		Macclesfield Town		Margate		Merthyr Tydfil	
	H	A	H	A	H	A	H	A	H	A	H	A	H	A	H	A	H	A
93-94					0-0	1-0	1-0	1-2					1-2	1-0			2-1	1-2
94-95					2-1	1-5	1-2	0-3					0-1	1-1			2-2	0-2
95-96	1-3	0-3			2-0	2-1	0-2	1-6					1-0	0-7				
96-97	1-0	1-1			2-1	1-4	2-3	0-3					3-3	0-1				
97-98	1-1	0-0	3-0	0-0	3-0	1-1	2-1	2-0	2-1	0-2								
98-02	-		-		-		-		-		-		-		-		-	
02-03			1-0	1-1	4-0	1-0					1-0	2-0			2-2	1-2		
03-04			1-2	1-7							2-1	1-1			0-1	0-2		

HALIFAX TOWN

	Morecambe		Northwich Victoria		Nuneaton Borough		Runcorn		Rushden & Diamonds		Scarborough		Shrewsbury Town		Slough Town		Southport	
	H	A	H	A	H	A	H	A	H	A	H	A	H	A	H	A	H	A
93-94			1-2	2-0			1-1	0-5							1-0	0-2	2-2	2-2
94-95			0-0	0-3			4-0	3-0							1-2	3-2	2-0	0-4
95-96	1-1	1-0	2-0	1-1			1-3	1-0							4-1	0-1	2-2	0-0
96-97	1-1	0-1	0-3	2-2							1-3	0-1			1-0	1-1	2-0	1-2
97-98	5-1	1-1	4-2	0-2							2-0	0-4					4-3	0-0
98-02	-		-		-		-		-		-		-		-		-	
02-03	1-0	0-2	0-5	2-0	3-1	0-2					2-1	1-0					3-4	0-2
03-04	1-0	0-2	5-3	1-0							1-0	0-1	0-0	0-2				

	Stafford Rangers		Stalybridge Celtic		Stevenage Borough		Tamworth		Telford United		Welling United		Witton Albion		Woking		Yeovil Town	
	H	A	H	A	H	A	H	A	H	A	H	A	H	A	H	A	H	A
93-94	1-1	1-1	2-1	1-1					6-0	2-3	1-1	2-0	0-0	2-2	2-3	6-2	1-1	0-0
94-95	6-0	1-0	1-1	1-1	0-2	0-1			1-1	1-1	4-0	1-1			4-0	3-1	2-1	1-3
95-96			2-3	0-1	2-3	0-2			0-0	1-1	2-1	0-0			2-2	0-2		
96-97			4-1	3-2	4-2	0-6			0-3	1-1	1-1	1-0			0-4	2-2		
97-98			3-1	1-0	4-0	2-1			6-1	3-0	1-0	2-6			1-0	2-2	3-1	1-0
98-02	-		-		-		-		-		-		-		-		-	
02-03					1-0	1-0			2-0	2-1					1-1	1-2	2-3	0-3
03-04					2-1	0-1	1-2	0-2	1-1	1-2					2-2	2-2		

Season 1994-95. Back row, left to right: William Griffiths, Andrew Hemingway, Chris Horsfall, Damian Place and Paul Hand. Middle Row: Darran Heyes, Danny Megson, Noel Horner, Lee Ludlow, Michael Midwood, Paul Stoneman, Michael Trotter, Gary Worthington, Elliott Beddard and Andy Woods. Front Row: Alan Russell Cox (Physio), Simon Johnson, Lee Wilson, Simon Thompson, John Bird (Manager), Jon Brown, Steve Prindiville, Kieran O'Regan and Geoge Mulhall(Assistant Manager).
Photo: Halifax Evening Courier.

Mark Bradshaw. Photo: Andrew Chitty.

Gary Brook. Photo: R.Sims.

Steve Burr. Photo: K. Gillard.

Darren Heyes. Photo: V.J.Robertson.

	Home						Away					
	P	W	D	L	F	A	P	W	D	L	F	A
ACCRINGTON S	1	0	1	0	1	1	1	0	0	1	1	2
ALDERSHOT T	1	0	0	1	1	2	1	0	0	1	1	3
ALTRINCHAM	4	0	4	0	3	3	4	0	1	3	4	8
BARNET	2	0	0	2	3	6	2	0	1	1	1	4
BATH C	4	2	1	1	11	8	4	0	3	1	3	4
BROMSGROVE R	4	3	1	0	9	3	4	2	0	2	2	4
BURTON A	2	0	0	2	1	5	2	0	2	0	4	4
CHELTENHAM T	1	0	1	0	1	1	1	0	0	1	0	4
CHESTER C	2	0	1	1	0	3	2	0	0	2	0	4
DAGENHAM & R	5	2	2	1	10	5	5	2	2	1	6	5
DONCASTER R	1	1	0	0	2	1	1	0	1	0	0	0
DOVER A	5	2	1	2	7	5	5	2	2	1	8	7
EXETER C	1	1	0	0	2	0	1	0	1	0	1	1
FARNBOROUGH T	6	4	1	1	7	1	6	1	1	4	2	10
FOREST GREEN R	2	0	1	1	1	2	2	2	0	0	4	1
GATESHEAD	5	5	0	0	12	3	5	2	1	2	8	8
GRAVESEND & N	2	2	0	0	3	1	2	0	0	2	0	2
HAYES	2	0	2	0	3	3	2	1	1	0	2	1
HEDNESFORD T	3	1	1	1	3	4	3	0	2	1	1	4
HEREFORD U	3	2	0	1	5	2	3	0	2	1	2	8
KETTERING T	6	5	1	0	13	2	6	3	1	2	7	11
KIDDERMINSTER H	5	2	0	3	6	8	5	1	0	4	4	14
LEEK T	1	1	0	0	2	1	1	0	0	1	0	2
LEIGH RMI	2	2	0	0	3	1	2	1	1	0	3	1
MACCLESFIELD T	4	1	1	2	5	6	4	1	1	2	2	9
MARGATE	2	0	1	1	2	3	2	0	0	2	1	4
MERTHYR T	2	1	1	0	4	3	2	0	0	2	1	4
MORECAMBE	5	3	2	0	9	3	5	1	1	3	2	6
NORTHWICH V	7	3	1	3	12	15	7	3	2	2	8	8
NUNEATON B	1	1	0	0	3	1	1	0	0	1	0	2
RUNCORN	3	1	1	1	6	4	3	2	0	1	4	5
RUSHDEN & D	2	1	0	1	3	3	2	0	0	2	0	5
SCARBOROUGH	2	2	0	0	3	1	2	1	0	1	1	1
SHREWSBURY T	1	0	1	0	0	0	1	0	0	1	0	2
SLOUGH T	4	3	0	1	7	3	4	1	1	2	4	6
SOUTHPORT	6	3	2	1	15	11	6	0	3	3	3	10
STAFFORD R	2	1	1	0	7	1	2	1	1	0	2	1
STALYBRIDGE C	5	3	1	1	12	7	5	2	2	1	6	5
STEVENAGE B	6	4	0	2	13	8	6	2	0	4	3	11
TAMWORTH	1	0	0	1	1	2	1	0	0	1	0	2
TELFORD U	7	3	3	1	16	6	7	2	3	2	11	9
WELLING U	5	3	2	0	9	3	5	2	2	1	6	7
WITTON A	1	0	1	0	0	0	1	0	1	0	2	2
WOKING	7	2	3	2	12	12	7	2	3	2	16	13
YEOVIL T	4	2	1	1	8	6	4	1	1	2	2	6
TOTAL	147	72	40	35	256	169	147	38	43	66	138	230

HALIFAX TOWN — APPEARANCES

	93-94	94-95	95-96	96-97	97-98	98-02	02-03	03-04	TOTAL
ADEKOLA David		2							2
ALLAN Jon								9+5	9+5
ANNAN Richard			20+1						20+1
ASHER Alistair							34+1		34+1
BARR Billy	39								39
BECKFORD Jason				3					3
BEDDARD Eliot		6+7	8+9						14+16
BENN Wayne			1						1
BOARDMAN Craig	28	32+1			4+1				64+2
BRACEY Lee	1								1
BRADSHAW Mark					42				42
BROOK Gary			11+3	34+4	18+4				63+11
BROWN Jimmy				7+2					7+2
BROWN Jonathan			33+1	31+2	37				**101+3**
BROWN Nick	3								3
BURR Steve	8								8
BUSHELL Steve							34	37+1	71+1
BUTLER Lee							37		37
CAMERON Dave								6+3	6+3
CAMERON Jim	2+1								2+1
CAMERON Mark				0+2					0+2
CARNEY David								2+1	2+1
CARTWRIGHT Mark								32	32
CIRCUIT Steve		1							1
CLARKSON Phil							38		38
COCHRANE Karl			16+6	2+2					18+8
COLLEY Karl								6+1	6+1
COLLINS Simon	1+2								1+2
CONSTABLE Sean	20+9		4+1						24+10
COSTELLO Peter	2								2
COX Paul				22+1					22+1
CRAVEN Peter	26								26
CROSBY Andy	0+1								0+1
CULLEN Jon								7	7
DAVIES Clint								8	8
DAVISON Bobby				11+14					11+14
DAWS Tony			5						5
DONALDSON Clayton								2+2	2+2
DUDGEON James								9+1	9+1
DUNPHY Sean		2							2
EDWARDS Elfyn	25+1								25+1
ELAM Lee								14+1	14+1
ELLIOTT Stuart							9+3		9+3
ELLISON Lee				1+1					1+1
FARRELL Andy							13+17	6+12	19+29
FILSON Martin	10+3								10+3
FITZPATRICK Ian							29+9		29+9
FLEMING Paul		23							23
FLOUNDERS Andy		9+2							9+2
FORD Stuaret		5							5

HALIFAX TOWN   APPEARANCES

	93-94	94-95	95-96	96-97	97-98	98-02	02-03	03-04	TOTAL
FOWLER Lee		12+3							12+3
FRANCE Darren	0+2								0+2
FRANCIS John				2					2
GARNETT Shaun							29	11	40
GEDMAN Paul							0+2		0+2
GERMAN Dave	20+8	22+6							42+14
GIBSON Paul				3					3
GOLDEN Ryan								0+1	0+1
GOULDING Derek				8+1					8+1
GRAHAM Deiniol			1						1
GRAY Ryan	0+1	0+2							0+3
GRAYSTON Neil							23+9		23+9
GREENWOOD Nigel	3								3
GREGORY Terry	5+1								5+1
GRIFFITHS Willie					0+2				0+2
HAIGH Phil							9+2		9+2
HALL David		4+1							4+1
HANSON Dave	12+1	26+4			6+4				44+9
HARDY Jason	5+3								5+3
HAROLD Ian				4					4
HART Ian			0+1						0+1
HARTFIELD Charlie							2		2
HENDRICK John			25+3	8+3					33+6
HERBERT Robert							0+3		0+3
HEYES Darren	18	28	17	1					64
HIGGINS David	2+3								2+3
HOCKENHULL Darren							27+4		27+4
HOOK Steve	1+1								1+1
HORNER Noel		1	17+7	27+10	10+8				55+25
HORSFIELD Geoff	6+3		19+5	40					65+8
HOYLE Matthew								0+1	0+1
HUDSON Danny								21+7	21+7
HULME Kevin				21	30				51
HURST Chris					2+1				2+1
HUTCHINSON Ian		9+2							9+2
INGLEDOW Jamie							0+1		0+1
INGRAM Denny								6	6
JACKSON Peter					8				8
JOHNSON Simon		4	15+2						19+2
JONES Alex	12	39							51
KELLY Tony				0+1					0+1
KERRIGAN Steve							4+5		4+5
KILCLINE Brian					23+1				23+1
KILLEEN Lewis							13	29+3	42+3
KIWOMYA Andy		29+1			0+5				29+6
LAMBERT Colin	20	38+1							58+1
LANCASTER Dave		21+3							21+3
LANGLEY Kevin		13+1							13+1
LEE Andy				8					8
LEE Christian								17+9	17+9

Geoff Horsfield. Photo: Peter Barnes.

Kevin Hulme. Photo: Peter Barnes.

Alex Jones. Photo: Gavin Ellis-Neville.

Brian Kilcline. Photo: Peter Barnes.

HALIFAX TOWN APPEARANCES

	93-94	94-95	95-96	96-97	97-98	98-02	02-03	03-04	TOTAL
LEE Glen			4+1						4+1
LEITCH Grant		11							11
LITTLE Colin								8	8
LORMOR Tony	7								7
LOWE Scott								2	2
LUCKETTI Chris	8								8
LUDLOW Lee			0+3						0+3
LYONS Darren				14+3	13+11				27+14
MALLON Ryan							16+2	29+8	45+10
MARTIN Dean		5+1		17					22+1
MARTIN Lee					32				32
MAY Rory							2+1		2+1
McAULEY Sean							6+4	11+4	17+8
McCOMBE Jamie								7	7
McINERNEY Ian				11+2					11+2
MEGSON Kevin	29+3								29+3
MIDGLEY Craig							35+3	28+10	63+13
MIDWOOD Michael			36+2	2+4	5				43+6
MONINGTON Mark							16	26+2	42+2
MORGAN Phil					1				1
MORGAN Tom							5		5
MUDD Paul			6	36+1					42+1
MURPHY Jamie				10	27+1				37+1
NAYLOR Peter								0+1	0+1
NORBURY Micky				30+1					30+1
O'REGAN Kieran			40	39	36+1				**115+1**
O'TOOLE Pat	5+2								5+2
OWEN Val								15+2	15+2
PARKE Simon							18+14	0+5	18+19
PARRY Craig								2	2
PATERSON Jamie	42	13+2			36				91+2
PEAKE Jason	27								27
PETTINGER Paul		7							7
PHILISKIRK Tony					4				4
PLACE Damian				0+2	0+1				0+3
PRICE Jamie								5	5
PRINDIVILLE Steve	17	39	17						73
QUAILEY Brian							26+8		26+8
QUINN Adam							20+5	21+4	41+9
RATHBONE Mick	2	5+1							7+1
RHODES Andy					8				8
RIDINGS Dave	15+1								15+1
RYAN Leon							0+5		0+5
SAGARE Jake								11+14	11+14
SANDWITH Kevin							20	31	51
SANSAM Chris			5						5
SAUNDERS Steve	14								14
SCAIFE Nicky			2						2
SENIOR Michael							9+4	0+4	9+8
SMITH Nigel	7+1								7+1

315

HALIFAX TOWN   APPEARANCES

	93-94	94-95	95-96	96-97	97-98	98--02	02-03	03-04	TOTAL
SMITH Paul			27						27
STONEMAN Paul			39	26+2	38		15	0+1	**118+3**
SUNLEY Mark		7+1							7+1
THACKERAY Andy					41				41
THOMPSON Simon			18+2						18+2
THORNBER Steve			1						1
THORNLEY Ben								1+2	1+2
TIMONS Chris			14						14
TOLSON Neil							2+1		2+1
TOZER Lewis								2+1	2+1
TROTTER Michael		18+2	36	8+1					62+3
WILMOT Richard	20	2							22
WILSON Lee			2+3						2+3
WOODS Andy			25	38	1				64
WORTHINGTON Gary		29+3	17+1	19+7					65+11
YATES Adam								12	12

Lee Martin. Photo: Keith Clayton.

Kieran O'Regan.

Jamie Patterson. Photo: Neil Thaler.

Michael Trotter. Photo: Peter Barnes.

HALIFAX TOWN   GOALSCORERS

	93-94	94-95	95-96	96-97	97-98	98--02	02-03	03-04	TOTAL
	90/91	91/92	92/93	93/94	94/95	95/96	96/97	97/98	TOTAL
ALLAN Jon								1	1
BARR Billy	4								4
BEDDARD Eliot		2	3						5
BRADSHAW Mark					5(1p)				5(1p)
BROOK Gary			4	8	3				15
BROWN Jimmy				1					1
BROWN Jonathan			1						1
BUSHELL Steve								3	3
CAMERON Dave								1	1
CLARKSON Phil							4		4
COCHRANE Karl			3						3
DAVISON Bobby				3					3
DAWS Tony			1						1
EDWARDS Elfyn	1								1
ELAM Lee							2		2
ELLISON Lee				1					1
FARRELL Andy							4	2	6
FILSON Martin	1								1
FITZPATRICK Ian							5		5
FLEMING Paul		1							1
FLOUNDERS Andy		1							1
GARNETT Shaun							1		1
GERMAN Dave		3							3
HANSON David	4	11			2				17
HATFIELD Charlie							2		2
HENDRICK John			2						2
HORNER Noel			1	3					4
HORSFIELD Geoff				9	30				**39**
HULME Kevin				2	8				10
HUTCHINSON Ian		1							1
JOHNSON Simon		1	6						7
JONES Alex		2							2
KERRIGAN Steve							1		1
KILCLINE Brian					2				2
KILLEEN Lewis							4	7	11
KIWOMYA Andy		13(1p)							13(1p)
LAMBERT Colin	7	3							10
LANCASTER Dave		7							7
LEE Christian								6	6
LEE Glen			1						1
LEITCH Grant		1							1
LITTLE Colin								2(1p)	2(1p)
LORMOR Tony	1								1
LUCKETTI Chris	1								1
LYONS Darren				4	3				7
MALLON Ryan							8(1p)	3	11(1p)
MARTIN Dean				2					2
McCOMBE Jamie								1	1
McINERNEY Ian				1					1

HALIFAX TOWN   GOALSCORERS

	93-94	94-95	95-96	96-97	97-98	98--02	02-03	03-04	TOTAL
MEGSON Kevin	3								3
MIDGLEY Craig							4(1p)	11(7p)	15(8p)
MIDWOOD Michael			10	1					11
MONINGTON Mark							2	1	3
MURPHY Jamie				2					2
NORBURY Mike				13(1p)					13(1p)
O'REGAN Kieran			4		1				5
OWEN Val								1	1
PARKE Simon							5		5
PATERSON Jamie	13(2p)	5			13(3p)				31(5p)
PEAKE Jason	6								6
PHILISKIRK Tony					2				2
PRINDIVILLE Steve		5							5
QUAILEY Brian							4		4
RATHBONE Mick		1							1
RIDINGS Dave	4								4
SAGARE Jake								1	1
SANDWITH Kevin							1	1	2
SANSAM Chris			1						1
SAUNDERS Steve	6								6
SMITH Nigel	2								2
STONEMAN Paul			3	2(1p)	2		3		10(1p)
THACKERAY Andy					2				2
TROTTER Michael			3	1					4
WORTHINGTON Gary		9(2p)	5	1					15(2p)

Season 2003-2004. Back row, left to right: Adam Quinn, Simon Peake, Ryan Poole, Shaun Garnett, Clint Davies, Christian Lee and Mark Monington. Middle Row: Tommy Geldert (Fitnes Coach), Michael Senior, Kevin Sandwith, Jon Cullen, Darren Hockenhull, Andy Farrell, Ryan Hindley and Alan Jackson (Club Physio). Front Row: Daniel Hudson, Craig Midgley, Lewis Killeen, Paul Stoneman, (Youth Team Manager), Chris Wilder (Manager), Sean McCauley (Assistant Manager), Steve Bushell Lee Elam and Ryan Mallon.

HAYES

PROMOTED FROM: Isthmian League 1995-96
RELEGATED TO: Isthmian League 2001-02
2004-2005 SEASON: Conference South

Hayes Squad 1998-99 — Photo: Ray Peploe

Back Row (L-R): Wayne Carter, Russell Townsend, Paul Moles, Mark Walsh, David Lynam, Danny Tilbury, Russell Meara, Deano Orange, Chris Payne, Steve Dell, Kevin Franklin.
Middle Row: Gag Sidhu (reserve manager), Dave Killick (Chief Scout), Steve Baker, Alvin Watts, Joe Lyons, Chris Sparks, Christian Metcalfe, Martin Randall, Jason Goodliffe, Andre Delisser, Darron Wilkinson, Derrick Matthews (Youth Dev. Officer), Ray Girvan (Reserve Coach).
Front Row: Karl Ballard (Sport Therapist), Terry Brown (Manager), Mark Hall, Nick Roddis, Neil Catlin, Lee Charles, Derek Goodall (Chairman), Barry Moore, Lee Flynn, Nathan Bunce, Alfredo Domingos, Willy Wordsworth (Asst. Manager), Kelly Monk (Reserve Physio)

SEASONS							
6							
TOTAL POINTS							
162							
HIGHEST POSITION							
3rd, 1998-99							
LOWEST POSITION							
20th, 2001-02							
HIGHEST ATTENDANCE							
2105 v Cheltenham T. 24.4.99							
LOWEST ATTENDANCE							
363 v Welling U. 24.9.96							
SEASON GOALSCORER							
Martin Randall 15(2p)							
CAREER GOALSCORER							
Martin Randall 38(5p)							
CAREER APPEARANCES							
Jason Goodliffe 143+3							

	HOME						AWAY						Position
	P	W	D	L	F	A	Pts	P	W	D	L	F	A	Pts	
96-97	21	7	7	7	27	21	28	21	5	7	9	27	34	22	15
97-98	21	10	4	7	36	25	34	21	6	6	9	26	27	24	12
98-99	21	12	3	6	34	25	39	21	10	5	6	29	25	35	3
99-00	21	7	3	11	24	28	24	21	9	5	7	33	30	32	11
00-01	21	5	6	10	22	31	21	21	7	4	10	22	40	25	18
01-02	21	6	2	13	27	45	20	21	7	3	11	26	35	24	20
Total	126	47	25	54	170	175	166	126	44	30	52	163	191	162	

HAYES

	Altrincham		Barnet		Barrow		Bath City		Boston United		Bromsgrove Rovers		Cheltenham Town		Chester City		Dagenham & Redbridge		Doncaster Rovers	
	H	A	H	A	H	A	H	A	H	A	H	A	H	A	H	A	H	A	H	A
96-97	3-1	2-0					0-1	1-3			1-0	2-2								
97-98													1-1	1-2						
98-99					1-0	1-0							3-2	3-3					2-0	1-0
99-00	1-1	2-1																	3-4	0-0
00-01									1-1	1-0					1-3	0-0	4-1	0-2	0-3	0-0
01-02			0-2	1-3					0-2	1-4					1-3	1-3	2-4	1-1	1-5	2-5

	Dover Athletic		Farnborough Town		Forest Green Rovers		Gateshead		Halifax Town		Hednesford Town		Hereford United		Kettering Town		Kidderminster H.	
	H	A	H	A	H	A	H	A	H	A	H	A	H	A	H	A	H	A
96-97	2-0	0-1	0-0	1-1			0-0	1-1	0-0	2-2	4-0	0-2			2-1	2-2	0-1	1-5
97-98	0-0	0-1	3-1	2-0			1-0	1-1	1-2	1-1	4-0	1-2	2-0	0-3	0-1	1-1	1-1	0-1
98-99	1-2	0-0	1-0	5-1	0-3	2-1					1-0	0-0	1-2	1-0	0-2	0-1	2-1	1-0
99-00	1-2	2-2			3-0	1-0					2-1	1-2	0-0	2-0	0-1	1-1	2-0	1-2
00-01	3-2	1-4			1-0	2-1					1-1	3-1	0-2	2-3	2-1	2-0		
01-02	2-1	2-3	0-3	2-1	1-1	1-2							4-1	1-0				

	Kingstonian		Leek Town		Leigh RMI		Macclesfield Town		Margate		Morecambe		Northwich Victoria		Nuneaton Borough		Rushden & Diamonds	
	H	A	H	A	H	A	H	A	H	A	H	A	H	A	H	A	H	A
96-97							0-2	0-1			2-3	4-2	1-1	1-2			1-1	2-2
97-98			3-1	2-1							0-3	2-0	1-1	1-1			1-2	3-1
98-99	3-0	1-1	2-0	4-1							1-2	3-2	1-0	1-2			2-1	0-5
99-00	1-2	3-1									0-1	4-1	2-1	0-0	3-0	1-2	0-5	0-1
00-01	1-1	1-0			1-2	0-4					1-1	0-4	2-2	4-3	0-0	1-1	0-3	0-4
01-02					2-1	1-1			2-4	0-1	3-1	1-2	1-2	0-1	1-2	2-0		

HAYES

	Scarborough		Slough Town		Southport		Stalybridge Celtic		Stevenage Borough		Sutton United		Telford United		Welling United		Woking		Yeovil Town	
	H	A	H	A	H	A	H	A	H	A	H	A	H	A	H	A	H	A	H	A
96-97			5-0	3-1	1-1	2-0	0-2	1-3	1-3	0-2			0-1	0-0	1-1	0-1	3-2	2-1		
97-98			0-1	0-0	2-0	2-0	1-2	1-1	1-3	5-1			2-1	0-1	3-1	0-2	3-0	0-3	6-4	3-4
98-99					3-0	2-1			2-2	1-2			4-3	0-2	1-2	2-0	2-2	0-2	1-1	1-1
99-00	0-1	1-4			0-2	1-4			1-2	0-3	1-0	2-2	1-2	2-1	1-0	2-1	0-0	3-0	2-3	4-2
00-01	0-1	0-2			1-0	0-2			0-1	3-3			0-1	0-2			1-2	2-1	2-3	0-3
01-02	1-2	2-1			1-0	3-2	0-0	0-1	0-2	1-1			1-4	2-1			4-1	1-0	0-4	1-2

	Home						Away					
	P	W	D	L	F	A	P	W	D	L	F	A
ALTRINCHAM	2	1	1	0	4	2	2	2	0	0	4	1
BARNET	1	0	0	1	0	2	1	0	0	1	1	3
BARROW	1	1	0	0	1	0	1	1	0	0	1	0
BATH C	1	0	0	1	0	1	1	0	0	1	1	3
BOSTON U	2	0	1	1	1	3	2	1	0	1	2	4
BROMSGROVE R	1	1	0	0	1	0	1	0	1	0	2	2
CHELTENHAM T	2	1	1	0	4	3	2	0	1	1	4	5
CHESTER CITY	2	0	0	2	2	6	2	0	1	1	1	3
DAGENHAM & R	2	1	0	1	6	5	2	0	1	1	1	3
DONCASTER R	4	1	0	3	6	12	4	1	2	1	3	5
DOVER A	6	3	1	2	9	7	6	0	2	4	5	11
FARNBOROUGH T	4	2	1	1	4	4	4	3	1	0	10	3
FOREST GREEN R	4	2	1	1	5	4	4	3	0	1	6	4
GATESHEAD	2	1	1	0	1	0	2	0	2	0	2	2
HALIFAX T	2	0	1	1	1	2	2	0	2	0	3	3
HEDNESFORD T	5	4	1	0	12	2	5	1	1	3	5	7
HEREFORD U	5	2	1	2	7	5	5	3	0	2	6	6
KETTERING T	5	2	0	3	4	6	5	1	3	1	6	5
KIDDERMINSTER H	4	2	1	1	5	3	4	1	0	3	3	8
KINGSTONIAN	3	1	1	1	5	3	3	2	1	0	5	2
LEEK T	2	2	0	0	5	1	2	2	0	0	6	2
LEIGH RMI	2	1	0	1	3	3	2	0	1	1	1	5
MACCLESFIELD T	1	0	0	1	0	2	1	0	0	1	0	1
MARGATE	1	0	0	1	2	4	1	0	0	1	0	1
MORECAMBE	6	1	1	4	7	11	6	4	0	2	14	11
NORTHWICH V	6	2	3	1	8	7	6	1	2	3	7	9
NUNEATON B	3	1	1	1	4	2	3	1	1	1	4	3
RUSHDEN & D	5	1	1	3	4	12	5	1	1	3	5	13
SCARBOROUGH	3	0	0	3	1	4	3	1	0	2	3	7
SLOUGH T	2	1	0	1	5	1	2	1	1	0	3	1
SOUTHPORT	6	4	1	1	8	3	6	4	0	2	10	9
STALYBRIDGE C	3	0	1	2	1	4	3	0	1	2	2	5
STEVENAGE B	6	0	1	5	5	13	6	1	2	3	10	12
SUTTON U	1	1	0	0	1	0	1	0	1	0	2	2
TELFORD U	6	2	0	4	8	12	6	2	1	3	4	7
WELLING U	4	2	1	1	6	4	4	2	0	2	4	4
WOKING	6	3	2	1	13	7	6	4	0	2	8	7
YEOVIL T	5	1	1	3	11	15	5	1	1	3	9	12
TOTALS	126	47	25	54	170	175	126	44	30	52	163	191

Left: Alvin Watts

Above: Jason Goodliffe

Below: Nathan Bunce

Photos: Andrew Chitty

LEADING APPEARANCES

	96-97	97-98	98-99	99-00	00-01	01-02	TOTAL
Jason Goodliffe	36+2	18	34+1	38	17		143+3
Lee Flynn	7+1	32+1	42	37	25		143+2
Nathan Bunce	24+5	27+8	31+1	32	6		120+14
Russell Meara	41	41	36				118
Alvin Watts		18	35+5	31+3	22+1	2+1	108+10
Darron Wilkinson	38+2	36	39				113+2
Martin Randall	26+6	31+6	32+6				89+18
Nick Roddis	19+3	17+7	20+6	27+4			83+20

HAYES   APPEARANCES

	96-97	97-98	98-99	99-00	00-01	01-02	TOTAL
ADAMS Kieran	7+2						7+2
ANSAH Andy	3						3
ANSELL Gary				4+1			4+1
ASHTON Jon						14+5	14+5
ASSELMAN Erwin			5+1				5+1
AUSTIN Gary						1	1
BAKER Steve	1						1
BAPTISTE Rocky					20+1		20+1
BARNES Steve					15+4		15+4
BARTLEY Carl	2+8						2+8
BECCLES Kevin		1					1
BEER Jamie		9+4					9+4
BEZHADI Bobby					8+6		8+6
BOOTHE Chris		19+3	4+6				23+9
BOSSU Bertrand					1	31	32
BOYCE Mark				24+9			24+9
BOYLAN Lee					10+2		10+2
BRADY Jon	37+2	38+2					75+4
BROAD Steve				3			3
BROWN Carlos						2	2
BRYSON Tom					1+1		1+1
BUGLIONE Martin			6+8				6+8
BULL Nicky						7	7
BUNCE Nathan	24+5	27+8	31+1	32	6		120+14
CARTER Wayne				1+2			1+2
CASE John						5+10	5+10
CATLIN Neil			5+4				5+4
CHARLES Anthony						14	14
CHARLES Lee			39+3	40+2			79+5
CLARK Dean						38+3	38+3
COATES Marc			1+1				1+1
COPPARD Dean				11+9	23+10	8+6	42+25
COX Andy	26+1	22+2					48+3
CRAFT Daryl		1+2					1+2
CURRIE Michael						12+5	12+5
DALY Steve						7	7
DELISSER Andre			9+6				9+6
DELL Steve		0+3					0+3
DIALLO Cherif						3+1	3+1

HAYES
APPEARANCES

	96-97	97-98	98-99	99-00	00-01	01-02	TOTAL
DICK Alex						3+2	3+2
DJEMAI Hadj		0+1					0+1
DOMINGOS Alfredo		6+3	1+5				7+8
DONOGHUE Corey	1						1
DUNCAN Iain	18+4	6+6					24+10
DYER Alex					1		1
DYER Kenny						38	38
ELVERSON Matt						9+2	9+2
EVERITT David					8	8+9	16+9
FLYNN Lee	7+1	32+1	42	37	25		143+2
FRANCIS Joe	13+3	10+10					23+13
GALLAGHER Kieron		3+2					3+2
GALLEN Brendan				6+4	12+4	13+3	31+11
GOODLIFFE Jason	36+2	18	34+1	38	17		143+3
GOTHARD Paul			32+1	25			57+1
GRANVILLE John					1		1
GREY Matthew						9+4	9+4
HALE Steve						8+4	8+4
HALL Mark	25+3	32+4	16+6				73+13
HAMMATT Bryan		11+13					11+13
HANNIGAN Al-James					3		3
HARRIS Glen						5+1	5+1
HAYNES Junior	19+13	9+14					28+27
HAYRETTIN Hakan	5+1						5+1
HEDGE Andy	0+1						0+1
HERBERT Craig					1		1
HIGHTON Bobby						2+3	2+3
HODGES Ian						31+5	31+5
HODSON Ben			20+7	5+7	10+10		35+24
HODSON Matt			6	6	16+2		28+2
HOLSGROVE Lee						1	1
HOLSGROVE Paul						25+1	25+1
HOLSGROVE Peter						8+18	8+18
HOOPER Dean	4						4
HYATT Freddie	9+11						9+11
JOLLY Richard						2+8	2+8
KELLY Warren	19						19
KODRA Ellis						4	4
LEWIS Karl	5+1						5+1
LILLINGTON Willie	5						5
McKIMM Steve				37+2			37+2
MEARA Russell	41	41	36				118
MEE Eddie	0+3						0+3
METCALFE Christian		12+1	14+7	12			38+8
METTIOUI Ahmed	0+1						0+1
MOLESLEY Mark				1	16+7	32+2	49+9
MOORE Barry			17+8	25+3	40+1		82+12
NEWTON Eddie					6		6
NORMAN Perry			8+5				8+5
NYAMAH Kofi					6+1		6+1
O'BRIEN Aiden				3			3

HAYES

APPEARANCES

	96-97	97-98	98-99	99-00	00-01	01-02	TOTAL
O'BRIEN Alex	0+1						0+1
ODETOYIABO Kunle	1						1
ONWERE Udo				3			3
PASSMORE Lee		0+1					0+1
PATTON Aaron				8+5			8+5
PAUL Kingsley			0+1				0+1
PICKETT Ross	2+1						2+1
PLUCK Colin					4		4
PRESTON Mark				2+5	17+10		22+15
PYE Mark		18+4					18+4
QUINN Jimmy					11		11
RANDALL Martin	26+6	31+6	32+6				89+18
ROBERTS Jason	19+9	7					26+9
ROBERTS Otis	0+1						0+1
RODDIS Nick	19+3	17+7	20+6	27+4			83+20
SCOTT Peter	2+1						2+1
SHIPPERLEY John						0+4	0+4
SLADE Steve						1	1
SLADEN Steve						3	3
SMITH Chris				4+1			4+1
SODJE Akpo						6	6
SPARKS Chris		27+1	35	0+2			62+3
SPENCER Ryan			5+2	14+12	25	24+3	68+17
STANT Phil						1+2	1+2
STERLING Dominic					36+2	39	75+2
STEVENS Dave				21	26+5	2+2	49+7
SUGRUE Jimmy	5+5						5+5
SULLIVAN Andy				0+1			0+1
TAYLOR Andy		11					11
TAYLOR Lee			2+2				2+2
TAYLOR Scott						3	3
TELEMAQUE Errol				6+3	1+16		7+19
TILBURY Danny				1			1
TOWN David					3+1		3+1
TREBBLE Neil				20+13			20+13
TUCKER Jason				2	2+2		4+2
ULASI Obinna	5						5
WARNER Dave					1+4		1+4
WARNER Kevin					39		39
WATTS Alvin		18	35+5	31+3	22+1	2+1	108+10
WHITBY Ian				0+2			0+2
WHITE Darren					5+4		5+4
WILKERSON Paul				4			4
WILKINSON Darron	38+2	36	39				113+2
WILLIAMS Gary	29+5						29+5
WISE James	2+1						2+1
WITTER Tony				2			2
WOTTON Gary	7+3						7+3

Left: Martin Randall   Photo: Peter Barnes

Below: Lee Charles   Photo: Garry Letts

Below

Left: Dave Stevens
Photo: Peter Barnes

Right: Dean Clark
Photo: Peter Barnes

GOALSCORERS

	96-97	97-98	98-99	99-00	00-01	01-02	TOTAL
ANSELL Gary				2			2
BAPTISTE Rocky					11		11
BARNES Steve					1		1
BOOTHE Chris		4(1p)					4(1p)
BOYLAN Lee					3		3
BRADY Jon		1					1
BUGLIONE Martin			1				1
BUNCE Nathan		4	3	2	1		10
CATLIN Neil			2				2
CHARLES Anthony						3	3
CHARLES Lee			17(1p)	13			30(1p)
CLARK Dean						14(1p)	14(1p)
COPPARD Dean					2		2
COX Andy	4	2					6
DOMINGOS Alfredo		1	1				2
DUNCAN Iain		1					1
DYER Kenny						1	1
EVERITT David					1	1	2
FLYNN Lee	2	5	4	6			17
FRANCIS Joe	2	1					3
GALLEN Brendan					1		1
GOODLIFFE Jason	6(5p)	1		1			8(5p)
GREY Matthew						1	1
HALE Steve						1	1
HALL Mark	4	7	3				14
HAMMATT Bryan		1					1
HAYNES Junior	9	3					12
HODGES Ian						12	12
HODSON Ben			7	2	4		13
HOLSGROVE Peter						5	5
LILLINGTON Willie	1						1
McKIMM Steve				5	1		6
METCALFE Christian		2	1				3
MOLESLEY Mark					1	5	6
MOORE Barry			2	6	4(1p)		6(1p)
NORMAN Perry			1				1
PRESTON Mark				1	1		2
QUINN Jimmy					6		6
RANDALL Martin	13(2p)	15(2p)	10(1p)				**38(5p)**
ROBERTS Jason	6	5					11
RODDIS Nick		3		1			4
SODJE Akpo						2	2
SPARKS Chris		1	3				4
SPENCER Ryan				1		1	2
STERLING Dominic						4	4
STEVENS Dave				11	5		16
TELEMAQUE Errol			2				2
TOWN David					1		1
TREBBLE Neil			1				1
WARNER Kevin						2	2
WATTS Alvin			3		1	1	5
WILKINSON Darren		2	2				4
WILLIAMS Gary	6						6

Left: Paul Gothard (Photo: Sportsfile)
and above in action against Kettering Town. (Photo: Paul Barnes)

Hayes 1999-200 L-R - Back Row: Lee Charles, Dean Coppard, Nathan Bunce, Neil Trebble, Jason Goodliffe, Ben Hodson, Alvin Watts, Ryan Spencer.   Front Row: Steve McKimm, Mark Boyce, Nick Roddis, Lee Flynn, Paul Gothard, Christian Metcalfe, Seb Proctor, Aaron Patton, Barry Moore.

Photo: Ray Peploe, Pisces Photography.

328

HEDNESFORD TOWN

PROMOTED FROM: Southern League 1994-95
RELEGATED TO: Southern League 2000-01
2004-2005 SEASON: Southern League Premier Division

Hednesford Town 1995-96   Photo: Eric Marsh

L-R - Back Row: Bernard McNally, Paul Carty, Mark Freeman, Scott Cooksey, Steve Essex, Colin Lambert, Stuart Lake, Gary Fitzpatrick, Keith Russell.
Front Row: Joe O'Connor, Gareth Jennings, Henry Wright, Steve Piearce, Steve Devine, Luke Yates.

SEASONS
6

TOTAL POINTS
342

HIGHEST POSITION
3rd 1995-96

LOWEST POSITION
22nd 2000-01

HIGHEST ATTENDANCE
2587 v Kidderminster H.
17.3.97

LOWEST ATTENDANCE
646 v Boston U. 23.4.01

SEASON GOALSCORER
Joe O'Connor 23 (95/96)

CAREER GOALSCORER
Joe O'Connor 48

CAREER APPEARANCES
Scott Cooksey 137

			HOME							AWAY					
	P	W	D	L	F	A	Pts	P	W	D	L	F	A	Pts	Position
95-96	21	13	3	5	38	21	42	21	10	4	7	33	25	34	3
96-97	21	10	7	4	28	17	37	21	6	5	10	24	33	23	8
97-98	21	14	4	3	28	12	46	21	4	8	9	31	38	20	7
98-99	21	9	8	4	30	24	35	21	6	8	7	19	20	26	10
99-00	21	10	3	8	27	23	33	21	5	3	13	18	45	18	17
00-01	21	2	6	13	24	38	12	21	3	7	11	22	48	16	22
Total	126	58	31	37	175	135	205	126	34	35	57	147	209	137	

HEDNESFORD TOWN

	Altrincham H	Altrincham A	Barrow H	Barrow A	Bath City H	Bath City A	Boston United H	Boston United A	Bromsgrove Rovers H	Bromsgrove Rovers A	Cheltenham Town H	Cheltenham Town A	Chester City H	Chester City A	Dagenham & Redbridge H	Dagenham & Redbridge A	Doncaster Rovers H	Doncaster Rovers A
95-96	2-1	1-2			2-1	0-1			4-2	4-1					0-0	2-1		
96-97	2-2	1-1			2-0	1-2			3-0	0-1								
97-98											0-1	0-1						
98-99			1-0	2-0							3-2	0-0					1-1	1-0
99-00	5-0	1-0															2-1	1-2
00-01							2-4	4-3					0-0	1-0	0-2	1-6	2-4	1-3

	Dover Athletic H	Dover Athletic A	Farnborough Town H	Farnborough Town A	Forest Green Rovers H	Forest Green Rovers A	Gateshead H	Gateshead A	Halifax Town H	Halifax Town A	Hayes H	Hayes A	Hereford United H	Hereford United A	Kettering Town H	Kettering Town A	Kidderminster H. H	Kidderminster H. A
95-96	2-2	3-1	4-1	3-1			0-1	3-0	3-0	3-1					1-0	0-2	1-3	1-3
96-97	1-1	2-2	0-1	0-1			0-0	1-0	1-1	0-1	2-0	0-4			0-0	2-0	1-4	1-2
97-98	1-0	3-1	1-0	3-1			3-0	5-2	0-0	1-1	2-1	0-4	1-1	1-2	1-1	1-2	3-0	1-1
98-99	1-2	0-0	0-0	1-0	1-1	0-1					0-0	0-1	3-1	0-0	0-2	0-1	2-1	2-1
99-00	1-0	1-4			1-0	0-3					2-1	1-2	0-1	0-3	1-1	2-4	0-2	0-3
00-01	0-0	0-4			1-1	2-0					1-3	1-1	0-3	1-1	1-2	0-2		

	Kingstonian H	Kingstonian A	Leek Town H	Leek Town A	Leigh RMI H	Leigh RMI A	Macclesfield Town H	Macclesfield Town A	Morecambe H	Morecambe A	Northwich Victoria H	Northwich Victoria A	Nuneaton Borough H	Nuneaton Borough A	Runcorn H	Runcorn A	Rushden & Diamonds H	Rushden & Diamonds A
95-96							0-1	1-1	1-2	1-0	2-1	2-0			2-0	2-2		
96-97							4-1	0-4	2-1	2-2	3-0	1-2					1-0	2-0
97-98			1-0	3-3					0-1	3-1	2-0	1-1					0-1	1-1
98-99	1-2	1-1	1-1	2-1					1-0	1-3	1-0	1-1					1-1	0-1
99-00	2-3	2-0							1-3	0-4	1-0	2-3	0-0	0-3			1-2	1-1
00-01	3-2	0-1			1-2	2-2			0-0	0-0	7-1	2-2	0-3	1-5			2-3	1-5

HEDNESFORD TOWN

	Scarborough H	A	Slough Town H	A	Southport H	A	Stalybridge Celtic H	A	Stevenage Borough H	A	Sutton United H	A	Telford United H	A	Welling United H	A	Woking H	A	Yeovil Town H	A
95-96			3-1	2-0	2-1	2-2	0-1	1-0	2-1	0-1			4-0	1-2	1-1	1-1	2-1	0-3		
96-97			2-1	2-2	0-1	2-1	2-1	2-1	0-0	2-3			0-0	1-1	0-3	2-1	2-0	0-2		
97-98			2-1	0-2	2-1	1-4	1-0	1-1	2-1	1-1			1-0	1-1	3-2	2-3	1-1	2-4	1-0	0-1
98-99					3-1	1-1			2-2	1-3			1-1	1-1	3-2	1-1	2-1	1-2	2-3	2-1
99-00	0-3	1-1			1-2	0-2			2-2	1-0	1-0	0-0	2-1	2-6	0-1	2-1	3-0	1-0	1-0	0-3
00-01	0-1	0-0			0-1	0-2			1-1	1-4			1-1	1-2			1-2	1-1	1-2	2-4

	Home P	W	D	L	F	A	Away P	W	D	L	F	A
ALTRINCHAM	3	2	1	0	9	3	3	1	1	1	3	3
BARROW	1	1	0	0	1	0	1	1	0	0	2	0
BATH C	2	2	0	0	4	1	2	0	0	2	1	3
BOSTON U	1	0	0	1	2	4	1	1	0	0	4	3
BROMSGROVE R	2	2	0	0	7	2	2	1	0	1	4	2
CHELTENHAM T	2	1	0	1	3	3	2	0	1	1	0	1
CHESTER CITY	1	0	1	0	0	0	1	1	0	0	1	0
DAGENHAM & R	2	0	1	1	0	2	2	1	0	1	3	7
DONCASTER R	3	1	1	1	5	6	3	1	0	2	3	5
DOVER A	6	2	3	1	6	5	6	2	2	2	9	12
FARNBOROUGH T	4	2	1	1	5	2	4	3	0	1	7	3
FOREST GREEN R	3	1	2	0	3	2	3	1	0	2	2	4
GATESHEAD	3	1	1	1	3	1	3	3	0	0	9	2
HALIFAX T	3	1	2	0	4	1	3	1	1	1	4	3
HAYES	5	3	1	1	7	5	5	0	1	4	2	12
HEREFORD U	4	1	1	2	4	6	4	0	2	2	2	6
KETTERING T	6	1	3	2	4	6	6	1	0	5	5	11
KIDDERMINSTER H	5	2	0	3	7	10	5	1	1	3	5	10
KINGSTONIAN	3	1	0	2	6	7	3	1	1	1	3	2
LEEK T	2	1	1	0	2	1	2	1	1	0	6	4
LEIGH RMI	1	0	0	1	1	2	1	0	1	0	2	2
MACCLESFIELD T	2	1	0	1	4	2	2	0	1	1	1	5
MORECAMBE	6	2	1	3	5	7	6	2	2	2	7	10
NORTHWICH V	6	6	0	0	16	2	6	1	3	2	9	9
NUNEATON B	2	0	1	1	0	3	2	0	0	2	1	8
RUNCORN	1	1	0	0	2	0	1	0	1	0	2	2
RUSHDEN & D	5	1	1	3	5	7	5	1	2	2	5	8
SCARBOROUGH	2	0	0	2	0	4	2	0	2	0	1	1
SLOUGH T	3	3	0	0	7	3	3	1	1	1	4	4
SOUTHPORT	6	3	0	3	8	7	6	1	2	3	6	12
STALYBRIDGE C	3	2	0	1	3	2	3	2	1	0	4	2
STEVENAGE B	6	2	4	0	9	7	6	1	1	4	6	12
SUTTON U	1	1	0	0	1	0	1	0	1	0	0	0
TELFORD U	6	3	3	0	9	3	6	0	3	3	7	13
WELLING U	5	2	1	2	7	9	5	2	2	1	8	7
WOKING	6	4	1	1	11	5	6	1	1	4	5	12
YEOVIL T	4	2	0	2	5	5	4	1	0	3	4	9
TOTALS	126	58	31	37	175	135	126	34	35	57	147	209

LEADING APPEARANCES

	95-96	96-97	97-98	98-99	99-00	00-01	TOTAL
Stuart LAKE	5+9	20+2	19+5	18+3	32+2	27+1	121+22
Scott COOKSEY	41	41	42	13			137
Gary FITZPATRICK	34	33+2	34	17+3			118+5
Andy COMYN		40	31	32	15		118
Paul CARTY	25+3	28+1	32+4	20+3			105+11
Joe O'CONNOR	40	37	25+3	4+2			106+5
Kevin COLLINS	37	35+1	29+2				101+3

Left:
Stuart Lake

Photo: Garry Letts

Below
Left:
Colin Lambert

Photo: Martin Wray

Right:
Kevin Collins

Photo: Paul Dennis

HEDNESFORD TOWN   APPEARANCES

	95-96	96-97	97-98	98-99	99-00	00-01	TOTAL
AIRDRIE Stewart					16+11	12+10	28+21
AMOS Nick				2+5	0+1		2+6
ANDERSON Dale			4+3				4+3
BAGSHAW Paul					9	31+5	40+5
BEESTON Carl			25	23			48
BETTNEY Scott					5		5
BIGNALL Mike				2+2			2+2
BLADES Paul			37+1	11			48+1
BONSALL Scott						11+11	11+11
BRADLEY Russell				30	16	31+3	77+3
BRANT Gavin		1					1
BRINDLEY Chris			14	39	36+1		89+1
BROADHURST Neil		2+1	2+3	0+1			4+5
BROWN Leon						6+8	6+8
BURR Steve	2+7						2+7
CARNEY Andrew						0+1	0+1
CARTER Nick						1	1
CARTY Paul	25+3	28+1	32+4	20+3			105+11
COATES Danny	0+1						0+1
COLKIN Lee			7	32	33	20+2	92+2
COLLINS Kevin	37	35+1	29+2				101+3
COMYN Andy		40	31	32	15		118
COOKSEY Scott	41	41	42	13			137
COOPER Mark						23+1	23+1
COTTERILL John		5+4					5+4
CRAVEN Dean						5	5
DANDY Richard		0+5	2				2+5
DAVIES Paul				1			1
DAVIS Neil				21+1	32	31+3	84+4
DENNISON Robbie			26+6	3+2			29+8
DEVINE Steve	37+2	18+6		1+1			56+9
ECCLESTON Tony		3	8+5				11+5
EDWARDS Paul		4					4
ESSEX Steve	40	26+7					66+7
EVANS Stuart					38+1	14	52+1
FITZPATRICK Gary	34	33+2	34	17+3			118+5
FORD Stuart					13	4	17
FOREMAN Darren	13+3						13+3
FRANCIS Delton		8+3	15+6	0+4			23+13
FREEMAN Mark	0+1						0+1
GARRATT Martin						1+1	1+1
GAYLE Mark						38	38
GOODWIN Scott					24+2	21+3	45+5
GRIFFITHS Tom						13+1	13+1
HACKETT Brendan	0+1						0+1
HANSON Dave	8						8
HARAN Mark						33+1	33+1
HARNETT Dave	2+3	1+4					3+7
HAYWARD Andy				15+2			15+2
HAYWARD Paul				1			1
HEMMINGS Tony		16+4	12+2				28+6
HIBBINS John					3		3

Andy Comyn   Photo: Andrew Chitty

Ged Kimmins   Photo: Keith Clayton

Scott Cooksey   Photo: Andrew Chitty

Wayne Simpson   Photo: Sportsfile

HEDNESFORD TOWN APPEARANCES

	95-96	96-97	97-98	98-99	99-00	00-01	TOTAL
HICKEY Ben				2+2			2+2
HOLMES David		2+1					2+1
HUNTER Colin				4+6			4+6
JACKSON Leon				1+2			1+2
JEFFERS John			0+1				0+1
JENNINGS Gareth	1+7						1+7
KELLY Jimmy				22+6	30		52+6
KIMMINS Ged				27+3	22+4		49+7
KNIGHT Lee			0+1				0+1
LAKE Stuart	5+9	20+2	19+5	18+3	32+2	27+1	121+22
LAMBERT Colin	27+2	29					56+2
LAMPKIN Kevin					1		1
LANDON Richard			3				3
LAWRENCE George		3+4					3+4
LEADBEATER Richard						4+1	4+1
MASON Richard		8+5					8+5
McKENZIE Christy		3+4	0+2				3+6
McNALLY Bernard	23	19+1					42+1
MEACHAM Robbie						0+1	0+1
MIKE Adie				13	16+3		29+3
MORGAN Phil				29	20		49
NIBLETT Nigel			6+3				6+3
NORBURY Micky			19+4		12+2	27+3	58+9
NORMAN John					8+8		8+8
NTAMARK Charlie			18+2				18+2
O'CONNOR Joe	40	37	25+3	4+2			106+5
O'CONNOR Sean				6+5	7+7		13+12
OWEN Val						28+2	28+2
PIEARCE Steve	1+4						1+4
POINTON Neil						20+2	20+2
RADBURN Colin	0+1						0+1
REECE Dominic				11+1	3+4		14+5
RHODES Ross					1+3	0+1	1+4
RIDINGS Dave	4+1						4+1
ROBINSON Ian					34+2	25+1	59+3
ROWLAND Steve		0+3					0+3
RUSSELL Keith	14	19+1				5+6	38+7
SEDGEMORE Jake			13	24+2	2+1	23+9	62+12
SHAKESPEARE Adam					0+1	8+3	8+4
SIMPSON Wayne	39	34	7+1				80+1
SMITH Neil			0+1				0+1
STEWART Billy					5		5
STREET Tyron	25+3	23+9					48+12
SZEWCZYK Paul				5+5	5+3		10+8
TAYLOR Steve		4+3					4+3
TITTERTON Dave	3+2						3+2
TWYNHAM Gary				4+1	14+11		18+12
WARE Paul			32	36+1			68+1
WILLIAMS Richard	1						1
WILSON Mark					3		3
WRIGHT Henry	8+19						8+19
YATES Luke	32+1	0+4					32+5

Top Left: Joe O'Connor
Photo: Sportsfile

Top Right: Micky Norbury
Photo: John Collings

Above: Tony Hemmings

Left:
Joe O'Connor in action.
Photo: John Collings

HEDNESFORD TOWN   GOALSCORERS

	95-96	96-97	97-98	98-99	99-00	00-01	TOTAL
ANDERSON Dale			3				3
BAGSHAW Paul						6	6
BEESTON Carl			1	1			2
BIGNALL Mike				1			1
BONSALL Scott						3	3
BRADLEY Russell				2			2
BRINDLEY Chris				2	1		3
BROWN Leon						1	1
BURR Steve	1						1
CARTY Paul	3(1p)	3(1p)	11(1p)	1			18(3p)
COLKIN Lee					1		1
COLLINS Kevin	1						1
COMYN Andy		2	3	2			7
COOPER Mark						4(2p)	4(2p)
COTTERILL John		1					1
DAVIS Neil				8(2p)	18(2p)	10(1p)	36(5p)
DENNISON Robbie			4(1p)				4(1p)
DEVINE Steve	5	1					6
ECCLESTON Tony			4				4
ESSEX Steve	4						4
FITZPATRICK Gary	2	3	7	2			14
FOREMAN Darren	4						4
FRANCIS Delton		3	3				6
GOODWIN Scott						2	2
HANSON Dave	3						3
HARAN Mark						1	1
HARNETT Dave		1					1
HAYWARD Andy				3			3
HEMMINGS Tony			1				1
KELLY Jimmy				1(1p)	1		2(1p)
KIMMINS Ged				8	7(2p)		15(2p)
LAKE Stuart	4	3	1	2	2	1	13
LAMBERT Colin	6	6					12
LAWRENCE George		1					1
MASON Richard		2(2p)					2(2p)
McNALLY Bernard	1	2(1p)					3(1p)
MIKE Adie				3	3		6
NORBURY Micky			6		1	8	15
NORMAN John					2		2
O'CONNOR Joe	23	15	8	2			48
O'CONNOR Sean				2			2
OWEN Val						3	3
RIDINGS Dave	2						2
ROBINSON Ian					6	2	8
RUSSELL Keith	4(1p)	5(2p)				1	10(3p)
SEDGEMORE Jake			1	2(2p)		2(1p)	5(3p)
SIMPSON Wayne	1						1
STREET Tyron	3	4					7
SZEWCZYK Paul				2	1		3
TWYNHAM Gary					1		1
WARE Paul			6	5			11
WRIGHT Henry	1						1
YATES Luke	2						2

Hednesford Town Squad 1997-98
L-R - **Back Row:** John Cotterill, Dave Harnett, Leighton Derry, Keith Russell, Paul Carty, Tyron Street, Luke Yates. **Middle Row:** Pete Windsor (Kit Man.), Stuart Lake, Steve Essex, Scott Cooksey, Gavin Brant, Andy Comyn, Colin Lambert, Don Drakeley (Physio). **Front Row:** Bernard McNally, Gary Fitzpatrick, Kevin Collins, John Baldwin (Manager), John Allen (Asst. Man.), Wayne Simpson, Steve Devine, Steve Taylor
Photo: Mr & Mrs C Rogers

Hednesford Town Squad 1999-00 - L-R - **Back Row:** Scott Goodwin, Dominic Reece, Stuart King, Iain Brunskill, Gary Twynham, Paul Szewcyck, Nick Amos, Jake Sedgemore, Noel Malcolm, Ross Rhodes. **Middle Row:** Don Drakeley (Physio), Stuart Evans, Adie Mike, Russell Beadley, Chris Brindley, Phil Morgan, Paul Hayward (Player-coach), Stuart Lake, Andy Comyn, Sean O'Connor, Peter Windsor (Kit Manager). **Front Row:** Ian Robinson, John Norman, Lee Colkin, James Kelly, John Baldwin (Manager), Steve Devine (Asst. Manager), Neil Davis, Ged Kimmins, Colin Hunter, Stewart Airdrie. **Grass:** Tom Griffiths, Tony Fierro.

HEREFORD UNITED

RELEGATED FROM: The Football League 1996-97
2004-2005 SEASON: The Conference

2003-04 Squad. Left to right: David Brown, Jordan King, Michael Rose, Paul Parry, Matthew Baker, Steve Quinn, Andrew Tretton, Richard Teesdale and Rob Sawyers. Front Row: Rob Purdie, Jamie Pitman, Richard O'Kelly (Coach), Graham Chairman (Chairman/ Director of Football), Tony Ford (Coach), Ben Smith and Danny Williams.

	HOME							AWAY							
	P	W	D	L	F	A	Pts	P	W	D	L	F	A	Pts	Position
97-98	21	11	7	3	30	19	40	21	7	6	8	26	30	27	6
98-99	21	9	5	7	25	17	32	21	6	5	10	24	29	23	13
99-00	21	9	6	6	43	31	33	21	6	8	7	18	21	26	8
00-01	21	6	12	3	27	19	30	21	8	3	10	33	27	27	11
01-02	21	9	6	6	28	15	33	21	5	4	12	22	38	19	17
02-03	21	9	5	7	36	22	32	21	10	2	9	28	29	32	6
03-04	21	14	3	4	42	20	45	21	14	4	3	61	24	46	2
Total	147	67	44	36	231	143	245	147	56	32	59	212	198	200	

SEASONS
7

TOTAL POINTS
445

HIGHEST POSITION
2nd 03-04

LOWEST POSITION
17th 01-02

HIGHEST ATTENDANCE
7240 v Chester C. 24.4.04

LOWEST ATTENDANCE
867 v Kingstonian 18.4.01

SEASON GOALSCORER
Steve Guinan 25 (03/4)

CAREER GOALSCORER
Steve Guinan 39

CAREER APPEARANCES
Tony James 172+6

	Accrington Stanley		Aldershot Town		Altrincham		Barnet		Barrow		Boston United		Burton Albion		Cheltenham Town		Chester City	
	H	A	H	A	H	A	H	A	H	A	H	A	H	A	H	A	H	A
96-97																		
97-98															3-2	2-1		
98-99									3-0	1-0					0-2	2-2		
99-00					2-2	1-2												
00-01											1-1	3-5					2-0	1-2
01-02							2-1	0-2			0-1	4-3					1-0	0-2
02-03							4-0	1-2					4-0	0-2			0-0	1-0
03-04	1-0	0-2	4-3	2-1			2-0	1-1					1-2	1-4			2-1	0-0

	Dagenham & Redbridge		Doncaster Rovers		Dover Athletic		Exeter City		Farnborough Town		Forest Green Rovers		Gateshead		Gravesend & N'fleet	
	H	A	H	A	H	A	H	A	H	A	H	A	H	A	H	A
96-97																
97-98					0-1	1-1			2-1	2-0			1-0	1-1		
98-99			1-0	1-3	2-0	1-3			2-0	4-0	4-0	1-2				
99-00			5-3	2-2	2-0	0-2					1-0	1-0				
00-01	0-1	1-2	0-1	1-2	4-2	0-1					3-1	1-1				
01-02	1-0	0-1	0-0	0-4	3-0	1-0			4-2	2-4	0-0	1-1				
02-03	2-1	0-1	2-4	0-2					2-1	2-2	1-1	3-1			3-0	0-3
03-04	1-1	9-0					1-1	1-0	2-0	5-0	5-1	7-1			3-3	5-2

	Halifax Town		Hayes		Hednesford Town		Kettering Town		Kidderminster H.		Kingstonian		Leek Town		Leigh RMI	
	H	A	H	A	H	A	H	A	H	A	H	A	H	A	H	A
96-97																
97-98	0-0	0-3	3-0	0-2	2-1	1-1	3-2	2-1	1-0	4-1			1-0	2-2		
98-99			0-1	2-1	0-0	1-3	0-2	1-1	1-3	0-1	2-0	0-2	1-0	2-3		
99-00			0-2	0-0	3-0	1-0	4-2	0-2	1-1	1-1	0-2	0-0				
00-01			3-2	2-0	1-1	3-0	0-0	2-0			0-0	3-0			1-1	1-2
01-02			0-1	1-4											0-1	1-0
02-03	1-1	0-1					2-0	3-2							0-1	2-0
03-04	7-1	2-1													0-1	5-0

HEREFORD UNITED

	Margate		Morecambe		Northwich Victoria		Nuneaton Borough		Rushden & Diamonds		Scarborough		Shrewsbury Town		Slough Town		Southport	
	H	A	H	A	H	A	H	A	H	A	H	A	H	A	H	A	H	A
96-97																		
97-98			1-0	5-1	2-2	2-0			1-1	0-1					1-1	0-3	1-1	0-0
98-99			2-0	0-1	2-2	0-1			3-2	1-1							2-2	0-0
99-00			1-1	2-3	3-0	0-0	1-1	1-0	4-0	0-0	4-4	0-3					2-1	1-0
00-01			2-2	1-1	0-0	0-1	1-1	2-1	3-1	0-1	1-1	4-2					0-0	1-1
01-02	3-0	2-2	0-2	2-2	1-0	0-1	1-1	0-2			6-0	2-3					0-0	1-1
02-03	2-3	2-0	1-2	1-3	1-2	2-2	2-1	3-0			0-1	1-2					0-2	2-1
03-04	2-1	3-1	3-0	2-2	1-0	5-1					2-1	3-3	2-1	1-4				

	Stalybridge Celtic		Stevenage Borough		Sutton United		Tamworth		Telford United		Welling United		Woking		Yeovil Town	
	H	A	H	A	H	A	H	A	H	A	H	A	H	A	H	A
96-97																
97-98	3-0	3-2	0-2	0-2					1-1	0-0	1-2	0-3	2-1	1-3	1-1	0-2
98-99			0-1	3-0					0-0	1-0	0-0	2-2	0-1	1-0	0-1	0-3
99-00			1-2	3-0	4-1	1-1			2-2	1-1	1-2	1-3	2-4	2-0	0-1	0-1
00-01			1-1	1-2					2-0	0-1			0-1	3-0	2-2	3-2
01-02	3-0	2-0	1-1	1-3					0-1	1-0			2-2	0-1	0-2	1-2
02-03			2-2	2-0					2-0	1-0			5-0	2-1	0-0	0-4
03-04			1-0	2-0			0-1	3-1	2-1	3-0			0-1	1-0		

Season 1997-98. Back Row, left to right: Gavin Mahon, Andy de Bont, Trevor Matthewson, Chris Mackenzie and Gary Cook. Middle Row: Simon Shakeshaft, Jamie Pitman, Brian McGorry, Neil Grayson, John Brough, Richard Walker, Chris Hargreaves, Rob Warne and Keith Downing. Front Row: Tony Agana, Ian Foster, David Norton, Graham Turner (Manager), Murray Fishlock, Roy Jordan and Ian Rodgerson.

	Home						Away					
	P	W	D	L	F	A	P	W	D	L	F	A
ACCRINGTON S	1	1	0	0	1	0	1	0	0	1	0	2
ALDERSHOT T	1	1	0	0	4	3	1	1	0	0	2	1
ALTRINCHAM	1	0	1	0	2	2	1	0	0	1	1	2
BARNET	3	3	0	0	8	1	3	0	1	2	2	5
BARROW	1	1	0	0	3	0	1	1	0	0	1	0
BOSTON U	2	0	1	1	1	2	2	1	0	1	7	8
BURTON A	2	1	0	1	5	2	2	0	0	2	1	6
CHELTENHAM T	2	1	0	1	3	4	2	1	1	0	4	3
CHESTER C	4	3	1	0	5	1	4	1	1	2	2	4
DAGENHAM & R	4	2	1	1	4	3	4	1	0	3	10	4
DONCASTER R	5	2	1	2	8	8	5	0	1	4	4	13
DOVER A	5	4	0	1	11	3	5	1	1	3	3	7
EXETER C	1	0	1	0	1	1	1	1	0	0	1	0
FARNBOROUGH T	5	5	0	0	12	4	5	3	1	1	15	6
FOREST GREEN R	6	4	2	0	14	3	6	3	2	1	14	6
GATESHEAD	1	1	0	0	1	0	1	0	1	0	1	1
GRAVESEND & N	2	1	1	0	6	3	2	1	0	1	5	5
HALIFAX T	3	1	2	0	8	2	3	1	0	2	2	5
HAYES	5	2	0	3	6	6	5	2	1	2	5	7
HEDNESFORD T	4	2	2	0	6	2	4	2	1	1	6	4
KETTERING T	5	3	1	1	9	6	5	3	1	1	8	6
KIDDERMINSTER H	3	1	1	1	3	4	3	1	1	1	5	3
KINGSTONIAN	3	1	1	1	2	2	3	1	1	1	3	2
LEEK T	2	2	0	0	2	0	2	0	1	1	4	5
LEIGH RMI	4	0	1	3	1	4	4	3	0	1	9	2
MARGATE	3	2	0	1	7	4	3	2	1	0	7	3
MORECAMBE	7	3	2	2	10	7	7	1	3	3	13	13
NORTHWICH V	7	3	3	1	10	6	7	2	2	3	9	6
NUNEATON B	4	1	3	0	5	4	4	3	0	1	6	3
RUSHDEN & D	4	3	1	0	11	4	4	0	2	2	1	3
SCARBOROUGH	5	2	2	1	13	7	5	1	1	3	10	13
SHREWSBURY T	1	1	0	0	2	1	1	0	0	1	1	4
SLOUGH T	1	0	1	0	1	1	1	0	0	1	0	3
SOUTHPORT	6	1	4	1	5	6	6	2	4	0	5	3
STALYBRIDGE C	2	2	0	0	6	0	2	2	0	0	5	2
STEVENAGE B	7	1	3	3	6	9	7	4	0	3	12	7
SUTTON U	1	1	0	0	4	1	1	0	1	0	1	1
TAMWORTH	1	0	0	1	0	1	1	1	0	0	3	1
TELFORD U	7	3	3	1	9	5	7	4	2	1	7	2
WELLING U	3	0	1	2	2	4	3	0	1	2	3	8
WOKING	7	2	1	4	11	10	7	5	0	2	10	5
YEOVIL T	6	0	3	3	3	7	6	1	0	5	4	14
TOTAL	147	67	44	36	231	143	147	56	32	59	212	198

Neil Grayson. Photo: Andrew Chitty. Chris Hargreaves. Photo: Andrew Chitty.

Tony James.

Chris Lane.   Photo: Francis Short.

HEREFORD UNITED ## LEADING APPEARANCES

	97-98	98-99	99-00	00-01	01-02	02-03	03-04	TOTAL
Tony JAMES		28	34+2	31+2	41	38+1	42	214+5
Paul PARRY	0+2	19+4	23+7	11+7	39	37	25	154+20
Ian WRIGHT		37	33	34	37	27+2		168+2
Gavin WILLIAMS	3+7	31+7	30+11	39	40			143+25
Ian RODGERSON	35+2	31+2	33+2	29+1	16			144+7
Matt CLARKE		7	28+2	36+2	36	32+2		139+6
John SNAPE		23+1	38+2	39+2	37+1			137+6
Matthew BAKER				2	37+1	42	42	123+1
Rob ELMES			29+8	29+9	26+10			84+27
Jamie PITMAN	29+1					37+1	39	105+2

Gavin Mahon.   Photo: Peter Barnes.   Phil Robinson puts in a challenge. Photo: Peter Barnes.

HEREFORD UNITED APPEARANCES

	97-98	98-99	99-00	00-01	01-02	02-03	03-04	TOTAL
AGANA Tony	17+5							17+5
BAKER Matthew				2	37+1	42	42	123+1
BARNES Neil					1			1
BARRICK Dean					7			7
BEALE Matthew			0+1					0+1
BEESLEY Mark							4+8	4+8
BETTS Rob							3+2	3+2
BODEN Chris		4						4
BROUGH John	31+1							31+1
BROWN David							25+13	25+13
BULL Steve				0+7				0+7
CAPALDI Tony					12			12
CAREY-BERTRAM Danny							2+18	2+18
CLARKE Matt		7	28+2	36+2	36	32+2		139+6
COLLINS Kevin		6						6
COOK Garry	7+10	14+14						21+24
COOKSEY Scott			17	40				57
CORREIA Alberto						4+2		4+2
COTTERILL John			0+3					0+3
COWE Steve		11+3						11+3
COZIC Bertrand							0+2	0+2
CRAVEN Dean							5+6	5+6
CROSS Matthew		3+5						3+5
CROWE Seamus				4				4
DAVIDSON Daniel					3+9			3+9
DE BONT Andy	2							2
DENNISON Robbie		17+2						17+2
DIAMOND Ross					1+2			1+2
DOWNING Keith		11+3						11+3
DRUCE Mark		14+5						14+5
DYER Wayne		2+4						2+4
ELMES Rob			29+8	29+9	26+10			84+27
ERIBENNE Chuki						3		3
EVANS Lee					0+1			0+1
EVANS Stuart		23+1						23+1
FEWINGS Paul		6+5	16+9					22+14
FISHLOCK Murray	37							37
FOSTER Ian	13+5							13+5
FOX James						0+4		0+4
GALLOWAY Mike						9		9
GARDINER Matt				7+7	1+2			8+9
GAYLE Mark	5							5
GIDDINGS Kerry				12+13				12+13
GOODWIN Scott					29+3			29+3
GRANT John						23+3		23+3
GRAYSON Neil	22+2							22+2
GREEN Ryan							38	38
GUINAN Steve						37+2	34	71+2
HANSON Craig			6+6	2+4				8+10
HARGREAVES Chris	38							38
HAWLEY Karl						5+1		5+1

HEREFORD UNITED APPEARANCES

	97-98	98-99	99-00	00-01	01-02	02-03	03-04	TOTAL
HILL Jon					1+2			1+2
HOLMES Richard					8			8
HUSBANDS Michael						0+5		0+5
JAMES Kristian					5+2			5+2
JAMES Tony		28	34+2	31+2	41	38+1	42	214+5
JONES Mark		4	16+1					20+1
JONES Stuart					4			4
JORDAN Roy	0+1							0+1
KEVAN Alex					2+1			2+1
KING Jordan							1+1	1+1
LANE Chris		36	27+2	24				87+2
LEADBEATER Richard	12	21+4						33+4
LOVETT Jay						8+2		8+2
MACKENZIE Chris	7							7
MAHON Gavin	42	16						58
MANSELL Craig	0+3							0+3
MARTIN Andy						0+1		0+1
MARTIN Dean		1						1
MATTHEWSON Trevor	27							27
MAY Leroy			20+9					20+9
McCUE James	5+3							5+3
McGORRY Brian	31+2							31+2
McINDOE Michael				27				27
MILNER Andy	8							8
MKANDAWIRE Tamika							14	14
MORAN Andrew				0+1				0+1
NORTON Dave	5							5
PALMER Chris							3	3
PARRY Paul	0+2	19+4	23+7	11+7	39	37	25	154+20
PIEARCE Steve		9+2	0+8	4+10				13+20
PITMAN Jamie	29+1					37+1	39	105+2
PLOTNEK Nick				0+1				0+1
PURDIE Robert						12+21	34+2	46+23
QUIGGIN Jimmy				13+2	13+8			26+10
QUINN Jimmy				2				2
QUY Andy	28	38	9					75
ROBERTS Christian		7+2						7+2
ROBINSON Phil				40	20+2			60+2
RODGERSON Ian	35+2	31+2	33+2	29+1	16			144+7
ROSE Michael						41	37+1	78+1
SAWYERS Robert						8+2	0+1	8+3
SEDGEMORE Jake					1+1			1+1
SHIRLEY John		0+2	0+2	10+1	10+5			20+10
SMITH Ben						22+2	28	50+2
SMITH Tom							7	7
SNAPE John		23+1	38+2	39+2	37+1			137+6
STURGESS Paul			32+2	22				54+2
TAYLOR Mark		40	35+1					75+1
TEESDALE Richard						7+8	4+8	11+16
TRAVIS Simon							5	5
TRETTON Andy						35+1	22	57+1

HEREFORD UNITED — APPEARANCES

	97-98	98-99	99-00	00-01	01-02	02-03	03-04	TOTAL
UDDIN Anwar							9	9
VOICE Scott					7+4	0+4		7+8
WALKER Richard	34	12						46
WALL James			11+3	9+1				20+4
WARNER Robert	24+7							24+7
WEBB Paul					12+1			12+1
WHITE Tom		16						16
WILLIAMS Danny						35+1	31+6	66+7
WILLIAMS Gavin	3+7	31+7	30+11	39	40			143+25
WILLIAMS Mark					12+1			12+1
WILLIS Scott							8	8
WRIGHT Ian		37	33	34	37	27+2		168+2

Above: John Snape. Photo: K. Gillard.
Right: Gavin Williams. Photo: Peter Barnes.

HEREFORD UNITED — GOALSCORERS

	97-98	98-99	99-00	00-01	01-02	02-03	03-04	TOTAL
AGANA Tony	7							7
BEESLEY Mark							2	2
BROUGH John	4							4
BROWN David							14	14
BULL Steve				2				2
CAREY-BERTRAM Danny							3	3
CLARKE Matt				3	1	4		8
COOK Garry	2	3						5
CORREIA Alberto						3		3
COWE Steve		2						2
DENNISON Robbie		2						2
DOWNING Keith		1						1
DRUCE Mark		2						2
DYER Wayne		1						1
ELMES Rob			13	14	9			36
EVANS Stuart		1						1
FEWINGS Paul		2	13					15
FISHLOCK Murray	2							2

HEREFORD UNITED   GOALSCORERS

	97-98	98-99	99-00	00-01	01-02	02-03	03-04	TOTAL
FOSTER Ian	3							3
GARDINER Matt			1					1
GIDDINGS Kerry			5					5
GOODWIN Scott					3			3
GRANT John						4		4
GRAYSON Neil	11(1p)							11(1p)
GREEN Ryan							1	1
GUINAN Steve						14	25	**39**
HANSON Craig			1	1				2
HARGREAVES Chris	4(1p)							4(1p)
HAWLEY Karl						1		1
JAMES Tony		1	2		1	1	9(9p)	14(9p)
LANE Chris			5(4p)					5(4p)
LEADBEATER Richard	7	6(2p)						13(2p)
LOVETT Jay						1		1
MAHON Gavin		3(2p)						3(2p)
MATTHEWSON Trevor	2							2
MAY Leroy			4					4
McGORRY Brian	1							1
McINDOE Michael				2				2
MILNER Andy	5							5
MKANDAWIRE Tamika							1	1
PARRY Paul		3	4	1	5	10	9	32
PIEARCE Steve			4	2	2			8
PITMAN Jamie	5					6	2	13
PURDIE Robert						1	8	9
QUIGGIN Jimmy				1	2			3
ROBERTS Christian		2						2
ROBINSON Phil				2	4			6
RODGERSON Ian		1	2	5	1			9
ROSE Michael						4	2	6
SAWYERS Robert						1		1
SHIRLEY John					1			1
SMITH Ben						5	13	18
SNAPE John		1	2	2	5			10
TAYLOR Mark		1(1p)	2					3(1p)
TEESDALE Richard							1	1
TRAVIS Simon							1	1
TRETTON Andy							2	2
UDDIN Anwar							2	2
VOICE Scott					2			2
WALKER Richard		3						3
WALL James			1					1
WILLIAMS Danny						5	5	10
WILLIAMS Gavin	1	6(1p)	6(3p)	8	10			31(4p)
WILLIAMS Mark					1(1p)			1(1p)
WILLIS Scott							2	2
WRIGHT Ian		7	6	3	3	2		21

1999-2000 Squad . Back Row (L-R): Paul Fewings, Leroy May, Rob Elmes, Andy Quy, James Wall, Chris Lane, Paul Parry. Middle Row: Craig Hanson, John Snape, Tony James, Matt Clarke, Steve Piearce, Gavin Williams, Mark Taylor. Front Row: Ian Rogerson, Tony Ford (Coach), Graham Turner (Manager), Thompson, Ian Wright.

2004-05 Squad. Back Row (L-R): Adam Stansfield, Tom Smith, Craig Stanley, Ben Scott, Andrew Tretton, Tamika Mkandawire, Andrew Williams. **Centre Row:** Bernard Day (Goalkeeper Coach), Ryan Green, Simon Travis, David Brown, Danny Carey-Bertram, Tony Ford (Fitness Adviser). **Front Row:** Rob Purdie, Jamie Pitman, Graham Turner (Manager), Tony James (Capt.), John Trewick (Coach), Danny Williams, Graham Hyde.

KETTERING TOWN

FOUNDER MEMBER elected from Southern League
RELEGATED TO: The Southern League 2001, 2003
PROMOTED FROM: The Southern League 2002
2004-2005 SEASON: Conference North

Kettering Town 1998-99 Back Row: Peter Costello, Bradley Sandeman, Tim Wilkes, David Moore, Dean Holliday, Rob Mutchell, Ian Ridgway, Chris Pearson. **Midle Row:** Julie Frost (Physio), Neil Lyne, Mickey Nuttell, Kevin Shoemake, Chris Taylor, Ray Van Dulleman, Mark Tucker, Paul Miles. **Front Row:** Paul Cox, Carl Adams, Steve Berry (Player/Manager), Craig Norman, Colin Vowden.

	HOME							AWAY							
SEASONS	**P**	**W**	**D**	**L**	**F**	**A**	**Pts**	**P**	**W**	**D**	**L**	**F**	**A**	**Pts**	**Position**
79-80	19	9	5	5	29	26	23	19	6	8	5	26	24	20	7
80-81	19	13	4	2	38	12	30	19	8	5	6	28	25	21	2
81-82	21	6	7	8	35	32	25	21	3	6	12	29	44	15	19
82-83	21	9	5	7	45	37	32	21	2	2	17	24	62	8	19
83-84	21	8	3	10	31	31	19	21	4	6	11	22	36	18	19
84-85	21	9	6	6	37	22	24	21	6	6	9	31	37	24	12
85-86	21	11	6	4	37	24	28	21	4	9	8	18	29	21	9
86-87	21	8	5	8	35	28	29	21	4	6	11	19	38	18	16
87-88	21	13	5	3	37	20	44	21	9	4	8	31	28	31	3
88-89	20	16	1	3	35	15	49	20	7	6	7	21	24	27	2
89-90	21	13	5	3	35	15	44	21	5	7	9	31	38	22	5
90-91	21	12	6	3	38	19	42	21	11	5	5	29	26	38	4
91-92	21	12	6	3	44	23	42	21	8	7	6	28	27	31	3
92-93	21	10	5	6	36	28	35	21	4	8	9	25	35	20	13
93-94	21	9	7	5	23	14	34	21	10	8	3	23	10	38	2
94-95	21	12	5	4	40	25	41	21	7	5	9	33	31	26	6
95-96	21	9	5	7	38	32	32	21	4	4	13	30	52	16	16
96-97	21	9	4	8	30	28	31	21	5	5	11	23	34	20	14
97-98	21	8	6	7	29	29	30	21	5	7	9	24	31	22	14
98-99	21	11	5	5	31	16	38	21	11	5	5	27	21	38	2
99-00	21	8	10	3	25	19	34	21	4	6	11	19	31	18	13
00-01	21	5	5	11	23	31	20	21	6	5	10	23	31	23	20
01-02															
02-03	21	4	3	14	23	39	15	21	4	4	13	14	34	16	22
Total	**478**	**224**	**119**	**135**	**774**	**565**	**741**	**478**	**137**	**134**	**207**	**578**	**748**	**531**	

SEASONS
23

TOTAL POINTS
1272

HIGHEST POSITION
2nd
(80/81) (88/89) (93/94) (98/99)

LOWEST POSITION
22nd (02/03)

HIGHEST ATTENDANCE
5039 v Rushden & D (27-3-99)

LOWEST ATTENDANCE
422 v Forest Green (8-4-03)

SEASON GOALSCORER
Robbie Cooke 28 (89/90)

CAREER GOALSCORER
Frank Murphy 71

CAREER APPEARANCES
Phil Brown 274 + 25

Kettering Town 1982-83
Back Row: Kevin Fox, Andy Wright, Malcolm Watts.
Middle Row: Jim Conde, Iori Jenkins, Alan Guy, Nicky Evans, Malcolm McIntosh, Peter Phipps, Paul Haverson, Eddie McGoldrick, Martin Forster, Phil Sysmie.   **Front Row:** David O'Reilly, David Hofbauer, Sean Suddards, Colin Clarke, Stuart Atkins, Frank Murphy, Derek Duggan

Kettering Town 1987-88
Back Row: Ian Wood, Billy Kellock, Steve Ward, Paul 'Tigger' Richardson, Paul Reece, Nick Goodwin, Ray Birch, Paul Curtiss, David Haywood, Ian Crawley, Russell Lewis.
Front Row: Billy Jefferies, Dougie Keast, Frankie Murphy, Mark Smith, Alan Buckley, Denis Mortimer, Mark Sciani, Arthur Mann, Malc Watts.

	Altrincham		A P Leamington		Aylesbury United		Bangor City		Barnet		Barrow		Bath City		Boston United		Bromsgrove Rovers	
	H	A	H	A	H	A	H	A	H	A	H	A	H	A	H	A	H	A
79-80	1-2	0-0	1-1	3-1			0-1	1-1	1-0	2-0	0-4	2-1	1-2	0-3	3-1	0-1		
80-81	1-1	1-4	3-0	3-3			3-1	1-0	2-1	1-0	0-1	1-2	2-2	0-0	0-0	1-2		
81-82	5-4	1-2	1-2	3-3					5-2	1-2	0-2	2-7	1-3	2-3	1-1	2-4		
82-83	3-2	1-3					3-4	2-4	3-1	3-2	3-1	0-2	4-2	1-2	2-0	1-2		
83-84	1-1	1-1					1-3	1-3	0-1	3-0			0-0	1-1	2-1	1-3		
84-85	1-2	1-2							4-0	2-4	0-0	1-0	1-2	6-1	2-1	1-3		
85-86	2-2	2-2							1-1	0-3	4-2	0-1	2-0	1-1	3-1	1-4		
86-87	0-2	1-4							1-1	2-1			2-0	2-1	1-2	1-2		
87-88	1-2	2-2							1-1	0-4			1-1	0-2	3-0	2-0		
88-89	0-1	2-1			5-2	1-0			3-1	2-3					1-2	1-1		
89-90	3-0	1-1							3-2	1-4	2-0	0-1			5-0	2-1		
90-91	1-1	2-3							1-3	1-0	2-0	1-0	1-1	3-3	1-1	2-1		
91-92	5-0	1-1									3-2	0-0	2-2	1-1	1-3	1-1		
92-93	1-1	0-3											0-1	0-0	3-3	1-0	3-2	1-1
93-94	1-0	1-1											0-1	3-0			0-1	4-0
94-95	2-2	4-2											0-0	0-2			0-1	4-2
95-96	4-2	3-1											3-0	1-3			2-2	2-3
96-97	3-1	3-4											1-0	2-0			2-0	2-1
97-98																		
98-99											2-0	0-0						
99-00	0-0	1-1																
00-01															2-2	3-4		
01-02																		
02-03									1-2	2-0								

	Burton Albion		Cheltenham Town		Chester City		Chorley		Colchester United		Dagenham		Dagenham & Redbridge 91-92 as Redbridge Forest		Darlington		Dartford	
	H	A	H	A	H	A	H	A	H	A	H	A	H	A	H	A	H	A
79-80																		
80-81																		
81-82											3-1	1-2					4-4	2-2
82-83											1-2	3-2						
83-84											2-2	0-2						
84-85											0-1	1-2					0-2	1-0
85-86			2-1	1-5							0-2	0-1					2-2	2-0
86-87			0-0	1-3							3-1	2-1						
87-88			1-1	2-1							3-0	5-0						
88-89			2-0	1-2			3-0	1-0										
89-90			1-0	1-1			2-1	2-2							1-3	1-2		
90-91			5-1	2-2					1-0	1-3								
91-92			3-0	3-0					2-2	1-3			3-2	0-4				
92-93													0-0	2-1				
93-94													1-1	3-2				
94-95													2-2	1-2				
95-96													2-0	2-1				
96-97																		
97-98			0-1	0-2														
98-99			0-2	0-3														
99-00																		
00-01					4-0	1-2									0-0	1-5		
01-02																		
02-03	1-2	0-2					0-1	0-0							1-3	1-3		

Above: Carl Shutt   Photo: Dennis Nicholson

Left: Andy Hunt   Photo: Mick Cheney

Below: Ernie Moss

	Doncaster Rovers		Dover Athletic		Enfield		Farnborough Town		Fisher Athletic		Forest Green Rovers		Frickley Athletic		Gateshead		Gravesend & N'fleet	
	H	A	H	A	H	A	H	A	H	A	H	A	H	A	H	A	H	A
79-80																	0-0	2-2
80-81													6-1	1-1			2-0	0-1
81-82					0-1	1-1							0-0	2-3			2-1	3-1
82-83					0-2	2-5							4-1	2-3				
83-84					1-0	2-2							0-1	1-1	3-0	2-1		
84-85					4-3	3-5							5-0	0-3	1-1	4-1		
85-86					2-1	1-1							2-0	0-3				
86-87					2-0	0-0							1-2	2-2	5-1	1-1		
87-88					2-1	0-2			2-1	1-1								
88-89					0-1	1-1			2-1	0-3								
89-90					3-2	3-0	1-1	1-1	3-0	1-3								
90-91									3-2	0-0					1-0	2-1		
91-92							1-2	3-1							1-1	0-0		
92-93							2-1	2-3							2-0	1-1		
93-94			1-0	1-0											0-0	0-0		
94-95			1-0	2-0			4-1	0-0							2-4	0-0		
95-96			2-2	1-2			0-2	1-1							1-0	1-1		
96-97			1-1	1-0			3-1	2-0							4-1	1-1		
97-98			2-1	0-0			2-1	2-3							3-0	0-2		
98-99	0-1	1-1	0-2	1-0							2-1	0-1						
99-00	2-2	1-2	1-2	1-1							1-0	0-2						
00-01	0-0	0-0	0-2	0-1							1-3	2-3						
01-02																		
02-03	0-2	0-1					1-4	1-0			2-3	0-1					1-1	2-0

	Halifax Town		Hayes		Hednesford Town		Hereford United		Kidderminster H.		Kingstonian		Leek Town		Leigh RMI		Lincoln City	
	H	A	H	A	H	A	H	A	H	A	H	A	H	A	H	A	H	A
79-80																		
80-81																		
81-82																		
82-83																		
83-84									4-2	1-3								
84-85									2-2	2-2								
85-86									2-2	0-0								
86-87									0-2	1-2								
87-88									1-1	1-2							2-0	1-0
88-89									2-1	1-1								
89-90									0-2	3-2								
90-91									4-1	0-3								
91-92									2-1	3-2								
92-93									1-2	0-0								
93-94	0-1	0-0							1-1	2-0								
94-95	5-1	1-2							0-0	3-1								
95-96	1-2	0-2			2-0	0-1			2-0	0-1								
96-97	4-1	1-2	2-2	1-2	0-2	0-0			3-1	0-4								
97-98	1-1	0-3	1-1	1-0	2-1	1-1	1-2	2-3	2-2	1-4			1-0	4-0				
98-99			1-0	2-0	1-0	2-0	1-1	2-0	1-1	1-1	2-0	2-1	2-1	2-1				
99-00			1-1	1-0	4-2	1-1	2-0	2-4	3-1	0-1	2-1	0-2						
00-01			0-2	1-2	2-0	2-1	0-2	0-0			3-1	1-0			0-1	0-1		
01-02																		
02-03	0-1	0-4					2-3	0-2							0-1	2-2		

Matt Fisher   Colin Vowden   Paul Cox

Photo: Peter Barnes

Richard Brown

Photo: M Close

Kevin Shoemake

Photo: Colin Stevens

	Macclesfield Town H	A	Maidstone United H	A	Margate H	A	Merthyr Tydfil H	A	Morecambe H	A	Northwich Victoria H	A	Nuneaton Borough H	A	Redditch United H	A	Runcorn H	A
79-80			1-1	3-1							1-0	2-2	1-1	2-2	2-1	1-0		
80-81			3-0	2-1							3-3	1-1	3-0	5-1				
81-82			2-2	0-2							0-0	0-2					0-0	2-3
82-83			1-3	1-5							1-4	1-2					3-1	0-6
83-84			0-2	0-1							1-0	0-4	3-4	0-1			1-0	1-4
84-85			2-0	0-3							2-2	2-1	1-1	1-1			3-0	2-2
85-86			2-0	0-0							2-1	0-0	1-4	3-0			0-0	1-0
86-87			1-2	0-3							1-0	0-0	2-2	0-0			1-1	0-1
87-88	3-2	0-0	0-2	3-2							3-1	1-0					0-3	0-1
88-89	1-0	1-0	3-3	0-0							2-1	1-1					2-0	1-2
89-90	0-0	1-3					2-0	2-3			3-1	2-2					1-1	1-3
90-91	2-0	2-1					2-0	3-1			1-0	1-0					3-0	1-2
91-92	2-0	2-0					3-1	1-4			1-0	3-4					3-0	0-0
92-93	1-0	0-1					1-3	1-2			2-1	2-2					3-3	2-2
93-94	0-1	0-0					0-0	1-0			0-0	1-1					2-2	0-0
94-95	1-0	0-1					4-1	1-2			3-3	2-3					3-0	2-1
95-96	2-2	1-1							2-3	3-5	2-2	2-6					4-0	2-4
96-97	1-4	0-2							0-2	2-5	1-0	1-2						
97-98									1-1	3-1	1-3	0-0						
98-99									6-0	1-3	0-0	0-4						
99-00									1-1	1-2	1-1	6-2	1-1	1-0				
00-01									1-5	2-0	2-3	2-1	1-2	1-1				
01-02																		
02-03					1-1	2-2			3-2	0-1	2-2	2-1	3-0	0-1				

	Rushden & Diamonds H	A	Scarborough H	A	Slough Town H	A	Southport H	A	Stafford Rangers H	A	Stalybridge Celtic H	A	Stevenage Borough H	A	Sutton United H	A	Telford United H	A
79-80			1-0	0-2					3-6	0-0							3-2	0-1
80-81			1-0	2-1					1-0	1-3							2-1	2-0
81-82			1-2	0-1					3-0	1-1							1-3	0-1
82-83			2-2	0-3					2-2	1-1							1-2	1-2
83-84			2-3	0-0													4-1	0-1
84-85			0-1	0-0													4-2	1-1
85-86			0-0	3-2					0-1	0-0							4-0	2-2
86-87			1-2	0-1					2-2	2-2					1-4	0-8	3-1	0-2
87-88									1-0	1-2					2-2	2-2	1-0	3-2
88-89									1-0	1-2					1-0	2-0	1-0	1-0
89-90									0-0	1-1					2-0	1-2	1-1	3-1
90-91					0-0	3-0			2-0	0-0					5-2	2-1	2-5	1-0
91-92					2-3	2-0			2-1	2-1							3-0	1-1
92-93					5-0	0-3			2-0	4-2	2-0	0-0					1-1	1-3
93-94					2-0	2-0	2-0	1-0	2-0	0-1	3-2	1-1					1-2	2-1
94-95							1-0	1-1	1-0	3-2	1-0	4-1	0-2	2-2			3-2	0-1
95-96					2-0	2-1	1-1	1-6			1-6	2-3	1-2	1-5			0-3	4-3
96-97	1-5	0-1			0-0	1-1	0-1	2-2			1-0	1-3	1-2	0-0			0-1	0-1
97-98	0-4	0-1			3-3	1-1	2-1	1-2			3-1	4-3	2-0	0-0			1-3	1-1
98-99	0-0	2-1					1-0	1-0					1-2	2-2			2-1	2-0
99-00	1-1	0-2	0-0	0-0			0-3	1-0					1-0	0-3	1-0	1-1	0-0	1-3
00-01	0-2	1-1	1-1	1-0			1-1	3-2					1-2	0-2			0-1	1-2
01-02																		
02-03			1-3	1-4			1-0	0-0					1-0	0-2			2-4	0-2

	Trowbridge Town		Wealdstone		Welling United		Weymouth		Witton Albion		Woking		Worcester City		Wycombe Wanderers		Yeovil Town	
	H	A	H	A	H	A	H	A	H	A	H	A	H	A	H	A	H	A
79-80			2-0	2-2			3-1	1-3					0-0	4-1			5-3	1-1
80-81			0-1	1-1			1-0	2-1					1-0	1-2			4-0	2-1
81-82	4-0	1-0					1-2	3-2					0-1	1-1			1-1	1-1
82-83	1-1	1-2	1-3	0-4			1-1	1-4					4-1	2-6			5-2	1-2
83-84	3-2	2-1	1-2	2-4			0-2	1-1					0-1	3-0			2-3	0-2
84-85			0-1	0-1			1-1	0-3					1-0	2-1			3-0	1-1
85-86			2-1	1-3			0-2	0-1							4-1	0-0		
86-87			0-2	1-2	5-1	3-0	3-0	0-2										
87-88			3-2	2-0	1-0	1-3	3-0	1-2							3-0	3-0		
88-89					2-1	1-2	1-0	0-3							2-1	1-0	1-0	2-2
89-90					0-1	0-3									1-0	2-2	1-0	2-0
90-91					0-0	0-0									0-1	1-5	1-1	1-0
91-92					1-1	3-2			1-1	0-1					1-1	0-1	2-0	1-0
92-93					2-4	1-1			2-1	2-4	0-1	2-3			0-4	2-1	3-0	1-2
93-94					2-2	0-2			1-0	1-0	3-0	0-0					1-0	0-1
94-95					4-3	1-2					0-1	1-3					3-2	1-1
95-96					1-3	0-1					3-0	1-1						
96-97					2-3	2-1					0-0	1-2						
97-98					0-1	2-2					0-1	1-0					1-1	0-2
98-99					1-1	2-0					3-0	0-0					1-2	1-2
99-00					2-1	0-1					0-0	1-1					1-2	0-2
00-01											2-0	1-1					2-1	0-2
01-02																		
02-03											0-3	1-2					0-1	0-4

Martin Roderick

	Home						Away					
	P	W	D	L	F	A	P	W	D	L	F	A
ALTRINCHAM	19	7	7	5	35	26	19	3	8	8	28	38
A P LEAMINGTON	3	1	1	1	5	3	3	1	2	0	9	7
AYLESBURY U	1	1	0	0	5	2	1	1	0	0	1	0
BANGOR C	4	1	0	3	7	9	4	1	1	2	5	8
BARNET	13	7	3	3	26	16	13	7	0	6	20	23
BARROW	10	6	1	3	16	12	10	3	2	5	7	14
BATH C	16	5	6	5	21	17	16	4	6	6	23	23
BOSTON U	15	7	5	3	30	18	15	4	2	9	20	29
BROMSGROVE R	5	2	1	2	7	6	5	3	1	1	13	7
BURTON A	1	0	0	1	1	2	1	0	0	1	0	2
CHELTENHAM T	9	5	2	2	14	6	9	2	2	5	11	19
CHESTER CITY	2	1	0	1	4	1	2	0	1	1	1	2
CHORLEY	2	2	0	0	5	1	2	1	1	0	3	2
COLCHESTER U	2	1	1	0	3	2	2	0	0	2	2	6
DAGENHAM	7	3	1	3	12	9	7	3	0	4	12	10
DAGENHAM & R	7	2	4	1	9	8	7	3	0	4	10	18
DARLINGTON	1	0	0	1	1	3	1	0	0	1	1	2
DARTFORD	3	0	2	1	6	8	3	2	1	0	5	2
DONCASTER R	4	0	2	2	2	5	4	0	2	2	2	4
DOVER A	8	3	2	3	8	10	8	4	2	2	7	4
ENFIELD	9	6	0	3	14	11	9	1	5	3	13	17
FARNBOROUGH T	9	5	1	3	18	14	9	4	3	2	15	10
FISHER A	4	4	0	0	10	4	4	0	2	2	2	7
FOREST GREEN R	4	2	0	2	6	7	4	0	0	4	2	7
FRICKLEY A	7	4	1	2	18	5	7	0	3	4	8	16
GATESHEAD	11	7	3	1	23	8	11	3	7	1	12	9
GRAVESEND & N	4	2	2	0	5	2	4	2	1	1	7	4
HALIFAX T	6	2	1	3	11	7	6	0	1	5	2	13
HAYES	5	1	3	1	5	6	5	3	0	2	6	4
HEDNESFORD T	6	5	0	1	11	5	6	2	3	1	6	4
HEREFORD U	5	1	1	3	6	8	5	1	1	3	6	9
KIDDERMINSTER H	17	7	7	3	30	22	17	4	5	8	19	29
KINGSTONIAN	3	3	0	0	7	2	3	2	0	1	3	3
LEEK T	2	2	0	0	3	1	2	2	0	0	6	1
LEIGH RMI	2	0	0	2	0	2	2	0	1	1	2	3
LINCOLN C	1	1	0	0	2	0	1	1	0	0	1	0
MACCLESFIELD T	10	6	2	2	13	9	10	3	3	4	7	9
MAIDSTONE U	10	3	3	4	15	15	10	3	2	5	9	18
MARGATE	1	0	1	0	1	1	1	0	1	0	2	2
MERTHYR T	6	4	1	1	12	5	6	2	0	4	9	12
MORECAMBE	7	2	2	3	14	14	7	2	0	5	12	17
NORTHWICH V	23	11	9	3	35	28	23	6	9	8	32	41
NUNEATON B	10	2	5	3	16	15	10	3	5	2	13	7
REDDITCH U	1	1	0	0	2	1	1	1	0	0	1	0
RUNCORN	15	8	6	1	29	11	15	2	4	9	15	31
RUSHDEN & D	5	0	2	3	2	12	5	1	1	3	3	6
SCARBOROUGH	11	2	4	5	10	14	11	3	3	5	7	14
SLOUGH T	7	3	3	1	14	6	7	4	2	1	11	6
SOUTHPORT	9	5	2	2	9	7	9	4	3	2	11	13
STAFFORD R	14	9	3	2	22	12	14	3	7	4	17	18
STALYBRIDGE C	6	5	0	1	11	9	6	2	2	2	12	11
STEVENAGE B	8	3	0	5	8	10	8	0	4	4	5	16
SUTTON U	6	4	1	1	12	8	6	2	2	2	8	14
TELFORD U	23	11	3	9	40	36	23	8	4	11	27	31
TROWBRIDGE T	3	2	1	0	8	3	3	2	0	1	4	3
WEALDSTONE	8	3	0	5	9	12	8	1	2	5	9	17
WELLING U	14	5	4	5	23	22	14	4	3	7	16	20
WEYMOUTH	10	5	2	3	14	9	10	2	1	7	9	22
WITTON A	3	2	1	0	4	2	3	1	0	2	3	5
WOKING	10	4	2	4	11	6	10	1	5	4	9	13
WORCESTER C	6	3	1	2	6	3	6	3	1	2	13	11
WYCOMBE W	7	4	1	2	11	8	7	3	2	2	9	9
YEOVIL T	18	11	3	4	37	19	18	4	5	9	15	26
TOTALS	478	224	119	135	774	565	478	137	134	207	578	748

KETTERING TOWN

APPEARANCES

LEADING APPEARANCES

Phil BROWN	274+25	(299)
Doug KEAST	261+34	(295)
Craig NORMAN	227+4	(231)
Colin VOWDEN	160+1	(161)
Russell LEWIS	150	(150)
Frank MURPHY	145+9	(154)
Jon GRAHAM	67+67	(134)
Carl ADAMS	122+6	(128)
Paul RICHARDSON	117+9	(126)
Nicky EVANS	120+1	(121)
Mark SMITH	112+6	(118)
Kevin SHOEMAKE	113+4	(117)
Sean SUDDARDS	117	(117)
Trevor SLACK	112+2	(114)
David HOFBAUER	93+20	(113)
Matt FISHER	108+5	(113)
Brett McNAMARA	91+21	(112)
Paul NICOL	107	(107)
Martin MATTHEWS	102+3	(105)
Billy JEFFREY	102+2	(104)
Derek DUGGAN	98+5	(103)
Paul COX	94+7	(101)

Kettering Town APPEARANCES

Player	79-80	80-81	81-82	82-83	83-84	84-85	85-86	86-87	87-88	88-89	89-90	90-91	91-92	92-93	93-94	94-95	95-96	96-97	97-98	98-99	99-00	00-01	01-02	02-03	TOTAL
ABRAHAMS Paul																					6+4				6+4
ADAMS Carl																			31	36+3	39+1	16+2			122+6
ADAMS Steve														8+2											8+2
ALEXANDER Keith						30+5	15+9																		45+14
ALFORD Carl																38+2	32						2+3		72+5
ARNOLD Ian																21	4+3								25+3
ASHBY Nicky															42	34									76
ASHBY Roger	37																								37
ASHDJAN John															1+5										1+5
ASOMBANG Victor																								12+10	12+10
ATKINS Stuart		19	26																						45
AYRES James																						0+1			0+1
BANCROFT Paul												40+1	28+5	11											79+6
BANTON Geoff				26+1	9+3																				35+4
BANYA Sam																					10+10				10+10
BARBER Fred														5											5
BARCLAY Dominic														2											2
BARKER Dean													4												4
BARNES Bobby															4+5										4+5
BARTLETT Paul									8																8

KETTERING TOWN **APPEARANCES**

Kettering Town APPEARANCES	79-80	80-81	81-82	82-83	83-84	84-85	85-86	86-87	87-88	88-89	89-90	90-91	91-92	92-93	93-94	94-95	95-96	96-97	97-98	98-99	99-00	00-01	01-02	02-03	TOTAL
BASTOCK Paul											2	3	24												29
BEASLEY Andy										8				2											10
BEAVON David					35+1																				35+1
BEECH Glenn										6+5	27+5														33+10
BENJAMIN Ian																	6+3								6+3
BENSTEAD Graham															34	22									56
BERRY Steve																		41	27+4						68+4
BIRCH Ray								4+2																	4+2
BLACKWELL Kevin												24													24
BLOODWORTH Darren													9+2												9+2
BOLTON Ian						28																			28
BOON Roy											0+2														0+2
BOWLING Ian																						25		32	59
BOYD Willie						16	11																		27
BOYLE-CHONG Michael																								7+4	7+4
BRADD Les					12																				12
BROOK Gary												1													1
BROOMES David																					0+1				0+1
BROWN Jim				10																					10
BROWN Phil									5+1	29	25+1	27+6	38+2	40+2	30+6	40+1	1								274+25
BROWN Richard																				37+1	32+5	30+2			60+2
BROWN Simon					1+5																				1+5
BROWNE Shaun												1													1
BROWNRIGG Andy																	3								3
BRYANT Steve			0+8																						0+8
BUTCHER Richard																								14+4	14+4
BUTTERWORTH Gary													8												8
CARTER Recky																		8							8
CAVENER Phil								25+1																	25+1
CHAMBERLAIN Glyn				35+2	30+2																				65+4
CHAMBERS Lewroy																					3				3
CHAPMAN Campbell							1+1																		1+1
CHARD Phil																6									6
CHERRY Steve																		3							3
CHESHIRE Blair			3+1																						3+1

Dougie Keast   Thsese two photograp[hs are a wonderful example of the late Mick Cheney's quality   Photo: Mick Cheney

Paul Bancroft   Photo: Mick Cheney

KETTERING TOWN APPEARANCES

Kettering Town APPEARANCES	79-80	80-81	81-82	82-83	83-84	84-85	85-86	86-87	87-88	88-89	89-90	90-91	91-92	92-93	93-94	94-95	95-96	96-97	97-98	98-99	99-00	00-01	01-02	02-03	TOTAL
CHILDS Chris					0+1																				0+1
CHRISTIE Trevor													19+1												19+1
CLARKE Colin	23	34	17																						74
CLARKE Lee																								8+1	8+1
CLARKE Peter			3																						3
CLARKE Simon														5	13+7	29+4									47+11
CLAYTON Roy	31	2																							33
CODNER Robert																						22			22
COLLEY Karl																								2+2	2+2
COLLIER Graham				2+5																					2+5
COLLINS Darren																						22			22
COLLINS Steve											38	18+1													56+1
CONROY Steve				3																					3
COOKE Robbie										31	39	23+2													93+2
COSTELLO Peter															6				31+3						37+3
COTTON Perry													4+2												4+2
COWLING Lee																						25+7			25+7
COX Paul													1				7+1		17+2	38+1	29+1	2+2			94+7
CRABB Neil					4																				4
CRAWLEY Ian							23+5	17+8	16+8																56+21
CREANE Gerard										24															24
CREASER Glyn					8																				8
CULLIP Danny																	3								3
CULPIN Paul													4												4
CUNNINGHAM Jamie														0+1											0+1
CURTIS Bob		25																							25
CURTIS Hamish													17												17
CURTIS Lenny																								2+1	2+1
CURTIS Paul									14+1																14+1
CURTISS Andy														3+4											3+4
DALEY Steve							12+4	15																	27+4
DANCY Steffan																								1+5	1+5
DAWSON Richard					10	30+5	27+4	3+3																	70+12
DE VITO Claudio																		1+2	9						10+2
DEMPSEY Mark															12										12

361

Kettering Town APPEARANCES	79-80	80-81	81-82	82-83	83-84	84-85	85-86	86-87	87-88	88-89	89-90	90-91	91-92	92-93	93-94	94-95	95-96	96-97	97-98	98-99	99-00	00-01	01-02	02-03	TOTAL
DENYER Peter					38+2	32+2																			70+4
DIUK Wayne																					30+6	24+5		28+6	82+17
DIVER Shaun				1+1	1+2																				2+3
DIXEY Richard	2+1																								2+1
DOANE Ben																					3				3
DOCKER Ian														15											15
DONALD Warren														21	40+1	19+1									80+2
DONN Nigel			4																						4
DONOVAN Neil														1+2	0+4										1+6
DOWLING Luke																	1+4	0+1							1+5
DUDFIELD Laurie																		3+9							3+9
DUGGAN Derek		26	33+5	38	1																				98+5
DUNPHY Shaun																1									1
DYER Wayne																					2				2
EASTHALL Freddie	29+2	22+1																							51+3
EASTWOOD Phil																				2+2					2+2
EDWARDS Colin																								0+3	0+3
EDWARDS Matt																	2								2
EDWARDS Neil									9+3	14+8	5+6														28+17
ELLIS Neil														0+1											0+1
EMMS Mick									1																1
EMSON Paul												10+2	2+1												12+3
EVANS Nicky	34	30	36	20+1																					120+1
FEE Greg						39	32+1	4+1																	75+2
FELTON Graham	13+3																								13+3
FISHER Matt																				34+1	33+4	31			108+5
FLANNAGAN John	35+1	32																							67+1
FLATTS Mark																		2							2
FORSTER Martyn		11	36	28+1																					75+1
FOSTER Barry				2+1																					2+1
FOTHERGILL Carl																						0+6			0+6
FOWLER John																	16								16
FOX Kevin			12																						12
FUCCILLO Lil										37+1															37+1
GALLAGHER Jackie										9+1															9+1

Kettering Town APPEARANCES	79-80	80-81	81-82	82-83	83-84	84-85	85-86	86-87	87-88	88-89	89-90	90-91	91-92	92-93	93-94	94-95	95-96	96-97	97-98	98-99	99-00	00-01	01-02	02-03	TOTAL
GAUNT Craig																		36	10						46
GAVIN Pat													15	3											18
GENOVESE Domenico								11+4			7+5														18+9
GERNON Irvin														31+1											31+1
GLEASURE Peter																15									15
GOODE Terry				23+2	1																				24+2
GOODWIN Mark												30+3													30+3
GOODWIN Nick					4	21	2	27	5																59
GOODWIN Scott																								29+1	29+1
GORDON Delroy																								8+1	8+1
GOULD Andy							6+4																		6+4
GOURLAY William																								2	2
GRAHAM Jon											0+11	11+29	30+8		18+6	8+13									67+67
GREENWOOD Roger														1+1											1+1
GRIFFITH Cohen										27+8	10														37+8
GUY Alan			6+1																						6+1
GUY Clint	15+8																								15+8
GYNN Micky																	13			1					14
HAILSTONE Ricky																					0+1				0+1
HAMILL Stewart				28																					28
HARAN Mark																								30+3	30+3
HARDING Paul																		4+2							4+2
HARMON Darren																	23+5	24+7							47+12
HARRIS Terry														3+4											3+4
HARRISON Andy							17																		17
HARRISON Mark						28		15																	43
HAVERSON Paul	17	30+1	34	2																					83+1
HAWORTH Robert																	8								8
HAYDON Nicky																				7	4+3				11+3
HAYES Adie																				5+5					5+5
HEFFERNAN Liam																	2								2
HERCOCK David																			7+2						7+2
HEYWOOD Dave								7+1	20+5	20															47+6
HICKTON Doug	3+1																								3+1
HILL Richard													41+1	13											54+1

Top left:
Trevor Christie
& Phil Brown
Photo: Mick Cheney

Top right:
Steve Holden,
Graham Benstead
& Nick Ashby

Middle left:
Andy Wright

Middle right:
Ernie Moss

Left:
Colin Vowden
Photo: Dennis Nicholson

KETTERING TOWN APPEARANCES

Kettering Town APPEARANCES	79-80	80-81	81-82	82-83	83-84	84-85	85-86	86-87	87-88	88-89	89-90	90-91	91-92	92-93	93-94	94-95	95-96	96-97	97-98	98-99	99-00	00-01	01-02	02-03	TOTAL
HINES Steve							22+3																		22+3
HODGES David														11+1											11+1
HODGSON Gary					2																				2
HOFBAUER David	2+5	14+4	24+3	18+6	35+2																				93+20
HOLDEN Steve															29	32	22								83
HOLYOAK Danny																								1	1
HONE Mark																				24+7					24+7
HOPE Chris														19											19
HOPKINS Craig																				0+2	6+9				6+11
HORWOOD Neil											9+3														9+3
HOULT Russell															7										7
HOWARTH Lee													6											24+1	30+1
HOWE Steve																6									6
HOWELLS Gareth														1											1
HUDSON Lee																				24+10	11+21				35+46
HUGHES Gary																								7+1	7+1
HUGHES Lyndon	11																								11
HUMPHRIES Steve				1	38	5								10											54
HUNT Andy												23+1													23+1
HUNTER Junior																	15								15
HUXFORD Richard												35+2	42												77+2
IBRAHIM Mustafa																8+3									8+3
INMAN Niall																						24+4		31+5	55+9
ITONGA Carlin																								1+1	1+1
IVEY Paul				2																					2
JAMES Micky								0+2																	0+2
JEFFREY Billy						40	42	20+2																	102+2
JENAS Dennis						22+4																			22+4
JENKINS Iori		15+1			33+1																				48+2
JONES David																	0+2								0+2
JONES Gary											12+1	19+7													31+8
JONES John		26+4																							26+4
JONES Paul													15+3												15+3
JUDGE Alan																	34	17+2							51+2
KABIA Jim							33+3	7																	40+3

365

Kettering Town APPEARANCES	79-80	80-81	81-82	82-83	83-84	84-85	85-86	86-87	87-88	88-89	89-90	90-91	91-92	92-93	93-94	94-95	95-96	96-97	97-98	98-99	99-00	00-01	01-02	02-03	TOTAL
KEARNS Ollie												1													1
KEAST Doug					12	19+8	22+1	26+12	37+3	38+1	41	40+1	26+8												261+34
KELLOCK Billy								30+4	22+2																52+6
KELLY Eddie				1																					1
KELLY Gavin																								7	7
KELLY Willie					17+1																				17+1
KING Eddie																	4+3								4+3
KING Jeff						9+1																			9+1
KIRK David					4+1																				4+1
LANE Frank	23																								23
LAWRENCE Les										4+4															4+4
LECZYNSKI Alex																			0+1						0+1
LEE Jason																						0+2			0+2
LENAGH Steve																						11+8			11+8
LEONARD Gary			5+1																						5+1
LEWIS Russell								39	41	39	31														150
LIM Harvey														7											16
LOCK Tony																					2				2
LOUGHLAN Terry															5										5
LYNCH Tony																		24+6							24+6
LYNE Neil																		19							19
MACKAY Roger									19+2																19+2
MAGEE John																0+2									0+2
MANN Arthur					9+1			41	34+1	6+1															84+2
MARCH Jamie																	17+11	23+8							40+19
MARSHALL Rob																		36+2							36+2
MARTIN Dean														5	18+7	9+4									32+11
MARTIN Dennis		30+3																							30+3
MARTIN Mick															1										1
MASON Andy																				4+3					4+3
MASSEY Richard										6+1															6+1
MASSON Don					5+1																				5+1
MATTHEWS Martin																				38+1		22+2		42	102+3
MAY Leroy																		10+1							10+1
MAYES Bobby											1+1														1+1

Kettering Town APPEARANCES	79-80	80-81	81-82	82-83	83-84	84-85	85-86	86-87	87-88	88-89	89-90	90-91	91-92	92-93	93-94	94-95	95-96	96-97	97-98	98-99	99-00	00-01	01-02	02-03	TOTAL
McGOLDRICK Eddie		8+2																							88+2
McGOWAN Andy							15																		15
McILROY Steve	8																								8
McILWAIN Alan							20+1																		20+1
McINTOSH Malcolm			41																						41
McKENZIE Michael																								6+12	6+12
McKERNON Craig													7+1												7+1
McMAHON Sam																		4							4
McNAMARA Brett																				34+5	29+5	28+11			91+21
McPARLAND Ian																	0+3								0+3
MIDDLETON Joe		1																							1
MILES Paul																	0+3	1+2	0+7						1+12
MILKINS John	14																								14
MILLER Chris																	0+1								0+1
MOODIE Mick	2																								2
MOORE David																			14						14
MORAN Richie												1													1
MORTIMER Dennis								22																	22
MOSS Ernie									32+3	33+3		5+1													70+7
MUCKLEBERG Terry															0+1										0+1
MUIR Maurice						3+5																			3+5
MURPHY Frank			35+3					9	29+2					8+2											145+9
MURPHY Gez																								19+1	19+1
MURPHY Matt															3+2										3+2
MURRAY Shaun																						3+2			3+2
MURRAY Shaun																								26+4	26+4
MUSTAFA Tarkan																	31	19+10							50+10
MUTCHELL Rob																			41	3+1					44+1
NAYLOR Stuart				2																					2
NEEDHAM Dave					16+1																				16+1
NEVILLE Chris												3													3
NEWMAN	0+1																								0+1
NICOL Paul												40	41	26											107
NIGHTINGALE Mark										40	34+2														74+2
NORMAN Craig																24+1	38	38	27+2	40	38	26+1		33	227+4

Kettering Town 1986-87
Back Row: Wood, Crawley, Fee, Tillson, Harrison, Wharton, Richardson, Kellock, Ward, Keast.
Front Row: Dawson, Lewis, Mann, Needham (Manager), Jeffries, Nixon (Asst. Man.), Kabia, Smith, Thacker
Photo: Malc Tompkins

Kettering Town 2001-02
Back Row: Andrew Speechley, Carl Lake, Brett McNamara, Chris Perkins, Jason Lee.
Midle Row: Peter Lake (Physio), Rob Yardy, Darren Collins, Steve Wilkinson, Ian Barling, Rob Wild, Steve Lenogh, Brad Piercewright, Gary Hughes. **Front Row:** Shaun Murray, Martin Matthews, Dale Watkins, Carl Shutt (Manager), Lee Carling, Craig Norman, Wayne Diuk

Kettering Town APPEARANCES	79-80	80-81	81-82	82-83	83-84	84-85	85-86	86-87	87-88	88-89	89-90	90-91	91-92	92-93	93-94	94-95	95-96	96-97	97-98	98-99	99-00	00-01	01-02	02-03	TOTAL
NORTH Marc													4+4	5											9+4
NUGENT Richard																		27							27
NUTTELL Micky														1					12+4						13+4
NYAMAH Kofi																	34	17							51
OKEEFE Terry					6+1																				6+1
OREILLY David			3+1																						3+1
OXBROW Darren														5	40	12	22+1								79+1
PALGRAVE Brian									0+1																0+1
PALMER Jem				40+1	17+7	0+4																			57+12
PARKER Simon																								11+3	11+3
PARSONS Mark																2	2+5								4+5
PAUL Mark																					0+2				0+2
PAWLUK Andy				0+1																					0+1
PEARSON Chris																		13+1	31+2						44+3
PEPPER Luke																								0+1	0+1
PERKINS Chris																					10+2	27+4		3+5	40+11
PERKINS Glen	3																								3
PETTINGER Paul																5									5
PHILLIPS Brendan		29																							29
PHILLIPS Ian												34+1													34+1
PHIPPS Peter	37	38	24																						99
PICK Gary																			5						5
PIERCEWRIGHT Brad																								19+3	19+3
POPE Neil																	37	14+1							51+1
POPLAR Dave				6+1																					6+1
POWNALL Dave		13+2		36+1	22+2																				71+5
PRICE Gareth													18+2	20+2	35	12+4									85+8
QUOW Trevor												13+4													13+4
QUY Andy																			2						2
RADFORD Mark														1											1
RADFORD Peter							0+4	0+1																	0+5
RAYMENT Pat																	6								6
RAYNOR Paul																				27					27
REA Simon																	4								4
REDDISH Shane														6											6

Kettering Town APPEARANCES	79-80	80-81	81-82	82-83	83-84	84-85	85-86	86-87	87-88	88-89	89-90	90-91	91-92	92-93	93-94	94-95	95-96	96-97	97-98	98-99	99-00	00-01	01-02	02-03	TOTAL
REECE Paul									37				6												43
REED Graham														16+1	29+1	18									63+2
RETALLICK Graham														2											2
REVELL Alex																								7	7
RICHARDSON Paul								36+1	26+5	22+3	33														117+9
RICKETTS Alan									1+12																1+12
RIDGWAY Ian																			25+6	1+6	22+7	8			56+19
RILEY David														25+2											25+2
RITCHIE David												1													1
ROBERTS Dave			9																						9
ROBERTS Steve			2																						2
RODERICK Martin														17+1	12+1										29+2
ROWE Zeke																			2						2
RUSSELL Glen														0+1											0+1
RYAN Peter	1		8	12																					21
SADDINGTON James																25	1+1								26+1
SANDEMAN Bradley																			23						23
SANDERCOCK Phil					22																				22
SCHIAVI Mark									11+4																11+4
SCOPE David											5+1														5+1
SCOTT IAN																	30+7								30+7
SELLERS John						0+6	14+1																		14+7
SETCHELL Gary																					24+7				24+7
SHANAHAN John																	1+1								1+1
SHEARER Mick														3+1											3+1
SHELTON Greg			23+3	1	1+2																				25+5
SHEPPARD Simon																			12						12
SHOEMAKE Kevin										23	38	12	18				8+3	13+1	1						113+4
SHRIEVES Terr						21+6	4+3																		25+9
SHUTT Carl																				17+8		17+4		8+17	42+29
SIMBA Amara																						2			2
SINDEN Sven																			1+1						1+1
SLACK Trevor											36+1	40	36+1												112+2
SLAWSON Steve																		15+1							15+1
SMALL Bryan																								7	7

KETTERING TOWN APPEARANCES

Kettering Town APPEARANCES	79-80	80-81	81-82	82-83	83-84	84-85	85-86	86-87	87-88	88-89	89-90	90-91	91-92	92-93	93-94	94-95	95-96	96-97	97-98	98-99	99-00	00-01	01-02	02-03	TOTAL
SMALLEY Mark														18+1											18+1
SMITH Mark						25+1	21+2	23+3	42					1											112+6
SMITH Paul																8									8
SMITH Scott																		4+1							4+1
SOLKHON Brett																								12	12
SOLLITT Adam																				32	42				74
SOMMER Jurgen														10											10
SOWDEN Shaun														6											6
STEBBING Gary														5											5
STOCK Russell																		13+7							13+7
STORER Paul																					5+2				5+2
STOTT Steve																	18								18
STRINGFELLOW Ian														1	12+2	31+1	16+5								60+8
SUDDARDS Sean	38	38	32	9																					117
SWAILES Chris														5											5
TALLANTYRE Dean																		2							2
TAYLOR Chris																			27						27
TAYLOR Robin														3	37+1	27+1									67+2
THACKER Tim						41	42	1																	84
THOMAS Anton															30+5	6+2									36+7
THOMPSON Paul																				0+3					0+3
THORPE Adrian															8+4										8+4
THROWER Nigel						38																			38
TILSON Andy								12	18																30
TINGAY Phil			22	14																					36
TOLSON Neil																								1	1
TOMLINSON David														8											8
TOMLINSON Paul																					1				1
TORRANCE Neil																					1				1
TOWN David																								4+2	4+2
TRIGG Simon																	1+2								1+2
TUCKER Mark																			33+1						33+1
TURLEY Billy																		9							9
TURNER Ian					1+6																				1+6
UNDERWOOD Simon													0+2												0+2

Kettering Town APPEARANCES	79-80	80-81	81-82	82-83	83-84	84-85	85-86	86-87	87-88	88-89	89-90	90-91	91-92	92-93	93-94	94-95	95-96	96-97	97-98	98-99	99-00	00-01	01-02	02-03	TOTAL
VAN DULLEMAN Ray																			10+1						10+1
VENABLES Dave																		10	3+3						13+3
VINTER Micky									0+1																0+1
VOWDEN Colin																			39+1	42	41	38			160+1
WADDICOR John				1+2																					1+2
WALKER Richard													5												5
WALLER David													2+4												2+4
WALSH Danny																								7+3	7+3
WALSH Mario													5												5
WALTERS Peter		38																							38
WALWYN Keith												7													7
WARD Simon																								1+1	1+1
WARD Steve								37+3	38																75+3
WARNE Paul																				4					4
WATKINS Dale																					23	32+8		8+3	63+11
WATSON Dave							10																		10
WHARTON Dave						42	37+1	17+2																	96+3
WHITEHOUSE Mark															6										6
WHITEHURST Billy														3+1											3+1
WILDE Adam																				2+3					2+3
WILKES Tim																		9+1	22+15	2+6					33+22
WILKINSON Steve																						3+5			3+5
WILLIAMS Steve																				7+4	0+2				7+6
WILLIAMSON Davey																								0+2	0+2
WILLIAMSON David																				1+3					1+3
WILLIS Roger																								2	2
WILSON Steve																				10	0+2	17			27+2
WOOD Garry				14																					14
WOOD Ian							18	36																	54
WOOD Shaun														25+1											25+1
WOODSFORD Jamie																		3							3
WRIGHT Andy			1+5	4+1						22+6	34+4	0+1													61+17
WRIGHT Ben																				5+6					5+6
WRIGHT Owen													14+3		24+4	8+5									46+12
YORK Paul								2+1																	2+1

Richard Huxford

Paul Nicol

Mark Goodwin

Ian Phillips

Trevor Slack

John Graham

Craig Norman

Steve Berry

Kevin Shoemake

LEADING GOALSCORERS

Leading Goalscorers	
Frank MURPHY	71
Phil BROWN	65
Nicky EVANS	50
Robbie COOKE	49(1p)
Craig NORMAN	46(27p)
David HOFBAUER	45
Mark SMITH	45
Carl ALFORD	45(4p)
Jon GRAHAM	41
Doug KEAST	36

Kettering Town GOALSCORERS

Player	79-80	80-81	81-82	82-83	83-84	84-85	85-86	86-87	87-88	88-89	89-90	90-91	91-92	92-93	93-94	94-95	95-96	96-97	97-98	98-99	99-00	00-01	01-02	02-03	TOTAL
ABRAHAMS Paul																									1
ADAMS Carl																			5(2p)	2(1p)		1			8(4p)
ALEXANDER Keith						9																			9
ALFORD Carl																23(4p)	22								45(4p)
ARNOLD Ian																11(1p)									11(1p)
ASHBY Nicky															1										1
ASHBY Roger	5(5p)																								5(5p)
ASOMBANG Victor																								2	2
ATKINS Stuart		9	13																						22
BANCROFT Paul												10(4p)	3	3											16(4p)
BANTON Geoff				8	2																				10
BANYA Sam																					1				1
BARTLETT Paul					1																				1
BEAVON David					1																				1
BEECH Glenn											2														2
BENJAMIN Ian																	3								3
BERRY Steve																		2	1						3
BOLTON Ian						1																			1
BRADD Les				2																					2
BROWN Phil																				8	4	2			65
BUTCHER Richard																								4	4
BUTTERWORTH Gary													1												1
CAVENER Phil								4																	4
CHAMBERLAIN Glyn				1																					1

Kettering Town GOALSCORERS	79-80	80-81	81-82	82-83	83-84	84-85	85-86	86-87	87-88	88-89	89-90	90-91	91-92	92-93	93-94	94-95	95-96	96-97	97-98	98-99	99-00	00-01	01-02	02-03	TOTAL
CHAMBERS Leroy																					1				1
CHRISTIE Trevor													5												5
CLARKE Colin		2																							2
CLARKE Lee																								1	1
CLARKE Simon															2	2									4
CLAYTON Roy	12																								12
CODNER Robert																						1			1
COLLIER Graham				2																					2
COLLINS Darren																						11			11
COLLINS Steve											3														3
COOKE Robbie										12(1p)	28	9													49(1p)
COSTELLO Peter															4				5						9
CRAWLEY Ian							11	4	9																24
CREANE Gerard										1															1
CURTIS Bob		4																							4
CURTIS Paul									1																1
DALEY Steve									2																2
DAWSON Richard					3		1																		4
DEMPSEY Mark															2										2
DENYER Peter					4																				4
DIUK Wayne																					2	2			4
DOCKER Ian														1											1
DONALD Warren														2	1										3
DONOVAN Neil														2											2
DOWLING Luke																	2								2
DUGGAN Derek		3	2	8																					13
EASTHALL Freddie	1	2																							3
EDWARDS Neil										5	1	1	1												8
EMSON Paul										2															2
EVANS Nicky	12	21	11	6																					50
FEE Greg																				2	4				6
FISHER Matt																						2			8
FLANNAGAN John	4																								4
FORSTER Martyn		1																							1

Andy Hunt

Gary Jones

Carl Alford

Frankie Murphy

Robbie Cooke

Photo: Mick Cheney

Photo: Mick Cheney

Kettering Town GOALSCORERS	79-80	80-81	81-82	82-83	83-84	84-85	85-86	86-87	87-88	88-89	89-90	90-91	91-92	92-93	93-94	94-95	95-96	96-97	97-98	98-99	99-00	00-01	01-02	02-03	TOTAL
FUCCILLO Lil										7(6p)															7(6p)
GALLAGHER Jackie										2															2
GAUNT Craig																		2							2
GAVIN Pat													3	1											4
GENOVESE Domenico								4			1														5
GOODE Terry				5																					5
GOODWIN Mark												5													5
GOODWIN Scott																								1	1
GRAHAM Jon											1	13	17		6	4									41
GRIFFITH Cohen										8	3														11
GUY Clint		5																							5
HAMILL Stewart				2																					2
HARMON Darren																	1	2							3
HARRIS Terry														3											3
HAVERSON Paul	1	1	3																						5
HAWORTH Robert																	2								2
HEYWOOD Dave									1																1
HICKTON Doug	1																								1
HILL Richard												16(8p)		3(1p)											19(9p)
HINES Steve							2																		2
HODGES David														3											3
HOFBAUER David	1	8	14	7	15																				45
HOLDEN Steve																3									3
HOPE Chris													3(1p)												3(1p)
HOWARTH Lee																								2	2
HOWE Steve																1									1
HUDSON Lee																			10		2	3			15
HUNT Andy											6														6
HUNTER Junior																	2								2
HUXFORD Richard											2		1												3
INMAN Niall																						4		5(1p)	9(1p)
JEFFREY Billy						16	8	7(4p)																	31(4p)
JENAS Dennis						7																			7
JONES Gary											3	4													7

Kettering Town GOALSCORERS	79-80	80-81	81-82	82-83	83-84	84-85	85-86	86-87	87-88	88-89	89-90	90-91	91-92	92-93	93-94	94-95	95-96	96-97	97-98	98-99	99-00	00-01	01-02	02-03	TOTAL
JONES John	4																								4
KABIA Jim							6																		6
KEAST Doug					3	5	7	3	8	3	2	4	1												36
KELLOCK Billy								9(1p)	3																12(1p)
KELLY Willie					3																				3
LAWRENCE Les									1																1
LENAGH Steve																						2			2
LEWIS Russell								1	4		2														7
LOUGHLAN Tony															1										1
LYNCH Tony																		7							7
LYNE Neil																		3							3
MARTIN Dean														2	4										6
MARTIN Dennis		3																							3
MASON Andy																				1					1
MASSON Don					1																				1
MATTHEWS Martin																				1					1
MAY Leroy																		2							2
McGOLDRICK Eddie				1	3																				4
McGOWAN Andy						4																			4
McILROY Steve	2																								2
McKENZIE Michael																								1	1
McNAMARA Brett																				12	4	2			18
MOODIE Mick	1																								1
MOSS Ernie										13	8	2													23
MUIR Maurice						1																			1
MURPHY Frank			15	23	11			4	12					6											**71**
MURPHY Gez																								4	4
MURRAY Shaun																								2(1p)	2(1p)
MUSTAFA Tarkan																	2	6							8
MUTCHELL Rob																			2						2
NEEDHAM Dave					2																				2
NICOL Paul												1	2												3
NIGHTINGALE Mark										1															1

Kettering Town GOALSCORERS	79-80	80-81	81-82	82-83	83-84	84-85	85-86	86-87	87-88	88-89	89-90	90-91	91-92	92-93	93-94	94-95	95-96	96-97	97-98	98-99	99-00	00-01	01-02	02-03	TOTAL
NORMAN Craig																	1	10(4p)	8(5p)	9(5p)	3(3p)			6(3p)	46(27p)
NORTH Marc													6												6
NUGENT Richard																		3							3
NUTTELL Micky														1					1						2
NYAMAH Kofi																	3	2							5
OXBROW Darren															2(1p)		5								7(1p)
PALMER Jem				1	1																				2
PARKER Simon																								3	3
PARSONS Mark																	1								1
PEARSON Chris																		4	14						18
PERKINS Chris																					1				1
PHILLIPS Brendan	2																								2
PHIPPS Peter	8	3	2																						13
POPE Neil																	6	2							8
POPLAR Dave				1																					1
POWNALL Dave		1		1																					2
PRICE Gareth														1	2(1p)										3(1p)
RAYNOR Paul																				2					2
REED Graham															2										2
REVELL Alex																								1	1
RICHARDSON Paul								2	4	2	3														11
RILEY David														9											9
RITCHIE David												1													1
ROBERTS Dave			1																						1
RODERICK Martin														1	2										3
SANDEMAN Bradley																		3							3
SANDERCOCK Phil					1																				1
SCOTT Ian																	7								7
SETCHELL Gary																					1				1
SHELTON Greg			2																						2
SHRIEVES Terry						7	1																		8
SHUTT Carl																					4				4
SLACK Trevor											5	2	1												8
SLAWSON Steve																		1							1

KETTERING TOWN GOALSCORERS

Kettering Town GOALSCORERS	79-80	80-81	81-82	82-83	83-84	84-85	85-86	86-87	87-88	88-89	89-90	90-91	91-92	92-93	93-94	94-95	95-96	96-97	97-98	98-99	99-00	00-01	01-02	02-03	TOTAL
SMITH Mark						13	8	8	16																45
SOLKHON Brett																								1	1
STOCK Russell																		3							3
STOTT Steve																	3								3
STRINGFELLOW Ian																6	6								12
TAYLOR Robin															5	4									9
THACKER Tim						3	1																		4
THOMAS Anton																8	1								9
THORPE Adrian															2										2
THROWER Nigel						1																			1
TILSON Andy								1	3																4
TOMLINSON David														1											1
TOWN David																								1	1
TUCKER Mark																			1						1
VAN DULLEMAN Ray																			1						1
VENABLES Dave																		1							1
VINTER Micky									1																1
VOWDEN Colin																			5	4	3				12
WALKER Richard													1												1
WALSH Danny																								1	1
WALWYN Keith												1													1
WARD Steve									2																2
WARNE Paul																				2					2
WATKINS Dale																					4	12(1p)			16(1p)
WATSON Dave							3																		3
WHARTON Dave						2		1																	3
WHITEHOUSE Mark															2										2
WILKES Tim																		2	7	1					10
WILLIAMS Steve																				3					3
WOOD Ian								3																	3
WOOD Shaun														1											1
WOODSFORD Jamie																		1							1
WRIGHT Andy				3						1	4														8
WRIGHT Owen														1											1

KIDDERMINSTER HARRIERS

PROMOTED FROM: Southern League 1993
PROMOTED TO: Football League (Div.3) 2003
2004-2005 SEASON: Football League Division 2

1999-2000 Squad. Back Row (L-R): Rene Petersen, Martin Weir, Steve Taylor, Stuart Brock, Phil King, Dean Bennett, Mark Druce.
Middle: Ginger Jordan (Kit Manager), Stuart Payne, Adie Smith, Craig Hinton, Andrew Brownrigg, Stewart Hadley, Steve Pope, Shaun Cunnington, Jim Conway (Physio).
Front: Thomas Skovbjerg, Les Hines, Jan Molby (Manager), Paul webb, Gary Barnett (Player Asst. Manager), Ian Foster, James Collins.

		HOME							AWAY						
	P	W	D	L	F	A	Pts	P	W	D	L	F	A	Pts	Position
83-84	21	7	9	5	32	30	23	21	7	5	9	22	31	26	10
84-85	21	8	4	9	40	38	20	21	9	4	8	39	39	31	8
85-86	21	12	4	5	51	28	28	21	12	3	6	48	34	39	3
86-87	21	10	4	7	46	34	34	21	7	0	14	31	47	21	12
87-88	21	11	8	2	42	28	41	21	7	7	7	33	38	28	7
88-89	20	10	4	6	32	32	34	20	11	2	7	36	25	35	5
89-90	21	7	6	8	37	33	27	21	8	3	10	27	34	27	13
90-91	21	8	5	8	33	30	29	21	6	5	10	23	37	23	13
91-92	21	8	6	7	35	32	30	21	4	3	14	21	45	15	19
92-93	21	9	5	7	26	30	32	21	5	11	5	34	30	26	9
93-94	21	13	5	3	31	12	44	21	9	4	8	32	23	31	1
94-95	21	6	5	10	28	29	23	21	10	4	7	35	32	34	11
95-96	21	13	4	4	49	26	43	21	5	6	10	29	40	21	7
96-97	21	14	4	3	48	18	46	21	12	3	6	36	24	39	2
97-98	21	6	8	7	32	31	26	21	5	6	10	24	32	21	17
98-99	21	9	4	8	32	22	31	21	5	5	11	24	30	20	15
99-00	21	16	3	2	47	16	51	21	10	4	7	28	24	34	1
Total	356	167	88	101	641	469	562	356	132	75	149	522	565	471	

SEASONS
17

TOTAL POINTS
562 + 471 = 1033

HIGHEST POSITION
1 (93/93) (99/00)

LOWEST POSITION
19 (91/92)

HIGHEST ATTENDANCE
6250 Rushden (8-4-00)

LOWEST ATTENDANCE
414 Altrincham (15-10-83)

SEASON GOALSCORER
Kim Casey 38(5p) (86/87)

CAREER GOALSCORER
Paul Davies 176(1p)
The Conference Record

CAREER APPEARANCES
Paul Davies 431+20

KIDDERMINSTER HARRIERS

	Home						Away					
	P	W	D	L	F	A	P	W	D	L	F	A
ALTRINCHAM	15	3	4	8	16	20	15	5	4	6	16	20
AYLESBURY U	1	1	0	0	4	3	1	1	0	0	5	1
BANGOR C	1	1	0	0	2	1	1	1	0	0	2	1
BARNET	8	1	2	5	7	18	8	5	1	2	16	12
BARROW	6	2	1	3	9	9	6	4	0	2	16	12
BATH C	12	6	3	3	24	16	12	5	2	5	23	25
BOSTON U	10	3	2	5	13	18	10	6	0	4	19	15
BROMSGROVE R	5	2	1	2	4	4	5	2	1	2	10	8
CHELTENHAM T	9	6	0	3	22	12	9	4	2	3	15	13
CHORLEY	2	1	0	1	3	3	2	1	0	1	3	2
COLCHESTER U	2	0	2	0	2	2	2	0	0	2	0	5
DAGENHAM	5	4	1	0	16	6	5	2	2	1	6	6
DAGENHAM & R	5	3	1	1	13	5	5	1	1	3	7	14
DARLINGTON	1	1	0	0	3	2	1	0	0	1	0	3
DARTFORD	2	1	1	0	5	2	2	0	0	2	2	7
DONCASTER R	2	1	1	0	4	3	2	1	0	1	2	2
DOVER A	7	3	3	1	13	7	7	4	0	3	13	6
ENFIELD	7	2	1	4	13	13	7	2	1	4	11	18
FARNBOROUGH T	8	3	2	3	14	14	8	2	2	4	13	15
FISHER A	4	1	3	0	7	6	4	0	2	2	3	7
FOREST GREEN R	2	0	2	0	5	5	2	0	0	2	2	8
FRICKLEY A	4	1	2	1	8	7	4	2	0	2	4	6
GATESHEAD	11	5	4	2	25	18	11	3	0	8	13	20
HALIFAX T	5	4	0	1	14	4	5	3	0	2	8	6
HAYES	4	3	0	1	8	3	4	1	1	2	3	5
HEDNESFORD T	5	3	1	1	10	5	5	3	0	2	10	7
HEREFORD U	3	1	1	1	3	5	3	1	1	1	4	3
KETTERING T	17	8	5	4	29	19	17	3	7	7	22	30
KINGSTONIAN	2	1	0	1	2	1	2	1	0	1	1	1
LEEK T	2	0	1	1	2	3	2	1	1	0	4	1
LINCOLN C	1	0	1	0	3	3	1	0	0	1	3	5
MACCLESFIELD T	10	3	4	3	11	14	10	5	5	0	12	5
MAIDSTONE U	6	3	2	1	12	11	6	3	0	3	11	12
MERTHYR T	6	3	1	2	9	6	6	3	0	3	12	11
MORECAMBE	5	3	1	1	14	11	5	2	0	3	7	10
NORTHWICH V	17	10	5	2	37	18	17	6	6	5	25	28
NUNEATON B	5	2	1	2	12	10	5	3	1	1	10	6
RUNCORN	13	7	3	3	23	15	13	5	3	5	22	22
RUSHDEN & D	4	2	1	1	4	2	4	0	2	2	6	11
SCARBOROUGH	5	3	0	2	11	7	5	1	1	3	7	9
SLOUGH T	7	1	3	3	10	12	7	2	1	4	13	14
SOUTHPORT	7	4	1	2	15	6	7	3	2	2	8	8
STAFFORD R	10	5	3	2	15	10	10	6	0	4	14	15
STALYBRIDGE C	6	5	1	0	15	4	6	2	2	2	11	11
STEVENAGE B	6	3	0	3	9	8	6	2	1	3	9	14
SUTTON U	6	3	3	0	7	4	6	3	1	2	9	8
TELFORD U	17	8	3	6	25	23	17	2	5	10	17	28
TROWBRIDGE T	1	0	1	0	1	1	1	1	0	0	2	1
WEALDSTONE	5	4	0	1	13	8	5	2	1	2	9	8
WELLING U	14	10	1	3	31	15	14	7	3	4	17	11
WEYMOUTH	6	2	2	2	7	7	6	2	2	2	7	7
WITTON A	3	0	2	1	0	1	3	0	1	2	3	6
WOKING	8	5	1	2	15	12	8	2	2	4	8	7
WORCESTER C	2	2	0	0	6	2	2	1	1	0	3	2
WYCOMBE W	7	3	0	4	13	12	7	3	2	2	13	11
YEOVIL T	12	5	4	3	23	13	12	2	5	5	11	16
TOTALS	356	167	88	101	641	469	356	132	75	149	522	565

	Altrincham		Aylesbury United		Bangor City		Barnet		Barrow		Bath City		Boston United		Bromsgrove Rovers		Cheltenham Town		Chorley	
	H	A	H	A	H	A	H	A	H	A	H	A	H	A	H	A	H	A	H	A
82-83																				
83-84	0-2	1-0			2-1	2-1	4-4	2-0			1-1	0-3	1-1	3-2						
84-85	0-2	1-2					1-4	4-2	0-1	3-1	2-2	2-0	2-0	3-2						
85-86	0-2	1-2					0-2	1-0	2-1	4-3	3-1	4-2	3-2	1-2			5-1	6-2		
86-87	3-0	1-3					0-3	2-5			2-4	2-3	1-2	1-2			5-1	2-1		
87-88	4-1	3-2					1-1	1-1			3-2	3-3	1-0	0-1			3-2	2-2		
88-89	2-3	1-3	4-3	5-1			1-0	2-0					0-2	2-0			3-2	1-4	0-2	3-1
89-90	1-2	1-0					0-1	1-2	2-2	1-2			1-3	3-2			1-2	1-2	3-1	0-1
90-91	0-1	2-1					0-3	3-2	3-1	3-1	3-2	1-4	3-3	1-3			2-0	0-0		
91-92	1-0	1-1							1-2	1-5	0-1	1-0	1-3	2-1			2-1	2-1		
92-93	0-1	2-2									1-0	1-2	0-2	3-0	1-0	2-2				
93-94	0-1	0-1									0-0	0-4			1-1	3-0				
94-95	2-2	0-2									2-1	5-3			0-1	3-4				
95-96	1-1	1-1									1-2	1-1			1-0	1-2				
96-97	1-1	1-0									6-0	3-0			1-2	1-0				
97-98																	1-2	1-0		
98-99									1-2	4-0							0-1	0-1		
99-00	1-1	0-0																		
00-01																				

	Colchester United		Dagenham		Dagenham & Redbridge		Darlington		Dartford		Doncaster Rovers		Dover Athletic		Enfield		Farnborough Town		Fisher Athletic	
	H	A	H	A	H	A	H	A	H	A	H	A	H	A	H	A	H	A	H	A
82-83																				
83-84			4-2	0-0											1-1	1-0				
84-85			5-1	2-2					1-1	1-2					1-3	2-5				
85-86			2-0	1-0					4-1	1-5					1-2	2-2				
86-87			4-2	1-3											3-4	0-3				
87-88			1-1	2-1											4-0	2-5			1-1	1-3
88-89															1-3	3-1			2-1	0-2
89-90							3-2	0-3							2-0	1-2	3-1	1-0	1-1	1-1
90-91	0-0	0-2															1-1	1-2	3-3	1-1
91-92	2-2	0-3			5-1	0-5														
92-93					0-1	2-3											1-5	2-2		
93-94					2-1	1-1							3-0	1-3						
94-95					1-1	2-1							0-0	0-1			0-1	0-1		
95-96					5-1	2-4							1-1	1-2			3-3	1-3		
96-97													4-1	5-0			2-3	1-2		
97-98													3-3	4-0			2-0	3-3		
98-99											3-3	0-1	1-0	1-0			2-0	4-2		
99-00											1-0	2-1	1-2	1-0						
00-01																				

1984-85 Squad. Back Row (L-R): J Chapman (Physio), N Bickley (Youth Coach), J Barton (Asst. Manager), M Kavanagh, T Garner, C Jones, J Horne, P davies, B Kenning (Coach), G Frisby (Youth Team Manager).
Middle: R Mercer (Secretary), G Lane (Director), P Fryar, (Director), D reynolds (Chairman), G Allner (Manager), M Morris (Director), C Youngjohns (Director), J Peutherer (Director).
Front: M Gavin, J Powell, K emson, G Mackenzie (Capt), A Richards, M Rosegreen, M woodall, A Ollis.

1986-87 Squad. Back Row (L-R):   Les Palmer, Richard Forsyth, Mark Yates, Jay Powell, Lee Hughes, Paul Webb, John Deakin, Delwyn Humphries.
Middle Row: Jim Conway (Physio), Mark Dearlove, Neil Cartwright, Darren Steadman, Kevin Rose, Jon Purdie, Martin Weir, Graham Allner (Manager).
Front Row: Paul Grainger, Chris Brindley, Simeon Hodson (Captian), Paul Davies, Paul Bancroft.

	Forest Green Rovers		Frickley Athletic		Gateshead		Halifax Town		Hayes		Hednesford Town		Hereford United		Kettering Town		Kingstonian		Leek Town	
	H	A	H	A	H	A	H	A	H	A	H	A	H	A	H	A	H	A	H	A
82-83																				
83-84			1-1	2-0	1-0	0-1									3-1	2-4				
84-85			2-4	0-3	3-0	1-4									2-2	2-2				
85-86			1-1	1-3											0-0	2-2				
86-87			4-1	1-0	3-1	4-2									2-1	2-0				
87-88															2-1	1-1				
88-89															1-1	1-2				
89-90															2-3	2-0				
90-91					2-3	1-2									3-0	1-4				
91-92					5-3	3-0									2-3	1-2				
92-93					3-3	0-1									0-0	2-1				
93-94					1-1	2-0	2-1	0-1							0-2	1-1				
94-95					2-3	0-1	3-0	2-1							1-3	0-0				
95-96					1-1	1-4	6-1	2-0			3-1	3-1			1-0	0-2				
96-97					3-2	1-3	3-0	3-2	5-1	1-0	2-1	4-1			4-0	1-3				
97-98					1-1	0-2	0-2	1-2	1-0	1-1	1-1	0-3	1-4	0-1	4-1	2-2			1-1	0-0
98-99	2-2	0-5							0-1	1-2	1-2	1-2	1-0	3-1	1-1	1-1	0-1	0-1	1-2	4-1
99-00	3-3	2-3							2-1	0-2	3-0	2-0	1-1	1-1	1-0	1-3	2-0	1-0		
00-01																				

	Lincoln City		Macclesfield Town		Maidstone United		Merthyr Tydfil		Morecambe		Northwich Victoria		Nuneaton Borough		Runcorn		Rushden & Diamonds		Scarborough	
	H	A	H	A	H	A	H	A	H	A	H	A	H	A	H	A	H	A	H	A
82-83																				
83-84					0-0	1-3					2-2	2-4	3-3	1-2	0-2	1-1			1-3	0-2
84-85					2-1	4-1					3-1	2-0	3-4	1-1	0-1	2-1			3-2	1-2
85-86					3-1	1-2					2-2	0-0	2-1	3-0	2-4	2-0			5-1	5-3
86-87					2-2	0-5					1-2	2-1	3-0	2-1	3-2	3-4			0-1	1-2
87-88	3-3	3-5	3-2	2-1	2-1	2-1					1-1	1-1			1-1	0-2				
88-89			0-1	1-1	3-6	3-0					1-1	4-2			2-1	3-1				
89-90			2-2	2-1			1-2	1-3			4-0	2-1			0-0	1-2				
90-91			0-0	0-0			1-2	2-1			3-1	1-1			3-1	1-5				
91-92			1-1	0-0			2-2	1-2			1-0	1-3			2-1	1-4				
92-93			2-1	1-1			1-0	3-4			5-3	1-0			2-0	0-0				
93-94			2-1	0-0			2-0	4-1			2-0	0-3			3-0	5-0				
94-95			1-2	3-1			2-0	1-0			1-2	4-3			1-1	2-2				
95-96			0-4	2-0					4-2	1-3	2-1	2-5			4-1	1-0				
96-97			0-0	1-0					2-2	3-2	1-0	1-1					1-0	1-1		
97-98									1-4	1-3	1-1	1-1					1-2	1-4		
98-99									5-2	1-2	4-0	0-1					0-0	1-1		
99-00									2-1	1-0	3-1	1-1	1-2	3-2			2-0	3-5	2-0	0-0
00-01																				

LEADING APPEARANCES

Paul DAVIES	431+20	451
Martin WEIR	385+11	396
Kim CASEY	195+30	225
Micky TUOHY	215+9	224
John BARTON	212	212
Richard FORSYTH	205+5	210
Paul WEBB	197+12	209
Chris BRINDLEY	207	207
Graham MACKENZIE	190+5	195
Mark YATES	185+2	187
John DEAKIN	151+33	184
Paul BANCROFT	170+2	172
Paul JONES	160	160
Darren STEADMAN	155+1	156
Peter HOWELL	130+15	145
Chris JONES	138+1	139
Delwyn HUMPHREYS	127+11	138
Simeon HODSON	131	131
Martin WOODALL	115+8	123
Kevin WILLETTS	113+5	118
Clive BOXALL	108+6	114
Dave BENTON	103+11	114
Lee HUGHES	98+10	108
Antone JOSEPH	92+12	104
Neil CARTWRIGHT	83+20	103

LEADING GOALSCORERS

Paul DAVIES	176(1p)
Kim CASEY	129(5p)
Micky TUOHY	53
Lee HUGHES	51(2p)
Richard FORSYTH	46(15p)
Peter HOWELL	41
John POWELL	38(1p)
Delwyn HUMPHREYS	33
Mark YATES	32

Ian Arnold. Photo: Paul Dennis.

Marcus Bignot.

Paul Bancroft. Photo: Dave West.

KIDDERMINSTER HARRIERS

	Slough Town		Southport		Stafford Rangers		Stalybridge Celtic		Stevenage Borough		Sutton United		Telford United		Trowbridge Town		Wealdstone		Welling United	
	H	A	H	A	H	A	H	A	H	A	H	A	H	A	H	A	H	A	H	A
82-83																				
83-84													1-0	0-3	1-1	2-1	3-1	0-2		
84-85													0-2	2-3			0-3	2-5		
85-86					1-1	2-3							3-0	1-0			3-1	3-0		
86-87					1-1	1-4			0-0	1-3	0-0	1-3	0-4	1-2			5-2	3-0	3-0	0-1
87-88					0-0	2-0					2-2	0-2	2-4	3-4			2-1	1-1	5-2	2-1
88-89					3-2	1-0					1-0	1-1	1-1	0-1					2-1	1-0
89-90					3-0	1-0					2-2	2-1	2-4	1-1					1-1	1-4
90-91	1-2	0-0			2-1	1-3					1-0	2-1	1-3	0-1					1-2	0-1
91-92	3-3	1-3			2-1	0-2							1-2	1-3					1-3	2-3
92-93	1-1	1-3			0-2	1-0	2-1	2-2					2-1	1-1					2-1	0-0
93-94	0-0	5-1	2-0	1-1	2-0	3-2	1-0	2-0					2-0	0-1					1-0	3-0
94-95			0-1	1-4	1-2	2-1	3-2	3-1	0-3	3-2			1-1	1-3					3-0	2-0
95-96	4-3	4-5	2-3	2-0			3-0	2-2	0-1	1-4			2-0	1-1					3-0	0-0
96-97	1-2	2-0	3-0	0-1					1-1	1-4	3-0	2-2	1-0	2-0					3-2	1-0
97-98	0-1	0-2	1-1	2-1			5-0	1-2			1-3	1-3	1-1	1-1					2-1	3-0
98-99			2-1	1-1							2-0	0-3	3-0	0-0					0-1	0-0
99-00			5-0	1-0					3-1	2-0	1-0	3-0	2-0	2-3					4-1	2-1
00-01																				

	Weymouth		Witton Albion		Woking		Worcester City		Wycombe Wanderers		Yeovil Town	
	H	A	H	A	H	A	H	A	H	A	H	A
82-83												
83-84	0-1	0-0					2-1	1-1			1-2	1-1
84-85	3-3	2-0					4-1	2-1			3-0	0-0
85-86	1-2	2-1							8-2	5-2		
86-87	1-1	1-2										
87-88	1-0	1-1							0-2	1-0		
88-89	1-0	1-3							2-0	0-1	2-2	3-1
89-90									0-2	3-3	3-2	1-3
90-91									1-2	3-2	0-0	0-2
91-92			0-1	1-2					1-0	0-2	1-1	1-1
92-93			0-0	2-2	1-3	5-1			1-4	1-1	1-1	2-2
93-94			0-0	0-2	3-1	0-1					2-3	1-0
94-95					1-3	0-0					3-0	1-1
95-96					2-0	0-0						
96-97					1-0	1-2						
97-98					1-1	1-0					3-1	0-1
98-99					3-2	1-2					0-1	1-3
99-00					3-2	0-1					4-0	0-1
00-01												

Chris Brindley. Photo: Eric Marsh.

Neil Cartwright. Photo: Dennis Nicholson.

John Deakin. Photo: John Collings.

Neil Doherty. Photo: John Collings.

KIDDERMINSTER H. APPEARANCES	82-83	83-84	84-85	85-86	86-87	87-88	88-89	89-90	90-91	91-92	92-93	93-94	94-95	95-96	96-97	97-98	98-99	99-00	TOTAL
ACTON Darren																			1
ARNOLD Ian																39	21+2		60+2
ARNOLD Jim					12	18													30
ATTWOOD Alan								1	4+5										5+5
BANCROFT Paul						17	38	39		20	0+1	36	20	20+1					**170+2**
BARBER Fred															18	3			21
BARNETT Dave									19	20									39
BARNETT Gary																		4+5	4+5
BARTON John			29	40	39	40	39	24	1										212
BEARD Matt																4+1	0+2		4+3
BENNETT Dean																	8+1	35+4	43+5
BENTON Dave								9+2	26+5	38+1	30+3								**103+11**
BIGNALL Mike																22+1	5+3		27+4
BIGNOT Marcus															39	4			43
BLAIR Andy								10											10
BOWATER Steve		33																	33
BOXALL Clive				17	37	31	8+4	15+2											**108+6**
BRADLEY Paul										0+1									0+1
BRADLEY Russell				2+2															2+2
BRAZIER Colin					18	14+1	32+1	14											78+2
BRENNAN Micky		6																	6
BRIGHTON Stewart																2+3			2+3
BRINDLEY Chris											42	42	26	39	36	22			207
BROCK Stuart																4	41	11+1	56+1
BROWNRIGG Andy																		16+4	16+4
BUCKLAND Mark				36	15														51
BURGESS Richard																		0+4	0+4
BURTON Chris							1	11	5+3										17+3
CAMPBELL Trevor			4	28	11														43
CANNING Andy					1+3	6+4													7+7
CARROLL Matthew									10+7	2+4									12+11
CARTWRIGHT Neil											8	30+6	18+7	22+3	2+4	3			83+20
CASEY Kim				38+1	40	22+1	8+2	36+1					6+1	36+5	6+11	3+8			**195+30**
CHAMBERS John		7																	7

389

Richard Forsyth. Photo: Paul Dennis.

Ian Foster. Photo: Eric Marsh.

Goalkeeper Ron Green. Photo: Paul Dennis.

Peter Howell. Photo: Gary Cave.

KIDDERMINSTER APPEARANCES

KIDDERMINSTER H. APPEARANCES	82-83	83-84	84-85	85-86	86-87	87-88	88-89	89-90	90-91	91-92	92-93	93-94	94-95	95-96	96-97	97-98	98-99	99-00	TOTAL
CLARKE Matt																10+1			10+1
CLARKE Tim																		29+1	29+1
CLARKSON Ian																		27+1	27+1
COLLINS James																		5	5
COLLINS Kevin					18	22													40
CONGRAVE Richard									1+1										1+1
COOGAN Marc										0+1									0+1
CUNNINGTON Shaun																	24+3	5+5	29+8
DALE Gareth		7+1																	7+1
DAVIES Ben																		0+1	0+1
DAVIES David													0+1						0+1
DAVIES Paul		29+1	40+1	35+1	39	38	36+1	1	29+3	30+3	30+3	34+1	28	38+1	9+4	14+1	1		**431+20**
DAVIS Matthew										3+1									3+1
DEAKIN John											30+2	13+8	14+3	25+3	13+6	30+4	26+7		**151+33**
DEARLOVE Mark							13+2	15					4+1	9+5	1+1				42+9
DOHERTY Neil															39+1	26+3			65+4
DRUCE Mark																	15	15+8	30+8
DULLESTON Alan		24																	24
EADES Gary													0+2	1+6					1+8
FORD Jon																	16		16
FORSYTH Richard							1	38+1	32+3	14+1	38	40	42						**205+5**
FOSTER Ian																		34+3	34+3
FRASER Jim																1+1			1+1
GARNER Tim		18	37	14															69
GAVIN Martin		36+1	23+1	22+3	9+2														90+7
GILLETT Craig										10+3	6+1	1+3							17+7
GLOVER Dean																	17		17
GORDON Colin											16	5							21
GRAINGER Paul										8	32+1	40+2	19						99+3
GREEN Ron										40	1								41
HACKETT Brendan										4									4
HADLEY Dave									16+1	18+2	25+3	4+2							63+8
HADLEY Stewart																	20+3	26+12	46+15

391

PAUL DAVIES

	83-84	84-85	85-86	86-87	87-88	88-89	89-90	90-91	91-92	92-93	93-94	94-95	95-96	96-97	97-98	98-99	99-00	TOTAL
Appearaces	29+1	40+1	35+1	39	38	36+1	1	29+3	30+3	30+3	34+1	28	38+1	9+4	14+1	1		431+20
Goals	8	19	21	15	24	20	-	6	4	11	14	11	14(1p)	4	5	-		176(1p)
	83-84	84-85	85-86	86-87	87-88	88-89	89-90	90-91	91-92	92-93	93-94	94-95	95-96	96-97	97-98	98-99	99-00	TOTAL

KIDDERMINSTER APPEARANCES

KIDDERMINSTER H. APPEARANCES	82-83	83-84	84-85	85-86	86-87	87-88	88-89	89-90	90-91	91-92	92-93	93-94	94-95	95-96	96-97	97-98	98-99	99-00	TOTAL
HANSON Jon										3+3	3+4								6+7
HATTON Mark					2														2
HAWKER Phil									3										3
HAYWARD Paul					5														5
HAZLEWOOD Malcolm					25+2	17+3													42+5
HINES Les																	16+1	6+5	22+6
HINTON Craig																	30+2	38+3	68+5
HODSON Simeon											6	42	42	40	1				131
HORNE John		35	22+1	15															72+1
HOWELL Peter						13+3	30+3	23+4	31+1	27+4	6								130+15
HUGHES Lee													29+6	32+3	37+1				98+10
HUMPHREYS Delwyn									23	35+2	8+4	27+3	34+2						127+11
JONES Chris		35+1	28	26	30	19													138+1
JONES Graham		10+5																	10+5
JONES Paul					14	24	40	41	41										160
JONES Robert						27+2	35+1	7											69+3
JOSEPH Antone								17+4	39+1	35+4	1+3								92+12
JUDD Robin					1+1														1+1
KAVANAGH Malcolm			15+1	14+1															29+2
KERBY Trevor		1+1																	1+1
KIMBERLEY Sean							3+1												3+1
KING Phil																		7+7	7+7
KURILA Alan									37+1	5+1									42+2
LANGFORD Tim													3						3
LATCHFORD Oliver								0+1											0+1
LILWALL Steve								1	35+1	24+4						4+3			64+8
LOWE Jason								21	8										29
MACAULEY Bob		18+1																	18+1
MACKENZIE Graham			25+1	42	31	40	7+3	34+1		11									190+5
MAFFEI Joe		5+4																	5+4
MARSH Mike																		23+1	23+1
MARTIN John		7	35																42
MAY Leroy														29+2			25+8		54+10
McCUE James															10+7	0+7			10+14

Lee Hughes. Photo: Alan Watson.

Paul Jones. Photo: Dave West.

Antone Joseph. Photo: Eric Marsh.

Tim Langford. Photo: Paul Dennis.

KIDDERMINSTER H. APPEARANCES	82-83	83-84	84-85	85-86	86-87	87-88	88-89	89-90	90-91	91-92	92-93	93-94	94-95	95-96	96-97	97-98	98-99	99-00	TOTAL
McGOWAN Andy		24	34+3																58+3
McGRATH John									27+2	35	36								98+2
MIDGLEY Neil																		4+1	4+1
MOORE Paul																0+2			0+2
MULDERS Jan					2+3	12+4	14+6	4+2											32+15
MULHOLAND Denis										5									5
MULLEN Phil		8+3																	8+3
NIBLETT Nigel																7			7
NICHOLLS Adam					0+1	1+2	0+2												1+5
O'DOWD Adrian				28	29+1	14+1													71+2
OLLIS Alan			22+1	8															30+1
OLNEY Ian															28+5	11			39+5
PALMER Les											19+5	12+11	5+11						36+27
PAYNE Stuart																	13+3		13+3
PEARSON Jon					10+5	21+3	35	1+2											67+10
PETERSEN Rene																		16+2	16+2
PHILLIPS Richard													0+2						0+2
PIGGOTT Gary											3								3
POPE Steve																12		15+5	27+5
POWELL Jay													14+7						14+7
POWELL John		35+2	39+1	7															81+3
PRINDIVILLE Steve															41	29			70
PURDIE Jon											18+1	35+3	14+4	0+1			4+2		71+11
RICHARDS Archie		34	18+1	14+2	13+1														79+4
RICHARDSON Paul											4								4
ROBERTS Elwyn		25	5+2																30+2
ROBINSON Anthony																6+9	2+3		8+12
ROBINSON Steve														5					5
ROGERS Darren											1								1
ROSE Kevin												42	27+1	4+1					73+2
ROSEGREEN Mark		2+1	5+4	5+3		7+1													19+9
SHEPHERD Mark														8+7	1	4			13+7
SHILVOCK Rob							29	6+2	7+3										42+5
SKELDING Jimmy																15	9		24

395

Mike Marsh. Photo: Peter Barnes.

Steve Pope. Photo: Colin Stevens.

Jon Purdie. Photo: Dennis Nicholson.

Adie Smith. Photo: Andrew Chitty.

KIDDERMINSTER APPEARANCES

KIDDERMINSTER H. APPEARANCES	82-83	83-84	84-85	85-86	86-87	87-88	88-89	89-90	90-91	91-92	92-93	93-94	94-95	95-96	96-97	97-98	98-99	99-00	TOTAL
SKOVBJERG Thomas																		30+1	30+1
SMITH Adie																23	22+2	42	87+2
SMITH Carl					2														2
STAMPS Scott																		34+1	34+1
STEADMAN Darren								1	1	2	41		15+1	38	24	33			**155+1**
STIRK Mark												0+1							0+1
STOKES Graham											1+5								1+5
SUGRUE Paul							8+2	12+5											20+7
SULLIVAN Kieron											1								1
SULLIVAN Roy			1																1
TAYLOR Justin									0+2	1+1									1+3
TAYLOR Steve																	26+2	4+7	30+9
THOMAS Clinton																	6+5		6+5
THOMAS Wayne																8			8
TUDOR Kevin					1														1
TUOHY Micky		7	41	40	41	36	37+1	13+8											215+9
WEBB Paul													42	33+2	35+1	23+4	31+3	33+2	**197+12**
WEIR Martin					2+3	21+4	26+1	38	38	37	40	40	21	18+1	41	28+2	34	1	**385+11**
WEST Mark																2			2
WESTHEAD Mark												1							1
WHITEHOUSE Mark								30+7	15+3	19+1									64+11
WILCOX Brett									12+4	30+2	5+2								47+8
WILLETTS Kevin														25+2	40	29+1	19+2		**113+5**
WILLIAMS Lee																		2	2
WILLIAMS Mick		3																	3
WILLIAMS Wayne											7	6+2							13+2
WILSON Herman		1+2																	1+2
WOLSEY Mark									2	6+4	2+1	2					8+11		20+16
WOOD Fraser		34	0+1																34+1
WOODALL Martin		18+1	39	31+1	8+2	9						10+4							115+8
YATES Mark											2		39+2	40	41	41	22		**185+2**

Mick Tuohy challenges the 'keeper.

Paul Webb. Photo: Dave West.

Martin Weir. Photo: David Watson.

KIDDERMINSTER GOALSCORERS

KIDDERMINSTER H. GOALSCORERS	82-83	83-84	84-85	85-86	86-87	87-88	88-89	89-90	90-91	91-92	92-93	93-94	94-95	95-96	96-97	97-98	98-99	99-00	TOTAL
ARNOLD Ian																9(3p)	5		14(3p)
ATTWOOD Alan												1							1
BANCROFT Paul						3	4					1							8
BARNETT Dave										2									2
BARNETT Gary																		2	2
BARTON John			2			1		1											4
BEARD Matt																1			1
BENNETT Dean																		10	10
BENTON Dave								1		1	1								3
BIGNALL Mike																11			11
BIGNOT Marcus															1				1
BLAIR Andy								1											1
BOWATER Steve		1																	1
BOXALL Clive						1	1												2
BRAZIER Colin						1													1
BRINDLEY Chris											1	2	2	2	2	1			10
BROWNRIGG Andy																		3	3
BUCKLAND Mark				6	3														9
BURTON Chris								5	1										6
CARROLL Matthew									1										1
CARTWRIGHT Neil											3	8		2		1			14
CASEY Kim				**36**	**38(5p)**	**17**	**3**	**16**					**2**	**14**	**3**				**129(5p)**
CONGRAVE Richard																			1
CUNNINGTON Shaun																	3		3
DAVIES Paul		**8**	**19**	**21**	**15**	**24**	**20**		**6**	**4**	**11**	**14**	**11**	**14(1p)**	**4**	**5**			**176(1p)**
DEAKIN John														4		2	2		12
DEARLOVE Mark													1	2					3
DOHERTY Neil															14(4p)	9(3p)			23(7p)
DRUCE Mark																	1	7	8
FORD Jon																	4		4
FORSYTH Richard								10	9(2p)	3(2p)	7(5p)	4(1p)	13(5p)						46(15p)
FOSTER Ian																		16(5p)	16(5p)

Mark Whitehouse heads for goal.

Mark Yates.
Photo: John Collings.

Below (L-R):
Delwyn Humphreys.
Kevin Rose.
Simeon Hodson.

KIDDERMINSTER GOALSCORERS

KIDDERMINSTER H. GOALSCORERS	82-83	83-84	84-85	85-86	86-87	87-88	88-89	89-90	90-91	91-92	92-93	93-94	94-95	95-96	96-97	97-98	98-99	99-00	TOTAL
GAVIN Martin	1	1																	3
GORDON Colin											3	1							4
GRAINGER Paul										4	6	2							12
HADLEY Dave									3	1	6								10
HADLEY Stewart																	6	12	18
HAZELWOOD Malcolm					2	3													5
HINES Les																	1		1
HINTON Craig																		3	3
HORNE John			1																1
HOWELL Peter						3	9	5	15	9									41
HUGHES Lee													9	12(1p)	30(1p)				51(2p)
HUMPHREYS Delwyn									4	7	1	13	8						33
JONES Chris		1	2	4	1	1													9
JONES Robert						4	2												6
JOSEPH Antone							1	1											2
KIMBERLEY Sean										1									1
KING Phil																		2	2
KURILA Alan										1									1
LILWALL Steve									1	3									4
MACKENZIE Graham			1	4	1	2		1											9
MARSH Mike																		4	4
MAY Leroy														13(1p)			11		24(1p)
McCUE James															1				1
McGOWAN Andy		4	12																16
McGRATH John									2		1								3
MIDGLEY Neil																		2	2
MULDERS Jan						2													2
MULLEN Phil		1																	1
ODOWD Adrian				7	5	3													15
OLLIS Alan			4	1															5
OLNEY Ian															7				7
PALMER Les											6	4	2						12

401

KIDDERMINSTER H. GOALSCORERS

GOALSCORERS	82-83	83-84	84-85	85-86	86-87	87-88	88-89	89-90	90-91	91-92	92-93	93-94	94-95	95-96	96-97	97-98	98-99	99-00	TOTAL
PAYNE Stuart																	4		4
PEARSON Jon							1												1
PETERSEN Rene																		3(1p)	3(1p)
PHILLIPS Richard													1						1
POPE Steve																		1	1
POWELL John		15(1p)	21	2															38(1p)
PRINDIVILLE Steve															1				1
PURDIE Jon											9	8							17
RICHARDS Archie		1																	1
ROBERTS Elwyn		9	1																10
ROBINSON Anthony																3	1		4
ROSEGREEN Mark				1															1
SHEPHERD Mark														4					4
SHILVOCK Rob							7		1										8
SKOVBJERG Thomas																		4	4
SMITH Adie																3		1	4
STAMPS Scott																		2	2
SUGRUE Paul							5	5											10
TAYLOR Steve																	4	1	5
THOMAS Clinton																	2		2
THOMAS Wayne																1			1
TUOHY Micky		5	11	12	8	6	10	1											53
WEBB Paul													2	1	6		1	1	11
WEIR Martin					1	2	2	5	5	4	1	3	1						24
WHITEHOUSE Mark								14	4	10(3p)									28(3p)
WILCOX Brett																		7	7
WILLETTS Kevin														2	4	2	7(4p)		15(4p)
WOOD Fraser		3(1p)																	3(1p)
WOODALL Martin		5(3p)	4	1	2														13(3p)
YATES Mark													10	8	7	5	2		32

KINGSTONIAN

PROMOTED FROM: Isthmian League 1998
RELEGATED TO: Isthmian League 2001
2004-2005 SEASON: Isthmian League Premier Division

Kingstonian Squad 1999-2000 (L-R)   **Back Row:** Clive Howse (Coach), Jim Pearce (Physio), Phil Wingfield, Gary Patterson, Simon Stewart, Mark Harris, Steve Farrelly, Richard Hurst, Matt Crossley, Derek Allan, Ian McDonald (Asst. Manager).   **Front Row:** Luke Basford, Junior Kadi, Tarkan Mustafa, Geoff Pitcher, Colin Luckett, Eddie Akuamoah, Dave Leworthy, Ronnie Green

David Leworthy, Matt Crossley and Gary Patterson.   Photo: Peter Barnes

SEASONS
3

TOTAL POINTS
165

HIGHEST POSITION
5th 1999-2000

LOWEST POSITION
21st 2000-01

HIGHEST ATTENDANCE
2694 v Woking 26.12.98

LOWEST ATTENDANCE
606 v Leek T. 23.2.99

SEASON GOALSCORER
David Leworthy 12 (99/00)

CAREER GOALSCORER
David Leworthy 22

CAREER APPEARANCES
Colin Luckett 114+1

	HOME							AWAY							
	P	W	D	L	F	A	Pts	P	W	D	L	F	A	Pts	Position
98-99	21	9	7	5	25	19	34	21	8	6	7	25	30	30	8
99-00	21	9	4	8	30	24	31	21	11	3	7	28	20	36	5
00-01	21	3	5	13	19	40	14	21	5	5	11	28	33	20	21
Total	63	21	16	26	74	83	79	63	24	14	25	81	83	86	

KINGSTONIAN

	Altrincham		Barrow		Boston United		Cheltenham Town		Chester City		Dagenham & Redbridge		Doncaster Rovers		Dover Athletic		Farnborough Town		Forest Green Rovers	
	H	A	H	A	H	A	H	A	H	A	H	A	H	A	H	A	H	A	H	A
98-99			5-1	1-0			1-2	0-1					2-1	1-0	1-0	1-5	1-1	2-4	0-1	0-1
99-00	2-2	3-1											0-1	0-1	4-1	1-0			0-1	3-0
00-01					0-0	1-2			1-3	0-0	2-3	2-1	1-1	2-0	0-0	3-1			0-1	1-3

	Hayes		Hednesford Town		Hereford United		Kettering Town		Kidderminster H.		Leek Town		Leigh RMI		Morecambe		Northwich Victoria		Nuneaton Borough	
	H	A	H	A	H	A	H	A	H	A	H	A	H	A	H	A	H	A	H	A
98-99	1-1	0-3	1-1	2-1	2-0	0-2	1-2	0-2	1-0	1-0	3-0	2-2			0-0	0-0	1-1	3-2		
99-00	1-3	2-1	0-2	3-2	0-0	2-0	2-0	1-2	0-1	0-2					0-0	2-1	3-3	3-0	2-0	0-2
00-01	0-1	1-1	1-0	2-3	0-2	0-0	0-1	1-3					0-2	1-2	1-6	2-3	1-0	1-2	2-2	1-2

	Rushden & Diamonds		Scarborough		Southport		Stevenage Borough		Sutton United		Telford United		Welling United		Woking		Yeovil Town	
	H	A	H	A	H	A	H	A	H	A	H	A	H	A	H	A	H	A
98-99	1-5	0-0			0-2	1-1	1-0	3-3			1-0	1-1	2-1	3-1	0-0	1-0	0-0	3-1
99-00	0-1	0-1	2-0	1-0	4-2	0-0	1-0	1-0	4-2	2-2	4-2	0-1	1-0	1-0	0-2	1-1	0-1	2-3
00-01	2-4	1-2	2-2	0-1	3-1	2-2	0-2	5-2			0-1	1-0			0-3	0-0	3-4	1-3

Gavin Holligan, heads for goal.

Photo: Eric Marsh

	Home						Away					
	P	W	D	L	F	A	P	W	D	L	F	A
ALTRINCHAM	1	0	1	0	2	2	1	1	0	0	3	1
BARROW	1	1	0	0	5	1	1	1	0	0	1	0
BOSTON U	1	0	1	0	0	0	1	0	0	1	1	2
CHELTENHAM T	1	0	0	1	1	2	1	0	0	1	0	1
CHESTER CITY	1	0	0	1	1	3	1	0	1	0	0	0
DAGENHAM & R	1	0	0	1	2	3	1	1	0	0	2	1
DONCASTER R	3	1	1	1	3	3	3	2	0	1	3	1
DOVER A	3	2	1	0	5	1	3	2	0	1	5	6
FARNBOROUGH T	1	0	1	0	1	1	1	0	0	1	2	4
FOREST GREEN R	3	0	0	3	0	3	3	1	0	2	4	4
HAYES	3	0	1	2	2	5	3	1	1	1	3	5
HEDNESFORD T	3	1	1	1	2	3	3	2	0	1	7	6
HEREFORD U	3	1	1	1	2	3	3	1	1	1	2	2
KETTERING T	3	1	0	2	3	3	3	0	0	3	2	7
KIDDERMINSTER H	2	1	0	1	1	1	2	1	0	1	1	2
LEEK T	1	1	0	0	3	0	1	0	1	0	2	2
LEIGH RMI	1	0	0	1	0	2	1	0	0	1	1	2
MORECAMBE	3	0	2	1	1	6	3	1	1	1	4	4
NORTHWICH V	3	1	2	0	5	4	3	2	0	1	7	4
NUNEATON B	2	1	1	0	4	2	2	0	0	2	1	4
RUSHDEN & D	3	0	0	3	3	10	3	0	1	2	1	3
SCARBOROUGH	2	1	1	0	4	2	2	1	0	1	1	1
SOUTHPORT	3	2	0	1	7	5	3	0	3	0	3	3
STEVENAGE B	3	2	0	1	2	2	3	2	1	0	9	5
SUTTON U	1	1	0	0	4	2	1	0	1	0	2	2
TELFORD U	3	2	0	1	5	3	3	1	1	1	2	2
WELLING U	2	2	0	0	3	1	2	2	0	0	4	1
WOKING	3	0	1	2	0	5	3	1	2	0	2	1
YEOVIL T	3	0	1	2	3	5	3	1	0	2	6	7
TOTAL	63	21	16	26	74	83	63	24	14	25	81	83

Phil Wingfield
Photo:
Mark Sandom

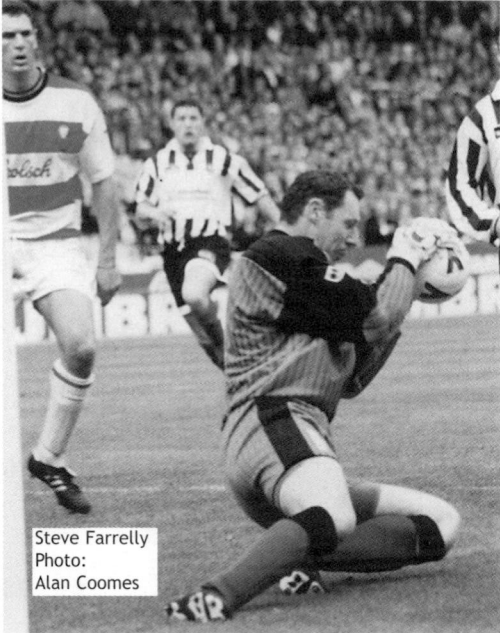

Steve Farrelly
Photo:
Alan Coomes

ABOVE:
Colin Luckett
Photo: Andrew Chitty

LEFT
TOP:
Mark Harris
Photo: Peter Barnes

MIDDLE
Geoff Pitcher
Photo: Garry Letts

BOTTOM:
David Leworthy
Photo: Andrew Chitty

APPEARANCES

	01-02	02-03	03-04	Total
AKUAMOAH Eddie	30+4	26+5	31+8	**87+17**
ALLAN Derek		28+1	30	58+1
ALLEN Lee			2+1	2+1
BARRETT Scott	6			6
BASFORD Luke		8+8	0+1	8+9
BASS David			22+6	22+6
BEARD Mark			23+1	23+1
BLAKE Adrian			5	5
BOYCE Mark			26+4	26+4
BOYLAN Lee	5	5+6		10+6
BROWN Kenny		2		2
BROWN Simon	3			3
BROWN Wayne	8+2			8+2
COATES Marc	1			1
CORBETT Scott	11+16			11+16
CROSSLEY Matt	35	37		72
CULVERHOUSE Ian	1			1
DIXON Frank	0+1			0+1
DREWETT Gary	0+2	4+4		4+6
DUERDEN Ian			14+1	14+1
FARRELLY Steve	22	40	6	68
FEWINGS Paul			2	2
FRANCIS Delton	7+10			7+10
FRANCIS Joe	6+4			6+4
GLASS Jimmy			14	14
GREEN Ronnie		4+2	12+23	16+25
HARRIOTT Marvin			4+1	4+1
HARRIS Mark	40	30+3	33	**103+3**
HENDRIE Iain		2+4		2+4
HOLLIGAN Gavin	5+12		9	14+12
HURST Richard		2	9+1	11+1
JOHN Jerome	11			11
JONES Mark			7+6	7+6
KADI Junior		8+8	2+4	10+12
KELLY Gavin			7	7
LANGLEY Simon	2			2
LESTER Mike	1+2	2+1		3+3
LEWORTHY David	33+2	25+6		58+8
LUCKETT Colin	41+1	33	40	**114+1**
LYTTLE Gerard		1		1
MARSHALL Dwight		8+4		8+4
MEAN Scott			2	2
MURRAY Matthew			1	1
MUSTAFA Tarkan	36	38+1		74+1
NEWMAN Dan		0+2		0+2
NYAMAH Kofi	4+1			4+1
O'CONNOR Joe		8+10		8+10
PATTERSON Gary	35	38	34+1	**107+1**
PITCHER Geoff	37	38+1	34+1	**109+2**
RATTRAY Kevin	25+8			25+8

APPEARANCES

	01-02	02-03	03-04	Total
SAUNDERS Eddie		9+2	26+3	35+5
SIMBA Amara		8	7+2	15+2
SMITH Danny	8+1	0+1		8+2
STEWART Simon	35	22+1	20+3	77+4
TAYLOR Robin		5+2		5+2
THOMAS Dean	1+2			1+2
THOMPSON Richard		1+1		1+1
THURGOOD Shaun			1	1
TRANTER Carl	3+5			3+5
WALKER Johnny		0+1		0+1
WALL Craig			0+1	0+1
WHITE Tom	4+1			4+1
WILKINSON Russell	0+1			0+1
WILLGRASS Alex	6+1			6+1
WINGFIELD Phil		30+4	12+3	42+7
WINSTON Sammy			27+9	27+9

GOALSCORERS

	01-02	02-03	03-04	Total
AKUAMOAH Eddie	7	8	3	18
ALLEN Derek		1	3	4
BASS David			1	1
BOYCE Mark			1	1
BOYLEN Lee	1			1
BROWN Wayne	1			1
CORBETT Scott	3			3
CROSSLEY Matt	2	1		3
DREWETT Gary		1		1
DUERDEN Ian			5	5
FRANCIS Joe	1			1
GREEN Ronnie			4	4
HARRIS Mark	1	4	1	6
HOLLIGAN Gavin	5		2	7
JONES Mark			1	1
KADI Junior			1	1
LEWORTHY David	10	12		22
LUCKETT Colin	5(4p)	2	7(5p)	14(9p)
MARSHALL Dwight		1		1
MUSTAFA Tarkan	3			3
O'CONNOR Joe		2		2
PATTERSON Gary	2		1	3
PITCHER Geoff	5	9	7	21
RATTRAY Kevin	2			2
SIMBA Amara		6	3	9
STEWART Simon	1	2	2	5
TRANTER Carl	1			1
WINGFIELD Phil		6	1	7
WINSTON Sammy			3	3

ABOVE: Tarkan Mustafa   Photo: Dennis Nicholson
RIGHT: Geoff Chapple   Photo: Francis Short

BELOW LEFT: Gary Patterson   Photo: Andrew Chitty
BELOW RIGHT: Eddie Akuamoah   Photo: Darren Thomas

LEEK TOWN

PROMOTED FROM: Northern Premier League 1997
RELEGATED TO: Northern Premier League 1999
2004-2005 SEASON: Northern Premier League, Premier Division

1998-1999 Squad. Back Row, left to right: Kenny Birch-Martin (Physio), Jan Hassell, Darren Baker, Aidan Callan, Jeff Parker, Dale Hawtin, Gary Germaine, Ray Newland, Neil Ellis, Ray Walker, Dean Trott, Wayne Biggins, amd Martin Parr (Assistant Physio). Front Row: Godfrey Heath (President), Steve Tobin, Stuart Leicester, Matt Beeby, John Diskin (captain), Ian Brunskill, Hugh McAuley, Dean Cunningham and Steve Soley.

SEASONS
2

TOTAL POINTS
52 + 24 = 76

HIGHEST POSITION
19th 97-98

LOWEST POSITION
21st 98-99

HIGHEST ATTENDANCE
1365 v Doncaster (2-1-99)

LOWEST ATTENDANCE
253 v Yeovil (29-4-99)

SEASON GOALSCORER
Hugh McAuley 18(5p) 98-99

CAREER GOALSCORER
Hugh McAuley 29(6p)

CAREER APPEARANCES
Hugh McAuley 67+7

Hugh McAuley loses out to Rushden's Michael McElhatton. Photo: Peter Barnes.

	HOME						AWAY						
	P	W	D	L	F	A	Pts	P	W	D	L	F	A	Pts	Position
97-98	21	8	8	5	34	26	32	21	2	6	13	18	41	12	19
98-99	21	5	5	11	34	42	20	21	3	3	15	14	34	12	21
Total	42	13	13	16	68	68	52	42	5	9	28	32	75	24	

Tony Agana. Photo: Peter Barnes.

John Diskin marking tightly v Rushden Photo: P. Barnes.

Chris James (left). v Farnborough Photo: Ian Morsman.

Wayne Biggins. Photo: Andrew Chitty.

	Barrow		Cheltenham Town		Doncaster Rovers		Dover Athletic		Farnborough Town		Forest Green Rovers		Gateshead		Halifax Town		Hayes	
	H	A	H	A	H	A	H	A	H	A	H	A	H	A	H	A	H	A
97-98			0-0	1-1			5-1	1-2	3-1	0-2			2-2	2-0	2-0	1-2	1-2	1-3
98-99	3-1	1-2	0-2	0-0	1-1	1-0	2-0	1-2	4-0	1-2	0-2	1-3					1-4	0-2
99-00																		

	Hednesford Town		Hereford United		Kettering Town		Kidderminster H.		Kingstonian		Morecambe		Northwich Victoria		Rushden & Diamonds		Slough Town	
	H	A	H	A	H	A	H	A	H	A	H	A	H	A	H	A	H	A
97-98	3-3	0-1	2-2	0-1	0-4	0-1	0-0	1-1			1-1	1-1	1-1	1-3	2-0	1-0	0-2	1-1
98-99	1-3	1-1	3-2	0-1	1-2	1-2	1-4	2-1	2-2	0-3	7-0	2-2	0-3	2-0	2-3	0-2		
99-00																		

	Southport		Stalybridge Celtic		Stevenage Borough		Telford United		Welling United		Woking		Yeovil Town	
	H	A	H	A	H	A	H	A	H	A	H	A	H	A
97-98	0-1	2-2	2-2	1-6	2-1	1-1	3-1	0-3	1-2	0-2	2-0	2-5	2-0	1-3
98-99	0-0	1-3			1-1	0-2	1-1	0-2	2-4	0-1	0-3	0-1	2-4	0-2
99-00														

	HOME						AWAY					
	P	W	D	L	F	A	P	W	D	L	F	A
BARROW	1	1	0	0	3	1	1	0	0	1	1	2
CHELTENHAM T	2	0	1	1	0	2	2	0	2	0	1	1
DONCASTER R	1	0	1	0	1	1	1	1	0	0	1	0
DOVER A	2	2	0	0	7	1	2	0	0	2	2	4
FARNBOROUGH T	2	2	0	0	7	1	2	0	0	2	1	4
FOREST GREEN R	1	0	0	1	0	2	1	0	0	1	1	3
GATESHEAD	1	0	1	0	2	2	1	1	0	0	2	0
HALIFAX T	1	1	0	0	2	0	1	0	0	1	1	2
HAYES	2	0	0	2	2	6	2	0	0	2	1	5
HEDNESFORD T	2	0	1	1	4	6	2	0	1	1	1	2
HEREFORD U	2	1	1	0	5	4	2	0	0	2	0	2
KETTERING T	2	0	0	2	1	6	2	0	0	2	1	3
KIDDERMINSTER H	2	0	1	1	1	4	2	1	1	0	3	2
KINGSTONIAN	1	0	1	0	2	2	1	0	0	1	0	3
MORECAMBE	2	1	1	0	8	1	2	0	2	0	3	3
NORTHWICH V	2	0	1	1	1	4	2	1	0	1	3	3
RUSHDEN & D	2	1	0	1	4	3	2	1	0	1	1	2
SLOUGH T	1	0	0	1	0	2	1	0	1	0	1	1
SOUTHPORT	2	0	1	1	0	1	2	0	1	1	3	5
STALYBRIDGE C	1	0	1	0	2	2	1	0	0	1	1	6
STEVENAGE B	2	1	1	0	3	2	2	0	1	1	1	3
TELFORD U	2	1	1	0	4	2	2	0	0	2	0	5
WELLING U	2	0	0	2	3	6	2	0	0	2	0	3
WOKING	2	1	0	1	2	3	2	0	0	2	2	6
YEOVIL T	2	1	0	1	4	4	2	0	0	2	1	5
TOTALS	42	13	13	16	68	68	42	5	9	28	32	75

APPEARANCES

	97/98	98/99	TOTAL
AGANA Tony		15+5	15+5
BAKER Darren		0+1	0+1
BAURESS Gary	2		2
BEEBY Matt	25+4	30+1	55+5
BIGGINS Wayne	32+5		32+5
BIRCH Mark	7		7
BRUNSKILL Iain	34+2	31+6	65+8
CALLAN Aiden	18+8	13+4	31+12
CIRCUIT Steve		36+1	36+1
CUNNINGHAM Dean	14+16	6	20+16
CUTLER Neil	11		11
DISKIN John	32	22+3	54+3
ELLIS Neil	33+2	19+6	52+8
FILSON Martin	12		12
GERMAINE Gary	10		10
HASSALL Jon	1+1		1+1
HAWKES Marc	0+2		0+2
HAWTIN Dale	30+3	18+4	48+7
HEVERIN Mike		2+5	2+5
INGHAM Gary		42	42
JAMES Chris		38+1	38+1
JONES Jason	0+2		0+2
KNOWLES Chris	1		1
LEICESTER Stuart	22+5		22+5
MARCH Jamie		22+4	22+4
McAULEY Hugh	30+6	37+1	67+7
McCORD Brian		15+2	15+2
MIKE Adie		25+1	25+1
MORGAN Lee		3+1	3+1
NEWLAND Ray	20		20
O'TOOLE Gavin		14+3	14+3
PARKER Jeff	12	20+1	32+1
PASCOE Jason		29+4	29+4
PRICE Steve		11+3	11+3
RILEY Kevin		7+5	7+5
SOLEY Steve	37		37
TOBIN Steve	24+7	1+4	25+11
TROTT Dean	20+8	3	23+8
WALKER Ray	35+1		35+1
WILLIAMS Scott		3+1	3+1

GOALSCORERS

	97/98	98/99	TOTAL
AGANA Tony		3	3
BEEBY Matt	2	1	3
BIGGINS Wayne	8(1p)		8(1p)
CALLAN Aidan		1	1
CIRCUIT Steve		1	1
CUNNINGHAM Dean	1	3	4
DISKIN John	1		1
ELLIS Neil	2	3	5
HAWTIN Dale	1	3	4
HEVERIN Mike		1	1
LEICESTER Stuart	1		1
McAULEY Hugh	11(1p)	18(5p)	29(6p)
MIKE Adie		10	10
MORGAN Lee		2	2
PARKER Jeff		1	1
SOLEY Steve	12		12
TOBIN Steve	5		5
TROTT Dean	5		5
WALKER Ray	2		2

LEIGH R.M.I.

PROMOTED FROM: The Northern Premier League 1999-2000
2004-2005 SEASON: The Conference

| SEASONS |
| 4 |

2002 Squad.
Back Row (L-R): Chris Scott, Dave Rydings, Marcus Hallows, Dave Felgate, Iain Swan, Andy Heald, Tony Black, Ged Kielly, Rick Harris, Steve Waywell.
Front Row: Dino Maamria, Ian Monk, Neil Durkin, Andy Farrell (captain), Neil Fisher, Nicky Spooner,Dave German, Mick Reynold and Dave Miller.

TOTAL POINTS
198

HIGHEST POSITION
5th 2000-01

LOWEST POSITION
21st 2003-04

HIGHEST ATTENDANCE
2002 v Chester C. 1.1.04

LOWEST ATTENDANCE
270 v Stevenage B. 14.2.04

SEASON GOALSCORER
David McNiven 25(4p) (03/4)

CAREER GOALSCORER
Dino Maamria 25(2p)
David McNiven 25(4p)

CAREER APPEARANCES
Ian Monk 107+2

	HOME							**AWAY**							
	P	W	D	L	F	A	Pts	P	W	D	L	F	A	Pts	Position
00-01	21	11	5	5	38	24	38	21	8	6	7	25	33	30	5
01-02	21	6	4	11	29	29	22	21	9	4	8	27	29	31	16
02-03	21	8	5	8	26	34	29	21	6	1	14	18	37	19	18
03-04	21	4	6	11	26	44	18	21	3	2	16	20	53	11	21
Total	**84**	**29**	**20**	**35**	**119**	**131**	**107**	**84**	**26**	**13**	**45**	**90**	**152**	**91**	

413

LEIGH R.M.I.

	Accrington Stanley		Aldershot Town		Barnet		Boston United		Burton Albion		Chester City		Dagenham & Redbridge		Doncaster Rovers		Dover Athletic	
	H	A	H	A	H	A	H	A	H	A	H	A	H	A	H	A	H	A
00-01							2-2	1-0			0-1	1-1	1-2	1-2	0-1	0-4	2-1	2-1
01-02					3-3	1-1	1-2	1-2			3-0	1-1	2-0	1-0	1-4	0-2	1-2	0-0
02-03					4-2	0-4			4-2	1-0	0-4	1-2	1-3	1-3	0-2	0-1		
03-04	1-2	1-4	2-2	0-2	1-4	1-2					0-1	2-3	2-6	0-5	2-1	2-1		

	Exeter City		Farnborough Town		Forest Green Rovers		Gravesend & N'fleet		Halifax Town		Hayes		Hednesford Town		Hereford United	
	H	A	H	A	H	A	H	A	H	A	H	A	H	A	H	A
00-01					1-1	1-3					4-0	2-1	2-2	2-1	2-1	1-1
01-02			3-0	0-3	1-2	2-1					1-1	1-2			0-1	1-0
02-03			3-2	0-1	1-0	1-4	0-0	3-1	0-2	0-1					0-2	1-0
03-04	1-1	2-3	0-2	1-1	1-2	2-2	1-2	1-3	1-1	1-2					0-5	1-0

	Kettering Town		Kingstonian		Margate		Morecambe		Northwich Victoria		Nuneaton Borough		Rushden & Diamonds		Scarborough	
	H	A	H	A	H	A	H	A	H	A	H	A	H	A	H	A
00-01	1-0	1-0	2-1	2-0			1-0	2-1	3-0	1-1	6-2	1-2	1-0	1-1	2-0	1-1
01-02					2-2	2-1	0-1	3-1	1-2	3-0	0-1	1-2			1-1	5-2
02-03	2-2	1-0			2-0	0-2	1-0	1-2	1-1	1-0	1-1	2-0			0-2	0-2
03-04					4-2	0-2	3-1	0-1	1-0	1-0					1-4	1-4

	Shrewsbury Town		Southport		Stalybridge Celtic		Stevenage Borough		Tamworth		Telford United		Woking		Yeovil Town	
	H	A	H	A	H	A	H	A	H	A	H	A	H	A	H	A
00-01			2-2	2-1			1-4	0-3			1-1	1-2	2-0	1-1	2-3	1-6
01-02			1-2	0-5	1-0	1-0	1-2	1-0			3-1	1-3	3-1	1-1	0-1	1-2
02-03			1-1	2-4			2-1	1-3			0-3	1-1	1-0	0-3	2-4	1-3
03-04	2-2	1-3					1-3	0-4	1-1	3-4	1-1	0-5	0-1	0-2		

	Home						Away					
	P	W	D	L	F	A	P	W	D	L	F	A
ACCRINGTON S	1	0	0	1	1	2	1	0	0	1	1	4
ALDERSHOT T	1	0	1	0	2	2	1	0	0	1	0	2
BARNET	3	1	1	1	8	9	3	0	1	2	2	7
BOSTON U	2	0	1	1	3	4	2	1	0	1	2	2
BURTON A	2	1	0	1	4	3	2	1	0	1	3	3
CHESTER C	4	1	0	3	5	11	4	0	2	2	3	9
DAGENHAM & R	4	2	0	2	6	6	4	2	0	2	5	6
DONCASTER R	3	0	0	3	1	7	3	0	0	3	0	7
DOVER A	2	1	0	1	3	3	2	1	1	0	2	1
EXETER C	1	0	1	0	1	1	1	0	0	1	2	3
FARNBOROUGH T	3	2	0	1	6	4	3	0	1	2	1	5
FOREST GREEN R	4	1	1	2	4	5	4	1	1	2	6	10
GRAVESEND & N	2	0	1	1	1	2	2	1	0	1	4	4
HALIFAX T	2	0	1	1	1	3	2	0	0	2	1	3
HAYES	2	1	1	0	5	1	2	1	0	1	3	3
HEDNESFORD T	1	0	1	0	2	2	1	1	0	0	2	1
HEREFORD U	4	1	0	3	2	9	4	3	1	0	4	1
KETTERING T	2	1	1	0	3	2	2	2	0	0	2	0
KINGSTONIAN	1	1	0	0	2	1	1	1	0	0	2	0
MARGATE	3	2	1	0	8	4	3	1	0	2	2	5
MORECAMBE	4	3	0	1	5	2	4	2	0	2	6	5
NORTHWICH V	4	2	1	1	6	3	4	3	1	0	6	1
NUNEATON B	3	1	1	1	7	4	3	1	0	2	4	4
RUSHDEN & D	1	1	0	0	1	0	1	0	1	0	1	1
SCARBOROUGH	4	1	1	2	4	7	4	1	1	2	7	9
SHREWSBURY T	1	0	1	0	2	2	1	0	0	1	1	3
SOUTHPORT	3	0	2	1	4	5	3	1	0	2	4	10
STALYBRIDGE C	1	1	0	0	1	0	1	1	0	0	1	0
STEVENAGE B	4	1	0	3	5	10	4	1	0	3	2	10
TAMWORTH	1	0	1	0	1	1	1	0	0	1	3	4
TELFORD U	4	1	2	1	5	6	4	0	1	3	3	11
WOKING	4	3	0	1	6	2	4	0	2	2	2	7
YEOVIL T	3	0	0	3	4	8	3	0	0	3	3	11
TOTAL	84	29	20	35	119	131	84	26	13	45	90	152

Tony Black. Photo: Colin Stevens.

Peter Cumiskey. Photo: Colin Stevens.

Neil Durkin.

LEIGH R.M.I.

	00-01	01-02	02-03	03-04	Total
ALFORD Carl				1	1
ARCHER William		0+1			0+1
ASHMOLE Ben			0+1		0+1
BARROWCLOUGH Carl				12+3	12+3
BENT Danny			3		3
BLACK Tony	36+1	24+2	9		69+3
BLACKMORE Clayton	1				1
BLAKEMAN Liam		0+3			0+3
BRODIE Steve			5		5
CAMPBELL Neil		11+1			11+1
COBURN Stuart			42	10	52
CORNELLY Chris			1+2		1+2
COURTNEY Ged			8+17	0+5	8+22
COYNE Liam				1+1	1+1
CRITCHLEY Neil	0+3				0+3
CUMISKEY Peter	7+2				7+2
DANIEL Mario				10+6	10+6
DERBYSHIRE Rob		0+1			0+1
DEVENNEY Michael	3+1				3+1
DOOTSON Craig	19	2			21
DOWNEY Chris				0+4	0+4
DURKIN Neil	20+4	42	41	37	**140+4**
ELLISON Gavin				4	4
FARRELL Andy	42	19+4			61+4
FELGATE David	23+1	7+1			30+2
FISHER Neil		25+4	8+7		33+11
FITZHENRY Neil			34+3		34+3
FITZPATRICK Ian			2		2
FITZPATRICK Lee		3+2			3+2
FORD Mark			12+1		12+1
FORREST Martyn				6	6
GARDNER Dave	1+5				1+5
GERMAN Dave	26+8	31+5			57+13
GUNBY Steve			8+2		8+2
HALLOWS Marcus		21+16	0+7		21+23
HARDY Lee			1		1
HARRIS Mike			1+2		1+2
HARRIS Rick	15+6	5			20+6
HARRISON Gerry		20	26+4	26+2	72+6
HAYDER Troy	2+8	1+5			3+13
HEALD Andy		10+12	20+10	3	33+22
HEFFERNAN Guy			1+3		1+3
HILL Nicky			3	9+1	12+1
HOLMES Gareth				11+1	11+1
JONES Steve	41+1				41+1
KELLY Gary				14	14
KIELTY Ged	39+1	22+6	25+4	7+3	93+14

APPEARANCES

	00-01	01-02	02-03	03-04	Total
LANCASTER Martyn			13	32+1	45+1
LANE Chris				2	2
LUDDEN Dominic			5		5
MAAMRIA Dino		25+5	25		50+5
MADEN Wayne			32+3	23+4	55+7
MARTIN Ian				16	16
MASON Andy	1+10				1+10
MATTHEWS Neil	3+10				3+10
McGILL Jon			0+3		0+3
McGRATH Chris				2+1	2+1
McHALE Kris				5+2	5+2
McNIVEN David				41	41
MILLIGAN Jamie				1	1
MONK Ian	28+2	42	37	14+7	121+9
MORRELL Mick	5+3				5+3
MURPHY Ged	1+1				1+1
ORR Adie				1+6	1+6
PENDLEBURY Ian			6+1	0+1	6+2
PEYTON Warren				27+7	27+7
PRICE Michael				4	4
PRINCE Neil			6		6
REDMOND Steve				22+4	22+4
REID Shaun	0+1				0+1
REYNOLDS Mick		0+3			0+3
REZAI Carl				16+4	16+4
RICKERS Paul				3	3
RIDINGS Dave	40	23			63
ROBERTSON John			4		4
ROBINSON Neil				9	9
ROSCOE Andy				30+3	30+3
SALISBURY James				2	2
SALT Phil		15	38+2		55+2
SCOTT Chris		8+6			8+6
SCOTT Gary	16				16
SCOTT Keith			9+2		9+2
SHEPHERD Paul				25+4	25+4
SKINNER Craig		5			5
SMITH Steve				1+2	1+2
SPENCER Steve		0+2			0+2
SPOONER Nicky	21+1	20+5	0+1		41+7
STARBUCK Phil				5+2	5+2
SWAN Iain	39	24+3			63+3
TENCH Graham				1+2	1+2
THOMPSON Steve		5+2			5+2
TICKLE Dave				2+2	2+2
TOLSON Neil			5		5
TREES Robert	18+5				18+5

APPEARANCES cont.

	00-01	01-02	02-03	03-04	Total
ALFORD Carl				1	1
ARCHER William		0+1			0+1
ASHMOLE Ben				0+1	0+1
BARROWCLOUGH Carl				12+3	12+3
BENT Danny			3		3
BLACK Tony	36+1	24+2	9		69+3
BLACKMORE Clayton	1				1
BLAKEMAN Liam			0+3		0+3
BRODIE Steve				5	5
CAMPBELL Neil		11+1			11+1
COBURN Stuart			42	10	52
CORNELLY Chris			1+2		1+2
COURTNEY Ged			8+17	0+5	8+22

GOALSCORERS

	00-01	01-02	02-03	03-04	Total
BARROWCLOUGH Carl				2	2
BLACK Tony	13(6p)	6(1p)	1		20(7p)
BRODIE Steve				4	4
COURTNEY Ged			2		2
CUMISKEY Peter	1(1p)				1(1p)
DANIEL Mario				3	3
DURKIN Neil				1	1
FISHER Neil		3			3
HALLOWS Marcus		8			8
HARRIS Rick	1				1
HARRISON Gerry			1		1
HAYDER Troy	1	1			2
HEALD Andy		2	4(1p)		6(1p)
JONES Steve	19(3p)				19(3p)
KIELTY Ged	5	1	4		10
LANCASTER Martyn			1	1	2
MAAMRIA Dino		13(1p)	12(1p)		25(2p)
MADEN Wayne			2	4	6
MASON Andy	2				2
MATTHEWS Neil	2				2
McNIVEN David				25(4p)	25(4p)
MONK Ian	5	5	6		16
PEYTON Warren				2	2
REDMOND Steve			1		1
RIDINGS Dave	11	2			13
ROBINSON Neil			1		1
ROSCOE Andy			1		1
SALT Phil			3		3
SCOTT Keith			3		3
SHEPHERD Paul			1		1
SWAN Iain	1				1
TOLSON Neil			1		1
TWISS Michael		14			14
WARD Chris			1		1
WHITTAKER Stuart			2		2

Above left: Steve Jones. Photo: Andrew Chitty.
Left: Ian Monk. Photo: Roger Turner.

1999-2000 Squad - Back Row (L-R): Derek Miles, Mick Higgins, Ian Bold, Peter Cumiskey, Dave Ridings, Dave Felgate, Ged Kielty, Rick Harris, Eddie Turkington, Mark O'Connor, Andy Mason. Front Row: Gerry Luska, Tony Black, Dave German, Ian Monk, Brian Butler, Mark Ward, Steve Jones, Brian Ross, Mick Wallace, Steve Wallace.

'What a feeling'. David Felgate, 'keeper and caption, leads the celebrations. Photo: Mark V. Sandom.

Simon Turpin (left) and Stuart Locke (right) keep a close eye on Fulham's Dirk Lehmann. Photo: Mark V. Sandom.

LINCOLN CITY

RELEGATED FROM: The Football League 1987
PROMOTED TO: The Football League1988
2004-2005 SEASON: The Football League Division 2

Back row, left to right: Gordon Simmonite (Player/Assistant Manager), Neil Franklin, John McGinlay, Lee Butler, Les Hunter, Michael Waitt, Trevor Marrhewson, Colin Murphy (Manager). Front row:Steve Buckley, Willie Gamble,Shane Nicholson (Apprentice), David Clarke and Philip Brown

SEASON 1987-88

HIGHEST ATTENDANCE
9432 Wycombe (2-5-88)
Conference Record

LOWEST ATTENDANCE
1995 Dagenham (29-8-87)

SEASON GOALSCORER
Phil Brown 16

SEASON APPEARANCES
Trevor Matthewson 40

	HOME						AWAY						
P	W	D	L	F	A	Pts	P	W	D	L	F	A	Pts	Position
21	16	4	1	53	13	52	21	8	6	7	33	35	30	1

APPEARANCES

	87-88
BATCH Nigel	32
BRESSINGTON Graham	9+4
BROWN Phil	38+2
BUCKLEY Steve	22
CASEY Paul	10
CLARKE David	26+4
CROMBIE Alan	1
CUMMING Bob	33
EVANS Clive	36

APPEARANCES cont.

	87-88
FRANKLIN Neil	3+1
GAMBLE Willie	1
HUNTER Les	3
MATTHEWSON Trevor	40
McGINLEY John	38
MOORE Andy	27+1
MOSSMAN David	20+1
NICHOLSON Shane	33
PARKIN David	0+1
SCOTT Chris	1+1
SERTORI Mark	18+10
SIMMONITE Gordon	13
SMITH Paul	33
WAITT Mick	15
WILSON Richard	10

GOALSCORERS

	87-88
BROWN Phil	16
CLARKE David	5
CUMMING Bob	7
EVANS Clive	8
HUNTER Les	1
MATTHEWSON Trevor	6
McGINLEY John	15(3p)
MOORE Andy	1
MOSSMAN David	2
NICHOLSON Shane	1
SERTORI Mark	6
SMITH Paul	8
WAITT Mick	8

The Lincoln defence survive this Boston United attack during their 2-1 Boxing Day win.

Photo: Bob Whitaker.

A record crowd of 9,432 watched Lincoln City clinch promotion against Wycombe Wanderers at Sincil Bank

LINCOLN CITY

	Altrincham		Barnet		Bath City		Boston United		Cheltenham Town		Dagenham		Enfield	
	H	A	H	A	H	A	H	A	H	A	H	A	H	A
86-87														
87-88	5-0	0-0	2-1	2-4	3-0	1-2	5-1	2-1	5-1	3-3	3-0	3-0	4-0	0-0

	Fisher Athletic		Kettering Town		Kidderminster Harriers		Macclesfield Town		Maidstone United		Northwich Victoria		Runcorn	
	H	A	H	A	H	A	H	A	H	A	H	A	H	A
86-87														
87-88	3-0	1-1	0-1	0-2	5-3	3-3	3-0	0-2	1-1	2-1	3-2	3-2	1-0	1-4

	Stafford Rangers		Sutton United		Telford United		Wealdstone		Welling United		Weymouth		Wycombe Wanderers	
	H	A	H	A	H	A	H	A	H	A	H	A	H	A
86-87														
87-88	2-1	4-1	1-1	1-4	0-0	1-0	3-0	0-0	2-1	4-1	0-0	0-3	2-0	2-1

	HOME						AWAY					
	P	W	D	L	F	A	P	W	D	L	F	A
ALTRINCHAM	1	1	0	0	5	0	1	0	1	0	0	0
BARNET	1	1	0	0	2	1	1	0	0	1	2	4
BATH C	1	1	0	0	3	0	1	0	0	1	1	2
BOSTON U	1	1	0	0	5	1	1	1	0	0	2	1
CHELTENHAM T	1	1	0	0	5	1	1	0	1	0	3	3
DAGENHAM	1	1	0	0	3	0	1	1	0	0	3	0
ENFIELD	1	1	0	0	4	0	1	0	1	0	0	0
FISHER A	1	1	0	0	3	0	1	0	1	0	1	1
KETTERING T	1	0	0	1	0	1	1	0	0	1	0	2
KIDDERMINSTER H	1	1	0	0	5	3	1	0	1	0	3	3
MACCLESFIELD T	1	1	0	0	3	0	1	0	0	1	0	2
MAIDSTONE U	1	0	1	0	1	1	1	1	0	0	2	1
NORTHWICH V	1	1	0	0	3	2	1	1	0	0	3	2
RUNCORN	1	1	0	0	1	0	1	0	0	1	1	4
STAFFORD R	1	1	0	0	2	1	1	1	0	0	4	1
SUTTON U	1	0	1	0	1	1	1	0	0	1	1	4
TELFORD U	1	0	1	0	0	0	1	1	0	0	1	0
WEALDSTONE	1	1	0	0	3	0	1	0	1	0	0	0
WELLING U	1	1	0	0	2	1	1	1	0	0	4	1
WEYMOUTH	1	0	1	0	0	0	1	0	0	1	0	3
WYCOMBE W	1	1	0	0	2	0	1	1	0	0	2	1
TOTAL	**21**	**16**	**4**	**1**	**53**	**13**	**21**	**8**	**6**	**7**	**33**	**35**

TEAM STRIPS
15 PLUS GOALIE

Green on White
Red on Yellow
Red on White
Yellow on Blue
Black on White

only £350.00

(inc. vat & delivery)

Blue on Yellow
White on Green
White on Blue
Blue on Sky Blue
White on Red

£60 EXTRA WITH SPONSORS NAME ON ALL 16 SHIRTS
£60 EXTRA FOR CLUB BADGE ON ALL 16 SHIRTS

MACCLESFIELD TOWN

PROMOTED FROM: Northern Premier League 1987
PROMOTED TO: Football League (Div.3) 1997
2004-2005 SEASON: Football League Division 2

1996-97: Back row.left to right: Cec Edey, Dave Norman, Mark Gardiner, Darren Tinson, Kevin Hulme, Steve Payne, Simon Hutchinson, Middle row: Darren Lyons, Steve Tobin, Mark Bradshaw, Ryan Price, Neil Sorvel, Steve Burr and Marc Coates. Front row: G.Prescott (Assistant Manager), Tony Hemmings, Phil Power, Sammy McIlroy (Manager), Neil Howarth, Paul Cavell and E.Campbell (Physio).

	HOME							AWAY							
	P	W	D	L	F	A	Pts	P	W	D	L	F	A	Pts	Position
87-88	21	10	5	6	36	27	35	21	8	4	9	28	35	28	11
88-89	20	9	5	6	31	26	32	20	8	5	7	32	31	29	7
89-90	21	11	6	4	35	16	39	21	6	9	6	21	25	27	4
90-91	21	11	4	6	38	22	37	21	6	8	7	25	30	26	7
91-92	21	7	7	7	25	21	28	21	6	6	9	25	29	24	13
92-93	21	7	9	5	23	20	30	21	5	4	12	17	30	19	18
93-94	21	7	8	6	24	18	29	21	9	3	9	24	31	30	7
94-95	21	14	3	4	39	18	45	21	10	5	6	31	22	35	1
95-96	21	12	5	4	32	16	41	21	10	4	7	34	33	34	4
96-97	21	15	4	2	41	11	49	21	12	5	4	39	19	41	1
Total	209	103	56	50	324	195	365	209	80	53	76	276	285	293	

SEASONS
10

TOTAL POINTS
365 + 293 = 658

HIGHEST POSITION
1 (94/95) (96/97)

LOWEST POSITION
18 (92/93)

HIGHEST ATTENDANCE
3143 Darlington (11-11-89)

LOWEST ATTENDANCE
338 Welling (22-4-92)

SEASON GOALSCORER
Steve Burr 21(1p) (88/89)

CAREER GOALSCORER
John Askey 75

CAREER APPEARANCES
John Askey 302+6

	Altrincham		Aylesbury United		Barnet		Barrow		Bath City		Boston United		Bromsgrove Rovers		Cheltenham Town		Chorley	
	H	A	H	A	H	A	H	A	H	A	H	A	H	A	H	A	H	A
87-88	1-0	3-1			2-2	1-2			0-2	4-3	2-1	2-0			1-0	0-1		
88-89	1-0	3-1	3-1	2-1	1-1	4-1					0-1	2-3			0-0	0-3	3-2	1-0
89-90	1-0	1-0			0-1	0-0	2-1	1-1			0-0	0-3			3-0	1-2	0-0	0-0
90-91	0-1	3-5			3-3	1-3	3-0	1-1	3-1	2-0	2-0	1-1			5-1	2-2		
91-92	1-1	1-3					0-1	0-2	0-0	1-1	0-1	5-1			3-3	3-2		
92-93	1-1	0-1							1-0	0-0	2-1	1-3	0-2	0-3				
93-94	1-0	1-0							0-0	1-5			4-3	0-3				
94-95	4-2	2-1							1-0	0-1			2-2	2-2				
95-96	2-3	4-0							0-1	1-1			2-1	0-1				
96-97	1-1	1-0							2-2	3-0			4-0	3-0				

	Colchester United		Dagenham		Dagenham & Redbridge (Redbridge Forest 91-92)		Darlington		Dover Athletic		Enfield		Farnborough Town		Fisher Athletic		Gateshead	
	H	A	H	A	H	A	H	A	H	A	H	A	H	A	H	A	H	A
87-88			3-1	0-0							0-3	2-1			2-4	2-1		
88-89											1-1	1-2			2-2	2-2		
89-90							0-0	1-1			4-0	1-1	0-0	2-1	0-1	3-1		
90-91	1-0	0-1													1-1	2-1	4-0	1-1
91-92	4-4	0-2			0-0	0-0							1-2	2-4			1-0	0-2
92-93					1-1	2-1							1-2	0-0			1-0	0-1
93-94					3-0	1-1			0-2	2-1							6-1	0-1
94-95					2-0	4-0			3-0	0-0			4-1	0-1			2-1	1-2
95-96					3-1	0-3			0-1	3-2			1-0	1-6			1-0	1-0
96-97									1-0	1-2			3-0	1-0			3-0	0-0

	Halifax Town		Hayes		Hednesford Town		Kettering Town		Kidderminster H.		Lincoln City		Maidstone United		Merthyr Tydfil		Morecambe	
	H	A	H	A	H	A	H	A	H	A	H	A	H	A	H	A	H	A
87-88							0-0	2-3	1-2	2-3	2-0	0-3	1-0	0-2				
88-89							0-1	0-1	1-1	1-0			4-3	3-3				
89-90							3-1	0-0	1-2	2-2					3-2	3-2		
90-91							1-2	0-2	0-0	0-0					0-1	2-0		
91-92							0-2	0-2	0-0	1-1					3-0	2-3		
92-93							1-0	0-1	1-1	1-2					0-1	2-1		
93-94	0-1	2-1					0-0	1-0	0-0	1-2					1-2	1-2		
94-95	1-1	1-0					1-0	0-1	1-3	2-1					0-0	2-1		
95-96	7-0	0-1			1-1	1-0	1-1	2-2	0-2	4-0							2-0	4-2
96-97	1-0	3-3	1-0	2-0	4-0	1-4	2-0	4-1	0-1	0-0							0-0	0-1

1994-95 Squad. Back Row (L-R): Gil Prescott (Assistant Manager), George Shepherd, Steve Payne, Mark Bradshaw, Phil Noon, Paul Kendal, Steve Farrelly, Darren Lyons, Ian Monk, Martin McDonald, Eric Campbell (Physio), Mark Lillis (Coach).
Front Row: Neil Sorvel, Steve Tobin, Dave Norman, Steve Wood, Neil Howarth (Captain), Sammy McIlroy (Manager), Phil Power, Stuart Locke, Paul Wright, John Askey.

A jubilant changing room with skipper Mickey Roberts (with spotted ball), Steve Burr, with the match ball after his hat trick and happy manager Peter Wragg, celebrate their wonderful 4-0 F.A.Cup victory over Rotherham United.

	Northwich Victoria		Runcorn		Rushden & Diamonds		Slough Town		Southport		Stafford Rangers		Stalybridge Celtic		Stevenage Borough		Sutton United	
	H	A	H	A	H	A	H	A	H	A	H	A	H	A	H	A	H	A
87-88	5-0	1-2	4-0	2-1							2-3	1-0					1-1	3-2
88-89	0-2	2-3	3-2	2-2							2-1	1-1					1-3	2-1
89-90	3-1	0-2	4-0	0-2							2-2	2-4					1-1	1-2
90-91	1-2	1-4	2-1	2-1			1-2	1-0			2-1	2-2					4-2	1-3
91-92	0-0	1-2	3-0	0-0			0-1	3-0			1-0	1-1						
92-93	1-2	3-1	1-1	2-1			1-2	1-2			4-1	0-1	1-0	1-2				
93-94	0-0	1-1	0-0	1-2			2-2	1-1	0-1	0-1	0-0	3-2	1-3	2-0				
94-95	3-1	3-1	0-1	2-2					3-0	3-2	1-2	3-0	3-0	2-2	0-3	1-1		
95-96	0-0	2-1	1-0	0-0			1-1	2-2	3-1	1-2			1-0	2-1	0-0	0-4		
96-97	0-1	1-2			2-1	1-1	2-0	0-0	3-2	5-1					2-0	1-0	2-1	3-2

	Telford United		Wealdstone		Welling United		Weymouth		Witton Albion		Woking		Wycombe Wanderers		Yeovil Town	
	H	A	H	A	H	A	H	A	H	A	H	A	H	A	H	A
87-88	1-1	0-0	3-2	1-1	3-2	1-3	1-2	1-1					1-1	0-5		
88-89	2-1	3-1			3-0	0-2	2-0	2-1					0-1	1-1	2-3	0-2
89-90	3-0	0-1			3-2	1-0							1-0	1-1	1-2	0-0
90-91	1-2	2-1			2-1	0-0							0-0	0-0	2-1	1-2
91-92	2-1	1-0			1-2	2-1			1-0	1-1			3-1	1-0	1-2	1-0
92-93	1-1	1-3			1-1	0-1			1-0	1-1	1-1	0-4	1-1	1-0	1-1	1-1
93-94	1-0	3-1			1-0	1-0			2-0	2-0	1-1	0-3			1-2	0-4
94-95	2-0	0-2			3-1	1-0					2-0	0-1			1-0	2-1
95-96	1-0	2-1			2-1	2-1					3-2	2-3				
96-97	2-1	3-0			1-1	3-0					5-0	3-2				

Phil Power.　　　　Conference Championship Trophy　　　　Neil Howarth

MACCLESFIELD TOWN

| | Home | | | | | | Away | | | | | |
	P	W	D	L	F	A	P	W	D	L	F	A
ALTRINCHAM	10	5	3	2	13	9	10	7	0	3	19	12
AYLESBURY U	1	1	0	0	3	1	1	1	0	0	2	1
BARNET	4	0	3	1	6	7	4	1	1	2	6	6
BARROW	3	2	0	1	5	2	3	0	2	1	2	4
BATH C	8	3	3	2	7	6	8	3	3	2	12	11
BOSTON U	6	3	1	2	6	4	6	2	1	3	11	11
BROMSGROVE R	5	3	1	1	12	8	5	1	1	3	5	9
CHELTENHAM T	5	3	2	0	12	4	5	1	1	3	6	10
CHORLEY	2	1	1	0	3	2	2	1	1	0	1	0
COLCHESTER U	2	1	1	0	5	4	2	0	0	2	0	3
DAGENHAM	1	1	0	0	3	1	1	0	1	0	0	0
DAGENHAM & R	5	3	2	0	9	2	5	2	2	1	7	5
DARLINGTON	1	0	1	0	0	0	1	0	1	0	1	1
DOVER A	4	2	0	2	4	3	4	2	1	1	6	5
ENFIELD	3	1	1	1	5	4	3	1	1	1	4	4
FARNBOROUGH T	6	3	1	2	10	5	6	2	1	3	6	12
FISHER A	4	0	2	2	5	8	4	3	1	0	9	5
GATESHEAD	7	7	0	0	18	2	7	1	2	4	3	7
HALIFAX T	4	2	1	1	9	2	4	2	1	1	6	5
HAYES	1	1	0	0	1	0	1	1	0	0	2	0
HEDNESFORD T	2	1	1	0	5	1	2	1	0	1	2	4
KETTERING T	10	4	3	3	9	7	10	2	2	6	9	13
KIDDERMINSTER H	10	0	5	5	5	12	10	3	4	3	14	11
LINCOLN C	1	1	0	0	2	0	1	0	0	1	0	3
MAIDSTONE U	2	2	0	0	5	3	2	0	1	1	3	5
MERTHYR T	6	2	1	3	7	6	6	4	0	2	12	9
MORECAMBE	2	1	1	0	2	0	2	1	0	1	4	3
NORTHWICH V	10	3	3	4	13	9	10	3	1	6	15	19
RUNCORN	9	6	2	1	18	5	9	3	4	2	11	11
RUSHDEN & D	1	1	0	0	2	1	1	0	1	0	1	1
SLOUGH T	6	1	2	3	7	8	6	2	3	1	8	5
SOUTHPORT	4	3	0	1	9	4	4	2	0	2	9	6
STAFFORD R	8	4	2	2	14	10	8	3	3	2	13	11
STALYBRIDGE C	5	4	0	1	8	3	5	3	1	1	8	5
STEVENAGE B	3	1	1	1	2	4	3	1	1	1	4	7
SUTTON U	4	1	2	1	7	7	4	2	0	2	7	8
TELFORD U	10	7	2	1	16	7	10	6	1	3	15	10
WEALDSTONE	1	1	0	0	3	2	1	0	1	0	1	1
WELLING U	10	7	2	1	20	11	10	6	1	3	11	8
WEYMOUTH	2	1	0	1	3	2	2	1	1	0	3	2
WITTON A	3	3	0	0	4	0	3	1	2	0	4	2
WOKING	5	3	2	0	12	4	5	1	0	4	5	13
WYCOMBE W	6	2	3	1	6	4	6	2	3	1	4	7
YEOVIL T	7	2	1	4	9	11	7	2	2	3	5	10
TOTALS	209	103	56	50	324	195	209	80	53	76	276	285

John Askeyshields the ball. Photo: John Rooney.

Marc Coates. Photo: Keith Clayton.

Phil Derbyshire.

Mike Doherty. Photo: Paul Dennis.

MACCLESFIELD TOWN   APPEARANCES

	79/86	87/88	88/89	89/90	90/91	91/92	92/93	93/94	94/95	95/96	96/97	97/03	TOTAL
ADAMS Steve								24+4					24+4
ALFORD Carl								34					34
ALLARDYCE Craig							2						2
ALLEN Gavin									2+1				2+1
ASKEY Bob		0+1		5+3									5+4
ASKEY John		41	34+1	32+1	39	33	31	29+1	30		34+3		303+6
BIMSON Stuart						12+1	32	36	21				101+1
BLAIN Colin						12+8							12+8
BLAKE Steve			1+1										1+1
BOUGHEY Darren					1+3								1+3
BRADSHAW Mark									15	30	12+9		57+9
BROWN Gary							1						1
BUNTER Steve						1							1
BURR Steve		42	29+1	34	28+2					3+2			136+5
BYRNE Chris										18			18
CAMDEN Chris				6+4									6+4
CARBERRY Jimmy						5+1							5+1
CAVELL Paul										25+6			25+6
CIRCUIT Steve											6+5		6+5
CLARK Martin										3+5			3+5
CLAYTON Paul					10+14								10+14
COATES Marc										26+7	4+4		30+11
COLEMAN John	3+8												3+8
CONNOR Jim	27	26+5	18+2	12+1									83+8
COYNE Peter			3										3
CRISP Mark								4+4					4+4
CUTLER Chris				2+1									2+1
DAVENPORT Peter											13+2		13+2
DAWSON Jason					5+11								5+11
DEMPSEY Mark					32+1	9+2	9+1						50+4
DERBYSHIRE Phil			30+1	11+5									41+6
DOHERTY Mick						15+2	10+8						25+10
EDEY Cec					2+4					20+4	26+3		48+11
EDWARDS Elfyn	37	31+1	38	37	38	39							220+1
ELLIS Ronnie			18+1	25+8	15+10								58+19
ESSER David	1+4												1+4
EVANS Gary										0+1			0+1
FARRELLY Mike			18+4	16+8	25+2	9+3							68+17
FARRELLY Steve				13	38	41	35	42					169
GARDINER Mark										20+2	14+3		34+5
GEE Danny											0+1		0+1
GERMAN Dave										11			11
GLENDON Kevin	10+4		1										11+4
GRANT David	18+3	3											21+3
GREEN Andy					25	1+1							26+1
GREEN Roy						9+1	2+3						11+4
HALLIDAY Mike						1+1							1+1
HANLON Steve		38+1	37	42	42	38							197+1

Mark Gardiner.

Colin Lambert. Photo: John Rooney.

Steve Hanlon, Elfyn Edwards and Peter Wragg. Photo: John Rooney.

MACCLESFIELD TOWN   APPEARANCES

	79/86	87/88	88/89	89/90	90/91	91/92	92/93	93/94	94/95	95/96	96/97	97/03	TOTAL
HARDMAN Mike	24+7	19+4	11+9				5+6						59+26
HEESOM Darren				21+5	11								32+5
HEMMINGS Tony										26	16+1		42+1
HERON Derek								2+1					2+1
HOPLEY Tony						2+3							2+3
HOWARTH Neil							23	39	38	39			139
HULME Kevin									16	0+1			16+1
HUMPHRIES Gareth		1+1											1+1
HUTCHINSON Simon									4+7				4+7
IMRIE John		13+7	32+3	25+2	1								71+12
JOHNSON Paul			33+1	26+1	33	11+3							103+5
KELSEY Andy				0+1									0+1
KENDALL Paul		37	24+1	25+6	14+1	33+3	25	11+2					169+13
KIRKHAM Paul			1										1
LAKE Mike	38	34+1	11										83+1
LAMBERT Colin				31+5	39+1	25+1							95+7
LANDON Richard										6			6
LEICESTER Stuart						31+4	4+2						35+6
LENNON Pat								3					3
LILLIS Mark						35+1	0+1						35+2
LOCKE Stuart							7	16+2	9+1				32+3
LODGE David	9+3	2											11+3
LYONS Darren			1+3					13+4	20+8	32+6			66+21
MARGINSON Karl									7	11+3			18+3
McDONALD Martin								24	38	13			75
McKEARNAN Ged	1												1
McMAHON John							21+5						21+5
MELROSE Jim				2+4									2+4
MIDDLEMASS Scott										2			2
MIDWOOD Michael									7				7
MITCHELL Neil											19+7		19+7
MITCHELL Richie							16+13	1+7					17+20
MONK Ian									16+7	0+1			16+8
MORGAN Phil										9	5		14
MOTTRAM Frank											5+6		5+6
MOUNTFORD Keith	11+11	3+4											14+15
MULLIGAN Jimmy						1							1
MURRAY Mark									6+3				6+3
NEATIS Alan	1+3												1+3
NORMAN Dave									13+1				13+1
OHANDJANIAN Demis										1			1
O'NEILL John						4							4
O'REILLY Justin										3			3
PARLANE Derek		9+17	1+1										10+18
PAYNE Steve									33	38	41		112
PEEL Nathan											0+2		0+2
PICKERING Sean							0+1						0+1
POLLITT Mike					1								1

Daren Lyons. Photo: John rooney.

Steve Payne (left) and Tony Hemming. Photo: Alan Coomes.

Ryan Price. Photo: Keith Clayton.

Micky Roberts. Photo: John Rooney.

MACCLESFIELD TOWN   APPEARANCES

	79/86	87/88	88/89	89/90	90/91	91/92	92/93	93/94	94/95	95/96	96/97	97/03	TOTAL
POWELL Gary							5+2						5+2
POWER Phil							25+2	39	21	33+3			118+5
PRICE Ryan									22	37			59
RIDDINGS Colin				1									1
RIDLER Colin				3									3
ROBERTS Graham							11						11
ROBERTS Micky	42	30+2	0+1										72+3
RUTTER Mark						1							1
SHARRATT Chris							24						24
SHAW Nigel	42	15+3											57+3
SHENTON Richard		0+1											0+1
SHEPHERD George				5	21	31	39	35	12				143
SORVEL Neil						35+5	38+4	38+2	42	42			195+11
SUTTON Stuart						1	1						2
THORPE Andy							3+2						3+2
TIMMONS John		13	25+7	17	31+5	40							126+12
TINSON Darren										15	36		51
TOBIN Graham	36+1	33+1	36	36+2	8+1								149+5
TOBIN Steve								14+10	1+1				15+11
TOMLINSON Dave			6+2										6+2
WALKER Gary							3						3
WILLIAMS Carwyn											12+15		12+15
WILLIAMS Karl									11				11
WILSON Phil			16										16
WOOD Steve							8+7	35+2	14+1	40+1			97+11
WORRALL Gary			3+15										3+15
WRIGHT Paul								4+4					4+4
ZELEM Alan		41	40	42	25	4+1							152+1

LEADING APPEARANCES

John ASKEY	303+6	(309)
Elfyn EDWARDS	220+1	(221)
Neil SORVEL	195+11	(206)
Steve HANLON	197+1	(198)
Paul KENDALL	169+13	(182)
Steve FARRELLY	169	(169)
Graham TOBIN	149+5	(154)
Alan ZELEM	152+1	(153)
George SHEPHERD	143	(143)
Steve BURR	136+5	(141)
Neil HOWARTH	139	(139)
John TIMMONS	126+12	(138)
Phil POWER	118+5	(123)
Steve PAYNE	112	(112)

Steve WOOD	97+11	(108)
Paul JOHNSON	103+5	(108)
Colin LAMBERT	95+7	(102)
Stuart BIMSON	101+1	(102)

LEADING GOALSCORERS

John ASKEY	75
Steve BURR	66(1p)
Phil POWER	51
Steve WOOD	27

John Timmons. Photo: John Rooney.

Alan Zelem punches clear.

MACCLESFIELD TOWN GOALSCORERS

	79/86	87/88	88/89	89/90	90/91	91/92	92/93	93/94	94/95	95/96	96/97	97/03	TOTAL
ADAMS Steve							1						1
ALFORD Carl							14(3p)						14(3p)
ASKEY Bob			1										1
ASKEY John	10	11	9	14	5	7	3	9			7		75
BIMSON Stuart					2								2
BLAIN Colin						3(1p)							3(1p)
BRADSHAW Mark										3	1		4
BURR Steve		19	21(1p)	16	10								66(1p)
BYRNE Chris											10		10
CAMDEN Chris				1									1
CAVELL Paul										9			9
CIRCUIT Steve											1		1
CLAYTON Paul					1								1
COATES Marc										11	1		12
COLEMAN John	1(1p)												1(1p)
CONNOR Jim	4												4
CUTLER Chris				1									1
DAVENPORT Peter											6(1p)		6(1p)
DAWSON Jason					1								1
DEMPSEY Mark					1(1p)	1							2(1p)
DERBYSHIRE Phil		13(1p)	4(1p)										17(2p)
DOHERTY Mick					6(1p)								6(1p)
EDWARDS Elfyn	5		4	2	3								14
ELLIS Ronnie			2(1p)	4	2								8(1p)
ESSER David	2												2
FARRELLY Mike					1(1p)	1							2(1p)
FARRELLY Steve							1						1
GARDINER Mark										1	1		2
GRANT David	2												2
GREEN Andy					7	1							8
GREEN Roy						1	2						3
HANLON Steve	6	4	5	7	2								24
HARDMAN Mike	1		1										2
HEESOM Darren				5(3p)									5(3p)
HEMMINGS Tony										2	2		4
HOPLEY Tom					2								2
HOWARTH Neil								3	11(1p)	2	3		19(1p)
HULME Kevin										4			4
HUTCHINSON Simon										1			1
IMRIE John		2	3	1									6
JOHNSON Paul					1(1p)	1(1p)							2(2p)
KENDALL Paul		1	2										3
LAMBERT Colin				4	9	8							21
LANDON Richard											3(2p)		3(2p)
LANE Mike	8	3	2										13
LEICESTER Stuart							2						2

Steve Burr.
Photo: John Rooney.

Neil Sorvel.
Photo:
Colin Stevens

MACCLESFIELD TOWN GOALSCORERS

	79/86	87/88	88/89	89/90	90/91	91/92	92/93	93/94	94/95	95/96	96/97	97/03	TOTAL
LYONS Darren							1	4	9(3p)				14(3p)
MARGINSON Karl									1	1			2
McDONALD Martin							1	3	1(1p)				5(1p)
MIDWOOD Michael								2					2
MITCHELL Neil										4			4
MITCHELL Ritchie						8(1p)							8(1p)
MONK Ian								3					3
MOTTRAM Frank											2(1p)		2(1p)
MOUNTFORD Kevin	2												2
NEATIS Alan	1												1
PARLANE Derek		2											2
PAYNE Steve									1	1			2
PAYNE Steve											2		2
POWELL Gary							2						2
POWER Phil								9	18	13	11		51
ROBERTS Graham								1					1
ROBERTS Micky	1												1
SHARRATT Chris								4					4
SHAW Nigel			1										1
SHEPHERD George									1				1
SORVEL Neil							3	5	5	4	5		22
TIMMONS John		2	3	8	4	4							21
TINSON Darren										1	1		2
TOBIN Graham	2	1		1									4
TOBIN Steve									2				2
WILLIAMS Carwyn											6(1p)		6(1p)
WILSON Phil			1										1
WOOD Steve							1		9	3	14		27
WORRALL Gary			1										1
WRIGHT Paul									1				1

MAIDSTONE UNITED

FOUNDER MEMBER
ELECTED FROM: Southern League 1979
PROMOTED TO: Football League (Div.4) 1989 Disbanded
Re-formed - Maidstone United played in the Kent League in season 2004-2005

1986-87 Squad - Back Row (L-R): Simon Brown, Tommy Boyle, Steve Clark, Micky Joyce, George Torrance, John Glover, Tony Lynch, Steve Clarke, Graham Humphries, Paul Hobbs, Richard Pearson.
Second Row: John Adams (Reserve Team Manager), Bernie Holden (Youth Team Coach), Andy Pearson, Ricky Bartholomew, Duncan Horton, Tony Pamphlett, Derek Richardson, Spencer Creedon, Steve Butler, Steve Galloway, Mark Hill, Frank Brooks (Trainer), Phil Debnam (Youth Team Manager). First Row: Nigel Donn, Malcolm Stewart, Jim Dawkins (Director), John Ryan (Assistant Manager), John Baxter (Vice Chairman), Bill Williams (General Manager), Steve Hatter (Captain), Jim Thompson (Chairman), Mick Mercer (Secretary), Mike Oldham (Director), Phil Hanford, Colin Barnes. Front: Mark Jones, Graham Stonestreet, Paul Weston, Russell Debman, Kevin McNab, Andy Baker.

		HOME						AWAY						
	P	W	D	L	F	A	Pts	P	W	D	L	F	A	Pts	Position
79-80	19	11	4	4	38	15	26	19	5	7	7	16	22	17	6
80-81	19	12	4	3	42	18	28	19	4	5	10	22	35	13	7
81-82	21	8	6	7	33	22	30	21	3	9	9	22	37	18	16
82-83	21	17	1	3	55	13	52	21	8	7	6	28	21	31	2
83-84	21	12	8	1	40	15	32	21	11	5	5	31	19	38	1
84-85	21	10	7	4	38	24	27	21	5	6	10	20	27	21	13
85-86	21	7	9	5	35	29	23	21	2	7	12	22	37	13	17
86-87	21	14	4	3	43	16	46	21	7	6	8	28	32	27	3
87-88	21	8	5	8	38	33	29	21	10	4	7	41	31	34	9
88-89	20	12	5	3	48	22	41	20	13	4	3	44	24	43	1
Total	205	111	53	41	410	207	334	205	68	60	77	274	285	255	

SEASONS
10

TOTAL POINTS
334 + 255 = 589

HIGHEST POSITION
1 (83/84) (88/89)

LOWEST POSITION
17 (85/86)

HIGHEST ATTENDANCE
2861 Kettering (18-3-89)

LOWEST ATTENDANCE
506 Chorley (15-10-88)

SEASON GOALSCORER
John Bartley 36 (82/83)

CAREER GOALSCORER
Steve Butler 81(10p)

CAREER APPEARANCES
Brian Thompson 211+6

Maidstone players and fans celebrate their Conference title.

1983-84 Squad: Nicky Terry, Richard Best, Ian Hamer, Steve Sutton, Dave Sowle, John Cook, Terry Jessop, Ashton Stirling, Steve Cobby, Gordon Milne, Ricky Gunn and Andy Douglas. Second row, George Cobby, David Holmes, John Bartley, Billy Hughes, Clive Green, Chris Kinnear, Kenny Hill, Jon Moore, Brian Thompson, Mark Penfold, Mark Newsome, Adrian Lemoine, John Watson and Frank Brookes. Serated: Scott McLachlan, Ray Holland, Tony Sitford, Duncan McLachlan, Bill Williams, Jim Thompson, Cyril Nicholls, Peter Hedgeland, Ray Clark and Harry Drury .Front row: Gary Bush, Kenny Wade, Jason Wheeler, Darren Genmtle, Stewart Ward and Mark Rayner.

MAIDSTONE UNITED

	Altrincham		A P Leamington		Aylesbury United		Bangor City		Barnet		Barrow		Bath City		Boston United		Cheltenham Town	
	H	A	H	A	H	A	H	A	H	A	H	A	H	A	H	A	H	A
79-80	2-2	0-1	0-0	2-0			0-1	0-1	2-0	1-0	2-0	2-0	6-0	1-1	1-0	1-1		
80-81	1-2	1-2	2-1	3-2			1-0	1-1	4-1	1-4	1-0	1-4	2-1	0-0	2-2	1-1		
81-82	0-0	2-1	4-0	1-1					0-0	1-1	1-0	0-2	1-0	1-1	0-2	0-6		
82-83	3-2	2-0					6-1	2-2	2-0	3-1	2-0	3-0	0-1	1-0	2-0	0-1		
83-84	1-0	0-1					2-0	2-0	1-1	4-0			1-1	2-1	2-2	0-1		
84-85	3-0	0-2							1-0	0-0	2-0	2-0	2-0	0-1	2-2	0-1		
85-86	1-2	0-1							2-2	3-3	0-0	1-1	3-2	1-1	1-2	2-2	1-0	1-2
86-87	3-0	0-4							1-0	1-3			0-0	0-1	2-2	3-0	1-1	0-2
87-88	2-2	0-0							2-1	0-2			3-0	3-1	1-2	3-3	2-2	2-2
88-89	7-2	1-0			1-1	2-1			3-2	1-2					3-0	4-1	2-0	4-0

	Chorley		Dagenham		Dartford		Enfield		Fisher Athletic		Frickley Athletic		Gateshead		Gravesend & N'fleet		Kettering Town	
	H	A	H	A	H	A	H	A	H	A	H	A	H	A	H	A	H	A
79-80															3-0	0-1	1-3	1-1
80-81											1-1	1-2			1-1	2-1	1-2	0-3
81-82			2-2	1-1	5-1	1-2	1-4	2-3			0-0	3-0			0-1	2-2	2-0	2-2
82-83			1-3	1-0			1-1	0-1			4-0	1-2					5-1	3-1
83-84			2-0	1-0			1-1	3-0			3-1	0-2	1-0	2-0			1-0	2-0
84-85			0-1	1-4	2-1	1-1	2-2	2-1			1-1	3-1	1-0	1-2			3-0	0-2
85-86			2-1	0-0	3-0	1-1	3-3	3-1			3-2	0-2					0-0	0-2
86-87			2-1	2-0			0-2	1-0			1-0	2-0	3-0	4-1			3-0	2-1
87-88			2-0	3-0			3-2	4-2	2-2	3-0							2-3	2-0
88-89	2-0	3-1					3-1	1-1	1-0	2-0							0-0	3-3

	Kidderminster H.		Lincoln City		Macclesfield Town		Northwich Victoria		Nuneaton Borough		Redditch United		Runcorn		Scarborough		Stafford Rangers	
	H	A	H	A	H	A	H	A	H	A	H	A	H	A	H	A	H	A
79-80							3-4	2-0	1-1	0-4	4-1	0-0			2-0	2-1	2-0	1-1
80-81							4-0	1-2	1-3	1-1					1-1	2-1	4-1	1-3
81-82							6-1	1-3					1-2	1-1	0-2	0-0	3-1	1-1
82-83							1-0	1-2	2-0	2-2			2-0	1-1	6-0	1-2	1-0	3-2
83-84	3-1	0-0					0-1	1-1	1-0	2-2			1-1	0-0	1-1	1-1		
84-85	1-4	1-2					1-0	0-0	2-2	2-3			5-1	4-1	2-2	0-1		
85-86	2-1	1-3					0-1	0-1	5-1	0-1			1-1	0-3	1-1	0-2	2-4	1-2
86-87	5-0	2-2					5-2	1-1	2-0	0-2			3-2	2-3	2-1	0-0	2-3	3-2
87-88	1-2	1-2	1-2	1-1	2-0	0-1	1-1	3-2					3-0	2-3			4-2	3-2
88-89	0-3	6-3			3-3	3-4	4-1	0-2					2-2	1-0			3-0	2-0

MAIDSTONE UNITED

	Sutton United H	A	Telford United H	A	Trowbridge Town H	A	Wealdstone H	A	Welling United H	A	Weymouth H	A	Worcester City H	A	Wycombe Wanderers H	A	Yeovil Town H	A
79-80			3-0	1-3			3-0	0-0			1-1	1-1	2-1	1-3			0-1	0-3
80-81			3-0	2-1			4-0	1-2			3-0	1-1	2-0	1-2			4-2	1-2
81-82			2-2	2-1	3-0	0-3					0-1	0-1	2-2	1-4			0-1	0-1
82-83			1-0	1-3	6-0	2-0	0-3	0-0			3-0	0-0	5-0	1-1			2-1	0-0
83-84			6-0	1-3	4-1	2-1	2-1	2-1			2-2	3-1	1-1	0-3			4-0	3-1
84-85			0-0	0-0			0-1	1-1			1-4	1-0	4-0	1-1			3-3	0-3
85-86			4-4	4-2			0-1	2-3			0-0	0-2			1-1	2-2		
86-87	0-1	1-3	0-0	1-1			1-0	0-0	4-0	2-2	3-1	1-4						
87-88	2-4	1-5	2-4	0-1			1-1	3-1	0-1	1-0	2-1	1-2			0-1	5-1		
88-89	1-1	1-1	1-3	2-1					3-0	0-0	3-0	3-1			1-3	3-2	5-0	2-1

	Home P	W	D	L	F	A	Away P	W	D	L	F	A
ALTRINCHAM	10	5	3	2	23	12	10	3	1	6	6	12
A P LEAMINGTON	3	2	1	0	6	1	3	2	1	0	6	3
AYLESBURY U	1	0	1	0	1	1	1	1	0	0	2	1
BANGOR C	4	3	0	1	9	2	4	1	2	1	5	4
BARNET	10	7	3	0	18	7	10	3	3	4	15	16
BARROW	6	5	1	0	8	0	6	3	1	2	9	7
BATH C	9	6	2	1	18	5	9	3	4	2	9	7
BOSTON U	10	3	4	3	16	14	10	2	4	4	14	17
CHELTENHAM T	4	2	2	0	6	3	4	1	1	2	7	6
CHORLEY	1	1	0	0	2	0	1	1	0	0	3	1
DAGENHAM	7	4	1	2	11	8	7	4	2	1	9	5
DARTFORD	3	3	0	0	10	2	3	0	2	1	3	4
ENFIELD	8	2	4	2	14	16	8	5	1	2	16	9
FISHER A	2	1	1	0	3	2	2	2	0	0	5	0
FRICKLEY A	7	4	3	0	13	5	7	3	0	4	10	9
GATESHEAD	3	3	0	0	5	0	3	2	0	1	7	3
GRAVESEND & N	3	1	1	1	4	2	3	1	1	1	4	4
KETTERING T	10	5	2	3	18	9	10	4	3	3	15	15
KIDDERMINSTER H	6	3	0	3	12	11	6	1	2	3	11	12
LINCOLN C	1	0	0	1	1	2	1	0	1	0	1	1
MACCLESFIELD T	2	1	1	0	5	3	2	0	0	2	3	5
NORTHWICH V	10	6	1	3	25	11	10	2	3	5	10	14
NUNEATON B	7	4	2	1	14	7	7	0	3	4	7	15
REDDITCH U	1	1	0	0	4	1	1	0	1	0	0	0
RUNCORN	8	4	3	1	18	9	8	2	3	3	11	12
SCARBOROUGH	8	3	4	1	15	8	8	2	3	3	6	8
STAFFORD R	8	6	0	2	21	11	8	4	2	2	15	13
SUTTON U	3	0	1	2	3	6	3	0	1	2	3	9
TELFORD U	10	4	4	2	22	13	10	4	2	4	14	16
TROWBRIDGE T	3	3	0	0	13	1	3	2	0	1	4	4
WEALDSTONE	8	4	1	3	11	7	8	2	4	2	9	8
WELLING U	3	2	0	1	7	1	3	1	2	0	3	2
WEYMOUTH	10	5	3	2	18	10	10	3	3	4	11	13
WORCESTER C	6	4	2	0	16	4	6	0	2	4	5	14
WYCOMBE W	3	0	1	2	2	5	3	2	1	0	10	5
YEOVIL T	7	4	1	2	18	8	7	2	1	4	6	11
TOTALS	205	111	53	41	410	207	205	68	60	77	274	285

MAIDSTONE UNITED   APPEARANCES

	79/80	80/81	81/82	82/83	83/84	84/85	85/86	86/87	87/88	88/89	89/90	TOTAL
AITKEN Glenn	31+2	13+1	1+1									45+4
ANDERSON Gary				6								6
ARCHBOLD John					1							1
ASHFORD Noel									27			27
AYRTON Neil			5+2			3+6						8+8
BAKER Sean						3						3
BALDRY Bill							3+1					3+1
BARNES Colin							31	1				32
BARTLEY Jon			41	40	17		12+4					110+4
BATES Jamie							6					6
BEATTIE Andy									22			22
BEENEY Mark							9	30	40			79
BERRY Les									40			40
BORG George							26+1					26+1
BRINKMAN Steve							7+2					7+2
BRISLEY Terry			18+1									18+1
BROWN Steve				2+6	2							4+6
BUDDEN Alan	19+3											19+3
BURNHAM Paul		1										1
BUTLER Steve							15	41	35+1	38		129+1
CARR David						19+3	8+1					27+4
CAWSTON Mervyn									10			10
CHARLERY Ken									10+1			10+1
CHURCHILL Peter							7+1					7+1
COBBY Steve			0+1									0+1
COLLINS Paul									1+1	12+1		13+2
COOPER Gary										2		2
COOPER Mark							4					4
CROWE Micky				15	32	30+2	14+1					91+3
CUGLEY Neil						2+1	7+5					9+6
DAUBNEY John	35+1	30+2	11+1									76+4
DINGWALL Micky					27+1	13						40+1
DOCKER John									14+2	8+4		22+6
DOHERTY Mick									23+2			23+2
DONN Nigel					29+6	15+2	18+4	32+5	41+1			135+18
DRIVER Phil						7+2						7+2
EDWARDS Billy	28	3										31
FARMER Julian							4+1					4+1
FERGUSSON Ian							23+5					23+5
FISHER Bobby							13					13
FOLEY Adrian		11+2	17+3									28+5
FORD Nigel		0+2										0+2
FUSCO Norman	34+1	2										36+1
GALL Mark									13+1	25+9		38+10
GALLOWAY Steve								24+5				24+15
GLOVER John						23	28+2	34	38+1			123+3

441

John Bartley.

Mark Gall (left).

John Glover.

Kenny Hill.

MAIDSTONE UNITED   APPEARANCES

	79/80	80/81	81/82	82/83	83/84	84/85	85/86	86/87	87/88	88/89	89/90	TOTAL
GOLLEY Mark										40		40
GOYETTE Paul								3+1	3+2			6+3
GREEN Clive			21+1	25+4	17+4	8+3	2+1					73+13
GREGORY Brian		10+1										10+1
GUY Dickie	38	37	42									117
HAMBERGER Steve		28	29+5									57+5
HANDFORD Phil							11+2					11+2
HARRISON Mark								22				22
HATTER Steve							17					17
HIGGINBOTTOM Andy							7	7+2				14+2
HILL Kenny	35+1	33	35	25								128+1
HILL Mark					42	33+6	39+1	28+3	31+1			173+11
HOLMES David	1	8+7	18+3	15+2								42+12
HORTON Duncan							36+1	33+1				69+2
HOYTE Kenny								7+3				7+3
HUGHES Billy				39	21+8	23+2						83+10
HUNT Peter		6										6
HUTTON John	24+1	36	24+2									84+3
IRONTON Nicky					5							5
JACQUES David								18+1	24+5			42+6
JELLY Paul			1									1
JOYCE Micky							27+6	5+7				32+13
JULIANS Gary			12									12
KINNEAR Chris	37+1	29	22+3	30+1								118+5
KNIGHT Graham	22	1										23
LAZARUS Paul					10+2	14+7						24+9
LEMOINE Adrian			8+1	4+7	1+5							13+13
LEWINGTON Colin					3	5						8
LYNCH Tony								21+2	5+8			26+10
MADDOCKS Kevin				25+1								25+1
MAHONEY Steve							4+3					4+3
MARSHALL Julian			4									4
MAY Warren								21+5				21+5
MEHMET Dave										9		9
MILLETT Kevin							8					8
MITCHELL Leon	3+2											3+2
MOORE Jon			40	40	38	8+1						126+1
MUNDEE Brian								3				3
NEWSON Mark	14	33+4	37	39	38	36+1						197+5
OVARD Frank	18+1	37	10+1	30+2	2	20+5						117+9
PAMPHLETT Tony								25	26	32		83
PARSONS Steve									4+1			4+1
PEARSON Andy							1					1
PEARSON Gerry					23+1		1					24+1
PENFOLD Mark			42	20								62
PITTAWAY Mike							18+4					18+4

Derek Richardson saves at the feet of Welling's Stuart White.

Brian Thompson.

MAIDSTONE UNITED   APPEARANCES

	79/80	80/81	81/82	82/83	83/84	84/85	85/86	86/87	87/88	88/89	89/90	TOTAL
QUINN Jimmy								3+2				3+2
RAGAN Steve			12									12
REYNOLDS Tony							27+5					27+5
RICHARDSON Derek				42	39	37	37	33				188
RISK Alan									37			37
ROAST Jesse								7+1	26+5	27+8		60+14
ROBBINS Terry				4+1								4+1
ROBERTS Gary									14+1			14+1
ROBINSON Keith		1										1
ROGERS Tony								1	20+5	9+8		30+13
ROLLINGS Andy				8								8
RYAN John						4						4
SAMSON Nicky		6										6
SCOTTING Alen									3+3			3+3
SHIELD Clay	1+1	8+3										9+4
SILLE John						25+4						25+4
SILVESTER Peter	7											7
SIMPSON M					0+2							0+2
SLOMAN Andy	1											1
SMELT Lee							5					5
SMITH Dave		7										7
SORRELL Tony									20+2			20+2
STARKEY Ian	4	1										5
STERLING Prince						1+2						1+2
STEWART Malcolm				34	26			27	25+2	18+1		130+3
STOCK Matt						7+3						7+3
SULLIVAN Terry								10+6				10+6
TAYLOR Peter				12	29	8+3						49+3
TERRY Nicky	2+1			0+1								2+2
THOMPSON Brian		33	36+2	42	39	33+3	28+1					211+6
TILTMAN Richard							13+7					13+7
TORRANCE George							7	30+3				37+3
TURNER Steve						3+2						3+2
VARRALL Tony									2			2
WALKER Ray									2			2
WALLACE Gary									0+1			0+1
WATSON John				35	17+2							52+2
WESTGARTH Dave		7+3										7+3
WHEELER Jason						7+1	1		11+5			19+6
WHITE Dean								15				15
WILTSHIRE Dave	34	12+1										46+1
WOLSEY S					0+1							0+1
WOODRUFF Mel									0+1			0+1
WOON Andy	30+3	25+1	17+2									72+6
YATES Paul					1							1

MAIDSTONE UNITED LEADING APPEARANCES

	79/80	80/81	81/82	82/83	83/84	84/85	85/86	86/87	87/88	88/89	89/90	TOTAL
THOMPSON Brian		33	36+2	42	39	33+3	28+1					211+6
NEWSON Mark	14	33+4	37	39	38	36+1						197+5
RICHARDSON Derek				42	39	37	37	33				188
HILL Mark						42	33+6	39+1	28+3	31+1		173+11
DONN Nigel					29+6	15+2	18+4	32+5	41+1			135+18
STEWART Malcolm					34	26		27	25+2	18+1		130+3
BUTLER Steve							15	41	35+1	38		129+1
HILL Kenny	35+1	33	35	25								128+1
MOORE Jon			40	40	38	8+1						126+1
GLOVER John					23		28+2	34	38+1			123+3
OVARD Frank	18+1	37	10+1	30+2	2	20+5						117+9
KINNEAR Chris	37+1	29	22+3	30+1								118+5
GUY Dickie	38	37	42									117
BARTLEY Jon				41	40	17		12+4				110+4

Steve Butler. Photo: Dave Goldsmith.

Mark Newson is presented with the Conference trophy.

MAIDSTONE UNITED   GOALSCORERS

	79/80	80/81	81/82	82/83	83/84	84/85	85/86	86/87	87/88	88/89	89/90	TOTAL
AITKEN Glenn	3(2p)	1										4(2p)
ASHFORD Noel										4		4
BARNES Colin							8(1p)					8(1p)
BARTLEY John				36	27(1p)	9		6				78(1p)
BEATTIE Andy									1			1
BERRY Les									1			1
BORG George							2					2
BUDDEN Alan	2											2
BUTLER Steve							9	24(5p)	22(1p)	26(4p)		**81(10p)**
CARR David						1						1
CHARLERY Ken									5			5
CHURCHILL Peter							2					2
COLLINS Paul									1			1
COOPER Mark							1					1
CROWE Micky					3	4						7
CUGLEY Neil					1	3						4
DAUBNEY John	21(1p)	15	4									40(1p)
DINGWALL Micky					7	3						10
DOCKER John									1	1		2
DOHERTY Mick									6			6
DONN Nigel					2				5			7
DRIVER Phil						2						2
EDWARDS Billy	1											1
FARMER Julian							1					1
FERGUSSON Ian							1(1p)					1(1p)
FISHER Bobby							1					1
FUSCO Norman	3											3
GALL Mark									14	26		40
GALLOWAY Steve							10					10
GLOVER John					3	5		2				10
GOLLEY Mark										7		7
GREEN Clive			9(1p)	7	12							28(1p)
GREGORY Brian		4										4
HAMBERGER Steve		3	4									7
HANDFORD Phil								1				1
HATTER Steve								2				2
HIGGINBOTTOM Andy								1	1			2
HILL Kenny	5	2	1	3								11
HILL Mark							2	1	2	4		9
HOLMES David		2	2	1								5
HUGHES Billy					1		1					2

447

MAIDSTONE UNITED   GOALSCORERS

	79/80	80/81	81/82	82/83	83/84	84/85	85/86	86/87	87/88	88/89	89/90	TOTAL
HUNT Peter		1(1p)										1(1p)
HUTTON John			1									1
IRONTON Nicky					1							1
JOYCE Micky							8	3				11
JULIANS Gary			2									2
KINNEAR Chris		3	4	1								8
LAZARUS Paul					1	6						7
LEMOINE Adrian			1									1
LYNCH Tony								2	2			4
MADDOCKS Kevin					1							1
MAHONEY Steve							1					1
MEHMET Dave										1		1
MOORE Jon			2	3								5
NEWSON Mark	2	6(4p)	8(4p)	6(2p)	1	11(2p)						34(12p)
OVARD Frank	5	17(2p)	6(3p)	8		3						39(5p)
PAMPHLETT Tony								3	5	4		12
PARSONS Steve									1			1
PEARSON Gerry						8						8
PENFOLD Mark			5	1								6
PITTAWAY Mike							1(1p)					1(1p)
RAGAN Steve			1									1
REYNOLDS Tony							6					6
ROAST Jesse									1	2		3
ROBERTS Gary									7			7
ROGERS Tony									7	3		10
ROLLINGS Andy					3							3
SAMSON Nicky		2										2
SILLE Jon						2						2
SILVESTER Peter	3											3
SORRELL Tony										3		3
STEWART Malcolm					3			4	1	3		11
SULLIVAN Terry								4				4
TAYLOR Peter				2	7	1						10
THOMPSON Brian		2	1	1			2					6
TILTMAN Richard							3					3
TORRANCE George							1	5				6
WATSON John				13(10p)	2(1p)							15(11p)
WESTGARTH Dave		1										1
WHEELER Jason						2			2			4
WHITE Dean								3(1p)				3(1p)
WILTSHIRE Dave	2	1										3
WOON Andy	7	4	4									15

MARGATE

PROMOTED FROM: The Southern League 2001
RESIGNED FROM Conference at end of the 2003-04 season.
2004-2005 SEASON: Conference South

Season 2001-02. Back row,left to right:Steve Hafner, Paul Lamb, Lee Williams, Dean Yorath, Paul Sykes, Mark Munday, Lee Turner, Charlie Mitten, Simon Beard, Graham Porter (Captain), Jay Saunders, Paul Lewis, Leon Braithwite, Tommy Tyne Front Row: Bill Edwards, Simon Ullathorne, Mo Takalogabhashi, Gary Blackford, Chris Kinnear (Manager), Kevin Raine (Asst. Manager), Phil Collins, John Keister, Mike Azzopardi and Robert Codner.

Season 2003-2004.Back Row. left to right: Paul Lamb, Eddie Youds, Charlie Mitten, Phil Smith, Warren Patmore and Iain O'Connell. Middle Row: Jay Saunders, Che Stadhart, Adrian Clarke, Simon Beard, Jake Leberl, Graham Porter, Greg Oates and John Michel Sigere. Front Row: Bill Edwards, Paul Abbott, Ian Pulman, Chris Kinnear (Manager), Kevin Raine (Asst Manager), Terry McFlynn, Darren Annon and John Keister.

SEASONS
3

TOTAL POINTS
165

HIGHEST POSITION
8th 2001-02

LOWEST POSITION
16th 2003-04

HIGHEST ATTENDANCE
3676 Dover A 26-12-01

LOWEST ATTENDANCE
255 v Forest Green R. 4.1.04
(at Dover Ath. FC)

SEASON GOALSCORER
Leon Braithwaite 16(5p) 01-02

CAREER GOALSCORER
Leon Braithwaite 27(6p)

CAREER APPEARANCES
Bill Edwards 103+6

			HOME							AWAY				
	P	W	D	L	F	A	Pts	P	W	D	L	F	A	Pts	Position
01-02	21	7	9	5	33	22	30	21	7	7	7	26	31	28	8
02-03	21	8	9	4	32	24	33	21	7	2	12	28	42	23	10
03-04	21	8	2	11	30	32	26	21	6	7	8	26	32	25	16
Total	**63**	**23**	**20**	**20**	**95**	**78**	**89**	**63**	**20**	**16**	**27**	**80**	**105**	**76**	

	Accrington Stanley		Aldershot Town		Barnet		Boston United		Burton Albion		Chester City		Dagenham & Redbridge		Doncaster Rovers		Dover Athletic		Exeter City	
	H	A	H	A	H	A	H	A	H	A	H	A	H	A	H	A	H	A	H	A
01-02					0-1	1-4	1-1	1-0			0-0	3-0	1-1	1-4	1-1	0-1	0-1	0-0		
02-03					2-2	1-0			0-0	1-0	0-1	0-5	0-1	0-3	2-1	1-3				
03-04	3-1	2-3	1-2	2-0	0-1	1-3			1-2	1-0	1-2	0-3	3-3	0-4					0-1	1-1

	Farnborough Town		Forest Green Rovers		Gravesend & N'fleet		Halifax Town		Hayes		Hereford United		Kettering Town		Leigh RMI		Morecambe		Northwich Victoria	
	H	A	H	A	H	A	H	A	H	A	H	A	H	A	H	A	H	A	H	A
01-02	2-1	0-0	1-1	3-3					1-0	4-2	2-2	0-3			1-2	2-2	1-1	1-2	1-2	1-1
02-03	0-0	1-4	3-0	1-4	4-2	2-1	2-1	2-2			0-2	3-2	2-2	1-1	2-0	0-2	1-1	0-3	4-4	0-1
03-04	3-0	1-1	2-0	2-1	1-3	1-2	2-0	1-0			1-3	1-2			2-0	2-4	1-1	3-3	3-1	3-0

	Nuneaton Borough		Scarborough		Shrewsbury Town		Southport		Stalybridge Celtic		Stevenage Borough		Tamworth		Telford United		Woking		Yeovil Town	
	H	A	H	A	H	A	H	A	H	A	H	A	H	A	H	A	H	A	H	A
01-02	1-1	0-0	1-1	1-0			2-0	2-1	8-0	2-2	2-1	1-3			3-1	0-2	4-3	1-0	0-1	2-1
02-03	1-1	2-3	3-1	2-3			1-0	2-0			1-1	3-1			1-1	0-1	2-1	5-1	1-2	1-2
03-04			0-2	1-0	0-2	1-1					1-4	1-2	3-2	1-1	1-0	1-1	1-2	0-0		

Leon Braithwaite. Photo: Garry Lets.

Phil Collins. Photo: Alan Coomes.

Billy Edwards. Photo: Roger Turner.   Lee Turner. Photo: Garry Letts.

	Home						Away					
	P	W	D	L	F	A	P	W	D	L	F	A
ACCRINGTON S	1	1	0	0	3	1	1	0	0	1	2	3
ALDERSHOT T	1	0	0	1	1	2	1	1	0	0	2	0
BARNET	3	0	1	2	2	4	3	1	0	2	3	7
BOSTON U	1	0	1	0	1	1	1	1	0	0	1	0
BURTON A	2	0	1	1	1	2	2	2	0	0	2	0
CHESTER C	3	0	1	2	1	3	3	1	0	2	3	8
DAGENHAM & R	3	0	2	1	4	5	3	0	0	3	1	11
DONCASTER R	2	1	1	0	3	2	2	0	0	2	1	4
DOVER A	1	0	0	1	0	1	1	0	1	0	0	0
EXETER C	1	0	0	1	0	1	1	0	1	0	1	1
FARNBOROUGH T	3	2	1	0	5	1	3	0	2	1	2	5
FOREST GREEN R	3	2	1	0	6	1	3	1	1	1	6	8
GRAVESEND & N	2	1	0	1	5	5	2	1	0	1	3	3
HALIFAX T	2	2	0	0	4	1	2	1	1	0	3	2
HAYES	1	1	0	0	1	0	1	1	0	0	4	2
HEREFORD U	3	0	1	2	3	7	3	1	0	2	4	7
KETTERING T	1	0	1	0	2	2	1	0	1	0	1	1
LEIGH R M I	3	2	0	1	5	2	3	0	1	2	4	8
MORECAMBE	3	0	3	0	3	3	3	0	1	2	4	8
NORTHWICH V	3	1	1	1	8	7	3	1	1	1	4	2
NUNEATON B	2	0	2	0	2	2	2	0	1	1	2	3
SCARBOROUGH	3	1	1	1	4	4	3	2	0	1	4	3
SHREWSBURY T	1	0	0	1	0	2	1	0	1	0	1	1
SOUTHPORT	2	2	0	0	3	0	2	2	0	0	4	1
STALYBRIDGE C	1	1	0	0	8	0	1	0	1	0	2	2
STEVENAGE B	3	1	1	1	4	6	3	1	0	2	5	6
TAMWORTH	1	1	0	0	3	2	1	0	1	0	1	1
TELFORD U	3	2	1	0	5	2	3	0	1	2	1	4
WOKING	3	2	0	1	7	6	3	2	1	0	6	1
YEOVIL T	2	0	0	2	1	3	2	1	0	1	3	3
TOTAL	63	23	20	20	95	78	63	20	16	27	80	105

APPEARANCES

	01-02	02-03	03-04	Total
ABBOTT Paul			0+6	0+6
ANNON Darren			38+3	38+3
AZZOPARDI Michael	1+5			1+5
BALTAZAR Bruno			1+1	1+1
BAPTISTE Rocky			12	12
BEARD Simon	25+3	10+1	1+1	36+5
BLACKFORD Gary	12+1			12+1
BOARDMAN Jon	3			3
BRAITHWAITE Leon	40+1	28+5		68+6
CLARKE Adrian		19+3	27+9	46+12
COLLINS Phil	15+6	23+5		38+11
EDWARDS Bill	41	35+1	27+5	**103+6**
GRAHAM Gareth	22+4			22+4
GRIFFITHS Leroy		1+2		1+2
HAFNER Steve	3+8			3+8
HANKIN San			3	3
HILAIRE Ian	0+2			0+2
JJUNJU Moses			0+2	0+2
KEISTER John	10+1	29+5	26+5	65+11
KWASHI Tostao			0+3	0+3
LAMB Paul	41	28+3		69+3
LEBERL Jake		32+2	39	71+2
LINCOLN Greg	1			1
McDONALD Charlie		5		5
McFLYNN Terry	21	18+11	10+1	49+12
MITTEN Charlie	18	20	0+1	38+1
MUNDAY Mark	33+5	2+5		35+10
MURPHY Danny			12	12
OATES Greg		39	36	75
O'CONNELL Iain	16+1	7+3	4+3	27+7
OMOYINMI Manny			13+1	13+1
PATMORE Warren			6	6
PIPER Lenny			7+2	7+2
PORTER Graham	38	29+4	35+3	**102+7**
PULLMAN Ian		0+3	2+9	2+12
RODDIS Nick	11+1			11+1
SAUNDERS Jay	36+2	38+1	36+1	110+4
SHEARER Lee		17+8		17+8
SIGERE Jean-Michel		13+8	18+13	31+21
SMITH Phil		22	42	64
SODJE Akpo	10+7			10+7
SODJE Sam		40	28+1	68+1
STADHART Che			19+15	19+15
TAKO Mo	0+2			0+2
TURNER Lee	24+1			24+1
WATSON Darren			9+12	9+12
WATTS Steve		7		7
WEBSTER Adrian		0+1		0+1
WHITBY Conrad			0+2	0+2
WILLIAMS Lee	35+2			35+2
YORATH Dean	6+2			6+2
ZORICICH Chris			11	11

GOALSCORERS

	01-02	02-03	03-04	Total
ANNON Darren		1		1
BALTAZAR Bruno		1		1
BAPTISTE Rocky			5	5
BEARD Simon	6	4		10
BOARDMAN Jon	1			1
BRAITHWAITE Leon	16(5p)	11(1p)		**27(6p)**
CLARKE Adrian			5(2p)	5(2p)
COLLINS Phil	3	6		9
GRAHAM Gareth	1			1
KEISTER John	6	4	1	11
LAMB Paul	1	1		2
LEBERL Jake		1	2	3
McDONALD Charlie		1		1
McFLYNN Terry	3	3	2	8
MUNDAY Mark	7	1		8
OATES Greg		3	1	4
OMOYINMI Manny			5	5
PATMORE Warren			1	1
PIPER Lenny			3	3
PORTER Graham	2	1	5	8
PULLMAN Ian			1	1
RODDIS Nick	2			2
SAUNDERS Jay	5	5	4	14
SHEARER Lee		1		1
SIGERE Jean-Michel		5	4	9
SODJE Akpo	3			3
SODJE Sam		6	2	8
STADHART Che			4	4
WATSON Darren			6	6
WATTS Steve		4(1p)		4(1p)
WILLIAMS Lee	1			1

MERTHYR TYDFIL

PROMOTED FROM: Southern League 1988-89
RELEGATED TO: Southern League 1994-95
2004-2005 SEASON: Southern League, Premier Division

1991-92 Squad - (Back Row (L-R): Steve Hookings, Terry Boyle, Gary Wager, Ian Thompson, George Wood, Eston Chiverton, Dave Webley.
Middle Row: Frank Hegarty (Trainer), Ryan James, Chris Hemming, Russell Lewis, Chris Summers, Tommy Hutchinson (Coach), Mark Williams, Cerri Williams, Wynford Hopkins (Manager).
Front Row: Phil Evans, Mike Pengelly, Chris Thomas, Kevin Rogers, Andy Beattie, Jon Morgan, David Burrows.
Photo: Les Williams.

SEASONS
6

TOTAL POINTS
334

HIGHEST POSITION
4 (91-92)

LOWEST POSITION
20 (93-94 & 94-95)

HIGHEST ATTENDANCE
3253 v Darlington (14-10-89)

LOWEST ATTENDANCE
317 v Altrincham (7-3-92)

SEASON GOALSCORER
Ian Thompson 20 (89/90)

CAREER GOALSCORER
Dave Webley 64(1p)

CAREER APPEARANCES
Gary Wager 216

	HOME							AWAY							
	P	W	D	L	F	A	Pts	P	W	D	L	F	A	Pts	Position
89-90	21	9	9	3	41	30	36	21	7	5	9	26	33	26	9
90-91	21	9	5	7	37	24	32	21	7	4	10	25	37	25	9
91-92	21	14	4	3	40	24	46	21	4	10	7	19	32	22	4
92-93	21	4	9	8	26	37	21	21	10	1	10	25	42	31	16
93-94	21	8	7	6	34	26	31	21	4	8	9	26	35	20	20
94-95	21	10	4	7	37	27	34	21	1	7	13	16	36	10	20
Total	126	54	38	34	215	168	200	126	33	35	58	137	215	134	

	Altrincham		Barnet		Barrow		Bath City		Boston United		Bromsgrove Rovers		Cheltenham Town		Chorley		Colchester United	
	H	A	H	A	H	A	H	A	H	A	H	A	H	A	H	A	H	A
88-89																		
89-90	0-0	1-4	2-1	0-4	3-3	5-1			1-0	2-2			1-1	2-0	1-0	0-1		
90-91	0-2	2-9	1-1	3-2	0-2	2-0	0-0	0-0	2-0	0-3			3-0	1-0			3-0	1-3
91-92	3-1	1-1			2-1	2-2	1-1	0-0	2-0	0-2			3-1	2-1			2-0	0-2
92-93	2-2	1-0					1-1	3-1	0-3	0-2	1-1	2-1						
93-94	0-0	0-3					1-1	3-0			2-1	3-3						
94-95	2-5	0-1					2-0	0-1			2-1	0-2						
96-97																		

	Dagenham & Redbridge		Darlington		Dover Athletic		Enfield		Farnborough Town		Fisher Athletic		Gateshead		Halifax Town		Kettering Town	
	H	A	H	A	H	A	H	A	H	A	H	A	H	A	H	A	H	A
88-89																		
89-90			1-1	0-0			5-1	0-2	1-1	1-0	1-4	2-1					3-2	0-2
90-91											1-0	0-0	3-1	0-1			1-3	0-2
91-92	2-2	1-1							1-0	0-0			1-4	1-0			4-1	1-3
92-93	0-2	1-6							1-3	1-2			1-1	0-4			2-1	3-1
93-94	0-0	1-0			0-0	0-1							3-0	0-0	2-1	1-2	0-1	0-0
94-95	2-0	1-2			2-3	2-2			1-1	1-2			1-2	0-2	2-0	2-2	2-1	1-4
96-97																		

	Kidderminster H.		Macclesfield Town		Northwich Victoria		Runcorn		Slough Town		Southport		Stafford Rangers		Stalybridge Celtic		Stevenage Borough	
	H	A	H	A	H	A	H	A	H	A	H	A	H	A	H	A	H	A
88-89																		
89-90	3-1	2-1	2-3	2-3	1-1	1-3	3-2	0-1					4-3	1-1				
90-91	1-2	2-1	0-2	1-0	3-2	3-0	0-0	1-2	3-0	2-1			1-1	0-2				
91-92	2-1	2-2	3-2	0-3	2-1	1-4	2-0	1-1	1-2	0-0			1-0	0-0				
92-93	4-3	0-1	1-2	1-0	3-0	2-1	0-3	3-2	1-1	1-2			0-0	1-0	1-1	2-2		
93-94	1-4	0-2	2-1	2-1	5-0	2-1	1-1	1-1	5-1	2-3	2-2	2-3	2-0	1-5	1-2	2-2		
94-95	0-1	0-2	1-2	0-0	2-0	0-2	3-0	0-0			1-2	1-3	4-1	1-2	4-2	1-1	2-2	0-0
96-97																		

MERTHYR TYDFIL

	Sutton United H	A	Telford United H	A	Welling United H	A	Witton Albion H	A	Woking H	A	Wycombe Wanderers H	A	Yeovil Town H	A
88-89														
89-90	2-3	1-1	0-0	1-1	4-0	3-0					1-1	2-1	2-2	0-4
90-91	3-0	1-1	2-3	1-3	1-0	1-2					2-4	1-2	1-1	3-3
91-92			2-2	2-1	2-1	2-1	1-0	2-3			1-2	0-4	2-2	1-1
92-93			4-0	0-5	1-1	0-5	0-2	1-3	1-5	2-0	1-4	0-4	1-1	1-0
93-94			0-3	0-1	0-1	1-1	4-3	2-2	2-3	1-2			1-1	2-2
94-95			3-1	1-1	0-2	1-2			1-1	1-4			0-0	3-1
96-97														

	Home						Away					
	P	W	D	L	F	A	P	W	D	L	F	A
ALTRINCHAM	6	1	3	2	7	10	6	1	1	4	5	18
BARNET	2	1	1	0	3	2	2	1	0	1	3	6
BARROW	3	1	1	1	5	6	3	2	1	0	9	3
BATH C	5	1	4	0	5	3	5	2	2	1	6	2
BOSTON U	4	3	0	1	5	3	4	0	1	3	2	9
BROMSGROVE R	3	2	1	0	5	3	3	1	1	1	5	6
CHELTENHAM T	3	2	1	0	7	2	3	3	0	0	5	1
CHORLEY	1	1	0	0	1	0	1	0	0	1	0	1
COLCHESTER U	2	2	0	0	5	0	2	0	0	2	1	5
DAGENHAM & R	4	1	2	1	4	4	4	1	1	2	4	9
DARLINGTON	1	0	1	0	1	1	1	0	1	0	0	0
DOVER A	2	0	1	1	2	3	2	0	1	1	2	3
ENFIELD	1	1	0	0	5	1	1	0	0	1	0	2
FARNBOROUGH T	4	1	2	1	4	5	4	1	1	2	3	4
FISHER A	2	1	0	1	8	4	2	1	1	0	2	1
GATESHEAD	5	2	1	2	9	8	5	1	1	3	1	7
HALIFAX T	2	2	0	0	4	1	2	0	1	1	3	4
KETTERING T	6	4	0	2	12	9	6	1	1	4	5	12
KIDDERMINSTER H	6	3	0	3	11	12	6	2	1	3	6	9
MACCLESFIELD T	6	2	0	4	9	12	6	3	1	2	6	7
NORTHWICH V	6	5	1	0	16	4	6	3	0	3	9	11
RUNCORN	6	3	2	1	9	6	6	1	3	2	6	7
SLOUGH T	4	2	1	1	10	4	4	1	1	2	5	6
SOUTHPORT	2	0	1	1	3	4	2	0	0	2	3	6
STAFFORD R	6	4	2	0	12	5	6	1	2	3	4	10
STALYBRIDGE C	3	1	1	1	6	5	3	0	3	0	5	5
STEVENAGE B	1	0	1	0	2	2	1	0	1	0	0	0
SUTTON U	2	1	0	1	5	3	2	0	2	0	2	2
TELFORD U	6	2	2	2	11	9	6	1	2	3	5	12
WELLING U	6	3	1	2	8	5	6	2	1	3	8	11
WITTON A	3	2	0	1	5	5	3	0	1	2	5	8
WOKING	3	0	1	2	4	9	3	1	0	2	4	6
WYCOMBE W	4	0	1	3	5	11	4	1	0	3	3	11
YEOVIL T	6	0	6	0	7	7	6	2	3	1	10	11
TOTALS	126	54	38	34	215	168	126	33	35	58	137	215

Gary Wager
Photo: V J Robertson

Andy Beattie
Photo: Duncan Cook

Mark Tucker and Dave Webley ready for the pass from Ceri Williams.   Photo: Mike Floate

MERTHYR TYDFIL — LEADING APPEARANCES

	89-90	90-91	91-92	92-93	93-94	94-95	TOTAL
Gary WAGER	39	37	31	30	38	41	216
Kevin ROGERS	15	41+1	27+5	32+4	27+9	38+1	180+20
Mark TUCKER	20	39	32+6	35+2	40		166+8
Dave WEBLEY	37+1	32	36+2	9+4		29+4	143+11
Andy BEATTIE	38	38	35+4	15+4		8+1	134+9
Ceri WILLIAMS	16+5	30+2	37+1	39+1	12		134+9
Mark WILLIAMS	1	8+1	36	38	35	19	137+1
Terry BOYLE		38+1	40	41		7+2	126+3
Ryan JAMES			36	39+1	33+3	4	112+4

MERTHYR TYDFIL — APPEARANCES

	89-90	90-91	91-92	92-93	93-94	94-95	TOTAL
ABRAHAM Gareth			8	7		24+1	39+1
ADEBOWALE Andy						10	10
BEATTIE Andy	38	38	35+4	15+4		8+1	134+9
BENBOW Ian				14	33+2		47+2
BOYLE Terry		38+1	40	41		7+2	126+3
CHIVERTON Eston			3+7	0+1			3+8
COATES Marc			7+2	30+7	18+5		55+14
COLE David				12+1			12+1
COSTA Lee						3+2	3+2
D'AURIA David		31+4	39				70+4
DAVEY Simon		6+2					6+2
DAVID Richard					3	2+1	5+1
DAVIES Mark				25+3	39	13+1	77+4
DOWNS Greg						7	7
DREWITT Ian					27+11		27+11
DYER Simon					16+1	29+6	45+7
EVANS Phil	37+2	6+3	8				51+5
FRENCH Ian						11+3	11+3
FRENCH Nigel	1+2						1+2
GILES Paul	34+3	21+9					55+12
GILL Craig				2+4			2+4
GORMAN Andy					6+1		6+1
GREEN Phil	16+22	12+7					28+29
HAIG Richard		0+1					0+1
HAMER Kevin	1+3						1+3
HEMMING Chris		11	10				21
HOLTHAM Matthew				12+2	28+4	29+3	69+9
HOLVEY Chris	9+1	4					13+1
HOPKINS Tony						13+1	13+1
HUNTER Paul						2	2
HUTCHINSON Tommy		8+3	29+4	7+4	1+4		45+15
JAMES Robbie					15	1	16

Above: Paul Sanderson

Top Left: Ian Drewitt

Photos: Dave West

Top Right: David D'Auria

MERTHYR TYDFIL — APPEARANCES

	89-90	90-91	91-92	92-93	93-94	94-95	TOTAL
JAMES Ryan			36	39+1	33+3	4	112+4
JARRETT Paul		0+1					0+1
JENKINS Anthony						19+8	19+8
JONES Lee						2+4	2+4
JONES Mark					8+2		8+2
JONES Nathan					29+1	36+2	65+3
JONES Peter	5+3						5+3
LEWIS Allan					10		10
LEWIS Dudley					29+3		29+3
LEWIS Richard		35					35
LEWIS Russell			23				23
LISSAMAN Jeff	24	14+4					38+4
LOSS Colin						11	11
MARSH Ian		2					2
MITCHELL Ian						21+6	21+6
MORGAN Jon			1+1				1+1
MORRIS Steve		2		12		1	15
MULLEN Richard	3	3					6
MULLEN Roger	10+12	10					20+12
NARBETT John						1	1
NEEDS Adrian				2+2		7+2	9+4
O'BRIEN Neil						13	13
OWEN Christian					0+2		0+2
POPHAM Philip						3+3	3+3
ROGERS Kevin	15	41+1	27+5	32+4	27+9	38+1	180+20
SANDERSON Paul	20	31+9				4+1	55+10
SCOTT Morrys						15+5	15+5
SHERWOOD Jeff			7+2				7+2
STEVENS Gary		0+2					0+2
STEVENSON Nigel	36+1	3+1					39+2
THOMPSON Ian	40	7	6+1				53+1
THRELFALL Dean						0+2	0+2
TONG David	21						21
TRICK Des				22+2	11		33+2
TUCKER Mark	20	39	32+6	35+2	40		166+8
TUPLING Steve	2						2
VOWLES Paul						3	3
WAGER Gary	39	37	31	30	38	41	216
WEBLEY Dave	37+1	32	36+2	9+4		29+4	143+11
WILLIAMS Ceri	16+5	30+2	37+1	39+1	12		134+9
WILLIAMS Chris	0+1						0+1
WILLIAMS Mark	1	8+1	36	38	35	19	137+1
WILLIAMS Morgan					4		4
WILLIAMS Steve	37+1	30+1					67+2
WITHERS David			2+2				2+2
WOOD George		11					11
WOOLGAR Matthew						3	3
YORK Andy						33	33

Ceri Williams (far right) scores.

Photo: Les Williams

Below: Dave Webley scores

MERTHYR TYDFIL GOALSCORERS

	89-90	90-91	91-92	92-93	93-94	94-95	TOTAL
ABRAHAM Gareth						2	2
ADEBOWALE Andy						1	1
BEATTIE Andy	2			1			3
BENBOW Ian				4	5		9
BOYLE Terry		2	2	1			5
CHIVERTON Eston			1				1
COATES Marc			1	9	7		17
D'AURIA David			5	2			7
DAVEY Simon			1				1
DAVIES Mark					2		2
DREWITT Ian					8(1p)		8(1p)
DYER Simon					10	9	19
FRENCH Ian						1	1
GILES Paul	2	2(1p)					4(1p)
GREEN Phil	7	10					17
HOLTAM Matthew					3	2	5
HUNTER Paul						2	2
HUTCHINSON Tommy			2				2
JAMES Robbie					2		2
JAMES Ryan					3		3
JENKINS Anthony						3	3
JONES Nathan						4(1p)	4(1p)
LEWIS Richard		2					2
LISSAMAN Jeff	2	1(1p)					3(1p)
MITCHELL Ian						6(1p)	6(1p)
MULLEN Roger	1						1
NEEDS Adrian				1			1
ROGERS Kevin	5	7(1p)	5(1p)	2	8(2p)	6	33(4p)
SANDERSON Paul	2	7					9
SCOTT Morrys						2	2
STEVENSON Nigel	2						2
THOMPSON Ian	20	2	1				23
TUCKER Mark	2	7	4	8	4		25
WEBLEY Dave	18	9	20	5		12(1p)	64(1p)
WILLIAMS Ceri	1(1p)	8	16(1p)	14(5p)	5(2p)		44(9p)
WILLIAMS Mark		1	1	3	3		8
WILLIAMS Steve	1	2					3
YORK Andy						1	1

1990-91 Squad. Back Row (L-R): Phil Green, Steve Williams, Jeff Lissaman, Terry Boyle, Kevin Rogers, Paul Sanderson.
Middle Row: Chris Holvey, Russell Lewis, Gary Wager, Ian Thompson, Nigel Stevenson.
Front Row: Paul Giles, Dave Webley, Andy Beattie (Captain), Ceri Williams, Mark Tucker.

Dave Webley.

462

MORECAMBE

PROMOTED FROM: The Northern Premier League 1994-95
2004-2005 SEASON: The conference

2002-2003 Squad. Back Row (L-R): Les Dewhirst (Kitman), Adrinao Rigoglioso, Garry Thompson,Stewart Drummond, Michael Stringfellow, Iain Swan, Jim Bentley, Wayne Curtis, Tommy Sawyer (Kitman).Middle Row: Claudia Manfredi (Sports Therapist), Nick Milner (Fitness Coach), Robbie Talbot, Lee Colkin, Dave McKearney, Craig Mawson, Danny Carlton, Neil Uberschar, Paul Oxborne, Jeff Udall (2nd Team Manager), Tony Gribbon (Asst. 2nd Team Manager). Front Row: Dave Edge (Sports Therapist), Michael Knowles, Ian Arnold, Andy Gouck, Jim Harvey (Manager), Ryan Zico Black, David Perkins, Nick Rogan,Andy Mutch (Assistant Manager).

		HOME							AWAY							
	P	W	D	L	F	A	Pts	P	W	D	L	F	A	Pts	Position
95-96	21	12	2	7	51	33	38	21	5	6	10	27	39	21	9
96-97	21	10	5	6	34	23	35	21	9	4	8	35	33	31	4
97-98	21	11	4	6	35	30	37	21	10	6	5	42	34	36	5
98-99	21	9	5	7	31	29	32	21	6	3	12	29	47	21	14
99-00	21	10	7	4	46	29	37	21	8	9	4	24	19	33	3
00-01	21	8	5	8	35	29	29	21	3	7	11	29	37	16	19
01-02	21	12	5	4	30	27	41	21	5	6	10	33	40	21	6
02-03	21	17	3	1	52	13	54	21	6	6	9	34	29	24	2
03-04	21	14	4	3	43	25	46	21	6	3	12	23	41	21	7
Total	189	103	40	46	357	238	349	189	58	50	81	276	319	224	

SEASONS
9

TOTAL POINTS
573

HIGHEST POSITION
2nd 02-03

LOWEST POSITION
19th 00-01

HIGHEST ATTENDANCE
3583 v Southport 26.12.99

LOWEST ATTENDANCE
635 v Farnborough T. 25.4.02

SEASON GOALSCORER
Justin Jackson 29(6p) (99/00)

CAREER GOALSCORER
John Norman 72(2p)

CAREER APPEARANCES
Dave McKearney 262+3

	Accrington Stanley		Aldershot Town		Altrincham		Barnet		Barrow		Bath City		Boston United		Bromsgrove Rovers		Burton Albion		Cheltenham Town	
	H	A	H	A	H	A	H	A	H	A	H	A	H	A	H	A	H	A	H	A
95-96					7-0	0-3					1-0	2-3					4-1	0-1		
96-97					2-1	1-0					1-2	1-2					1-0	3-2		
97-98																			1-0	1-2
98-99									3-2	1-2									0-2	1-4
99-00					3-3	2-2														
00-01													2-0	1-2						
01-02							1-0	0-1					0-0	1-2						
02-03							1-1	1-1									5-0	4-1		
03-04	1-0	0-1	2-0	2-2			1-3	1-2									2-1	1-0		

	Chester City		Dagenham & Redbridge		Doncaster Rovers		Dover Athletic		Exeter City		Farnborough Town		Forest Green Rovers		Gateshead		Gravesend & N'fleet	
	H	A	H	A	H	A	H	A	H	A	H	A	H	A	H	A	H	A
95-96			2-2	2-2			3-1	3-2			2-3	1-3			2-3	0-3		
96-97							3-1	0-3			1-1	2-2			4-0	3-0		
97-98							3-3	3-2			1-1	2-0			2-0	4-1		
98-99					1-2	1-2	0-4	3-2			1-0	6-1	3-1	2-2				
99-00					2-1	1-0	2-0	1-3					1-1	2-1				
00-01	0-2	0-1	2-3	2-3	2-1	0-1	1-2	2-2					0-2	0-0				
01-02	0-3	1-1	1-1	2-3	2-1	3-3	2-1	1-1			1-1	1-2	2-0	1-3				
02-03	1-1	1-2	2-1	1-1	3-0	1-1					1-1	3-2	4-0	0-1			2-0	2-3
03-04	0-1	1-2	3-2	3-1					0-3	0-4	3-2	4-2	4-0	2-1			2-2	0-6

	Halifax Town		Hayes		Hednesford Town		Hereford United		Kettering Town		Kidderminster H.		Kingstonian		Leek Town		Leigh RMI	
	H	A	H	A	H	A	H	A	H	A	H	A	H	A	H	A	H	A
95-96	0-1	1-1			0-1	2-1			5-3	3-2	3-1	2-4						
96-97	1-0	1-1	2-4	3-2	2-2	1-2			5-2	2-0	2-3	2-2						
97-98	1-1	1-5	0-2	3-0	1-3	1-0	1-5	0-1	1-3	1-1	3-1	4-1			1-1	1-1		
98-99			2-3	2-1	3-1	0-1	1-0	0-2	3-1	0-6	2-1	2-5	0-0	0-0	2-2	0-7		
99-00			1-4	1-0	4-0	3-1	3-2	1-1	2-1	1-1	0-1	1-2	1-2	0-0				
00-01			4-0	1-1	0-0	0-0	1-1	2-2	0-2	5-1			3-2	6-1			1-2	0-1
01-02			2-1	1-3			2-2	2-0									1-3	1-0
02-03	2-0	0-1					3-1	2-1	1-0	2-3							2-1	0-1
03-04	2-0	0-1					2-2	0-3									1-0	1-3

MORECAMBE

	Macclesfield Town		Margate		Northwich Victoria		Nuneaton Borough		Runcorn		Rushden & Diamonds		Scarborough		Shrewsbury Town		Slough Town	
	H	A	H	A	H	A	H	A	H	A	H	A	H	A	H	A	H	A
95-96	2-4	0-2			2-2	1-2			3-1	3-1							1-2	1-1
96-97	1-0	0-0			2-0	0-1					2-0	1-2					0-0	2-1
97-98					3-1	0-5					3-1	3-3					2-1	3-3
98-99					3-1	1-1					2-3	1-3						
99-00					5-0	0-0	1-1	1-1			0-0	2-0	0-1	2-0				
00-01					4-0	0-1	4-2	1-5			2-1	1-4	4-4	2-2				
01-02			2-1	1-1	2-1	3-4	1-0	3-2					2-0	2-0				
02-03			3-0	1-1	3-1	2-3	3-2	1-1					3-1	0-1				
03-04			3-3	1-1	3-0	1-1							2-1	0-1	3-3	0-2		

	Southport		Stalybridge Celtic		Stevenage Borough		Sutton United		Tamworth		Telford United		Welling United		Woking		Yeovil Town	
	H	A	H	A	H	A	H	A	H	A	H	A	H	A	H	A	H	A
95-96	4-3	1-1	2-0	2-0	1-0	1-1					2-0	2-2	1-0	0-1	4-5	0-3		
96-97	2-1	1-3	0-0	1-2	1-2	2-4					0-1	3-2	1-2	4-1	1-2	2-1		
97-98	2-0	1-1	3-1	1-3	0-2	3-0					1-0	3-1	4-2	2-2	1-2	2-0	1-0	3-2
98-99	1-1	0-1			1-1	0-2					0-1	3-2	2-1	2-3	0-1	3-0	1-1	1-0
99-00	3-3	1-1			3-3	2-1	6-2	1-0			5-2	2-3	2-1	0-0	1-0	0-0°	1-1	0-2
00-01	1-3	2-1			1-2	1-1					0-0	0-2			3-0	1-3	0-0	2-3
01-02	2-2	1-1	1-0	3-4	0-3	1-3					2-1	1-4			3-1	3-1	1-5	1-1
02-03	3-0	3-2			3-1	1-1					1-0	3-0			5-0	6-0	1-2	0-2
03-04					2-1	1-0			4-0	3-2	1-0	1-2			2-1	1-4		

Lee Colkin. Photo: Peter Barnes.

Stuart Drummond.

	Home						Away					
	P	W	D	L	F	A	P	W	D	L	F	A
ACCRINGTON S	1	1	0	0	1	0	1	0	0	1	0	1
ALDERSHOT T	1	1	0	0	2	0	1	0	1	0	2	2
ALTRINCHAM	3	2	1	0	12	4	3	1	1	1	3	5
BARNET	3	1	1	1	3	4	3	0	1	2	2	4
BARROW	1	1	0	0	3	2	1	0	0	1	1	2
BATH C	2	1	1	0	2	1	2	0	0	2	3	5
BOSTON U	2	1	1	0	2	0	2	0	0	2	2	4
BROMSGROVE R	2	2	0	0	5	1	2	1	0	1	3	3
BURTON A	2	2	0	0	7	1	2	2	0	0	5	1
CHELTENHAM T	2	1	0	1	1	2	2	0	0	2	2	6
CHESTER C	4	0	1	3	1	7	4	0	1	3	3	6
DAGENHAM & R	5	2	2	1	10	9	5	1	2	2	10	10
DONCASTER R	5	4	0	1	10	5	5	1	2	2	6	7
DOVER A	7	4	1	2	14	12	7	3	2	2	13	15
EXETER C	1	0	0	1	0	3	1	0	0	1	0	4
FARNBOROUGH T	7	2	4	1	10	9	7	4	1	2	19	12
FOREST GREEN R	6	4	1	1	14	4	6	2	2	2	7	8
GATESHEAD	3	2	0	1	8	3	3	2	0	1	7	4
GRAVESEND & N	2	1	1	0	4	2	2	0	0	2	2	9
HALIFAX T	5	3	1	1	6	2	5	0	2	3	3	9
HAYES	6	2	0	4	11	14	6	4	1	1	11	7
HEDNESFORD T	6	2	2	2	10	7	6	3	1	2	7	5
HEREFORD U	7	3	3	1	13	13	7	2	2	3	7	10
KETTERING T	7	5	0	2	17	12	7	3	2	2	14	14
KIDDERMINSTER H	5	3	0	2	10	7	5	1	1	3	11	14
KINGSTONIAN	3	1	1	1	4	4	3	1	2	0	6	1
LEEK T	2	0	2	0	3	3	2	0	1	1	1	8
LEIGH RMI	4	2	0	2	5	6	4	1	0	3	2	5
MACCLESFIELD T	2	1	0	1	3	4	2	0	1	1	0	2
MARGATE	3	2	1	0	8	4	3	0	3	0	3	3
NORTHWICH V	9	8	1	0	27	6	9	0	3	6	8	18
NUNEATON B	4	3	1	0	9	5	4	1	2	1	6	9
RUNCORN	1	1	0	0	3	1	1	1	0	0	3	1
RUSHDEN & D	5	3	1	1	9	5	5	1	1	3	8	12
SCARBOROUGH	5	3	1	1	11	7	5	2	1	2	6	4
SHREWSBURY T	1	0	1	0	3	3	1	0	0	1	0	2
SLOUGH T	3	1	1	1	3	3	3	1	2	0	6	5
SOUTHPORT	8	4	3	1	18	13	8	2	4	2	10	11
STALYBRIDGE C	4	3	1	0	6	1	4	1	0	3	7	9
STEVENAGE B	9	3	2	4	12	15	9	3	3	3	12	13
SUTTON U	1	1	0	0	6	2	1	1	0	0	1	0
TAMWORTH	1	1	0	0	4	0	1	1	0	0	3	2
TELFORD U	9	6	1	2	12	5	9	4	1	4	18	18
WELLING U	5	4	0	1	10	6	5	1	2	2	8	7
WOKING	9	5	0	4	20	12	9	5	1	3	18	12
YEOVIL T	6	1	3	2	5	9	6	2	1	3	7	10
TOTAL	189	103	40	46	357	238	189	58	50	81	276	319

Justin Jackson. Photo: Andrew Chitty.   Michael Knowles. Photo: Martin Wray.

MORECAMBE — LEADING APPEARANCES

	95-96	96-97	97-98	98-99	99-00	00-01	01-02	02-03	03-04	TOTAL
Dave McKEARNEY		37	33	33+2	41	42	39	37+1	26+8	288+11
Stuart DRUMMOND	1+1	1+2	19+8	32+6	39	40	36	42	31	241+17
John NORMAN	14+10	40+1	40+2	39+3	11+1	29+7	22+15			195+39
Paul BURNS	39	27+5	25+8	31+4	23+3					145+20
Garry THOMPSON					14+8	11+8	27+1	31+4	29+6	112+27
Michael KNOWLES	27+9	34+4	10+9	8+1	18+3	1+3		6+1		104+30
Craig MAWSON							41	42	39+1	122+1
Andy FENSOME			11	40	39	24+5				114+5
Adriano RIGOGLIOSO						19+10	19+18	32+4	13	83+32
Steve McILHARGEY	15	35	28	25	9					112
Wayne CURTIS			4	7+12	0+1		10+13	30+7	18+5	69+38
Ryan - Zico BLACK					0+6	20+13	14+15	13+16	0+4	47+54

MORECAMBE APPEARANCES

	95-96	96-97	97-98	98-99	99-00	00-01	01-02	02-03	03-04	TOTAL
ALTY Stephen						0+2				0+2
ANNAN Richard		17+1								17+1
ARMSTRONG Robbie	13+1									13+1
ARNOLD Ian							23+4			23+4
BALDWIN Kevin						0+1				0+1
BANKS Andy	8	7	14	17	33+2	6+1				85+3
BANKS Andy C				5+1						5+1
BENTLEY Jim								23	36	59
BIGNALL Mike		12	7+3							19+3
BLACK Ryan - Zico					0+6	20+13	14+15	13+16	0+4	47+54
BLACKBURN Chris									4+1	4+1
BROWN Greg				6+1	13+4	8+3				27+8
BURNS Paul	39	27+5	25+8	31+4	23+3					145+20
CAIN Ian	30+4	9+7								39+11
CARLTON Danny							4+7	7+19	28+10	39+36
CERAOLO Mark	14+15	6+5	8+10	9+14						37+44
COLEMAN John	26+1									26+1
COLKIN Lee							28+1	24+1		52+2
COLLINS Lee								6	10+2	16+2
COMSTIVE Paul	21+7									21+7
CRUMBLEHULME Danny							5+3			5+3
CURTIS Wayne			4	7+12	0+1		10+13	30+7	18+5	69+38
DODGSON Lee									0+3	0+3
DOWE Julian					7					7
DRUMMOND Stuart	1+1	1+2	19+8	32+6	39	40	36	42	31	241+17
DULLAGHAN Gary	7+5									7+5
DUNBAVIN Ian									3	3
EASTWOOD Phil					25+7	18+11	2+10			45+28
ELAM Lee								37+3		37+3
FARRELL Andy					30+1					30+1
FENSOME Andy				11	40	39	24+5			114+5
FOLEY Steve	7									7
GARDNER David				9+13	4+3					13+16
GARNETT Shaun									12	12
GOUCK Andy							24+4	4+10		28+14
GRIMSHAW Andy	29+3	23+4	24							76+7
HADDOW Paul				3+2						3+2
HALL Dave				24						24
HALLAM Tony								0+1		0+1
HARDIKER John				1	18+4	31	18			68+4
HARDY Niell					17+14					17+14
HARVEY Jim	1+3									1+3
HAY Alex							2			2
HEALD Andrew				0+5	7+5	2+8				9+18
HEALY Brian		15+1	39	17+1						71+2
HILL Keith								19+1		19+1
HODGSON Steve	0+1	11+1	6+4							17+6
HORRIGAN Ian	3+2									3+2
HOWELL Dean									24+6	24+6
HUGHES Darren			8+2							8+2
HUGHES Tony	29+3	23	8	18+1						78+4

MORECAMBE — APPEARANCES

	95-96	96-97	97-98	98-99	99-00	00-01	01-02	02-03	03-04	TOTAL
HUNT Steve			1+3							1+3
HUNTER Colin						6+7				6+7
HUNTER Garry									8+7	8+7
JACKSON Justin	5+4	22+1		4	38					69+5
JOHNSTONE Glen	19									19
KEELING Barrie				13+10	3+19	1				17+29
KENNEDY John			13	20						33
KNOWLES Michael	27+9	34+4	10+9	8+1	18+3	1+3		6+1		104+30
LANE Chris								15+1		15+1
LAVELLE Ben	25+1	17+2								42+3
LEAVER David		19+1								19+1
LEE David						12				12
LIGHTFOOT Chris							15			15
LOWE David			4+2							4+2
LYONS Andy						27+2				27+2
LYONS Darren				28+1	23+2					51+3
MADDOCK Wayne	10+2									10+2
MAWSON Craig							41	42	39+1	122+1
MAYERS Kenny			26+15	27+4						53+19
McCLUSKIE Jim	25+11	3+24								28+35
McFLYNN Terry								16+3		16+3
McGUIRE Paul				0+1	8+11	5+9	32+2			45+23
McILHARGEY Steve	15	35	28	25	9					112
McKEARNEY Dave		37	33	33+2	41	42	39	37+1	26+8	288+11
MILLER David		13+1	16							29+1
MILNER Andy			21	3	0+4					24+4
MITCHELL Neil			2+4							2+4
MONK Ian	25+2	34+3	31+3							90+8
MORGAN Alan								2+4		2+4
MORTON Neil				4+2	2+1					6+3
MURPHY Jamie						21+6	16+4	8+11	22+5	67+26
NORMAN John	14+10	40+1	40+2	39+3	11+1	29+7	22+15			195+39
OSBOURNE Paul									5+2	5+2
PARKINSON Stuart			4+15							4+15
PERKINS David						4	19+2	17+4	39	79+6
PORTER Alex							1+5			1+5
POTTS Colin						1				1
PRICE Chris						2+1				2+1
QUAYLE Mark						15+3	1+1			16+4
RIGOGLIOSO Adriano						19+10	19+18	32+4	13	83+32
ROBINSON Craig							3+1			2+1
ROGAN Nick								0+10	3+21	3+31
RUSHTON Paul	23+1	16+4	25+3	12+8	1+1					77+17
SANG Nneil	7+1	4+3								11+4
SHIRLEY Mark		17+2	38+1	27+5						82+8
SMITH Leon					5+11	5				10+11
SMITH Mark						36				36
STANFORD Carl							0+3			0+3
STIMPSON Barrie	2									2
STRINGFELLOW Michael						6+3	3+5	30+5	26+3	65+16
SUGDEN Ryan									13+20	13+20

2003-2004 Squad.
Back Row (L-R): Dean Howell, Jim Bentley, Stewart Drummond, Michael Stringfellow, Iain Swan, Adriano Rigoglioso, Wayne Curtis.
Middle Row: Nik Rogan, Chris Lane, Garry Thompson, Craig Mawson, Keiron Walmsley, Danny Carlton, Dale Gordon.
Front Row: Gary Hunter, Paul Osborne, Jim Harvey (Manager), Andy Mutch (Assistant Manager), Lee Dodgson, David Perkins.

Wayne Curtis.   Paul Osbourne.

MORECAMBE — APPEARANCES

	95-96	96-97	97-98	98-99	99-00	00-01	01-02	02-03	03-04	TOTAL
SWAN Iain								39+2	14+5	53+7
SWANNICK David		2		1+1	3+2					6+3
TAKANO Keisuke			6+1	19+13	19+3	10+7				54+24
TALBOT Robbie						10+11	25	6+11		41+22
TAYLOR Paul	0+2									0+2
TAYLOR Perry								0+1		0+1
THOMPSON Garry					14+8	11+8	27+1	31+4	29+6	112+27
THOMSON Peter							2+2			2+2
TOMLINSON Paul	26									26
UBERSCHAR Neil							2+1	6+3	7+6	15+10
UDALL Jamie		2								2
WALLER Micky				8						8
WALMSLEY Keiron									27	27
WALTERS Steve						20+2				20+2
WARD Peter					1					1
WEST Paul	9	15+6								24+6
WILLCOCK Iain							1			1
WILLIAMS Gary		3+7	2+7							5+14
WITHERS Peter	2+4									2+4
WRIGHT Andrew						2+2				2+2
WRIGHT Mark					19	1				20

MORECAMBE — GOALSCORERS

	95-96	96-97	97-98	98-99	99-00	00-01	01-02	02-03	03-04	TOTAL
ARMSTRONG Robbie	1									1
ARNOLD Ian							7(4p)			7(4p)
BANKS Andy C			1							1
BENTLEY Jim								3	4	7
BIGNALL Mike		6	5							11
BLACK Ryan-Zico						5	5	5(1p)		15(1p)
BROWN Greg					1					1
BURNS Paul	7(6p)	7(5p)	2		4(1p)					20(12p)
CAIN Ian	9	2								11
CARLTON Danny							1	7	17(1p)	25(1p)
CEROALO Mark	11	3	7	5						26
COLEMAN John	11									11
COLLINS Lee								1		1
COMSTIVE Paul	1									1
CURTIS Wayne			2	3			8	18(1p)	8(2p)	39(3p)
DRUMMOND Stuart			1	5	4	7	4	11(2p)	5(1p)	37(3p)
DULLAGHAN Gary	1									1
EASTWOOD Phil					11(1p)	10(3p)				21(4p)
ELAM Lee								13		13
GARDNER Dave				2	1					3

MORECAMBE — GOALSCORERS

	95-96	96-97	97-98	98-99	99-00	00-01	01-02	02-03	03-04	TOTAL
GOUCK Andy							3(1p)	1		4(1p)
GRIMSHAW Andy	3	3	2							8
HARDY Niell					8					8
HEALD Andrew				1		2				3
HEALY Brian		3	7	2						12
HODGSON Steve		1								1
HOWELL Dean								3		3
HUGHES Darren			1							1
HUNTER Colin							1			1
JACKSON Justin	2	15		6	29(6p)					**52(6p)**
KEELING Barrie				1						1
KNOWLES Michael	2	1			1					4
LANE Chris								1		1
LIGHTFOOT Chris							2			2
LYONS Andy						1				1
LYONS Darren				6	3					9
MAYERS Kenny			3	2						5
McCLUSKIE Jim	11	6								17
McFLYNN Terry								3		3
McGUIRE Paul				1						1
McKEARNEY Dave		3(2p)	4(3p)	1	1	4(2p)		1		14(7p)
MILLER David		1								1
MILNER Andy			8	1						9
MONK Ian	9	6	2							17
MURPHY Jamie						1		1	1	3
NORMAN John	8	7	18(1p)	19(1p)	4	10	6			**72(2p)**
PARKINSON Stuart			1							1
QUAYLE Mark							8			8
RIGOGLIOSO Adriano						2	4	10	3(2p)	19(2p)
ROGAN Nick									4	4
RUSHTON Paul			1							1
SHIRLEY Mark		1	10	2						13
SMITH Leon					1					1
STRINGFELLOW Mike								2	1	3
SUGDEN Ryan									6	6
SWAN Iain								1		1
TAKANO Keisuke				2						2
TALBOT Robbie						7	15(1p)	3		25(1p)
THOMPSON Garry					1	4	7	5	6	23
THOMSON Peter							1			1
TOMLINSON Paul	1									1
UDALL Jamie		1								1
WALMSLEY Keiron									2	2
WALTERS Steve						1				1
WEST Paul	1									1

NEWPORT COUNTY

RELEGATED FROM: The Football League 1988

Folded during the season and all records were expunged, however, to ensure that this book contained ALL the players who have played in the Conference during the 25 years we have included them. 2004-2005 SEASON: A new club, Newport AFC, was formed in 1989 which now plays in the Conference South once again under the name of Newport County.

	HOME						AWAY					
	P	W	D	L	F	A	P	W	D	L	F	A
ALTRINCHAM							1	0	0	1	0	1
AYLESBURY U	1	0	1	0	2	2						
BARNET	1	0	0	1	1	7	1	0	0	1	1	4
BOSTON U	1	0	1	0	1	1	1	0	1	0	1	1
CHELTENHAM T	1	0	0	1	0	1	1	0	0	1	2	3
CHORLEY	1	1	0	0	2	0	1	1	0	0	2	0
ENFIELD							1	0	0	1	0	3
FISHER A							1	0	0	1	2	3
KETTERING T	1	0	0	1	1	2						
KIDDERMINSTER H	1	0	0	1	1	2	1	0	1	0	1	1
MACCLESFIELD T							1	0	0	1	0	3
MAIDSTONE U	1	1	0	0	2	1	1	0	0	1	1	2
NORTHWICH V							1	0	0	1	1	3
RUNCORN							1	0	1	0	0	0
STAFFORD R							1	0	0	1	0	3
SUTTON U							1	0	1	0	1	1
TELFORD U	1	0	0	1	0	3	1	0	0	1	1	3
WELLING U	1	0	0	1	0	1						
WEYMOUTH	1	1	0	0	4	0						
WYCOMBE W	1	0	0	1	3	5	1	0	0	1	0	5
YEOVIL T	1	0	1	0	1	1						
TOTAL	13	3	3	7	18	26	16	1	4	11	13	36

APPEARANCES

88-89

ABBRUZZESE David	8+3
ANDREWS Kheri	17+2
BANKS Chris	15+5
BENNETT Sean	0+2
BICKERTON Dave	2+1
BIRD Tony	29
BRIGNULL Phil	13
EVANS Richard	11+2
FOLEY Will	7+3
FORD Francis	16+1
GIBBINS Roger	2
GILES David	3
GRIPTON Mark	1+1
HAMER Kevin	1+1
JONES Gareth	2
KING Andy	1
KING Jamie	2
MARUSTIK Chris	14
McLAUGHLIN Jim	2

APPEARANCES cont.

88-89

MILLETT Glynne	12+2
MILLS Sean	0+1
MORGAN Steve	1+1
NUTTELL Mike	5
PEACOCK Darren	14
PREECE Ryan	0+2
RICHARDS Gary	14
ROGERS Graham	4+2
SANDERSON Paul	24+1
SHERLOCK Steve	26
SUGRUE Paul	13+1
TAYLOR Robbie	1
THOMPSON Ian	2+1
THOMPSON Max	15
WALKER Shane	2+1
WILLIAMS Phil	22
WITHERS David	18+2

GOALSCORERS

88-89

ANDREWS Keri	1
BANKS Chris	1
BRIGNULL Phil	1
EVANS Richard	2
FOLEY Will	1
FORD Francis	2
GILES David	2
MARUSTIK Chris	3
MILLETT Glynne	1
NUTTELL Mike	1
RICHARDS Gary	2
SANDERSON Paul	5
SUGRUE Paul	2(1p)
THOMPSON Ian	1
WILLIAMS Phil	2
WITHERS David	4

Last ever squad photo of Newport County before the club closed down.
Back Row (L-R): Glyn Jones (Youth Coach), Max Thompson, Steve Sherlock, Darren Peacock, Phil Williams, Tony Bird, Paul Sanderson, Graham Rogers, Shane Walker, Mark Gibbs, Tony Gilbert (Trainer).
Front Row: David Williams (Assistant Manager), Chris Banks, Francis Ford, Keri Andrews, John Mahoney (Manager), Richard Evans, David Withers, Glynne Millett.

Newport County see this attack cleared by the Macclesfield 'keeper.

NORTHWICH VICTORIA

FOUNDER MEMBER - elected from the Northern Premier League
2004-2005 SEASON: The Conference

1980-81. Back row, left to right: Stan Storton (Manager), Terry Owen, Keith Braithwaite, Jeff Forsham, Colin Williams, Dave Ryan, Albie Nieman, Paul Mayman, and Brian Dainteth (Trainer).Front row: John Denham, Steve Eaton, Ken Jones, Tony Murphy and Brian Hall. Photo: Northwich Chronicle

		HOME						AWAY						
		P	W	D	L	F	A	Pts	P	W	D	L	F	A	Pts	Position

	P	W	D	L	F	A	Pts	P	W	D	L	F	A	Pts	Position
79-80	19	11	5	3	31	14	27	19	5	5	9	19	24	15	8
80-81	19	12	4	3	32	13	28	19	5	7	7	21	27	17	4
81-82	21	12	6	3	35	17	42	21	8	3	10	21	29	27	6
82-83	21	15	5	1	48	22	50	21	3	5	13	20	41	14	8
83-84	21	11	8	2	35	18	30	21	5	6	10	19	29	21	7
84-85	21	9	4	8	22	19	22	21	7	7	7	28	27	28	9
85-86	21	5	6	10	24	25	16	21	5	6	10	18	29	21	16
86-87	21	6	7	8	25	23	25	21	4	7	10	28	46	19	17
87-88	21	8	6	7	30	25	30	21	2	11	8	16	32	17	17
88-89	20	8	5	7	31	30	29	20	6	6	8	33	35	24	10
89-90	21	9	3	9	29	30	30	21	6	2	13	22	37	20	15
90-91	21	8	7	6	33	30	31	21	5	6	10	32	45	21	12
91-92	21	10	4	7	40	25	34	21	6	2	13	23	33	20	11
92-93	21	5	6	10	24	29	21	21	11	2	8	44	26	35	11
93-94	21	7	9	5	26	19	30	21	4	10	7	18	26	22	15
94-95	21	7	8	6	39	30	29	21	7	7	7	38	36	28	10
95-96	21	9	3	9	38	35	30	21	7	9	5	34	29	30	8
96-97	21	11	5	5	31	20	38	21	6	7	8	30	34	25	6
97-98	21	8	9	4	34	24	33	21	7	6	8	29	35	27	9
98-99	21	11	3	7	29	21	36	21	8	6	7	31	30	30	7
99-00	21	10	8	3	33	25	38	21	3	4	14	20	53	13	18
00-01	21	8	7	6	31	24	31	21	3	6	12	18	43	15	17
01-02	21	9	4	8	32	34	31	21	7	3	11	25	36	24	13
02-03	21	6	5	10	26	34	23	21	7	7	7	40	38	28	14
03-04	21	2	8	11	15	38	14	21	2	3	16	15	42	9	22
Total	520	217	145	158	773	624	748	520	139	143	238	642	862	550	

SEASONS
25

TOTAL POINTS
1298

HIGHEST POSITION
4th 1980-81

LOWEST POSITION
22nd 2003-04

HIGHEST ATTENDANCE
2897 v Witton A. 27.12.93
at Drill Field
3268 v Shrewsbury T. 1.1.04
at Wincham Park

LOWEST ATTENDANCE
367 v Dagenham 3.5.86

SEASON GOALSCORER
Colin Williams 26(1p) (80/81)

CAREER GOALSCORER
Malcolm O'Connor 97(8p)

CAREER APPEARANCES
Dave Ryan 432

	Accrington Stanley		Aldershot Town		Altrincham		A P Leamington		Aylesbury United		Bangor City		Barnet		Barrow		Bath City	
	H	A	H	A	H	A	H	A	H	A	H	A	H	A	H	A	H	A
79-80					1-0	0-0	2-1	2-2			4-0	3-0	2-0	2-0	6-3	0-1	6-1	0-0
80-81					1-0	1-1	2-0	1-1			2-1	0-0	4-1	0-1	0-0	1-2	3-1	0-0
81-82					2-0	2-0	3-0	2-0					1-1	1-0	2-0	1-6	2-1	1-1
82-83					2-1	0-3					1-4	1-1	1-0	2-4	1-0	0-0	3-0	0-3
83-84					1-1	1-1					2-1	1-0	0-0	1-2			3-2	0-2
84-85					1-2	2-2							2-0	1-1	1-0	0-0	3-1	3-0
85-86					1-2	1-2							0-1	0-1	0-1	2-1	1-2	0-0
86-87					1-1	1-1							1-2	0-4			1-1	1-1
87-88					1-2	0-2							2-1	1-4			2-1	0-0
88-89					4-3	2-2			1-1	0-2			1-1	0-2				
89-90					2-3	2-0							0-2	0-1	1-0	0-1		
90-91					1-1	2-0							0-2	1-1	2-2	2-2	2-0	1-4
91-92					1-2	1-0									6-1	2-0	1-3	0-2
92-93					1-2	0-0											3-1	5-0
93-94					2-0	2-2											3-1	0-0
94-95					1-1	3-1											1-1	2-2
95-96					2-1	4-3											2-2	3-0
96-97					2-2	3-2											1-0	2-3
97-98																		
98-99															1-0	1-0		
99-00					1-1	0-2												
00-01																		
01-02													0-3	0-1				
02-03													1-1	4-3				
03-04	3-3	2-2	1-1	3-4									1-1	0-1				

	Boston United		Bromsgrove Rovers		Burton Albion		Cheltenham Town		Chester City		Chorley		Colchester United		Dagenham		Dagenham & Redbridge	
	H	A	H	A	H	A	H	A	H	A	H	A	H	A	H	A	H	A
79-80	0-1	0-2																
80-81	3-1	3-2																
81-82	1-0	0-2													3-0	1-2		
82-83	1-1	0-1													3-0	1-3		
83-84	3-1	1-3													3-1	1-3		
84-85	1-0	4-3													0-1	1-2		
85-86	3-4	0-3					3-1	0-2							0-1	0-1		
86-87	4-0	1-0					1-0	2-5							2-3	3-3		
87-88	6-0	1-0					0-0	1-1							1-0	0-1		
88-89	0-1	1-2					1-0	2-2			0-4	1-3						
89-90	1-0	3-1					0-0	3-2			0-1	2-1						
90-91	3-1	1-4					5-2	1-1					2-2	0-4				
91-92	1-1	2-0					3-1	0-1					1-1	0-1			0-2	3-4
92-93	3-3	5-3	0-1	2-1													1-1	1-4
93-94			1-1	0-0													2-2	1-1
94-95			3-1	4-1													5-0	2-1
95-96			2-2	1-1													1-0	3-0
96-97			1-0	5-0														
97-98							2-1	2-3										
98-99							1-0	1-0										
99-00																		
00-01	0-3	1-1							1-1	1-1							3-0	0-1
01-02	1-2	2-3							3-1	2-1							1-2	1-1
02-03					1-3	1-1			1-1	3-2							0-2	0-2
03-04					1-2	1-0			0-4	0-4							0-1	0-2

NORTHWICH VICTORIA

	Darlington		Dartford		Doncaster Rovers		Dover Athletic		Enfield		Exeter City		Farnborough Town		Fisher Athletic		Forest Green Rovers	
	H	A	H	A	H	A	H	A	H	A	H	A	H	A	H	A	H	A
79-80																		
80-81																		
81-82			3-4	1-0					2-1	0-1								
82-83									3-1	1-2								
83-84									3-1	2-1								
84-85			0-1	0-1					1-1	2-3								
85-86			2-0	0-2					2-2	0-1								
86-87									2-0	2-1								
87-88									1-1	1-0					1-2	0-0		
88-89									2-2	2-1					3-0	4-2		
89-90	1-0	0-4							1-0	0-2			0-2	1-0	2-1	0-1		
90-91																	0-0	2-5
91-92													1-1	4-2				
92-93													3-0	3-0				
93-94							0-1	0-2										
94-95							1-3	1-3					1-2	1-2				
95-96							1-2	1-0					1-3	1-0				
96-97							2-0	2-2					1-1	2-2				
97-98							2-1	0-4					3-3	3-2				
98-99					1-3	2-2	2-0	0-0					3-0	6-1			1-0	1-3
99-00					2-1	0-2	1-1	1-4									0-0	1-5
00-01					1-1	2-0	2-0	0-3									0-0	0-1
01-02					2-3	2-2	2-1	1-2					1-2	1-4			2-2	0-2
02-03					1-2	2-1							2-2	2-3			2-1	0-1
03-04											1-1	0-2	1-1	0-2			0-4	0-0

	Frickley Athletic		Gateshead		Gravesend & N'fleet		Halifax Town		Hayes		Hednesford Town		Hereford United		Kettering Town		Kidderminster H.	
	H	A	H	A	H	A	H	A	H	A	H	A	H	A	H	A	H	A
79-80					0-0	1-2									2-2	0-1		
80-81	1-3	1-0			4-0	1-0									1-1	3-3		
81-82	0-0	0-1			1-0	1-0									2-0	0-0		
82-83	2-1	0-0													2-1	4-1		
83-84	1-1	1-4	3-1	3-1											4-0	0-1		
84-85	3-0	0-4	2-0	6-2											1-2	2-2	0-2	1-3
85-86	2-3	0-1													0-0	1-2	0-0	2-2
86-87	1-1	1-1			1-2	1-1									0-0	0-1	1-2	2-1
87-88													0-1	1-3			1-1	1-1
88-89													1-1	1-2	2-4	1-1		
89-90															2-2	1-3	1-2	0-4
90-91			3-2	4-0									0-1	0-1	1-1	1-3		
91-92			1-1	0-2											4-3	0-1	3-1	0-1
92-93			0-0	2-0											2-2	1-2	0-1	3-5
93-94			1-2	0-1			0-2	2-1							1-1	0-0	3-0	0-2
94-95			1-1	0-4			3-0	0-0							3-2	3-3	3-4	2-1
95-96			1-2	1-1			1-1	0-2			0-2	1-2			6-2	2-2	5-2	1-2
96-97			4-2	1-5			2-2	3-0	2-1	1-1	2-1	0-3			2-1	0-1	1-1	0-1
97-98			1-1	2-2			2-0	2-4	1-1	1-1	1-1	0-2	0-2	2-2	0-0	3-1	1-1	1-1
98-99									2-1	0-1	1-1	0-1	1-0	2-2	4-0	0-0	1-0	0-4
99-00									0-0	1-2	3-2	0-1	0-0	0-3	2-6	1-1	1-1	1-3
00-01									3-4	2-2	2-2	1-7	1-0	0-0	1-2	3-2		
01-02									1-0	2-1			1-0	0-1				
02-03					1-2	1-1	0-2	5-0							2-2	2-1	1-2	2-2
03-04					0-0	2-2	0-1	3-5					1-5	0-1				

477

1983-84 Squad.
Back Row (L-R): Brian Morley, Tony Murphy, Dave Ryan, John Anderson, and Dave Fretwell. Middle Row: John King (Manager), Paul Reid, Colin Chesters, Phil Jones, Graham Abel, Steve Craven, and George Connelly (Kit Man) . Front Row: Jeff Forshaw, Paul Bennett, Ken Jones(Captain), Phil Wilson and Mark Ward.

1985-86 Squad: Back row, left to right:Tim Burton (Team Secretary), Mike Seaman (Director), Ken Edwards (Vice-President), Terry Murphy (Manager) and Graham Rathbone (Director). Middle row: Dave Thomas (CommercialManager), Jim Rafferty (Director),Graham Abel, Glyn Stephens, Mark Dean, Dave Ryan, Steve Craven, Mark Emmerson, George Connelly (Dressing room attendant), John Horton (President), Jim Burton (Chairman) and Derek Nuttall (Vice-Chairman). Front row: Phil Sheridon (CompanySecretary), Dave Essex, Ray Redshaw, Eddie Bishop, Tony Murphy, Ken Jones,Paul Reid, Dave Fretwell and Ron Reddy (Physio).

478

NORTHWICH VICTORIA

	Kingstonian H	A	Leek Town H	A	Leigh RMI H	A	Lincoln City H	A	Macclesfield Town H	A	Maidstone United H	A	Margate H	A	Merthyr Tydfil H	A
79-80											0-2	4-3				
80-81											2-1	0-4				
81-82											3-1	1-6				
82-83											2-1	0-1				
83-84											1-1	1-0				
84-85											0-0	0-1				
85-86											1-0	1-0				
86-87											1-1	2-5				
87-88							2-3	2-3	2-1	0-5	2-3	1-1				
88-89									3-2	2-0	2-0	1-4				
89-90									2-0	1-3					3-1	1-1
90-91									4-1	2-1					0-3	2-3
91-92									2-1	0-0					4-1	1-2
92-93									1-3	2-1					1-2	0-3
93-94									1-1	0-0					1-2	0-5
94-95									1-3	1-3					2-0	0-2
95-96									1-2	0-0						
96-97									2-1	1-0						
97-98			3-1	1-1												
98-99	2-3	1-1	0-2	3-0												
99-00	0-3	3-3														
00-01	2-1	0-1					1-1	0-3								
01-02					0-3	2-1							1-1	2-1		
02-03					0-1	1-1							1-0	4-4		
03-04					0-1	0-1							0-3	1-3		

	Morecambe H	A	Nuneaton Borough H	A	Redditch United H	A	Runcorn H	A	Rushden & Diamonds H	A	Scarborough H	A	Shrewsbury Town H	A	Slough Town H	A
79-80			2-1	1-2	1-0	1-0					1-1	1-2				
80-81			2-0	0-2							0-1	0-0				
81-82							1-1	1-0			2-1	4-0				
82-83			2-2	1-2			2-0	1-1			1-1	1-5				
83-84			1-1	0-1			0-1	0-0			3-1	1-1				
84-85			1-0	2-2			0-1	0-0			1-1	0-0				
85-86			0-3	3-1			1-1	3-2			0-0	0-0				
86-87			1-2	1-0			1-2	3-7			0-1	1-2				
87-88							2-0	1-2								
88-89							0-1	1-3								
89-90							1-1	1-2								
90-91							1-4	1-3							1-0	4-2
91-92							3-0	1-3							3-0	1-0
92-93							3-2	1-0							0-1	4-0
93-94							1-1	2-1							1-1	2-2
94-95							4-1	2-2								
95-96	2-1	2-2					4-3	4-3							0-3	1-1
96-97	1-0	0-2							1-2	1-1					0-1	4-3
97-98	5-0	1-3							2-4	1-0					0-1	0-3
98-99	1-1	1-3							2-1	2-1						
99-00	0-0	0-5			3-1	1-3			2-1	0-6	2-0	0-3				
00-01	1-0	0-4			2-2	1-3			0-0	1-2	3-0	0-4				
01-02	4-3	1-2			3-0	1-0					1-1	2-1				
02-03	3-2	1-3			3-1	4-1					0-2	1-4				
03-04	1-1	0-3									1-1	0-1	0-2	1-3		

(above) Graham Bennett. Photo: Pay Campion.

(left) Dele Adebola. Photo: Keith Clayton.

Season 1996-97. Back row, left to right: Wesley Simpson, Mark Jones, Darren Vicary, Lee Steel and Roy Sweeney. Middle Row: P.Lea (Physio), Chris Duffy, PaulTait, George Oghani, Trevor Ball, Dean Greygoose, Dave Burgess, Steve Walters, Graham Abel and T.Martin (Coach).Front row: Ian Cooke, Carwyn Williams, Brian Butler, Brian Kettle (Manager), John Williams (Assistant Manager), Delwyn Humphries and DerekWard.

1997-98 Squad. Back row, left to right: Don Page, Steve Walters,Wayne Fairclough, Wes Simpson, Chris Duffy, Dean Greygoose, Paul Tait, Delwyn Humphreys, Ian Cooke, Eddie Bishop and Phil Lea (Physio). Front row: John Stannard, Darren Vicary, Dominic Crookes, Phil Wilson (Manager), John Williams (Director od Football), Lee Steele, Derek Ward and Shane Reddish.   Photo: Northwich Chronicle.

NORTHWICH VICTORIA

	Southport		Stafford Rangers		Stalybridge Celtic		Stevenage Borough		Sutton United		Tamworth		Telford United		Trowbridge Town	
	H	A	H	A	H	A	H	A	H	A	H	A	H	A	H	A
79-80			1-0	1-4									2-1	0-0		
80-81			2-1	0-2									1-0	3-1		
81-82			1-2	2-2									2-2	1-2	0-0	0-1
82-83			2-1	1-1									2-1	0-3	6-3	2-0
83-84													0-0	2-0	0-2	1-1
84-85													1-0	1-0		
85-86			2-0	2-1									0-1	0-4		
86-87			1-1	1-4					0-1	1-2			1-0	0-1		
87-88			1-1	0-3					1-4	1-1			1-2	1-1		
88-89			1-1	1-0					4-2	3-3			1-0	4-1		
89-90			4-3	0-1					2-3	1-2			0-2	1-2		
90-91			1-1	0-0					1-0	2-2			2-4	0-1		
91-92			1-2	1-2									0-1	4-1		
92-93			1-2	0-1	1-3	6-0							1-0	0-1		
93-94	2-1	0-0	0-0	1-3	2-0	1-1							1-0	1-2		
94-95	2-1	2-0	0-1	3-1	2-2	1-2	0-1	1-1					1-1	0-1		
95-96	1-2	2-2			1-0	5-1	1-3	1-5					2-0	0-1		
96-97	5-1	0-0			0-1	1-0	0-1	0-2					1-0	2-2		
97-98	0-0	2-0			1-0	1-0	1-1	3-1					2-2	1-2		
98-99	1-2	2-2					0-1	3-1					1-1	0-3		
99-00	0-1	1-0					3-3	1-3	2-0	2-2			2-1	1-0		
00-01	0-2	1-1					3-2	1-3					0-1	3-2		
01-02	3-1	1-5			1-0	1-1	2-1	0-1					2-2	0-1		
02-03	2-1	1-1					1-1	2-2					2-1	0-1		
03-04							1-2	0-1			1-0	1-2	1-0	1-0		

	Wealdstone		Welling United		Weymouth		Witton Albion		Woking		Worcester City		Wycombe Wanderers		Yeovil Town	
	H	A	H	A	H	A	H	A	H	A	H	A	H	A	H	A
79-80	0-0	1-0			0-0	0-2					1-0	1-2			0-1	1-1
80-81	0-0	1-1			0-0	3-4					3-0	1-2			1-2	2-1
81-82					0-2	0-1					3-0	1-0			1-1	1-4
82-83	3-3	1-2			1-1	0-3					3-0	0-3			5-0	4-2
83-84	1-1	0-1			1-0	1-1					1-0	0-2			0-0	0-2
84-85	0-2	1-1					0-3	0-1			2-2	1-0			2-0	1-0
85-86	2-2	0-0					0-1	2-2					4-0	1-1		
86-87	2-1	1-1	2-1	2-3			1-1	2-2								
87-88	0-0	2-2	0-0	1-1			2-1	0-0					2-1	1-1		
88-89			0-2	0-0			2-0	2-2					2-3	4-1	1-2	1-2
89-90			2-3	0-2									3-0	3-3	1-4	2-1
90-91			1-2	5-4									1-1	0-3	2-0	1-1
91-92			1-2	1-6			3-0	1-1					0-1	0-2	1-0	1-2
92-93			1-1	5-1			1-3	3-1	1-0	0-1			0-0	0-1	0-1	1-1
93-94			3-1	1-0			0-1	1-1	0-0	1-2					1-1	3-0
94-95			1-1	5-1					2-2	1-1					2-2	4-4
95-96			1-2	1-1					3-0	0-0						
96-97			0-0	1-1					1-2	1-3						
97-98			5-1	1-0					0-2	0-1					2-1	2-2
98-99			3-0	3-2					0-3	1-2					1-2	2-1
99-00			3-2	3-1					3-1	1-1					3-0	2-3
00-01									4-0	1-1					1-2	0-1
01-02									0-3	1-3					1-3	3-2
02-03									1-3	3-2					1-2	1-2
03-04									1-4	0-3						

Mark Birch. Photo: Andrew Chitty.

Tony Bullock. Photo: Martin Wray.

Ian Cooke. Photo: John L. Newton.

Alan Crompton. Photo: Pat Campion.

		Home							Away				
	P	W	D	L	F	A	P	W	D	L	F	A
ACCRINGTON S	1	0	1	0	3	3	1	0	1	0	2	2
ALDERSHOT T	1	0	1	0	1	1	1	0	0	1	3	4
ALTRINCHAM	19	7	6	6	28	25	19	8	7	4	27	23
A P LEAMINGTON	3	3	0	0	7	1	3	1	2	0	5	3
AYLESBURY U	1	0	1	0	1	1	1	0	0	1	0	2
BANGOR C	4	3	0	1	9	6	4	2	2	0	5	1
BARNET	15	5	5	5	16	16	15	3	2	10	13	26
BARROW	10	7	2	1	20	7	10	3	3	4	9	13
BATH C	16	11	3	2	37	18	16	3	8	5	18	18
BOSTON U	16	8	3	5	31	19	16	7	1	8	25	30
BROMSGROVE R	5	2	2	1	7	5	5	3	2	0	12	3
BURTON A	2	0	0	2	2	5	2	1	1	0	2	1
CHELTENHAM T	9	7	2	0	16	5	9	2	3	4	12	17
CHESTER C	4	1	2	1	5	7	4	2	1	1	6	8
CHORLEY	2	0	0	2	0	5	2	1	0	1	3	4
COLCHESTER U	2	0	2	0	3	3	2	0	0	2	0	5
DAGENHAM	7	4	0	3	12	6	7	0	1	6	7	15
DAGENHAM & R	9	3	2	4	13	10	9	2	2	5	11	16
DARLINGTON	1	1	0	0	1	0	1	0	0	1	0	4
DARTFORD	3	1	0	2	5	5	3	1	0	2	1	3
DONCASTER R	5	1	1	3	7	10	5	2	2	1	8	7
DOVER A	9	5	1	3	13	9	9	1	2	6	6	20
ENFIELD	9	5	4	0	17	9	9	4	0	5	10	12
EXETER C	1	0	1	0	1	1	1	0	0	1	0	2
FARNBOROUGH T	11	2	5	4	17	17	11	6	1	4	24	18
FISHER A	4	2	1	1	6	3	4	1	1	2	6	8
FOREST GREEN R	6	2	3	1	5	7	6	0	1	5	2	12
FRICKLEY A	7	2	3	2	10	9	7	1	2	4	3	11
GATESHEAD	11	4	4	3	18	14	11	4	3	4	20	19
GRAVESEND & N	5	2	2	1	6	2	5	2	2	1	6	5
HALIFAX T	7	2	2	3	8	8	7	3	1	3	15	12
HAYES	6	3	2	1	9	7	6	1	3	2	7	8
HEDNESFORD T	6	2	3	1	9	9	6	0	0	6	2	16
HEREFORD U	7	3	2	2	6	9	7	1	3	3	6	10
KETTERING T	23	8	9	6	41	32	23	3	9	11	28	35
KIDDERMINSTER H	17	5	6	6	28	25	17	2	5	10	18	37
KINGSTONIAN	3	1	0	2	4	7	3	0	2	1	4	5
LEEK T	2	1	0	1	3	3	2	1	1	0	4	1
LEIGH RMI	4	0	1	3	1	6	4	1	1	2	3	6
LINCOLN C	1	0	0	1	2	3	1	0	0	1	2	3
MACCLESFIELD T	10	6	1	3	19	15	10	4	3	3	9	13
MAIDSTONE U	10	5	3	2	14	10	10	3	1	6	11	25
MARGATE	3	1	1	1	2	4	3	1	1	1	7	8
MERTHYR T	6	3	0	3	11	9	6	0	1	5	4	16
MORECAMBE	9	6	3	0	18	8	9	0	1	8	6	27
NUNEATON B	11	6	3	2	20	13	11	4	1	6	15	17
REDDITCH U	1	1	0	0	1	0	1	1	0	0	1	0
RUNCORN	15	6	4	5	24	19	15	5	4	6	22	29
RUSHDEN & D	5	2	1	2	7	8	5	2	1	2	5	10
SCARBOROUGH	13	4	6	3	15	11	13	2	4	7	11	23
SHREWSBURY T	1	0	0	1	0	2	1	0	0	1	1	3
SLOUGH T	7	2	1	4	5	7	7	4	2	1	16	11
SOUTHPORT	10	5	1	4	16	12	10	3	6	1	12	11
STAFFORD R	14	5	5	4	18	16	14	3	3	8	13	25
STALYBRIDGE C	7	4	1	2	8	6	7	4	2	1	16	5
STEVENAGE B	10	2	3	5	12	16	10	2	2	6	12	20
SUTTON U	6	3	0	3	10	10	6	0	4	2	10	12
TAMWORTH	1	1	0	0	1	0	1	0	0	1	1	2
TELFORD U	25	13	6	6	29	23	25	8	3	14	26	33
TROWBRIDGE T	3	1	1	1	6	5	3	1	1	1	3	2
WEALDSTONE	8	1	6	1	8	9	8	1	5	2	7	8
WELLING U	14	5	4	5	23	18	14	7	4	3	29	23
WEYMOUTH	10	3	4	3	7	9	10	0	5	5	10	18
WITTON A	3	1	0	2	4	4	3	1	2	0	5	3
WOKING	12	4	2	6	16	20	12	1	4	7	10	20
WORCESTER C	6	5	1	0	13	2	6	2	0	4	4	9
WYCOMBE W	7	3	2	2	12	6	7	1	3	3	9	12
YEOVIL T	19	6	4	9	26	24	19	7	5	7	32	32
TOTAL	520	217	145	158	773	624	520	139	143	238	642	862

Northwich Victoria LEADING APPEARANCES	79-80	80-81	81-82	82-83	83-84	84-85	85-86	86-87	87-88	88-89	89-90	90-91	91-92	92-93	93-94	94-95	95-96	96-97	97-98	98-99	99-00	00-01	01-02	02-03	03-04	TOTAL
Dave RYAN	38	37	42	42	42	41	42	41	42	40	25															432
Mark JONES									35	38	37	32	41	20+5	39	33+2	21+3									296+10
Malcolm O'CONNOR										38+1	27+4	37	40	41	26+5	31+6										240+16
Ken JONES	34	35	39	40	41	40	1+2																			230+2
Darren VICARY																9+1	37	36+3	23+10	30+6	38+2	14+3				187+25
Tony MURPHY	12	37	36	38	20	27+2	35+2																			205+4
Mark DEVLIN																		15+3	35+1		41		33	41	35	200+4
Ian COOKE																25+10	31+4	28+4	28+9	8+14	27+3	1+7				148+51
Jeff FORSHAW	32	35	32	34	34	29																				196
Graham ABEL		6	19+9	22	26+2	41	15									33+1	21+1									183+13
David YOUNG						32+2	28	35	28+1	26+2	26	16														191+5
Dean GREYGOOSE															11	42	35	37	42	22						189
Brian BUTLER													34+1	38	35+1	37	39+1									183+3
Wesley SIMPSON																16	23+5	37+1	36	32+2	29+1	16+1				173+10
Steve WALTERS																16	27	34+1	40	31	27+1					175+2
Chris DUFFY																26	33+4	33+5	29+5	30+8						151+22
Paul REID	6+5	30+1		25	37+1	40		6	11+7																	155+14
Phil WILSON	33	35+1		36	37+2				10																	151+3
Jeff PARKER										28+1		16+1		33+3	30+1	31										138+6
Mark HANCOCK											12	26+2	32	30	37											137+2
Dave FRETWELL		31+1	39	37		28																				135+1
John ANDERSON	29	40	30+1	29+6																						128+7
Richard NORRIS																						38+1	22+8	28+9	10+17	98+35
Dominic CROOKES																		38+3	37+2	24+1	17+5					116+11
Paul TAIT																	8+1	24+9	36+4	33+5						101+19
Eddie BISHOP						17+1	32+1	11		3								30	16+8							109+10
Paul MAGUIRE										37	39	35+5														111+5
Steve GARVEY																							33+8	25+13	30+5	88+26
Derek WARD																27+1		31+8	26+7	6+8						90+24
Carwyn WILLIAMS																24+5	32+7	16+8	9+11							81+31
Colin BLAIN																										100+10
John ROBERTSON																				35+1	34+1	34+1				103+3
Val OWEN																				23+1	26+4		17+2	17	8+5	91+12

NORTHWICH VICTORIA APPEARANCES

Northwich Victoria	79-80	80-81	81-82	82-83	83-84	84-85	85-86	86-87	87-88	88-89	89-90	90-91	91-92	92-93	93-94	94-95	95-96	96-97	97-98	98-99	99-00	00-01	01-02	02-03	03-04	TOTAL
ABEL Graham	6		19+9	22	26+2	41	15									33+1	21+1									183+13
ABERCROMBIE Simon															3											3
ADAMS Christian																0+4										0+4
ADEBOLA Dele															15+1											15+1
AINSWORTH Gareth													14	5												19
ALLAN Jon																								26+3	15+1	41+4
ANDERS Jason															3											3
ANDERSON John		29	40	30+1	29+6																					128+7
ANDERTON Steve												8+1														8+1
ARMSTRONG Terry							9																			9
ASHWORTH Lawrence									0+1																	0+1
ASPINALL John											5															5
ASPINALL Wayne							18+1																			18+1
ATKINSON Paul												6+3														6+3
BAAH Peter																5										5
BAILEY Mark																					12+3	26+7	12+1			50+11
BAILEY Terry	31+1																									31+1
BALL Trevor												40	8				5									53
BARDSLEY David																						2				2
BARNARD Mark																						23	39	8		70
BARNES Peter												2+7														2+7
BARNES Rob												5+1														5+1
BASTABLE Gary	3																									3
BATES Jamie																				26+3	30+3	21+2				77+8
BENNETT Chris																									0+1	0+1
BENNETT Graham								24	8+7																	32+7
BENNETT Mike														5+2												5+2
BENNETT Paul			32+5		40		17+2																			89+7
BERKS John															1											1
BERRYMAN Steve													12	3												15
BETTS M		1																								1
BILLING Peter																		14+1								14+1
BIRCH Mark																				42	32+3					74+3
BIRCH Trevor								4+2																		4+2
BIRCHALL Michael															2+2											2+2

485

Gordon Davies. Photo: V.J.Robertson.

Steve Davis. Photo: James Wood.

Paul Donnelly. Photo: Paul Dennis.

Chris Duffy. Photo: Colin Stevens.

486

Northwich Victoria
APPEARANCES

Name	79-80	80-81	81-82	82-83	83-84	84-85	85-86	86-87	87-88	88-89	89-90	90-91	91-92	92-93	93-94	94-95	95-96	96-97	97-98	98-99	99-00	00-01	01-02	02-03	03-04	TOTAL
BISHOP Eddie					17+1	32+1	11			3								30	16+8							109+10
BISHOP John													1+1													1+1
BLACK Ryan Zico																									2+4	2+4
BLACKBURN Chris																									25+3	25+3
BLACKHURST Jimmy								6+5	0+2																	6+7
BLAIN Colin											34+2	36+3	24+3	6+2												100+10
BLEASE Rory					1+5	11+5																				12+10
BLUNDELL Chris													36	12+9												48+9
BLUNDELL Gregg																						15+1	41	34		90+1
BOWERING Martin								1																		1
BOYD Charlie													28		39	30+2										97+2
BRADLEY Dave	37+1	16			11+2	6+2																				70+5
BRADLEY Lee	5+1																									5+1
BRAITHWAITE Keith	13+1	19+3																								32+4
BRAMHALL Neil							2+1																			2+1
BRAZIER Phil																									34+2	34+2
BRISCOE Ben																									1+5	1+5
BROUGH Lee																									3+2	3+2
BROWN Karl																									6	6
BROWNRIGG Andy																							5+2			5+2
BULLOCK Tony												1	22	35	31	0+1										89+1
BUNTER Steve															24											24
BURGESS Dave																	36+3	6+2								42+5
BURKE Gary																						29+4	26+6			55+10
BURKE Jordan																					1+1					1+1
BURKE Marshall						11																				11
BUTLER Brian													34+1	38	35+1	37	39+1									183+3
BUTTERWORTH Dean																									1+4	1+4
BUXTON Steve												13+2	0+1													13+3
CALLAGHAN Ian											18+8	33+6														51+14
CAME Shaun																								10+2	13+2	23+4
CARROLL Mike											0+2															0+2
CARROLL Tony																			4+12							4+12
CEGIELSKI Wayne								31+1																		31+1
CHALLENDER Greg																						3+4				3+4

NORTHWICH VICTORIA APPEARANCES

Northwich Victoria	79-80	80-81	81-82	82-83	83-84	84-85	85-86	86-87	87-88	88-89	89-90	90-91	91-92	92-93	93-94	94-95	95-96	96-97	97-98	98-99	99-00	00-01	01-02	02-03	03-04	TOTAL
CHARNOCK Keiran																									21+6	21+6
CHESTERS Colin				34	27																					61
CHRISTIE Dave															6											6
CLARKE Mike												4														4
CLAYTON Paul																	14+1									14+1
CLYNCH Stuart					3	0+1																				3+1
COLLIER Jim	14+2																									14+2
COLLINS James																		5+3					9+8			14+11
CONNETT Ben																								4	10	14
CONNOR Jim		16+5																								16+5
CONSTANTINE Dave								25																		25
COOK Alan		1																								1
COOKE Ian																25+10	31+4	28+4	28+9	8+14	27+3	1+7				148+51
COOPER Graham												1														1
COOPER Lee																	0+1									0+1
CORRIGAN Frank			12+1																							12+1
COYLE Tony											9+6															9+6
CRAVEN Steve				8+3	21	39	22+1																			90+4
CROMPTON Alan									24	32+1	10															66+1
CROOKES Dominic																		38+3	37+2	24+1	17+5					116+11
CROSSLEY Richard											2															2
CUMISKEY Peter																	1									1
CUTLER Chris												0+1														0+1
DANSKIN Jason										19+4																19+4
DAVIES Dai				0+2																						0+2
DAVIES Geoff						2																				2
DAVIES Gordon														35+1												35+1
DAVIES Steve										6+1								0+1								6+2
DAVIS Steve																						18	1	9		28
DAWSON Jon																							0+3			0+3
DEAN Mark				31+2	38+1	7+1	8+1																			84+5
DEELEY Nigel																0+1										0+1
DEGG Brenton									0+1																	0+1
DENHAM John	13	14+9	23																							50+9
DEVLIN Mark																				15+3	35+1	41	33	41	35	200+4

NORTHWICH VICTORIA APPEARANCES

Northwich Victoria	79-80	80-81	81-82	82-83	83-84	84-85	85-86	86-87	87-88	88-89	89-90	90-91	91-92	92-93	93-94	94-95	95-96	96-97	97-98	98-99	99-00	00-01	01-02	02-03	03-04	TOTAL
DOHERTY Martin																					0+1					0+1
DONNELLY Paul													8+6	6+1												14+7
DONNELLY Peter															13+6											13+6
DORAN Ian												2+1														2+1
DOWELL Wayne																			0+1							0+1
DUFFY Chris																26	33+4	33+5	29+5	30+8						151+22
DULSON Gary	8																									8
DUNCALF Kevin					1+2																					1+3
DUNN Mark							10+2		2+2																	12+4
EASTER Graham												4+2	14+1	1												19+3
EATOCK David																					0+2					0+2
EATON Steve		31																								31
EDWARDS Mike																	2									2
EDWARDS Paul											15															15
EDWARDS Rob											1															1
EDWARDS Steve									0+1																	0+1
EDWARDSON Barry													4+2													4+2
ELI Roger										10+1																10+1
ELLIOTT Andy				0+1																						0+1
ELLIS Neil																					14+9	8+3				22+12
EMMERSON Mark						2+4	7+1	23+1																		32+6
ESSER Dave						13																				13
FAIRCLOUGH Wayne																		26+4	33+1							59+5
FEELEY Andy													13													13
FENLON Paul			1+1																							1+1
FERGUSON Mark							3+3																			3+3
FILSON Martin																				3+1						3+1
FLETCHER Gary																					11+8	20+3				31+11
FOGG Mark								1																		1
FORAN Mark																								36+3		36+3
FORSHAW Jeff	32	35	32	34	34	29																				196
FRASER Bobby											7+1															7+1
FREEMAN David		1																								1
FRETWELL Dave		31+1	39	37	28																					135+1
GALLAGHER Jason															22+4											22+4

Neil Ellis. Photo: Keith Clayton.

Mark Gardener. Photo: Eric Marsh.

Andy Graham. Photo: Colin Stevens.

Neill Hardy. Photo: Paul Dennis.

Northwich Victoria APPEARANCES	79-80	80-81	81-82	82-83	83-84	84-85	85-86	86-87	87-88	88-89	89-90	90-91	91-92	92-93	93-94	94-95	95-96	96-97	97-98	98-99	99-00	00-01	01-02	02-03	03-04	TOTAL
GAMBLE Frank								4+1																		4+1
GANN John																					1+1					1+1
GARDINER Mark																			21	0+2	4+3					25+5
GARDNER Phil							12		34+4																	46+4
GARNETT Steve							1																			1
GARVEY Steve																							33+8	25+13	30+5	88+26
GIBSON Paul																							42	12		54
GLENDON Kevin								19+1																		19+1
GRAHAM Andy											16		13+6													29+6
GRANT John																							11			11
GRAY David																					9+10					9+10
GRESTY Simon													0+3													0+3
GREYGOOSE Dean															11	42	35	37	42	22						189
GRIFFITHS Neil											1															1
GRIFFITHS Peter										0+4																0+4
GRIGGS Danny																						1		5+11		6+11
HACKETT Lee														1												1
HALL Brian		32+1																								32+1
HALL Dave	8+3																									8+3
HALOM Vic			6																							6
HANCHARD Martin										31+6	19															50+6
HANCOCK Mark										12	26+2	32	32	30	37											137+2
HANCOCK Tony												2														2
HANKIN Sean																									1	1
HARDY Neill														7+1	27+12	11+8										45+21
HARRISON Kevin								5																		5
HARWOOD Carl																	0+1									0+1
HEALY John									3+3																	3+3
HEATH Seamus						11+6																				11+6
HEMMINGS Tony											12		34+5	35												86+5
HENDERSON Peter				6+2																						6+2
HENNIGAN Martin							3+3																			3+3
HENRY Tony																						3+1				3+1
HILL Gordon								27	17	7																51
HILTON Robbie															2		7+1									9+1

NORTHWICH VICTORIA APPEARANCES

Northwich Victoria	79-80	80-81	81-82	82-83	83-84	84-85	85-86	86-87	87-88	88-89	89-90	90-91	91-92	92-93	93-94	94-95	95-96	96-97	97-98	98-99	99-00	00-01	01-02	02-03	03-04	TOTAL
HOLCROFT Peter																						10+7				10+7
HOLDEN Steve								1+2																		1+2
HOLDEN Steve																	1									1
HOLLAND Steve												2+1	7+3													9+4
HOLLIS Chris											1															1
HOLT Michael																					5					5
HOOTON Russ								8																		8
HORTON Bob							12+3																			12+3
HOUGHTON Mike																						0+1				0+1
HOUSTON Graham									6+2																	6+2
HOWARD Mark											5															5
HUGHES Graham																	0+6									0+6
HUGHES James																		0+2								0+2
HUGHES Ross																		4								4
HUMPHREYS Delwyn																	12+3	19+10								31+13
HUSSIN Eddie																			4+4							4+4
HUTCHINSON Simon																		2								2
HYNETT Kevin					0+1																					0+1
ILLMAN Neil																			14	25+9	1+5		4+6			44+20
IMRIE John									20+1	1																21+1
INGRAM Denny																							22	35		57
IRWIN Colin									1																	1
JARRETT Danny	0+1																									0+1
JAYCOCK Billy																								0+1		0+1
JOHNSON Steve												1+2														1+2
JONES Garry		11+1																								11+1
JONES Graham									18+5																	18+5
JONES Ken	34	35	39	40	41	40	1+2																			230+2
JONES Marcus																							11			11
JONES Mark									35	38	37	32	41	20+5	39	33+2	21+3									296+10
JONES Phil				9+2																						9+2
JONES Terry															4+1											4+1
JONES Trevor	6+1																									6+1
KEIGHLEY Paul										0+1																0+1
KELLY Gary																								7		7

Northwich Victoria	79-80	80-81	81-82	82-83	83-84	84-85	85-86	86-87	87-88	88-89	89-90	90-91	91-92	92-93	93-94	94-95	95-96	96-97	97-98	98-99	99-00	00-01	01-02	02-03	03-04	TOTAL
KENNEDY Alan										11																11
KEY Lance																				18	18	33				69
KIDD Andy														0+1												0+1
KIMMINS Ged																						4+3				4+3
KING Alan	7+1																									7+1
KNOWLES Darren																							13+4			13+4
LAMBERT Colin								1+1																		1+1
LAMPKIN Ricky																			0+1							0+1
LAURIE Carl																						1+8				1+8
LENTON Darren													2+2	0+1												2+3
LEWIN Craig															3+7											3+7
LEWIS Colin																		2								2
LEWIS Graham																						8+4				8+4
LLOYD Darren							1+2																			1+2
LLOYD Tommy															2+1											2+1
LOCKE Stuart													42	32+1												74+1
LOGAN Matthew																	0+1									0+1
LUCKETTI Chris												2														2
MACOWAT Ian											15+1															15+1
MAGUIRE Paul										37	39	35+5														111+5
MALKIN Chris									14	3																17
MARSH John	9+1																									9+1
MATTHEWS Rob																								3+3		3+3
MAYMAN Paul		34	37																							71
McADAM Neil			1																							1
McAUGHTRIE Dave											32+1															32+1
McAULEY Hugh																4+11									0+1	4+12
McCARRICK Mark													5													5
McCLATCHEY Derek									0+1																	0+1
McCOY James																									0+2	0+2
McDERMOTT Wayne																						1+2				1+2
McDONALD Rod									1																	1
McGHEE Tony													2+4		2											4+4
McGROGAN Jim		1																								1
McGUIRE Jamie	0+1																							3	4	7

493

NORTHWICH VICTORIA APPEARANCES

Northwich Victoria	79-80	80-81	81-82	82-83	83-84	84-85	85-86	86-87	87-88	88-89	89-90	90-91	91-92	92-93	93-94	94-95	95-96	96-97	97-98	98-99	99-00	00-01	01-02	02-03	03-04	TOTAL
McGUIRE Mark																								0+1		0+1
McGUIRE Paul																								5+3	5+3	5+3
McHALE Ray								2																		2
McILROY Sammy													7	1												8
McKEARNEY Dave											3															3
McKENZIE Mike							14+2																			14+2
McMULLAN Dave			4+8																							4+8
McNEILIS Steve									24+5	36																60+5
McNIVEN David																								17+7		17+7
McRAE Peter									1																	1
MEAKER Michael																							5+3			5+3
MIKE Ade																						31+4	17+3			48+7
MILLIGAN Mark																			10+2							10+2
MILLS Brian																										3
MILNER Andy																					2+2					2+2
MITCHELL Craig																									3	3
MITCHELL Richard																						4+13	1+5			5+18
MITTEN Paul																0+2										0+2
MORGAN Dave										1																1
MORLEY Brian				14+9																						14+9
MORTON Neil										15+2	38+1	9+1														62+4
MULLIGAN Jamie															2											2
MUNDY Damian						1																				1
MURPHY Phil			3+2																							3+2
MURRAY Tony	12	37	36	38	20	27+2	35+2																			205+4
MURRAY Eddie																										2
MURRAY Karl																									3	3
NASSARI Derek														1+1												1+1
NELSON Steve							41																			41
NESBITT Carl																2										2
NEWALL Andy																	2									2
NEWHOUSE Aiden																						0+1				0+1
NICHOLAS Steve																									12	12
NIEMAN Albie	33+1	1+1																								34+2
NIXON Craig														2												2

NORTHWICH VICTORIA APPEARANCES

Northwich Victoria	79-80	80-81	81-82	82-83	83-84	84-85	85-86	86-87	87-88	88-89	89-90	90-91	91-92	92-93	93-94	94-95	95-96	96-97	97-98	98-99	99-00	00-01	01-02	02-03	03-04	TOTAL
NOLAN Ian										22+6	18+3															40+9
NORMAN Dave															24+4	8+1										32+5
NORRIS Richard																						38+1	22+8	28+9	10+17	98+35
O'CONNOR Malcolm										38+1	27+4	37	40	41	26+5	31+6										240+16
OGDEN Neil																	2									2
OGHANI George																29+8	2+21									31+29
O'GORMAN Dave												3	7+1													10+1
OMAR Vince								0+1																		0+1
O'NEILL David	14+3																									14+3
ORR Peter						5+1																				5+1
OTOOLE John																				2						2
OWEN Gareth																								3+1		3+1
OWEN Terry		6+2																								6+2
OWEN Val																				23+1	26+4		17+2	17	8+5	91+12
PAGE Don							14	4+3										0+4								18+7
PAGE Faz								14+2																		14+2
PARKER Derrick									21	37+1	20+10	3+7														81+18
PARKER Jeff										28+1	16+1			33+3	30+1	31										138+6
PARKER Stuart								13	39+2	3+1																55+3
PARKIN Rick								1																		1
PARRY Matthew																								19		19
PATTERSON Kevin																	0+1									0+1
PAWSEY Charlie								21+2																		21+2
PAXTON Dave													4+11		1											5+11
PEARSON David																					0+2					0+2
PEARSON Stuart								1																		1
PEEL Nathan																				10+1	3+4					13+5
PEJIC Mike							1+1																			1+1
PELL Robert																					4					4
PINNINGTON Dave						1+1																				1+1
POLAND Lee																					5+4	3+7				8+11
PORTER Andy																							9			9
POTTS Colin																									10+1	10+1
POWELL John							2																			2
POWER Mike							2																			2

Tony Hemmings. Photo: Colin Stevens.

Gordon Hill. Photo: Pat Campion.

Paul Lodge.

Chris Malkin.

Northwich Victoria APPEARANCES	79-80	80-81	81-82	82-83	83-84	84-85	85-86	86-87	87-88	88-89	89-90	90-91	91-92	92-93	93-94	94-95	95-96	96-97	97-98	98-99	99-00	00-01	01-02	02-03	03-04	TOTAL
POWER Phil				8+7	7+7																					15+14
PRENDERGAST Rory																					6+2					6+2
PRICE John						7																				7
PYE Alan						3+2																				3+2
QUIGLEY Mike																						0+1				0+1
QUINN Jimmy																						7	13+16	8+12		28+28
RACHEL Adam																						1				1
RALPH Andy																									9	9
RATCLIFFE Robert																0+3										0+3
REDDISH Shane																		35+3								35+3
REDSHAW Ray						11+2	33+1	7+5																		51+8
REID Paul		6+5	30+1	25	37+1	40		6	11+7																	155+14
RIGBY Malcom																					23	8				31
RIOCH Greg																								34	7	41
RITCHIE Bob	15+1																									15+1
RITCHIE Dave												0+1														0+1
ROBERTS Brian					3+2																					3+2
ROBERTSON John																				35+1	34+1	34+1				103+3
ROBERTSON Lammie			9																							9
ROBINSON Ian																						2				2
ROBINSON Liam																					14+1					14+1
ROCHE Paddy											1															1
ROSE Colin																						8+3				8+3
ROSS Neil																									3	3
ROYLE Chris																					0+2		9	35	30+3	74+5
RUSSELL Mark							7+5																			7+5
RUTTER Mark														1+1												1+1
RYAN Dave	38	37	42	42	42	41	42	41	42	40	25															432
SALATHIEL Neil												14+1														14+1
SALMON Austin									14+1																	14+1
SANDEMAN Bradley																			5+1							5+1
SAUNDERS Steve																										5+1
SAWTELL Michael							3+1																			3+1
SAYER Peter								35+3	7+5															2		42+8
SCARBOROUGH Kevin							7+2																			7+2

497

Northwich Victoria	79-80	80-81	81-82	82-83	83-84	84-85	85-86	86-87	87-88	88-89	89-90	90-91	91-92	92-93	93-94	94-95	95-96	96-97	97-98	98-99	99-00	00-01	01-02	02-03	03-04	TOTAL
SCOTT Bob							11																			11
SEASMAN John										7+3																7+3
SEDDON Gareth																								1		1
SEDGEMORE Jake																							18+5	33+3		51+8
SENIOR John												0+1														0+1
SEWELL Jim															0+4											0+4
SHAW Mark											2+3															2+3
SIDDALL Barry														2												2
SIMMS Mark														34	20+3											54+3
SIMPSON Gary						1																				1
SIMPSON Wesley																	23+5	37+1	36	32+2	29+1	16+1				173+10
SKILLEN Keith		1																								1
SKINNER Craig																							4+2			4+2
SMITH Barry															5											5
SMITH Graham	33																									33
SMITH John														12												12
SMITH Nigel								39																		39
SMITH Ossie											9+2															9+2
SMITH Sean											5															5
SMITH Tommy							10+1																			10+1
SNOWDEN Trevor															7	9+1										16+1
SPROSON Phil												11+1														11+1
SROMEK Frank	11+3																									11+3
STANNARD John																		7+9	16+13							23+22
STEELE Lee																	8+2	32+9								40+11
STEPHENS Glyn						19	41	6+1																		66+1
STEWART Gary								23+1																		23+1
STIMPSON Barrie										2																2
STREET Kevin																								12+1		12+1
STRINGER John											8+1	16+3	20+1	2+1												46+6
SUNDERLAND Jon																	3									3
SWEENEY Roy																	5+2									5+2
TAAFFE Steve																						1				1
TAIT Paul																	8+1	24+9	36+4	33+5						101+19
TALBOT Gary																						19	38			57

Northwich Victoria	79-80	80-81	81-82	82-83	83-84	84-85	85-86	86-87	87-88	88-89	89-90	90-91	91-92	92-93	93-94	94-95	95-96	96-97	97-98	98-99	99-00	00-01	01-02	02-03	03-04	TOTAL
TAYLOR Andy																								15+16		15+16
TEALE Shaun								13	6																5+1	24+1
TEATHER Paul																								3+4		3+4
TELFORD Billy			6																							6
TERRY Stuart																				34+4	19+10					53+14
THELWELL Kevin														2												2
THOMAS Scott																					1+3					1+3
THOMPSON Chris																									1+9	1+9
THOMPSON Max								1																		1
THOMSON Dave								12	5																	17
TINSON Darren															20+1	34+1	24									78+2
TOLLEY Glenn																									5	5
TURNER Andy																								0+2		0+2
TURPIN Simon																3										3
VAUGHAN Gary													21+4													21+4
VICARY Darren																9+1	37	36+3	23+10	30+6	38+2	14+3				187+25
WADDINGTON Steve								2																		2
WAIN Les	3+1																									3+1
WAKENSHAW Rob										1																1
WALKER Richard																					10					10
WALLING Dean																						8+6				8+6
WALSH Steve																					2	3+10	4+4	13+1		22+15
WALTERS Steve																16	27	34+1	40	31	27+1					175+2
WARD Chris																									15+10	15+10
WARD Derek																	27+1	31+8	26+7	6+8						90+24
WARD Mark		36		37															7+1							80+1
WEBSTER Jamie																				4+5						4+5
WELLINGS Barry					17																					17
WELSH Paul							1+1																			1+1
WEST Colin																					2					2
WESTRAY Kane														24+1	25+6											49+7
WESTRAY Shaun						0+1																				0+1
WESTWOOD Kevin						16																				16

Northwich Victoria	79-80	80-81	81-82	82-83	83-84	84-85	85-86	86-87	87-88	88-89	89-90	90-91	91-92	92-93	93-94	94-95	95-96	96-97	97-98	98-99	99-00	00-01	01-02	02-03	03-04	TOTAL
WHITBREAD Barry								0+2																		0+2
WHITEHEAD Damien																								3+2		3+2
WHYTE Dave			9+1																							9+1
WILKINSON Colin						1+1																				1+1
WILKINSON Damien																	0+1									0+1
WILLIAMS Carvyn																24+5	32+7		16+8	9+11						81+31
WILLIAMS Colin	26+1	35																								61+1
WILLIAMS Damien									5																	5
WILLIAMS Gary										3																3
WILLIAMS Jamie														0+1												0+1
WILLIAMS Paul												0+1														0+1
WILLIAMS Paul																					0+1					0+1
WILLIAMS Phil						2																				2
WILLIS Scott																									4	4
WILSHAW Steve	19																									19
WILSON Alan	1																									1
WILSON Andy										0+1																0+1
WILSON Eugene								3																		3
WILSON Phil		33	35+1	36	37+2																					151+3
WINDRIDGE Dave									2																	2
WINTERSGILL Dave											6															6
WOODS Andy																									23	23
WOODS Phil																		1								1
WOODS Ray							4																			4
WOODWARD Andy																								7+1		7+1
WOODYATT Lee																									19	19
WRENCH Mark											3+1	31+1	1+1													35+3
WRIGHT Peter																									20+2	20+2
WROE Mark								10+2																		10+2
YOUNG David				32+2			28	35	28+1	26+2	26	16														191+5
YOUNG Nicky																									6+3	6+3

NORTHWICH VICTORIA GOALSCORERS

Northwich Victoria LEADING GOALSCORERS	79-80	80-81	81-82	82-83	83-84	84-85	85-86	86-87	87-88	88-89	89-90	90-91	91-92	92-93	93-94	94-95	95-96	96-97	97-98	98-99	99-00	00-01	01-02	02-03	03-04	TOTAL
O'CONNOR Malcolm										14/1p	7/1p	13	18/2p	21/2p	6/2p	18										97/8p
REID Paul		3	19	13	12	14		2	4																	67
COOKE Ian																13	6	6	8	3	7	1				44
TAIT Paul																	1	10/1p	12	15						38/1p
PARKER Derrick									9/1p	18	4	4														35/1p
WALTERS Steve																1	6	6/1p	7/3p	10/5p	5/1p					35/10p
BUTLER Brian											3/2p	4			5/1p	7/1p	15/6p									34/10p
WILLIAMS Carwyn																10	17		4		2					33

Northwich Victoria APPEARANCES	79-80	80-81	81-82	82-83	83-84	84-85	85-86	86-87	87-88	88-89	89-90	90-91	91-92	92-93	93-94	94-95	95-96	96-97	97-98	98-99	99-00	00-01	01-02	02-03	03-04	TOTAL
ABEL Graham	1		2	2	6	6	1									2										20
ADEBOLA Dele															7											7
AINSWORTH Gareth													4													4
ALLAN Jon																							10	2		12
ANDERS Jason															1											1
ANDERSON John		6	4	4	5																					19
ANDERTON Steve							1																			1
ARMSTRONG Terry												1														1
BAILEY Mark																					1	1				2
BAILEY Terry	3																									3
BARNARD Mark																						1	2(1p)			3(1p)
BATES Jamie																					1	2(1p)				3(1p)
BENNETT Graham								12	1(1p)																	13(1p)
BENNETT Paul				6(2p)	2	3(1p)																				11(3p)
BIRCH Mark																				1						1
BIRCHALL Michael										1																1
BISHOP Eddie																		3(1p)	4							19(1p)
BLAIN Colin											3	4(2p)	6	1												14(2p)
BLEASE Rory							1																			1
BLUNDELL Chris													1													1

Derek Parker heads for goal. Photo: Pat Campion

(Left) Paul Reid. Photo: Pat Campion.

Liam Robinson. Photo: D.Nicholson.

Northwich Victoria GOALSCORERS	79-80	80-81	81-82	82-83	83-84	84-85	85-86	86-87	87-88	88-89	89-90	90-91	91-92	92-93	93-94	94-95	95-96	96-97	97-98	98-99	99-00	00-01	01-02	02-03	03-04	TOTAL
BLUNDELL Gregg																						4	16	19(3p)		39(3p)
BOYD Charlie														2												3
BRADLEY Dave		3	9	7																						19
BRAITHWAITE Keith	2					1																				5
BROWNRIGG Andy																							1			1
BUNTER Steve															5											5
BURKE Gary																						1	2			3
BURKE Marshall							1																			1
BUTLER Brian													3(2p)	4	5(1p)	7(1p)	15(6p)									34(10p)
BUXTON Steve												3														3
CALLAGHAN Ian											1	4														5
CARROLL Tony																			1							1
CEGIELSKI Wayne									1																	1
CHESTERS Colin				17	12																					29
CLAYTON Paul																	4									4
COLLINS James																			3							3
CONSTANTINE Dave								2(2p)						.												2(2p)
COOKE Ian																13	6	6	8	3	7	1				44
CORRIGAN Frank			6																							6
COYLE Tony											1															1
CRAVEN Steve				1	3	6	2																			12
CROMPTON Alan									4	2																6
CROOKES Dominic																		3	3	1						7
DANSKIN Jason										3																3
DAVIES Geoff						2																				2
DAVIES Gordon														12												12
DAVIES Steve										1																1
DAVIS Steve																						1				1
DENHAM John	1	1																								2
DEVLIN Mark																				2	4	8	3(1p)	6	3	26(1p)
DONNELLY Paul														1												1
DONNELLY Peter															2											2
DUFFY Chris																1	1	2	1							5
DULSON Gary	1																									1

503

Dave Ryan. Photo: Mick Cheney.

John Smith. Photo: Paul Dennis.

Lee Steele.

Paul Tait. Photo: Colin Stevens.

NORTHWICH VICTORIA GOALSCORERS

Northwich Victoria	79-80	80-81	81-82	82-83	83-84	84-85	85-86	86-87	87-88	88-89	89-90	90-91	91-92	92-93	93-94	94-95	95-96	96-97	97-98	98-99	99-00	00-01	01-02	02-03	03-04	TOTAL
DUNCALF Kevin					1																					1
DUNN Mark							2																			2
EASTER Graham													3													3
EATON Steve		1																								1
EDWARDSON Barry													1													1
ELI Roger										1																1
ELLIS Neil																					3					3
ESSER Dave						1																				1
FEELEY Andy													1													1
FILSON Martin																				1						1
FLETCHER Gary																					3	8				11
FORAN Mark																									2	2
FORSHAW Jeff	4				1	2															2					9
GARDINER Mark																			1							1
GARDNER Phil									2																	2
GARVEY Steve																							5	4	5(1p)	14(1p)
GLENDON Kevin								2																		2
GRAHAM Andy												4	3													7
GRANT John																							4			4
GRAY David																					3					3
HALL Brian	1																									1
HALL Dave	1																									1
HALOM Vic			1																							1
HANCHARD Martin											14(1p)	8														22(1p)
HANCOCK Mark														3	1											4
HARDY Niell														1	8	3										12
HARRISON Kevin								1																		1
HEMMINGS Tony												2	11(4p)	15(3p)	1											29(7p)
HILL Gordon								13(5p)	4(1p)	4																21(6p)
HOLCROFT Peter																						1				1
HOLDEN Steve								1																		1
HOLLAND Steve												1	2													3
HORTON Bob							1																			1
HOUSTON Graham									1																	1

Northwich Victoria	79-80	80-81	81-82	82-83	83-84	84-85	85-86	86-87	87-88	88-89	89-90	90-91	91-92	92-93	93-94	94-95	95-96	96-97	97-98	98-99	99-00	00-01	01-02	02-03	03-04	TOTAL
HOWARD Mark											1															1
HUMPHREYS Delwyn																	1	3(2p)								4(2p)
ILLMAN Neil																			9(1p)	10			2			21(1p)
JOHNSON Steve												1														1
JONES Garry			4																							4
JONES Graham									1																	1
JONES Ken	1				1	6(6p)																				8(6p)
JONES Marcus																							1			1
JONES Mark																	1									1
LEWIN Craig															1											1
LEWIS Graham																						2				2
LOCKE Stuart													1													1
MAGUIRE Paul										8(5p)	6(2p)	9(6p)														23(13p)
MALKIN Chris									5	2																7
MAYMAN Paul	5	4																								9
McAUGHTRIE Dave											1															1
McAULEY Hugh																	2									2
McMULLAN Dave			1																							1
McNEILIS Steve									2	3																5
McNIVEN David																								6(1p)		6(1p)
MEAKER Michael																							1			1
MIKE Ade																						9	4			13
MILLIGAN Mark																			1							1
MILLS Brian												2														2
MITCHELL Richard																						2	1			3
MORLEY Brian				2																						2
MORTON Neil										2	10	3														15
MURPHY Phil			1																							1
MURPHY Tony	2	1		3			1																			9
NELSON Steve							1																			1
NICHOLAS Steve																									1	1
NOLAN Ian										2																2
NORRIS Richard																						1	3	4	1	9
OCONNOR Malcolm										14(1p)	7(1p)	13	18(2p)	21(2p)	6(2p)	18										97(8p)

NORTHWICH VICTORIA GOALSCORERS

Northwich Victoria	79-80	80-81	81-82	82-83	83-84	84-85	85-86	86-87	87-88	88-89	89-90	90-91	91-92	92-93	93-94	94-95	95-96	96-97	97-98	98-99	99-00	00-01	01-02	02-03	03-04	TOTAL
OGHANI George																12(5p)	1(1p)									13(6p)
OGORMAN Dave												2	2													4
ONEILL David	2																									2
OWEN Terry		2																								2
OWEN Val																				3	11		1	2		17
PAGE Don							4	1																		5
PAGE Faz								3																		3
PARKER Derrick									9(1p)	18	4	4														35(1p)
PARKER Jeff										2				2	2	1										7
PARKER Stuart									4	1																5
PAXTON Dave														1												1
PEEL Nathan																				1						1
PELL Robert																					1					1
POLAND Lee																					3					3
POTTS Colin																									1	1
POWELL John								1																		1
POWER Phil					3																					3
QUINN Jimmy																						4	6	2(1p)		12(1p)
REDSHAW Ray						5	11																			16
REID Paul		3	19	13	12	14		2	4																	67
RIOCH Greg																		1								1
ROBERTSON John																					1					1
ROBINSON Liam																					3(1p)					3(1p)
ROSS Neil																									1	1
RYAN Dave								1																		1
SALMON Austin									1																	1
SAYER Peter									5																	5
SCOTT Bob							1																			1
SIMPSON Gary						1																				1
SIMPSON Wesley																		1				1				1
SKILLEN Keith																				2	3					8
SMITH Graham	2																									2
SMITH John	22																									22
SMITH Ossie											1															1

507

Val Owen.

Steve Walters. Photo: Peter Barnes.

Mark Ward.

Carwyn Williams. Photo: Keith Gillard.

NORTHWICH VICTORIA GOALSCORERS

Northwich Victoria	79-80	80-81	81-82	82-83	83-84	84-85	85-86	86-87	87-88	88-89	89-90	90-91	91-92	92-93	93-94	94-95	95-96	96-97	97-98	98-99	99-00	00-01	01-02	02-03	03-04	TOTAL
SMITH Tommy							4																			4
SNOWDEN Trevor															3(1p)	1										4(1p)
STANNARD John																		3	3							6
STEELE Lee																	5	16								21
STEPHENS Glyn						1	3																			4
STEWART Gary								6																		6
STREET Kevin																								6		6
STRINGER John												2	6													8
TAIT Paul																	1	10(1p)	12	15						38(1p)
TALBOT Gary																						1	3			4
TAYLOR Andy																								1		1
TEATHER Paul																								1		1
TELFORD Billy			1																							1
TERRY Stuart																				4						4
THOMPSON Chris																									3	3
THOMSON Dave								1																		1
TURNER Andy																								1		1
TURPIN Steve															1											1
VICARY Darren																4	9	5	2	5	3	1				29
WALTERS Steve																1	6	6(1p)	7(3p)	10(5p)	5(1p)					35(10p)
WARD Chris																									6	6
WARD Derek																	2	1								3
WARD Mark			1	9																						10
WELLINGS Barry														1												1
WESTRAY Kane															1											2
WESTWOOD Kevin						3																				3
WILLIAMS Carwyn																10	17		4	2						33
WILLIAMS Colin	3	26(1p)																								29(1p)
WILSHAW Steve	1																									1
WILSON Phil		3	4	2	3				1																	13
WRIGHT Peter																									4	4
WROE Mark								1																		1
YOUNG Dave											1															1

Class of '98. Back Row (L-R): Phil Lea (Physio), Mark Birch, Ian Cooke, Chris Duffy, John Robertson, Dean Greygoose, Martin Filson, Paul Tait, Wes Simpson, Mark Gardiner, Val Owen, Paul Bennett (coach). Front Row: Stuart Terry, Neil Illman, Steve Walters, John Williams (Director of Football), Phil Wilson (Manager), Darren Vicory, Derek Ward, Carwyn Williams.

2000-01 Squad. Back Row (L-R): Mark devlin, Adie Mike, Lance Key, Malcolm Rigby, Gary Burke, Steve Davies. Middle Row: Lee Poland, Mark Bailey, Neil Ellis, Wes Simpson, John robertson, Ian Cooke, Gary Fletcher, Ged Kimmins, Steve Walsh, Richard Norris, Darren Vicary. Front Row: dave Gillett (Asst. Kit Manager), Peter Holcroft, Carl Laurie, Mark Gardiner (Player-Manager), Phil Lea (Physio), Colin Rose, Jamie Bates, Jason Avison (Kit Manager)

2002-03 Squad. Back Row (L-R): Kevin Street, Phil Trainer, Paul Gibson, Chris Grassie, Andy Woodward, Chris Royle. Middle: Phil Lea (Physio), Steve Walsh, denny Ingram, Richard Norris, Jake Sedgemore, Dave Cooke (Asst. Manager), Rob Matthews, Greg Blundell, David McNiven, Steve Davis (Player/Coach). Front: Mark Devlin, Greg Rioch, Andy Taylor, Jimmy Quinn (Manager), Val Owen, Danny Griggs, Steve Garvey.

NUNEATON BOROUGH

FOUNDER MEMBER
ELECTED FROM: Southern League 1979
PROMTED FROM: Southern League 1982, 1999
RELEGATED TO: Southern League 1981, 1987, 2003
2004-2005 SEASON: Conference North

Promotion winning side from 1981-82- Back Row (L-R): D.Brown, J.Glover, A.Dulleston, R.Dixey, B.Lowe.
Middle Row: M.McFarlane, R.Parker, P.Sandercock, A.Hoult, J.Jones, T.Robson, D.Looms (Trainer).
Front Row: G.Dale, G.Carr (Manager), J.Sammels (Coach), R.Stockley.

	HOME						AWAY						
	P	W	D	L	F	A	Pts	P	W	D	L	F	A	Pts	Position

SEASONS
11

TOTAL POINTS
541

HIGHEST POSITION
2nd (83/84) (84/85)

LOWEST POSITION
20th (02/03)

HIGHEST ATTENDANCE
4490 v Rushden & D (2-11-99)

LOWEST ATTENDANCE
369 Weymouth (1-2-86)

SEASON GOALSCORER
Paul Culpin 41(5p) (83/84)

CAREER GOALSCORER
Paul Culpin 90(8p)

CAREER APPEARANCES
Willie Gibson 193

	P	W	D	L	F	A	Pts	P	W	D	L	F	A	Pts	Position
79-80	19	12	5	2	41	16	29	19	1	8	10	17	28	10	10
80-81	19	6	5	8	27	31	17	19	4	4	11	22	34	12	18
81-82															
82-83	21	11	6	4	36	20	39	21	4	7	10	21	40	19	11
83-84	21	14	6	1	44	17	34	21	10	5	6	26	23	35	2
84-85	21	13	8	0	55	23	34	21	6	6	9	30	30	24	2
85-86	21	8	3	10	27	27	19	21	5	2	14	31	46	17	18
86-87	21	6	8	7	23	28	26	21	4	6	11	25	45	18	18
1987-1999															
99-00	21	7	6	8	28	25	27	21	5	9	7	21	28	24	15
00-01	21	9	5	7	35	26	32	21	4	10	7	25	34	22	13
01-02	21	9	3	9	33	27	30	21	7	6	8	24	30	27	10
02-03	21	9	4	8	27	32	31	21	4	3	14	24	46	15	20
Total	227	104	59	64	376	272	318	227	54	66	107	266	384	223	

	Altrincham		A P Leamington		Bangor City		Barnet		Barrow		Bath City		Boston United		Burton Albion		Cheltenham Town	
	H	A	H	A	H	A	H	A	H	A	H	A	H	A	H	A	H	A
79-80	2-0	1-3	1-1	0-0	2-2	0-1	2-1	1-2	3-0	0-1	1-1	1-1	2-0	2-2				
80-81	0-0	3-0	3-0	1-0	3-2	5-2	0-1	0-1	3-1	0-1	0-0	0-0	0-2	1-3				
81-82																		
82-83	3-1	2-1			2-1	2-5	1-0	0-1	1-1	2-2	5-0	0-3	1-2	1-1				
83-84	0-1	1-0			3-0	2-1	2-2	2-1			5-2	1-0	4-0	0-3				
84-85	4-1	0-1					1-1	1-1	5-2	0-0	0-0	0-1	4-2	3-2				
85-86	0-0	4-7					4-1	1-0	0-1	0-2	2-3	2-0	0-1	2-3			0-1	3-5
86-87	2-2	2-2					1-3	1-4			1-0	3-2	1-5	1-2			0-0	1-1
1987-1999																		
99-00	3-1	2-2																
00-01													3-1	1-4				
01-02							2-3	1-0					1-1	1-4				
02-03							3-2	1-2							1-2	0-1		

	Chester City		Dagenham		Dagenham & Redbridge		Dartford		Doncaster Rovers		Dover Athletic		Enfield		Farnborough Town		Forest Green Rovers	
	H	A	H	A	H	A	H	A	H	A	H	A	H	A	H	A	H	A
79-80																		
80-81																		
81-82																		
82-83			1-1	0-0									0-2	1-1				
83-84			1-1	2-4									4-0	1-0				
84-85			2-2	1-2			5-1	2-2					2-2	0-1				
85-86			1-2	2-3			3-1	1-0					1-5	2-3				
86-87			3-3	1-3									2-0	1-3				
1987-1999																		
99-00									0-0	1-0	0-2	1-3					2-3	2-1
00-01					2-0	1-1			1-0	1-1	1-2	1-2					2-0	0-0
01-02					2-0	0-2			2-3	2-2	3-0	2-1			1-1	1-2	2-1	2-1
02-03					1-3	2-1			0-3	1-1					0-2	2-0	3-2	1-6

Top: Early action against Maidstone United in front of a crowd of 3,592. Photo: D Beaton.
Below: Nuneaton's defence is kept busy by Dagenham & Redbridge Photo: Peter Singh.

Chris McKenzie saves.

Photo: Keith Clayton

	Frickley Athletic		Gateshead		Gravesend & N'fleet		Halifax Town		Hayes		Hednesford Town		Hereford United		Kettering Town		Kidderminster H.	
	H	A	H	A	H	A	H	A	H	A	H	A	H	A	H	A	H	A
79-80					3-1	2-2									2-2	1-1		
80-81	0-1	3-4			1-2	0-4									1-5	0-3		
81-82																		
82-83	5-1	1-2													0-0	0-0		
83-84	1-0	3-1	3-2	1-1											1-0	4-3	2-1	3-3
84-85	0-0	1-1	3-0	2-0											1-1	1-1	1-1	4-3
85-86	0-1	2-2													0-3	4-1	0-3	1-2
86-87	2-1	1-1	1-1	2-3											0-0	2-2	1-2	0-3
1987-1999																		
99-00									2-1	0-3	3-0	0-0	0-1	1-1	0-1	1-1	2-3	2-1
00-01									1-1	0-0	5-1	3-0	1-2	1-1	1-1	2-1		
01-02									0-2	2-1			2-0	1-1				
02-03					0-1	1-4	2-0	1-3					0-3	1-2	1-0	0-3		

	Kingstonian		Leigh RMI		Maidstone United		Margate		Morecambe		Northwich Victoria		Redditch United		Runcorn		Rushden & Diamonds	
	H	A	H	A	H	A	H	A	H	A	H	A	H	A	H	A	H	A
79-80					4-0	1-1					2-1	1-2	5-1	0-1				
80-81					1-1	3-1					2-0	0-2						
81-82																		
82-83					2-2	0-2					2-1	2-2			0-2	1-3		
83-84					2-2	0-1					1-0	1-1			2-2	1-0		
84-85					3-2	2-2					2-2	0-1			2-1	0-1		
85-86					1-0	1-5					1-3	3-0			1-0	1-3		
86-87					2-0	0-2					0-1	2-1			1-0	1-1		
1987-1999																		
99-00	2-0	0-2							1-1	1-1	3-1	1-3					1-1	1-1
00-01	2-1	2-2			2-1	2-6			5-1	2-4	3-1	2-2					1-1	1-2
01-02			2-1	1-0			0-0	1-1	2-3	0-1	0-1	0-3						
02-03			0-2	1-1			3-2	1-1	1-1	2-3	1-4	1-3						

NUNEATON BOROUGH

	Scarborough		Southport		Stafford Rangers		Stalybridge Celtic		Stevenage Borough		Sutton United		Telford United		Trowbridge Town		Wealdstone	
	H	A	H	A	H	A	H	A	H	A	H	A	H	A	H	A	H	A
79-80	3-1	1-2			3-1	1-0							1-1	1-2			0-1	2-2
80-81	0-4	1-2			2-2	2-2							3-3	2-2			2-0	0-0
81-82																		
82-83	0-2	0-3			1-1	2-1							2-1	0-2	2-0	2-0	1-1	2-1
83-84	3-0	0-1											1-1	0-1	2-1	2-0	1-1	0-0
84-85	5-2	2-3											2-1	1-2			1-0	1-3
85-86	3-1	1-2			3-0	0-2							1-1	1-1			0-0	0-1
86-87	3-0	0-1			0-0	1-3					1-1	3-2	0-2	1-1			1-1	0-6
1987-1999																		
99-00	1-1	1-1	0-2	0-2					0-1	1-2	2-0	2-1	1-1	0-1				
00-01	1-2	0-0			1-2	2-1			0-3	1-1			1-1	1-2				
01-02	1-2	2-1			3-0	1-1			2-1	2-2			1-2	2-0				
02-03	1-1	1-4			3-2	0-1	3-1	2-4	3-0	1-3			1-0	2-1				

	Welling United		Weymouth		Woking		Worcester City		Wycombe Wanderers		Yeovil Town	
	H	A	H	A	H	A	H	A	H	A	H	A
79-80			1-2	0-2			1-0	1-1			3-0	1-2
80-81			1-4	0-1			2-3	0-1			3-0	1-5
81-82												
82-83			2-0	0-3			2-0	1-1			3-1	2-6
83-84			3-0	1-0			1-0	1-1			2-1	0-1
84-85			4-2	3-1			3-0	4-1			5-0	2-1
85-86			3-0	0-2					3-0	0-2		
86-87	1-2	2-1	0-4	0-1								
1987-1999												
99-00	4-3	0-0			0-1	1-1					1-1	3-1
00-01					1-1	2-0					0-2	0-0
01-02					2-0	0-0					1-2	1-2
02-03					1-1	1-2					1-1	2-3

Rob Straw   Photo: Keith Clayton   Dave Hanson   Photo: Keith Clayton

Paul Bancroft   Photo: Mick Cheney   Eddie McGoldrick

NUNEATON BOROUGH

	Home						Away					
	P	W	D	L	F	A	P	W	D	L	F	A
ALTRINCHAM	8	4	3	1	14	6	8	3	2	3	15	16
A P LEAMINGTON	2	1	1	0	4	1	2	1	1	0	1	0
BANGOR C	4	3	1	0	10	5	4	2	0	2	9	9
BARNET	9	4	2	3	16	14	9	3	1	5	8	12
BARROW	5	3	1	1	12	5	5	0	2	3	2	6
BATH C	7	3	3	1	14	6	7	3	2	2	7	7
BOSTON U	9	4	1	4	16	14	9	1	2	6	12	24
BURTON A	1	0	0	1	1	2	1	0	0	1	0	1
CHELTENHAM T	2	0	1	1	0	1	2	0	1	1	4	6
CHESTER CITY	3	1	0	2	3	5	3	1	0	2	2	6
DAGENHAM	5	0	4	1	8	9	5	0	1	4	6	12
DAGENHAM & R	3	2	0	1	5	3	3	1	1	1	3	4
DARTFORD	2	2	0	0	8	2	2	1	1	0	3	2
DONCASTER R	4	1	1	2	3	6	4	1	3	0	5	4
DOVER A	3	1	0	2	4	4	3	1	0	2	4	6
ENFIELD	5	2	1	2	9	9	5	1	1	3	5	8
FARNBOROUGH T	2	0	1	1	1	3	2	1	0	1	3	2
FOREST GREEN R	4	3	0	1	9	6	4	2	1	1	5	8
FRICKLEY A	6	3	1	2	8	4	6	1	3	2	11	11
GATESHEAD	3	2	1	0	7	3	3	1	1	1	5	4
GRAVESEND & N	3	1	0	2	4	4	3	0	1	2	3	10
HALIFAX T	1	1	0	0	2	0	1	0	0	1	1	3
HAYES	3	1	1	1	3	4	3	1	1	1	2	4
HEDNESFORD T	2	2	0	0	8	1	2	1	1	0	3	0
HEREFORD U	4	1	0	3	3	6	4	0	3	1	4	5
KETTERING T	10	2	5	3	7	13	10	3	5	2	15	16
KIDDERMINSTER H	5	1	1	3	6	10	5	2	1	2	10	12
KINGSTONIAN	2	2	0	0	4	1	2	0	1	1	2	4
LEIGH RMI	3	2	0	1	4	4	3	1	1	1	4	7
MAIDSTONE U	7	4	3	0	15	7	7	1	2	4	7	14
MARGATE	2	1	1	0	3	2	2	0	2	0	2	2
MORECAMBE	4	1	2	1	9	6	4	0	1	3	5	9
NORTHWICH V	11	6	1	4	17	15	11	2	3	6	13	20
REDDITCH U	1	1	0	0	5	1	1	0	0	1	0	1
RUNCORN	5	3	1	1	6	5	5	1	1	3	4	8
RUSHDEN & D	2	0	2	0	2	2	2	0	1	1	2	3
SCARBOROUGH	11	5	2	4	21	16	11	1	2	8	9	20
SOUTHPORT	4	2	0	2	7	6	4	1	1	2	3	5
STAFFORD R	5	2	3	0	9	4	5	2	1	2	6	8
STALYBRIDGE C	1	1	0	0	3	1	1	0	0	1	2	4
STEVENAGE B	4	2	0	2	5	5	4	0	2	2	5	8
SUTTON U	2	1	1	0	3	1	2	2	0	0	5	3
TELFORD U	11	3	6	2	14	14	11	2	3	6	11	15
TROWBRIDGE T	2	2	0	0	4	1	2	2	0	0	4	0
WEALDSTONE	7	2	4	1	6	4	7	1	3	3	5	13
WELLING U	2	1	0	1	5	5	2	1	1	0	2	1
WEYMOUTH	7	4	0	3	14	12	7	2	0	5	4	10
WOKING	4	1	2	1	4	3	4	1	2	1	4	3
WORCESTER C	5	4	0	1	9	3	5	1	3	1	7	5
WYCOMBE W	1	1	0	0	3	0	1	0	0	1	0	2
YEOVIL T	9	5	2	2	19	8	9	2	1	6	12	21
TOTAL	227	104	59	64	376	272	227	54	66	107	266	384

NUNEATON BOROUGH   APPEARANCES

	79-80	80-81	81-82	82-83	83-84	84-85	85-86	86-87	1988	1999	99-00	00-01	01-02	02-03	TOTAL
ALFORD Carl													7+2		7+2
ANDERSON T							0+1								0+1
ANGUS Terry											34	35+1	37	32	138+1
ARMSTRONG Terry					5										5
BACON Carl												12+1			12+1
BAILEY Tim					1+2										1+2
BANCROFT Paul					1+1										1+1
BARNES Paul												9			9
BARRICK Dean													11		11
BATEMAN Lee							0+1								0+1
BEALE Mick				2	7										9
BELL Colin			1												1
BENNYWORTH Ian				15	37										52
BIRCH Gary												5			5
BLACKBURN Colin			5												5
BLAKE Marvin											1+8				1+8
BLYTH Jim					14										14
BOTTERILL Dave			1												1
BRADLEY Peter				0+1	0+1	29+2									29+4
BRADSHAW Mark											5				5
BRENNAN Karl											1+3	8+4			9+7
BRODIE Steve													11		11
BROUGHTON Drewe											10				10
BROWN Derek			3												3
BROWN Jon											28+2				28+2
BROWN Micky													10		10
BROWN Paul				13		2+1									15+1
BURGESS Richard												3+3			3+3
BURKE Micky			7+1	0+3											7+4
CAMPBELL Cliff	2+2														2+2
CARR Everton					35	14+2	34+1	30					·		113+3
CARR Steve		1+1													1+1
CARTWRIGHT Les						4									4
CARTY Paul											1+1				1+1
CHARLES Lee												34+5	28+4		62+9
CLARKSON Ian													10+2		10+2
CLAY Steve					2										2
CLIFFORD Mark													4		4
COFFEY Mike							1								1
COFFILL Peter					1										1
CONVEY Steve		4													4
COOPER Adam												7+5	11+4		18+9
CORDER Peter					16	21									37
CRAWLEY Ian	7+2														7+2

NUNEATON BOROUGH APPEARANCES

	79-80	80-81	81-82	82-83	83-84	84-85	85-86	86-87	1988	1999	99-00	00-01	01-02	02-03	TOTAL
CROSS Roy	18+1	20													38+1
CROWLEY Dave											22	30+4	26+2		78+6
CULPIN Paul			24	40	42										106
CUNNINGHAM Mark							6								6
DALE Gareth	18	20	35	1+2											74+2
DANIEL Paul							1								1
DAVIES Clint														4	4
DENYER Peter						16									16
DIXEY Richard		5	36	37	37	11	38								164
DONOGHUE Laurie							0+2								0+2
DOYLE Daire													7+3		7+3
DUCROS Andy								31+5					10		41+5
DUGGAN Derek				26+2	1+3										27+5
DULLESTON Alan			41				2								43
DUNKLEY Roy												2+6			2+6
DYSON John													10		10
EVERITT Leigh								0+1							0+1
FALLON Tommy	29+1	2													31+1
FARNDON Paul	5+1	4													9+1
FEARY Graham							11+1								11+1
FLETCHER Mark							1								1
FRANCIS Delton											19+13	15+10			34+23
FRY Norman						2									2
GALLAGHER Stuart	29	14													43
GARDNER Duncan					1+1										1+1
GARNER Tim			1												1
GENOVESE Domenic						7+4									7+4
GIBSON Willie			33	41	41	39	39								193
GITTENS Jon												11+2			11+2
GLOVER John		35	40	38+1	9+1										122+2
GORDON Russell			3												3
GORMAN Tommy							3								3
GRAY Steve	14														14
GREGORY Ade						3+5									3+5
HALL Ken	35	38													73
HALL Stuart			9												9
HAMILL Stewart					34+3	35+1	11+1								80+5
HANNEY Joseph												0+3			0+3
HANSON Dave								21+4							21+4
HARKIN Maurice													13+1		13+1
HARRIS Alan						5									5
HARRIS Jason													11+2	1+9	12+11
HEAD Maurice	19+1														19+1
HENDRY Ian				39+1	5		1								45+1

NUNEATON BOROUGH   APPEARANCES

	79-80	80-81	81-82	82-83	83-84	84-85	85-86	86-87	1988	1999	99-00	00-01	01-02	02-03	TOTAL
HILL Richard				8+2	19+2	36									63+4
HODGSON Steve													1+2		1+2
HOGAN Eddie		16													16
HOLMES Gareth													0+1		0+1
HOLMES Jimmy							19	12+1							31+1
HORMANTSCHUCK Peter							2								2
HOULT Alan	30+2	17+4													47+6
HOWEY Lee												10	7		17
HOWLES Martin						0+1									0+1
HUNTER Roy														3	3
HUTCHINSON Mark							25+5	18+2							43+7
IPPOLITO Mario						2									2
JENAS Dennis				2+4											2+4
JOHNSON Gary							1+2	11+10							12+12
JOHNSON Steve				2+2											2+2
JONES Gary													13+2		13+2
JONES John		9													9
KELLY Leon												3			3
KENNERDALE Nicky												0+3	0+2		0+5
KENNEY Dave							2+1								2+1
KING Ian												15+8			15+8
KINGSTON Andy				14											14
KOTYLO Kristof											1+3	3+2			4+5
LANE Gavin	6														6
LAVERY Richard												29+5	24+4		53+9
LEADBEATER Richard												3+9			3+9
LENTON Jamie													11+5		11+5
LEWIS Dave	11	12+3													23+3
LEWIS Mark							1								1
LOVE Michael											35+4	40+1	35+3		110+8
LOWE Barry				25	8										33
MACKENZIE Chris											41	33	42	37	153
MANNING Allan						0+1									0+1
MANSELL Lee													5		5
MARTIN Eddie							1								1
McDERMOTT Wayne											14+1				14+1
McFARLANE Mike		29+4		5											34+4
McGOLDRICK Eddie					40	42									82
McGRANAGHAN Andy							13								13
McGREGOR Marc												25	17+1	13+12	55+13
McKENNA John							5								5
MITCHELL Gary							3+4								3+4
MITCHELL Richard												1+4			1+4
MORLEY Trevor		13		36	39	38									126

APPEARANCES

	79-80	80-81	81-82	82-83	83-84	84-85	85-86	86-87	1988	1999	99-00	00-01	01-02	02-03	TOTAL
MORRISON Lance							14	24+1							38+1
MOSS Paul								22+1							22+1
MUIR Ian											13+7				13+7
MURPHY Frank					8	40	36+4	25+1							109+5
MURPHY Ged											12+5				12+5
MURPHY Gez													10		10
NARDIELLO Don				0+1											0+1
NEALE Mark	26+1	29+5													55+6
NEWITT Tony		0+1													0+1
O'BRIEN Aiden											1+1				1+1
O'CONNOR Joe											11+3				11+3
PARKER Bobby	1	1+1	19+8	10+2											31+11
PARR Trevor						20+2									20+2
PASCHALIS Eliot														3	3
PEAKE Jason												21+1	22+2	14	57+3
PENN Don				3											3
PEYTON Warren												31+3	6+5		37+8
PHILLIPS Brendan				27		3+1									30+1
PHIPPS Peter				3											3
POOLE Andy					42	38									80
PRENDERGAST Rory											3+3				3+3
PRINDIVILLE Steve											30+1	1			31+1
PUGH Eamonn	11+9	3+7													14+16
QUAYLE Mark													29		29
RATCLIFFE Mark		23+2													23+2
REAY Simon							14+7								14+7
REED Ian											8+5				8+5
RICHARDSON Paul				41											41
RICKETTS Alan							14								14
RICKETTS Sam													11		11
ROBSON Tommy			5+1												5+1
RYDER Stuart											20				20
SALL Abdou													3		3
SAMMELS Jon	23	25													48
SANDERCOCK Phil		7													7
SAXBY Steve					0+3										0+3
SHEARER Peter							7								7
SHOTTON Malcolm	30														30
SIMPSON Wayne											30+3	30+5			60+8
SMITH Dean		4													4
SMITH Steve				7											7
SMITHERS Tim	37				26	42	42	16							163
SQUIRES Jamie													19		19
STARKEY Wayne							12								12

521

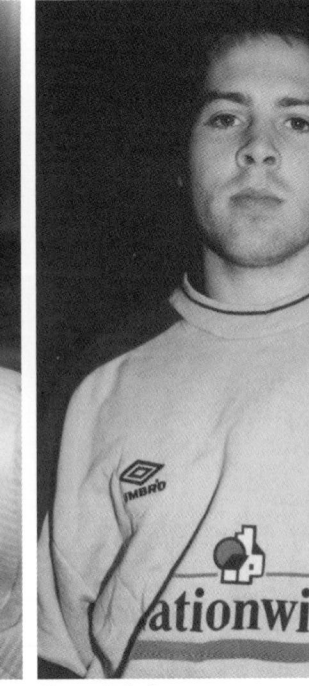

Above: Lee Charles
Photo: Neil Thaler

Above: Andy Ducros

Below: Mark Quayle

Below: Marc McGregor
Photo: Peter Barnes

NUNEATON BOROUGH APPEARANCES

	79-80	80-81	81-82	82-83	83-84	84-85	85-86	86-87	1988	1999	99-00	00-01	01-02	02-03	TOTAL
STEPHENS Kirk							9								9
STIRLAND Gary				11											11
STOCKLEY Bob	38	33	13												84
STRAW Rob											2+3				2+3
STURRIDGE Mick							5								5
SUGRUE Paul	16+1		3												19+1
SULLIVAN Lee			4+2	0+3											4+5
SYKES Alex												10+15	19+3		29+18
TAYLOR Mark												19+1			19+1
THACKERAY Andy											37	21+2	35+2	27+2	120+6
THOMAS Dean	8	20+2													28+2
THOMAS Paul						1+1									1+1
THURMAN Mick					14+1	33	31+1								78+2
TRICKETT Kenny					2+1										2+1
TULLIN Chris													1		1
TURNER Andy													2+1		2+1
TURNER John													8+1	15+10	23+11
TURNER Tony		16													16
WADDLE Alan				1											1
WALKER Derek		18													18
WALLE Paddy			1												1
WALLING Dean													1		1
WARD Dave							26								26
WARD Eric	2	0+2													2+2
WARE Paul											3				3
WATERS Adrian			1												1
WEATHERSTONE Ross														9	9
WEAVER Simon											4+2	27+1	24+4		55+7
WELSH Peter				1											1
WHALLEY Dave						12+1									12+1
WHITE Gary												0+3			0+3
WHITEHALL Steve													10+6		10+6
WHITEHOUSE Carl							2								2
WHITTAKER Stuart														2+2	2+2
WILDING Paul	3														3
WILLIAMS Barry											32+1	22+7	18+7	27+2	99+17
WILLIAMS Danny														1+19	1+19
WILLIAMS Jamie													19+3	13+1	32+4
WILLIAMS Paul							4								4
WINTERS John				1											1
WOODLEY Craig													8+1		8+1
WRAY Shaun											26+5	17+1			43+6
WRIGHT Mark													3+3		3+3
YOUNG Ryan											1	9+1			10+1

Trevor Peake
Photo: D J Gregory

Paul Culpin

Barry Williams
Photo: Peter Barnes

Warren Peyton

NUNEATON BOROUGH   GOALSCORERS

	79-80	80-81	81-82	82-83	83-84	84-85	85-86	86-87	1988	1999	99-00	00-01	01-02	02-03	TOTAL
ALFORD Carl													2(1p)		2(1p)
ANGUS Terry											1	4	1		6
BARNES Paul												10			10
BENNYWORTH Ian					2										2
BIRCH Gary												3			3
BRADLEY Peter							1								1
BRODIE Steve													4		4
BROUGHTON Drewe											2				2
BROWN Micky													2		2
BROWN Paul				1	2										3
CHARLES Lee												5	10		15
CRAWLEY Ian	1														1
CULPIN Paul			13	41(5p)	36(3p)										90(8p)
CUNNINGHAM Mark							2								2
DALE Gareth	5	5	5	1											16
DENYER Peter						5									5
DIXEY Richard			2	1		2	4								9
DUCROS Andy											9		1		10
DUNKLEY Roy												1			1
FALLON Tommy	1														1
FRANCIS Delton											6	5			11
GALLAGHER Stewart	7	2													9
GENOVESE Dominic						1									1
GIBSON Willie			1	1		1									3
GLOVER John		2	1	3	2										8
GRAY Steve	3														3
HAMILL Stewart				2	1	2									5
HANSON Dave											3				3
HARKIN Maurice												1			1
HARRIS Jason												5	1		6
HEAD Maurice	2														2
HENDRY Ian			10(6p)	1											11(6p)
HILL Richard			2		2										4
HOGAN Eddie		2(1p)													2(1p)
HOLMES Jimmy						3(1p)									3(1p)
HOULT Alan	8	10													18
HUTCHINSON Mark						3	3								6
JONES Gary													4		4
KING Ian												4(1p)			4(1p)
LAVERY Richard													1		1
LEADBEATER Richard												1			1
LEWIS Dave		1													1
LOVE Michael												1			1
LOWE Barry			4(3p)												4(3p)
MANSELL Lee													2		2
McDERMOTT Wayne											2				2
McFARLANE Mike		1	1												2
McGOLDRICK Eddie					2	2									4
McGRANAGHAN Mark							1								1
McGREGOR Marc												13(1p)	8(2p)	3	24(3p)

525

NUNEATON BOROUGH   GOALSCORERS

	79-80	80-81	81-82	82-83	83-84	84-85	85-86	86-87	1988	1999	99-00	00-01	01-02	02-03	TOTAL
MORLEY Trevor		8		9	8	6									31
MORRISON Lance							2	9							11
MOSS Paul								3							3
MUIR Ian											3(3p)				3(3p)
MURPHY Frank				5		21(1p)	15(2p)	10(2p)							51(5p)
MURPHY Ged											1				1
MURPHY Gez													3(1p)		3(1p)
NEALE Mark	12	9													21
O'CONNOR Joe											3				3
PARKER Bobby				1											1
PARR Trevor							1								1
PASCHALIS Eliot													1		1
PEAKE Jason												4			4
PENN Don				1											1
PEYTON Warren												9(5p)			9(5p)
PHILLIPS Brendan				3											3
PRINDIVILLE Steve											2(1p)				2(1p)
PUGH Eamonn	7	1													8
QUAYLE Mark													14		14
REAY Simon							3								3
RICHARDSON Paul				3											3
RICKETTS Alan							6								6
RICKETTS Sam													1		1
RYDER Stuart											1				1
SAMMELS Jon	2	5(3p)													7(3p)
SHOTTON Malcolm	4(2p)														4(2p)
SMITH Steve				2											2
SMITHERS Tim	2			1		12(3p)	14(5p)	3(1p)							32(9p)
SQUIRES Jamie													1		1
STIRLAND Gary				1											1
STRAW Rob											1				1
SUGRUE Paul	3														3
SULLIVAN Lee				2											2
SYKES Alex												3	3		6
THACKERAY Andy											3	2	5	1	11
THURMAN Mick					1	1									2
TURNER John													1	1	2
WADDLE Alan					1										1
WALKER Derek		2													2
WALLING Dean													1		1
WARD Dave							1								1
WARE Paul											3				3
WHALLEY Dave						2									2
WHITEHALL Steve													7		7
WILLIAMS Barry											3	3		3	9
WILLIAMS Jamie												2	1		3
WILLIAMS Paul							2								2
WOODLEY Craig													3		3
WRAY Shaun											4	3			7
WRIGHT Mark													1		1

REDDITCH UNITED

FOUNDER MEMBER: elected from the Southern League
RELEGATED TO: Southern League 1979-80
2004-2005 SEASON: Conference North

1979-80 Squad - Back Row (L-R): Mick Williams, John Tidmarsh, Nigel Casley, Ron Skinner, Phil Caldecott, Chris Sharp, Ian Clark, Dave Clements, Roger Grice. Front: Mick Brennan, Ray Taylor, Noel Finglas, Chris Cotton, Gary Bastable, Steve Shaw, Martin Woolridge.

SEASON														
1979-80														

	HOME						AWAY						Position
	P	W	D	L	F	A	Pts	P	W	D	L	F	A	Pts	
	19	4	5	10	18	29	13	19	1	3	15	8	40	5	20

HIGHEST ATTENDANCE
936 v Worcester C. 4.3.80

LOWEST ATTENDANCE
150 v Maidstone U 29.12.79

SEASON GOALSCORER
Roger Grice 7

SEASON APPEARANCES
Ron Taylor 38

APPEARANCES

	03-04
BARNES Keith	8
BASTABLE Gary	9
BRENNAN Micky	22
CASLEY Nigel	7+3
CLARKE Ian	13+3
CLEMENTS Dave	19
COTTON Chris	16
DEEHAN Kevin	17+2
FINGLASS Noel	10
GRICE Roger	37
HAINES Graham	1

APPEARANCES cont.

	03-04
LATCHFORD Dave	9
LOLLEY Martin	2
MARTIN David	1
NEAL Tim	10+1
NORWOOD Darrel	8+2
SHARP Chris	29+3
SHAW Roger	11
SHAW Steve	3
SKIDMORE Jim	22+1
SKINNER Ron	34
SMART Brian	28
SYKES Bobby	5
TAYLOR Ray	38
TIDMARSH John	1
WALKER Dave	29
WILKINSON Paul	0+2
WILLIAMS Mick	13
WOOLDRIDGE Martin	12+3
WRIGHT Les	4

GOALSCORERS

	03-04
BASTABLE Gary	1
BRENNAN Micky	5
COTTON Chris	2
DEEHAN Kevin	2
GRICE Roger	7
NEAL Tim	1
SHAW Roger	3
SKIDMORE Jim	2
SKINNER Ron	1
TAYLOR Ray	1
WRIGHT Les	1

REDDITCH UNITED

	Altrincham		A P Leamington		Bangor City		Barnet		Barrow		Bath City		Boston United	
	H	A	H	A	H	A	H	A	H	A	H	A	H	A
02-03														
03-04	0-1	0-2	3-1	2-0	1-5	0-1	1-0	0-0	1-3	0-2	1-1	1-1	0-2	0-2

	Gravesend & Northfleet		Kettering Town		Maidstone United		Northwich Victoria		Nuneaton Borough		Scarborough		Stafford Rangers	
	H	A	H	A	H	A	H	A	H	A	H	A	H	A
02-03														
03-04	0-2	0-1	0-1	1-2	0-0	1-4	0-1	0-1	1-0	1-5	1-2	0-3	0-2	1-1

	Telford United		Wealdstone		Weymouth		Worcester City		Yeovil Town	
	H	A	H	A	H	A	H	A	H	A
02-03										
03-04	2-2	1-2	4-1	0-2	0-2	0-6	1-1	0-3	2-2	0-2

	HOME						AWAY					
	P	W	D	L	F	A	P	W	D	L	F	A
ALTRINCHAM	1	0	0	1	0	1	1	0	0	1	0	2
A P LEAMINGTON	1	1	0	0	3	1	1	1	0	0	2	0
BANGOR C	1	0	0	1	1	5	1	0	0	1	0	1
BARNET	1	1	0	0	1	0	1	0	1	0	0	0
BARROW	1	0	0	1	1	3	1	0	0	1	0	2
BATH C	1	0	1	0	1	1	1	0	1	0	1	1
BOSTON U	1	0	0	1	0	2	1	0	0	1	0	2
GRAVESEND & N	1	0	0	1	0	2	1	0	0	1	0	1
KETTERING T	1	0	0	1	0	1	1	0	0	1	1	2
MAIDSTONE U	1	0	1	0	0	0	1	0	0	1	1	4
NORTHWICH V	1	0	0	1	0	1	1	0	0	1	0	1
NUNEATON B	1	1	0	0	1	0	1	0	0	1	1	5
SCARBOROUGH	1	0	0	1	1	2	1	0	0	1	0	3
STAFFORD R	1	0	0	1	0	2	1	0	1	0	1	1
TELFORD U	1	0	1	0	2	2	1	0	0	1	1	2
WEALDSTONE	1	1	0	0	4	1	1	0	0	1	0	2
WEYMOUTH	1	0	0	1	0	2	1	0	0	1	0	6
WORCESTER C	1	0	1	0	1	1	1	0	0	1	0	3
YEOVIL T	1	0	1	0	2	2	1	0	0	1	0	2
TOTAL	19	4	5	10	18	29	19	1	3	15	8	40

RUNCORN

PROMOTED FROM: Northern PremierLeague 1981
RELEGATED TO: Northern Premier League 1996
2004-2005 SEASON: Conference North (as Runcorn FC Halton)

Runcorn Squad 1981-82 - Back Row (L-R): Ray Pritchard, Mark Hodder, Bobby Fraser, Peter Eales, Gary Jones. Middle Row: Peter Goodwin (Trainer), Terry Murphy (Assistant Manager), Tim Rutter, Mike Roberts, Efyn Edwards, Brian Parker, Leo Skeete, Mike Kilduff, Ben Seddon, John Williams (Manager). Front Row: Alan Crompton, Ossie Smith, David Robins (Mascot), Mike Scott, Stevie Joel, Karl Green.

SEASONS
15

TOTAL POINTS
920

HIGHEST POSITION
1st (81/82)

LOWEST POSITION
21st (95/96)

HIGHEST ATTENDANCE
1682 v Enfield (26-1-82)

LOWEST ATTENDANCE
165 v Telford (7-12-94)

SEASON GOALSCORER
Mark Carter 30(4p) (86/87)

CAREER GOALSCORER
Mark Carter 143 (10p)

CAREER APPEARANCES
Mark Carter 249+6

	HOME							AWAY							Position
	P	W	D	L	F	A	Pts	P	W	D	L	F	A	Pts	
81-82	21	17	2	2	48	18	53	21	11	7	3	27	19	40	1
82-83	21	15	5	1	50	21	50	21	7	3	11	23	32	24	4
83-84	21	11	8	2	34	18	30	21	9	5	7	27	27	32	5
84-85	21	6	9	6	27	21	21	21	7	6	8	21	26	27	14
85-86	21	11	6	4	40	17	28	21	8	8	5	30	27	32	6
86-87	21	12	7	2	45	23	43	21	6	6	9	26	35	24	8
87-88	21	14	4	3	42	20	46	21	7	7	7	26	27	28	4
88-89	20	11	3	6	39	22	36	20	8	5	7	38	31	29	6
89-90	21	16	3	2	52	20	51	21	3	10	8	27	42	19	3
90-91	21	12	4	5	44	29	40	21	4	6	11	25	38	18	8
91-92	21	5	11	5	26	26	26	21	6	2	13	24	37	20	16
92-93	21	8	3	10	32	36	27	21	5	7	9	26	40	22	19
93-94	21	12	6	3	41	26	42	21	2	13	6	22	31	19	5
94-95	21	11	7	3	39	28	40	21	5	3	13	20	43	18	9
95-96	21	4	5	12	25	43	17	21	3	5	13	23	44	18	21
Total	314	165	83	66	584	368	550	314	93	91	130	385	499	370	

John Carroll (tackling Welling's Trevor Booker)
Photo: Keith Gillard

Mark Carter

Ray McBride gathers well

RUNCORN

	Altrincham		A P Leamington		Aylesbury United		Bangor City		Barnet		Barrow		Bath City		Boston United		Bromsgrove Rovers	
	H	A	H	A	H	A	H	A	H	A	H	A	H	A	H	A	H	A
79-81																		
81-82	5-4	2-2	3-0	1-1					1-0	3-1	0-0	1-1	5-1	2-0	4-0	1-0		
82-83	1-0	1-2					1-2	2-1	2-0	0-2	2-1	2-1	1-0	1-2	3-2	4-2		
83-84	0-0	3-1					0-2	3-2	2-0	0-2			2-1	1-1	3-1	2-1		
84-85	1-2	1-0							1-2	1-1	0-0	1-1	0-0	1-0	1-2	0-2		
85-86	2-1	1-1							0-0	2-1	3-1	4-0	2-0	1-0	3-0	1-2		
86-87	1-1	0-0							1-1	0-3			0-1	2-1	3-1	0-2		
87-88	1-1	0-2							0-1	2-1			2-1	1-0	3-0	2-2		
88-89	3-0	2-1			5-0	2-1			3-0	2-3					1-32	6-0		
89-90	0-0	2-1							2-2	2-2	4-3	2-2			3-1	2-3		
90-91	1-3	0-1							3-2	0-2	3-1	1-2	1-1	1-6	2-1	2-2		
91-92	2-2	2-2									2-2	3-2	0-2	1-3	2-2	1-2		
92-93	0-1	2-0											1-3	1-1	1-2	0-0	2-1	0-0
93-94	2-1	1-2											0-0	0-0			4-1	0-0
94-95	3-0	2-3											1-1	3-4			3-1	0-1
95-96	0-1	2-2											1-0	0-3			0-0	0-2
96-04																		

	Cheltenham Town		Chorley		Colchester United		Dagenham		Dagenham & Redbridge		Darlington		Dartford		Dover Athletic		Enfield	
	H	A	H	A	H	A	H	A	H	A	H	A	H	A	H	A	H	A
79-81																		
81-82							1-0	1-0			.		4-2	2-1			2-0	0-2
82-83							5-1	1-3									2-2	0-0
83-84							1-0	2-0									0-0	1-0
84-85							3-0	1-2					1-1	1-1			1-1	1-1
85-86	5-0	1-1					1-1	3-2					5-0	1-0			1-1	0-2
86-87	1-0	1-1					4-0	2-3									1-1	0-5
87-88	2-2	0-0					2-1	4-1									2-2	3-1
88-89	2-1	1-2	3-0	3-1													1-2	3-0
89-90	2-4	2-2	3-2	2-0							2-1	1-1					9-0	2-3
90-91	2-2	3-1			0-3	2-2												
91-92	2-1	1-4			1-3	1-2			1-0	2-1								
92-93									1-0	1-5								
93-94									2-1	1-2					2-1	3-2		
94-95									0-0	2-3					3-3	1-1		
95-96									2-0	3-2					1-3	2-4		
96-04																		

531

Ian Brady

Jamie Bates
Photo: V.J. Robertson.

	Farnborough Town		Fisher Athletic		Frickley Athletic		Gateshead		Gravesend & N'fleet		Halifax Town		Hednesford Town		Kettering Town		Kidderminster H.	
	H	A	H	A	H	A	H	A	H	A	H	A	H	A	H	A	H	A
79-81																		
81-82					1-0	0-2			1-0	4-2					3-2	0-0		
82-83					3-3	2-0									6-0	1-3		
83-84					2-1	1-2	4-2	1-1							4-1	0-1	1-1	2-0
84-85					0-0	1-1	1-1	3-0							2-2	0-3	1-2	1-0
85-86					2-2	1-3									0-1	0-0	0-2	4-2
86-87					1-0	2-0	4-0	3-1							1-0	1-1	4-3	2-3
87-88			5-1	2-0											1-0	3-0	2-0	1-1
88-89			1-1	1-0											2-1	0-2	1-3	1-2
89-90	3-2	3-6	4-0	1-0											3-1	1-1	2-1	0-0
90-91			5-1	1-0			2-0	1-3							2-1	0-3	5-1	1-3
91-92	1-1	2-0					1-1	1-1							0-0	0-3	4-1	1-2
92-93	1-4	3-2					4-2	1-4							2-2	3-3	0-0	0-2
93-94							1-1	2-2			5-0	1-1			0-0	2-2	0-5	0-3
94-95	1-0	4-0					3-2	0-4			0-3	0-4			1-2	0-3	2-2	1-1
95-96	0-3	1-0					1-1	0-1			0-1	3-1	2-2	0-2	4-2	0-4	0-1	1-4
96-04																		

RUNCORN

	Lincoln City		Macclesfield Town		Maidstone United		Merthyr Tydfil		Morecambe		Northwich Victoria		Nuneaton Borough		Scarborough		Slough Town	
	H	A	H	A	H	A	H	A	H	A	H	A	H	A	H	A	H	A
79-81																		
81-82					1-1	2-1					0-1	1-1			2-0	0-3		
82-83					1-1	0-2					1-1	0-2	3-1	2-0	2-1	2-3		
83-84					0-0	1-1					0-0	1-0	0-1	2-2	2-0	1-2		
84-85					1-4	1-5					0-0	1-0	1-0	1-2	1-1	0-0		
85-86					3-0	1-1					2-3	1-1	3-1	0-1	0-0	1-1		
86-87					3-2	2-3					7-3	2-1	1-1	0-1	0-2	2-1		
87-88	4-1	0-1	1-2	0-4	3-2	0-3					2-1	0-2						
88-89			2-2	2-3	0-1	2-2					3-1	1-0						
89-90			2-0	0-4			1-0	2-3			2-1	1-1						
90-91			1-2	1-2			2-1	0-0			3-1	4-1					3-1	1-2
91-92			0-0	0-3			1-1	0-2			3-1	0-3					1-0	0-1
92-93			1-2	1-1			2-3	3-0			0-1	2-3					0-3	1-1
93-94			2-1	0-0			1-1	1-1			1-2	1-1					3-2	0-3
94-95			2-2	1-0			0-0	0-3			2-2	1-4						
95-96			0-0	0-1					1-3	1-3	3-4	3-4					4-3	1-0
96-04																		

	Southport		Stafford Rangers		Stalybridge Celtic		Stevenage Borough		Sutton United		Telford United		Trowbridge Town		Wealdstone		Welling United	
	H	A	H	A	H	A	H	A	H	A	H	A	H	A	H	A	H	A
79-81																		
81-82			1-0	1-0							2-3	1-1	2-0	0-0				
82-83			4-1	1-0							0-0	0-4	3-2	2-1	2-1	0-1		
83-84											0-0	1-1	2-0	1-0	4-2	2-4		
84-85											3-0	1-3			2-0	0-1		
85-86			3-0	1-1							1-0	3-2			1-1	1-1		
86-87			3-1	0-2					3-2	1-1	3-0	2-2			1-1	3-0	2-2	0-3
87-88			1-1	1-2					1-0	2-2	2-1	1-2			1-0	1-0	4-0	1-1
88-89			4-1	4-0					2-1	1-3	0-0	1-1					1-2	0-4
89-90			3-0	1-1					1-0	0-3	3-0	1-2					0-1	1-1
90-91			1-0	1-1					5-1	3-1	0-0	0-2					2-3	2-2
91-92			0-0	0-1							0-2	0-1					2-2	2-1
92-93			0-2	1-0	2-1	0-0					3-1	1-2					3-0	2-3
93-94	3-0	0-1	2-2	2-2	1-1	2-1					3-2	1-1					2-4	1-1
94-95	2-1	0-5	3-1	2-1	0-3	0-0	3-1	1-0			4-1	0-2					3-2	2-1
95-96	1-1	1-1			0-1	0-2	0-8	1-4			2-3	2-1					1-3	1-1
96-04																		

LEADING APPEARANCES

Mark CARTER	249+6
Ossie SMITH	229+4
Mike ROBERTS	192+6
Alan CROMPTON	188+10
Gary ANDERSON	190+5
John CARROLL	188
Ray McBRIDE	188
John IMRIE	173+12
Jamie BATES	163+3
Peter BYRNE	160+6
Bobby FRASER	160+5
Tommy MILLER	145+8
Arthur WILLIAMS	144
Ian HAROLD	137
Ian BRADY	127+7
Elfyn EDWARDS	124
Brian KETTLE	124
Graham HILL	116+3
Steve JOEL	102+12
Ian McINERNEY	93+19
Brian PARKER	107
Paul ROBERTSON	101+6
Peter WITHERS	78+29
Paul ROWLANDS	102+3

	Weymouth		Witton Albion		Woking		Worcester City		Wycombe Wanderers		Yeovil Town	
	H	A	H	A	H	A	H	A	H	A	H	A
79-81												
81-82	3-1	1-0					5-2	1-0			2-1	3-1
82-83	1-0	1-1					3-1	0-1			4-1	1-1
83-84	1-1	1-3					2-1	0-3			4-4	1-0
84-85	3-1	2-0					1-2	0-2			3-0	3-1
85-86	1-2	2-5							2-1	1-0		
86-87	1-1	1-1										
87-88	2-1	0-0							1-2	2-2		
88-89	1-0	1-1							2-3	3-3	2-1	2-2
89-90									2-0	0-5	1-1	1-1
90-91									1-1	1-1	0-3	0-1
91-92			0-1	3-1					1-2	0-1	2-2	4-1
92-93			4-4	3-0	2-3	0-4			2-1	1-5	1-0	0-4
93-94			1-0	1-1	2-1	1-1					4-0	2-4
94-95					1-0	0-2					2-1	0-1
95-96					2-3	1-2						
96-04												

Below: Neil Parker (shoots against Slough)
Photo: Ray Grainger, Runcorn Weekly News

RUNCORN

	Home						Away					
	P	W	D	L	F	A	P	W	D	L	F	A
ALTRINCHAM	15	6	5	4	22	17	15	5	5	5	21	20
A P LEAMINGTON	1	1	0	0	3	0	1	0	1	0	1	1
AYLESBURY U	1	1	0	0	5	0	1	1	0	0	2	1
BANGOR C	2	0	0	2	1	4	2	2	0	0	5	3
BARNET	10	5	3	2	15	8	10	3	2	5	12	18
BARROW	7	4	3	0	14	8	7	3	3	1	14	9
BATH C	13	6	4	3	16	11	13	5	3	5	15	21
BOSTON U	12	8	1	3	29	14	12	4	3	5	21	18
BROMSGROVE R	4	3	1	0	9	3	4	0	2	2	0	3
CHELTENHAM T	7	4	2	1	16	10	7	1	4	2	9	11
CHORLEY	2	2	0	0	6	2	2	2	0	0	5	1
COLCHESTER U	2	0	0	2	1	6	2	0	1	1	3	4
DAGENHAM	7	6	1	0	17	3	7	4	0	3	14	11
DAGENHAM & R	5	4	1	0	6	1	5	2	0	3	9	13
DARLINGTON	1	1	0	0	2	1	1	0	1	0	1	1
DARTFORD	3	2	1	0	10	3	3	2	1	0	4	2
DOVER A	3	1	1	1	6	7	3	1	1	1	6	7
ENFIELD	9	2	6	1	19	9	9	3	2	4	10	14
FARNBOROUGH T	5	2	1	2	6	10	5	4	0	1	13	8
FISHER A	4	3	1	0	15	3	4	4	0	0	5	0
FRICKLEY A	6	3	3	0	9	6	6	2	1	3	7	8
GATESHEAD	9	5	4	0	21	10	9	2	3	4	12	17
GRAVESEND & N	1	1	0	0	1	0	1	1	0	0	4	2
HALIFAX T	3	1	0	2	5	4	3	1	1	1	4	6
HEDNESFORD T	1	0	1	0	2	2	1	0	0	1	0	2
KETTERING T	15	9	4	2	31	15	15	1	6	8	11	29
KIDDERMINSTER H	13	5	3	5	22	22	13	3	3	7	15	23
LINCOLN C	1	1	0	0	4	1	1	0	0	1	0	1
MACCLESFIELD T	9	2	4	3	11	11	9	1	2	6	5	18
MAIDSTONE U	8	3	3	2	12	11	8	1	3	4	9	18
MERTHYR T	6	2	3	1	7	6	6	1	2	3	6	9
MORECAMBE	1	0	0	1	1	3	1	0	0	1	1	3
NORTHWICH V	15	6	4	5	29	22	15	5	4	6	19	24
NUNEATON B	5	3	1	1	8	4	5	1	1	3	5	6
SCARBOROUGH	6	3	2	1	7	4	6	1	2	3	6	10
SLOUGH T	5	4	0	1	11	9	5	1	1	3	3	7
SOUTHPORT	3	2	1	0	6	2	3	0	1	2	1	7
STAFFORD R	12	8	3	1	25	9	12	5	4	3	15	11
STALYBRIDGE C	4	1	1	2	3	6	4	1	2	1	2	3
STEVENAGE B	2	1	0	1	3	9	2	1	0	1	2	4
SUTTON U	5	5	0	0	12	4	5	1	2	2	7	10
TELFORD U	15	8	4	3	26	13	15	2	5	8	15	27
TROWBRIDGE T	3	3	0	0	7	2	3	2	1	0	3	1
WEALDSTONE	6	4	2	0	11	5	6	2	1	3	7	7
WELLING U	10	3	2	5	20	19	10	2	5	3	12	18
WEYMOUTH	8	5	2	1	13	7	8	2	4	2	9	11
WITTON A	3	1	1	1	5	5	3	2	1	0	7	2
WOKING	4	2	0	2	7	7	4	0	1	3	2	9
WORCESTER C	4	3	0	1	11	6	4	1	0	3	1	6
WYCOMBE W	7	3	1	3	11	10	7	1	3	3	8	17
YEOVIL T	11	7	3	1	25	14	11	4	3	4	17	17
TOTALS	314	165	83	66	584	368	314	93	91	130	385	499

RUNCORN APPEARANCES

RUNCORN APPEARANCES	79-81	81-82	82-83	83-84	84-85	85-86	86-87	87-88	88-89	89-90	90-91	91-92	92-93	93-94	94-95	95-96	TOTAL
ABRAHAMS Tony												0+3					0+3
ALLEN Gavin																8	8
ALLEN Mark					6+1												6+1
ALMAN Steve			2														2
ANDERSON Dave				4+2													4+7
ANDERSON Gary								37	27	28+1			37	30+3	30	1+1	190+5
ANDERSON John					7												7
ARMFIELD John							21	3									24
ASPINALL Wayne							9										9
BALDWIN Mark														1			1
BARNETT Dave							23+1	6+3									29+4
BATES Jamie												27	26+3	41	39	30	163+3
BIGNALL Mike																35+3	35+3
BIRCH Trevor			23+8														23+8
BISHOP John							10+7	5									15+7
BLEASE Rory					0+1												0+1
BOYD Charlie													0+1				0+1
BRABIN Gary												31	30+3	34			95+3
BRADLEY Gary							1		2+1								3+1
BRADSHAW Steve					0+2			1									1+2
BRADY Ian											27+3	7+1	25	34	16+1	18+2	127+7
BRAMHALL Neil				2+1													2+1
BROCKBANK Andy			4		13+4	10+1											27+5
BROWN Jimmy													26+1	5+2			31+3
BUTLER John				39	3												42
BYRNE Peter							24	30+4	36+1		31+1	19	5				160+6
BYRNE Stephen															34	36+1	55+1
CAMDEN Chris				0+1													0+1
CARPENTER Jamie																11	11
CARRODUS Frank						24+1											24+1
CARROLL John								38	37	37	35	20	14	7			188
CARTER Mark					36+2	31+4	41	42	40	34	25						249+6
CARTER Steve												1					1
CARTWRIGHT Mark																6	6
CLARKE Tony				4+8													4+8

	79-81	81-82	82-83	83-84	84-85	85-86	86-87	87-88	88-89	89-90	90-91	91-92	92-93	93-94	94-95	95-96	TOTAL
CLOWES Lee																13+18	13+18
COLEMAN John								4+2									4+2
CONNOR Joe													16+2	38+1	31		85+3
COTTON Simon													2+3				2+3
CROMPTON Alan		37+1	40	41	38	27+8	5+1										188+10
CROMPTON Steve					8	30+4	8+2										46+6
CUMMINS Marty								4+1									4+1
CURTIS Ray															2+1		2+1
DALEY Peter																2	2
DAVISON John							17										17
DEELEY Nigel			3+4														3+4
DENSMORE Peter								37	26+1								75+1
DIGGLE Andrew												1+1					1+1
DISLEY Martin												2					2
DOHERTY Mick										33+3							33+3
DOHERTY Mick																25+2	25+2
DOHERTY Neil															10+11	21	31+11
DONNERY Andrew													0+1				0+1
DOONER Gary										0+1	3+3						3+4
DUFF Peter		1															1
DWYER Alan			4														4
EALES Peter		6			1	9											16
EDWARDS Elfyn		41	41	42													124
EDWARDS Tony										26	34+1						60+1
ELLIS Peter															6	35+1	41+1
ELLIS Ronnie			20+4														20+4
EYRE Stephen																19+1	19+1
FAGAN Mike				2													2
FALLON Shaun											1+1						1+1
FARRELL Terry								11+1	8+1								19+2
FARRINGTON Mark																5	5
FERGUSON Mark									1+2	0+5							1+7
FIELDING Mark			9														13
FIELDING Mike							4										4
FINLEY Alan															25	23	48

RUNCORN APPEARANCES	79-81	81-82	82-83	83-84	84-85	85-86	86-87	87-88	88-89	89-90	90-91	91-92	92-93	93-94	94-95	95-96	TOTAL
FRASER Bobby		20+4															160+5
FURLONG Carl																1+1	1+1
GALLAGHER Mick													13				14
GALLOWAY Dave									9+3	24+2							33+5
GAYNOR Dave					1												1
GLASSER Tony			2														2
GODFREY Warren															0+2		0+2
GREEN Karl		9+4															9+4
HAGAN Kevin												1+1					1+1
HAIGH Ian									3								3
HANCHARD Martin												5					5
HARDMAN Mick				16+8	18+1												34+9
HAROLD Ian										39	41	32	25				137
HAW Steve			6+5														6+5
HAWKINS Kevin							5+3	5+5									10+8
HAWTIN Craig										26+4		8+5					34+9
HENDERSON Peter				3+2													3+2
HENSHAW Gary												2+2					2+2
HENSHAW Mark											8+3	5+2					13+5
HIGHDALE Derek									1+4	10+8	15+1						26+13
HILL Graham											10	36	18	26+2	26	0+1	116+3
HILL Paul				0+4	0+3												0+7
HIRST Alan						0+1											0+1
HODDER Mark		7+1															7+1
HODGETT Carl											1						1
HOLDEN Steve						20+16	1										21+16
HOPLEY Tony											6+1						6+1
HOUGHTON Peter									0+14		1						1+14
HUGHES Mark															39+1		39+1
HUGHES Paul											10+1	2					12+1
IMRIE John		7+3	42	31+3	28+4	34+1	28+1					3					173+12
JACKSON Ian					0+3												0+3
JACKSON Mike													1				1
JACQUES Kevin									1+2								1+2
JOEL Steve		39+1	36+2	20+1	3+3	2	2+5										102+12

RUNCORN

APPEARANCES

	79-81	81-82	82-83	83-84	84-85	85-86	86-87	87-88	88-89	89-90	90-91	91-92	92-93	93-94	94-95	95-96	TOTAL
JOHNSTON Jimmy																	1
JONES Gary		31	1+6	0+6													32+12
JONES Graham					37	40											77
JONES Mark				0+1													0+1
JONES Steve					6+2												6+2
KELLY Dave		6															6
KEOGH Danny					1+1												1+1
KETTLE Brian			41	42	36												124
KILDUFF Mike						5											5
KILSHAW Ron				7+4													7+4
KING Tommy										0+1	1+3	0+1					1+5
KNAPMAN Steve																0+4	0+4
LEE Andy						18+2								26+2	13+1	12	69+5
LEWIS Karl		3															3
LIVINGSTONE Richie																1	1
LOMAX Simon										0+10							0+10
LOOKER Damien							6+1										6+1
LUNDON Sean												11+5	10+1				21+6
MATHER Dave						21+6	31+2	3+1									55+9
McBRIDE Ray				2	41	31	8	39	37	19	11						188
McCARRICK Mark							26										26
McCARTY Darrell												24	16				40
McINERNEY Ian													11+8	36+1	30+5	16+5	93+19
McKENNA Ken								8					15	35+4			58+4
McMAHON John								21+1	23+2								44+3
McNALLY Paul										12+5							12+5
McRAE Peter				4+2	3+4												7+6
MILLER Tommy							40+1	36+2	36+1	31+4	2						145+8
MITCHELL Jimmy								0+2									0+2
MORRIS Mark															40	26	66
MULLEN Paul												36	6+2				42+2
MURPHY Colin										1+1	2+6						3+7
MURPHY Colin															2		2
O'BRIEN Kevin			11														11
O'BRIEN Steve														3+1			3+1

539

Joey Dunn
Photo: Andrew Chitty

Garry Brabin

Joe Connor

Arthur Williams
Photo: Paul Dennis

RUNCORN APPEARANCES

RUNCORN APPEARANCES	79-81	81-82	82-83	83-84	84-85	85-86	86-87	87-88	88-89	89-90	90-91	91-92	92-93	93-94	94-95	95-96	TOTAL
OKORIE Kelechi																2+1	2+1
PACEY Jon											2						2
PAGE Don							35	12+1	33								80+1
PALLIDINO Joe												16					16
PARKER Brian		36	31	40													107
PARKER Neil													16+8	9+6			25+14
PARKER Stuart					22+1	2+4											24+5
PARRY Peter		12+4															12+4
PENNELL Dave							6										6
PRITCHETT Kevin					1+1												1+1
PUGH Dave								33+1	16+1								49+2
PUGH Steve															4+3		4+3
REDMAN Ian												18+6					18+6
REID Andy								6	34								40
RICHARDS Alan													1+1				1+1
RICHARDS Francis												14+5					14+5
RIGBY Tony												0+2					0+2
ROBERTS Mike		36+2	42	40	39+2	35+2											192+6
ROBERTSON Paul													22	29+6	35	15	101+6
RODAWAY Billy								8									8
RODWELL Tony									37+1	12							49+1
ROGERS John				28+4													28+4
ROONEY Andy								36+2	26+2								62+4
ROUTLEDGE John												2	16				18
ROWLANDS Paul					3	31+2	36	26	3+1					3			102+3
RUDGE Simon										23	34+1						57+1
RUFFER Carl															16+5	31+6	47+11
RUTTER Tim		32+1	1+1														33+2
SANG Russell											8+2		5+1				13+3
SAUNDERS Steve											34	35					69
SCOTT Mike		32															32
SEASMAN John										26+1	2						28+2
SEDDON Ben		38															38
SHAUGHNESSY Steve											14+1	37+2	38+3				89+6
SHAW Nigel													2	8+3	6		16+3

RUNCORN APPEARANCES

RUNCORN APPEARANCES	79-81	81-82	82-83	83-84	84-85	85-86	86-87	87-88	88-89	89-90	90-91	91-92	92-93	93-94	94-95	95-96	TOTAL
SKEETE Leo		22	29+4														51+4
SKEETE Steve						20+15	1+5										21+20
SMITH Mike														10+6	24+15	7+3	41+24
SMITH Ossie		42	32+1	42	39	36+3	38										229+4
STANT Robbie																2+1	2+1
STEPHENS Glyn							17	8									25
STRINGER John				16+2	7+1												23+3
TAIT Paul																4	4
TAYLOR Andrew													9+4				9+4
TAYLOR Colin															0+3	28+5	28+8
TELFER George			5														5
THOMAS Karl														40	34+1	4+4	78+5
THOMAS Kevin						2											2
THOMPSON Stuart			0+1														0+1
THOMSON Alan																10	10
THORNTON Geoff							13										13
TRAYNOR Steve							4										4
VARDEN Paul												0+6					0+6
VERNON Ian					0+1												0+1
WALL Justin												10	29	4+1			43+1
WANN Dennis					1												1
WARDER Aiden																17+1	17+1
WARING John												0+2					0+2
WELLINGS Barry												9+6	0+1				9+7
WHITBREAD Barry					5+4												5+4
WILKINSON Paul					10												10
WILLIAMS Arthur										23	29	24	26	42			144
WILLIAMS Colin								3+2									3+2
WILLIAMS David									4+2	21+5	4						29+7
WILLIS Peter											1+3						1+3
WILSON Gus											15		2+1				17+1
WILTON J					1												1
WITHERS Peter										25+4	29+11	24+14					78+29
WOAN Ian										26+3							26+3
WOODS Ray					11+6												11+6

Cheshire Senior Cup Final squad April 1988
Back Row (L-R): A.Reid, K.McKenna, P.Rowlands, R.McBride, J.Carroll, J.Armfield, T.Miller, D.Pugh, P.Byrne, A.Williams.
Front Row: G.Anderson, D.Page, K.Hawkins, M.Carter (Captain), J.McMahon, P.Densmore, A.Rooney, T.Farrell. Photo: W.Leigh.

Runcorn Squad 1990-91 (L-R) **Back Row:** T Edwards, D Highdale, R McBride, D Williams, A Williams, J Carroll, T Miller. **Middle:** J Graham (Physio), M Ferguson, M Doherty, S Lomax, P Withers, D Galloway, G Dooner, J Seasman, T Brett (Kit Man). **Front:** C Murphy, I Harold, B Whitbread (Manager), M Carter (Captain), J Owens (Asst. Manager), S Rudge, P McNally

Above: Mark Carter scores (against Maidstone United)
Photo: James Coogan, Runcorn Weekly News

Opposite: Mark Carter & Ken McKenna celebrate
Photo: W Leigh

Below: Ken McKenna at Wembley
Photo: Paul Dennis

RUNCORN GOALSCORERS

RUNCORN GOALSCORERS	79-81	81-82	82-83	83-84	84-85	85-86	86-87	87-88	88-89	89-90	90-91	91-92	92-93	93-94	94-95	95-96	TOTAL
ALLEN Gavin																3	3
ALLEN Mark					1(1p)												1(1p)
ALMAN Steve			1														1
ANDERSON Gary								5	5	4			4(1p)	1	6		25(1p)
ANDERSON John					1												1
BATES Jamie															2	1	3
BIGNALL Mike																15(1p)	15(1p)
BIRCH Trevor			2														2
BISHOP John								2									2
BRABIN Gary												3	4	3			10
BRADY Ian											12(5p)	1	1	4	4		22(5p)
BROCKBANK Andy					1												1
BROWN Jimmy													6				6
BUTLER John				4													4
BYRNE Peter								2(1p)	2(1p)								5(2p)
BYRNE Stephen											1						1
CARRODUS Frank						1											1
CARROLL John									4	2	2	1	1				14
CARTER Mark					11(1p)	21(1p)	30(4p)	22(1p)	23(1p)	19	18(2p)						144(10p)
CLOWES Lee																3	3
COLEMAN John								1									1
CONNOR Joe													2	6	4		12
COTTON Simon													1				1
CROMPTON Alan		9	14(1p)	12(2p)	9(1p)	5	3										52(4p)
CROMPTON Steve					3	2	4										9
DISLEY Martin												1					1
DOHERTY Mick										18(5p)							18(5p)
DOHERTY Neil															1	4	5
DWYER Alan			1														1
EDWARDS Elfyn		2	5	3													10
EDWARDS Tony											1						1
ELLIS Ronnie			6														6
EYRE Stephen																4(2p)	4(2p)
FARRELL Terry								3									3
FARRINGTON Mark																3	3
FERGUSON Mark										1							1
FINLEY Alan															1	1	2
FRASER Bobby		3	2	3		1											10

545

Steve Shaughnessy (outpacing Stalybridge's Lee Coathup)

Joe Connor (denied by Witton's Keith Mason)

RUNCORN GOALSCORERS	79-81	81-82	82-83	83-84	84-85	85-86	86-87	87-88	88-89	89-90	90-91	91-92	92-93	93-94	94-95	95-96	TOTAL
GALLAGHER Mick																	2
GALLOWAY Dave													2				4
GREEN Karl		3															3
HANCHARD Martin												1					1
HAROLD Ian											4						5
HAW Steve			1														1
HAWKINS Kevin								1									1
HAWTIN Craig											2						2
HIGHDALE Derek										1	1						2
HILL Graham											1	2		1	1		5
HODDER Mark		2															2
HOLDEN Steve						7											7
HOPLEY Tony											1						1
HUGHES Mark															16		16
IMRIE John		1	7	4	1	6	2										21
JOEL Steve		12	10	7(1p)	2												31(1p)
JONES Gary		8															8
KELLY Dave		1															1
KETTLE Brian			2	3	3(1p)												8(1p)
KILDUFF Mike		1															1
LEE Andy						4(3p)								1			5(3p)
LOOKER Damien							1										1
LUNDON Sean												2	1				3
MATHER Dave						7	1										8
McCARRICK Mark							2										2
McCARTY Darrell												9	2				11
McINERNEY Ian														8			13
McKENNA John								3						9	3		12
McMAHON John								4	3(1p)								7(1p)
McNALLY Paul										1							1
MILLER Tommy										1	1						2
MURPHY Colin											1						1
PAGE Don							15	5	21								41
PARKER Neil													3	1			4
PARKER Stuart					3												3
PARRY Peter		3															3
PENNELL Dave							1										1
PUGH Dave								7	3								10

RUNCORN GOALSCORERS

RUNCORN GOALSCORERS	79-81	81-82	82-83	83-84	84-85	85-86	86-87	87-88	88-89	89-90	90-91	91-92	92-93	93-94	94-95	95-96	TOTAL
PUGH Steve																	1
REDMAN Ian												2					2
REID Andy									3								3
ROBERTSON Paul														1		1	2
RODWELL Tony									7	2							9
ROGERS John				7													7
ROONEY Andy								3	1								4
ROWLANDS Paul							4	3	1								8
RUDGE Simon										2	1						3
RUFFER Carl																	1
SANG Russell													1				1
SAUNDERS Steve											12	12(3p)					24(3p)
SCOTT Mike		8(2p)															8(2p)
SEASMAN John										4(2p)							4(2p)
SEDDON Ben		1															1
SHAUGHNESSY Steve											6	11	11				28
SHAW Nigel														2	3(3p)		5(3p)
SKEETE Leo		6	12														18
SKEETE Steve						8	1										9
SMITH Mike														1	4	1	6
SMITH Ossie		14	9	10	6	5	5										49
STRINGER John				6	2												8
TAYLOR Andrew													1(1p)				1(1p)
TAYLOR Colin																9	9
TELFER George			1														1
THOMAS Karl												1		23(4p)	11(1p)		35(5p)
TRAYNOR Steve							1										1
WALL Justin												1	1				2
WARDER Aiden																1	1
WELLINGS Barry												1					1
WHITBREAD Barry					2												2
WILKINSON Paul					1												1
WILLIAMS David										2							2
WILSON Gus													1				1
WITHERS Peter										9	4	3(1p)					16(1p)
WOAN Ian										11							11
WOODS Ray					1												1

RUSHDEN & DIAMONDS

PROMOTED FROM: Southern League 1996
PROMOTED TO: Football League (Div.3) 2001
2004-2005 SEASON: Football League Division 2

2000-2001.Back row, left to right; Mark Peters, John Hamsher, Duane Darby, Stuart Naylor, Billy Turley, Michael Bertocchi, Michael McElhatton, Darren Bradshaw and Simon Wormull.Middle row: Jean-Michel Sigere, Gary Butterworth, Gary Setchell, Justin Jackson, Jim Rodwell, Mark Sale, Richard Butcher and Matthew Stowell.
Front row: Simon Parsell (Physio), Paul Underwood, Gary Mills, Jon Brady, Ray Warburton (captain), Brian Talbot (Manager), Darren Collins, Tarkan Mustafa, Andrew Burgess, David Town and Terry Westley (coach).

SEASONS
5

TOTAL POINTS
198 + 163 = 361

HIGHEST POSITION
1 (00/01)

LOWEST POSITION
12 (96/97)

HIGHEST ATTENDANCE
6312 Cheltenham (3-4-99)

LOWEST ATTENDANCE
1459 Welling (28-4-98)

SEASON GOALSCORER
Darren Collins 29(1p) (97/98)

CAREER GOALSCORER
Darren Collins 65(2p)

CAREER APPEARANCES
Gary Butterworth 168+3

			HOME							AWAY					
	P	W	D	L	F	A	Pts	P	W	D	L	F	A	Pts	Position
96-97	21	8	8	5	30	25	32	21	6	3	12	31	38	21	12
97-98	21	12	4	5	44	26	40	21	11	1	9	35	31	34	4
98-99	21	11	4	6	41	22	37	21	9	8	4	30	20	35	4
99-00	21	11	8	2	37	18	41	21	10	5	6	34	24	35	2
00-01	21	14	6	1	41	13	48	21	11	5	5	37	23	38	**1**
Total	105	56	30	19	193	104	198	105	47	22	36	167	136	163	

Darren Collins, Adrian Foster and Paul Underwood combine to clear the danger.

RUSHDEN & DIAMONDS

	Altrincham		Barrow		Bath City		Boston United		Bromsgrove Rovers		Cheltenham Town		Chester City		Dagenham & Redbridge		Doncaster Rovers	
	H	A	H	A	H	A	H	A	H	A	H	A	H	A	H	A	H	A
96-97	3-2	3-4			4-1	2-3			1-2	1-0								
97-98											4-1	0-2						
98-99			4-0	2-0							1-2	0-1					1-3	1-1
99-00	1-0	2-1															0-0	1-0
00-01							0-0	1-1					2-0	2-1	2-1	2-0	0-0	2-3

	Dover Athletic		Farnborough Town		Forest Green Rovers		Gateshead		Halifax Town		Hayes		Hednesford Town		Hereford United		Kettering Town	
	H	A	H	A	H	A	H	A	H	A	H	A	H	A	H	A	H	A
96-97	1-1	1-1	0-2	2-2			0-4	0-1	1-0	3-1	2-2	1-1	0-2	0-1			1-0	5-1
97-98	4-1	3-0	5-5	0-2			3-2	1-2	4-0	0-2	1-3	2-1	1-1	1-0	1-0	1-1	1-0	4-0
98-99	2-2	1-1	1-0	2-1	4-0	2-0					5-0	1-2	1-0	1-1	1-1	2-3	1-2	0-0
99-00	1-1	4-0			3-2	0-1					1-0	5-0	1-1	2-1	0-0	0-4	2-0	1-1
00-01	2-1	1-4			0-0	0-0					4-0	3-0	5-1	3-2	1-0	1-3	1-1	2-0

	Kidderminster H.		Kingstonian		Leek Town		Leigh RMI		Macclesfield Town		Morecambe		Northwich Victoria		Nuneaton Borough		Scarborough	
	H	A	H	A	H	A	H	A	H	A	H	A	H	A	H	A	H	A
96-97	1-1	0-1							1-1	1-2	2-1	0-2	1-1	2-1				
97-98	4-1	2-1			0-1	0-2					3-3	1-3	0-1	4-2				
98-99	1-1	0-0	0-0	5-1	2-0	3-2					3-1	3-2	1-2	1-2				
99-00	5-3	0-2	1-0	1-0							0-2	0-0	6-0	1-2	1-1	1-1	0-0	1-0
00-01			2-1	4-2			1-1	0-1			4-1	1-2	2-1	0-0	2-1	1-1	1-0	3-0

Nick Ashby. Photo: Keith Clayton.

Jon Brady. Photo: Peter Barnes.

Andy Burgess. Photo: Peter Barnes.

Gary Butterworth. Photo: Peter Barnes.

RUSHDEN & DIAMONDS

	Slough Town H	A	Southport H	A	Stalybridge Celtic H	A	Stevenage Borough H	A	Sutton United H	A	Telford United H	A	Welling United H	A	Woking H	A	Yeovil Town H	A
96-97	2-2	0-5	3-0	1-2	1-1	0-2	0-1	1-4			2-0	5-0	3-0	1-0	1-1	2-4		
97-98	0-1	2-1	1-0	2-3	3-0	4-2	2-0	1-2			3-2	2-4	0-1	1-0	2-1	2-0	2-2	2-1
98-99			3-1	1-0			2-1	0-0			2-3	2-2	3-1	1-0	2-0	1-1	1-2	1-0
99-00			4-2	1-2			2-1	2-2	4-0	4-0	1-1	1-1	2-0	3-0	1-3	3-1	1-1	1-5
00-01			4-0	3-1			2-2	2-0			3-0	2-1			2-0	4-1	1-2	0-0

	Home						Away					
	P	W	D	L	F	A	P	W	D	L	F	A
ALTRINCHAM	2	2	0	0	4	2	2	1	0	1	5	5
BARROW	1	1	0	0	4	0	1	1	0	0	2	0
BATH C	1	1	0	0	4	1	1	0	0	1	2	3
BOSTON U	1	0	1	0	0	0	1	0	1	0	1	1
BROMSGROVE R	1	0	0	1	1	2	1	1	0	0	1	0
CHELTENHAM T	2	1	0	1	5	3	2	0	0	2	0	3
CHESTER CITY	1	1	0	0	2	0	1	1	0	0	2	1
DAGENHAM & R	1	1	0	0	2	1	1	1	0	0	2	0
DONCASTER R	3	0	2	1	1	3	3	1	1	1	4	4
DOVER A	5	2	3	0	10	6	5	2	2	1	10	6
FARNBOROUGH T	3	1	1	1	6	7	3	1	1	1	4	5
FOREST GREEN R	3	2	1	0	7	2	3	1	1	1	2	1
GATESHEAD	2	1	0	1	3	6	2	0	0	2	1	3
HALIFAX T	2	2	0	0	5	0	2	1	0	1	3	3
HAYES	5	3	1	1	13	5	5	3	1	1	12	4
HEDNESFORD T	5	2	2	1	8	5	5	3	1	1	7	5
HEREFORD U	4	2	2	0	3	1	4	0	1	3	4	11
KETTERING T	5	3	1	1	6	3	5	3	2	0	12	2
KIDDERMINSTER H	4	2	2	0	11	6	4	1	1	2	2	4
KINGSTONIAN	3	2	1	0	3	1	3	3	0	0	10	3
LEEK T	2	1	0	1	2	1	2	1	0	1	3	4
LEIGH RMI	1	0	1	0	1	1	1	0	0	1	0	1
MACCLESFIELD T	1	0	1	0	1	1	1	0	0	1	1	2
MORECAMBE	5	3	1	1	12	8	5	1	1	3	5	9
NORTHWICH V	5	2	1	2	10	5	5	2	1	2	8	7
NUNEATON B	2	1	1	0	3	2	2	0	2	0	2	2
SCARBOROUGH	2	1	1	0	1	0	2	2	0	0	4	0
SLOUGH T	2	0	1	1	2	3	2	1	0	1	2	6
SOUTHPORT	5	5	0	0	15	3	5	2	0	3	8	8
STALYBRIDGE C	2	1	1	0	4	1	2	1	0	1	4	4
STEVENAGE B	5	3	1	1	8	5	5	1	2	2	6	8
SUTTON U	1	1	0	0	4	0	1	1	0	0	4	0
TELFORD U	5	3	1	1	11	6	5	2	2	1	12	8
WELLING U	4	3	0	1	8	2	4	4	0	0	6	0
WOKING	5	3	1	1	8	5	5	3	1	1	12	7
YEOVIL T	4	0	2	2	5	7	4	2	1	1	4	6
TOTALS	105	56	30	19	193	104	105	47	22	36	167	136

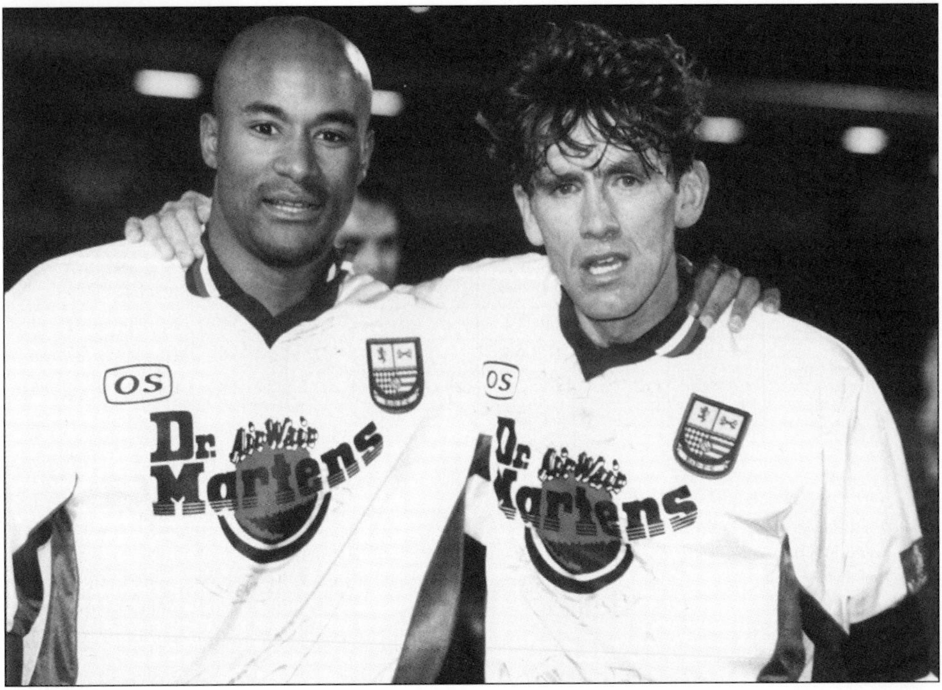

Mequel Desouza and David Lowe. Photo: Peter Barnes.

Brendan Hackett. Photo: Peter Barnes.

John Hamsher. Photo: Peter Barnes.

LEADING APPEARANCES

	96-97	97-98	98-99	99-00	00-01	TOTAL
Gary BUTTERWORTH	41	28	18+2	41	40+1	168+3
Jim RODWELL	41	12+3	29	32+1	28+2	142+6
Darren COLLINS	33+3	39	31	22+8	0+1	125+12
Paul UNDERWOOD		25+4	40	41	23+2	129+6
Jon BRADY			33+4	23+4	39+2	95+10

RUSHDEN & DIAMONDS   APPEARANCES

	96-97	97-98	98-99	99-00	00-01	TOTAL
ALDRIDGE Martin				1		1
ALFORD Carl	32+4	4+2				36+6
ALLARDYCE Craig	0+1					0+1
ARCHER Lee			1+2			1+2
ASHBY Nick	20					20
AYORINDE Sam	2					2
BAILEY Richard	4+1					4+1
BARNWELL-EDINBORO Jamie		4+1				4+1
BENSTEAD Graham	6					6
BERRY Steve			1+1			1+1
BRADSHAW Darren		28	34	12+3	0+1	74+4
BRADY Jon			33+4	23+4	39+2	95+10
BRANSTON Guy		10+1	10			20+1
BULLOCK Darren				4		4
BURGESS Andy				12+7	37+3	49+10
BUTTERWORTH Gary	41	28	18+2	41	40+1	168+3
CANN Adam		0+1				0+1
CAPONE Julian	11	18+12				29+12
CAREY Shaun					32+1	32+1
CHAPMAN Andy		0+2				0+2
CHERRY Steve	10	8				18
COLLETT Andy			4			4
COLLINS Darren	33+3	39	31	22+8	0+1	125+12
COOPER Mark		9+5	17+1	11+3		37+9
CORRY Steve			1			1
COTTERILL Leo		1				1
CRAMMAN Kenny	37+2	36+1	2	5+3		80+6
CROSBY Gary		4				4
CROSSLEY Matt	2					2
DARBY Duane				38		38
DAVIES Martin	26					26
DE SOUZA Miquel			19+5	21+9		40+14
ESSANDOH Roy				0+2		0+2
FEUER Ian			3			3
FOSTER Adrian		14+6	19+5			33+11
FUFF Glen		4				4
FURNELL Andy	2+6					2+6
GAYLE Mark			14			14
GRAY Stuart					4+2	4+2
HACKETT Brendan	23+7	23+6				46+13
HAMSHER John		21+8	11+4	18+2		50+14
HANLON Ritchie			1+4			1+4
HANNIGAN Al-James	2					2

Carl Heggs.

Ian King. Photo: Peter Barnes.

Steve Lilwall. Photo: Peter Barnes.

Michael McElhatton. Photo: Peter Barnes.

RUSHDEN & DIAMONDS — APPEARANCES

	96-97	97-98	98-99	99-00	00-01	TOTAL
HEGGS Carl			21+3	1+8		22+11
HODSON Simeon	21	4				25
HOLDEN Steve	7					7
IGA Andrew					0+1	0+1
JACKSON Justin					40	40
KELLY Warren		11+4				11+4
KING John	11+10					11+10
KIRKUP Andy	0+7					0+7
LEWORTHY David	18					18
LILWALL Steve	4					4
LOWE David				12		12
McELHATTON Michael			29+3	30		59+3
MEHEW David		5+5	1+1			6+6
MILLS Gary				8+8	12+9	20+17
MISON Michael		29	13+2	7+4		49+6
MORRISON David	2+3					2+3
MUSTAFA Tarkan					41	41
NAYLOR Stuart				2	0+1	2+1
NDAH Jamie		4+1				4+1
NDEKWE Malcolm		0+2	0+2			0+4
O'SHEA Danny		1				1
PEAKS Andy	19+2	5				24+2
PETERS Mark				27+4	20+2	47+6
RAWLE Mark		0+8	0+2			0+10
RODWELL Jim	41	12+3	29	32+1	28+2	142+6
ROGERS Kristian					1	1
SALE Mark				6+2	0+2	6+4
SETCHELL Gary					19+10	19+10
SIGERE Jean-Michel				6+1	5+15	11+16
SMITH Craig		1+1				1+1
SMITH Mark		30	20			50
SMITH Neil	7+1					7+1
SOLKHON Brett					1	1
STAPLETON Simon	5+3	2				7+3
STERLING Worrall		0+1				0+1
STOTT Steve	31	2+2				33+2
STOWELL Matt				5+1		5+1
TOWN David				13+5	1+2	14+7
TUCKER Mark	6					6
TURLEY Billy				40	41	81
UNDERWOOD Paul		25+4	40	41	23+2	129+6
VAN DER VELDEN Karel			12			12
WARBURTON Ray			10	39	37	86
WATTS Darren		4				4
WEST Colin		14+1	12+3	0+4		26+8
WHYTE Chris		34	17+2			51+2
WILKIN Kevin	13+8					13+8
WILSON Paul			14			14
WILSON Terry	9					9
WOODING Tim	17+1	28	25+5	14+3		84+9
WORMULL Simon				9+2	3+5	12+7

557

Tarkan Mustafa. Photo: Peter Barnes.

Andy Peaks. Photo: Paul Dennis.

Jean-Michel Sigere. Photo: Peter Barnes.

Tim Wooding and Michael Mison. Photo: Peter Barnes.

RUSHDEN & DIAMONDS — GOALSCORERS

	96-97	97-98	98-99	99-00	00-01	TOTAL
ALFORD Carl	13(1p)	2				15(1p)
BAILEY Richard	1					1
BARNWELL-EDINBORO Jamie		3				3
BRADY Jon			2	3	11	16
BURGESS Andy				5	7	12
BUTTERWORTH Gary	2	1		1	1	5
CAPONE Julian	3	2				5
CAREY Shaun					1	1
COLLINS Darren	8	29(1p)	17	11(1p)		**65(2p)**
COOPER Mark		3	6	1(1p)		10(1p)
CRAMMAN Kenny	6	2(1p)				8(1p)
DARBY Duane					24(4p)	24(4p)
DE SOUZA Miquel			7	7		14
FOSTER Adrian		9	15			24
HACKETT Brendan	3	3				6
HAMSHER John		1	1(1p)	2(2p)		4(3p)
HANLON Ritchie			1			1
HEGGS Carl			3			3
JACKSON Justin					18(1p)	18(1p)
KING John	2					2
LEWORTHY David	8					8
LOWE David				4		4
McELHATTON Michael			4	11		15
MEHEW David		1				1
MISON Michael		7	1	1		9
NDAH Jamie		1				1
PETERS Mark				5	2	7
RAWLE Mark		1				1
RODWELL Jim	4		2	1		7
SETCHELL Gary					1	1
SIGERE Jean-Michel				4	6	10
STAPLETON Simon	2					2
STOTT Steve	2					2
TOWN David				5	1	6
UNDERWOOD Paul		6	2	4	3(2p)	15(2p)
WARBURTON Ray				3	1	4
WEST Colin		6	3	1		10
WHYTE Chris			1			1
WILKIN Kevin	4					4
WILSON Terry	1					1
WOODING Tim			3(1p)			3(1p)
WORMULL Simon					1	1

Darren Collins. Photo: Peter Barnes.

Duane Darby. Photo: Paul Dennis.

Justin Jackson. Photo: Peter Barnes.

David Town. Photo: Peter Barnes.

SCARBOROUGH

FOUNDER MEMBER - elected from The Northern Premier League
PROMOTED TO: The Football League 1986-87
RELEGATED FROM: The Football League 1998-99
2004-2005 SEASON: The Conference

Scarborough manager Neil Warnock holds the Conference trophy aloft as Boro fans celebrate on the pitch at the Athletic Ground.

	HOME							AWAY							Position
	P	W	D	L	F	A	Pts	P	W	D	L	F	A	Pts	
79-80	19	8	8	3	32	14	24	19	4	7	8	15	24	15	11
80-81	19	10	7	2	25	11	27	19	7	6	6	24	18	20	3
81-82	21	11	6	4	34	20	39	21	8	5	8	31	32	29	7
82-83	21	10	6	5	39	23	36	21	7	6	8	32	35	27	9
83-84	21	10	10	1	32	16	30	21	4	6	11	20	39	18	13
84-85	21	10	7	4	35	20	27	21	7	6	8	34	42	27	6
85-86	21	10	4	7	35	31	24	21	3	7	11	19	35	16	15
86-87	21	12	7	2	31	19	43	21	15	3	3	33	14	48	1
1987 to 1999															
99-00	21	10	6	5	36	14	36	21	9	6	6	24	21	33	4
00-01	21	7	9	5	29	25	30	21	7	7	7	27	29	28	10
01-02	21	9	6	6	27	22	33	21	5	8	8	28	41	23	12
02-03	21	12	3	6	41	28	39	21	6	7	8	22	26	25	7
03-04	21	8	9	4	32	25	33	21	4	6	11	19	29	18	15
Total	269	127	88	54	428	268	421	269	86	80	103	328	385	327	

SEASONS
13

TOTAL POINTS
747
1 pt deducted season 01/02

HIGHEST POSITION
1st 1986-87

LOWEST POSITION
15th 85-86, 03-04

HIGHEST ATTENDANCE
5450 v Weymouth 2.5.87)

LOWEST ATTENDANCE
443 v Northwich V. 29.2.84

SEASON GOALSCORER
Colin Williams 26(4p) (81-82)

CAREER GOALSCORER
Dave Bowman 36

CAREER APPEARANCES
Neil Sellers 261+11

Scarborough players enjoy an open-top bus ride through the town to celebrate winning the Conference championship of 1986-87.

1982-83 Squad.Back Row, left to right: Harry Dunn, Mitch Cook, Ma I Wright, Malcolm Smith, Brian Magee, Peter.Walters, Chris Topping, Colin Williams, Neil Sellars, J.McAnearney. Front Row: Geoff Bowman, N eil Parker, Dave Bowman, Peter Howey, Pat Olney, Kenny Dennis, Ian Smith and John Watson.

SCARBOROUGH

	Accrington Stanley		Aldershot Town		Altrincham		A P Leamington		Bangor City		Barnet		Barrow		Bath City		Boston United		Burton Albion	
	H	A	H	A	H	A	H	A	H	A	H	A	H	A	H	A	H	A	H	A
79-80					1-1	0-2	5-0	1-1	0-0	0-1	0-0	0-0	2-0	0-0	6-1	0-1	2-4	2-2		
80-81					1-0	3-4	0-0	0-2	1-1	3-0	3-0	2-1	0-0	1-0	1-0	1-0	3-2	3-0		
81-82					1-3	0-2	6-1	2-1			1-0	1-1	2-0	2-3	1-1	0-2	1-1	1-2		
82-83					1-1	1-2			2-0	3-0	0-2	3-2	1-1	2-1	0-1	3-2	0-0	0-1		
83-84					3-1	0-2			3-0	1-1	1-0	1-0					0-0	1-4	2-0	1-1
84-85					2-1	0-3					1-1	2-1	1-1	1-1	2-0	1-2	1-0	3-3		
85-86					1-0	0-2					3-1	0-1	3-1	4-2	2-1	0-0	2-1	1-2		
86-87					2-2	0-1					0-0	2-2			1-1	3-0	0-0	3-1		
1987	-		-		-		-		-		-		-		-		-		-	
1999	-		-		-		-		-		-		-		-		-		-	
99-00					1-0	1-2														
00-01																	2-2	2-2		
01-02											3-0	1-1					2-0	2-2		
02-03											1-1	0-3							4-1	1-1
03-04	2-1	0-1	1-0	2-1							2-2	0-0							1-2	0-2

	Cheltenham Town		Chester City		Dagenham		Dagenham & Redbridge		Dartford		Doncaster Rovers		Dover Athletic		Enfield		Exeter City		Farnborough Town	
	H	A	H	A	H	A	H	A	H	A	H	A	H	A	H	A	H	A	H	A
79-80																				
80-81																				
81-82					1-1	2-2			2-0	1-0					1-4	4-1				
82-83					1-1	1-1									0-2	3-5				
83-84					0-0	1-1									0-4	1-2				
84-85					5-0	2-0			1-3	1-3					2-3	4-3				
85-86	1-0	1-5			2-1	0-0			1-1	1-1					1-3	0-4				
86-87	1-3	3-2			2-1	2-0									1-1	1-0				
1987	-		-		-		-		-		-		-		-		-		-	
1999	-		-		-		-		-		-		-		-		-		-	
99-00											0-0	1-0	1-2	1-1						
00-01			0-2	2-3			0-1	0-1			3-1	2-0	2-0	2-0						
01-02			2-1	0-0			0-0	2-4			1-0	3-4	1-1	2-0					1-0	2-4
02-03			0-1	0-0			0-1	0-1			2-5	1-0							1-0	1-1
03-04			2-2	0-1			0-0	0-1									2-3	0-0	2-1	2-1

	Forest Green Rovers		Frickley Athletic		Gateshead		Gravesend & N'fleet		Halifax Town		Hayes		Hednesford Town		Hereford United		Kettering Town	
	H	A	H	A	H	A	H	A	H	A	H	A	H	A	H	A	H	A
79-80							1-1	0-3									2-0	0-1
80-81			2-1	0-1			1-0	1-1									1-2	0-1
81-82			0-1	3-2			5-0	0-3									1-0	2-1
82-83			1-2	1-2													3-0	2-2
83-84			3-1	1-2	1-1	1-1											0-0	3-2
84-85			1-2	3-2	5-1	1-3											0-0	1-0
85-86			2-3	1-2													2-3	0-0
86-87			4-2	2-0	3-2	1-0											1-0	2-1
1987	-		-		-		-		-		-		-		-		-	
1999	-		-		-		-		-		-		-		-		-	
99-00	5-0	1-0									4-1	1-0	1-1	3-0	3-0	4-4	0-0	0-0
00-01	1-0	3-2									2-0	1-0	0-0	1-0	2-4	1-1	0-1	1-1
01-02	1-1	2-2									1-2	2-1			3-2	0-6		
02-03	3-0	0-0					3-2	2-5	0-1	1-2					2-1	1-0	4-1	3-1
03-04	2-2	0-4					2-0	1-1	1-0	0-1					3-3	1-2		

	Kidderminster H.		Kingstonian		Leigh RMI		Maidstone United		Margate		Morecambe		Northwich Victoria		Nuneaton Borough		Redditch United	
	H	A	H	A	H	A	H	A	H	A	H	A	H	A	H	A	H	A
79-80							1-2	0-2					2-1	1-1	2-1	1-3	3-0	2-1
80-81							1-2	1-1					0-0	1-0	2-1	4-0		
81-82							0-0	2-0					0-4	1-2				
82-83							2-1	0-6					5-1	1-1	3-0	2-0		
83-84	2-0	3-1					1-1	1-1					1-1	1-3	1-0	0-3		
84-85	2-1	2-3					1-0	2-2					0-0	1-1	3-2	2-5		
85-86	3-5	1-5					2-0	1-1					0-0	0-0	2-1	1-3		
86-87	2-1	1-0					0-0	1-2					2-1	1-0	1-0	0-3		
1987	-		-		-		-		-		-		-		-		-	
1999	-		-		-		-		-		-		-		-		-	
99-00	0-0	0-2	0-1	0-2							0-2	1-0	3-0	0-2	1-1	1-1		
00-01			1-0	2-2	1-1	0-2					2-2	4-4	4-0	0-3	0-0	2-1		
01-02					2-5	1-1			0-1	1-1	0-2	0-2	1-2	1-1	1-2	2-1		
02-03					2-0	2-0			3-2	1-3	1-0	1-3	4-1	2-0	4-1	1-1		
03-04					4-1	4-1			0-1	2-0	1-0	1-2	1-0	1-1				

SCARBOROUGH

	Runcorn		Rushden & Diamonds		Shrewsbury Town		Southport		Stafford Rangers		Stalybridge Celtic		Stevenage Borough		Sutton United		Tamworth	
	H	A	H	A	H	A	H	A	H	A	H	A	H	A	H	A	H	A
79-80									0-0	1-3								
80-81									0-0	1-3								
81-82	3-0	0-2							1-0	1-1								
82-83	3-2	1-2							2-1	0-0								
83-84	2-1	0-2																
84-85	0-0	1-1																
85-86	1-1	0-0							2-4	3-0								
86-87	1-2	2-0							2-0	0-0					2-1	2-0		
1987	-		-		-		-		-		-		-		-		-	
1999	-		-		-		-		-		-		-		-		-	
99-00			0-1	0-0			3-0	2-2					1-3	1-0	3-0	2-1		
00-01			0-3	0-1			1-1	1-3					2-2	1-1				
01-02							2-0	0-1			1-1	3-2	1-1	0-2				
02-03							2-2	1-1					1-2	1-1				
03-04					0-1	0-0							2-2	2-2			1-1	1-4

	Telford United		Trowbridge Town		Wealdstone		Welling United		Weymouth		Woking		Worcester City		Wycombe Wanderers		Yeovil Town	
	H	A	H	A	H	A	H	A	H	A	H	A	H	A	H	A	H	A
79-80	1-2	1-0			0-0	4-2			0-0	1-0			4-1	0-0			0-0	1-1
80-81	1-1	0-0			4-0	2-2			2-0	1-1			0-0	0-2			2-1	0-0
81-82	0-0	1-1	3-1	3-1					2-1	1-3			1-0	4-2			2-2	0-0
82-83	1-1	2-0	5-2	1-1	1-2	2-2			2-0	0-2			4-1	3-1			2-2	1-2
83-84	3-0	0-1	0-0	0-1	1-1	1-1			1-1	1-6			4-4	0-3			3-0	2-1
84-85	4-1	2-1			1-1	0-1			0-0	2-1			1-2	1-4			2-1	2-2
85-86	3-1	0-1			0-1	3-0			1-1	1-4					1-2	1-2		
86-87	0-0	0-0			2-1	3-1	2-0	3-1	2-1	1-0								
1987	-		-		-		-		-		-		-		-		-	
1999	-		-		-		-		-		-		-		-		-	
99-00	2-0	0-1					0-0	1-2			3-2	2-0					5-0	2-1
00-01	1-1	0-1									3-2	1-1					2-2	1-0
01-02	3-1	0-3									1-0	2-1					0-0	2-2
02-03	1-4	2-0									1-1	1-2					2-1	0-1
03-04	1-1	1-2									2-2	1-2						

Kevin Blackwell - Ex-Boston United and Barnet 'keeper, whose arrival at Scarborough coincided with a record-breaking run which helped Boro to win the Conference championship in 1987.

A handshake from Ray McHale (left) after Scarborough's Stewart Mell had put Boro 1-0 up in their final game of the 1986-87 season against Weymouth. These two players were to become Boro's first ever scorers in the Football League the following season, as Boro drew 2-2 with Wolverhampton Wanderers.

Neil Thompson - Long-serving Scarborough full-back who did not miss a single game in Boro's championship winning season. Later went on to a long Football League career at Ipswich, Barnsley and York City. Returned briefly as Boro manager before leaving to join Boston United.

Neil Warnock - The manager who took Scarborough into the Football League. Later managed Notts County in the top flight of English football before embarking on a long stay at Sheffield United.

	Home						Away					
	P	W	D	L	F	A	P	W	D	L	F	A
ACCRINGTON S	1	1	0	0	2	1	1	0	0	1	0	1
ALDERSHOT T	1	1	0	0	1	0	1	1	0	0	2	1
ALTRINCHAM	9	5	3	1	13	9	9	0	0	9	5	20
A P LEAMINGTON	3	2	1	0	11	1	3	1	1	1	3	4
BANGOR C	4	2	2	0	6	1	4	2	1	1	7	2
BARNET	11	5	5	1	15	7	11	4	5	2	12	12
BARROW	6	3	3	0	9	3	6	3	2	1	10	7
BATH C	8	4	3	1	13	5	8	3	1	4	9	11
BOSTON U	10	5	4	1	15	10	10	2	5	3	18	16
BURTON A	2	1	0	1	5	3	2	0	1	1	1	3
CHELTENHAM T	2	1	0	1	2	3	2	1	0	1	4	7
CHESTER C	4	1	1	2	4	6	4	0	2	2	2	4
DAGENHAM	6	3	3	0	11	4	6	2	4	0	8	4
DAGENHAM & R	4	0	2	2	0	2	4	0	0	4	2	7
DARTFORD	3	1	1	1	4	4	3	1	1	1	3	4
DONCASTER R	4	2	1	1	6	6	4	3	0	1	7	4
DOVER A	3	1	1	1	4	3	3	2	1	0	5	1
ENFIELD	6	0	1	5	5	17	6	3	0	3	13	15
EXETER C	1	0	0	1	2	3	1	0	1	0	0	0
FARNBOROUGH T	3	3	0	0	4	1	3	1	1	1	5	6
FOREST GREEN R	5	3	2	0	12	3	5	2	2	1	6	8
FRICKLEY A	7	3	0	4	13	12	7	3	0	4	11	11
GATESHEAD	3	2	1	0	9	4	3	1	1	1	3	4
GRAVESEND & N	5	4	1	0	12	3	5	0	2	3	4	13
HALIFAX T	2	1	0	1	1	1	2	0	0	2	1	3
HAYES	3	2	0	1	7	3	3	3	0	0	4	1
HEDNESFORD T	2	0	2	0	1	1	2	2	0	0	4	0
HEREFORD U	5	3	1	1	13	10	5	1	2	2	7	13
KETTERING T	11	5	3	3	14	7	11	5	4	2	14	10
KIDDERMINSTER H	5	3	1	1	9	7	5	2	0	3	7	11
KINGSTONIAN	2	1	0	1	1	1	2	0	1	1	2	4
LEIGH RMI	4	2	1	1	9	7	4	2	1	1	7	4
MAIDSTONE U	8	3	3	2	8	6	8	1	4	3	8	15
MARGATE	3	1	0	2	3	4	3	1	1	1	4	4
MORECAMBE	5	2	1	2	4	6	5	1	1	3	7	11
NORTHWICH V	13	7	4	2	23	11	13	3	6	4	11	15
NUNEATON B	11	8	2	1	20	9	11	4	2	5	16	21
REDDITCH U	1	1	0	0	3	0	1	1	0	0	2	1
RUNCORN	6	3	2	1	10	6	6	1	2	3	4	7
RUSHDEN & D	2	0	0	2	0	4	2	0	1	1	0	1
SHREWSBURY T	1	0	1	0	1	1	1	0	0	1	1	4
SOUTHPORT	4	2	2	0	8	3	4	0	2	2	4	7
STAFFORD R	6	3	2	1	7	5	6	1	3	2	6	6
STALYBRIDGE C	1	0	1	0	1	1	1	1	0	0	3	2
STEVENAGE B	5	0	3	2	7	10	5	1	3	1	5	6
SUTTON U	2	2	0	0	5	1	2	2	0	0	4	1
TAMWORTH	1	0	0	1	0	1	1	0	1	0	0	0
TELFORD U	13	5	6	2	21	13	13	4	3	6	9	11
TROWBRIDGE T	3	2	1	0	8	3	3	1	1	1	4	3
WEALDSTONE	7	2	3	2	9	6	7	3	3	1	15	9
WELLING U	2	1	1	0	2	0	2	1	0	1	4	3
WEYMOUTH	8	4	4	0	10	4	8	3	1	4	8	17
WOKING	5	3	2	0	10	7	5	2	1	2	7	6
WORCESTER C	6	3	2	1	14	8	6	2	1	3	8	12
WYCOMBE W	1	0	0	1	1	2	1	0	0	1	1	2
YEOVIL T	10	5	5	0	20	9	10	3	5	2	11	10
TOTAL	269	127	88	54	428	268	269	86	80	103	328	385

SCARBOROUGH LEADING APPEARANCES

	79-80	80-81	81-82	82-83	83-84	84-85	85-86	86-87	87-99	99-00	00-01	01-02	02-03	03-04	TOTAL
Neil SELLERS	38	37	36+1	32+2	24+3	33	36	25+5							261+11
Kenny DENNIS	14	35	29+1	41	17+1	36	34+2	3+1							209+5
Neil THOMPSON				32+1	40	40	42		9	18					181+1
Brian MAGEE	14	29	42	34	40	12									171
Andy WOODS									34	36	37	38			145
Gareth STOKER									35	31+7	24+4	35+4			125+15
Mitch COOK		1	19	36	40+1			31+4							127+5
Dave BOWMAN	3	5+1	21+5	10+1	23+1	32+5	17								111+13
Richard DAWSON				14	40	28	33+2								115+2
Shaun RENNISON									25+6	32+2	38+1	12			107+9
David POUNDER										33+6	29+7	30+10			92+23
Harry DUNN	25+1	19+1	15	8		26	16+3								109+5
Pat OLNEY	7	19+4	21+4	26+3	7+2	6+4	4+5								90+22

Shaun Rennison. Photo: Roger Turner.

Neil Sellers.

SCARBOROUGH LEADING GOALSCORERS

	79-80	80-81	81-82	82-83	83-84	84-85	85-86	86-87	87-99	99-00	00-01	01-02	02-03	03-04	TOTAL
Dave BOWMAN	1	2	9	2	6	11	5								36
Mitch COOK			2	12(6p)	8		13(4p)								35(10p)
Steve BRODIE										13	10	4			27
Colin WILLIAMS			26(4p)												26(4p)
John HANSON				13	12										25
Neil SELLERS	3	3	5	5	2	2	2	2							24
Bob GAUDEN	16	6													22
David POUNDER											9	4	9		22
Neil THOMPSON					4	5(2p)	6(1p)	4		1	2(1p)				22(4p)
Marshall BURKE						12(1p)	5								17(1p)

SCARBOROUGH

APPEARANCES

	79-80	80-81	81-82	82-83	83-84	84-85	85-86	86-87	87-99	99-00	00-01	01-02	02-03	03-04	TOTAL
ABBEY Derek	11+1														11+1
ALKHATIB Mounir										0+4					0+4
APPLETON Leigh	4														4
ATKINSON Paul										15+1	13+1				28+2
BAKER Steve											14+4	3+1	18+1		35+6
BARNWELL-EDINBORO Justin												2+2			2+2
BARRATT Roger	11+1														11+1
BASS David										17+2					17+2
BATCHELOR Chris													0+1		0+1
BELFIORE Ivan	3														3
BELL Charlie					14										14
BENNETT Gary										1					1
BENNYWORTH Ian							39+1								39+1
BETTS Simon									38	21					59
BLACK John				2+2											2+2
BLACKMAN Lloyd													5+1		5+1
BLACKWELL Kevin							25								25
BLUNT Jason										10	40	7+8			57+8
BOGAN Darren									1+1						1+1
BOWMAN Dave	3	5+1	21+5	10+1	23+1	32+5	17								111+13
BOWMAN Geoff H			1		5+1	11+1	1								18+2
BOWMAN J C	1														1
BOYLAN Tony	13														13
BRADSHAW Gary													2		2
BRASSART Olivier												27+4			27+4
BRODIE Steve										36	28+2	17+1			81+3
BROLLY Mike							9+7								9+7
BROUGHTON Mark			14												14
BROWN Steve				1+1											1+1
BROWNRIGG Andy													2+1		2+1
BRUNTON Danny										0+1	30+1	0+1			30+3
BURKE Marshall						37	18+1								55+1
BURLEY Adam												3			3
BURNS David			18+2												18+2
BURT Jamie											10+4	3+4		1	14+8
CAMMACK Steve						2									2
CAMPBELL Neil												12+11			12+11
CAPPER Stephen													18+2		18+2
CARDWELL Harry			5+6												5+6
CARR Graham									1+1						1+1
CHAPMAN Dave					3										3
COHEN Gary												7+1			7+1
COLEBY Dave					21										21
COLEBY Stuart					41										41
CONNELL Darren												1+6	0+5		1+11
COOK Mitch		1	19	36	40+1		31+4								127+5
COOPER Lee						1+1	1								2+1
COTTAM John			40	32	12										84
COX Mark				5+5											5+5
CRAWFORD Andy				0+1											0+1

	79-80	80-81	81-82	82-83	83-84	84-85	85-86	86-87	87-99	99-00	00-01	01-02	02-03	03-04	TOTAL
CRAWFORD Graeme				42	36	15									93
CRAWFORD Richard											0+1	0+1			0+2
CRYAN Colin													2	10	12
DAVIDSON Iain													2		2
DAVIS Ian					7	11+1									18+1
DAWSON Andrew										1+5					1+5
DAWSON Dick			26	8+3											34+3
DAWSON Richard			14	40	28	33+2									115+2
DEMPSEY Paul													11+2		11+2
DENNIS Kenny	14	35	29+1	41	17+1	36	34+2	3+1							209+5
DIALLO Cherif							15+6								15+6
DILELLA Gustavo							3+1								3+1
DIXEY Richard	24	22													46
DONALDSON Clayton													2		2
DONOGHUE Gerry	26+5	17+1													43+6
DOWNEY Glen													14+1		14+1
DRYDEN Richard											4	20+2			24+2
DUDGEON James													0+1		0+1
DUNCAN John		0+1													0+1
DUNN Harry	25+1	19+1	15	8		26	16+3								109+5
DUNN Harry 'A'	23+2	27+1													50+3
DYAMOND Trevor	2														2
EARNSHAW Joe							1+2								1+2
ECCLES Terry			12+3												12+3
ELLENDER Paul									23	36					59
ELLIOTT Stuart											6+2				6+2
EXLEY Derek	1			2+6											3+6
FAIRLESS Keith						11									11
FATOKUN Bimbo												16+9			16+9
FAURE Romain										12+4	16+3				28+7
FEAR Keith				12	0+1										12+1
FERGUSON Mark						7	7+4								14+4
FICKLING Ashley											7				7
FITZSIMMONS Peter											16+1				16+1
FOUNTAIN Charlie	10														10
FRENCH Steve							1+7	1+1							2+8
GALLAGHER Barry								8							8
GAUDEN Bob	33	15+2													48+2
GILDEA Alex									1+8	0+4					1+12
GILL Wayne													28+7		28+7
GILROY Keith													7	5+7	12+7
GOODWILL Robbie					6										6
GOSLING Steve			3	3											6
GOTHARD Steve					0+1										0+1
GRAHAM Tommy							39								39
GRAYDON Keith													0+1		0+1
GREENWOOD Roy					7										7
HACKWORTH Tony													11		11
HAIRE Gary						13+1									13+1
HALL Danny													1		1

SCARBOROUGH   APPEARANCES

	79-80	80-81	81-82	82-83	83-84	84-85	85-86	86-87	87-99	99-00	00-01	01-02	02-03	03-04	TOTAL
HALL Howard	11														11
HAMILL Stewart							9+1								9+1
HANNAH John				7											7
HANSON John			38	34+3											72+3
HARRIOTT Marvin										20+5					20+5
HARRIS Martin	24+1	20+1													44+2
HARRISON Andy							14+13								14+13
HARTLEY Graham			2	16	21	38	4+12								81+12
HENDERSON David												0+2			0+2
HENRY Nick													13+1	8	21+1
HOGG Tim												0+1			0+1
HOLBROOK Steve	4+1														4+1
HOLDSWORTH David												16			16
HOOLEY Gary						11+1									11+1
HOTTE Mark											17+1	29+4	37+1		83+6
HOWEY Peter			30	5+1											35+1
HUTCHINS Don			2												2
INGRAM Denny										11	25	13			49
JAMESON Tim				12	0+1										12+1
JEWELL Adam											1	0+5			1+5
JONES Brynley				26+2											26+2
JONES Marcus										35+1	15+1	6+1			56+3
JORDAN Scott											5+3	20+1	8+4		33+8
KAYE David							17								17
KEEGAN John											2	5			7
KELLY Jimmy														30	30
KENDALL Paul							42								42
KERR Scott													9	36+1	45+1
KETCHANKE Bertrand														5	5
LAYBOURNE Keith	4														4
LETHERAN Glan				25											25
LEWIS Jack		12+1													12+1
LIVESEY Gordon	37														37
LORD Malcolm		1													1
LYTH Ashley											5			22+5	27+5
MAGEE Brian	14	29	42	34	40	12									171
MALLON Ryan													6+1		6+1
MANN Neil												2			2
MARCELLE Clint														26+3	26+3
MARSHALL Sean	33+2	35													68+2
MARTIN Kevin							8								8
McALINDON Gareth										11+3					11+3
McGINTY Brian							8								8
McHALE Ray							16+1								16+1
McKECHNIE Ian		2													2
McNAUGHTON Michael										1+7					1+7
McNIVEN David										5					5
McSWEENEY Leon														0+3	0+2
MELL Stewart							39+1								39+1
MIDDLEMASS Scott										9+1					9+1

Conference action against Rushden & Diamonds. Photo: Peter Barnes.

Gus Di Lella and Ashley Lyth. Photo: Peter Barnes.

Gareth Stoker and Mark Tyrell put the pressure on.

1983-84 Squad. Back Row , left to right: John Cottam, Neil Sellars, Malcolm Smith, Glen Letheran, Harry Dunn, Mitch Cooke and John Hanson.
Front Row: Pat Olney, John Steepley, Kenny Dennis, Dick Dawson and Kevin Pickard.   Photo: W.Leigh

SCARBOROUGH   APPEARANCES

	79-80	80-81	81-82	82-83	83-84	84-85	85-86	86-87	87-99	99-00	00-01	01-02	02-03	03-04	TOTAL
MILBOURNE Ian										2+4					2+4
MITCHELL Ken							9+1								9+1
MORRIS Andy										6+3					6+3
MORRIS Stewart										5+17	1+16				6+33
MURPHY John	19														19
NESOVIC Alex													0+1		0+1
NEWTON Paul												1			1
NICHOLSON Kevin													13		13
NIX Peter		1													1
OAKLEY Dave					1										1
OLNEY Pat	7	19+4	21+4	26+3	7+2	6+4	4+5								90+22
OMONI Phil							6+3								6+3
O'NEILL Paul												1			1
O'RIORDAN Martin										0+1					0+1
ORMEROD Anthony												24+6			24+6
PALIOS Mark					5										5
PARKER Neil			31	4											35
PATTERSON Mark											17+2	3+1			20+3
PECK Brian	1														1
PHILLIPS Brendan				37+2	25+3	15+1									77+6
PICKARD Kevin			3												3
PIERCEWRIGHT Brad											1+3				1+3
PODD Cec								33							33
POLLARD Brian					15+2										15+2
POUNDER David											33+6	29+7	30+10		92+23
PRICE Michael												8	12+4		20+4
PRIESTLEY Phil											6				6
QUAYLE Mark													35+1		35+1
QUINN Andrew										1+3					1+3
RAW Tom													3+1	7+4	10+5
REDMILE Matt														22	22
REED Martin											2+1				2+1
RENNISON Shaun										25+6	32+2	38+1	12		107+9
RICHARDS Steve								31							31
RIDLER David													7		7
ROBERTS Darren										28+7					28+7
ROBINSON Gerard											4+1				4+1
ROBINSON Len			15												15
ROBINSON Mark													2		2
ROSE Karl												12+4	15+8	23+4	50+16
ROSE Nigel			4+5			13+7	14+7								31+19
RUSSELL Matthew										19	18+1				37+1
SALT Phil											11				11
SAVIC Sinisa										2					2
SCOTT Keith												27+1			27+1
SELLERS Neil	38	37	36+1	32+2	24+3	33	36	25+5							261+11
SENIOR Chris													7+33		7+33
SESTANOVICH Ashley													7		7
SHEPHERD Paul												10	35+1		45+1
SHERLOCK Jamie													1+6		1+6

SCARBOROUGH   APPEARANCES

	79-80	80-81	81-82	82-83	83-84	84-85	85-86	86-87	87-99	99-00	00-01	01-02	02-03	03-04	TOTAL
SHERWOOD Ben												1+5			1+5
SHIELDS Dean												9			9
SHORT Chris												5			5
SHORT Craig						5									5
SHUTTLEWORTH Barry											2				2
SILLAH Mohammed													14+1		14+1
SINNOTT Lee										22					22
SMITH Ian		36+1	25+4	5+2											66+7
SMITH Malcolm		13	7	15											35
SMITH Mark												4			4
SMITH Trevor	9	8+5													17+5
SOLLITT Adam														7+2	7+2
SPRINGETT Peter		36													36
STAMP Darryn											1	28+3			29+3
STEEPLES John				23											23
STOKER Gareth										35	31+7	24+4	35+4		125+15
SUGDEN Ryan												9+4			9+4
SUTCLIFFE Peter					10+5										10+5
SWALES Mark												3+4			3+4
TATE Chris										22	8+3				30+3
TAYLOR Cleveland													11+1		11+1
TAYLOR Peter	4+1														4+1
THOMPSON Neil				32+1	40	40	42			9	18				181+1
TOONE Leigh											0+1				0+1
TOPPING Chris			15+1												15+1
TRACEY Richard												0+1			0+1
TRURAN Gary						3									3
TURLEY James												0+5			0+5
TYRRELL Mark										9+3					9+3
WALKER Johnny										0+1					0+1
WALKER Leigh													4+1	35	39+1
WALKER P		1													1
WALKER Phil								32+1							32+1
WALTERS Peter			24												24
WATSON John		10+1	26												36+1
WHITMAN Tristram														4+2	4+2
WIGGAN Trenton					30+6	30+3	24+1								84+10
WILFORD Aaron												9+1			9+1
WILLIAMS Colin			42												42
WILLIAMS Gareth										20	32+2				52+2
WILLIAMS Jacques														6+6	6+6
WINDROSS Andy											1+4	5+6			6+10
WINTERSGILL Dave							12+2								12+2
WOOD Neil	4														4
WOODS Andy										34	36	37	38		145
WRIGHT Andy												4			4
WRIGHT Mally	5	17	38												60

SCARBOROUGH GOALSCORERS

	79-80	80-81	81-82	82-83	83-84	84-85	85-86	86-87	87-99	99-00	00-01	01-02	02-03	03-04	TOTAL
ABBEY Derek	1														1
BAKER Steve												1(1p)			1(1p)
BARRATT Roger	2														2
BASS David								1							1
BELL Charlie				2											2
BENNYWORTH Ian							4								4
BETTS Simon										6(2p)	4(3p)				10(5p)
BLUNT Jason													6	2	8
BOWMAN Dave	1	2	9	2	6	11	5								36
BOYLAN Tony	3														3
BRASSART Olivier												1			1
BRODIE Steve										13	10	4			27
BROLLY Mick							1								1
BROWN Steve				1											1
BURKE Marshall					12(1p)	5									17(1p)
BURNS David				1											1
BURT Jamie												2	1		3
CAMMACK Steve							1								1
CAMPBELL Neil													4		4
COHEN Gary													2		2
CONNELL Darren												2			2
COOK Mitch			2	12(6p)	8		13(4p)								35(10p)
COOPER Lee						1									1
COTTAM John				4	1										5
CRYAN Colin													1		1
DAWSON Dick				13	2										15
DAWSON Richard					4	3									7
DENNIS Kenny		1													1
DIALLO Cherif										8					8
DIXEY Richard	2	2													4
DONOGHUE Gerry	1	1(1p)													2(1p)
DOWNEY Glen													1		1
DRYDEN Richard												2	1		3
DUNN Harry	1	1		1											3
DUNN Harry "A"	5(2p)	5													10(2p)
ECCLES Terry			7												7
ELLENDER Paul										6					6
ELLIOTT Stuart												1			1
FAIRLESS Keith						1									1
FATOKUN Bimbo													8		8
FEAR Keith				1											1
FERGUSON Mark					1	1									2
GALLAGHER Barry							1(1p)								1(1p)
GAUDEN Bob	16	6													22
GILL Wayne														1	1
GILROY Keith													1(1p)	3(1p)	4(2p)
GRAHAM Tommy							3								3
GREENWOOD Ricky					1										1
HACKWORTH Tony														3	3

SCARBOROUGH GOALSCORERS

	79-80	80-81	81-82	82-83	83-84	84-85	85-86	86-87	87-99	99-00	00-01	01-02	02-03	03-04	TOTAL
HAIRE Graham							4								4
HALL Howard	3														3
HAMILL Stewart							2								2
HANNAH John					2										2
HANSON John			13	12											25
HARRIOTT Marvin										1					1
HARRIS Martin	5	5													10
HARTLEY Graham				1	2	4									7
HENRY Nick													1	1	2
HOLBROOK Steve	1														1
HOLDSWORTH David													1		1
HOOLEY Gary							7(2p)								7(2p)
HOTTE Mark													1		1
HOWEY Peter			1												1
INGRAM Denny											1				1
JONES Brynley			3(1p)												3(1p)
JONES Marcus										1					1
JORDAN Scott											2	1			3
KELLY Jimmy														2(1p)	2(1p)
KETCHANKE Bertrand														1	1
LEWIS Jack		5													5
MAGEE Brian		1	2	2	1	2									8
MALLON Ryan													1		1
MARCELLE Clint														4	4
MARSHALL Sean		1													1
McALINDON Gareth										3					3
McHALE Ray							1								1
McNAUGHTON Michael										1					1
McNIVEN David										2					2
MELL Stewart								16							16
MITCHELL Ken						1									1
MORRIS Andy										2					2
MORRIS Stewart										2					2
MURPHY John	1														1
NICHOLSON Kevin													1		1
OLNEY Pat	2	4	2	6	1										15
ORMEROD Anthony												2			2
PALIOS Mark					1										1
PHILLIPS Brendan				5	5	2									12
POLLARD Brian				5(4p)											5(4p)
POUNDER David										9	4	9			22
PRICE Michael													1		1
QUAYLE Mark													14(5p)		14(5p)
QUINN Andrew										1					1
RAW Tom													1		1
REDMILE Matt														3	3
RENNISON Shaun										2	2	3			7
RICHARDS Steve							2								2
ROBERTS Darren										9(2p)					9(2p)
ROSE Karl											6	2		4	12
ROSE Nigel			1		7	5									13

576

SCARBOROUGH GOALSCORERS

	79-80	80-81	81-82	82-83	83-84	84-85	85-86	86-87	87-99	99-00	00-01	01-02	02-03	03-04	TOTAL
ABBEY Derek	1														1
BAKER Steve											1(1p)				1(1p)
BARRATT Roger	2														2
BASS David										1					1
BELL Charlie				2											2
BENNYWORTH Ian							4								4
BETTS Simon										6(2p)	4(3p)				10(5p)
BLUNT Jason												6	2		8
BOWMAN Dave	1	2	9	2	6	11	5								**36**
BOYLAN Tony	3														3
BRASSART Olivier													1		1
BRODIE Steve										13	10	4			27
BROLLY Mick							1								1
BROWN Steve			1												1
BURKE Marshall					12(1p)	5									17(1p)
BURNS David			1												1
BURT Jamie											2	1			3
CAMMACK Steve							1								1
CAMPBELL Neil													4		4
COHEN Gary													2		2
CONNELL Darren												2			2
COOK Mitch			2	12(6p)	8		13(4p)								35(10p)
COOPER Lee							1								1
COTTAM John				4	1										5
CRYAN Colin														1	1
DAWSON Dick				13	2										15
DAWSON Richard						4	3								7

Colin Williams.

Andy Woods.

1999-2000 Squad.

2001-2002 Squad.

Back Row, left to right; Mitch Cook, Danny Brunton, John Keegan, Paul Ellender, Romain Faure, Paul Newton, Andy Woods, Darryn Stamp, Shaun Rennison, Paul Atkinson, David Pounder and Mick Tarney.

Front Row: Steve Brodie, Adam Jewell, Gareth Stoker, Ray McHale, Neil Thompson, Ian Kerr, James Burt, Denny Ingram and Jason Blunt.

SHREWSBURY TOWN

RELEGATED FROM: The Football League 2002-03
PROMOTED TO (via the play-offs): The Football League Division 2, 2003-04
2004-2005 SEASON: The Football League Division 2

Back row, left to right: Darren Tinson, Jamie Tolley, Darren Moss, Mark Cartwright, Colin Cramb, Ian Dunbavin, Steve Watts, Sam Aiston and Martin O'Connor. Middle Row: Dave Timmons (GK Coach), Chic Bates (Coach), Chris Packer, Dave Edwards, Jake Sedgemoor, Danny March, Neville Thompson, Karl Murray, Steve Jagielka, Alan Rivers (Kit Manager) and Rachael Greenley (Physio). Front Row: Ross Stephens, Dave Ridler, Leon Drysdale, Luke Rodgers, Jimmy Quinn (Mnager), Dave Cook (Asst Manager), Ryan Lowe, Gregor Rioch and Glenn Tolley

SEASON 2003-04

HIGHEST ATTENDANCE
6738 v Telford Utd. 9.12.03

LOWEST ATTENDANCE
2869 v Gravesend & N. 20.4.04

SEASON GOALSCORER
Luke Rodgers 13 (1p)

SEASON APPEARANCES
Darren Tinson 38+1

HOME							AWAY							
P	W	D	L	F	A	Pts	P	W	D	L	F	A	Pts	Position
21	13	6	2	38	14	45	21	7	8	6	29	28	29	3

APPEARANCES

	03-04
AISTON Sam	30+2
BANIM Jody	7+9
BELL Lee	1+2
CHALLIS TREVOR	7+1
CRAMB Colin	24+10
DARBY Duane	20+4
DRYSDALE Leon	1
DUNBAVIN Ian	3
EDWARDS David	7+9
FITZPATRICK Ian	3+4
HART Joe	2
HOWIE Scott	37+1
JAGIELKA Steve	8+3

APPEARANCES cont.

	03-04
LAWRENCE Lee	6+1
LOWE Ryan	20+14
MOSS Darren	37+1
MURRAY Karl	4+2
O'CONNOR Martyn	35+1
POTTER Graham	4+1
QUINN Jimmy	8+8
RIDLER David	39
RIOCH Greg	18+2
RODGERS Luke	26+8
SEDGEMORE Jake	27+8
STEPHENS Ross	0+1
STREET Kevin	20+8
TINSON Darren	38+1
TOLLEY Glenn	0+1
TOLLEY Jamie	26+1
WATTS Steve	4+4

GOALSCORERS

	03-04
BANIM Jody	2
CRAMB Colin	12(1p)
DARBY Duane	10
JAGIELKA Steve	1
LAWRENCE Lee	2
LOWE Ryan	9
O'CONNOR Martyn	2
QUINN Jimmy	4
RIDLER David	2
RODGERS Luke	13(1p)
SEDGEMORE Jake	2(1p)
STREET Kevin	2
TINSON Darren	1
TOLLEY Jamie	3
WATTS Steve	1

SHREWSBURY TOWN

	Accrington Stanley		Aldershot Town		Barnet		Burton Albion		Chester City		Dagenham & Redbridge		Exeter City	
	H	A	H	A	H	A	H	A	H	A	H	A	H	A
02-03														
03-04	0-0	1-0	1-2	1-1	0-1	1-0	1-0	1-0	0-0	1-2	2-1	0-5	2-2	2-3

	Farnborough Town		Forest Green Rovers		Gravesend & N'fleet		Halifax Town		Hereford United		Leigh RMI		Margate	
	H	A	H	A	H	A	H	A	H	A	H	A	H	A
02-03														
03-04	3-0	3-1	2-0	1-1	1-1	3-0	2-0	0-0	4-1	1-2	3-1	2-2	1-1	2-0

	Morecambe		Northwich Victoria		Scarborough		Stevenage Borough		Tamworth		Telford United		Woking	
	H	A	H	A	H	A	H	A	H	A	H	A	H	A
02-03														
03-04	2-0	3-3	3-1	2-0	4-1	1-1	3-1	0-2	3-1	1-1	0-0	0-1	1-0	3-3

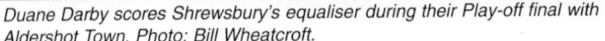

Duane Darby scores Shrewsbury's equaliser during their Play-off final with Aldershot Town. Photo: Bill Wheatcroft.

Ryan Lowe.

SLOUGH TOWN

PROMOTED FROM: The Isthmian League 1990, 1995
RELEGATED TO: The Isthmian League 1994   RESIGNED from Conference 1998
2004-2005 SEASON: The Isthmian League Premier Division

1992-93 Squad. Back row, left to right: Alan Pluckrose, Carlton Fairweather, Steve Scott, Trevor Bunting, Paul McKinnon, Ian Hazel, Mark Fiore and Darren Anderson. Front row: Brian Lee, George Friel, Les Briley, Steve Whitby, David Greene, Mark Quamina and Andy Sayer.

Photo: Dave West

SEASONS
7

TOTAL POINTS
208 + 155 = 363

HIGHEST POSITION
5 (92/93)

LOWEST POSITION
21 (93/94)

HIGHEST ATTENDANCE
4500 Wycombe (13-4-93)

LOWEST ATTENDANCE
385 Welling (10-9-98)

SEASON GOALSCORER
Mark West 21(4p) (95/96)

CAREER GOALSCORER
Mark West 35(4p)

CAREER APPEARANCES
Trevor Bunting 146

	HOME							AWAY							
	P	W	D	L	F	A	Pts	P	W	D	L	F	A	Pts	Position
90-91	21	9	4	8	31	29	31	21	4	2	15	20	51	14	19
91-92	21	7	3	11	26	39	24	21	6	3	12	30	43	21	20
92-93	21	12	3	6	39	28	39	21	6	8	7	21	27	26	5
93-94	21	8	8	5	30	24	32	21	3	6	12	14	34	15	21
94-95															
95-96	21	4	6	11	35	44	18	21	9	2	10	28	32	29	17
96-97	21	7	7	7	42	32	28	21	5	7	9	20	33	22	16
97-98	21	10	6	5	34	21	36	21	8	4	9	24	28	28	8
Total	147	57	37	53	237	217	208	147	41	32	74	157	248	155	

Action from Slough's 0-1 defeat by Gateshead in the 1990-91 season.

Steve Thompson scores to give Slough a 2-1 league victory over Stafford Rangers during the 1990-91 season.

Trevor Bunting collects whilst Mark Foran looks on.

SLOUGH TOWN

	Altrincham		Barnet		Barrow		Bath City		Boston United		Bromsgrove Rovers		Cheltenham Town		Colchester United		Dagenham & Redridge		Dover Athletic	
	H	A	H	A	H	A	H	A	H	A	H	A	H	A	H	A	H	A	H	A
90-91	3-3	0-3	1-3	1-6	3-0	1-2	2-0	0-4	2-0	1-0			0-3	0-2	0-2	1-2				
91-92	2-3	1-3			1-0	4-3	2-2	1-2	3-1	1-3			1-3	0-1	2-4	0-4	4-0	0-4		
92-93	1-4	1-1					1-1	1-0	3-0	0-0	1-3	1-0					2-0	4-4		
93-94	0-2	0-2					0-0	0-3			1-1	1-0					3-1	0-1	1-0	0-0
94-95																				
95-96	1-2	1-0					1-1	1-3			2-3	0-0					5-0	3-1	3-2	1-0
96-97	0-1	1-0					5-2	0-0			2-0	1-4							2-2	0-0
97-98													1-2	1-1					2-4	1-2

	Farnborough Town		Fisher Athletic		Gateshead		Halifax Town		Hayes		Hednesford Town		Hereford United		Kettering Town		Kidderminster H.	
	H	A	H	A	H	A	H	A	H	A	H	A	H	A	H	A	H	A
90-91			1-0	1-1	1-1	0-1									0-3	0-0	0-0	2-1
91-92	0-5	1-2			2-0	1-2									0-2	3-2	3-1	3-3
92-93	3-1	0-1			1-0	0-1									3-0	0-5	3-1	1-1
93-94					2-1	0-0	2-0	0-1							0-2	0-2	1-5	0-0
94-95																		
95-96	1-1	1-0			1-2	1-2			2-3	2-1	0-2	1-3			1-2	0-2	5-4	3-4
96-97	1-1	1-2			0-1	1-2	1-0	1-4	1-3	0-5	2-2	1-2			1-1	0-0	0-2	2-1
97-98	1-0	0-1			1-0	1-5	1-1	0-1	0-0	1-0	2-0	1-2	3-0	1-1	1-1	3-3	2-0	1-0

	Leek Town		Macclesfield Town		Merthyr Tydfil		Morecambe		Northwich Victoria		Runcorn		Rushden & Diamonds		Southport		Stafford Rangers	
	H	A	H	A	H	A	H	A	H	A	H	A	H	A	H	A	H	A
90-91			0-1	2-1	1-2	0-3			2-4	0-1	2-1	1-3					2-1	4-3
91-92			0-3	1-0	0-0	2-1			0-1	0-3	1-0	0-1					2-2	1-1
92-93			2-1	2-1	2-1	1-1			0-4	1-0	1-1	3-0					2-1	0-1
93-94			1-1	2-2	3-2	1-5			2-2	1-1	3-0	2-3			0-0	0-1	3-0	0-0
94-95																		
95-96			2-2	1-1			1-1	2-1	1-1	3-0	0-1	3-4			2-5	0-2		
96-97			0-0	0-2			1-2	0-0	3-4	1-0			5-0	2-2	1-1	1-0		
97-98	1-1	2-0					3-3	1-2	3-0	1-0			1-2	1-0	1-0	2-1		

Trevor How heads the first of four at Staines watched by Tommy Langley.

Gary Abbott. Photo: Andrew Chitty.

George Friel. Photo: E. Joy Griffiths.

SLOUGH TOWN

	Stalybridge Celtic H	A	Stevenage Borough H	A	Sutton United H	A	Telford United H	A	Welling United H	A	Witton Albion H	A	Woking H	A	Wycombe Wanderers H	A	Yeovil Town H	A
90-91					1-2	2-5	2-0	1-2	3-0	0-2					3-3	1-2	2-0	2-7
91-92							0-3	2-2	0-3	2-0	2-1	1-2			0-1	0-3	1-4	0-1
92-93	2-3	0-0					2-0	1-1	4-2	1-2	2-3	1-1	0-1	2-1	1-1	0-1	3-0	1-5
93-94	2-3	1-0					0-0	1-4	1-1	2-6	0-1	0-1	0-0	1-2			5-2	2-0
94-95																		
95-96	2-1	1-0	2-6	1-3			1-2	0-2	0-0	3-0			2-3	0-3				
96-97	4-1	2-2	1-6	2-2			6-0	2-0	3-3	2-3			3-0	0-2				
97-98	4-0	1-0	3-1	2-4			1-0	1-0	1-2	1-1			1-3	1-2			1-1	1-2

	Home						Away					
	P	W	D	L	F	A	P	W	D	L	F	A
ALTRINCHAM	6	0	1	5	7	15	6	3	1	2	10	9
BARNET	1	0	0	1	1	3	1	0	0	1	1	6
BARROW	2	2	0	0	4	0	2	1	0	1	5	5
BATH C	6	2	4	0	11	6	6	1	1	4	3	12
BOSTON U	3	3	0	0	8	1	3	1	1	1	2	3
BROMSGROVE R	4	1	1	2	6	7	4	2	1	1	3	4
CHELTENHAM T	3	0	0	3	2	8	3	0	1	2	1	4
COLCHESTER U	2	0	0	2	2	6	2	0	0	2	1	6
DAGENHAM & R	4	4	0	0	14	1	4	1	1	2	7	10
DOVER A	4	2	1	1	8	8	4	1	2	1	2	2
FARNBOROUGH T	5	2	2	1	6	8	5	1	0	4	3	6
FISHER A	1	1	0	0	1	0	1	0	1	0	1	1
GATESHEAD	7	4	1	2	8	5	7	0	1	6	4	13
HALIFAX T	4	2	1	1	6	4	4	1	0	3	3	7
HAYES	2	0	1	1	1	3	2	1	0	1	1	5
HEDNESFORD T	3	1	1	1	4	4	3	0	0	3	1	7
HEREFORD U	1	1	0	0	3	0	1	0	1	0	1	1
KETTERING T	7	1	2	4	6	11	7	1	3	3	6	14
KIDDERMINSTER H	7	4	1	2	14	13	7	3	3	1	12	10
LEEK T	1	0	1	0	1	1	1	1	0	0	2	0
MACCLESFIELD T	6	1	3	2	5	8	6	3	2	1	8	7
MERTHYR T	4	2	1	1	6	5	4	1	1	2	4	10
MORECAMBE	3	0	2	1	5	6	3	1	1	1	3	3
NORTHWICH V	7	1	2	4	11	16	7	4	1	2	7	5
RUNCORN	5	3	1	1	7	3	5	1	0	4	9	11
RUSHDEN & D	2	1	0	1	6	2	2	1	1	0	3	2
SOUTHPORT	4	1	2	1	4	6	4	2	0	2	3	4
STAFFORD R	4	3	1	0	9	4	4	1	2	1	5	5
STALYBRIDGE C	5	3	0	2	14	8	5	3	2	0	5	2
STEVENAGE B	3	1	0	2	6	13	3	0	1	2	5	9
SUTTON U	1	0	0	1	1	2	1	0	0	1	2	5
TELFORD U	7	4	1	2	12	5	7	2	2	3	8	11
WELLING U	7	2	3	2	12	11	7	2	1	4	11	14
WITTON A	3	1	0	2	4	5	3	0	1	2	2	4
WOKING	5	1	1	3	6	7	5	1	0	4	4	10
WYCOMBE W	3	0	2	1	4	5	3	0	0	3	1	6
YEOVIL T	5	3	1	1	12	7	5	1	0	4	6	15
TOTALS	147	57	37	53	237	217	147	41	32	74	157	248

Sean Latiff foils Andy Hunt.

Paul McKinnon heads for goal with Mick Punam watching on.

Mark Quamina holds off Altrincham's Ian Thompson.

SLOUGH TOWN   APPEARANCES

	90/91	91/92	92/93	93/94	94/95	95/96	96/97	97/98	TOTAL
ABBOTT Gary							37+1	29+7	66+8
ADAMS Mark	3+2								3+2
ALSFORD Julian			5						5
ANDERSON Darren	34+1	36+1	37						107+2
ANGUS Terry								33	33
BAILEY Danny								40	40
BARCLAY Dominic							1+2		1+2
BARON Trevor						26			26
BASHIR Naseem	7+7								7+7
BATEMAN Steve						17+4	37		54+4
BLACKFORD Gary							34+1		34+1
BLACKMAN Garfield						21+12			21+12
BLUNDEN Mark						0+3			0+3
BOLT Danny							18+8	39+1	57+9
BOOK Steve			2						2
BOOKER Trevor		4							4
BRAZIL Gary							12	36+2	48+2
BRESSINGTON Graham						6			6
BRILEY Les			37	23					60
BROWN Jimmy		0+1							0+1
BROWN Stuart	0+2								0+2
BROWNE Corey								26+6	26+6
BUNTING Trevor	32	27	40	40		7			146
BURNS Phil		3							3
BUSHAY Ansil						26+5			26+5
CASH Stuart							4		4
CATLIN Neil						35+3			35+3
CLARKE Dwain						1			1
CLEMENT Andy						27	20+2		47+2
CONNOR Brian						1+1			1+1
DELL Tony	28+1	4+1							32+2
DENNIS Tony	2								2
DODD Gary	3								3
DONNELLAN Gary	20	27							47
DOWSON Alan				39					39
DUFFY Gary								0+2	0+2
EATON Grant							2+3		2+3
EDWARDS Russell			10	4					14
EMBERSON Carl			2						2
FAIRWEATHER Carlton			6+1						6+1
FIELDER Colin		38	0+1						38+1
FIORE Mark			26+1	40		38+2	24+9	8+3	136+15
FORAN Mark			23						23
FRIEL George			14+16						14+16
GRAY Andy						5+3			5+3
GREENE David			0+2						0+2

SLOUGH TOWN — LEADING APPEARANCES

	90/91	91/92	92/93	93/94	94/95	95/96	96/97	97/98	TOTAL
Mark FIORE			26+1	40		38+2	24+9	8+3	136+15 (151)
Trevor BUNTING	32	27	40	40		7			146 (146)
Neil STANLEY	29+2	18+10	21+6	23+8					91+26 (117)
Darren ANDERSON	34+1	36+1	37						107+2 (109)

SLOUGH TOWN — APPEARANCES

	90/91	91/92	92/93	93/94	94/95	95/96	96/97	97/98	TOTAL
HANCOCK Darren			0+1	25+1					25+2
HARDYMAN Paul							10	28+1	38+1
HARVEY Lee						28+3			28+3
HAZEL Ian			37+2	32+3					69+5
HEMSLEY Stuart		11+1	8						19+1
HERCULES Cliff						16	30	37	83
HICKEY Steve		2+6							2+6
HILL Mark	27	31+1							58+1
HONOR Christian						10+1			10+1
HORNER Duncan						0+1			0+1
HOW Trevor	33+1								33+1
HOWELL Dave	3								3
HUNT John	4+3								4+3
IMBER Noel							5		5
JOHNSON Robbie	3								3
JOSEPH Francis		4+2							4+2
KNIGHT Tony	41	22							63
LANGLEY Tommy	23+4								23+4
LATIFF Sean	10								10
LAY David						4+1			4+1
LEE Brian			8	35+1		31+5			74+6
LOMAS Andy						1			1
LYNCH Tony		1							1
MALLINSON Mark	28+2	29+1							57+3
MANNING Paul				26+1					26+1
MARGERRISON Lee				3+1					3+1
MAXWELL Paul			3						3
McDERMOTT Brian						2+4			2+4
McGINNIS Gary							30+2	23+1	53+3
McKAY Paul				3+1					3+1
McKINNON Paul		35	36+4						71+4
McMINN Ted							9		9
McPHERSON Gavin				1+1					1+1
McVIE Graeme						1			1
MERNAGH Gavin							1+6		1+6
MICKLEWHITE Gary							15		15

SLOUGH TOWN APPEARANCES

	90/91	91/92	92/93	93/94	94/95	95/96	96/97	97/98	TOTAL
MILES Ben						15	16	11	42
MOUSSADIK Chuck		3				3			6
MURPHY Frank	4								4
MURPHY Michael							6+4		6+4
NOLAN Tony						4	2	3	9
O'CONNOR Eamonn		14+6							14+6
OWUSU Lloyd							6+9	16+11	22+20
PARIS Alan						21			21
PARIS Robert							0+2		0+2
PETERS Robbie				14					14
PICKETT Ross						8+19			8+19
PLUCKROSE Alan		36	42						78
PRATT Vernon	7+2								7+2
PREDDIE Delroy						16			16
PUTNAM Michael		6+2							6+2
PYE Mark						21+1	7+4		28+5
QUAMINA Mark			21+2	35+1					56+3
RAKE Barry	10+11	1				13+8			24+19
RANDALL Lee								10+5	10+5
ROWE Kevin	5								5
SANSOM Kenny						6			6
SAYER Andy			42	31+3					73+3
SCOTT Morrys				34+4					34+4
SCOTT Steve		11+4	12+6	26+5					49+15
SIMPSON Derek							10+4	9+3	19+7
SISSONS Jon	20+3								20+3
SITTON John		4							4
SMART Garry						8	39	42	89
SMITH Brett				2+4					2+4
SMITH Robert						2+3	22+1	4+4	28+8
STACEY Phil	28	33							61
STANLEY Neil	29+2	18+10	21+6	23+8					91+26
STAPLETON Simon							22+2		22+2
STONE Martin						1+1			1+1
STOWELL Matthew								23+3	23+3
THOMPSON Steve	38	23							61
TURKINGTON Mark	11+2	10							21+2
WALKER Lee				1+6					1+6
WALTON Byron							6+7		6+7
WATKISS Richard		9							9
WEST Mark						41	16+1	14+10	71+11
WHITBY Steve		20+3	37	14					71+3
WILKERSON Paul							21	31	52
WILSON Junior	9								9
WRIGHT Dale				4					4

Jon Sissons scores past Wycombe's John Granville.

Paul Wilkerson.

Neal Stanley scores against Runcorn.

SLOUGH TOWN GOALSCORERS

	90/91	91/92	92/93	93/94	94/95	95/96	96/97	97/98	TOTAL
ABBOTT Gary							18	9	27
ALSFORD Julian				1					1
ANDERSON Darren	1	8(4p)	2						11(4p)
ANGUS Terry								1	1
BARCLAY Dominic							1		1
BARON Trevor						4			4
BASHIR Naseem	2								2
BATEMAN Steve						1	2		3
BLACKFORD Gary							3		3
BLACKMAN Garfield						6			6
BOLT Danny							3(2p)	11(2p)	14(4p)
BRAZIL Gary							3	4	7
BRILEY Les			2						2
BROWNE Corey							4(1p)		4(1p)
BUSHAY Ansil						8			8
CATLIN Neil						5			5
CLEMENT Andy						2	1		3
DENNIS Tony	1								1
DONNELLAN Gary	3	4							7
FAIRWEATHER Carlton			1						1
FIORE Mark			7	3		2	2	2	16
FORAN Mark			2						2
FRIEL George			3						3
HANCOCK Darren				1					1
HARDYMAN Paul							1	2	3
HARVEY Lee						1			1
HAZEL Ian		4(1p)	5(1p)						9(2p)
HERCULES Cliff						7	5	7	19
HILL Mark	1								1
HOW Trevor	3								3
JOSEPH Francis		2							2
KNIGHT Terry	1								1
LANGLEY Tommy	4								4
LAY David						2(1p)			2(1p)
LEE Brian				1					1
MALLINSON Mark	1	1							2
MANNING Paul				1					1
McKINNON Paul		15	13						28
MERNAGH Gavin							1		1
MURPHY Frank	1								1
MURPHY Michael							1		1
O'CONNOR Eamonn		3(2p)							3(2p)
OWUSU Lloyd							5	9	14
PETERS Robbie				3					3
PICKETT Ross						2			2
PLUCKROSE Alan		6	3						9

591

SLOUGH TOWN   GOALSCORERS

	90/91	91/92	92/93	93/94	94/95	95/96	96/97	97/98	TOTAL
PRATT Vernon	1								1
RAKE Barry	1								1
RANDALL Lee								2	2
SAYER Andy			19	7					26
SCOTT Morrys				14					14
SCOTT Steve		2	2	1					5
SISSONS Jon	8								8
SMART Garry						1	1	1	3
SMITH Robert							1		1
STACEY Phil		1							1
STANLEY Neil	7	2	1	4					14
STAPLETON Simon							3		3
STOWELL Matthew								1	1
THOMPSON Steve	14(1p)	10							24(1p)
TURKINGTON Mark	1	1							2
WALKER Lee				1					1
WALTON Byron							1		1
WEST Mark						21(4p)	9	5	**35(4p)**
WILSON Junior	1								1

Andy Sayer evades this challenge.

Mark West.

Photo: Dave West.

SOUTHPORT

PROMOTED FROM: Northern Premier League 1993
RELEGATED TO: Northern Premier League 2003
2004-2005 SEASON: Conference North

Southport 1995-96 - **Back Row** (L-R): Max Thompson, Peter Davenport, David Gamble, Derek Goulding, John McKenna, Peter Guarsdale, Ian Blackstone, Andy Whittaker, Leroy Dove, Steve Joel (Asst. Man.). **Front Row:** Martin Clark, Jimmy Blackhurst, Steve Haw, Roy Morris (Secretary), Charlie Clapham (Chairman), Billy Ayre (Manager), Paul Lodge, Gary Thomas, Bryan Griffiths. **Photo:** Gordon Whiting

SEASONS
10

TOTAL POINTS
579

HIGHEST POSITION
3rd (94/95)

LOWEST POSITION
21st (02/03)

HIGHEST ATTENDANCE
2447 v Chester (30.11.02)

LOWEST ATTENDANCE
560 v Woking (1.5.97)

SEASON GOALSCORER
Andy Whittaker 19 (96/97)

CAREER GOALSCORER
David Gamble 49 (16p)

CAREER APPEARANCES
Martin Clark 242+8

	HOME						AWAY						
	P	W	D	L	F	A	Pts	P	W	D	L	F	A	Pts	Position
93-94	21	10	7	4	26	21	37	21	8	5	8	31	30	29	4
94-95	21	13	4	4	46	21	43	21	8	5	8	22	29	29	3
95-96	21	10	7	4	42	25	37	21	8	5	8	35	39	29	6
96-97	21	8	5	8	27	28	29	21	7	5	9	24	33	26	11
97-98	21	9	5	7	32	26	32	21	4	6	11	24	32	18	16
98-99	21	6	9	6	29	28	27	21	4	6	11	18	31	18	18
99-00	21	10	5	6	31	21	35	21	5	8	8	24	35	23	9
00-01	21	9	5	7	33	24	32	21	11	4	6	25	22	37	4
01-02	21	9	6	6	40	26	33	21	4	8	9	13	23	20	15
02-03	21	6	8	7	31	32	26	21	5	4	12	23	37	19	21
Total	210	90	61	59	337	252	331	210	64	56	90	239	311	248	

SOUTHPORT

	Altrincham		Barnet		Barrow		Bath City		Boston United		Bromsgrove Rovers		Burton Albion		Cheltenham Town		Chester City	
	H	A	H	A	H	A	H	A	H	A	H	A	H	A	H	A	H	A
93-94	3-1	2-1					1-1	1-2			1-2	2-2						
94-95	1-4	0-0					3-1	2-1					2-1	1-1				
95-96	1-2	1-1					2-1	0-4					1-2	1-4				
96-97	1-3	0-1					3-1	2-0					0-0	1-0				
97-98															1-2	0-2		
98-99					0-4	0-0									0-2	0-3		
99-00	2-0	0-3																
00-01									3-1	0-1							1-0	1-0
01-02			0-1	0-0					2-3	0-0							3-2	2-0
02-03			2-1	1-3									2-2	0-1			1-3	0-2

	Dagenham & Redbridge		Doncaster Rovers		Dover Athletic		Farnborough Town		Forest Green Rovers		Gateshead		Gravesend & N'fleet		Halifax Town		Hayes	
	H	A	H	A	H	A	H	A	H	A	H	A	H	A	H	A	H	A
93-94	0-0	3-3			3-2	2-0					1-1	3-1			2-2	2-2		
94-95	1-1	1-5			2-2	2-1	0-1	4-1			5-0	1-0			4-0	0-2		
95-96	2-1	2-1			0-0	1-0	7-1	0-1			1-0	2-2			0-0	2-2		
96-97					0-1	1-0	0-3	3-3			1-1	2-2			2-1	0-2	0-2	1-1
97-98					0-1	1-3	3-1	2-3			3-1	2-0			0-0	3-4	0-2	0-2
98-99			3-2	1-0	3-0	1-2	2-2	1-1	1-1	0-1							1-2	0-3
99-00			1-0	1-1	1-2	1-1			2-0	0-1					4-1	2-0		
00-01	0-1	1-0	1-0	0-1	2-1	1-0			1-1	0-2					2-0	0-1		
01-02	2-2	1-1	1-0	0-1	0-2	1-0	2-5	1-0	5-1	1-2							0-1	2-3
02-03	2-3	3-0	0-4	0-0			0-0	1-2	2-2	2-0			1-1	3-1	2-0	4-3		

	Hednesford Town		Hereford United		Kettering Town		Kidderminster H.		Kingstonian		Leek Town		Leigh RMI		Macclesfield Town		Margate	
	H	A	H	A	H	A	H	A	H	A	H	A	H	A	H	A	H	A
93-94					0-1	0-2	1-1	0-2							1-0	1-0		
94-95					1-1	0-1	4-1	1-0							2-3	0-3		
95-96	2-2	1-2			6-1	1-1	0-2	3-2							2-1	1-3		
96-97	1-2	1-0			2-2	1-0	1-0	0-3							1-5	2-3		
97-98	4-1	1-2	0-0	1-1	2-1	1-2	1-2	1-1			2-2	1-0						
98-99	1-1	1-3	0-0	2-2	0-1	0-1	1-1	1-2	1-1	2-0	3-1	0-0						
99-00	2-0	2-1	0-1	1-2	0-1	3-0	0-1	0-5	0-0	2-4								
00-01	2-0	1-0	1-1	0-0	2-3	1-1			2-2	1-3			1-2	2-2				
01-02			1-1	0-0									5-0	2-1			1-2	0-2
02-03			1-2	2-0	0-0	0-1							4-2	1-1			0-2	0-1

	Merthyr Tydfil		Morecambe		Northwich Victoria		Nuneaton Borough		Runcorn		Rushden & Diamonds		Scarborough		Slough Town		Stafford Rangers	
	H	A	H	A	H	A	H	A	H	A	H	A	H	A	H	A	H	A
93-94	3-2	2-2			0-0	1-2			1-0	0-3					1-0	0-0	0-2	2-0
94-95	3-1	2-1			0-2	1-2			5-0	1-2							3-0	1-1
95-96			1-1	3-4	2-2	2-1			1-1	1-1					2-0	5-2		
96-97			3-1	1-2	0-0	1-5							2-1	0-3	0-1	1-1		
97-98			1-1	0-2	0-2	0-0							3-2	0-1	1-2	0-1		
98-99			1-0	1-1	2-2	2-1							0-1	1-3				
99-00			1-1	3-3	0-1	1-0	2-0	2-0			2-1	2-4	2-2	0-3				
00-01			1-2	3-1	1-1	2-0	1-2	2-1			1-3	0-4	3-1	1-1				
01-02			1-1	2-2	5-1	1-3	1-1	0-3					1-0	0-2				
02-03			2-3	0-3	1-1	1-2	1-0	2-3					1-1	2-2				

	Stalybridge Celtic		Stevenage Borough		Sutton United		Telford United		Welling United		Witton Albion		Woking		Yeovil Town	
	H	A	H	A	H	A	H	A	H	A	H	A	H	A	H	A
93-94	0-2	1-3					1-0	3-1	2-1	2-0	2-1	2-0	2-1	0-1	1-1	2-3
94-95	3-1	1-1	2-1	2-1			2-1	0-0	1-0	1-3			2-0	0-3	0-0	1-0
95-96	5-3	4-1	0-1	3-1			3-2	1-2	2-0	1-0			2-2	0-4		
96-97	3-0	2-2	0-0	1-2			0-1	0-1	3-2	3-2			4-1	1-0		
97-98	4-2	3-1	1-0	0-1			1-2	2-2	3-1	5-3			0-0	1-1	2-1	0-0
98-99			1-1	0-0			2-1	0-1	5-2	1-2			0-0	3-2	2-3	1-3
99-00			2-1	1-1	1-1	1-1	1-3	0-0	3-2	1-4			4-1	0-0	1-1	1-1
00-01			2-2	3-1			3-0	3-2					0-1	2-1	3-0	1-0
01-02	3-1	0-0	0-0	1-2			0-0	1-1					2-0	0-2	3-0	0-0
02-03			3-2	0-3			1-1	0-2					5-1	1-1	0-1	0-6

Paul Comstive's free kick gave Southport their first ever Conference goal at Haig Avenue.   **Photo:** Rob Ruddock

Below:
'Keeper Steve Dickinson & Martin Clark (7) combine to deny Rushden striker Jean-Michel Sigere.
Photo: Peter Barnes

Above:
Leroy Dove
Photo: V J Robertson

David Gamble scores against Merthyr Tydfil.

Photo: Paul Maher

| | Home | | | | | | Away | | | | | |
	P	W	D	L	F	A	P	W	D	L	F	A
ALTRINCHAM	5	2	0	3	8	10	5	1	2	2	3	6
BARNET	2	1	0	1	2	2	2	0	1	1	1	3
BARROW	1	0	0	1	0	4	1	0	1	0	0	0
BATH C	4	3	1	0	9	4	4	2	0	2	5	7
BOSTON U	2	1	0	1	5	4	2	0	1	1	0	1
BROMSGROVE R	4	1	1	2	4	5	4	1	2	1	5	7
BURTON A	1	0	1	0	2	2	1	0	0	1	0	1
CHELTENHAM T	2	0	0	2	1	4	2	0	0	2	0	5
CHESTER CITY	3	2	0	1	5	5	3	2	0	1	3	2
DAGENHAM & R	6	1	3	2	7	8	6	3	2	1	11	10
DONCASTER R	5	4	0	1	6	6	5	1	2	2	2	3
DOVER A	9	3	2	4	11	11	9	6	1	2	11	7
FARNBOROUGH T	7	2	2	3	14	13	7	2	2	3	12	11
FOREST GREEN R	5	2	3	0	11	6	5	1	0	4	3	6
GATESHEAD	5	3	2	0	11	3	5	3	2	0	10	5
GRAVESEND & N	1	0	1	0	1	1	1	1	0	0	3	1
HALIFAX T	6	3	3	0	10	3	6	1	2	3	11	15
HAYES	6	2	0	4	9	10	6	1	1	4	3	8
HEDNESFORD T	6	3	2	1	12	6	6	3	0	3	7	8
HEREFORD U	6	0	4	2	3	5	6	1	4	1	6	5
KETTERING T	9	2	3	4	13	11	9	2	2	5	7	9
KIDDERMINSTER H	7	2	2	3	8	8	7	2	1	4	6	15
KINGSTONIAN	3	0	3	0	3	3	3	1	0	2	5	7
LEEK T	2	1	1	0	5	3	2	1	1	0	1	0
LEIGH RMI	3	2	0	1	10	4	3	1	2	0	5	4
MACCLESFIELD T	4	2	0	2	6	9	4	1	0	3	4	9
MARGATE	2	0	0	2	1	4	2	0	0	2	0	3
MERTHYR T	2	2	0	0	6	3	2	1	1	0	4	3
MORECAMBE	8	2	4	2	11	10	8	1	3	4	13	18
NORTHWICH V	10	1	6	3	11	12	10	4	1	5	12	16
NUNEATON B	4	2	1	1	5	3	4	2	0	2	6	7
RUNCORN	3	2	1	0	7	1	3	0	1	2	2	6
RUSHDEN & D	5	3	0	2	8	8	5	0	0	5	3	15
SCARBOROUGH	4	2	2	0	7	4	4	0	2	2	3	8
SLOUGH T	4	2	0	2	4	3	4	1	2	1	6	4
STAFFORD R	2	1	0	1	3	2	2	1	1	0	3	1
STALYBRIDGE C	6	5	0	1	18	9	6	2	3	1	11	8
STEVENAGE B	9	4	4	1	11	8	9	3	2	4	11	12
SUTTON U	1	0	1	0	1	1	1	0	1	0	1	1
TELFORD U	10	5	2	3	14	11	10	2	4	4	10	12
WELLING U	7	7	0	0	19	8	7	4	0	3	14	14
WITTON A	1	1	0	0	2	1	1	1	0	0	2	0
WOKING	10	6	3	1	21	7	10	3	3	4	8	15
YEOVIL T	8	3	3	2	12	7	8	2	3	3	6	13
TOTALS	210	90	61	59	337	252	210	64	56	90	239	311

Left:
(L - R)
Kevin Formby,
Brian Butler,
Andy Whittaker
&
Ged Kielty

Photo:
Southport Visitor

Below:
Steve Whitehall
scores against
Woking.

Photo:
Bill Wheatcroft

SOUTHPORT — LEADING APPEARANCES

	93-94	94-95	95-96	96-97	97-98	98-99	99-00	00-01	01-02	02-03	TOTAL
MartinCLARK		37	29+1	34			35+2	34+2	41	32+3	242+8
David GAMBLE	36+3	31+6	31+6	33+8	27+7	31+2					189+32
Steve DICKINSON							42	42	42	31	157
Andy FARLEY	5+1		26+1	32+4	36	34+2					133+8
Leroy DOVE	34+1	36	39	13+4	7						129+5
Billy STEWART				42	37	40					119
Phil BOLLAND					23+3	26+2	35	33+1			117+6
Tim RYAN					36+1	38	39				113+1
Neil GRAYSTON							34+7	39+2	36		109+9
Scott GUYETT						34	39	36			109
Lee ELAM						26+1	31+10	14+13	37+2		108+26
Derek GOULDING	28+1	39	39								106+1

SOUTHPORT — APPEARANCES

	93-94	94-95	95-96	96-97	97-98	98-99	99-00	00-01	01-02	02-03	TOTAL
ANDERSON Lee				14+3							14+3
APPLETON Steve	1										1
ARNOLD Ian						5	40+1	33+3			78+4
ASHCROFT Lee									11		11
BAGNALL John				5	2						7
BAURESS Gary								9+3	1+4		10+7
BLACKHURST Jimmy	0+2	16+11	3								19+13
BLACKSTONE Ian			8+6								8+6
BLAKEMAN Chris			1+1	8+4	0+1						9+6
BLISSETT Luther	5										5
BLYTHE Tony					1+1						1+1
BOLLAND Phil					23+3	26+2	35	33+1			117+6
BORWICK Chris				0+1							0+1
BRADSHAW Mark								2			2
BRENNAN Mark	4+1										4+1
BURKE Jordan								0+2			0+2
BUTLER Brian				31	35	22+2					88+2
CARDEN Adam									0+1		0+1
CARROLL Dave				8+2							8+2
CAVANAGH Andy			1+9								1+9
CHADWICK Dave	0+1										0+1
CHALLENDER Greg		5+1	2+1								7+2
CHARNOCK Kieran										2+1	2+1
CLARK Martin		37	29+1	34			35+2	34+2	41	32+3	242+8
CLARKE Paul					1+2						1+2
COCHRAN Stuart			17+2								17+2
COMSTIVE Paul	28+4	24+5									52+9
CONNELLY James										1+3	1+3
CONNOLLY James							0+1				0+1
COOPER Lee		0+1									0+1
COURTNEY Gerard						0+1	0+2				0+3

SOUTHPORT APPEARANCES

	93-94	94-95	95-96	96-97	97-98	98-99	99-00	00-01	01-02	02-03	TOTAL
CROASDALE Peter			8								8
CUNNINGHAM Harvey		27+6	9+2								36+8
DAVENPORT Peter			34+5	15+4							49+9
DAVIS Earl										8	8
DEARY John					13						13
DEVEREUX Robbie							3+4				3+4
DICKINSON Steve							42	42	42	31	157
DOBBIN Jim						3					3
DOVE Leroy	34+1	36	39	13+4	7						129+5
DUERDEN Ian			11								11
EASTWOOD Phil									5+8		5+8
EDWARDS Elfyn	10	5									15
EDWARDS Paul										4+1	4+1
ELAM Lee						26+1	31+10	14+13	37+2		108+26
ELLISON Kevin			2+2								2+2
ELLISON Lee							8+8				8+8
EYRE Stephen			2+1								2+1
FARLEY Andy	5+1		26+1	32+4	36	34+2					133+8
FORMBY Kevin					35	20+9	16+5				71+14
FULLER Dave	37+2	31	25+4								93+6
FURLONG Lee						17+5	9+20	13+11			39+36
FUTCHER Paul					37+1	12+2					49+3
GAMBLE David	36+3	31+6	31+6	33+8	27+7	31+2					189+32
GIBSON Neil										24+4	24+4
GOUCK Andy						34	30+1	26			80+1
GOULDING Derek	28+1	39	39								106+1
GRAVES Stuart						1+2					1+2
GRAYSTON Neil							34+7	39+2	36		109+9
GRIFFITHS Bryan			23+7	1+5							24+12
GUMMER Sean							0+1				0+1
GUYETT Scott						34	39	36			109
HALLIDAY Mick	5										5
HARVEY Jim	7										7
HAW Steve	39+1	30+5	19+10	7+6							95+22
HOGAN Barry										0+1	0+1
HORNBY Gary										2	2
HORNER Phil			11	38+1	22	28+3					99+4
HORNER Richard				17							17
HOWARD Stephen			1								1
HOWELL Dean									20+1	34+6	54+7
JONES Alex				17							17
JONES Barry									36+1	40	76+1
JONES Matthew								2			2
JONES Paul					11+10						11+10
JONES Steve									36+2	33+5	69+7
KELLY Mark			1+1								1+1
KENWORTHY Jon			2								2
KIELTY Ged					33+4						33+4
LALLY Tony						0+1					0+1

SOUTHPORT
APPEARANCES

	93-94	94-95	95-96	96-97	97-98	98-99	99-00	00-01	01-02	02-03	TOTAL
LAMB Tom										1+1	1+1
LANE Chris								18	35+1	36	89+1
LEADBETTER Kevin									0+5		0+5
LINIGHAN David								15+4			15+4
LLOYD-WILLIAMS Marc										15+3	15+3
LODGE Paul	25+1	38	36								99+1
LYONS Darren	13+2						0+1				13+3
MAAMRIA Noureddine								15+10			15+10
MACAULEY Carl								12+1	23+5		35+6
MARSH Mike						1		35			36
MAYERS Kenny				4							4
McAULEY Scott								1			1
McDONALD Alan	31+7	17+7									48+14
McDONALD Martin			19+2								19+2
McDONALD Rod				12							12
McGORRY Brian									7+5		7+5
McGUIRE Liam									12+1		12+1
McKENNA John		42	33								75
McNALLY John		1+2									1+2
McNIVEN David							8+4				8+4
MIKE Adie							9+6				9+6
MITCHELL Neil			8								8
MITCHELL Richard	6+4										6+4
MITTEN Paul				2	14+11						16+11
MOONEY Kevin	25										25
MOORE Michael					2+4						2+4
MOORE Neil										16	16
MOORE Paul	42										42
MORAN Steve				13+1	0+1						13+2
MORGAN Joe					2+2	1					3+2
MORGAN John				1+5							1+5
MORGAN Phil									0+1		0+1
MORLEY Dominic							32+3				32+3
MORRIS Steve					5+5						5+5
MULLEN Paul	3+3										3+3
MULVANEY Lee									0+3	8+4	8+7
MUTCH Andy						0+1					0+1
NEWMAN John						2+3					2+3
NOLAN Ian										8+1	8+1
OBONG Ben								2+3			2+3
OBONG Sam									2+1		2+1
O'BRIEN Mick								2+1			2+1
O'DONNELL Karl									0+1		0+1
O'REILLY Justin					10+1	12+1					22+2
OWEN Val									3		3
PARKE Simon								29+5	40+1		69+6
PELL Robert							6+3	0+3		7+4	13+10
PENMAN John		9+11									9+11
PEPPER Julian					0+4						0+4

Above: **Billy Stewart** Photo: Andrew Chitty
Below: **Steve Haw** Photo: V J Robertson

Andy Farley Photo: Peter Barnes
Brian Butler Photo: Peter Barnes

SOUTHPORT   APPEARANCES

	93-94	94-95	95-96	96-97	97-98	98-99	99-00	00-01	01-02	02-03	TOTAL
PICKFORD Steve										30+1	30+1
PILLING Andy	3+2										3+2
POWELL Frannie				0+1	0+1						0+2
PREECE Roger				9							9
PRINCE Neil										0+1	0+1
PRITCHARD Brian		7+1									7+1
QUINLAN Phil	10+14	0+1									10+15
QUINN Stuart						4+9					4+9
ROBERTSON John									21+2		21+2
ROGERS David				22+1							22+1
ROSS Brian					20+7	12+10					32+17
RYAN Tim					36+1	38	39				113+1
SCOTT Andy									3+3		3+3
SCOTT Andy										16+12	16+12
SHARRATT Chris				25+2							25+2
SIMMS Mark		11									11
SLOAN Martin		0+2									0+2
SOLEY Steve										18+2	18+2
SPEARRITT Tom										0+1	0+1
STEWART Billy				42	37	40					119
STUART Mark						9	35+1	19+4			63+5
SULLIVAN Tony									9+12	2+11	11+23
SYMONS Paul		1+2									1+2
TAKANO Kenny							2+2				2+2
TAYLOR Paul					0+1	2+1	0+1				2+3
TEALE Shaun								26+8	35+1		61+9
THOMAS Gary		24+5	7+3								31+8
THOMPSON Dave					28+9	25+15					53+24
THOMSON Peter										25+5	25+5
TODHUNTER Stuart	0+1										0+1
TRUNDLE Lee						20+1	0+5				20+6
TURNER Mike				5+3							5+3
UNDERWOOD Jeff								1			1
VICKERS Ian				1+7							1+7
WALMSLEY Chris	28+9										28+9
WARD Chris									3		3
WARD Derek		31	3+2								34+2
WELSBY Kevin										11	11
WHEATCROFT Paul										6+2	6+2
WHITEHALL Steve									16+2	5+13	21+15
WHITTAKER Andy			29+6	41	22+2	1+4					93+12
WHITTAKER Stuart								13+15	0+9		13+24
WILLIAMS Gary									3+1		3+1
WILLIAMS Lee	3+5										3+5
WINSTANLEY Mark										23	23
WITHERS Peter	34+3										34+3
WOODS Neil							9+4				9+4

Above: **Tim Ryan** Photo: Andrew Chitty

Andy Whittaker Photo: Andrew Chitty

Below: **Lee Elam** Photo: Garry Letts

Brian Ross Photo: Andrew Chitty

SOUTHPORT GOALSCORERS

	93-94	94-95	95-96	96-97	97-98	98-99	99-00	00-01	01-02	02-03	TOTAL
ANDERSON Lee				1							1
ARNOLD Ian						2	14(6p)	13(2p)			29(8p)
ASHCROFT Lee										2	2
BAURESS Gary										1	1
BLACKHURST Jimmy		6									6
BLACKSTONE Ian			3								3
BLISSETT Luther	2										2
BOLLAND Phil					1	5	3				9
BUTLER Brian				4	4						8
CHALLENDER Greg		1									1
CLARK Martin		3	2	1			1	2			9
COMSTIVE Paul	2	9									11
CONNOLLY James									1		1
CUNNINGHAM Harvey		5									5
DAVENPORT Peter			13	5							18
DEARY John					4						4
DOVE Leroy		3	2	2							7
EASTWOOD Phil									2		2
EDWARDS Paul									1		1
ELAM Lee						7	11	1	4		23
FARLEY Andy			3	1							4
FORMBY Kevin					3						3
FULLER Dave			2								2
FURLONG Lee						4	3	1			8
GAMBLE David	15(6p)	12(2p)	7(2p)	9(4p)	4(1p)	2(1p)					49(16p)
GIBSON Neil									1		1
GOUCK Andy						1	2	1			4
GOULDING Derek	2	3	1								6
GRAYSTON Neil							1	1	1		3
GRIFFITHS Bryan			6								6
GUYETT Scott						6	5	2			13
HAW Steve	10	12	9	1							32
HORNER Phil			1	2	1	2					6
HOWELL Dean									1	3	4
JONES Alex			3								3
JONES Barry									3		3
JONES Matthew								1			1
JONES Steve									8	2	10
KIELTY Ged					5						5
LANE Chris								2	4(1p)	1	7(1p)
LEADBETTER Kevin									1		1
LINIGHAN David								2			2
LLOYD-WILLIAMS Marc										3	3

605

SOUTHPORT   GOALSCORERS

	93-94	94-95	95-96	96-97	97-98	98-99	99-00	00-01	01-02	02-03	TOTAL
LODGE Paul	1	1	1								3
MAAMRIA Noureddine								3			3
MARSH Mike								7(5p)			7(5p)
McDONALD Alan	2	3									5
McDONALD Martin			4(2p)								4
McNIVEN David							1				1
MIKE Adie							1				1
MITCHELL Neil		4									4
MITCHELL Richard	1										1
MITTEN Paul					4						4
MORLEY Dominic							1				1
MORRIS Steve					1						1
MULVANEY Lee										4	4
NOLAN Ian										1	1
OBONG Ben								2			2
O'REILLY Justin					6	5					11
PARKE Simon								13	16		29
PELL Robert							2			3	5
PENMAN John		2									2
PICKFORD Steve										4	4
QUINLAN Phil	6										6
QUINN Stuart						1					1
ROGERS David				1							1
ROSS Brian					6	3					9
RYAN Tim					1	1					2
SHARRATT Chris				1							1
SOLEY Steve										7	7
STUART Mark					1	7	2				10
SULLIVAN Tony									2	1	3
TEALE Shaun									5		5
THOMAS Gary		6									6
THOMPSON Dave					3	1					4
THOMSON Peter										12(2p)	12(2p)
TRUNDLE Lee						4					4
WALMSLEY Chris	4										4
WARD Derek		2	1								3
WHEATCROFT Paul									1		1
WHITEHALL Steve									6	4	10
WHITTAKER Andy		16	19	8	1						44
WHITTAKER Stuart								5			5
WINSTANLEY Mark										1	1
WITHERS Peter	11										11
WOODS Neil							2				2

STAFFORD RANGERS

FOUNDER MEMBER elected from The Southern League
RELEGATED TO: The Southern League 1983, 1995
PROMOTED FROM: The Southern League 1985
2004-2005 SEASON: Conference North

Stafford Rangers 1985-86. Back Row: P Derbyshire, M Hanchard, P Upton, P Titley, M Gill, F Wood.
Middle: B Whittaker (Physio), P Carr, D Field, G Simpson, P Pritchard, G Bennett, M Meddings (Asst. Manager), R Walters (Trainer) **Front:** P Johnson, B Lowe, J Ridley, R Reid (Manager), K Beech, K Mooney, R Mountain

SEASONS		HOME						AWAY						
14		P	W	D	L	F	A	Pts	P	W	D	L	F	A	Pts	Position
	79-80	19	4	7	8	20	21	15	19	2	3	14	21	36	7	19
TOTAL POINTS	**80-81**	19	10	4	5	34	22	24	19	1	11	7	22	34	13	11
665	**81-82**	21	7	8	6	22	19	29	21	5	8	8	26	28	23	14
HIGHEST POSITION	**82-83**	21	4	8	9	22	30	20	21	1	6	14	18	45	9	22
6th (87/88) (92/93)	**83-84**															
LOWEST POSITION	**84-85**															
22nd (82/83)	**85-86**	21	10	7	4	30	22	27	21	9	6	6	31	32	33	7
	86-87	21	9	5	7	32	25	32	21	5	6	10	26	35	21	13
HIGHEST ATTENDANCE	**87-88**	21	12	4	5	43	25	40	21	8	5	8	36	33	29	6
2658 v Altrincham (28-4-91)	**88-89**	20	7	4	9	27	32	25	20	4	3	13	22	42	15	19
LOWEST ATTENDANCE	**89-90**	21	9	6	6	25	23	33	21	3	6	12	25	39	15	17
390 v Bromsgrove (14-2-95)	**90-91**	21	7	9	5	30	26	30	21	5	5	11	18	25	20	15
SEASON GOALSCORER	**91-92**	21	7	8	6	25	24	29	21	3	8	10	16	35	17	17
Phil Derbyshire 24(1p) (87/88)	**92-93**	21	7	6	8	22	24	27	21	11	4	6	33	23	37	6
CAREER GOALSCORER	**93-94**	21	10	7	4	39	22	37	21	4	8	9	17	30	20	9
Phil Derbyshire 49(5p)	**94-95**	21	5	5	11	29	34	20	21	4	6	11	24	45	18	21
CAREER APPEARANCES	**Total**	**289**	**108**	**88**	**93**	**400**	**349**	**388**	**289**	**65**	**85**	**139**	**335**	**482**	**277**	
Fraser Wood 311+26																

STAFFORD RANGERS

	Altrincham		A P Leamington		Aylesbury United		Bangor City		Barnet		Barrow		Bath City		Boston United		Bromsgrove Rovers	
	H	A	H	A	H	A	H	A	H	A	H	A	H	A	H	A	H	A
79-80	1-2	1-3	1-1	0-2			0-1	1-1	1-2	1-2	1-1	1-2	4-0	1-2	0-0	2-3		
80-81	1-3	2-4	1-1	1-1			4-0	0-0	1-0	1-1	1-0	1-5	0-2	0-0	2-3	2-2		
81-82	2-0	1-0	3-1	5-1					1-0	2-0	1-1	1-1	2-0	1-1	0-0	1-2		
82-83	2-3	0-4					1-1	0-1	1-0	0-1	2-0	1-2	1-1	1-5	0-2	1-1		
83-84																		
84-85																		
85-86	1-1	3-1							0-0	2-0	1-0	1-0	1-0	1-0	2-1	1-1		
86-87	2-3	0-2							0-3	2-1			0-1	2-4	0-1	0-2		
87-88	3-0	0-2							1-1	2-2			1-0	3-0	3-4	1-4		
88-89	0-2	1-2			3-1	1-1			1-2	2-1					4-1	1-2		
89-90	3-1	1-3							1-1	1-1	1-1	1-2			0-0	0-2		
90-91	2-1	0-0							2-2	0-2	2-2	0-2	2-1	1-0	1-2	2-0		
91-92	1-2	0-3									0-0	0-0	2-0	1-0	0-1	2-2		
92-93	0-0	5-1											3-2	1-2	0-0	1-0	3-4	3-2
93-94	0-1	0-0											2-0	3-2			0-0	3-3
94-95	0-1	1-5											0-2	3-3			1-1	1-2

	Cheltenham Town		Chorley		Colchester United		Dagenham		Dagenham & Redbridge		Darlington		Dartford		Dover Athletic		Enfield	
	H	A	H	A	H	A	H	A	H	A	H	A	H	A	H	A	H	A
79-80																		
80-81																		
81-82							0-0	2-2					0-3	2-2			0-1	0-2
82-83							1-2	3-3									0-3	1-0
83-84																		
84-85																		
85-86	2-0	0-2					3-1	1-1					5-1	3-3			1-1	1-3
86-87	0-1	1-2					1-1	0-1									0-3	0-2
87-88	2-2	3-2					4-0	4-2									3-1	0-0
88-89	1-1	2-1	3-2	1-3													3-1	2-4
89-90	0-1	3-1	1-0	1-1							0-4	1-2					1-0	1-4
90-91	2-2	2-1			0-2	0-2												
91-92	2-2	0-0			3-3	0-2			2-1	3-4								
92-93									0-1	1-0								
93-94									2-0	0-1					2-2	0-2		
94-95									1-2	3-3					1-0	2-3		

STAFFORD RANGERS

	Farnborough Town H	A	Fisher Athletic H	A	Frickley Athletic H	A	Gateshead H	A	Gravesend & N'fleet H	A	Halifax Town H	A	Kettering Town H	A	Kidderminster H. H	A	Lincoln City H	A
79-80									0-1	0-2			0-0	6-3				
80-81					3-3	2-3			2-3	1-1			3-1	0-1				
81-82					0-0	0-2			1-0	1-1			1-1	0-3				
82-83					1-1	0-3							1-1	2-2				
83-84																		
84-85																		
85-86					0-0	0-3							0-0	1-0	3-2	1-1		
86-87					2-0	1-2	1-0	2-2					2-2	2-2	4-1	1-1		
87-88			3-2	2-1									2-1	0-1	0-2	0-0	1-4	1-2
88-89			0-1	1-0									2-1	0-1	0-1	2-3		
89-90	3-2	3-3	1-3	2-0									1-1	0-0	0-1	0-3		
90-91			2-0	3-1			0-1	1-2					0-0	0-2	3-1	1-2		
91-92	0-1	1-1					1-3	0-0					1-2	1-2	2-0	1-2		
92-93	2-2	1-1					2-1	1-0					2-4	0-2	0-1	2-0		
93-94							3-3	0-0			1-1	1-1	1-0	0-2	2-3	0-2		
94-95	1-1	0-0					3-1	1-1			0-1	0-6	2-3	0-1	1-2	2-1		

Ryan Price saves against Bath City.

Photo: Alan Casse

	Macclesfield Town		Maidstone United		Merthyr Tydfil		Northwich Victoria		Nuneaton Borough		Redditch United		Runcorn		Scarborough		Slough Town	
	H	A	H	A	H	A	H	A	H	A	H	A	H	A	H	A	H	A
79-80			1-1	0-2			4-1	0-1	0-1	1-3	1-1	2-0			3-1	0-0		
80-81			3-1	1-4			2-0	1-2	2-2	2-2					2-1	0-0		
81-82			1-1	1-3			2-2	2-1					0-1	0-1	1-1	0-1		
82-83			2-3	0-1			1-1	1-2	1-2	1-1			0-1	1-4	0-0	1-2		
83-84																		
84-85																		
85-86			2-1	4-2			1-2	0-2	2-0	0-3			1-1	0-3	0-3	4-2		
86-87			2-3	3-2			4-1	1-1	3-1	0-0			2-0	1-3	0-0	0-2		
87-88	0-1	3-2	2-3	2-4			3-0	1-1					2-1	1-1				
88-89	1-1	1-2	0-2	0-3			0-1	1-1					0-4	1-4				
89-90	4-2	2-2			1-1	3-4	1-0	3-4					1-1	0-3				
90-91	2-2	1-2			2-0	1-1	0-0	1-1					1-1	0-1			3-4	1-2
91-92	1-1	0-1			0-0	0-1	2-1	2-1					1-0	0-0			1-1	2-2
92-93	1-0	1-4			0-1	0-0	1-0	2-1					0-1	2-0			1-0	1-2
93-94	2-3	0-0			5-1	0-2	3-1	0-0					2-2	2-2			0-0	0-3
94-95	0-3	2-1			2-1	1-4	1-3	1-0					1-2	1-3				

Ryan Price under pressure against Dagenham & Redbridge

Photo: John Collinge

STAFFORD RANGERS

	Southport		Stalybridge Celtic		Stevenage Borough		Sutton United		Telford United		Trowbridge Town		Wealdstone		Welling United		Weymouth	
	H	A	H	A	H	A	H	A	H	A	H	A	H	A	H	A	H	A
79-80									0-1	2-2			0-1	1-2			1-5	1-2
80-81									0-1	1-1			3-0	1-1			2-0	1-2
81-82									1-2	3-2	0-2	1-1					3-0	1-1
82-83									1-1	0-2	3-2	3-5	2-1	2-3			1-2	0-0
83-84																		
84-85																		
85-86									0-3	0-0			2-1	3-2			2-3	1-1
86-87							4-2	0-3	1-1	0-0			1-0	3-0	3-1	4-2	0-0	3-1
87-88							2-0	0-2	1-1	2-1			5-2	2-4	2-0	5-0	0-0	0-2
88-89							1-1	0-2	1-3	2-2					3-0	3-1	1-0	0-1
89-90							3-1	0-1	2-0	2-0					0-2	0-1		
90-91							1-2	3-0	1-1	0-0					1-0	1-2		
91-92									3-2	1-4					0-0	1-1		
92-93			0-0	0-1					2-1	0-0					4-3	2-1		
93-94	0-2	2-0	2-2	2-1					1-1	1-2					3-0	1-2		
94-95	1-1	0-3	5-0	3-2	0-3	0-1			2-2	0-0					1-1	1-3		

	Witton Albion		Woking		Worcester City		Wycombe Wanderers		Yeovil Town	
	H	A	H	A	H	A	H	A	H	A
79-80					0-0	0-1			2-1	1-3
80-81					1-0	1-1			1-1	4-3
81-82					0-2	1-1			3-1	1-2
82-83					0-0	0-3			1-3	0-0
83-84										
84-85										
85-86							1-1	4-2		
86-87										
87-88							3-0	4-0		
88-89							1-1	1-6	2-6	0-2
89-90							1-0	1-2	0-1	0-0
90-91							2-1	0-2	1-1	0-0
91-92	3-2	0-6					0-2	0-3	0-0	1-0
92-93	1-1	5-2	0-0	3-0			0-1	2-2	0-1	0-2
93-94	1-0	1-1	3-0	0-4					4-2	1-0
94-95			2-3	2-2					4-1	0-1

STAFFORD RANGERS

	Home						Away				
	P	W	D	L	F	A	P	W	D	L	F	A
ALTRINCHAM	14	4	2	8	18	20	14	3	2	9	15	30
A P LEAMINGTON	3	1	2	0	5	3	3	1	1	1	6	4
AYLESBURY U	1	1	0	0	3	1	1	0	1	0	1	1
BANGOR C	3	1	1	1	5	2	3	0	2	1	1	2
BARNET	10	3	4	3	9	11	10	4	3	3	13	11
BARROW	8	3	5	0	9	5	8	1	2	5	6	14
BATH C	12	8	1	3	18	9	12	5	3	4	18	19
BOSTON U	12	2	4	6	12	15	12	2	4	6	14	21
BROMSGROVE R	3	0	2	1	4	5	3	1	1	1	7	7
CHELTENHAM T	7	1	4	2	9	9	7	4	1	2	11	9
CHORLEY	2	2	0	0	4	2	2	0	1	1	2	4
COLCHESTER U	2	0	1	1	3	5	2	0	0	2	0	4
DAGENHAM	5	2	2	1	9	4	5	1	3	1	10	9
DAGENHAM & R	4	2	0	2	5	4	4	1	1	2	7	8
DARLINGTON	1	0	0	1	0	4	1	0	0	1	1	2
DARTFORD	2	1	0	1	5	4	2	0	2	0	5	5
DOVER A	2	1	1	0	3	2	2	0	0	2	2	5
ENFIELD	7	3	1	3	8	10	7	1	1	5	5	15
FARNBOROUGH T	4	1	2	1	6	6	4	0	4	0	5	5
FISHER A	4	2	0	2	6	6	4	4	0	0	8	2
FRICKLEY A	5	1	4	0	6	4	5	0	0	5	3	13
GATESHEAD	6	4	0	2	10	7	6	1	4	1	5	5
GRAVESEND & N	3	1	0	2	3	4	3	0	2	1	2	4
HALIFAX T	2	0	1	1	1	2	2	0	1	1	1	7
KETTERING T	14	4	7	3	18	17	14	2	3	9	12	22
KIDDERMINSTER H	10	4	0	6	15	14	10	2	3	5	10	15
LINCOLN C	1	0	0	1	1	4	1	0	0	1	1	2
MACCLESFIELD T	8	2	3	3	11	13	8	2	2	4	10	14
MAIDSTONE U	8	2	2	4	13	15	8	2	0	6	11	21
MERTHYR T	6	3	2	1	10	4	6	0	2	4	5	12
NORTHWICH V	14	8	3	3	25	13	14	4	5	5	16	18
NUNEATON B	5	2	1	2	8	6	5	0	3	2	4	9
REDDITCH U	1	0	1	0	1	1	1	1	0	0	2	0
RUNCORN	12	3	4	5	11	15	12	1	3	8	9	25
SCARBOROUGH	6	2	3	1	6	6	6	1	2	3	5	7
SLOUGH T	4	1	2	1	5	5	4	0	1	3	4	9
SOUTHPORT	2	0	1	1	1	3	2	1	0	1	2	3
STALYBRIDGE C	3	1	2	0	7	2	3	2	0	1	5	4
STEVENAGE B	1	0	0	1	0	3	1	0	0	1	0	1
SUTTON U	5	3	1	1	11	6	5	1	0	4	3	8
TELFORD U	14	3	6	5	16	20	14	3	8	3	14	14
TROWBRIDGE T	2	1	0	1	3	4	2	0	1	1	4	6
WEALDSTONE	6	5	0	1	13	5	6	2	1	3	12	12
WELLING U	9	6	2	1	17	7	9	4	1	4	18	13
WEYMOUTH	8	3	2	3	10	10	8	1	3	4	7	10
WITTON A	3	2	1	0	5	3	3	1	1	1	6	9
WOKING	3	1	1	1	5	3	3	1	1	1	5	6
WORCESTER C	4	1	2	1	1	2	4	0	2	2	2	6
WYCOMBE W	7	3	2	2	8	6	7	2	1	4	12	17
YEOVIL T	11	4	3	4	18	18	11	3	3	5	8	13
TOTALS	289	108	88	93	400	349	289	65	85	139	335	482

STAFFORD RANGERS — LEADING APPEARANCES

	79/80	80/81	81/82	82/83	83-85	85/86	86/87	87/88	88/89	89/90	90/91	91/92	92/93	93/94	94/95	TOTAL
Fraser WOOD	34	34	30	17		10+1	29+4	15+2	21+2	23+2	39+1	38+1	19+11	2+2		311+26
Ryan PRICE							38	42	42	42	42	40				246
Wayne SIMPSON							5	37	39	39	37	38	29			224
Steve ESSEX								40	39	37	40	34+1				190+1
Paul UPTON			12		36	37	27+1	37	36							185+1
Mark BRADSHAW										13	34+3	41	42	27		157+3
Phil TITLEY					38+1	42	37	10+4								127+5
Steve BURR		8	26+5	40+1								23	18			115+6
Trevor DANCE		34	41	42												117
Darren BOUGHEY												33+5	37+4	35+2		105+11
Martin HANCHARD		8	28+2	31+2	22+2	18+1										107+7
Phil DERBYSHIRE					31+1	37	39									107+1
Russell TURLEY								14+4	23+10	16+9	25+5					78+28
John RIDLEY					42	27	12+3	19+1								100+4
Stuart CHAPMAN	27	20+1	33	21												101+1

STAFFORD RANGERS — APPEARANCES

	79/80	80/81	81/82	82/83	83-85	85/86	86/87	87/88	88/89	89/90	90/91	91/92	92/93	93/94	94/95	TOTAL
ABBISHAW David														2+1		2+1
ADAMS Steve						5+1										5+1
ANASTASI Savvas											24+11	4+1				28+12
ARNOT Chris			10+2													10+2
ATKINSON Paul											7					7
BAILEY Terry		33+2														33+2
BAINBRIDGE Richard								0+2								0+2
BAKER Karl												0+2				0+2
BARNES Bobby											4+1					4+1
BARNETT Dave		5														5
BASTABLE Gary	14+1															14+1
BECKETT Michael			25													25
BEECH Kenny						35+5	32+4	18								85+9
BENNETT Graham						16+1	13+1									29+2
BENTLEY Bill		18+2														18+2
BERKS John												2+1				2+1
BERKS Peter												11+5				11+5
BERRY George												7	29+3	14+6	6+6	56+15
BERRY Gwynne														4		4
BODKIN Martin													21+2			21+2
BOOTH Matthew												7+1				7+1
BOUGHEY Darren												33+5	37+4	35+2		105+11
BOWLING Ian					9	3										12
BOYLE Lee												3				3
BRADSHAW Mark										13	34+3	41	42	27		157+3
BREMNER Des										32+1	7					39+1
BRIGGS Malcolm	11															11

Above: **Danny Williams** Photo: Paul Dennis   **Stan Collymore**

Below: **Mark Bradshaw**   **Phil Derbyshire**

STAFFORD RANGERS   APPEARANCES

	79/80	80/81	81/82	82/83	83-85	85/86	86/87	87/88	88/89	89/90	90/91	91/92	92/93	93/94	94/95	TOTAL
BRINDLE Keith		32+1	3													35+1
BRISSETT T				11												11
BROUGH John											5					5
BROWN Gary														6+2		6+2
BROWN Ian					1+1	0+1	27+9	21+5	11		5+1					65+17
BROWN Tony				11												11
BROWNBILL Derek		26+4														26+4
BURNS Kenny										5						5
BURR Steve		8	26+5	40+1									23	18		115+6
BURTON Chris														6		6
BUTLER David			4+1													4+1
BUTTERWORTH Steve											19	1				20
CALLAGHAN Nigel											7	5				12
CAMDEN Chris							33+2	38+1								71+3
CAMPBELL Winston							7+1	8+3								15+4
CANTELLO Len				3												3
CARR Peter					38+3	33+2										71+5
CAVELL Paul						19	27+2	31+2								77+4
CHADWICK Colin	19+9															19+9
CHAMBERLAIN Neville							12+1									12+1
CHAPMAN Stuart	27	20+1	33	21												101+1
CHARLESWORTH Mick	10	2														12
CIRCUIT Steve												9+1				9+1
CLAYTON Paul												22+8	9+7			31+15
COCKERILL John						35										35
COFFEY Mike	14	1+2														15+2
COLLYMORE Stan								10+8	17							27+8
COOKE Jason														1+1		1+1
COOPER Mark	1															1
CORBETT Steve														1+1		1+1
CORRIGAN Frank			11													11
CREANE Ged				3												3
CRISP Mark														6		6
CROSS Kevin					3+1											3+1
CROWLEY David														8+2		8+2
CULLERTON Mick	21+1	8+8														29+9
CUNNINGHAM Sylvester				8												8
DANCE Trevor		34	41	42												117
DAVIES Martin													2	13		15
DAWSON Dougie														8+1		8+1
DAWSON Jason											8+1	12+2				20+3
DEANE Brian	10+1															10+1
DEAVILLE Mark	12	3														15
DERBYSHIRE Phil					31+1	37	39									107+1
DEVLIN Paul										19+5	26					45+5
DOYLE Maurice								1								1
DREWITT Ian														30		30
DRUMMOND Brendan			17+1													17+1
DUFFIN Stuart														14		14
DULSON Gary	7	27														34

STAFFORD RANGERS APPEARANCES

	79/80	80/81	81/82	82/83	83-85	85/86	86/87	87/88	88/89	89/90	90/91	91/92	92/93	93/94	94/95	TOTAL
DUNCALF Kevin	3															3
DUNKLEY Malcolm						21										21
DUNNE Nick										1						1
ECCLES Peter							2									2
ECCLESTON Stuart				3+1												3+1
EDENSOR John														1		1
EDWARDS Dean												2				2
EDWARDS Keith									7							7
EDWARDS Reg	17															17
ESSEX Steve									40	39	37	40	34+1			190+1
EVANS Neil	1+1															1+1
EVANS Tony					14+2											14+2
FENOUGHTY Nick		13														13
FIELD Dave	9	1		35	33											78
FINNEY Kevin													9			9
FISHER Mark												7+2				7+2
FORD S				3												3
FOREMAN Darren											10					10
FOY David													22+3	10		32+3
GALLAGHER Stuart		12	12													24
GARNER Richard										1						1
GILL Martyn				17+6		14+1		28+1								59+8
GORDON Russell							22+1	2+1								24+2
GREAVES Phil								35+2								35+2
GRIFFITHS Neil			14													14
GRIFFITHS Peter								9+1								9+1
GRIFFITHS Tony									16+1	3		12+4	10+10	17+7		58+22
HAMLETT Gordon		11														11
HANCHARD Martin		8	28+2	31+2	22+2	18+1										107+7
HANLON Steve													13			13
HARLE David											5					5
HARMON Darren											4					4
HARRIS Dave			24	18												42
HARRIS Kevin	11+2															11+2
HARRISON Mark						39										39
HARRISON Mark														2		2
HARRISON Mick												1				1
HASSALL Jon														23+3		23+3
HAWKINS Richard														0+2		0+2
HEGGS Carl											4					4
HEMMING Chris											22	29+3	22			73+3
HENDRY Ian										6						6
HENLEY Russell										1+3						1+3
HENRY Tony												2				2
HEYWOOD Dave								5+2								5+2
HICKS Nathan														1+2		1+2
HIGNETT Craig							12+1									12+1
HILL Gordon						18										18
HODKINSON Andy											3					3
HOLLIER Vic											1					1

STAFFORD RANGERS   APPEARANCES

	79/80	80/81	81/82	82/83	83-85	85/86	86/87	87/88	88/89	89/90	90/91	91/92	92/93	93/94	94/95	TOTAL
HOPE Darren										8+10						8+10
HOPE Mark													11+7			11+7
INGRAM Peter			1													1
JACKSON Phil	8															8
JENNINGS Kirk	2															2
JOHNSON Cory							0+1									0+1
JOHNSON Paul				31+1	3											34+1
JONES B			4													4
JONES Graham					1											1
JONES Marcus												6+1				6+1
JONES Mark						15+2	0+5	11								26+7
JONES Paul									9	34+2						43+2
JONES Steve	3+2															3+2
KABIA Jason													3			3
KABIA Jim		31+2	14													45+2
KELLY Keith		4+1	1+1	0+2												5+4
KERSLEY Colin	33+3	34+1	1+2													68+6
KHAN Changez									11+9							11+9
KILBANE Farrell														14		14
KING Peter								19								19
KITCHEN Dave							9									9
KNIGHT Terry							16+1	1+2								17+3
KURILA Alan								40								40
LAW Marcus														5		5
LEEMING Dan														9		9
LINDSEY Scott										8+3						8+3
LIPPITT Paul			15													15
LLOYD Tommy									2							2
LOCKETT Corrigan			6+1													6+1
LODGE Ivan				1	0+2											1+2
LOSKA Tony	16															16
LOVE Craig									0+1							0+1
LOWE Barry				27+3	28+2											55+5
LUBY Seamus													3+2	1		4+2
LUNDON Sean								4+1								4+1
LYONS Steve											0+1					0+1
MACKENZIE Steve														16+2		16+2
MALLABURN Dave			19													19
MARDENBOROUGH Steve													11	11		
MARSH Everton						22+1										22+1
MASKERY Chris					5			2								7
MASSEY Andy													5+1			5+1
MAY Leroy													8	36+1		44+1
McKENNA Ken					4											4
MEE Andy													10+6	2+4		12+10
MERCHANT Shaun								2+7								2+7
METTIOUI Ahmed												6	27+2			33+2
MEYER Chris									0+3							0+3
MILLER Ian											12+1					12+1
MILSOM Paul														6		6

617

Above:**Ian Drewitt** (Stevenage's Rudi Henman) Photo: Paul Dennis

Stan Collymore

Below:**Steve Essex** (thwarting Telford's Ken McKenna)

Steve Jones Photo: Chris Elsey

STAFFORD RANGERS APPEARANCES

	79/80	80/81	81/82	82/83	83-85	85/86	86/87	87/88	88/89	89/90	90/91	91/92	92/93	93/94	94/95	TOTAL
MOLLOY Paul														8+1		8+1
MOONEY Kevin			6	3+1												9+1
MORGAN Andy		1+1														1+1
MORRISON Lance									4+1							4+1
MOSSMAN Dave								2+1								2+1
MOUNTAIN Bob				21+1	10+5											31+6
MOWER Kenny												2				2
NARDIELLO Don			5													5
NEAL Tim	0+1															0+1
NELSON Denis		16+3														16+3
NEWMAN Darren											3+3					3+3
NEWTON Stan								12+2								12+2
NIEMAN Albie		33	24													57
NIXON Chris	15+2															15+2
NIXON Chris					2											2
O'CONNOR Joe									7+10							7+10
O'NEILL Dave	4															4
O'TOOLE Pat														15		15
OWEN Mark			2	5												7
PAGE Don				14+2												14+2
PALGRAVE Brian										37	15+2	29+3	4+1			85+6
PEACOCK John			42													42
PEARSON Jon										26	27+4	16				69+4
PENNY Andy														10+1		10+1
PERRY Mike						19+14										19+14
POWER Mike				3+1												3+1
PRICE Ryan								38	42	42	42	42	40			246
PRITCHARD Paul				7												7
PROUDLOVE Andy	13+1															13+1
REECE Andy				9												9
REES Mark														4+1		4+1
REID Tony							7		12							19
RICH Micky			13	27+2												40+2
RICHARDS Archie							3+2									3+2
RICHARDSON Kevin			28	29												57
RIDLEY John						42	27	12+3	19+1							100+4
RITCHIE Bob	14	17														31
ROBERTS Darren												1				1
ROONEY Simon												5+1				5+1
RYLANDS Dave		10														10
SADLER Stuart									1							1
SALMON Sylvan								3+5								3+5
SARGEANT Jim	16+1															17+1
SAXBY Gary								0+1								0+1
SECKER Wayne	29+1	9		5+1												43+2
SEDDON Ben	30															30
SHELLEY Mark									5							5
SHEPHERD Glyn									2							2
SHEPSTONE Paul														15	3	18
SIMPSON Gary						30	30	36								96

STAFFORD RANGERS   APPEARANCES

	79/80	80/81	81/82	82/83	83-85	85/86	86/87	87/88	88/89	89/90	90/91	91/92	92/93	93/94	94/95	TOTAL
SIMPSON Wayne									5	37	39	39	37	38	29	224
SKIPPER Peter													5			5
SMITH Jim		18														18
SMITH Mark														2		2
SMITH Paul	3															3
SMITH Robert														9+1		9+1
SPROSON Phil										2						2
SQUIRES Jamie														8		8
STRAW Robert											1+3					1+3
TAYLOR Andrew					0+1											0+1
THACKER Colin							34									34
THOMSON Andy	16															16
THORNLEY Mark							2									2
TIMONS Chris														5		5
TITLEY Phil				38+1	42	37	10+4									127+5
TUOHY Micky										24+1	12					36+1
TURLEY Russell						14+4	23+10	16+9	25+5							78+28
TYRRELL Alan								1								1
UPTON Paul			12		36	37	27+1	37	36							185+1
VICKERS Ian												1				1
WALKER Gary														20		20
WALSH Matthew					2+3											2+3
WAREING Gary											0+2					0+2
WASSELL Kim								2								2
WELLS Mark											6+1					6+1
WESTWOOD Kevin			30+4	23+9												53+13
WHARTON David						18	28+3	9+1	20							75+4
WHITEHOUSE Mark										4						4
WHITEHOUSE Phil											1+1					1+1
WHITEHURST Billy													2			2
WHITTLE Maurice	2															2
WILKINSON Don										1+1						1+1
WILLIAMS Danny													35+3	31+4		66+7
WILLIAMS Jos			28+1													28+1
WILLIAMSON Charlie							39	1+1								40+1
WILLIS Dave	1															1
WILSON Harry		1														1
WILSON Phil											5					5
WITHE Jason											2					2
WOLVERSON Jason											6					6
WOOD Alf	15+1															15+1
WOOD Fraser	34	34	30	17		10+1	29+4	15+2	21+2	23+2	39+1	38+1	19+11	2+2		311+26
WOOD Richard							1		1+3	4						6+3
WOODWARD Andy														2+1		2+1
WOOLFALL Alan	10															10
WRIGHT Evran														1+1		1+1
WYNN Steve						2+3										2+3
YOULL L					1+2											1+2

STAFFORD RANGERS   GOALSCORERS

	79/80	80/81	81/82	82/83	83-85	85/86	86/87	87/88	88/89	89/90	90/91	91/92	92/93	93/94	94/95	TOTAL
ANASTASI Savvas										11						11
ATKINSON Paul								1								1
BAILEY Terry		10														10
BASTABLE Gary	3															3
BECKETT Michael			1													1
BEECH Kenny				2		2										4
BENNETT Graham					8	3										11
BENTLEY Bill		1														1
BERKS Peter											1					1
BERRY George											1(1p)	4(1p)	1(1p)	1		7(3p)
BODKIN Martin													2			2
BOOTH Matthew											1					1
BOUGHEY Darren												7	2			9
BRADSHAW Mark											2	3	1	1		7
BRIGGS Malcolm	3															3
BRINDLE Keith		3														3
BROWN Ian						4	1									5
BROWN Tony				3												3
BROWNBILL Derek		5														5
BURR Steve		2	15	13								6	7			43
BURTON Chris													1			1
BUTLER David			3													3
BUTTERWORTH Steve										1						1
CALLAGHAN Nigel												1				1
CAMDEN Chris						23(3p)	10(1p)									33(4p)
CAMPBELL Winston								1								1
CANTELLO Len			1													1
CARR Peter					4	1										5
CAVELL Paul						12	8	11								31
CHADWICK Colin	1															1
CHAMBERLAIN Neville								3								3
CHAPMAN Stuart	4	3														7
CLAYTON Paul													9	4		13
COCKERILL John						6(6p)										6(6p)
COLLYMORE Stan								4	7							11
CORRIGAN Frank			1													1
CRISP Mark														2		2
CROSS Kevin					1											1
CULLERTON Mick	8	3(1p)														11(1p)
DAWSON Jason												1	2			3
DEANE Bryan	1															1
DERBYSHIRE Phil					12(2p)	13(2p)	24(1p)									49(5p)
DEVLIN Paul								4	3							7
DREWITT Ian														5(2p)		5(2p)
DRUMMOND Brendan				3												3
DUFFIN Stuart														6		6

621

Above: Chris Camden scores against Rushall

Below: Phil Derbyshire evades Telford United 'keeper Kevin Charlton before scoring.

STAFFORD RANGERS   GOALSCORERS

	79/80	80/81	81/82	82/83	83-85	85/86	86/87	87/88	88/89	89/90	90/91	91/92	92/93	93/94	94/95	TOTAL
DULSON Gary	1															1
DUNKLEY Malcolm						9										9
ECCLESTON Stuart			1													1
EDWARDS Keith											3					3
ESSEX Steve								3	2	1	3	1				10
EVANS Tony				8												8
FENOUGHTY Nick	2															2
FINNEY Kevin													1			1
FISHER Mark												1				1
FOREMAN Darren										5						5
FOY David													2			2
GALLAGHER Stuart	3	1														4
GILL Martyn				3			6									9
GORDON Russell					8											8
GRIFFITHS Tony							1					1		1		3
HANCHARD Martin	4	4		7(2p)	8											23(2p)
HANLON Steve													1			1
HARRIS Dave			1													1
HEGGS Carl										1						1
HEMMING Chris												2				2
HENRY Tony												1				1
HIGNETT Craig								3								3
HILL Gordon						5(1p)										5(1p)
HODKINSON Andy											1(1p)					1(1p)
HOPE Darren											1					1
JACKSON Phil	1															1
JOHNSON Cory									1							1
JONES Mark									1	1						2
JONES Paul												2				2
JONES Steve	1															1
KABIA Jim		8	1													9
KELLY Keith			1													1
KERSLEY Colin	6	5														11
KHAN Changez									1							1
KILBANE Farrell														3		3
LIPPITT Paul			1													1
LLOYD Tommy										1						1
LOCKETT Corrigan			1													1
LOWE Barry						2(1p)										2(1p)
MACKENZIE Steve														1		1
MARDENBOROUGH Steve														4		4
MARSH Everton									1							1
MAY Leroy														8	21(1p)	29(1p)
McKENNA Ken						2										2
MEE Andy													1			1
MERCHANT Shaun										1						1

STAFFORD RANGERS   GOALSCORERS

	79/80	80/81	81/82	82/83	83-85	85/86	86/87	87/88	88/89	89/90	90/91	91/92	92/93	93/94	94/95	TOTAL
METTIOUI Ahmed													3	11		14
MEYER Chris										1						1
MILLER Ian											1					1
MILSOM Paul															2	2
MOUNTAIN Bob				11	2											13
NARDIELLO Don			2													2
NELSON Denis		2														2
NEWTON Stan								2								2
NIEMAN Albie		2	1													3
O'CONNOR Joe									1							1
PAGE Don				4												4
PALGRAVE Brian										1	2	4	1			8
PERRY Mike						7										7
PROUDLOVE Andy	3															3
REID Tony						1		1								2
RICH Micky			5	3												8
RIDLEY John				2												2
SALMON Sylvan								2								2
SARGEANT Jim			1													1
SECKER Wayne	2		1													3
SEDDON Ben	3															3
SHEPSTONE Paul														2	1	3
SIMPSON Gary				3	1	4										8
SIMPSON Wayne											3(3p)	6(5p)	3	7(3p)	1	20(11p)
SMITH Jim		5(1p)														5(1p)
SMITH Paul	1															1
THACKER Colin								2								2
TIMONS Chris														1		1
TITLEY Phil				2	1											3
TUOHY Micky											7	2				9
TURLEY Russell							2	3(1p)	2	1						8(1p)
UPTON Paul				2			1	1	1							5
WESTWOOD Kevin			1	4												5
WHARTON David							1	2		1						4
WILLIAMS Danny														2	2	4
WILLIAMS Jos				1												1
WILLIAMSON Charlie							1									1
WITHE Jason												1				1
WOLVERSON Jason												2				2
WOOD Alf	3															3
WOOD Fraser	4	4	1	2		2(1p)			4	4	3	2	1			27(1p)
WOOD Richard									1	1						2
WOOLFALL Alan	1															1

STALYBRIDGE CELTIC

PROMOTED FROM: The Northern Premier League 1992, 2001
RELEGATED TO: The Northern Premier League 1998, 2002
2004-2005 SEASON: Conference North

1996-97 Squad - Back Row (L-R): Dave Pover (Physio), Simon Heaton, Craig Powell, Ian Arnold, Greg Chellender, Harvey Willetts, Mark Powell, David Frain, Dave Denby (Assistant Manager).
Middle Row: Steve O'Shaughnessy, Dean Trott, Steve Charles, Peter Wragg (Manager), Brenan Burke, Steve Jones, Craig Boardman.
Front Row: Mark Hine, Jamie Bates, Darren Vine, Lee Coathup.

SEASONS
7

TOTAL POINTS
336

HIGHEST POSITION
12th (92/93)

LOWEST POSITION
22nd (97/98)

HIGHEST ATTENDANCE
1694 v Wycombe (23-1-93)

LOWEST ATTENDANCE
274 v Gateshead (4-3-97)

SEASON GOALSCORER
Brendan Burke 16 (97/98)

CAREER GOALSCORER
Brendan Burke 42(3p)

CAREER APPEARANCES
Lee Coathup 172+6

			HOME							AWAY				
	P	W	D	L	F	A	Pts	P	W	D	L	F	A	Pts	Position
92-93	21	7	10	4	25	26	31	21	6	7	8	23	29	25	12
93-94	21	6	6	9	27	30	24	21	8	6	7	27	25	30	14
94-95	21	9	6	6	29	27	33	21	2	8	11	23	45	14	18
95-96	21	9	3	9	29	37	30	21	7	4	10	30	31	25	14
96-97	21	9	5	7	35	29	32	21	5	5	11	18	29	20	13
97-98	21	6	5	10	33	38	23	21	1	3	17	15	55	6	22
98-99															
99-00															
00-01															
01-02	21	7	6	8	26	32	27	21	4	4	13	14	37	16	21
Total	147	53	41	53	204	219	200	147	33	37	77	150	251	136	

STALYBRIDGE CELTIC

	Altrincham		Barnet		Bath City		Boston United		Bromsgrove Rovers		Cheltenham Town		Chester City		Dagenham & Redbridge		Doncaster Rovers		Dover Athletic	
	H	A	H	A	H	A	H	A	H	A	H	A	H	A	H	A	H	A	H	A
92-93	1-0	0-0			1-1	1-1	2-1	1-1	0-1	0-4					0-3	2-1			0-3	2-1
93-94	1-3	0-0			1-3	1-1			0-2	0-2					5-0	1-0			5-0	1-0
94-95	2-1	0-1			0-1	3-2			1-1	1-2					1-0	2-2			1-0	2-2
95-96	1-0	0-1			1-0	4-0			2-1	1-1					2-1	1-4			2-1	1-4
96-97	1-0	0-1			2-2	2-0			3-0	1-0										
97-98											1-4	0-2								
98-01																				
01-02			1-1	2-1			2-1	1-4					0-4	0-0	2-3	1-2	1-0	1-0	2-3	1-2

	Farnborough Town		Forest Green Rovers		Gateshead		Halifax Town		Hayes		Hednesford Town		Hereford United		Kettering Town		Kidderminster H.		Leek Town	
	H	A	H	A	H	A	H	A	H	A	H	A	H	A	H	A	H	A	H	A
92-93	2-0	2-1			2-1	0-0									0-0	0-2	2-2	1-2		
93-94					2-1	1-2	1-1	1-2							1-1	2-3	0-2	0-1		
94-95	4-1	0-0			0-1	0-0	1-1	1-1							1-4	0-1	1-3	2-3		
95-96	2-2	1-1			0-2	0-1	1-0	3-2			0-1	1-0			3-2	6-1	2-2	0-3		
96-97	2-0	0-1			2-5	2-0	2-3	1-4	3-1	2-0	1-2	1-2			3-1	0-1	4-1	1-1		
97-98	1-1	0-6			2-2	3-3	0-1	1-3	1-1	2-1	1-1	0-1	2-3	0-3	3-4	1-3	2-1	0-5	6-1	2-2
98-01																				
01-02	1-1	0-2	2-1	2-0					1-0	0-0			0-2	0-3						

	Leigh RMI		Macclesfield Town		Margate		Merthyr Tydfil		Morecambe		Northwich Victoria		Nuneaton Borough		Runcorn		Rushden & Diamonds		Scarborough	
	H	A	H	A	H	A	H	A	H	A	H	A	H	A	H	A	H	A	H	A
92-93			2-1	0-1			2-2	1-1			0-6	3-1			0-0	1-2				
93-94			0-2	3-1			2-2	2-1			1-1	0-2			1-2	1-1				
94-95			2-2	0-3			1-1	2-4			2-1	2-2			0-0	3-0				
95-96			1-2	0-1					0-2	0-2	1-5	0-1			2-0	1-0				
96-97			0-1	0-2							2-1	0-0	0-1	1-0			2-0	1-1		
97-98									3-1	1-3	0-1	0-1					2-4	0-3		
98-01																				
01-02	0-1	0-1			2-2	0-8			4-3	0-1	1-1	0-1	4-2	1-3					2-3	1-1

	Slough Town		Southport		Stafford Rangers		Stevenage Borough		Telford United		Welling United		Witton Albion		Woking		Wycombe Wanderers		Yeovil Town	
	H	A	H	A	H	A	H	A	H	A	H	A	H	A	H	A	H	A	H	A
92-93	0-0	3-2			1-0	0-0			3-3	2-0	0-0	4-1	1-2	0-2	3-0	1-2	2-2	0-4	1-1	1-1
93-94	0-1	3-2	3-1	2-0	1-2	2-2			1-0	2-0	2-1	2-1	2-1	3-0	2-2	0-3			1-2	0-0
94-95			1-1	1-3	2-3	0-5	1-0	1-5	1-0	1-1	1-3	3-3			2-1	1-4			3-1	0-3
95-96	0-1	1-2	1-4	3-5			2-5	2-2	2-2	1-0	2-1	1-1			2-4	1-2				
96-97	2-2	1-4	2-2	0-3			0-3	1-1	0-0	1-1	0-0	0-2			0-2	2-3				
97-98	0-1	0-4	1-2	2-4			1-1	1-1	1-2	0-1	2-1	0-1			0-3	1-3			3-2	0-2
98-01																				
01-02			0-0	1-3			2-0	0-2	0-2	1-3					0-2	1-1			1-1	2-0

	Home						Away					
	P	W	D	L	F	A	P	W	D	L	F	A
ALTRINCHAM	5	4	0	1	6	4	5	0	2	3	0	3
BARNET	1	0	1	0	1	1	1	1	0	0	2	1
BATH C	5	1	2	2	5	7	5	3	2	0	11	4
BOSTON U	2	2	0	0	4	2	2	0	1	1	2	5
BROMSGROVE R	5	2	1	2	6	5	5	1	1	3	3	9
CHELTENHAM T	1	0	0	1	1	4	1	0	0	1	0	2
CHESTER C	1	0	0	1	0	4	1	0	1	0	0	0
DAGENHAM & R	5	3	0	2	10	7	5	2	1	2	7	9
DONCASTER R	1	1	0	0	1	0	1	1	0	0	1	0
DOVER A	6	4	1	1	9	5	6	1	2	3	6	8
FARNBOROUGH T	6	3	3	0	12	5	6	1	2	3	3	11
FOREST GREEN R	1	1	0	0	2	1	1	1	0	0	2	0
GATESHEAD	6	2	1	3	8	12	6	1	3	2	6	6
HALIFAX T	5	1	2	2	5	6	5	1	1	3	7	12
HAYES	3	2	1	0	5	2	3	2	1	0	4	1
HEDNESFORD T	3	0	1	2	2	4	3	1	0	2	2	3
HEREFORD U	2	0	0	2	2	5	2	0	0	2	0	6
KETTERING T	6	2	2	2	11	12	6	1	0	5	9	11
KIDDERMINSTER H	6	2	2	2	11	11	6	0	1	5	4	15
LEEK T	1	1	0	0	6	1	1	0	1	0	2	2
LEIGH RMI	1	0	0	1	0	1	1	0	0	1	0	1
MACCLESFIELD T	5	1	1	3	5	8	5	1	0	4	3	8
MARGATE	1	0	1	0	2	2	1	0	0	1	0	8
MERTHYR T	3	0	3	0	5	5	3	1	1	1	5	6
MORECAMBE	4	3	0	1	9	7	4	0	1	3	1	6
NORTHWICH V	7	1	2	4	5	16	7	2	1	4	6	8
NUNEATON B	1	1	0	0	4	2	1	0	0	1	1	3
RUNCORN	4	1	2	1	3	2	4	2	1	1	6	3
RUSHDEN & D	2	1	0	1	4	4	2	0	1	1	1	4
SCARBOROUGH	1	0	0	1	2	3	1	0	1	0	1	1
SLOUGH T	5	0	2	3	2	5	5	2	0	3	8	14
SOUTHPORT	6	1	3	2	8	11	6	1	0	5	9	18
STAFFORD R	3	1	0	2	4	5	3	0	2	1	2	7
STEVENAGE B	5	2	1	2	6	9	5	0	3	2	5	11
TELFORD U	7	2	3	2	8	9	7	3	2	2	8	6
WELLING U	6	3	2	1	7	6	6	2	2	2	10	9
WITTON A	2	1	0	1	3	3	2	1	0	1	3	2
WOKING	7	2	1	4	9	14	7	0	1	6	7	18
WYCOMBE W	1	0	1	0	2	2	1	0	0	1	0	4
YEOVIL T	5	2	2	1	9	7	5	1	2	2	3	6
TOTALS	147	53	41	53	204	219	147	33	37	77	150	251

Above: Dominic Crookes
Photo: Peter Barnes

Below: Lee Coathup
Photo: GM Ellis-Neville

Above: Sammy Ayorinde
Photo: Francis Short

Below: Gary Bauress
Photo: Paul Dennis

STALYBRIDGE CELTIC   LEADING APPEARANCES

	92/93	93/94	94/95	95/96	96/97	97/98	1998 to 2001	01/02	TOTAL
Lee COATHUP		35	38	40	32+3	27+3			172+6
Brendan BURKE			21	41	34	37+1			133+1
David HALL			13	37+2	38+1	21+1			109+4
Russ HUGHES	42	42	26						110
Steve JONES				29+2	33+3	42			104+5

STALYBRIDGE CELTIC   APPEARANCES

	92/93	93/94	94/95	95/96	96/97	97/98	1998 to 2001	01/02	TOTAL
ALLEN Paul		2							2
ANDERSON Lee						0+1			0+1
ANDERSON Stewart	12	38	26+6						76+6
ARNOLD Ian		16		28	31+2				75+2
ASPINALL John	34	34							68
AYORINDE Sam								19	19
BARKER Glyn								0+1	0+1
BATES Jamie					24+3	29+3			53+6
BATTY Jason								4	4
BAURESS Gary	30+3		33+4	18					81+7
BEESLEY Paul								26	26
BENNETT Paul	35+1	28+2	9+3						72+6
BLACKMAN Ricky	1								1
BLAIN Colin		6+3							6+3
BOARDMAN Craig					38+1				38+1
BOOTH Kevin	22+2	24+1	6+3	1					53+6
BOYLE Gary	19+3	4+1							23+4
BRIEN Tony						3			3
BROWN Jimmy		5+4							5+4
BROWN John	36+2	9+4							45+6
BROWN Richard				6					6
BROWNRIGG Andy						10+1			10+1
BUNN Frank	10+2	9+6							19+8
BURKE Brendan			21	41	34	37+1			133+1
BURRELL Mark	5+2								5+2
BUSHELL Steve								16+2	16+2
BUTLER John						4			4
CHALLENDER Greg				6+3	11+7				17+10
CHARLES Steve					35+3	2+4			37+7
CHERRY Steve						10			10
CLAYTON Paul		17	34+1						51+1
CLEMENTS Matt								2	2
COATHUP Lee		35	38	40	32+3	27+3			172+6
COOKSEY Scott			13						13

STALYBRIDGE CELTIC   APPEARANCES

	92/93	93/94	94/95	95/96	96/97	97/98	1998 to 2001	01/02	TOTAL
COURTNEY Ged								33+5	33+5
CRANE Tim					2+7				2+7
CROOKES Dominic								5+1	5+1
CROSSLEY Richard						7			7
CURTIS Len						4			4
CUTLER Neil						7			7
DALY Matt						8			8
DIXON Kenneth				1					1
DIXON Paul	33	28+1	11						72+1
DOLBY Chris						11+4			11+4
DOVE Leroy						16+2			16+2
DULSON Craig		0+1							0+1
EDEY Cec						2			2
EDMONDS Neil	25+3	16	28+2	12+7					81+12
EDWARDS Mark	33+8								33+8
EDWARDS Mike		3							3
ELLIS Neil			2+1	12+5					14+6
ELLISON Lee				3+1					3+1
EVAND Andy								0+3	0+3
FILSON Martin	34+1								34+1
FISH David								22+3	22+3
FRAIN David			7	31+3	3+2				41+5
FUTCHER Ben								26	26
GOLDBOURNE Ronnie					4+3	7+5			11+8
GOODACRE Sammy				21+7	1				22+7
HALL David			13	37+2	38+1	21+1			109+4
HAMMOND Andy						2+1			2+1
HAROLD Ian		15							15
HEATH Steve						8			8
HEATON Simon					0+3				0+3
HIGGINBOTTOM Paul	5+5			10+7					15+12
HIGHFIELD Mark						12			12
HILL Jonathan	12+4	2+1							14+5
HINE Mark					36+2	21+4			57+6
HOE Mike						0+3			0+3
HORNER Richard						3			3
HUGHES Russ	42	42	26						110
INGHAM Gary						8		6	14
JACKSON Robert		11+12	11+11		0+1				22+24
JONES Alex				25					25
JONES Steve				29+2	33+3	42			104+5
KELLY Leon								8	8
KING Peter	4+1								4+1
KIRKHAM Paul	27+5	21+5	0+2						48+12
LEICESTER Stuart		21+11	1+1						22+12
LEVENDIS Andy						0+1			0+1
LIVINGSTONE Richard			2+1						2+1
LOCKE Stuart		14+1						1	15+1
LONERGAN Darren						2			2
LUTKEVITCH Mike		9+1							9+1
MARIVAT Boris								0+4	0+4

STALYBRIDGE CELTIC   APPEARANCES

	92/93	93/94	94/95	95/96	96/97	97/98	1998 to 2001	01/02	TOTAL
MARSH Neil						0+2			0+2
MARTIN Dean						11+1			11+1
McCORD Brian						2			2
McNEIL Matt								5+9	5+9
MEGSON Kevin			25+4	20+4					45+8
MIKE Adie								2+5	2+5
MORGAN Steve	13+4								13+4
MURPHY Gerard								32+6	32+6
NICHOLLS Alan				1					1
OGLEY Mark		25	35						60
O'SHAUGHNESSY Steve			11	28	4				43
PARR Kevin								31	31
PATTERSON Ian			19	2+1					21+1
PEACOCK Richard								29+1	29+1
PEARSON Gary				4+3					4+3
PEARSON John				3+1					3+1
PERKINS Chris								21+6	21+6
PICKFORD Steve								32	32
PICKLES Jon						1+1			1+1
POWELL Craig				3+2	1+3				4+5
POWELL Mark					27+9	32+1			59+10
POWER Phil	21+4	6							27+4
PRIEST Eric	3+3								3+3
PROKAS Richard		0+1							0+1
QUY Andy				4					4
RAMSEY John						2			2
RAWSTRON Mark						0+1			0+1
RICHARDS Alan		2							2
ROBINSON Phil			2+1						2+1
RYAN John			31	25+1					56+1
SCOTT Andy								17+3	17+3
SHANDRAN Tony								6+1	6+1
SHAUGHNESSY Steve		16+6	29+7	1+1					46+14
SHAW Nigel				7+5					7+5
SHEARER Lee						0+1			0+1
SHERWOOD Steve				9					9
STATHAM Mark						16			16
STEELE Winfield								1+3	1+3
STOREY Brett						8+2			8+2
SULLIVAN Tony						19+9			19+9
SUNLEY Mark			2						2
THOMAS Gary					21+1	8+1			29+2
THOMAS Karl					4+3				4+3
TODD Mark					4+2				4+2
TOMLINSON Dave	4+1								4+1
TRAINER Phil								3+1	3+1
TREES Robert						18+6			18+6
TROTT Dean					31+1				31+1
TRUNDLE Lee						19+3			19+3
TURLEY James								4+5	4+5
UTLEY Darren						1			1

631

Matthew McNeil   Photo: Peter Barnes   Russ Hughes   Photo: G Ellis-Neville

Below: Steve Pickford against Stevenage Borough   Photo: Peter Barnes

STALYBRIDGE CELTIC APPEARANCES

	92/93	93/94	94/95	95/96	96/97	97/98	1998 to 2001	01/02	TOTAL
VARADI Imre						0+1			0+1
VINE Darren					7+8	3+10			10+18
WALKER Gavin						3			3
WALKER Leigh								10+1	10+1
WALSH David								1+5	1+5
WARD Derek								7	7
WARD Richard		1							1
WATSON John						1			1
WESTHEAD Mark					9				9
WHARTON Nathan								1+6	1+6
WHEELER Paul			26+8	6+12					32+20
WHITTAKER Stuart						3+1			3+1
WILLETTS Harvey			27	12					39
WILLIAMS Carwyn						10			10
WILLIAMS David				20					20
WILLIAMSON Matt								10+7	10+7
WILSON Paddy				1+6					1+6
WOOD Steve	2+2							38	40+2
WOODHEAD Robert								8	8
WOODS Kenny		3							3
WOODS Matt								36+1	36+1
WRIGHTSON Jeff						2			2
ZELEM Alan			1						1

1995-96 Squad - Back Row (L-R): David Pover (Physio), Kevin Megson, Ian Patterson, Alex Jones, Matt Smith, Steven Jones, Steven O'Shaughnessy, Sammy Goodacre, David Denby (Assistant Manager).
Middle: Gary Bauress, David Hall, Lee Coathup, Peter Wragg (Manager), Brendan Burke, Paul Wheeler, John Ryan.
Front: David Frain, Neil Edmonds, Nigel Shaw, Paul Higginbottom.

Kevin Parr
Photo: Peter Barnes

Brendan Burke
Photo: Peter Barnes

John Brown
Photo: Colin Stevens

STALYBRIDGE CELTIC GOALSCORERS

	92/93	93/94	94/95	95/96	96/97	97/98	1998 to 2001	01/02	TOTAL
ANDERSON Stewart	3	5	2						10
ARNOLD Ian		7		6(1p)	13(1p)				26(2p)
ASPINALL John	1	1							2
AYORINDE Sam								6	6
BATES Jamie						1			1
BAURESS Gary	1		4						5
BENNETT Paul		1							1
BLAIN Colin		1							1
BROWN John	2	3							5
BUNN Frank	3	2							5
BURKE Brendan			3	12(2p)	11(1p)	16			42(3p)
BUSHELL Steve								1	1
CHARLES Steve					11	1			12
CLAYTON Paul		6	6						12
COATHUP Lee				2					2
COURTNEY Ged								10	10
CRANE Tim					1				1
DIXON Paul	1	2	2						5
DOLBY Chris						1			1
EDMONDS Neil		3	2						5
EDWARDS Mark	12(1p)								12(1p)
EDWARDS Mike		1							1
ELLIS Neil				1					1
ELLISON Lee				1					1
EVANS Andy								2	2
FILSON Martin	2								2
FRAIN David			2	2					4
FUTCHER Ben								1	1
GOLDBOURNE Ronnie					1				1
GOODACRE Sammy				11					11
HALL David			1		3	1			5
HAROLD Ian		1							1
HEATH Steve						1			1
HIGGINBOTTOM Paul	1		3						4
HIGHFIELD Mark						1			1
HINE Mark						1			1
JACKSON Robert		4	6						10
JONES Alex				2					2
JONES Steve				5	5	4			14
KELLY Leon								3	3
KIRKHAM Paul	9	10(3p)							19(3p)
LEICESTER Stuart		2	1						3
MARTIN Dean						1			1
MEGSON Kevin			3	1					4
MORGAN Steve	2								2
MURPHY Gerard								1	1

STALYBRIDGE CELTIC   GOALSCORERS

	92/93	93/94	94/95	95/96	96/97	97/98	1998 to 2001	01/02	TOTAL
O'SHAUGHNESSY Steve				2					2
PARR Kevin								3	3
PEACOCK Richard								5	5
PICKFORD Steve								3(1p)	3(1p)
POWELL Craig				3					3
POWELL Mark						2			2
POWER Phil	8	1							9
PRIEST Eric	1								1
RAMSEY John						1			1
RYAN John			4	3					7
SHANDRAN Tony								1	1
SHAUGHNESY Steve		3	8						11
SHAW Nigel				1					1
STEELE Winfield								2	2
STOREY Brett						1			1
SULLIVAN Tony						6			6
THOMAS Gary						1			1
TREES Robert						1			1
TROTT Dean					6				6
TRUNDLE Lee						7(2p)			7(2p)
TURLEY James								1	1
VINE Darren					1				1
WHEELER Paul			7(2p)	4					11(2p)
WILLIAMS Carwyn						1			1
WOOD Steve	1								1
WOODS Matt								1	1

Stalybridge Celtic Squad 1992-93

STEVENAGE BOROUGH

PROMOTED FROM: Isthmian League 1993-94

2004-2005 SEASON: The Conference

1996-97 Squad - Back Row, left to right: Brian Hierons (Physio), Miguel Luque (Res.Manager), Bill Bannister (Res. Asst. Man), Efetobar Sodje, Des Gallagher, Nicholas Grime, Neil Trebble, Dave Venables, Riochard Wiilmot, Corey Browne, Eric Richards (Kit), and Robbie Scott (Scout). Middle Row: Shaun Stevens, Matthew Vier, Mike Bignall, Paul Fairclough (Manager), Noel Blackwell (Ciach), KennyWebster, DominicGrime, and Barry Hayles. Front Row: Alan Paris, Mark Smith, Neil Catlin, Scott Gretton, Start Beevor, Gary Crawshaw, Paul Barrowcliff, Ron Mutchell and John Ugbah.

		HOME						AWAY						
	P	**W**	**D**	**L**	**F**	**A**	**Pts**	**P**	**W**	**D**	**L**	**F**	**A**	**Pts**	**Position**
94-95	21	10	4	7	40	27	34	21	10	3	8	28	22	33	5
95-96	21	13	6	2	51	20	45	21	14	4	3	50	24	46	1
96-97	21	15	4	2	53	23	49	21	9	6	6	34	30	33	3
97-98	21	8	8	5	35	27	32	21	5	4	12	24	36	19	15
98-99	21	9	9	3	37	23	36	21	8	8	5	25	22	32	6
99-00	21	8	5	8	26	20	29	21	8	4	9	34	34	28	10
00-01	21	8	7	6	36	33	31	21	7	11	3	35	28	32	7
01-02	21	10	4	7	36	30	34	21	5	6	10	21	30	21	11
02-03	21	7	6	8	31	25	27	21	7	4	10	30	30	25	12
03-04	21	10	5	6	29	22	35	21	8	4	9	29	30	28	8
Total	210	98	58	54	374	250	352	210	81	54	75	310	286	297	

SEASONS
10

TOTAL POINTS
649

HIGHEST POSITION
1st 95-96

LOWEST POSITION
15th 97-98

HIGHEST ATTENDANCE
6,489
v Kidderminster H. 25.1.97

LOWEST ATTENDANCE
879 v Stalybridge C. 18.3.95

SEASON GOALSCORER
Barry Hayles 29 (95/96)

CAREER GOALSCORER
Barry Hayles 58

CAREER APPEARANCES
Mark Smith 266+1

	Accrington Stanley		Aldershot Town		Altrincham		Barnet		Barrow		Bath City		Boston United		Bromsgrove Rovers		Burton Albion		Cheltenham Town	
	H	A	H	A	H	A	H	A	H	A	H	A	H	A	H	A	H	A	H	A
94-95					4-2	2-1					3-0	1-2			1-0	1-2				
95-96					1-1	2-0					2-0	2-1			3-3	1-1				
96-97					2-1	2-1					2-1	0-0			3-0	1-1				
97-98																			1-2	1-1
98-99									1-2	1-0									2-2	0-3
99-00					1-1	1-0														
00-01													3-2	3-3						
01-02							3-2	3-0					1-2	0-0						
02-03							1-2	2-0									0-1	2-1		
03-04	2-1	1-2	0-1	0-2			1-2	0-0									1-0	1-1		

	Chester City		Dagenham & Redbridge		Doncaster Rovers		Dover Athletic		Exeter City		Farnborough Town		Forest Green Rovers		Gateshead		Gravesend & N'fleet		Halifax Town	
	H	A	H	A	H	A	H	A	H	A	H	A	H	A	H	A	H	A	H	A
93-94			3-1	1-0			0-3	0-2			3-1	1-1			2-3	2-1			1-0	2-0
94-95			1-0	2-1			3-2	2-1			0-0	2-2			1-1	2-2			2-0	3-2
96-97							4-1	3-3			3-1	1-3			4-1	2-2			6-0	2-4
97-98							2-2	1-1			5-0	2-1			6-1	1-2			1-2	0-4
98-99					2-0	0-0	1-0	1-1			3-1	0-1	1-1	2-1						
99-00					3-0	2-1	3-1	2-4					1-1	2-3						
00-01	1-2	1-1	0-2	0-3	0-0	0-0	1-1	0-1					3-1	3-2						
01-02	2-1	1-5	1-3	0-1	0-0	0-2	1-3	1-0			1-2	1-6	4-1	0-0						
02-03	0-1	0-2	2-0	2-3	2-3	0-0					5-0	1-0	0-0	3-0			1-0	1-2	0-1	0-1
03-04	0-0	2-1	0-2	2-1					2-2	0-1	3-2	0-2	2-1	1-3			2-2	3-2	1-0	1-2

	Hayes		Hednesford Town		Hereford United		Kettering Town		Kidderminster H.		Kingstonian		Leek Town		Leigh RMI		Macclesfield Town		Margate	
	H	A	H	A	H	A	H	A	H	A	H	A	H	A	H	A	H	A	H	A
93-94							2-2	2-0	2-3	3-0							1-1	3-0		
94-95			1-0	1-2			5-1	2-1	4-1	1-0							4-0	0-0		
96-97	2-0	3-1	3-2	0-0			0-0	2-1	2-2	0-3							2-3	1-2		
97-98	1-5	3-1	1-1	1-2	2-0	2-0	0-0	0-2	3-1	3-1			1-1	1-2						
98-99	2-1	2-2	3-1	2-2	0-3	1-0	2-2	2-1	3-0	0-2	3-3	0-1	2-0	1-1						
99-00	3-0	2-1	0-1	2-2	0-3	2-1	3-0	0-1	0-2	1-3	0-1	0-1								
00-01	3-3	1-0	4-1	1-1	2-1	1-1	2-0	2-1					2-5	2-0	3-0	4-1				
01-02	1-1	2-0			3-1	1-1									0-1	2-1			3-1	1-2
02-03					0-2	2-2	2-0	0-1							3-1	1-2			1-3	1-1
03-04					0-2	0-1									4-0	3-1			2-1	4-1

STEVENAGE BOROUGH

	Merthyr Tydfil		Morecambe		Northwich Victoria		Nuneaton Borough		Runcorn		Rushden & Diamonds		Scarborough		Shrewsbury Town		Slough Town	
	H	A	H	A	H	A	H	A	H	A	H	A	H	A	H	A	H	A
93-94	0-0	2-2			1-1	1-0			0-1	1-3								
94-95			1-1	0-1	5-1	3-1			4-1	8-0							3-1	6-2
96-97			4-2	2-1	2-0	1-0					4-1	1-0					2-2	6-1
97-98			0-3	2-0	1-3	1-1					2-1	0-2					4-2	1-3
98-99			2-0	1-1	1-3	1-0					0-0	1-2						
99-00			1-2	3-3	3-1	3-3	2-1	1-0			2-2	1-2	0-1	3-1				
00-01			1-1	2-1	3-1	2-3	1-1	3-0			0-2	2-2	1-1	2-2				
01-02			3-1	3-0	1-0	1-2	2-2	1-2					2-0	1-1				
02-03			1-1	1-3	2-2	1-1	3-1	0-3					1-1	2-1				
03-04			0-1	1-2	1-0	2-1							2-2	2-2	2-0	1-3		

	Southport		Stafford Rangers		Stalybridge Celtic		Sutton United		Tamworth		Telford United		Welling United		Woking		Yeovil Town	
	H	A	H	A	H	A	H	A	H	A	H	A	H	A	H	A	H	A
93-94	1-2	1-2	1-0	3-0	5-1	0-1					4-3	2-1	1-2	0-1	0-1	0-3	5-0	0-0
94-95	1-3	1-0			2-2	5-2					0-1	3-1	4-1	3-0	4-0	1-4		
96-97	2-1	0-0			1-1	3-0					3-0	3-2	2-1	0-2	0-3	1-3		
97-98	1-0	0-1			1-1	1-1					1-1	0-3	0-0	0-1	0-0	3-5	2-1	1-2
98-99	0-0	1-1									2-2	3-0	1-1	1-1	5-0	2-1	1-1	3-1
99-00	1-1	1-2					1-0	2-0			2-0	1-2	0-1	1-2	0-1	2-0	0-0	2-2
00-01	1-3	2-2									5-3	2-2			0-3	1-1	0-0	1-1
01-02	2-1	0-0			2-0	0-2					1-1	1-2			1-4	1-1	2-3	1-2
02-03	3-0	2-3									1-3	3-1			1-1	5-1	2-2	1-2
03-04									3-1	2-1	0-1	2-0			1-1	1-1		

2003-2004. Back row, left to right: Jamie Cook, Lee Flynn, Justin Richards, Sam McMahon, Simon Travis, Simon Wormull, Micky Warner. Middle row: Anthony Elding, Tony Battersby, Peter Costelo, Mark Westhead, Lionel Perez, Barry Laker, Rocky Baptiste and Jamie Gould. Front row: Graham Pearce (Asst. Man), Danny Carroll, Jason Goodliffe, Graham Westley (Manager), Steve Watson, Gary Holloway and Graham Benstead (Coach)

	Home						Away					
	P	W	D	L	F	A	P	W	D	L	F	A
ACCRINGTON S	1	1	0	0	2	1	1	0	0	1	1	2
ALDERSHOT T	1	0	0	1	0	1	1	0	0	1	0	2
ALTRINCHAM	4	2	2	0	8	5	4	4	0	0	7	2
BARNET	3	1	0	2	5	6	3	2	1	0	5	0
BARROW	1	0	0	1	1	2	1	1	0	0	1	0
BATH C	3	3	0	0	7	1	3	1	1	1	3	3
BOSTON U	2	1	0	1	4	4	2	0	2	0	3	3
BROMSGROVE R	3	2	1	0	7	3	3	0	2	1	3	4
BURTON A	2	1	0	1	1	1	2	1	1	0	3	2
CHELTENHAM T	2	0	1	1	3	4	2	0	1	1	1	4
CHESTER C	4	1	1	2	3	4	4	1	1	2	4	9
DAGENHAM & R	6	3	0	3	7	8	6	3	0	3	7	9
DONCASTER R	5	2	2	1	7	3	5	1	3	1	2	3
DOVER A	8	4	2	2	15	13	8	2	3	3	10	13
EXETER C	1	0	1	0	2	2	1	0	0	1	0	1
FARNBOROUGH T	8	6	1	1	23	7	8	2	2	4	8	16
FOREST GREEN R	6	3	3	0	11	5	6	3	1	2	11	9
GATESHEAD	4	2	1	1	13	6	4	1	2	1	7	7
GRAVESEND & N	2	1	1	0	3	2	2	1	0	1	4	4
HALIFAX T	6	4	0	2	11	3	6	2	0	4	8	13
HAYES	6	3	2	1	12	10	6	5	1	0	13	5
HEDNESFORD T	6	4	1	1	12	6	6	0	4	2	7	9
HEREFORD U	7	3	0	4	7	12	7	3	3	1	9	6
KETTERING T	8	4	4	0	16	5	8	5	0	3	10	8
KIDDERMINSTER H	6	3	1	2	14	9	6	3	0	3	8	9
KINGSTONIAN	3	0	1	2	5	9	3	1	0	2	2	2
LEEK T	2	1	1	0	3	1	2	0	1	1	2	3
LEIGH RMI	4	3	0	1	10	2	4	3	0	1	10	5
MACCLESFIELD T	3	1	1	1	7	4	3	1	1	1	4	2
MARGATE	3	2	0	1	6	5	3	1	1	1	6	4
MERTHYR T	1	0	1	0	0	0	1	0	1	0	2	2
MORECAMBE	9	3	3	3	13	12	9	4	2	3	15	12
NORTHWICH V	10	6	2	2	20	12	10	5	3	2	16	12
NUNEATON B	4	2	2	0	8	5	4	2	0	2	5	5
RUNCORN	2	1	0	1	4	2	2	1	0	1	9	3
RUSHDEN & D	5	2	2	1	8	6	5	1	1	3	5	8
SCARBOROUGH	5	1	3	1	6	5	5	2	3	0	10	7
SHREWSBURY T	1	1	0	0	2	0	1	0	0	1	1	3
SLOUGH T	3	2	1	0	9	5	3	2	0	1	13	6
SOUTHPORT	9	4	2	3	12	11	9	1	4	4	8	11
STAFFORD R	1	1	0	0	1	0	1	1	0	0	3	0
STALYBRIDGE C	5	2	3	0	11	5	5	2	1	2	9	6
SUTTON U	1	1	0	0	1	0	1	1	0	0	2	0
TAMWORTH	1	1	0	0	3	1	1	1	0	0	2	1
TELFORD U	10	4	3	3	19	15	10	6	1	3	20	14
WELLING U	6	2	2	2	8	6	6	1	1	4	5	7
WOKING	10	2	3	5	12	14	10	3	3	4	17	20
YEOVIL T	7	2	4	1	12	7	7	1	3	3	9	10
TOTAL	210	98	58	54	374	250	210	81	54	75	310	286

STEVENAGE BOROUGH — LEADING APPEARANCES

	94-95	95-96	96-97	97-98	98-99	99-00	00-01	01-02	02-03	03-04	TOTAL
Mark SMITH	41	39	40	31	42	38+1	35			12+2	278+3
Robin TROTT				40	17+2	21	28+1	22+4	19		147+7
Ryan KIRBY			27	31	18+1	35+6	18+4				129+11
Stuart BEEVOR	24+4	14+6	28+7	26+4	20+3						112+24
Des GALLAGHER	29+2	23+1	31	31	6	1					121+3
Efetobor SODJE	23+5	37+1	39+1								99+7
Barry HAYLES	35	38	24+6								97+6
Sam McMAHON						9	27	35+3	21+2		92+5
Michael LOVE				26+1	30+4	33+3					89+8
Gary CRAWSHAW	5	12+4	22+9	36+3							75+16
Dave VENABLES	37	29+4	9+4								75+8
Paul BARROWCLIFF		36+3	36+2	5							77+5
Carl ALFORD					40+1	38+1					78+2

Mark Smith. Photo: Keith Clayton.

Carl Alford. Photo: Keith Clayton.

STEVENAGE BOROUGH — LEADING GOALSCORERS

	94-95	95-96	96-97	97-98	98-99	99-00	00-01	01-02	02-03	03-04	TOTAL
HAYLES Barry	13	29	16								58
ALFORD Carl					26(2p)	24(3p)					50(5p)
CRAWSHAW Gary	1	4(2p)	12(2p)	11(1p)							28(5p)
BROWNE Corey		15	10								25
ELDING Anthony								7	17		24
HAY Darran						15	6				21
VENABLES Dave	8	10	1								19
LYNCH Tony	8	9									17

STEVENAGE BOROUGH   APPEARANCES

	94-95	95-96	96-97	97-98	98-99	99-00	00-01	01-02	02-03	03-04	TOTAL
ABBEY Ben								0+1			0+1
ABBEY Nathan										6	6
ABBOTT Paul							2+3				2+3
ADAMS Carl			7+6								7+6
ALFORD Carl					40+1	38+1					78+2
ALLEN Malcolm				0+1							0+1
ARCHER Arron				0+1							0+1
ARMSTRONG Paul						0+3	25+16	4+12			29+31
ARNOTT Ady								7			7
AYRES James						6	2				8
BAPTISTE Rocky										9+11	9+11
BARNARD Lee										2+2	2+2
BARNWELL-EDINBORO Jamie					14						14
BARR Gordon					1	0+1					1+1
BARROWCLIFF Paul		36+3	36+2	5							77+5
BASS David						9					9
BATES Marvin	0+2	0+3	1								1+5
BATTERSBY Tony									4+2	10+4	14+6
BEDROSSIAN Ara	5										5
BEEKE Scott		1+4									1+4
BEEVOR Stuart	24+4	14+6	28+7	26+4	20+3						112+24
BELL Leon									2+2		2+2
BERRY Steve		37			27						64
BIGNALL Mike			8+2								8+2
BLACKWOOD Michael									17+1		17+1
BOYD George									1	4+7	5+7
BOYLAN Lee							1				1
BRADSHAW Darren							7				7
BRADY Jon										13+7	13+7
BRENNAN Dean										13+4	13+4
BRIDGE Mark							0+3				0+3
BRISSETT Jason							1+1				1+1
BROCK Kevin	5+1										5+1
BROOKER Paul					10						10
BROUGH Michael										11	11
BROUGHTON Drewe							4				4
BROWNE Corey		31+1	23+12				0+1				54+14
BUNCE Nathan							24+1		11	24	59+1
BUTLER Steve					6+3						6+3
CAMARA Ben										0+1	0+1
CAMPBELL Dudley J								18+3	0+2		18+5
CAMPBELL Jamie								8+1	25		33+1
CAMPBELL Sean				1							1
CAREY Shaun								3			3
CARROLL Danny									15	15+5	30+5
CASH Stuart	5										5
CASTLE Steve								5+2			5+2
CATLIN Neil			21+2	8							29+2
CLARKE Adrian							34+2	27+5	3+1		64+8

STEVENAGE BOROUGH APPEARANCES

	94-95	95-96	96-97	97-98	98-99	99-00	00-01	01-02	02-03	03-04	TOTAL
CODNER Robert				4							4
COLLINS Chris						4+1					4+1
CONROY Stuart	3										3
COOK Jamie									7+6	15+11	22+17
CORT Leon							8+1				8+1
COSTELLO Peter										8+4	8+4
CRACKNELL Dean										0+1	0+1
CRAWSHAW Gary	5	12+4	22+9	36+3							75+16
CRETTON Scott	0+1	6+8	5+1								11+10
DEAN Phil				2+2							2+2
DEAN Tony								0+1			0+1
DILLNUTT James				9+3	5						14+3
DILLON Kevin	12										12
DIXON Gary				1+3							1+3
DREYER John								24	2		26
DUCKETT Mark							0+1				0+1
DYER Wayne							2+2				2+2
ELAD Efan				1+2							1+2
ELDING Anthony									12+2	33+3	45+5
ENDERSBY Lee		2									2
EVERS Sean								6+2			6+2
FENTON Darren				5+5							5+5
FIELD Lewis						0+1					0+1
FISHER Matt								13+3	15		28+3
FITZPATRICK Lee								1+1			1+1
FLACK Jo									0+1	0+1	0+2
FLYNN Lee										22	22
FORBES Steve						4+2					4+2
FORTUNE-WEST Leo	13+4										13+4
FRASER Stuart								5	12+5		17+5
FURNESS Adam								0+1			0+1
FUTCHER Andy					2						2
GALLAGHER Des	29+2	23+1	31	31	6	1					121+3
GALLEN Joe				0+4							0+4
GENTLE Dominic			8+2								8+2
GEORGE Liam								3+1			3+1
GITTINGS Martin	10+2										10+2
GOODLIFFE Jason								32	31+3	9	72+3
GOULD Jamie										26+1	26+1
GRAHAM Mark							9+1				9+1
GRAY Phil									0+2		0+2
GRAZIOLI Giulliano				11+1							11+1
GREGORY Justin									4		4
GREYGOOSE Dean								18			18
GRIDELET Phil					1						1
GRIME Dominic		0+1	2								2+1
GRIME Nicholas		1+1									1+1
HAAG Kelly		0+1									0+1
HAMSHER John							18	28+1			46+1

643

Dudley Campbell. Photo: Peter Barnes.

Adrian Clarke. Photo: Peter Barnes.

Gary Crawshaw. Photo: Mark Sandom.

Matt Fisher. Photo: Peter Barnes.

Leo Fortune-West.

Barry Hayles. Photo: Eric Marsh.

STEVENAGE BOROUGH — APPEARANCES

	94-95	95-96	96-97	97-98	98-99	99-00	00-01	01-02	02-03	03-04	TOTAL
HARRISON Ross					13	10+10					23+10
HARVEY Lee				7+4	33	30+1					70+5
HASELL James					2						2
HAY Darran							24+4	12+10			36+14
HAYLES Barry	35	38	24+6								97+6
HEDMAN Rudi	31+2										31+2
HIGHTON Bobby					0+1						0+1
HOCKTON Danny						18+2	0+1				18+3
HODGSON Richard										3+3	3+3
HOLDEN Steve				8+4							8+4
HOLLOWAY Gary									6+3	13+10	19+13
HOOPER Dean			21								21
HOUGHTON Ray						3					3
HOUGHTON Scott								5+2	3+3		8+5
HOWARTH Lee				31+3	35+2						66+5
HOWELL Dave		1									1
HOWELL Richard								2	3+4		5+4
ILLMAN Neil							24+10	5+11			29+21
INMAN Niall				1+4							1+4
JACKSON Elliot					7						7
JACKSON Kirk								11+6	16+3		27+9
JOHANSEN Thomas				3+1							3+1
JOYCE Tony	2										2
KALDJOB Simon				0+1							0+1
KALOGERACOS Vasili	2+1										2+1
KEAN Robbie					1+2						1+2
KELLY Warren				6+1							6+1
KERSEY Lee						3+1					3+1
KING Ian						16+1					16+1
KIRBY Ryan			27	31	18+1	35+6	18+4				129+11
LAKER Barry									14	35	49
LANGSTON Matt									1+2		1+2
LEADBEATER Richard				11+1	15+20	5+1					31+22
LINCOLN Greg								1			1
LOMAS Andy	12										12
LOVE Michael				26+1	30+4	33+3					89+8
LUCKETT Colin								1			1
LUQUE Miguel	4+4										4+4
LYNCH Tony	28+7	25+1									53+8
MAAMRIA Dino									8+3	25	33+3
MAHORN Paul				2+4							2+4
MANUEL Billy	2										2
MARCELLE Clint										0+3	0+3
MARCH Jamie				30+2							30+2
MARSHALL Rob				1							1
MARSHALL Shaun		9+17									9+17
MARTIN Dean						20+3	28+2				48+5
McAREE Rodney				3							3
McDONALD Charlie									13+3		13+3

Kirk Jackson. Photo: Peter Barnes.

Tony Lynch. Photo: V.J.Robertson.

Sam McMahon. Photo: Peter Barnes.

Steve Perkins. Photo: Peter Barnes.

Efetobar Sodje. Photo: Alan Coomes.

Paul Sturgess. Photo: Peter Barnes.

STEVENAGE BOROUGH APPEARANCES

	94-95	95-96	96-97	97-98	98-99	99-00	00-01	01-02	02-03	03-04	TOTAL
McDONALD Gary									5+3		5+3
McGHEE David						0+2					0+2
McMAHON Sam						9	27	35+3	21+2		92+5
MEAH Jeran				3+2							3+2
METCALFE Christian							6+2				6+2
MIDSON Jack								1+3	0+6		1+9
MILLER Robert						8+1	24+8				32+9
MISON Michael			9								9
MORGAN John							12+6	2+4			14+10
MORRISON David						3+1					3+1
MUSTOE Neil									0+2		0+2
MUTCHELL Rob		35+1	32+3								67+4
NAYLOR Dominic					17+6						17+6
NUGENT Richard	27+1	10+1				1+1					38+3
NYAMAH Kofi	6						5+4				11+4
OMEGBEHIN Colin	1+1										1+1
OPARA Louis									0+1		0+1
OUGHAM James						0+1					0+1
PACQUETTE Richard									6+1		6+1
PARIS Alan		5	11+2								16+2
PARKER Adam	7+7										7+7
PEARSON Chris					10+8	1+6	0+4				11+18
PEEL Nathan					2+2						2+2
PENNYFATHER Glenn	3+1										3+1
PEREZ Leonel									4+1	27	31+1
PERKINS Steve				25+1	3+2						28+3
PHILLIPS David							18+2				18+2
PHILLIPS Mark	1										1
PITCHER Geoff										4+1	4+1
PLUCK Colin						3					3
PLUMMER Dwayne					18+5	2+4					20+9
RATTLE Jon	20										20
REINELT Robbie					7+3						7+3
RICHARDS Justin									12+7	9+16	21+23
RIDDLE Louis								5	6+1		11+1
ROBERTS Graham	11										11
ROGERS Darren				1	8+3						9+3
ROGERS Mark										4	4
RUDGLEY Simon	1										1
SAMPANY Kwame				0+1							0+1
SAMUELS Dean					6+3						6+3
SAMUELS Junior						13+9					13+9
SANDEMAN Bradley				8+1							8+1
SCOTT Richard									4+1	2+4	6+5
SEARLE Steve							5				5
SHIELDS Tony								1+1			1+1
SIGERE Jean-Michel								18+3	7+9		25+12
SIMPSON Phil	22	10+1									32+1
SIMPSON Robert				1+2							1+2

David Venables. Photo: Keith Clayton.

Martin Williams. Photo: Peter Barnes.

Simon Wormull. Photo: Peter Barnes.

STEVENAGE BOROUGH

APPEARANCES

	94-95	95-96	96-97	97-98	98-99	99-00	00-01	01-02	02-03	03-04	TOTAL
SMART Garry	18+1										18+1
SMITH Dean								0+1			0+1
SMITH Leon								0+4			0+4
SMITH Mark	41	39	40	31	42	38+1	35			12+2	278+3
SMITH Neil									4+4		4+4
SODJE Akpo							0+1				0+1
SODJE Efetobor	23+5	37+1	39+1								99+7
SODJE Sam								8	17+3		25+3
SOLOMAN Jason			10	27+4							37+4
STAPLETON Simon				3+1							3+1
STATHAM Brian					3						3
STEVENS Shaun			0+1								0+1
STEVENS Tim				7+3							7+3
STIRLING Jude								8+3	9+1		17+4
STROUTS Jimmy					17+1	18+1					35+2
STURGESS Paul								24+1			24+1
TAGRO Baroan								0+1			0+1
TATE Chris								6			6
TAYLOR Chris					29	39	15				83
TELEMAQUE Errol					1+6						1+6
THOMPSON Paul				5+4	3+10						8+14
TOMLINSON Graeme									2+8		2+8
TRAVIS Simon									37+3	20+2	57+5
TREBBLE Neil		6+2	10+17	31+5							47+24
TROTT Robin				40	17+2	21	28+1	22+4	19		147+7
UGBAH John			8+5								8+5
VAN DER VELDEN Carel				1							1
VENABLES Dave	37	29+4	9+4								75+8
VIER Matthew		0+1									0+1
WALTERS Steve							7	10			17
WARNER Michael									10+1	30+5	40+6
WATSON Steve									15	26+1	41+1
WATTS Alvin								2			2
WEATHERSTONE Ross										2+2	2+2
WEBSTER Kenny	13+1	38	17								68+1
WESTHEAD Mark									37	9+1	46+1
WHITMARSH Paul	1+4										1+4
WILKERSON Paul							27	24			51
WILLIAMS Darren										0+1	0+1
WILLIAMS Dean	3+2										3+2
WILLIAMS Martin								26+7	15		41+7
WILLIS Roger									1		1
WILMOT Richard		19+1	11+1	11							41+2
WILSON Phil									1+2		1+2
WORDSWORTH Dean				15+5							15+5
WORMULL Simon								22+1	23+7	20+1	65+9
WORRALL Ben						1					1
WRAIGHT Gary					22+5	8					30+5

STEVENAGE BOROUGH   GOALSCORERS

	94-95	95-96	96-97	97-98	98-99	99-00	00-01	01-02	02-03	03-04	TOTAL
ADAMS Carl			4								4
ALFORD Carl					26(2p)	24(3p)					50(5p)
ARMSTRONG Paul							8	1			9
BAPTISTE Rocky										4	4
BARNARD Lee										1	1
BARNWELL-EDINBORO Jamie					4						4
BARROWCLIFF Paul		6	5(3p)								11(3p)
BATES Marvin	1		1								2
BATTERSBY Tony									3(1p)	3(1p)	6(2p)
BEEVOR Stuart	3	2	3	4	3						15
BERRY Steve		2			1						3
BIGNALL Mike			4								4
BLACKWOOD Michael									2		2
BOYD George										1	1
BRENNAN Dean										2	2
BROCK Kevin	1										1
BROOKER Paul					1						1
BROUGH Michael										2	2
BROUGHTON Drewe							3				3
BROWNE Corey		15	10								25
BUNCE Nathan							1		1	1	3
BUTLER Steve					3						3
CAMPBELL Dudley J								3			3
CAMPBELL Jamie								1			1
CARROLL Danny									4	1	5
CATLIN Neil			7	2							9
CLARKE Adrian							9(3p)	6(1p)			15(4p)
CONROY Steve	1										1
COOK Jamie									1	1	2
COSTELLO Paul									1		1
CRAWSHAW Gary	1	4(2p)	12(2p)	11(1p)							28(5p)
DILLON Kevin	2(1p)										2(1p)
ELDING Anthony									7	17	24
FISHER Matt								2			2
FLACK Jo										1	1
FORBES Steve						1					1
FORTUNE-WEST Leo	7										7
FRASER Stuart									1		1
GITTINS Martin	2										2
GOODLIFFE Jason								3	4(2p)	1	8(2p)
GOULD Jamie										1	1
GRAHAM Mark							1				1
GRAZIOLI Giuiliano				7							7
HAMSHER John							1(1p)	3(3p)			4(4p)
HARRISON Ross					1						1
HAY Darran							15	6			21
HAYLES Barry	13	29	16								58
HEDMAN Rudi	2										2

650

STEVENAGE BOROUGH GOALSCORERS

	94-95	95-96	96-97	97-98	98-99	99-00	00-01	01-02	02-03	03-04	TOTAL
HOCKTON Danny						6					6
HOLLOWAY Gary										3	3
HOOPER Dean			1								1
HOUGHTON Scott									1(1p)		1(1p)
HOWARTH Lee					1	1					2
ILLMAN Neil							11				11
JACKSON Kirk								7	5		12
KALOGERACOS Vasili	1										1
KEAN Robbie					1						1
KIRBY Ryan		2		1		3	1				7
LAKER Barry									1	1	2
LEADBEATER Richard					4	5	2				11
LOVE Michael				1	3	2					6
LYNCH Tony	8	9									17
MAAMRIA Dino									5	9(3p)	14(3p)
MARSHALL Shaun		4									4
MARTIN Dean						3	4				7
McDONALD Charlie									3		3
McMAHON Sam						1	2	4	2		9
MIDSON Jack									1		1
MILLER Robert						1					1
MISON Michael			5								5
MORGAN John							2				2
MORRISON David						1					1
MUTCHELL Rob		1(1p)									1(1p)
NUGENT Richard	2	2									4
NYAMAH Kofi	1										1
OMEGBEHIN Colin	1										1
PACQUETTE Richard									2		2
PEARSON Chris					3	1	2				6
PERKINS Steve				4							4
PHILLIPS David							1				1
PLUMMER Dwayne					2						2
RATTLE Jon	1										1
RICHARDS Justin								6(1p)	3		9(1p)
ROBERTS Graham	1(1p)										1(1p)
ROGERS Mark										1	1
SAMUELS Junior						5					5
SHIELDS Tony								1			1
SIGERE Jean-Michel								10	3		13
SIMPSON Phil	2(1p)										2(1p)
SMART Gary	1										1
SMITH Mark	4	6		2							12
SODJE Akpo							1				1
SODJE Efetobor	1	4	4								9
SODJE Sam								2			2
SOLOMAN Jason			3	3							6
STEVENS Tim				3							3

651

STEVENAGE BOROUGH   GOALSCORERS

	94-95	95-96	96-97	97-98	98-99	99-00	00-01	01-02	02-03	03-04	TOTAL
STIRLING Jude								1			1
STROUTS Jimmy					5	3					8
TATE Chris								2			2
TELEMAQUE Errol					1						1
THOMPSON Paul				1(1p)	1						2(1p)
TRAVIS Simon										1	1
TREBBLE Neil		2	5	8							15
TROTT Robin				3	2	1	2		1		9
UGBAH John			1								1
VENABLES Dave	8	10	1								19
WALTERS Steve							2				2
WEBSTER Kenny		4(2p)	2(2p)								6(4p)
WILLIAMS Dean	3										3
WILLIAMS Martin								3	2		5
WORDSWORTH Dean				8(4p)							8(4p)
WORMULL Simon								3(1p)	4	2	9(1p)
WRAIGHT Gary						2	1				3

Giuliano Grazioli and Jason Soloman.   Photo: Peter Barnes.

SUTTON UNITED

PROMOTED FROM: The Isthmian League 1986, 1999
RELEGATED TO: The Isthmian League 1991, 2000
2004-2005 SEASON: Conference South

1987-88 Squad.
Back Row (L-R): Bill Webb (Matchday Assistant), Nigel golley, Francis Awartefe, Micky Joyce, Trevor Roffey, Vernon Pratt, Mark Golley, Paul McKinnon, Danny Keenan (Physio), Dave Wall (Liaison Officer), Barrie Williams (General Manager).
Front Row: Stuart Hemsley, Robyn Jones, Richard Pope, Mike Cornwell, Tony Rains, Paul Rogers, Micky Stephens.

	HOME							AWAY							
	P	W	D	L	F	A	Pts	P	W	D	L	F	A	Pts	Position
86-87	21	12	4	5	52	24	40	21	7	7	7	29	27	28	7
87-88	21	9	8	4	41	25	35	21	7	10	4	36	29	31	8
88-89	20	10	5	5	43	26	35	20	2	10	8	21	28	16	12
89-90	21	14	2	5	42	24	44	21	5	4	12	26	40	19	8
90-91	21	6	6	9	29	33	24	21	4	3	14	33	49	15	21
91-92															
92-93															
93-94															
94-95															
95-96															
96-97															
97-98															
98-99															
99-00	21	4	8	9	23	32	20	21	4	2	15	16	43	14	22
Total	125	55	33	37	230	164	198	125	29	36	60	161	216	123	

SEASONS
6

TOTAL POINTS
198 + 123 = 321

HIGHEST POSITION
7   (86/87)

LOWEST POSITION
22   (99/00)

HIGHEST ATTENDANCE
1496   Colchester (26-1-91)

LOWEST ATTENDANCE
445   Frickley (28-3-87)

SEASON GOALSCORER
Efan Ekoku 25 (89/90)

CAREER GOALSCORER
Paul McKinnon 65(10p)

CAREER APPEARANCES
Paul Rogers 187+3

SUTTON UNITED

	Altrincham		Aylesbury United		Barnet		Barrow		Bath City		Boston United		Cheltenham Town		Chorley		Colchester United	
	H	A	H	A	H	A	H	A	H	A	H	A	H	A	H	A	H	A
86-87					3-1	2-1			7-2	3-1	3-1	0-0	0-0	2-1				
87-88					0-1	2-6			3-1	4-0	1-2	0-0	3-0	1-1				
88-89			5-2	0-1	5-1	1-1					0-0	1-3	1-1	3-2	1-2	1-2		
89-90					1-3	1-4	3-3	0-1			2-0	1-3	0-2	0-2	3-0	2-3		
90-91					0-1	0-1	2-1	1-3	1-1	2-2	0-0	2-2	2-3	2-3			0-1	0-1
91																		
/																		
99																		
99-00																		

	Dagenham		Darlington		Doncaster Rovers		Dover Athletic		Enfield		Farnborough Town		Fisher Athletic		Forest Green Rovers		Frickley Athletic	
	H	A	H	A	H	A	H	A	H	A	H	A	H	A	H	A	H	A
86-87	1-0	1-2							0-1	0-0							3-0	1-1
87-88	1-1	1-0							3-3	3-2			2-0	1-1				
88-89									3-1	1-1			2-1	1-1				
89-90			2-1	0-2					2-0	3-2	2-3	3-1	2-1	2-1				
90-91													3-1	1-1				
91																		
/																		
99																		
99-00					1-0	0-1	0-1	1-1							3-2	2-1		

	Gateshead		Hayes		Hednesford Town		Hereford United		Kettering Town		Kidderminster H.		Kingstonian		Lincoln City		Macclesfield Town	
	H	A	H	A	H	A	H	A	H	A	H	A	H	A	H	A	H	A
86-87	3-0	1-1							8-0	4-1	3-1	0-0						
87-88									2-2	2-2	2-0	2-2			4-1	1-1	2-3	1-1
88-89									0-2	0-1	1-1	0-1					1-2	3-1
89-90									2-1	0-2	1-2	2-2					2-1	1-1
90-91	3-3	9-0							1-2	2-5	1-2	0-1					3-1	2-4
91																		
/																		
99																		
99-00			2-2	0-1	0-0	0-1	1-1	1-4	1-1	0-1	0-3	0-1	2-2	2-4				

	Maidstone United		Merthyr Tydfil		Morecambe		Northwich Victoria		Nuneaton Borough		Runcorn		Rushden & Diamonds		Scarborough		Slough Town	
	H	A	H	A	H	A	H	A	H	A	H	A	H	A	H	A	H	A
86-87	3-1	1-0					2-1	1-0	2-3	1-1	1-1	2-3			0-2	1-2		
87-88	5-1	4-2					1-1	4-1			2-2	0-1						
88-89	1-1	1-1					3-3	2-4			3-1	1-2						
89-90			1-1	3-2			2-1	3-2			3-0	0-1						
90-91			1-1	0-3			2-2	0-1			1-3	1-5					5-2	2-1
91 / 99																		
99-00					0-1	2-6	2-2	0-2	1-2	0-2			0-4	0-4	1-2	0-3		

	Southport		Stafford Rangers		Stevenage Borough		Telford United		Wealdstone		Welling United		Weymouth		Woking		Wycombe Wanderers		Yeovil Town	
	H	A	H	A	H	A	H	A	H	A	H	A	H	A	H	A	H	A	H	A
86-87			3-0	2-4			2-2	2-0	2-2	1-2	2-0	1-3	2-3	2-2						
87-88			2-0	0-2			2-1	3-3	1-1	0-0	1-1	4-1	0-1	1-2			2-2	1-1		
88-89			2-0	1-1			1-2	0-0			0-1	1-1	3-1	2-2			3-0	2-2	5-2	0-0
89-90			1-0	1-3			6-1	1-1			1-0	0-1					1-2	2-3	3-1	1-3
90-91			0-3	2-1			0-3	2-4			1-1	2-1					1-0	1-4	1-0	1-2
91 / 99																				
99-00	1-1	1-1			0-2	0-1	2-1	0-2			2-3	3-2			1-1	2-1			0-1	2-1

SUTTON UNITED LEADING APPEARANCES

	86/87	87/88	88/89	89/90	90/91	91/92 - 98/99	99/00	TOTAL
ROGERS Paul	39+1	38	40	29+1	41+1			187+3
RAINS Tony	39	42	34	42	21			178
GOLLEY Nigel	34	32	38	23	36+1			163+1
McKINNON Paul	9	22+1	26	38	34+5			129+6
HEMSLEY Stuart	41	35	19	27	6+1			128+1
DENNIS Lenny	28+3	32+1	38	1	15+1			114+5
DAWSON Phil	29+4	9+5	32+3	15	19			104+12

Gwynne Berry.

Danny Brooker. Photo: Dennis Nicholson.

Mike Cornwell. Photo: Jo Corkett.

Phil Dawson. Photo: Eric Marsh.

SUTTON UNITED

	Home						Away					
	P	W	D	L	F	A	P	W	D	L	F	A
ALTRINCHAM	6	1	3	2	7	10	6	1	1	4	5	18
ALTRINCHAM	6	4	0	2	13	9	6	1	1	4	3	10
AYLESBURY U	1	1	0	0	5	2	1	0	0	1	0	1
BARNET	5	2	0	3	9	7	5	1	1	3	6	13
BARROW	2	1	1	0	5	4	2	0	0	2	1	4
BATH C	3	2	1	0	11	4	3	2	1	0	9	3
BOSTON U	5	2	2	1	6	3	5	0	3	2	4	8
CHELTENHAM T	5	1	2	2	6	6	5	2	1	2	8	9
CHORLEY	2	1	0	1	4	2	2	0	0	2	3	5
COLCHESTER U	1	0	0	1	0	1	1	0	0	1	0	1
DAGENHAM	2	1	1	0	2	1	2	1	0	1	2	2
DARLINGTON	1	1	0	0	2	1	1	0	0	1	0	2
DONCASTER R	1	1	0	0	1	0	1	0	0	1	0	1
DOVER A	1	0	0	1	0	1	1	0	1	0	1	1
ENFIELD	4	2	1	1	8	5	4	2	2	0	7	5
FARNBOROUGH T	1	0	0	1	2	3	1	1	0	0	3	1
FISHER A	4	4	0	0	9	3	4	1	3	0	5	4
FOREST GREEN R	1	1	0	0	3	2	1	1	0	0	2	1
FRICKLEY A	1	1	0	0	3	0	1	0	1	0	1	1
GATESHEAD	2	1	1	0	6	3	2	1	1	0	10	1
HAYES	1	0	1	0	2	2	1	0	0	1	0	1
HEDNESFORD T	1	0	1	0	0	0	1	0	0	1	0	1
HEREFORD U	1	0	1	0	1	1	1	0	0	1	1	4
KETTERING T	6	2	2	2	14	8	6	1	1	4	8	12
KIDDERMINSTER H	6	2	1	3	8	9	6	0	3	3	4	7
KINGSTONIAN	1	0	1	0	2	2	1	0	0	1	2	4
LINCOLN C	1	1	0	0	4	1	1	0	1	0	1	1
MACCLESFIELD T	4	2	0	2	8	7	4	1	2	1	7	7
MAIDSTONE U	3	2	1	0	9	3	3	2	1	0	6	3
MERTHYR T	2	0	2	0	2	2	2	1	0	1	3	5
MORECAMBE	1	0	0	1	0	1	1	0	0	1	2	6
NORTHWICH V	6	2	4	0	12	10	6	3	0	3	10	10
NUNEATON B	2	0	0	2	3	5	2	0	1	1	1	3
RUNCORN	5	2	2	1	10	7	5	0	0	5	4	12
RUSHDEN & D	1	0	0	1	0	4	1	0	0	1	0	4
SCARBOROUGH	2	0	0	2	1	4	2	0	0	2	1	5
SLOUGH T	1	1	0	0	5	2	1	1	0	0	2	1
SOUTHPORT	1	0	1	0	1	1	1	0	1	0	1	1
STAFFORD R	5	4	0	1	8	3	5	1	1	3	6	11
STEVENAGE B	1	0	0	1	0	2	1	0	0	1	0	1
TELFORD U	6	3	1	2	13	10	6	1	3	2	8	10
WEALDSTONE	2	0	2	0	3	3	2	0	1	1	1	2
WELLING U	6	2	2	2	7	6	6	3	1	2	11	9
WEYMOUTH	3	1	0	2	5	5	3	0	2	1	5	6
WOKING	1	0	1	0	1	1	1	1	0	0	2	1
WYCOMBE W	4	2	1	1	7	4	4	0	2	2	6	10
YEOVIL T	4	3	0	1	9	4	4	1	1	2	4	6
TOTALS	125	55	33	37	230	164	125	29	36	60	161	216

Lenny Dennis.

Stuart Massey.

Paul McKinnon. Photo: Paul Dennis.

Paul Rogers.

SUTTON UNITED   GOALSCORERS

	86/87	87/88	88/89	89/90	90/91	91/92 - 98/99	99/00	TOTAL
ANDERSON Carey				2				2
AWARITEFE Francis	10	5						15
BARNES Andy					12			12
CORNWELL Mike	3	5	2					10
DACK Jimmy							4	4
DAWSON Phil	1		2	1				4
DENNIS Lenny	13	19	20(1p)		7			59(1p)
EKOKU Efan			4	25				29
ELLIOTT Gary					1			1
EVANS Peter					2			2
FORRESTER Scott							1	1
FOWLER Steve		1		3				4
GILL Martyn					4			4
GOLLEY Mark	14(3p)	3						17(3p)
GOLLEY Nigel	5	6	3	1	2			17
HANLAN Matthew		4	5	5				14
HARFOED Paul							2	2
HARLOW David							1	1
HEMSLEY Stuart		2		1				3
HUTCHINSON Ed							4	4
JONES Robyn		2	1					3
JOYCE Micky	10	5						15
LAKER Barry							2	2
MACKAY Roger	1							1
MASSEY Stuart				5	9(2p)			14(2p)
McKINNON Paul	12	15(6p)	11(1p)	15(2p)	12(1p)			**65(10p)**
NEWHOUSE Aidan							3	3
NEWMAN Zak					3			3
PRATT Vernon		4	5					9
RAINS Tony	1		2(1p)	2				5(1p)
RILEY Andy							1	1
ROBSON Neil	1							1
ROGERS Paul	4	4(1p)	2	1	3			14(1p)
ROWLANDS Keith							1	1
SEAGROATT Robin				6	6			12
SHEPHERD David	1							1
SKELLY Richard							1	1
STEPHENS Micky		1	4					5
THORNTON Paul	3							3
TUTT Steve	1							1
WATSON Mark							11	11
WINSTON Sammy							8(3p)	8(3p)

Efan Ekoku.

Scott Forrester. Photo: Garry Letts.

Matthew Hanlan. Photo: Jo Corkett.

Paul Harford. Photo: Garry Letts.

SUTTON UNITED   APPEARANCES

	86/87	87/88	88/89	89/90	90/91	91/92 - 98/99	99/00	TOTAL
ADAM Paul				6+2	14+1			20+3
ANDERSON Carey			3+2	12+7	3+4			18+13
ANDREWS Stuart			0+1					0+1
AWARITIFE Francis	15	22+2						37+2
BAKER Joe							0+2	0+2
BARCLAY Dominic							0+5	0+5
BARKER Micky	0+1							0+1
BARNES Andy					26			26
BARWICK Steve				0+3				0+3
BERRY Gwynne				30	34+1		33	97+1
BRODRICK Darren							7+4	7+4
BROOKER Danny							30+2	30+2
CORNWELL Mike	26+1	32	12	0+1				70+2
COSTELLO Mark				0+1	16+1			16+2
DACK Jimmy					5+8		28+2	33+10
DAWSON Phil	29+4	9+5	32+3	15	19			104+12
DENNIS Lenny	28+3	32+1	38	1	15+1			114+5
DOBINSON Robin				3+1				3+1
EDWARDS Lee			3+3					3+3
EKOKU Efan			14+1	39				53+1
EKOKU Nko							22+14	22+14
ELLIOTT Gary					13+3			13+3
EVANS Peter					18+3			18+3
FEARON Ron	42							42
FENTON Jason				4+4				4+4
FLANAGAN Tony				8				8
FORRESTER Scott							1+17	1+17
FOWLER Steve		1	6+3	5+1				12+4
GATES Paul				36	34+2			70+2
GILL Martyn					19+1			19+1
GOLDING Paul			3					3
GOLLEY Mark	38	25+1						63+1
GOLLEY Nigel	34	32	38	23	36+1			163+1
GUARD Tony	3							3
HANLAN Matthew	0+5	17+6	27+2	31+3				75+16
HARFORD Paul							33+1	33+1
HARLOW David							40	40
HAWKINS John				18+3	0+1			18+4
HEMSLEY Stuart	41	35	19	27	6+1			128+1
HOPKINS Neil					7			7
HORNER Justin			6+1					6+1
HOWELL Dave					2			2
HOWELLS Gareth							41	41
HUTCHINSON Ed							10+6	10+6
JENKINS Neil					3+5			3+5
JONES Robyn	11	41	36					88
JOYCE Micky	17	17+2						34+2
KENNEDY John			0+2					0+2
LAKER Barry							30+1	30+1

Dave Harlow. Photo: Peter Barnes.

Robyn Jones. Photo: Paul Dennis.

Mickey Joyce.

John Mackie.

	86/87	87/88	88/89	89/90	90/91	91/92 - 98/99	99/00	TOTAL
LEE Matt							5	5
LITTLE Andy							1	1
MACKAY Roger	36							36
MACKIE John							10	10
MASSEY Stuart	3+4			30+1	36+3			69+8
McCANN Gary					11			11
McCORMACK Frank							1+1	1+1
McKINNON Paul	9	22+1	26	38	34+5			129+6
METAXA Ned	1+1							1+1
MORRIS Graham			9+1	1+4				10+5
NEWHOUSE Aidan							17+1	17+1
NEWMAN Zak					4+7			4+7
POPE Richard		1+5						1+5
PRATT Vernon		21+3	29+5	7				57+8
RAINS John	12+1							12+1
RAINS Tony	39	42	34	42	21			178
RILEY Andy							21+1	21+1
ROBSON Neil	13			2+1				15+1
ROFFEY Trevor		29	33					62
ROGERS Paul	39+1	38	40	29+1	41+1			187+3
RONDEAU Ian			2+1	6				8+1
ROWLANDS Keith							8+13	8+13
SALAKO Andy							4+2	4+2
SCOTT Andy					0+3			0+3
SEAGROATT Robin				7+6	11+6			18+12
SEARS Paul							14+5	14+5
SHEPHERD David	1	2						3
SIMPSON Colin							4+1	4+1
SKELLY Richard							41	41
STEPHENS Micky	14+1	31+3	18	0+1				63+5
SULLIVAN Nicky				42	31			73
SWAIN Glen	2+1							2+1
THORNTON Paul	8+2							8+2
THURLOW Steve					3+1			3+1
TURNER Steve			3+4					3+4
TUTT Steve	1+1							1+1
VAN SLIEDREGT Arjon			2+1					2+1
VINCENT John		12	7					19
VINES Francis							0+5	0+5
WATSON Mark							25+12	25+12
WEBB Paul		1						1
WEBB Steve				0+1				0+1
WESTCOTT John							1	1
WINSTON Sammy							35+4	35+4

Tony Rains.

Mickey Stephens. Photo: Bob Thomas.

Joff Vansittart. Photo: Garry Letts.

Sammy Winston. Photo: Peter Barnes.

TAMWORTH

PROMOTED FROM: The Southern League 2002-03
2004-2005 SEASON: The Conference

2003-04 Squad: Bck row.left to right: Andy Watson, Mark Barnard, Rob Warner, Scott Rickards, James Lindley, Phil Whitehead, Joe Taylor, Marc McGregor, G ary Setchell and Darren Coillins. Insert Phil Trainer. Front row: A Danylyk, Joe Hanney, Richard Follett, Dave Robinson, MarkCooper, DarrenGee, L.ee Wilson, Matt Fisher, Karl Johnson, Brett Darby and Mark Turner.

SEASON 2003-04

HIGHEST ATTENDANCE
2535 v Burton Alb. 1.1.04

LOWEST ATTENDANCE
905 v Leigh RMI 7.2.04

SEASON GOALSCORER
Mark Cooper 15 (2p)

SEASON APPEARANCES
Rob Warner 34+5

HOME							AWAY							
P	W	D	L	F	A	Pts	P	W	D	L	F	A	Pts	Position
21	9	6	6	32	30	33	21	4	4	13	17	38	16	17

GOALSCORERS   03-04

BARNES Paul	4
BLUNT Jason	1
BROOKS Jamie	1
COOPER Mark	15(2p)
DRYDEN Richard	2
EBDON Marcus	1
FOLLETT Richard	3
POWELL Paul	1
RICKARDS Scott	3(1p)
ROBINSON Dave	3
SCULLY Tony	1
SETCHELL Gary	2(1p)
SMITH Nick	2
SYLLA Norman	4
WATSON Andy	2
WHITMAN Tristram	3

APPEARANCES   03-04

AYRES Lee	23
BARNARD Mark	3+3
BARNES Paul	17+1
BLUNT Jason	26+1
BROOKS Jamie	1
BRUSH Richard	10
COLKIN Lee	9
COLLINS Darren	4+2
COOPER Mark	35+3
DARBY Brett	13+13
DRYDEN Richard	22
EBDON Marcus	13+1
FISHER Matt	14+1
FOLLETT Richard	27+5
FOX James	0+1
GOODWIN Scott	2+2
HANNEY Joe	0+2
HENDERSON Wayne	3
JOHN-BAPTISTE Alex	4
JOHNSON Karl	6+5
JORDAN Tom	17+2
LANGMEAD Kelvin	2
LINDLEY James	6
McGREGOR Marc	4+3

APPEARANCES cont.   03-04

NOON Mark	5+2
ONE Armand	4
POWELL Paul	5
PRICE Ryan	8
QUAILEY Brian	14+3
RICKARDS Scott	13+6
ROBINSON Dave	24+1
RODWELL Jim	6
SCOTT Keith	4
SCULLY Tony	1
SETCHELL Gary	17
SMITH Adie	3+1
SMITH Nick	6+5
STANFORD Edward	6+1
SYLLA Norman	12+13
TAYLOR Joe	5+1
TRAINER Phil	5+1
TURNER Mark	3+5
WARNER Rob	34+5
WATSON Andy	6+1
WHITEHEAD Phil	15
WHITMAN Tristram	5+2
WILSON Lee	0+1

TAMWORTH

	Accrington Stanley		Aldershot Town		Barnet		Burton Albion		Chester City		Dagenham & Redbridge		Exeter City	
	H	A	H	A	H	A	H	A	H	A	H	A	H	A
02-03														
03-04	1-1	0-3	3-3	1-1	2-0	0-1	1-1	1-0	1-5	0-1	2-0	0-0	2-1	2-3

	Farnborough Town		Forest Green Rovers		Gravesend & N'fleet		Halifax Town		Hereford United		Leigh RMI		Margate	
	H	A	H	A	H	A	H	A	H	A	H	A	H	A
02-03														
03-04	2-1	3-3	1-0	1-2	1-3	0-2	2-0	2-1	1-3	1-0	4-3	1-1	1-1	2-3

	Morecambe		Northwich Victoria		Scarborough		Shrewsbury Town		Stevenage Borough		Telford United		Woking	
	H	A	H	A	H	A	H	A	H	A	H	A	H	A
02-03														
03-04	2-3	0-4	2-1	0-1	0-0	1-0	1-1	1-3	1-2	1-3	0-1	0-2	2-0	0-4

Mark Turner controls the ball despite close attention from an opposing player. Photo: Paul Barber.

TELFORD UNITED

FOUNDER MEMBER
2004-2005 SEASON: Telford Utd folded at the end of the 2003-04 season.
A new club AFC Telford Utd. was formed and plays in the Northern Premier League Division 1

1986-87 Squad - Back Row (L-R): L. Lloyd (Trainer), H. Wiggins, S. Eaton, L. Halton, K. McKenna, M. Hancock, K. Charlton, S. Nelson, C. Williams, A. griffiths, G. Holland, K. Lewis, S. Day. Front: J. Powell, T. Morgan, J. McGinty, S. Storton, E. Hogan, J. Alcock, A. Joseph, T. Turner, J. Stringer.

	HOME P	W	D	L	F	A	Pts	AWAY P	W	D	L	F	A	Pts	Position
79-80	19	9	3	7	31	27	21	19	4	5	10	21	33	13	13
80-81	19	7	6	6	25	23	20	19	6	3	10	22	36	15	13
81-82	21	13	4	4	38	20	43	21	10	4	7	32	31	34	3
82-83	21	16	3	2	46	17	51	21	4	8	9	23	31	20	6
83-84	21	13	3	5	32	19	29	21	4	8	9	18	39	20	11
84-85	21	10	7	4	36	24	27	21	5	7	9	23	30	22	10
85-86	21	13	5	3	42	24	31	21	5	5	11	26	42	20	8
86-87	21	12	5	4	41	23	41	21	6	5	10	28	36	23	9
87-88	21	11	5	5	33	23	38	21	9	5	7	32	27	32	5
88-89	20	5	5	10	17	24	20	20	8	4	8	20	19	28	16
89-90	21	8	7	6	31	29	31	21	7	6	8	25	34	27	12
90-91	21	11	3	7	30	21	36	21	9	4	8	32	31	31	6
91-92	21	10	4	7	32	31	34	21	9	3	9	30	35	30	6
92-93	21	9	5	7	31	24	32	21	5	5	11	24	36	20	15
93-94	21	8	7	6	24	22	31	21	5	5	11	17	27	20	17
94-95	21	9	9	3	30	20	36	21	1	7	13	23	42	10	19
95-96	21	8	7	6	27	23	31	21	7	3	11	24	33	24	13
96-97	21	6	7	8	21	30	25	21	10	3	8	25	26	33	9
97-98	21	6	7	8	25	31	25	21	4	5	12	28	45	17	20
98-99	21	7	8	6	24	24	29	21	3	8	10	20	36	17	17
99-00	21	12	4	5	34	21	40	21	2	5	14	22	45	11	16
00-01	21	13	1	7	33	23	40	21	6	7	8	18	28	25	6
01-02	21	8	6	7	34	31	30	21	6	9	6	29	27	27	9
02-03	21	7	2	12	20	33	23	21	7	5	9	34	36	26	15
03-04	21	10	3	8	28	28	33	21	5	7	9	21	23	22	12
Total	520	241	126	153	765	615	797	520	147	136	237	617	828	567	

SEASONS
25

TOTAL POINTS
1364

HIGHEST POSITION
3rd 1981-82

LOWEST POSITION
20th 1997-98

HIGHEST ATTENDANCE
4337 Shrewsbury (6-4-04)

LOWEST ATTENDANCE
518 v Morecambe 29.11.97
at Bucks Head
281 v Leigh 16.9.00
at Worcester

SEASON GOALSCORER
Steve Norris 24(3p) (87/8)

CAREER GOALSCORER
Dave Mather 84

CAREER APPEARANCES
Kevin Charlton 395+1

	Accrington Stanley		Aldershot Town		Altrincham		A P Leamington		Aylesbury United		Bangor City		Barnet		Barrow		Bath City	
	H	A	H	A	H	A	H	A	H	A	H	A	H	A	H	A	H	A
79-80					3-2	0-2	0-1	1-2			2-0	1-1	1-2	1-4	3-2	0-2	3-1	1-1
80-81					3-2	2-0	2-3	0-5			1-1	0-2	0-0	1-2	5-2	1-0	2-1	1-0
81-82					4-3	0-3	2-0	2-0					3-0	0-1	0-0	0-2	0-2	2-1
82-83					1-1	0-1					2-0	1-1	3-0	2-0	1-3	5-0	2-0	0-0
83-84					2-1	1-1					2-1	0-4	0-0	0-0			3-2	1-1
84-85					0-2	1-0							1-0	1-0	3-1	1-2	3-1	1-2
85-86					2-1	0-1							2-2	2-1	3-1	0-1	1-0	0-3
86-87					4-0	1-2							0-1	2-2			4-2	1-3
87-88					1-0	3-0							2-4	2-0			3-1	2-1
88-89					0-1	0-0			0-1	0-2			0-3	3-1				
89-90					1-3	1-0							1-3	1-2	3-0	0-3		
90-91					1-2	1-2							1-1	0-0	0-1	1-2	2-2	1-0
91-92					2-1	3-2									4-2	0-3	0-2	2-1
92-93					2-1	3-0											0-0	1-4
93-94					0-2	0-2											0-0	0-3
94-95					2-3	1-3											3-0	1-1
95-96					2-0	0-1											3-1	3-0
96-97					0-0	3-2											1-1	3-2
97-98																		
98-99															1-1	1-1		
99-00					0-1	3-3												
00-01																		
01-02													1-2	0-0				
02-03													2-1	0-3				
03-04	1-0	5-1	2-5	1-3									1-2	0-2				

	Boston United		Bromsgrove Rovers		Burton Albion		Cheltenham Town		Chester City		Chorley		Colchester United		Dagenham		Dagenham & Redbridge	
	H	A	H	A	H	A	H	A	H	A	H	A	H	A	H	A	H	A
79-80	4-1	1-3																
80-81	2-0	3-5																
81-82	4-1	2-4													0-2	2-3		
82-83	3-2	0-4													3-0	1-1		
83-84	3-2	3-2													3-1	2-1		
84-85	1-1	3-1													1-1	0-1		
85-86	2-1	2-2					3-0	1-1							2-1	4-1		
86-87	5-2	3-2					3-1	1-3							0-2	1-3		
87-88	2-1	1-1					0-1	0-3							1-0	1-0		
88-89	0-1	0-1					2-0	1-0			2-1	0-2						
89-90	4-2	2-2					0-0	2-1			0-4	2-1						
90-91	1-0	1-2					1-2	1-0					2-0	0-2				
91-92	0-2	2-1					2-1	1-2					0-3	0-2				
92-93	0-1	2-2	0-1	0-0													0-1	2-0
93-94			0-0	5-0													0-0	1-4
94-95			2-2	1-0													0-4	2-3
95-96			0-0	2-0													0-0	1-1
96-97			3-1	1-2														
97-98							0-0	1-3										
98-99							0-3	0-2										
99-00																		
00-01	3-2	1-2							3-0	0-1							0-1	0-0
01-02	2-2	1-3							0-3	2-2							1-4	5-1
02-03					0-2	7-4			0-1	1-4							1-2	1-1
03-04					2-2	1-2			0-2	0-0							1-0	1-1

TELFORD UNITED

	Darlington		Dartford		Doncaster Rovers		Dover Athletic		Enfield		Exeter City		Farnborough Town		Fisher Athletic		Forest Green Rovers	
	H	A	H	A	H	A	H	A	H	A	H	A	H	A	H	A	H	A
79-80																		
80-81																		
81-82			2-0	0-2					0-0	4-3								
82-83									4-3	2-6								
83-84									0-3	1-3								
84-85			1-2	0-0					2-0	0-0								
85-86			2-1	1-2					2-2	0-4								
86-87									2-1	1-3								
87-88									4-0	4-1					2-1	1-0		
88-89									3-0	1-0					1-1	1-0		
89-90	0-1	1-1							1-1	2-1			4-2	1-2	3-1	3-1		
90-91															3-1	0-2		
91-92													1-2	2-2				
92-93													6-3	1-0				
93-94							0-1	1-0										
94-95							1-1	0-2					1-1	3-5				
95-96							1-0	0-1					3-2	1-2				
96-97							1-0	4-1					2-0	2-0				
97-98							0-1	3-6					0-1	0-1				
98-99					0-2	1-2	1-1	1-1					3-1	1-3			2-1	1-1
99-00					0-2	0-2	1-0	0-3									2-0	2-5
00-01					1-0	2-1	0-2	3-1									1-0	1-1
01-02					1-1	0-1	4-3	1-0					0-1	1-1			0-0	1-1
02-03					4-4	3-1							0-2	2-2			0-1	1-1
03-04											2-0	3-0	2-4	1-2			0-2	0-0

	Frickley Athletic		Gateshead		Gravesend & N'fleet		Halifax Town		Hayes		Hednesford Town		Hereford United		Kettering Town		Kidderminster H.	
	H	A	H	A	H	A	H	A	H	A	H	A	H	A	H	A	H	A
79-80					1-2	2-1									1-0	2-3		
80-81	1-0	1-4			0-0	2-2									0-2	1-2		
81-82	7-1	0-0			1-0	2-0									1-0	3-1		
82-83	1-1	2-2													2-1	2-1		
83-84	0-1	1-1	4-0	1-2											1-0	1-4	3-0	0-1
84-85	5-3	2-1	1-1	1-1											1-1	2-0	3-2	2-0
85-86	2-1	1-3													2-2	0-4	0-1	0-3
86-87	4-1	2-4	2-1	2-0											2-0	1-3	2-1	4-0
87-88															2-3	0-1	4-3	4-2
88-89															0-1	0-1	1-0	1-1
89-90															1-3	1-1	1-1	4-2
90-91			1-2	1-5											0-1	5-2	1-0	3-1
91-92			1-1	2-0											1-1	0-3	3-1	2-1
92-93			1-0	1-0											3-1	1-1	1-1	1-2
93-94			0-0	2-0			3-2	0-6							1-2	2-1	1-0	0-2
94-95			3-1	0-0			1-1	1-1							1-0	2-3	3-1	1-1
95-96			0-0	2-1			1-1	0-0			2-1	0-4			3-4	3-0	1-1	0-2
96-97			0-3	3-2			1-1	3-0	0-0	1-0	1-1	0-0			1-0	1-0	0-2	0-1
97-98			4-4	2-0			0-3	1-6	1-0	1-1	1-1	0-1	0-0	1-1	1-1	3-1	1-1	1-1
98-99									2-0	3-4	1-1	1-1	0-1	0-0	0-2	1-2	0-0	0-3
99-00									1-2	2-1	6-2	1-2	1-1	2-2	3-1	0-0	3-2	0-2
00-01									2-0	1-0	2-1	1-1	1-0	0-2	2-1	1-0		
01-02									1-2	4-1			0-1	1-0				
02-03					2-1	2-0	1-2	0-2					0-1	0-2	2-0	4-2		
03-04					1-1	2-1	2-1	1-1					0-3	1-2				

1984-85 Squad. Back Row (L-R): Kevin Charlton, Harry Wiggins, Paul Bennett, Steve Ecton, Mark Hancock, Colin Williams, Liam Halton, John McGinty, John Stringer, John Alcock, Len Lloyd.
Front: Ken McKenna, Antone Joseph, Tony Turner, Dave Mather, Adrian Jones, Kevin Cross.

1987-88 Squad. Back Row (L-R): Lennie Lloyd (trainer), Paul Mayman, Steve Norris, Trevor Storton, Mark Cunningham, Peter Darby, Steve Nelson, Kevin Charlton, Andy Kerr, Tom Lloyd, Iain Sankey, Steve Biggins, Stan Day (Physio). Front: Antone Joseph, Tony Griffiths, John McGinty, Harry Wiggins, Kevin Laws (Asst. Manager), Stan Storton (Manager), Mark Hancock, John Alcock, Andy Lee, John Stringer.

1991-92 Squad. Back Row (L-R): Lennie Lloyd (Trainer), Ken McKenna, John McGinty, Ian Crawley, Kevin Charlton, Steve Nelson, Chris Brindley, Tony Griffths, Kevin Lewis (Coach). Front: Iain Sankey, Tommy Lloyd, Antone Joseph, Stan Storton (Manager), Harry Wiggins, Mark Hancock, Paul Grainer.

	Kingstonian		Leek Town		Leigh RMI		Lincoln City		Macclesfield Town		Maidstone United		Margate		Merthyr Tydfil	
	H	A	H	A	H	A	H	A	H	A	H	A	H	A	H	A
79-80											3-1	0-3				
80-81											1-2	0-3				
81-82											1-2	2-2				
82-83											3-1	0-1				
83-84											3-1	0-6				
84-85											0-0	0-0				
85-86											2-4	4-4				
86-87											1-1	0-0				
87-88							0-1	0-0	0-0	1-1	1-0	4-2				
88-89									1-3	1-2	1-2	3-1				
89-90									1-0	0-3					1-1	0-0
90-91									1-2	2-1					3-1	3-2
91-92									0-1	1-2					1-2	2-2
92-93									3-1	1-1					5-0	0-4
93-94									1-3	0-1					1-0	3-0
94-95									2-0	0-2					1-1	1-3
95-96									1-2	0-1						
96-97									0-3	1-2						
97-98			3-0	1-3												
98-99	1-1	0-1	2-0	1-1												
99-00	1-0	2-4														
00-01	0-1	1-0			2-1	1-1										
01-02					3-1	1-3							2-0	1-3		
02-03					1-1	3-0							1-0	1-1		
03-04					5-0	1-1							1-1	0-1		

	Morecambe		Northwich Victoria		Nuneaton Borough		Redditch United		Runcorn		Rushden & Diamonds		Scarborough		Shrewsbury Town	
	H	A	H	A	H	A	H	A	H	A	H	A	H	A	H	A
79-80			0-0	1-2	2-1	1-1	2-1	2-2					0-1	2-1		
80-81			1-3	0-1	2-2	3-3							0-0	1-1		
81-82			2-1	2-2					1-1	3-2			1-1	0-0		
82-83			3-0	1-2	2-0	1-2			4-0	0-0			0-2	1-1		
83-84			0-2	0-0	1-0	1-1			1-1	0-0			1-0	0-3		
84-85			0-1	0-1	2-1	1-2			3-1	0-3			1-2	1-4		
85-86			4-0	1-0	1-1	1-1			2-3	0-1			1-0	1-3		
86-87			1-0	0-1	1-1	2-0			2-2	0-3			0-0	0-0		
87-88			1-1	2-1					2-1	1-2						
88-89			1-4	0-1					1-1	0-0						
89-90			2-1	2-0					2-1	0-3						
90-91			1-0	4-2					2-0	0-0						
91-92			1-4	1-0					1-0	2-0						
92-93			1-0	0-1					2-1	1-3						
93-94			2-1	0-1					1-1	2-3						
94-95			1-0	1-1					2-0	1-4						
95-96	2-2	0-2	1-0	0-2					1-2	3-2						
96-97	2-3	1-0	2-2	0-1							0-5	0-2				
97-98	1-3	0-1	2-1	2-2							4-2	2-3				
98-99	2-3	1-0	3-0	1-1							2-2	3-2				
99-00	3-2	2-5	0-1	1-2			1-0	1-1			1-1	1-1	1-0	0-2		
00-01	2-0	0-0	2-3	1-0	2-1	1-1					1-2	0-3	1-0	1-1		
01-02	4-1	1-2	1-0	2-2	0-2	2-1							3-0	1-3		
02-03	0-3	0-1	1-0	1-2	1-2	0-1							0-2	4-1		
03-04	2-1	0-1	0-1	0-1									2-1	1-1	1-0	0-0

1996-97 Squad. Back Row (L-R): Mark Turner, Brian Caswell, Steve Eccleston, Brett Wilcox, Brian Gray, Derek Dudley, Darren Simkin, Nigel Niblett, Steve Foster, Chris Harnson, Mark Keorney. Front: Lee Fowler, Kevin Ashley, Justin Ellitts, Brian Taylor, Wayne Clarke, Tony Esp, Lee robinson, Tim Langford, Jon Purdie.

2000-01 Squad. Back Row (L-R): Gez Murphy, Chris Malkin, Dean Williams, Brian McGorry, Martin Poole, Jon Ford, Kevin Sandwith. Middle: Suzanne Jones, Stuart Corns, Scott Huckerby, Steve Palmer, gary Fitzpatrick, Martyn Naylor, Ben Henshaw. Front: Carl Macauley, Maurice Doyle, Alan Lewer, Jim Bentley, Andy Mutch, Lee Fowler, Simon Travis.

2002-03 Squad. Back Row (L-R): Gary Fitzpatrick, Matthew Bloomer, Peter Smith, Grant Brown, Paul Edwards, Craig Jones, Tony Lormor, Mark Foran, Richard Scott.. Front Row: David Brown, Gareth Hanmer, Paul Moore, Kevin Jobling, Jake King, Steve Palmer, Ashley Wooliscroft, Jordan King, Kevin Davies.

TELFORD UNITED

	Slough Town		Southport		Stafford Rangers		Stalybridge Celtic		Stevenage Borough		Sutton United		Tamworth		Trowbridge Town	
	H	A	H	A	H	A	H	A	H	A	H	A	H	A	H	A
79-80					2-2	1-0										
80-81					1-1	1-0										
81-82					0-3	2-1									2-0	2-1
82-83					2-0	1-1									3-1	0-2
83-84															1-0	2-2
84-85																
85-86					0-0	3-0										
86-87					0-0	1-1					0-2	2-2				
87-88					1-2	1-1					3-3	1-2				
88-89					2-2	3-1					0-0	2-1				
89-90					0-2	0-2					1-1	1-6				
90-91	2-1	0-2			0-0	1-1					4-2	3-0				
91-92	2-2	3-0			4-1	2-3										
92-93	1-1	0-2			0-0	1-2	0-2	3-3								
93-94	4-1	0-0	1-3	0-1	2-1	1-1	0-2	0-1								
94-95			0-0	1-2	0-0	2-2	1-1	0-1	1-2	3-4						
95-96	2-0	2-1	2-1	2-3			0-1	2-2	1-3	1-0						
96-97	0-2	0-6	1-0	1-0			1-1	0-0	2-3	0-3						
97-98	0-1	0-1	2-2	2-1			1-0	2-1	3-0	1-1						
98-99			1-0	1-2					0-3	2-2						
99-00			0-0	3-1					2-1	0-2	2-0	1-2				
00-01			2-3	0-3					2-2	3-5						
01-02			1-1	0-0			3-1	2-0	2-1	1-1						
02-03			2-0	1-1					1-3	3-1						
03-04									0-2	1-0			2-0	1-0		

	Wealdstone		Welling United		Weymouth		Witton Albion		Woking		Worcester City		Wycombe Wanderers		Yeovil Town	
	H	A	H	A	H	A	H	A	H	A	H	A	H	A	H	A
79-80	1-3	0-0			3-3	2-3					0-1	1-2			0-3	2-0
80-81	2-1	0-4			1-0	0-1					1-2	3-0			0-1	2-1
81-82					2-0	1-0					3-2	1-2			2-1	2-1
82-83	0-0	0-2			2-0	0-0					2-0	0-1			3-2	4-3
83-84	0-1	0-4			0-1	3-2					2-0	1-0			2-2	0-1
84-85	4-2	2-2			0-0	2-3					1-1	0-0			3-1	3-3
85-86	2-1	1-1			4-1	2-5							3-1	2-1		
86-87	1-3	1-0	2-1	3-1	5-1	0-3										
87-88	1-1	2-2	2-0	1-4	1-0	0-1							0-0	1-2		
88-89			0-0	1-0	1-0	0-0							1-2	0-1	0-1	3-4
89-90			0-0	1-1									4-1	1-1	1-1	0-1
90-91			2-1	1-1									1-0	2-3	1-2	2-1
91-92			2-1	1-3			2-1	1-1					1-0	1-6	1-0	2-0
92-93			0-1	3-1			0-3	1-2	3-3	2-3			2-3	0-4	1-0	0-1
93-94			2-0	0-0			2-2	0-0	2-0	0-0					1-1	0-1
94-95			4-2	0-1					0-0	1-2					1-0	1-1
95-96			0-0	1-3					1-2	1-5						
96-97			2-0	1-2					1-2	0-0						
97-98			0-3	1-4					0-3	1-1					1-4	3-5
98-99			0-0	1-0					1-0	0-3					2-2	0-4
99-00			2-1	0-2					1-2	0-1					3-1	1-2
00-01									3-1	0-3					1-2	0-2
01-02									3-3	1-1					2-2	1-1
02-03									1-0	0-3					0-5	0-3
03-04									1-0	1-3						

Telford's defence prepare to clear the danger. Photo: A. Millar.

Ryan Price punches clear. Photo: Peter Barnes.

Telford's Kevin Charlton gives his team mate a friendly tap on the head whilst trying to clear the ball. Photo: Paul Lewis.

	Home						Away					
	P	W	D	L	F	A	P	W	D	L	F	A
ACCRINGTON S	1	1	0	0	1	0	1	1	0	0	5	1
ALDERSHOT T	1	0	0	1	2	5	1	0	0	1	1	3
ALTRINCHAM	19	10	2	7	30	26	19	7	3	9	23	25
A P LEAMINGTON	3	1	0	2	4	4	3	1	0	2	3	7
AYLESBURY U	1	0	0	1	0	1	1	0	0	1	0	2
BANGOR C	4	3	1	0	7	2	4	0	2	2	2	8
BARNET	15	4	4	7	18	21	15	5	4	6	15	18
BARROW	10	6	2	2	23	13	10	2	1	7	9	16
BATH C	16	10	4	2	30	16	16	7	4	5	20	23
BOSTON U	16	11	2	3	36	21	16	4	4	8	27	37
BROMSGROVE R	5	1	3	1	5	4	5	3	1	1	9	2
BURTON A	2	0	1	1	2	4	2	1	0	1	8	6
CHELTENHAM T	9	4	2	3	11	8	9	3	1	5	8	15
CHESTER C	4	1	0	3	3	6	4	0	2	2	3	7
CHORLEY	2	1	0	1	2	5	2	1	0	1	2	3
COLCHESTER U	2	1	0	1	2	3	2	0	0	2	0	4
DAGENHAM	7	4	1	2	10	7	7	3	1	3	11	10
DAGENHAM & R	9	1	3	5	6	15	9	2	4	3	13	12
DARLINGTON	1	0	0	1	0	1	1	0	1	0	1	1
DARTFORD	3	2	0	1	5	3	3	0	1	2	1	4
DONCASTER R	5	1	2	2	6	9	5	2	0	3	6	7
DOVER A	9	3	3	3	9	10	9	4	1	4	13	15
ENFIELD	9	5	3	1	18	10	9	4	1	4	15	21
EXETER C	1	1	0	0	2	0	1	1	0	0	3	0
FARNBOROUGH T	11	5	1	5	22	19	11	2	3	6	15	20
FISHER A	4	3	1	0	9	4	4	3	0	1	5	3
FOREST GREEN R	6	3	1	2	5	4	6	0	5	1	6	9
FRICKLEY A	7	5	1	1	20	8	7	1	3	3	9	15
GATESHEAD	11	4	5	2	17	13	11	7	2	2	17	11
GRAVESEND & N	5	2	2	1	5	4	5	4	1	0	10	4
HALIFAX T	7	2	3	2	9	11	7	1	3	3	6	16
HAYES	6	3	1	2	7	4	6	4	0	2	12	8
HEDNESFORD T	6	3	3	0	13	7	6	0	3	3	3	9
HEREFORD U	7	1	2	4	2	7	7	1	3	3	5	9
KETTERING T	23	11	4	8	31	27	23	9	3	11	36	40
KIDDERMINSTER H	17	10	5	2	28	17	17	6	3	8	23	25
KINGSTONIAN	3	1	1	1	2	2	3	1	0	2	3	5
LEEK T	2	2	0	0	5	0	2	0	1	1	2	4
LEIGH RMI	4	3	1	0	11	3	4	1	2	1	6	5
LINCOLN C	1	0	0	1	0	1	1	0	1	0	0	0
MACCLESFIELD T	10	3	1	6	10	15	10	1	2	7	7	16
MAIDSTONE U	10	4	2	4	16	14	10	2	4	4	13	22
MARGATE	3	2	1	0	4	1	3	0	1	2	2	5
MERTHYR T	6	3	2	1	12	5	6	2	2	2	9	11
MORECAMBE	9	4	1	4	18	18	9	2	1	6	5	12
NORTHWICH V	25	14	3	8	33	26	25	6	6	13	23	29
NUNEATON B	11	6	3	2	15	11	11	2	6	3	14	14
REDDITCH U	1	1	0	0	2	1	1	0	1	0	2	2
RUNCORN	15	8	5	2	27	15	15	3	4	8	13	26
RUSHDEN & D	5	1	2	2	8	12	5	1	1	3	6	11
SCARBOROUGH	13	6	3	4	11	9	13	2	6	5	13	21
SHREWSBURY T	1	1	0	0	1	0	1	0	1	0	0	0
SLOUGH T	7	3	2	2	11	8	7	2	1	4	5	12
SOUTHPORT	10	4	4	2	12	10	10	3	2	5	11	14
STAFFORD R	14	3	8	3	14	14	14	5	6	3	20	16
STALYBRIDGE C	7	2	2	3	6	8	7	2	3	2	9	8
STEVENAGE B	10	3	1	6	14	20	10	3	3	4	15	19
SUTTON U	6	2	3	1	10	8	6	2	1	3	10	13
TAMWORTH	1	1	0	0	2	0	1	1	0	0	1	0
TROWBRIDGE T	3	3	0	0	6	1	3	1	1	1	4	5
WEALDSTONE	8	3	2	3	11	12	8	1	4	3	6	15
WELLING U	14	8	4	2	18	10	14	4	3	7	15	23
WEYMOUTH	10	7	2	1	19	6	10	2	2	6	10	18
WITTON A	3	1	1	1	4	6	3	0	2	1	2	3
WOKING	12	5	3	4	17	16	12	0	4	8	7	25
WORCESTER C	6	3	1	2	9	6	6	2	1	3	6	5
WYCOMBE W	7	4	1	2	12	7	7	1	1	5	7	18
YEOVIL T	19	7	5	7	25	31	19	6	3	10	26	35
TOTAL	520	241	126	153	765	615	520	147	136	237	617	828

TELFORD UNITED LEADING APPEARANCES

TELFORD UNITED LEADING APPEARANCES

Player	79-80	80-81	81-82	82-83	83-84	84-85	85-86	86-87	87-88	88-89	89-90	90-91	91-92	92-93	93-94	94-95	95-96	96-97	97-98	98-99	99-00	00-01	01-02	02-03	03-04	TOTAL
Kevin CHARLTON	13	35	42	41	38	42	29+1	42	39	24	38	11	1													395+1
John ALCOCK	35	36	32	37	28+4	17	36	37+2	20+5	8+2																286+13
Eddie HOGAN	34	18	39	41	30+3	40+1	33+1	41																		276+5
Antone JOSEPH			36	29	18+6	12+6	29+3	28+7	34+3	33	14															240+29
Tony TURNER		13	42	36	40+1	42	33+2	7+3																		213+6
Martin MYERS												39	38	33+2	34+3	34+1	33+2									211+8
Steve NELSON								27+1	36+1	25+6	29+8	39	35													191+16
Lee FOWLER																8+1	21+3	35+1	32	29+2	26+1	21	23			195+8
Dave MATHER	12	33	38+2	38+1	35+3	21+13	0+7																			177+26
Steve PALMER																			21+12	28+7	28+4	38	28+2	32+2		175+27
Harry WIGGINS						5	32+3	36+3	33+2	34+2	41+1															181+11
John McGINTY							40+2	35	28+3	14+2	25	38														180+7
Dave BARNETT		18	29	38+1	38+1	25+2	18+2																			166+6
Steve EATON		7	32	32+3	25+1	28	18+5	1																		143+9
Ken McKENNA						31+4	23+6	40		15+2	26+3															135+15
Marcus BIGNOT														40	41+1	37	28+2									146+3
Jim BENTLEY																			34	35+1	25	23	28			145+1
Nigel NIBLETT														21	37+1	23	24+1	37+1								142+3
Chris BRINDLEY										24	40	40	39+1													143+1
Gary FITZPATRICK																				17	34+2	5+5	31+7	39		127+15
Mark HANCOCK									13	19	15															139+2
Paul MAYMAN				23+1	23+2	24+8	23+1	32+1																		125+13
Alan WALKER	13	35	41	36	11																					136
John STRINGER									16+5	17+1	15	11+3	35+1	22												118+17
Tim LANGFORD																	22+6	16+4	7+6							113+20
Colin WILLIAMS				20	29	15																				124+7
Tony GRIFFITHS						10	27		35+2	31+4	18+1															121+7
Brian GRAY																	41	38	25+9	2+9						106+18
Paul GRAINGER										18	35	34+1	27													114+1
Gez MURPHY																			9	28+11	29+9	17+12				83+32
Mark TURNER																	25	27+5	39+2	10+3						101+10
John MARTIN	14	33	22+2	17	19																					105+2
Steve FOSTER														17+3	34+2	36+1	14									101+6

TELFORD UNITED APPEARANCES

TELFORD UNITED APPEARANCES

	79-80	80-81	81-82	82-83	83-84	84-85	85-86	86-87	87-88	88-89	89-90	90-91	91-92	92-93	93-94	94-95	95-96	96-97	97-98	98-99	99-00	00-01	01-02	02-03	03-04	TOTAL
ACTON Darren												3	38	39	16											96
ADAMS Carl																13+5	27									40+5
ALBRIGHTON Mark																					18	25+2	30+1			73+3
ALCOCK John	35	36	32	37	28+4	17	36	37+2	20+5	8+2																286+13
ALLEYNE Robert													6+2													6+2
AMOS Gary													1													1
ANDERSON John						5																				5
ANDERSON Michael																			0+1							0+1
ARNOT Chris							2+1																			2+1
ASHLEY Kevin																		24+4	19							43+4
ATKINSON Craig																			1							1
AULERT John	5+6																									5+6
BAILEY Danny																				7						7
BAILEY Mal					20+1																					20+1
BARLOW Martin																								31		31
BARNETT Dave		18	29	38+1	38+1	25+2	18+2																			166+6
BEAUMONT Nigel													25+5													25+5
BEAZLEY Adam																				2						2
BENBOW Ian												27+1	34+2	24+2												85+5
BENNETT Dave																			2							2
BENNETT G		0+2																								0+2
BENNETT Paul						24+4	6+1																			30+5
BENTLEY Jim																			34	35+1	25	23	28			145+1
BIGGINS Steve								5+3	25+6	2+1																32+10
BIGNOT Marcus														40	41+1	37	28+2									146+3
BLACKWELL Kevin											3															3
BLACKWOOD Michael																									25+11	25+11
BLOOMER Matt																								14		14
BOURTON Alan	3																									3
BOWEN Stewart														19	2											21
BRADBURY Shaun															3+2											3+2
BRANCH John	10+2	6+5																								16+7
BRAY Justin																					7+2					7+2
BRENNAN Mick	29+1		2+2																							31+3
BRIDGE Dean												1														1

677

Darren Acton. Photo: John Collinge.

Ian Benbow scores. Photo: Steve Holloway.

Steve Biggins. Photo: Jeff Mimward.

Marcus Bignot (8). Photo: Paul Dennis.

Justin Bray reaches for the ball. Photo: K Gillard.

TELFORD UNITED APPEARANCES

TELFORD UNITED APPEARANCES

	79-80	80-81	81-82	82-83	83-84	84-85	85-86	86-87	87-88	88-89	89-90	90-91	91-92	92-93	93-94	94-95	95-96	96-97	97-98	98-99	99-00	00-01	01-02	02-03	03-04	TOTAL
BRIDGWATER David																					0+1	1+3				1+4
BRINDLEY Chris										24	40	40	39+1													143+1
BROUGH John																6+1										6+1
BROWN David																								34+2		34+2
BROWN Grant																								37		37
BROWN Ian										15+1	17+8	6+4														38+13
BROWN Jimmy					3																					3
BURKE Dennis													2													2
BUTTRESS Mike	34	9																								43
BUXTON Steve											14															14
BYTHEWAY Matt																			11+1	4+5						15+6
BYWATER Paul																			18	2						20
CADETTE Nathan																				3						3
CADMAN Dave				1																						1
CAMERON David																								6		6
CAMPBELL Neil																				4						4
CARR Cliff													1			17+2										18+2
CARTWRIGHT Jamie																						3+4				3+4
CARTWRIGHT Neil																		14+6		2						16+6
CASTLEDINE Gary															3+3											3+3
CASWELL Peter	22																									22
CHALLINOR Paul																	18	15+3	18+7							51+10
CHALLIS Trevor																									33	33
CHARLESWORTH Mike		4																								4
CHARLTON Asa																		4+3								4+3
CHARLTON Kevin	13	35	42	41	38	42	29+1	42	39	38	38															395+1
CLARKE Brian	23																									23
CLARKE Matt																									29+5	29+5
CLARKE Stuart										0+2	4		20+5	14+2												38+9
CLARKE Wayne																	15+4									15+4
COLCOMBE Scott																			17+2							17+2
COLLEY Nick																			4+16							4+16
COLLINS Tony																			1+3							1+3
COOKE Andy												3+8		5+3												8+11
COOKE Tim				1																						1

Ian Crawley. Photo: Mick Cheney.

Chris Brindley heads clear. Photo: Mick Cheney.

Steve Eaton.

Lee Fowler. Photo: Peter Barnes.

Brian Gayle. Photo: Peter Barnes.

TELFORD UNITED APPEARANCES

	79-80	80-81	81-82	82-83	83-84	84-85	85-86	86-87	87-88	88-89	89-90	90-91	91-92	92-93	93-94	94-95	95-96	96-97	97-98	98-99	99-00	00-01	01-02	02-03	03-04	TOTAL
COOPER Mark																					5					5
CORNES Stuart																				6+3	0+6					6+9
COSTELLO Peter																4+1										4+1
CRAWLEY Ian										24+7	14+4	16+4														54+15
CRISP Richard																27+4										27+4
CROFT Brian																		0+1								0+1
CROMPTON Alan								16+2	8																	24+2
CROOKES Dominic																25+8	8+1									33+9
CROWE Seamus																							0+1			0+1
CULPIN Paul													1													1
CUNNINGHAM Mark									6+1	6+2																12+3
DALEY Ryan																			5+9							5+9
DALY Gerry											19+1	7+4														26+5
DANCE Trevor							11																			11
DANIELS John																									0+1	0+1
DARBY Peter									3																	3
DAVIDSON Jonathan														9		15+2	6									30+2
DAVIDSON Mick											10	7+1														17+1
DAVIES Kevin																						31+1	21+6	29+5		81+12
DAVIS Craig																				4						4
DAY Nicky					6+2																					6+2
DEGG David	3																									3
DONNELLY Steve																3+1										3+1
DOUGHERTY Paul																2										2
DOWNES Chris													1													1
DOYLE Maurice																				30+1	18+7					48+8
DUDLEY Craig																				1						1
DUDLEY Derek																	1	4+1	6							11+1
DUERDEN Ian																			5+2							5+2
DUFFY Darryl												1+1														1+1
DYSON Paul											36+1		35													71+1
EASTWOOD Phil																			8							8
EATON Steve	7	32	32+3	25+1		28	18+5	1																		143+9
ECCLESTON Steve																	17+1	19+11	23+3							59+15
EDWARDS Dean				6+5	26+11	14+8	0+1																			46+25

Martin Gavin collects under pressure.

Nick Goodwin claims the ball. Photo: Alan Coomes

Paul Grainger. Photo: Malcolm Couzens

Brian Gray is congratulated by Steve Palmer and Evran Wright.

TELFORD UNITED APPEARANCES

	79-80	80-81	81-82	82-83	83-84	84-85	85-86	86-87	87-88	88-89	89-90	90-91	91-92	92-93	93-94	94-95	95-96	96-97	97-98	98-99	99-00	00-01	01-02	02-03	03-04	TOTAL
EDWARDS Jake																					23+4	23+8	23+5			69+17
EDWARDS Neil									4+2																	4+2
EDWARDS Paul																							21	39		60
EDWARDS Steve																						0+1				0+1
ELLISON Steve							2																			2
ELLITTS Justin																	6+7									6+7
EUSTACE Scott																									6	6
EVANS Paul		2+5																								2+5
EVES Mel											18+3															18+3
FARRINGTON Mark																	2									2
FEE Greg																				18+1						18+1
FEREDAY Wayne																	5									5
FERGUSSON Steve													23+1	30	35											88+1
FITZPATRICK Gary													1+1							17	34+2	5+5	31+7	39		127+15
FORAN Mark																								39		39
FORD Gary															24	13										37
FORD Jon																					30+4					30+4
FORSYTH Richard													9													9
FOSTER George															2											2
FOSTER Steve															17+3	34+2	36+1	14								101+6
FOWLER Lee																8+1	21+3	35+1	32	29+2	26+1	21	23			195+8
FRANCE John					0+2																					0+2
FRANCIS Sean														23+11												23+11
FRISBY Steve															0+2											0+2
GARDINER Nathan																	4+4									4+4
GARDNER Duncan			16+11	14+9	1																					31+20
GARRATT Anthony													5+3	1+4												6+7
GAUNT Craig														9												9
GAVIN Martin	36																									36
GAYLE Brian																					9	18				27
GERMAINE Gary																	10									10
GERNON Irvin															11+6											11+6
GILMAN Shaun													7+1													7+1
GOODWIN Nick																39	14+1									53+1

683

TELFORD UNITED **APPEARANCES**

	79-80	80-81	81-82	82-83	83-84	84-85	85-86	86-87	87-88	88-89	89-90	90-91	91-92	92-93	93-94	94-95	95-96	96-97	97-98	98-99	99-00	00-01	01-02	02-03	03-04	TOTAL
GRAINGER Paul										18	35	34+1	27													114+1
GRANGE Damien														3												3
GRANT John																									20+15	20+15
GRAY Brian																	41	38	25+9	2+9						106+18
GREEN Roy														16+2												16+2
GREEN Scott																									16+4	16+4
GREENHOUGH Ricky										4																4
GRIFFITHS Bryan																16+1										16+1
GRIFFITHS Tony							10	27	35+2	31+4	18+1															121+7
HACKETT Brendan													7+3													7+3
HALTON Liam						15+1	26+6	9+2																		50+9
HANCHARD Martin										4+1																4+1
HANCOCK Mark						37	23+1	32+1	13	19	15															139+2
HANMER Gareth																							42	38+3		80+3
HARPER Phil	1+3																									1+3
HARRIS Alan	24	1																								25
HARRIS Andy											5+1															5+1
HARRISON Mark										16																16
HARTFIELD Charlie																					19+2					19+2
HATELEY Gary																							2			2
HENDERSON Peter				7																						7
HINDMARSH Rob															1											1
HODGIN Chris														5+5												5+5
HODSON Simeon																			20	5+1						25+1
HOGAN Eddie	34	18	39	41	30+3	40+1	33+1	41																		276+5
HOLDEN Mark																5+1										5+1
HOLMES Michael															7+5											7+5
HOWARTH Neil																									26	26
HOWELL Peter																10+5										10+5
HOWELLS																0+1										0+1
HUCKERBY Scott																				33+8	1+18	4+12				38+38
HUGHES Ken															26	3	15	7+1								51+1
HUGHES Phil												1														1
HULBERT Robin																								21+1		21+1
HUMPHREYS John												41	30+5													71+5

TELFORD UNITED APPEARANCES

TELFORD UNITED APPEARANCES	79-80	80-81	81-82	82-83	83-84	84-85	85-86	86-87	87-88	88-89	89-90	90-91	91-92	92-93	93-94	94-95	95-96	96-97	97-98	98-99	99-00	00-01	01-02	02-03	03-04	TOTAL
HUMPHRIES Steve												22														22
HUNT David											7															7
HUNTER Paul														1	0+4											1+4
HURST Martin												1+3														1+3
JACKSON Paul				2	19+7		12+1																			33+8
JEFFRIES Derek			21																							21
JOBLING Kevin																						41	32+1	9+7		82+8
JONES Craig																								0+2		0+2
JONES John		20																								20
JONES Marcus																			13	23+5						36+5
JONES Mark																		31+2	28	1						60+2
JONES Roger	11+1																									11+1
JOSEPH Antone			36	29	18+6	12+6	29+3	28+7	34+3	33	14				0+2			4+1	3+1							240+29
KEARNEY Mark																38	29+2	32+1								99+3
KERR Andy								20+1																		20+1
KERRIGAN Steve																								4		4
KING Jordan																							6+7	15+14		21+21
LANCASTER Dave												1+1														1+1
LANGFORD Tim												11+3	35+1				22+6	16+4	7+6							113+20
LAVERY Richard																									23+8	23+8
LEE Andy									18+2	36+1			32													86+3
LEMON Paul															0+3											0+3
LEWIS Kevin				28	28+1	34+2																				90+3
LITTLEJOHN Colin								2																		2
LLOYD Tommy									8+6	17+9	1+9															26+24
LORMOR Tony																								3+2		3+2
LYNE Neil																				6+1						6+1
LYNEX Steve											3	3+1														6+1
MACAULEY Carl																				15	32+3					47+3
MACKENZIE Chris																									39	39
MALCOLM Ken	35																									35
MALKIN Chris																					19+13	14+7				33+20
MANEY Gary	12+2	24+4	0+1																							36+7
MANN Arthur							6+1																			6+1
MARTIN John	14	33	22+2	17	19																					105+2

685

TELFORD UNITED APPEARANCES

	79-80	80-81	81-82	82-83	83-84	84-85	85-86	86-87	87-88	88-89	89-90	90-91	91-92	92-93	93-94	94-95	95-96	96-97	97-98	98-99	99-00	00-01	01-02	02-03	03-04	TOTAL
MARTIN Lee																		1+1								1+1
MARTINDALE Gary																					5+1	28+4	11+10			44+15
MATHER Dave	12	33	38+2	38+1	35+3	21+13	0+7																			177+26
MAY Leroy														0+4												0+4
MAYMAN Paul			31	23+1	23+2	24+8	1		8+1	15+1																125+13
McBEAN Peter														7+1												7+1
McCORD Brian																				4+1						4+1
McDONOUGH Seamus												6														6
McGINTY John							40+2	35	28+3	14+2	25	38														180+7
McGORRY Brian																					32	35				67
McKENNA Ken					31+4	23+6		40		15+2	26+3															135+15
McNALLY Bernard																			0+1							0+1
MEREDITH Neil										0+1																0+1
MILLER Carlton															1+1											1+1
MILLS Lee																									26	26
MITCHELL Ian															6+3											6+3
MOONEY Kevin			2+2																							2+2
MOORE Christian																									10+9	10+9
MOORE Kevin	4																									4
MOORE Michael														9+1			0+2		8							17+3
MOORE Neil																					4	37	40			81
MOORE Paul																							4+22	34+4	8+4	46+30
MORGAN Tom								8+9																		8+9
MORLEY Ben																								5		5
MOUNTFORD Bob					0+1																					0+1
MUIR John															2											2
MULLENDER Andy											1															1
MULLIGAN James														7												7
MURPHY Chris																									15+9	15+9
MURPHY Gez																			9	28+11	29+9	17+12				83+32
MUTCH Andy																				3+1	0+1					3+2
MUTCHELL Rob																	4									4
MYERS Martin												39	38	33+2	34+3	34+1	33+2									211+8
NARDIELLO Don			6																							6
NAYLOR Martin																		16+4		20+3	6+14					42+21

TELFORD UNITED APPEARANCES

TELFORD UNITED APPEARANCES

	79-80	80-81	81-82	82-83	83-84	84-85	85-86	86-87	87-88	88-89	89-90	90-91	91-92	92-93	93-94	94-95	95-96	96-97	97-98	98-99	99-00	00-01	01-02	02-03	03-04	TOTAL
NAYLOR Tony																									16+5	16+5
NEALE Mark			25+8	15+9																						40+17
NELSON Steve								27+1	36+1	25+6	29+8	35	31	8												191+16
NIBLETT Nigel														21	37+1	23	24+1	37+1								142+3
NIELD Danny									2																	2
NORBURY Micky																		6+2		8+6						14+8
NORMAN David																				4+1						4+1
NORRIS Steve									40+1																	40+1
OAKLEY Andy											2+3															2+3
OCONNOR A								2																		2
OGLEY Mark														0+3												0+3
OSBOURNE Gary											19+3	7+4														26+7
PAGE Don																		10+1								10+1
PALMER Steve																			21+12	28+7	28+4	38	28+2	32+2		175+27
PARRISH Sean													15+1	33	41											89+1
PERKS Martin													1													1
PETTINGER Paul																								3		3
PHILLIPS Hilton		4+1																								4+1
PREECE Roger																		8			9	9+5	5+4			31+9
PRICE Ryan																					18	21	19			58
PRITCHARD Dave																										64
PUGH Mark		2+2																								2+2
PURDIE Jon																	5+4	31+4	5+3							41+11
QUAYLE Mark																							22+2			22+2
RAMSEY Paul																	3									3
READ Dave																				10						10
RICHARDS Archie	15	4+1																								19+1
RICHARDS Carl												5														5
RICKETTS Sam																									39+2	39+2
ROBERTS Darren															10	10										20
ROBERTS Matt											0+2															0+2
ROBERTS P		1																								1
ROBERTSON Jim													1													1
ROBINSON Lee																	17+3	27								44+3
RODOSTHENOUS Michael																		4								4

Paul Mayman.

Jim McDonagh. Photo: Mick Cheney.

Ken McKenna.

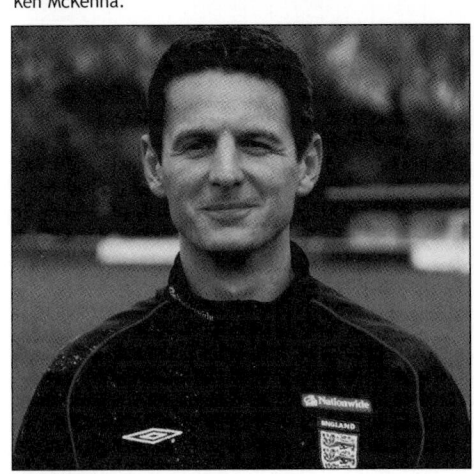

Neil Moore.

Gez Murphy.

TELFORD UNITED APPEARANCES

TELFORD UNITED APPEARANCES	79-80	80-81	81-82	82-83	83-84	84-85	85-86	86-87	87-88	88-89	89-90	90-91	91-92	92-93	93-94	94-95	95-96	96-97	97-98	98-99	99-00	00-01	01-02	02-03	03-04	TOTAL
ROLLASON Lee														6+3												6+3
ROSS Brian													3													3
ROWE Justin																									2+6	2+6
RUGGIERO John		21+3																								21+3
RUSHBURY Andy																									8+2	8+2
RUSSELL Damon																		7+8								7+8
RUTTER Tim					19+3	8																				27+3
RYAN Darren													1													1
SALATHIEL Neil												15														15
SANDWITH Kevin																				12	19+4	13+3				44+7
SANKEY Iain								4+1	31+1	26+6	13+5															74+13
SAYER Ronnie																								3+4		3+4
SCOTT Richard																							21+5	2+1		23+6
SHAKESPEARE Craig																			8	27+2						35+2
SHELDON Kevin							4																			4
SILLE Jon							2																			2
SIMKIN Darren																	8	4+2								12+2
SIMPSON Fitzroy																									28+3	28+3
SIMPSON Paul																			7							7
SLEEUWENHOEK Kris															4+7											4+7
SMITH Peter																							25+8	26+13		51+21
SPINK Dean																								3		3
SROMEK Frank		4																								4
STANLEY Craig																									11+1	11+1
STATHAM Derek															33+1											33+1
STEVENS Gary											21															21
STORTON Trevor								29	33+2	28+1						4										94+3
STRANEY Paul																	2+1									2+1
STRINGER John					22+3	23+3	25+5	16+5	17+1	15																118+17
TAYLOR Colin															33+7											37+7
TAYLOR Gary	3																									3
TAYLOR I	1																									1
TAYLOR Martin																									3	3
TAYLOR Steve																			14							14
THOMPSON Kevin										0+1		3														3+1

689

TELFORD UNITED APPEARANCES

TELFORD UNITED APPEARANCES

Player	79-80	80-81	81-82	82-83	83-84	84-85	85-86	86-87	87-88	88-89	89-90	90-91	91-92	92-93	93-94	94-95	95-96	96-97	97-98	98-99	99-00	00-01	01-02	02-03	03-04	TOTAL
TODD Mark																		1								1
TOTTEY Phil		2																								2
TRAVIS Simon																					29+8	34+2				63+10
TREHERNE Jason																1+2										1+2
TURNER Jamie																				1+3						1+3
TURNER Mark																	25	27+5	39+2	10+3						101+10
TURNER Tony	13		42	36	40+1	42	33+2	7+3																		213+6
UDDIN Anwar																									6	6
WALKER Alan	13	35	41	36	11																					136
WALTON Russell	8	28+1	1																							37+1
WARD Nicky																			2							2
WARNER Ashley																11+3										11+3
WARNER Michael																	10									10
WASSELL Kim		2																								3
WEIR Phil		1																								1
WESTHEAD Mark																			8							8
WHITEHEAD Stewart																									36+1	36+1
WHITEHOUSE Mark															21+7											21+7
WHITEHOUSE Phil													4													4
WHITTINGHAM Steve							1																			1
WHITTINGtON Trevor														25												25
WIGGINS Harry						5	32+3	36+3	33+2	34+2	41+1															181+11
WILCOX Brett																24+3	23+1	21+2	13+3							81+9
WILCOX Richard	1																									1
WILDING Peter																		13								13
WILKES Tim																				3+2						3+2
WILKEY Peter	32	7+4																								39+4
WILKINSON Andy																									8	8
WILLIAMS Colin	6			20	29	15	40+2	14+5																		124+7
WILLIAMS Dean																				37	17	21+1				75+1
WILLIAMS Jimmy		28+2																								28+2
WILLIAMS Lee																									8+5	8+5
WILLIAMS Mark	1																									1
WILLIAMS Mark																		2+5								2+5
WILLIAMS P					2																					2

TELFORD UNITED APPEARANCES

	79-80	80-81	81-82	82-83	83-84	84-85	85-86	86-87	87-88	88-89	89-90	90-91	91-92	92-93	93-94	94-95	95-96	96-97	97-98	98-99	99-00	00-01	01-02	02-03	03-04	TOTAL
WILLIAMS Wayne											13															13
WILSHAW Steve	3																									3
WILSON Lee															12	34+4										46+4
WINSTONE Simon																3										3
WITHE Jason													5+5													5+5
WOLVERSON Jason														0+2												0+2
WOOD Justin																0+2										0+2
WOODS Ray																		11+3								11+3
WOOLISCROFT Ashley																							28+2	17+1		45+3
WORRALL Steve												18+1	4+5													22+6
WRIGHT Evran																			7							7
WRIGHT Martin					2																					2

Above: Steve Nelson. Photo: John Rooney.
Below: Steve Norris. Photo: John Rooney.

TELFORD UNITED LEADING GOALSCORERS

Alan Walker.

TELFORD UNITED LEADING GOALSCORERS

	79-80	80-81	81-82	82-83	83-84	84-85	85-86	86-87	87-88	88-89	89-90	90-91	91-92	92-93	93-94	94-95	95-96	96-97	97-98	98-99	99-00	00-01	01-02	02-03	03-04	TOTAL
MATHER Dave	9	13	22	21	8	11																				84
McKENNA Ken							19	23	8	4	12															66
WILLIAMS Colin	2		11		11	4	10	4																		42
LANGFORD Tim												4	12	6			6	4	5							37
MYERS Martin												9	10	3		6	9									37
STRINGER John						5	11	6	1	5	7															35
GRAY Brian																	10	13	10	1						34
MURPHY Gez																			8	8	10(2p)	7				33(2p)
BENBOW Ian												13	12(2p)	7												32(2p)
ALCOCK John	2	9	5	5	3	5	2																			31
HOGAN Eddie	7	1(1p)	5	1	3	3	5	3	2																	30(1p)

TELFORD UNITED GOALSCORERS

TELFORD UNITED GOALSCORERS	79-80	80-81	81-82	82-83	83-84	84-85	85-86	86-87	87-88	88-89	89-90	90-91	91-92	92-93	93-94	94-95	95-96	96-97	97-98	98-99	99-00	00-01	01-02	02-03	03-04	TOTAL
ADAMS Carl																	4(1p)									4(1p)
ALBRIGHTON Mark																					1	2	5			8
ALCOCK John	2	9	2	5	3	5	2	1	2																	31
ALLEYNE Robert													1													1
ASHLEY Kevin																		2	1							3
AULERT John	3																									3
BARLOW Martin																								2		2
BARNETT Dave		1	4	3	5	1	1																			15
BEAUMONT Nigel													1													1
BENBOW Ian											13	12(2p)	7													32(2p)
BENNETT Paul						3																				3
BENTLEY Jim																			5	4	4	2	8			23
BIGGINS Steve								2	15(2p)																	17(2p)
BIGNOT Marcus														4	4	3	3									14
BLACKWOOD Michael																									3	3
BOURTON Alan	1																									1
BOWEN Stewart														1												1
BRANCH John	3	3																								6
BRENNAN Mick		3(1p)																								3(1p)
BRINDLEY Chris											3	1	6			1										11
BROUGH John										1																1
BROWN David																								16(1p)		16(1p)
BROWN Ian											3	1	1													5
BUTTRESS Mike	3																									3
BUXTON Steve												2														2
CAMPBELL Neil													1													1
CLARKE Stuart														3	1											4
CLARKE Wayne																	5(1p)									5(1p)
COLLEY Nick																			1							1
COOKE Andy													1	2												3
COOPER Mark																1										1
COSTELLO Peter																					1					1
CRAWLEY Ian										7	6	5														18
CROMPTON Alan								5																		5
CROOKES Dominic																2										2
CULPIN Paul												2														2

693

TELFORD UNITED GOALSCORERS

Name	79-80	80-81	81-82	82-83	83-84	84-85	85-86	86-87	87-88	88-89	89-90	90-91	91-92	92-93	93-94	94-95	95-96	96-97	97-98	98-99	99-00	00-01	01-02	02-03	03-04	TOTAL
CUNNINGHAM Mark										1																1
DALEY Ryan																			1							1
DALY Gerry								2				2														4
DAVIES Kevin																						1	1	1		3
DEGG David	1																									1
DONNELLY Steve																2										2
DOYLE Maurice																				1						1
DYSON Paul											3		5													8
EASTWOOD Phil																			2							2
EATON Steve		1																								1
ECCLESTON Steve																	1									1
EDWARDS Dean				3	11	6																				20
EDWARDS Jake																					9	10	8			27
EDWARDS Neil									1																	1
EVES Mel											4															4
FEREDAY Wayne																	1									1
FERGUSSON Steve													3(2p)	8(4p)	3(2p)											14(8p)
FITZPATRICK Gary																				4	4		5	3		16
FORAN Mark																								5		5
FORD Gary															2	1										3
FORD Jon																					3(1p)					3(1p)
FOSTER Steve																		1								1
FOWLER Lee																		5(4p)	3(1p)	1						9(5p)
FRANCIS Sean														7												7
GARDNER Duncan			7	2																						9
GAVIN Martin	2																									2
GRAINGER Paul										2	5	4														11
GRANT John																									6	6
GRAY Brian																	10	13	10	1						34
GREEN Roy														3												3
GREEN Scott																									3	3
GREENHOUGH Ricky										2																2
GRIFFITHS Bryan																2										2
GRIFFITHS Tony							3	7	2	3	1															16
HALTON Liam							3	1																		4
HANCHARD Martin										1																1

694

TELFORD UNITED GOALSCORERS

TELFORD UNITED GOALSCORERS

	79-80	80-81	81-82	82-83	83-84	84-85	85-86	86-87	87-88	88-89	89-90	90-91	91-92	92-93	93-94	94-95	95-96	96-97	97-98	98-99	99-00	00-01	01-02	02-03	03-04	TOTAL
HANCOCK Mark							1	1		1																3
HANMER Gareth																							4	1		5
HARPER Phil	1																									1
HARRIS Andy											1															1
HATSFIELD Charlie																				3(3p)						3(3p)
HENDERSON Peter				1																						1
HODGIN Chris														1												1
HOGAN Eddie	7	1(1p)	5	5	1	3	5	3																		30(1p)
HOLDEN Mark																1										1
HOWELL Peter																2										2
HUCKERBY Scott																				11	2	2				15
HULBERT Robin																									1	1
HUMPHREYS John												4														4
HURST Mark												1														1
JACKSON Paul				1	3																					4
JOBLING Kevin																						4	1	1		6
JONES John		3																								3
JONES Marcus																				1						1
JONES Roger	2																									2
JOSEPH Antone			3	1			2	4																		11
KEARNEY Mark																5										5
KERR Andy									1																	1
KING Jordan																							1	2		3
LANGFORD Tim												4	12	6			6	4	5							37
LAVERY Richard																									1	1
LEE Andy										4(2p)																4(2p)
LLOYD Tommy									7	4	1										1					12
MACAULEY Carl																					1					1
MALCOLM Ken	2																									2
MALKIN Chris																					5	4				9
MANEY Gary	1	1																								2
MARTIN John					1																					1
MARTINDALE Gary																					4(1p)	7(2p)	4(1p)			15(4p)
MATHER Dave	9	13	22	21	8	11																				84
MAYMAN Paul		5		1	6																					12
McGINTY John						7(1p)		4	2(2p)		4(1p)	4(2p)														21(6p)

695

TELFORD UNITED GOALSCORERS

	79-80	80-81	81-82	82-83	83-84	84-85	85-86	86-87	87-88	88-89	89-90	90-91	91-92	92-93	93-94	94-95	95-96	96-97	97-98	98-99	99-00	00-01	01-02	02-03	03-04	TOTAL
McGORRY Brian																					1					1
McKENNA Ken						8	19	23		4	12															66
MILLS Lee																									9	9
MITCHELL Ian															1											1
MOORE Christian																									1	1
MOORE Michael																		2	2							4
MOORE Neil																						3	2			5
MOORE Paul																							2	14		16
MORGAN Tom								6																		6
MULLIGAN James														3												3
MURPHY Chris																									7	7
MURPHY Gez																			8	8	10(2p)	7				33(2p)
MYERS Martin												9	10	3		6	9									37
NARDIELLO Don			1																							1
NAYLOR Martin																				1	1					2
NAYLOR Tony																									11	11
NEALE Mark			8	5																						13
NELSON Steve								1	4	1		3														9
NIBLETT Nigel														1	1	2	3		1	2						10
NORBURY Micky																		3								3
NORRIS Steve									24(3p)																	24(3p)
OAKLEY Andy											1															1
PAGE Don																		1								1
PALMER Steve																			4	7	4	5	1	1		22
PARRISH Shaun													1	4	2											7
PREECE Roger																	1					1				2
PRITCHARD Dave														1												1
PURDIE Jon																2		4								6
QUAYLE Mark																							13(1p)			13(1p)
RICKETTS Sam																									4	4
ROBERTS Darren														5(1p)		5										10(1p)
ROBINSON Lee																	1	1								2
RODOSTHENOUS Michael																	1									1
ROSS Brian												1														1
RUSSELL Damon																		3								3

TELFORD UNITED GOALSCORERS

TELFORD UNITED GOALSCORERS

	79-80	80-81	81-82	82-83	83-84	84-85	85-86	86-87	87-88	88-89	89-90	90-91	91-92	92-93	93-94	94-95	95-96	96-97	97-98	98-99	99-00	00-01	01-02	02-03	03-04	TOTAL
SALATHIEL Neil												1														1
SANDWITH Kevin																					1					1
SANKEY Iain									5	1																6
SAYER Ronnie																								1		1
SCOTT Richard																							1			1
SHAKESPEARE Craig																			1							1
SHELDON Kevin							2																			2
SIMKIN Darren																	1									1
SLEEUWENHOEK Kris															2											2
SMITH Peter																							5	7		12
SROMEK Frank	1																									1
STANLEY Craig																									1	1
STEVENS Gary											4															4
STRINGER John						5	11	6	1	5	7															35
TAYLOR Colin															11	1										12
TAYLOR Steve																			2							2
TRAVIS Simon																						2				2
TURNER Mark																	3	3	4	3						13
TURNER Tony			11	6	4	5																				26
WALKER Alan		1	1	3	1																					6
WALTON Russell	1	1																								2
WARNER Ashley																6(1p)										6(1p)
WHITEHEAD Stewart																								1		1
WHITEHOUSE Mark															6(1p)											6(1p)
WHITTINGTON Trevor													4													4
WILCOX Brett																2	1									3
WILDING Peter																		2								2
WILKEY Peter	11	4																								15
WILLIAMS Colin	2			11	11	4	10	4																		42
WILLIAMS Jimmy		5																								5
WILLIAMS Lee																										1
WILSON Lee															4	9(1p)										13(1p)
WOODS Ray																										3
WORRALL Steve												3														3
WRIGHT Evran																		2								2

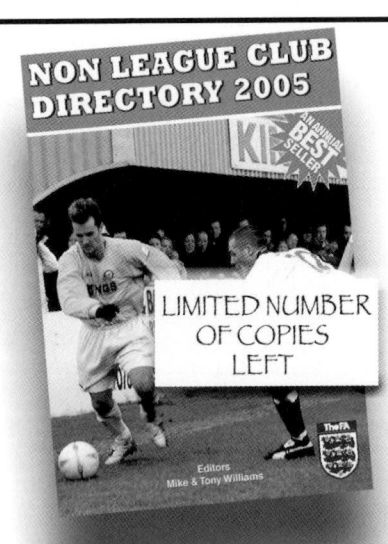

1982-83 F.A. Trophy winners.

TROWBRIDGE TOWN

PROMOTED FROM: The Southern League 1981
RELEGATED TO: The Southern League 1984
2004-2005 SEASON: Hellenic League Division One West

SEASONS
3

TOTAL POINTS
109

HIGHEST ATTENDANCE
1967 v Bath C. 26.12.83

LOWEST ATTENDANCE
204 v Bangor C. 28.4.84

SEASON GOALSCORER
John Evans 14 (82/83)
Bernie Wright 14(1p) (82/83)

CAREER GOALSCORER
Bernie Wright 29(4p)

CAREER APPEARANCES
Bernie Wright 115+1

1981-82 Squad - Back Row (L-R): T. Beasley, P. Hunt, P. Collicutt, S. Harding, I. Harris, J. Smeulders, P. Rose, S. Strong, S. Scarrott, J. Gough.
Front: D. Cunningham, M. Williams, A. Feeley, A. Birchenall (Player/Manager), T. Senter (general Manager), K. Tanner, K. Davies, P. Fielding, S. Peters (Physio).

	HOME							AWAY							
	P	W	D	L	F	A	Pts	P	W	D	L	F	A	Pts	Position
81-82	21	8	7	6	26	23	31	21	4	4	13	12	31	16	17
82-83	21	9	5	7	31	30	32	21	3	2	16	25	58	11	18
83-84	21	3	4	14	15	34	10	21	2	3	16	18	53	9	22
Total	63	20	16	27	72	87	73	63	9	9	45	55	142	36	

	Altrincham		A P Leamington		Bangor City		Barnet		Barrow		Bath City		Boston United		Dagenham		Dartford	
	H	A	H	A	H	A	H	A	H	A	H	A	H	A	H	A	H	A
81-82	0-2	2-1	2-1	1-0			1-1	0-0	2-0	0-1	1-1	1-1	1-0	0-1	0-1	2-1	2-1	0-1
82-83	3-2	0-2			3-2	3-4	0-2	3-1	2-1	2-3	1-1	0-2	1-2	0-3	2-2	1-0		
83-84	0-0	0-4			1-2	0-4	0-4	1-2			1-2	1-2	0-2	0-2	1-4	0-6		

	Enfield		Frickley Athletic		Gateshead		Gravesend & N'fleet		Kettering Town		Kidderminster H.		Maidstone United		Northwich Victoria		Nuneaton Borough	
	H	A	H	A	H	A	H	A	H	A	H	A	H	A	H	A	H	A
81-82	2-2	1-2	2-0	0-2			2-1	1-1	0-1	0-4			3-0	0-3	1-0	0-0		
82-83	2-1	0-2	2-0	2-2					2-1	1-1			0-2	0-6	0-2	3-6	0-2	0-2
83-84	0-0	1-2	0-1	0-2	0-2	2-2			1-2	2-3	1-2	1-1	1-2	1-4	1-1	2-0	0-2	1-2

	Runcorn		Scarborough		Stafford Rangers		Telford United		Wealdstone		Weymouth		Worcester City		Yeovil Town	
	H	A	H	A	H	A	H	A	H	A	H	A	H	A	H	A
81-82	0-0	0-2	1-3	1-3	1-1	2-0	1-2	0-2			1-1	0-1	1-1	1-3	2-4	0-2
82-83	1-2	2-3	1-1	2-5	5-3	2-3	2-0	1-3	0-0	0-4	0-0	1-2	2-3	1-4	2-1	1-0
83-84	0-1	0-2	1-0	0-0			2-2	0-1	1-2	0-6	1-2	1-0	2-1	2-5	1-0	1-3

	HOME						AWAY					
	P	W	D	L	F	A	P	W	D	L	F	A
ALTRINCHAM	3	1	1	1	3	4	3	1	0	2	2	7
A P LEAMINGTON	1	1	0	0	2	1	1	1	0	0	1	0
BANGOR C	2	1	0	1	4	4	2	0	0	2	3	8
BARNET	3	0	1	2	1	7	3	1	1	1	4	3
BARROW	2	2	0	0	4	1	2	0	0	2	2	4
BATH C	3	0	2	1	3	4	3	0	1	2	2	5
BOSTON U	3	1	0	2	2	4	3	0	0	3	0	6
DAGENHAM	3	0	1	2	3	7	3	2	0	1	5	7
DARTFORD	1	1	0	0	2	1	1	0	0	1	0	1
ENFIELD	3	1	2	0	4	3	3	0	0	3	2	6
FRICKLEY A	3	2	0	1	4	1	3	0	1	2	2	6
GATESHEAD	1	0	0	1	0	2	1	0	1	0	2	2
GRAVESEND & N	1	1	0	0	2	1	1	0	1	0	1	1
KETTERING T	3	1	0	2	3	4	3	0	1	2	3	8
KIDDERMINSTER H	1	0	0	1	1	2	1	0	1	0	1	1
MAIDSTONE U	3	1	0	2	4	4	3	0	0	3	1	13
NORTHWICH V	3	1	1	1	2	3	3	1	1	1	5	6
NUNEATON B	2	0	0	2	0	4	2	0	0	2	1	4
RUNCORN	3	0	1	2	1	3	3	0	0	3	2	7
SCARBOROUGH	3	1	1	1	3	4	3	0	1	2	3	8
STAFFORD R	2	1	1	0	6	4	2	1	0	1	4	3
TELFORD U	3	1	1	1	5	4	3	0	0	3	1	6
WEALDSTONE	2	0	1	1	1	2	2	0	0	2	0	10
WEYMOUTH	3	0	2	1	2	3	3	1	0	2	2	3
WORCESTER C	3	1	1	1	5	5	3	0	0	3	4	12
YEOVIL T	3	2	0	1	5	5	3	1	0	2	2	5
TOTALS	63	20	16	27	72	87	63	9	9	45	55	142

TROWBRIDGE TOWN

	APPEARANCES 81/82	82/83	83/84	TOTAL	GOALS 81/82	82/83	83/84	TOTAL
ANENIH C			1	1				
ARMSTRONG George		17		17		1		1
ASHTON Stuart			15	15				
ASHWORTH Simon			1	1				
BARTLEY Danny			38	38			1	1
BEASLEY Tony	5			5	1			1
BIRCHENALL Alan	42	15		57	2			2
BOOTON Chris	1			1				
BRAY Marcus			19+6	19+6				
BUTLER Geoff		3+1		3+1				
CHALKLIN Geoff		18	8	26				
COLLICUTT Paul	42	41		83	3	1		4
CUNNINGHAM Dave	28+4	8+10		36+14	1			1
DAVIES Kevin	26+2			26+2				
DAVIES Paul	23	12+1		35+1	7			7
DAVIS Peter			5+2	5+2			1	1
DEAN Steve	4+4	23+1		27+5		1		1
EVANS John		31	21+2	52+2		14	4	18
FEELEY Andy	38	23	23+1	84+1	3	4	5	12
FIELDING Peter	0+1			0+1				
GODDARD Howard			2	2				
GOUGH Jimmy	9+3			9+3	2			2
GUTHRIE Chris		9		9		3		3
HARDING Steve	38	11		49	1	1		2
HARRIS Gary	36	39	28+5	103+5		7		7
HARRIS I	1			1	1			1
HOLDER Phil	2+1			2+1				
HUGHES Tony			8	8				
HUNT Paul	13+1			13+1	1			1
JONES D			1	1				
KANE Tony		6+1		6+1				
KEMBER Steve		3		3				
KILKELLY Tom	1			1				
KINZETT Gary		5		5				
LAYTON John		13	21	34		1	4	5

TROWBRIDGE TOWN

	APPEARANCES				GOALS			
	81/82	82/83	83/84	TOTAL	81/82	82/83	83/84	TOTAL
MARSHALL Julian		4		4				
MAYNARD Stanley		0+1		0+1				
McCAFFERTY Jimmy		3+1		3+1				
MERRICK Neil		23		23				
MITCHELL Dave			6+1	6+1				
MOONEY Dean			3	3				
MOSS Craig		2	23+5	25+5			2	2
NEAT Paul			2+4	2+4				
PALMER Andy	10+2			10+2	2			2
PREECE Brian		9+2		9+2		3		3
PULIS Ray			10+4	10+4			1	1
RITCHIE Steve			34+1	34+1			3	3
ROBERTS Dave			16	16			1	1
ROSE Paul	3	2+1		5+1				
ROSS Duncan			14+1	14+1				
ROUND Steve			8+3	8+3			1	1
RUSTELL Micky		1+1		1+1				
SAMMELS Jon		3		3				
SANKEY Martin			6+3	6+3				
SCARROTT Steve	8+2			8+2	1(1p)			1(1p)
SECKER Wayne		6+3		6+3				
SHRUBSOLE Ian		1	4	5				
SMEULDERS John	42	41		83				
SMITH Steve			27	27				
SPITTLE Paul			11	11			1	1
STEVENS Mark			3	3				
STRONG Steve	19+2			19+2	1			1
SWEENEY Gerry	1			1				
SYMONDS Paul		1+3		1+3				
TAINTON Trevor		41+1	39+1	80+2		3	2(2p)	5(2p)
TANNER Keith	7+4	7		14+4				
THOMAS Martin			14+5	14+5				
THOMSON Barrie			8	8				
WILLIAMS Mark	28+8			28+8	1(1p)			1(1p)
WRIGHT Bernie	35	41	39+1	115+1	11(3p)	14(1p)	4	29(4p)

702

WEALDSTONE

FOUNDER MEMBER
ELECTED from: Southern League
RELEGATED TO: The Isthmian League 1981, 1988
PROMOTED FROM: The Isthmian League 1982
2004-2005 SEASON: The Isthmian League Premier Division

The double winning squad of 1984-85 - Back Row (L-R): Steve Tapley, Robin Wainwright, Andy Graham, Vinny Jones, Steve McCargo. Middle: Les Reed (Coach), Brian Greenway, Alan Cordice, Bob Iles, Neil Cordice, Mark Graves, Arnold Reed (Physio). Front: Gary Donnellan, Lee Holmes, Paul Bowgett (Captain), Brian Hall (Manager), Dennis Byatt, Nigel Johnson, Derek Doyle.

SEASONS
8

TOTAL POINTS
212 +175 = 387

HIGHEST POSITION
1st 1984-85

LOWEST POSITION
21st 1987-88

HIGHEST ATTENDANCE
1556 v Barnet 19.3.88

LOWEST ATTENDANCE
304 v Stafford R. 1.5.86

SEASON GOALSCORER
Mark Graves 31(7p) (83/84)

CAREER GOALSCORER
Mark Graves 89(8p)

CAREER APPEARANCES
Paul Bowgett 262+2
Robin Wainwright 261+13

	HOME						AWAY						
	P	W	D	L	F	A	Pts	P	W	D	L	F	A	Pts	Position
79-80	19	5	9	5	26	25	19	19	4	6	9	16	29	14	15
80-81	19	6	8	5	27	19	20	19	3	3	13	10	37	9	19
81-82														
82-83	21	13	5	3	45	17	44	21	9	8	4	35	24	35	3
83-84	21	15	4	2	48	14	34	21	6	10	5	27	22	28	4
84-85	21	8	8	5	31	26	24	21	12	2	7	33	28	38	1
85-86	21	10	5	6	35	28	25	21	6	4	11	22	28	22	10
86-87	21	7	5	9	26	34	26	21	4	5	12	24	36	17	19
87-88	21	3	11	7	20	33	20	21	2	6	13	19	43	12	21
Total	164	67	55	42	258	196	212	164	46	44	74	186	247	175	

WEALDSTONE

	Altrincham		A P Leamington		Bangor City		Barnet		Barrow		Bath City		Boston United		Cheltenham Town		Dagenham	
	H	A	H	A	H	A	H	A	H	A	H	A	H	A	H	A	H	A
79-80	1-4	1-2	1-2	0-0	0-0	0-1	2-1	3-1	2-1	0-1	1-1	4-4	1-1	0-0				
80-81	1-2	0-2	1-2	1-1	1-1	2-0	2-0	0-3	2-0	0-1	0-1	0-2	3-0	1-2				
81-82																		
82-83	1-1	1-0			2-0	2-2	6-0	0-0	4-0	2-0	1-1	2-3	0-0	0-0			3-1	2-1
83-84	3-1	0-1			5-0	0-0	3-0	1-1			0-3	0-0	1-1	1-1			1-0	0-1
84-85	1-0	2-1					1-2	0-7	2-2	1-2	0-1	1-3	0-1	1-1			0-0	2-1
85-86	2-2	0-1					2-0	0-1	4-0	1-1	0-1	3-2	7-2	0-1	0-0	2-1	0-4	2-0
86-87	0-2	2-1					0-0	1-2			1-2	0-2	0-4	0-2	1-0	1-0	2-2	0-1
87-88	0-0	0-1					0-6	1-5			1-1	0-0	1-1	1-0	1-4	1-1	2-3	2-1

	Dartford		Enfield		Fisher Athletic		Frickley Athletic		Gateshead		Gravesend & N'fleet		Kettering Town		Kidderminster H.		Lincoln City	
	H	A	H	A	H	A	H	A	H	A	H	A	H	A	H	A	H	A
79-80											0-0	0-3	2-2	0-2				
80-81							0-2	1-1			3-1	1-0	1-1	1-0				
81-82																		
82-83	1-3	1-0					2-0	2-2					4-0	3-1				
83-84	2-1	2-0					0-0	5-2	4-0	1-1			4-2	2-1	2-0	1-3		
84-85	0-0	3-2	1-2	0-2			1-1	2-0	4-2	2-1			1-0	1-0	5-2	3-0		
85-86	2-1	2-1	2-4	0-1			2-0	1-2					3-1	1-2	0-3	1-3		
86-87			0-3	2-4			2-1	1-3	2-2	1-1			2-1	2-0	0-3	2-5		
87-88			1-0	2-5	2-1	1-3							0-2	2-3	1-1	1-2	0-0	0-3

	Macclesfield Town		Maidstone United		Northwich Victoria		Nuneaton Borough		Redditch United		Runcorn		Scarborough		Stafford Rangers		Sutton United	
	H	A	H	A	H	A	H	A	H	A	H	A	H	A	H	A	H	A
79-80			0-0	0-3	0-1	0-0	2-2	1-0	2-0	1-4			2-4	0-0	2-1	1-0		
80-81			2-1	0-4	1-1	0-0	0-0	0-2					2-2	0-4	1-1	0-3		
81-82																		
82-83			0-0	3-0	2-1	3-3	1-2	1-1			1-0	1-2	2-2	2-1	3-2	1-2		
83-84			1-2	1-2	1-0	1-1	0-0	1-1			4-2	2-4	1-1	1-1				
84-85			1-1	1-0	1-1	2-0	3-1	0-1			1-0	0-2	1-0	1-1				
85-86			3-2	1-0	0-0	2-2	1-0	0-0			1-1	1-1	0-3	1-0	2-3	1-2		
86-87			0-0	0-1	1-1	1-2	6-0	1-1			0-3	1-1	1-3	1-2	0-3	0-1	2-1	2-2
87-88	1-1	2-3	1-3	1-1	2-2	0-0					0-1	0-1			4-2	2-5	0-0	1-1

WEALDSTONE

	Telford United		Trowbridge Town		Welling United		Weymouth		Worcester City		Wycombe Wanderers		Yeovil Town	
	H	A	H	A	H	A	H	A	H	A	H	A	H	A
79-80	0-0	3-1					1-1	0-4	2-4	1-2			5-0	1-1
80-81	4-0	1-2					1-1	1-2	1-2	1-4			1-1	0-4
81-82														
82-83	2-0	0-0	4-0	0-0			2-4	1-4	2-0	3-1			2-0	5-1
83-84	4-0	1-0	6-0	2-1			2-0	4-0	3-1	1-1			1-0	0-0
84-85	2-2	2-4					3-2	3-0	3-3	4-0			0-3	2-0
85-86	1-1	1-2					1-0	2-4			2-0	0-1		
86-87	0-1	3-1			3-1	1-1	3-1	2-3						
87-88	2-2	1-1			1-1	0-4	0-2	1-2			0-0	0-1		

	Home						Away					
	P	W	D	L	F	A	P	W	D	L	F	A
ALTRINCHAM	8	2	3	3	9	12	8	3	0	5	6	9
A P LEAMINGTON	2	0	0	2	2	4	2	0	2	0	1	1
BANGOR C	4	2	2	0	8	1	4	1	2	1	4	3
BARNET	8	5	1	2	16	9	8	1	2	5	6	20
BARROW	5	4	1	0	14	3	5	1	1	3	4	5
BATH C	8	0	3	5	4	11	8	1	3	4	10	16
BOSTON U	8	2	4	2	13	10	8	1	4	3	4	7
CHELTENHAM T	3	1	1	1	2	4	3	2	1	0	4	2
DAGENHAM	6	2	2	2	8	10	6	4	0	2	8	5
DARTFORD	2	1	1	0	2	1	2	2	0	0	5	3
ENFIELD	6	2	0	4	7	13	6	2	0	4	7	12
FISHER A	1	1	0	0	2	1	1	0	0	1	1	3
FRICKLEY A	6	3	2	1	7	4	6	2	2	2	12	10
GATESHEAD	3	2	1	0	10	4	3	1	2	0	4	3
GRAVESEND & N	2	1	1	0	3	1	2	1	0	1	1	3
KETTERING T	8	5	2	1	17	9	8	5	0	3	12	9
KIDDERMINSTER H	5	2	1	2	8	9	5	1	0	4	8	13
LINCOLN C	1	0	1	0	0	0	1	0	0	1	0	3
MACCLESFIELD T	1	0	1	0	1	1	1	0	0	1	2	3
MAIDSTONE U	8	2	4	2	8	9	8	3	1	4	7	11
NORTHWICH V	8	2	5	1	8	7	8	1	6	1	9	8
NUNEATON B	7	3	3	1	13	5	7	1	4	2	4	6
REDDITCH U	1	1	0	0	2	0	1	0	0	1	1	4
RUNCORN	6	3	1	2	7	7	6	0	2	4	5	11
SCARBOROUGH	7	1	3	3	9	15	7	2	3	2	6	9
STAFFORD R	6	3	1	2	12	12	6	1	0	5	5	13
SUTTON U	2	1	1	0	2	1	2	0	2	0	3	3
TELFORD U	8	3	4	1	15	6	8	3	2	3	12	11
TROWBRIDGE T	2	2	0	0	10	0	2	1	1	0	2	1
WELLING U	2	1	1	0	4	2	2	0	1	1	1	5
WEYMOUTH	8	4	2	2	13	11	8	2	0	6	14	19
WORCESTER C	5	2	1	2	11	10	5	2	1	2	10	8
WYCOMBE W	2	1	1	0	2	0	2	0	0	2	0	2
YEOVIL T	5	3	1	1	9	4	5	2	2	1	8	6
TOTALS	164	67	55	42	258	196	164	46	44	74	186	247

Above: Alan Cordice   Photo:Roger Price Ltd

Below: Danny Bailey   Photo: Eric Marsh

Above: John Watson.   Photo: Roger Price Ltd

Below: Stuart Pearce   Photo: Eric Marsh

WEALDSTONE   APPEARANCES

	79-80	80-81	81-82	82-83	83-84	84-85	85-86	86-87	87-88	TOTAL
ADAMS Mark	17+1	8+4								25+5
BADDELEY Kevin						4				4
BAILEY Danny									12	12
BALDWIN Tommy		3								3
BARWICK Fred	29	35+1		38	10					112+1
BATE Frank								5		5
BENNETT Anthony	6+1	13+3								19+4
BOWGETT Paul		32		41	39	39	39	36+2	36	262+2
BOYLE Terry	13+3									13+3
BRANNIGAN Paul	32+2	26+1								58+3
BYATT Dennis		8		41	36	34	22	20+2	14+2	175+4
CLEAVELEY Les							1			1
CORDICE Alan		36		36	40	38+1	16		11+2	177+3
CORDICE Neil	37	23		32	5+8	22+8	25+6	25+4	9+1	178+27
COTTER Paul						4				4
CRANSTONE Ian	31	38								69
CROSS Don								2+1		2+1
DAVIES Roy				36		37+2	1			74+2
DAVIS Bert								1		1
DAVIS Paul								12		12
DEVLIN Mark								0+1		0+1
DIBBLE Chris					25	2+1				27+1
DOLLING Gary								0+2		0+2
DONNELLAN Gary					28+4	38+1	24+1	20		110+6
DOWE Hughy						1			5	6
DOYLE Derek							26+2	30+1		56+3
ELLIOTT Mark				0+1						0+1
ENGLISH Tom									21+3	21+3
EVANS Dylan		11								11
EVANS Terry								2		2
FERGUSON Mick								10+1		10+1
FILBY Malcolm	1									1
FORDE Clevere		19+5								19+5
FOSTER Kevin								5		5
FURSDON Alan	27+3	14								41+3
GALLOWAY Steve							3			3
GODDARD Ray				41	5	8				54
GRAHAM Andy						11+2	11+8			22+10
GRAVES Mark				40	40+1	31+5	35+2	32+5		178+13
GREENAWAY Brian					32+3	33+1	36	31+5		132+9
GREENHALGH Brian	5+4									5+4
HARDMAN Colin		15								15
HARRIOT Les		5								5
HARRISON Mark								16		16
HATTER Steve							11	13		24
HAXTON Andy							5			5
HIRST Martin								5+1	25+5	30+6
HIRST Steve									2	2
HOLMES Lee						34+1	35	16+1		85+2
HORGAN Seamus	28									28
ILES Bob					37	27	38	37		139
ISAACS Tony								3+2		3+2
JACKSON Phil								1		1
JAMES Tommy	4+1									4+1
JOHNSON Colin	10+1									10+1
JOHNSON Nigel	33	26+3		26+2	38	7+8				130+13

WEALDSTONE

APPEARANCES

	79-80	80-81	81-82	82-83	83-84	84-85	85-86	86-87	87-88	TOTAL
JONES Paul							3			3
JONES Vinny						8+4	11+15			19+19
KING Gary								0+1		0+1
KNOWLES Ray			3+1							3+1
KOTEY Peter								0+1		0+1
LA RONDE Everald								16		16
LARNER Keith		3+1								3+1
LOWE Barry								5+2		5+2
LYNCH Tony								21		21
MADDISON Lee								12		12
MARGERRISON John				19						19
McCARGO Steve					28+1	26	34+2			88+3
McCARTHY Paddy							5	39+1		44+1
McCLURE Doug							8	38+1		46+1
McGUINNESS Wilf						3				3
MEADOWS Toni								0+1	5+4	5+5
MILLER Paul								10+1		10+1
MORRIS Mark					1					1
MOSS Bobby	24+1									24+1
MUTPHY Tom		11+4								11+4
O'KEEFE Robert							1+3		7	8+3
OLALEYE Samson									13+2	13+2
PEARCE Dave	0+1									0+1
PEARCE Stuart	37+1	37		35	10					119+1
PERKINS Steve		14		38	32+1	16	11+2			111+3
PERRY Mick									8+5	8+5
PITTAWAY Mike									28+1	28+1
PRICE David					25+2					25+2
PRIDDY Paul				1						1
RAGAN Steve								3+7		3+7
RICHARDSON Jimmy					2+1					2+1
RIVERO Francisco									20+2	20+2
ROBINSON Paul	10+3									10+3
RUTTER Steve							15+3			15+3
SEAGRAVES Chris							2+1			2+1
SMURTHWAITE Tony								1		1
SOLOMON Gerry									8+1	8+1
SPERRIN Mark		1								1
STAGG Billy									1+3	1+3
SWEETZER Jimmy		7								7
TAPLEY Steve							40	37		77
TAYLOR Bob	4									4
TONGE Keith							1+6	5+10		6+16
TOOGOOD John	1									1
TURNER Paul									1	1
TUTT Graham	2									2
WADDOCK Andy				4	3					7
WAINWRIGHT Robin	37	24+1		27+2	26+6	39	42	40	26+4	261+13
WAITES Paul				4+3	0+3					4+6
WALLACE Andy								19+3		19+3
WALTON Byron								6+2	14+2	20+4
WATSON John	30	9								39
WEDDERBURN Kevin						0+1				0+1
WELSH Alex									37	37
ZACHARIA Greg									8+3	8+3

Brian Hall

Les Reed

Left: Andy Graham   Photo: Martin Dalton

Below: Vinny Jones

WEALDSTONE   GOALSCORERS

	79-80	80-81	81-82	82-83	83-84	84-85	85-86	86-87	87-88	TOTAL
ADAMS Mark	1									1
BARWICK Fred		1			1					2
BATE Frank									4	4
BOWGETT Paul		8		2(1p)	8	1	2	1	1	23(1p)
BRANNIGAN Paul	1	1								2
BYATT Dennis				5(3p)		1	1	1	1	9(3p)
CORDICE Alan		4		13	6	11	1		3	38
CORDICE Neil	10	9		11	1	7	6	1		45
DAVIES Ray				5						5
DIBBLE Chris					4					4
DONNELLAN Gary					4	5	2	3		14
DOYLE Derek							5(1p)	5(3p)		10(4p)
ENGLISH Tom									10	10
FERGUSON Mick									3	3
FORDE Clevere		1								1
GALLOWAY Steve								2		2
GRAHAM Andy						4	7			11
GRAVES Mark				23	31(7p)	15(1p)	8	12		89(8p)
GREENAWAY Brian					10(1p)	3	6	2(1p)		21(2p)
HARRISON Mark									1	1
HATTER Steve									1	1
HIRST Martin									1	1
HOLMES Lee						7	6	3		16
HORGAN Seamus	8									8
JOHNSON Nigel	8	5		11	7	3				34
JONES Vinny							2			2
LA RONDE Everald								1		1
LYNCH Tony								3		3
MARGERRISON John				4						4
McCARGO Steve					1	3	2			6
McCARTHY Paddy								1		1
MILLER Paul								4		4
MOSS Bobby	5									5
OLALEYE Samson									4	4
PEARCE Stuart	2	2		4(1p)						8(1p)
RAGAN Steve								1		1
ROBINSON Paul	1									1
RUTTER Steve								1		1
SPERRIN Martin		2								2
SWEETZER Jimmy		1								1
TONGE Keith								1		1
WAINWRIGHT Robin	3	1		1		2	8	5	1	21
WALLACE Andy								7		7
WALTON Byron								1	3	4
WATSON John	1	2								3
ZACHARIA Greg									1	1

WELLING UNITED

PROMOTED FROM: Southern League 1986
RELEGATED TO: Southern League 2000
2004-2005 SEASON: Conference South

1989-90 Squad.
Back Row: Stuart White, Ray Burgess, Tony Reynolds, Paul Barron, Mark Hone, John Glover, Roy Hales, Duncan Horton. Front Row: Phil Handford, Terry Robbins, Neil Clemmence, Trevor Booker, Martin Buglione, Nigel Ransom. Photo: Keith Gillard

	HOME							AWAY							
	P	W	D	L	F	A	Pts	P	W	D	L	F	A	Pts	Position
86-87	21	8	4	9	39	38	28	21	2	6	13	22	46	12	20
87-88	21	8	4	9	33	32	28	21	3	5	13	17	40	14	19
88-89	20	8	6	6	27	16	30	20	6	5	9	18	30	23	11
89-90	21	11	6	4	36	16	39	21	7	4	10	26	34	25	6
90-91	21	7	10	4	33	27	31	21	6	5	10	22	30	23	11
91-92	21	8	6	7	40	38	30	21	6	6	9	29	41	24	12
92-93	21	8	6	7	34	37	30	21	4	6	11	23	35	18	20
93-94	21	7	7	7	25	23	28	21	6	5	10	22	26	23	16
94-95	21	9	3	9	31	33	30	21	4	7	10	26	41	19	17
95-96	21	6	8	7	21	23	26	21	4	7	10	21	30	19	19
96-97	21	9	2	10	24	26	29	21	4	7	10	26	34	19	18
97-98	21	11	5	5	39	27	38	21	6	4	11	25	35	22	10
98-99	21	4	7	10	18	30	19	21	5	7	9	26	35	22	20
99-00	21	6	5	10	27	32	23	21	7	3	11	27	34	24	20
Total	293	110	79	104	427	398	409	293	70	77	146	330	491	287	

SEASONS
14

TOTAL POINTS
696

HIGHEST POSITION
6th (89/90)

LOWEST POSITION
20 (86/87) (92/93) (98/99) (99/00)

HIGHEST ATTENDANCE
2621 v Darlington (5-5-90)

LOWEST ATTENDANCE
400 v Hednesford (12-3-96)

SEASON GOALSCORER
Terry Robbins 29 (1p) (91/92)

CAREER GOALSCORER
Terry Robbins 139 (12p)

CAREER APPEARANCES
Nigel Ransom 327+4

es for good

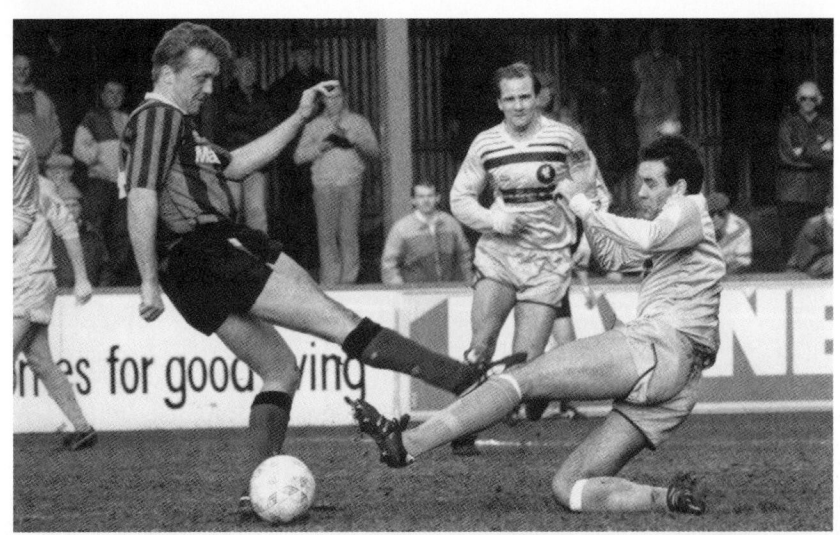

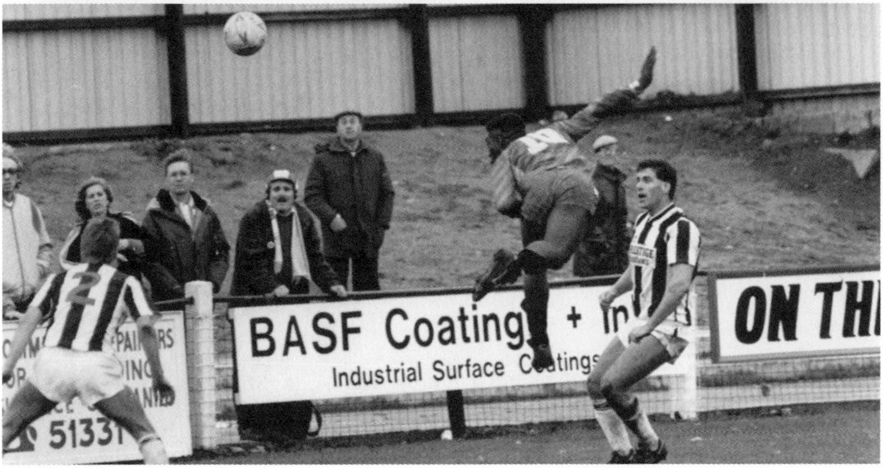
BASF Coating
Industrial Surface
ON TH
5133

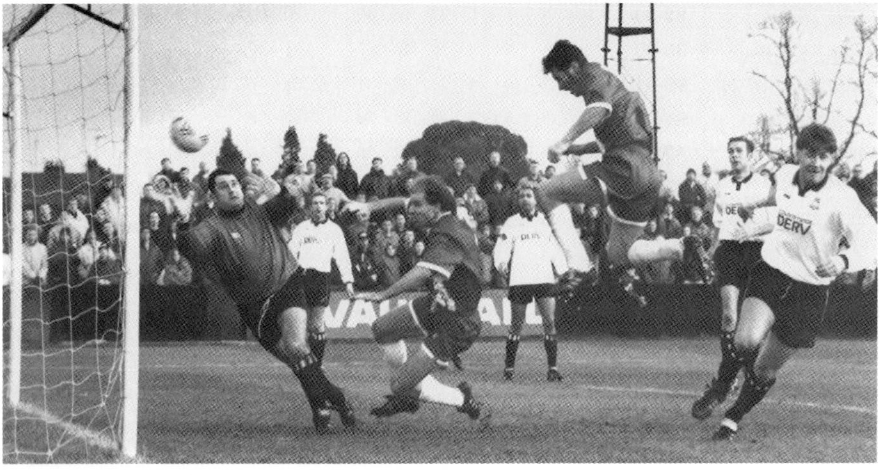
DERV

WELLING UNITED

	Altrincham		Aylesbury United		Barnet		Barrow		Bath City		Boston United		Bromsgrove Rovers		Cheltenham Town		Chorley	
	H	A	H	A	H	A	H	A	H	A	H	A	H	A	H	A	H	A
86-87	0-1	1-1			1-1	1-1			1-1	1-1	4-2	3-4			1-3	0-2		
87-88	0-1	0-1			0-2	2-5			2-1	0-0	3-1	2-1			0-1	2-2		
88-89	0-0	1-3	5-0	0-0	1-1	3-2					3-2	0-2			0-2	1-1	1-0	1-1
89-90	1-1	0-4			3-1	1-1	0-0	1-1			6-0	1-2			1-1	2-3	3-1	0-4
90-91	2-2	1-0			1-4	2-3	4-2	1-1	2-1	1-2	0-0	0-0			0-0	0-3		
91-92	2-2	2-1					5-3	1-6	0-5	3-0	1-3	1-5			1-1	2-3		
92-93	2-0	0-2							0-3	1-1	2-2	1-2	4-2	2-2				
93-94	2-1	0-2							0-0	0-0			1-1	1-1				
94-95	0-0	1-1							1-5	0-2			1-2	1-4				
95-96	1-1	0-1							2-1	1-1			5-2	1-1				
96-97	1-0	1-1							2-0	1-3			1-2	0-1				
97-98															2-1	1-1		
98-99															2-1	0-0		
99-00	2-2	1-0																

	Colchester United		Dagenham		Dagenham & Redbridge 91-92 as Redbridge Forest		Darlington		Doncaster Rovers		Dover Athletic		Enfield		Farnborough Town		Fisher Athletic	
	H	A	H	A	H	A	H	A	H	A	H	A	H	A	H	A	H	A
86-87			1-0	1-1									2-3	2-0				
87-88			6-1	2-1									1-1	0-1			1-1	0-1
88-89													0-0	1-0			3-1	3-1
89-90							0-1	0-1					3-0	3-2	4-3	1-3	2-0	3-1
90-91	1-1	1-2															1-1	1-1
91-92	4-1	1-3			2-2	0-2									1-0	1-1		
92-93					0-2	0-1									3-1	2-3		
93-94					0-0	0-2					2-0	1-0			1-3	2-1		
94-95					4-1	0-0					0-1	1-1			0-1	1-0		
95-96					0-0	1-1					1-0	1-2			0-2	1-2		
96-97											1-0	1-2			1-0	0-0		
97-98											2-2	1-2			0-0	1-1		
98-99									1-1	1-4	0-3	2-1						
99-00									0-1	1-1	1-1	1-2						

Opposite page photo captions.

TOP: Welling's Duncan Horgan dispossessing Altrincham's Paul Rowlands.

MIDDLE: An athletic Trevor Booker heading Welling's second goal against Stafford Rangers.

BOTTOM: Another headed goal - this time Tony Reynolds scoring against Dover Athletic.

Photos: Keith Gillard

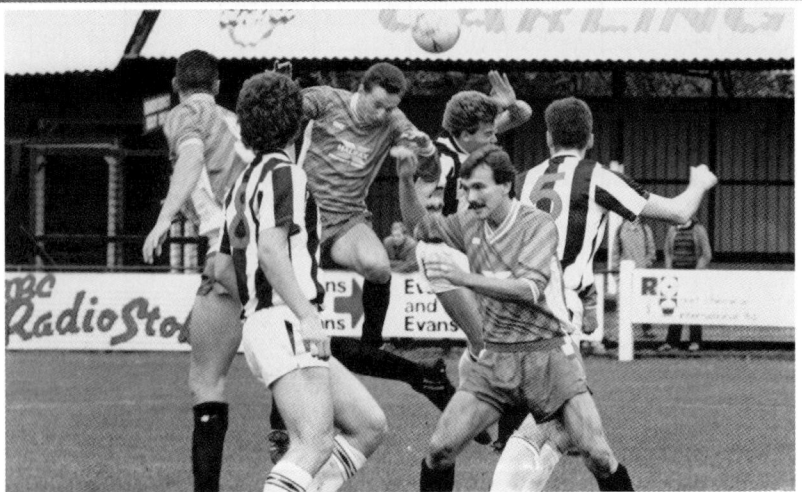

WELLING UNITED

	Forest Green Rovers		Frickley Athletic		Gateshead		Halifax Town		Hayes		Hednesford Town		Hereford United		Kettering Town		Kidderminster H.	
	H	A	H	A	H	A	H	A	H	A	H	A	H	A	H	A	H	A
86-87			3-2	1-3	3-4	1-1									0-3	1-5	1-0	0-3
87-88															3-1	0-1	1-2	2-5
88-89															2-1	1-2	0-1	1-2
89-90															3-0	1-0	4-1	1-1
90-91					6-0	3-0									0-0	0-0	1-0	2-1
91-92					2-2	1-1									2-3	1-1	3-2	3-1
92-93					2-1	2-1									1-1	4-2	0-0	1-2
93-94					1-2	0-1	0-2	1-1							2-0	2-2	0-3	0-1
94-95					3-0	0-2	1-1	0-4							2-1	3-4	0-2	0-3
95-96					1-2	1-1	0-0	1-2			1-1	1-1			1-0	3-1	0-0	0-3
96-97					2-0	2-1	0-1	1-1	1-0	1-1	1-2	3-0			1-2	3-2	0-1	2-3
97-98					2-0	1-2	6-2	0-1	2-0	1-3	3-2	2-3	3-0	2-1	2-2	1-0	0-3	1-2
98-99	0-2	2-3							0-2	2-1	1-1	2-3	2-2	0-0	0-2	1-1	0-0	1-0
99-00	1-1	2-1							1-2	0-1	1-2	1-0	3-1	2-1	1-0	1-2	1-2	1-4

	Kingstonian		Leek Town		Lincoln City		Macclesfield Town		Maidstone United		Merthyr Tydfil		Morecambe		Northwich Victoria		Nuneaton Borough	
	H	A	H	A	H	A	H	A	H	A	H	A	H	A	H	A	H	A
86-87									2-2	0-4					3-2	1-2	1-2	2-1
87-88					1-4	1-2	3-1	2-3	0-1	1-0					1-1	0-0		
88-89							2-0	0-3	0-0	0-3					0-0	2-0		
89-90							0-1	2-3			0-3	0-4			2-0	3-2		
90-91							0-0	1-2			2-1	0-1			4-5	2-1		
91-92							2-1	2-1			1-2	1-2			6-1	2-1		
92-93							1-0	1-1			5-0	1-1			1-5	1-1		
93-94							0-1	0-1			1-1	1-0			0-1	1-3		
94-95							0-1	1-3			2-1	2-0			1-5	1-1		
95-96													1-0	0-1	1-1	2-1		
96-97							0-3	1-1					1-4	2-1	1-1	0-0		
97-98			2-0	2-1									2-2	2-4	0-1	1-5		
98-99	1-3	1-2	1-0	4-2									3-2	1-2	2-3	0-3		
99-00	0-1	0-1											0-0	1-2	1-3	2-3	0-0	3-4

Opposite page photo captions.

TOP: Nigel Ransom's acrobatic headed goal against Cheltenham was unfortunately disallowed.

MIDDLE: Dereck Browne sliding in to tackle Dagenham & Redbridge's Dominic Crookes.

BOTTOM: Mark Honegets his head to this corner against Stafford Rangers.

Photos: Keith Gillard

WELLING UNITED

	Runcorn		Rushden & Diamonds		Scarborough		Slough Town		Southport		Stafford Rangers		Stalybridge Celtic		Stevenage Borough		Sutton United	
	H	A	H	A	H	A	H	A	H	A	H	A	H	A	H	A	H	A
86-87	3-0	2-2			1-3	0-2					2-4	1-3					3-1	0-2
87-88	1-1	0-4									0-5	0-2					1-4	1-1
88-89	4-0	2-1									1-3	0-3					1-1	1-0
89-90	1-1	1-0									1-0	2-0					1-0	0-1
90-91	2-2	3-2					2-0	0-3			2-1	0-1					1-2	1-1
91-92	1-2	2-2					0-2	3-0			1-1	0-0						
92-93	3-2	0-3					2-1	2-4			1-2	3-4	1-4	0-0				
93-94	1-1	4-2					6-2	1-1	0-2	1-2	2-1	0-3	1-2	1-2				
94-95	1-2	2-3							3-1	0-1	3-1	1-1	3-3	3-1	1-0	2-1		
95-96	1-1	3-1					0-3	0-0	0-1	0-2			1-1	1-2	0-3	1-4		
96-97			0-1	0-3			3-2	3-3	2-3	2-3			2-0	0-0	2-0	1-2		
97-98			0-1	1-0			1-1	2-1	3-5	1-3			1-0	1-2	1-0	0-0		
98-99			0-1	1-3					2-1	2-5					1-1	1-1		
99-00			0-3	0-2	2-1	0-0			4-1	2-3					2-1	1-0	2-3	3-2

	Telford United		Wealdstone		Weymouth		Witton Albion		Woking		Wycombe Wanderers		Yeovil Town	
	H	A	H	A	H	A	H	A	H	A	H	A	H	A
86-87	1-3	1-2	1-1	1-3	5-0	2-3								
87-88	4-1	0-2	4-0	1-1	0-2	0-4					1-0	1-3		
88-89	0-1	0-0			4-0	0-1					0-1	1-1	0-2	0-4
89-90	1-1	0-0									0-0	0-1	0-1	4-0
90-91	1-1	1-2									1-1	1-4	0-3	1-0
91-92	3-1	1-2					1-1	2-2			1-3	0-4	1-0	0-3
92-93	1-3	1-0					2-2	1-0	1-1	0-1	2-2	0-3	0-3	0-1
93-94	0-0	0-2					2-1	5-0	2-2	2-0			2-0	1-0
94-95	1-0	2-4							1-2	1-1			2-1	3-3
95-96	3-1	0-0							1-2	2-3				
96-97	2-1	0-2							1-1	1-2				
97-98	4-1	3-0							1-1	1-3			1-3	1-1
98-99	0-1	0-0							0-1	0-0			1-2	3-1
99-00	2-0	1-2							1-2	3-2			2-5	1-1

WELLING UNITED

	Home						Away					
	P	W	D	L	F	A	P	W	D	L	F	A
ALTRINCHAM	12	3	7	2	13	11	12	3	3	6	8	17
AYLESBURY U	1	1	0	0	5	0	1	0	1	0	0	0
BARNET	5	1	2	2	6	9	5	1	2	2	9	12
BARROW	4	2	2	0	10	6	4	0	2	2	4	10
BATH C	9	4	2	3	10	17	9	1	5	3	8	10
BOSTON U	7	4	2	1	19	10	7	1	1	5	8	16
BROMSGROVE R	5	2	1	2	12	9	5	0	3	2	5	9
CHELTENHAM T	8	2	3	3	7	10	8	0	4	4	8	15
CHORLEY	2	2	0	0	4	1	2	0	1	1	1	5
COLCHESTER U	2	1	1	0	5	2	2	0	0	2	2	5
DAGENHAM	2	2	0	0	7	1	2	1	1	0	3	2
DAGENHAM & R	5	1	3	1	6	5	5	0	2	3	1	6
DARLINGTON	1	0	0	1	0	1	1	0	0	1	0	1
DONCASTER R	2	0	1	1	1	2	2	0	1	1	2	5
DOVER A	7	3	2	2	7	7	7	2	1	4	8	10
ENFIELD	4	1	2	1	6	4	4	3	0	1	6	3
FARNBOROUGH T	8	4	1	3	10	10	8	2	3	3	9	11
FISHER A	4	2	2	0	7	3	4	2	1	1	7	4
FOREST GREEN R	2	0	1	1	1	3	2	1	0	1	4	4
FRICKLEY A	1	1	0	0	3	2	1	0	0	1	1	3
GATESHEAD	9	5	1	3	22	11	9	3	3	3	11	10
HALIFAX T	5	1	2	2	7	6	5	0	2	3	3	9
HAYES	4	2	0	2	4	4	4	1	1	2	4	6
HEDNESFORD T	5	1	2	2	7	8	5	2	1	2	9	7
HEREFORD U	3	2	1	0	8	3	3	2	1	0	4	2
KETTERING T	14	7	3	4	20	16	14	5	4	5	22	23
KIDDERMINSTER H	14	4	3	7	11	17	14	3	1	10	15	31
KINGSTONIAN	2	0	0	2	1	4	2	0	0	2	1	3
LEEK T	2	2	0	0	3	0	2	2	0	0	6	3
LINCOLN C	1	0	0	1	1	4	1	0	0	1	1	2
MACCLESFIELD T	10	4	1	5	9	10	10	1	2	7	11	20
MAIDSTONE U	3	0	2	1	2	3	3	1	0	2	1	7
MERTHYR T	6	3	1	2	11	8	6	2	1	3	5	8
MORECAMBE	5	2	2	1	7	8	5	1	0	4	6	10
NORTHWICH V	14	3	4	7	23	29	14	5	4	5	18	23
NUNEATON B	2	0	1	1	1	2	2	1	0	1	5	5
RUNCORN	10	3	5	2	18	12	10	5	2	3	19	20
RUSHDEN & D	4	0	0	4	0	6	4	1	0	3	2	8
SCARBOROUGH	2	1	0	1	3	4	2	0	1	1	0	2
SLOUGH T	7	4	1	2	14	11	7	2	3	2	11	12
SOUTHPORT	7	3	0	4	14	14	7	0	0	7	8	19
STAFFORD R	9	4	1	4	13	18	9	1	2	6	7	17
STALYBRIDGE C	6	2	2	2	9	10	6	1	2	3	6	7
STEVENAGE B	6	4	1	1	7	5	6	2	2	2	6	8
SUTTON U	6	2	1	3	9	11	6	2	2	2	6	7
TELFORD U	14	7	3	4	23	15	14	2	4	8	10	18
WEALDSTONE	2	1	1	0	5	1	2	0	1	1	2	4
WEYMOUTH	3	2	0	1	9	2	3	0	0	3	2	8
WITTON A	3	1	2	0	5	4	3	2	1	0	8	2
WOKING	8	0	4	4	8	12	8	2	2	4	10	12
WYCOMBE W	6	1	3	2	5	7	6	0	1	5	3	16
YEOVIL T	10	3	0	7	9	20	10	4	3	3	14	14
TOTALS	293	110	79	104	427	398	293	70	77	146	330	491

WELLING UNITED   LEADING APPEARANCES

	86-87	87-88	88-89	89-90	90-91	91-92	92-93	93-94	94-95	95-96	96-97	97-98	98-99	99-00	TOTAL
Nigel RANSOM	31	41	30+1	41	41	39+1	36+1	34+1	34						327+4
Terry ROBBINS	24+3	22+4	33	37	40+1	42	42	40	42						322+8
Stuart WHITE	37+1	38+1	32	41	33+6	40	34+3	41+1	15						311+12
Duncan HORTON		39	38	38	27				25+1	42	38	30			277+1
Tony REYNOLDS	40	10+4	35	41	34+1	31+2	12	35+2	2						240+9
Neil CLEMMENCE	24+8	16+6	21+10	37+2	30+5	29+7	27+5	19+2							203+45
Mike RUTHERFORD							12	23	35	39	38	37	37+3		221+3
Gary ABBOTT	38+1	14			38+3	37+1	42	35+2							204+7
Mark HONE				30	32	30+4	39	41							172+4
Lew WATTS										27+4	33+1	39	40	32	171+5
Paul COPLEY							32+1	27	41	40+1	29				169+2
Steve ROBINSON				18+3	32+1	30+1	41+1	32							153+6
John FARLEY								26+2	32+6	19+2	33+7	23+2	1+2		134+21
John GLOVER			39	41	38+1	21+1	13								152+2
Wayne BROWN			6+1	3+8	2	24+7	6	28+1	38	19	7+1				133+18
Ray BURGESS	42	32+1	29+2	18+6	1+2	7+2		1+2	0+1						130+16
Trevor BOOKER		30+9	35+1	30+2	29+6	1+3									125+21
Phil HANDFORD	8	22	35+1	34+2	39										138+3
Paul BARRON			39	36	25	25									125
Dereck BROWN										23+1	41	13+4	35+4		112+9
Glen KNIGHT											39	40	41		120

WELLING UNITED   APPEARANCES

	86-87	87-88	88-89	89-90	90-91	91-92	92-93	93-94	94-95	95-96	96-97	97-98	98-99	99-00	TOTAL
ABBOH Dennis					1										1
ABBOTT Gary	38+1	14			38+3	37+1	42	35+2							204+7
ABBOTT Stuart											0+9				0+9
ADAMS Danny													3+1		3+1
ADAMS Darren												16+2			16+2
ALLARDYCE Craig												3			3
ANDERSON Luke												6			6
APPIAH Sam									3	0+4	9	8+13			20+17
ASH Jason									20+6						20+6
BAILEY Danny													19+3		19+3
BAKER Joe													2+6		2+6
BARNES Steve							7+6	24+11	10				8		49+17
BARRETT Chris								15+1							15+1
BARRON Paul			39	36	25	25									125
BARTLEY John	10														10
BATTRAM Paul			13+15												13+15
BERRY Gwynne									41						41
BERRY Les				3	29+1										32+1
BOOKER Trevor		30+9	35+1	30+2	29+6	1+3									125+21
BRAITHWAITE Leon												5	30+4		35+4
BROWN Dereck										23+1	41	13+4	35+4		112+9
BROWN Wayne			6+1	3+8	2	24+7	6	28+1	38	19	7+1				133+18

WELLING UNITED   APPEARANCES

	86-87	87-88	88-89	89-90	90-91	91-92	92-93	93-94	94-95	95-96	96-97	97-98	98-99	99-00	TOTAL
BROWNE Stafford												22+4			22+4
BUDDEN John													25		25
BUGLIONE Martin			1+8	7+11											8+19
BURGESS Ray	42	32+1	29+2	18+6	1+2	7+2		1+2	0+1						130+16
CANT Cliff	8+1														8+1
CHAPMAN Danny											33+1		30+3		63+4
CLARKE Chris													2+3		2+3
CLEEVELY Les								10							10
CLEMMENCE Neil	24+8	16+6	21+10	37+2	30+5	29+7	27+5	19+2							203+45
COLLINS Paul							34+2	6	2+3						42+5
COOKSEY Scott								5							5
COOPER Gary										30					30
COOPER Geoff					5										5
COOPER Mark											35	20+4			55+4
COPLEY Paul							32+1	27	41	40+1	29				169+2
CORBYN Richard										1					1
COTTER Micky	5+11	3+15													8+26
CROWE Micky		34+2													34+2
DENNIS Kevin												4	16+3		20+3
DENNIS Lenny						19+16	0+2			34+1					53+19
DICHIO Danny							3								3
DIMMOCK Richard									3+3	2+11	0+6				5+20
DOLBY Tony											32+2	21+8			53+10
EDWARDS Russell													35+1		35+1
EVANS Danny										0+1					0+1
FARLEY John								26+2	32+6	19+2	33+7	23+2	1+2		134+21
FERGUSON Ian		6													6
FINNAN Steve						11+11	14+5								25+16
FRANCIS Joe			5+8	15+13	23	0+1									43+22
FRIAR Paul		2													2
GAMBLE Bradley								0+1	3						3+1
GLOVER John		39	41	38+1	21+1	13									152+2
GOLLEY Mark					27+3										27+3
GORMAN Dave								17	2+5						19+5
GRITT Steve									2						2
HALES Kevin							26+3	28+2	1	1					56+5
HALES Roy				17+11											17+11
HANCOCK Darren								5+1							5+1
HANDFORD Phil	8	22	35+1	34+2	39										138+3
HANLON Ritchie											31+4	7	20		58+4
HANSON Dave								12							12
HARFORD Paul												1			1
HARLE Michael												7	23+1		30+1
HARNEY Michael													10+4		10+4
HARRIS Andy									35			1	8		44
HARRISON Lee					7	10									17
HAVERSON Paul		10+6	0+1												10+7
HAYES Curtis		6													6
HENRY Liburd								14+2							14+2
HODDY Kevin						18+7									18+7

719

TOP LEFT: **Ray Burgess** receiving a presentation tankard to mark his 1000th game for the club from Gen. Manager Graham Hobbins..
TOP RIGHT: **Steve Robinson** & **Mike Rutherford** thwart another attack.
BOTTOM LEFT: YTS player, **Steve Finnan**, became the first player to sign professional forms for Welling watched by Secretary Barrie Hobbins and player/manager Terry Robbins.
BOTTOM RIGHT: **Steve Barnes**, another YTS product in action against Northwich.

WELLING UNITED APPEARANCES

	86-87	87-88	88-89	89-90	90-91	91-92	92-93	93-94	94-95	95-96	96-97	97-98	98-99	99-00	TOTAL
HOLMAN Mark						4									4
HONE Mark			30	32	30+4	39	41								172+4
HOPPING Andy							12								12
HORTON Duncan		39	38	38	27			25+1	42	38	30				277+1
HORWOOD Neil		19													19
HOWELL Greg					7										7
HUMPHRIES Steve				14											14
HUNTER Alvin												9+1			9+1
HYNES Mark											14+2	14+1			28+3
ILIC Sasa											2				2
IRONTON Nicky		2													2
JACOMET Etienne	0+1														0+1
JONES David			0+1												0+1
JONES Murray										4					4
KIMBLE Gary							11								11
KING Tyrone										0+3	4+3	1			5+6
KNIGHT Glen										39	40	41			120
LAKIN Barry										28+4	9				37+4
LEMOINE Adrian	34														34
LEWINGTON Ray										2					2
LEWIS Ben												0+1			0+1
LINDSAY Dave	8	40	13+2												61+2
LINDSEY Scott											1				1
LINGER Paul												12+10			12+10
LUFF Neil		3													3
MACDONALD Tony			39												39
MARGERRISON John		3													3
MARTIN Dave											6				6
MARTIN Elliott							3								3
MARTIN Jae													14		14
MAY Andy									1						1
McDONALD Dave												18			18
MILES Philip	3+4	0+1													3+5
MONTICE David					0+1										0+1
MORAH Ollie									34	39					73
MUNDEN Maurice	1														1
NAPIER Matthew								1							1
NEWMAN Dave						12+2									12+2
O'KEEFE Sean							0+1								0+1
OMIGIE Joe											0+1				0+1
O'SULLIVAN Donal														0+1	0+1
PARRY John	14+2														14+2
PARSONS Jeremy				5	3	1									9
PERKINS Steve											4+1				4+1
PIPER Lenny												1+1			1+1
POWELL Ray												3+7			3+7
QUAMINA Mark								31+4							31+4
RANSOM Nigel	31	41	30+1	41	41	39+1	36+1	34+1	34						327+4
RATTRAY Kevin											7				7
REYNOLDS Tony	40	10+4	35	41	34+1	31+2	12	35+2	2						240+9

WELLING UNITED   APPEARANCES

	86-87	87-88	88-89	89-90	90-91	91-92	92-93	93-94	94-95	95-96	96-97	97-98	98-99	99-00	TOTAL
RICHARDSON Derek		35													35
RIVERE Anthony													13+3	29+5	42+8
ROBBINS Terry	24+3	22+4	33	37	40+1	42	42	40	42						322+8
ROBERTS Gary	12														12
ROBINSON Louis	0+2														0+2
ROBINSON Steve				18+3	32+1	30+1	41+1	32							153+6
ROGERS Alan	4														4
ROSSATI Jerry			0+1												0+1
ROWE Zeke												10	35		45
RUTHERFORD Mike							12	23	35	39	38	37	37+3		221+3
SALAKO Andy						18+2									18+2
SAWYER Paul	40	34	1+1												75+1
SHEAD Ian		1		1											2
SHOEMAKE Kevin	7														7
SIDE Charley										0+1		0+1	4+16		4+18
SIMPSON Colin										0+1					0+1
SKIVERTON Terry											29	36			65
SLATER Steve							0+8								0+8
SMELT Lee	30														30
SMITH Danny							4+7	5+12	6+12	10+15					25+46
SMITH David	1														1
SMITH Gary						22+1									22+1
STANDEN Dean													1+1		1+1
STAPLEY Glen					2										2
STARKEY Ian	41														41
STEFFE Paul							4+1								4+1
SULLIVAN Nicky					7	5									12
SYKES Paul									4+10						4+10
TIERLING Lee									23	5					28
TIVEY Mark						7+2									7+2
TREBBLE John												16			16
TROTT Robin										41					41
TURNER Lee						1									1
TWIN Danny													0+1		1+1
UGBAH John												19+2			19+2
VERCESI Richard											11+14	10+2			21+16
WALKER Ray			1												1
WASTELL James								3+1	7+1	1					11+2
WATSON Mark											15+9				15+9
WATTS Lew									27+4	33+1	39	40	32		171+5
WATTS Steve													3+1		3+1
WATTS Stuart										0+6	0+1				0+7
WHITE Stuart	37+1	38+1	32	41	33+6	40	34+3	41+1	15						311+12
WILD Rob						1									1
WILKERSON Paul													34		34
WILLIAMS Darren						25	42	12							79
WITTER Tony												8			8
WORDSWORTH Dean									22						22
ZORICICH Chris										1					1

WELLING UNITED GOALSCORERS

	86-87	87-88	88-89	89-90	90-91	91-92	92-93	93-94	94-95	95-96	96-97	97-98	98-99	99-00	TOTAL
ABBOTT Gary	23(5p)	6(2p)			11(1p)	19(1p)	17	5							81(9p)
ADAMS Darren													6(1p)		6(1p)
APPIAH Sam											2	1			3
BAILEY Danny														2	2
BARNES Steve								5	3					2	10
BARTLEY John	6(2p)														6(2p)
BATTRAM Paul			2(1p)												2(1p)
BERRY Gwynne									1						1
BOOKER Trevor		7	10	7	5										29
BRAITHWAITE Leon											1		6		7
BROWN Dereck									2			2			4
BROWN Wayne					3		1	3		1					8
BROWNE Stafford												6			6
BUDDEN John													1(1p)		1(1p)
BUGLIONE Martin				2(1p)											2(1p)
BURGESS Ray	1	2	7	3											13
CLEMMENCE Neil	1			2	2	1	1								7
COOPER Gary										1					1
COOPER Mark											18	3			21
COPLEY Paul							2	6	2	1	4				15
COTTER Micky	1	3													4
CROWE Micky		1													1
DENNIS Kevin													3		3
DENNIS Lenny						9				21(6p)					30(6p)
DICHIO Danny							6(1p)								6(1p)
DIMMOCK Richard									1						1
DOLBY Tony												7(4p)	6(3p)		13(7p)
EDWARDS Russell													1		1
FARLEY John								3	3	1	1	1			9
FINNAN Steve								1							1
FRANCIS Joe				1	1										2
GAMBLE Bradley									2						2
GLOVER John			5	7	7	1									20
GOLLEY Mark					2										2
GORMAN Paul								13(4p)	1						14(4p)
HALES Roy				4											4
HANDFORDS Phil		1	2	1	1										5
HANLON Ritchie											15	4(1p)	12(4p)		31(5p)
HANSON Dave									3						3
HAVERSON Paul		1(1p)													1(1p)
HENRY Liburd									4						4
HONE Mark				5	2(1p)	1	2	3					2		15(1p)
HORTON Duncan		1													1
HORWOOD Neil		5													5
HOWELL Greg					1										1
HYNES Mark												6	3		9
LAKIN Barry										5					5
LINDSAY Dave		3(1p)	1(1p)												4(2p)
LINGER Paul													3		3
MARTIN Jae														4	4

220 Conference goals
between them for Welling

Above: **Gary Abbott**

Below: **Terry Robbins**

and on opposite page **Stuart White**

Photos: Keith Gillard

WELLING UNITED GOALSCORERS

	86-87	87-88	88-89	89-90	90-91	91-92	92-93	93-94	94-95	95-96	96-97	97-98	98-99	99-00	TOTAL
MORAH Ollie									11(3p)	9					20(3p)
NEWMAN Dave						1									1
PARRY John	3														3
QUAMINA Mark								2							2
RANSOM Nigel	2	2	2	2	3	3	1		5						20
REYNOLDS Tony	3	1		7	2	1		5	1						20
RIVERE Anthony													3		3
ROBBINS Terry	11	6	12(1p)	17(2p)	18(2p)	29(1p)	19(3p)	17(3p)	10						**139(12p)**
ROBERTS Gary	4														4
ROBINSON Steve								3							3
ROWE Zeke													2	11(2p)	13(2p)
RUTHERFORD Mike						1				2	4	2	1	3	13
SALAKO Andy					1										1
SAWYER Paul		2													2
SKIVERTON Terry												2			2
SMITH Danny								2			1				3
STARKEY Ian	1														1
TREBBLE Neil													3		3
TROTT Robin											3				3
UGBAH John												1			1
VERCESI Richard											3	1			4
WATSON Mark											2				2
WATTS Lew											1				1
WATTS Steve													2		2
WATTS Stuart											1				1
WHITE Stuart	5	6	3(1p)	5		4	4	4	2						33(1p)
WORDSWORTH Dean									3						3

Stuart White hurdles a desperate Cheltenham lunge. Photo: Keith Gillard

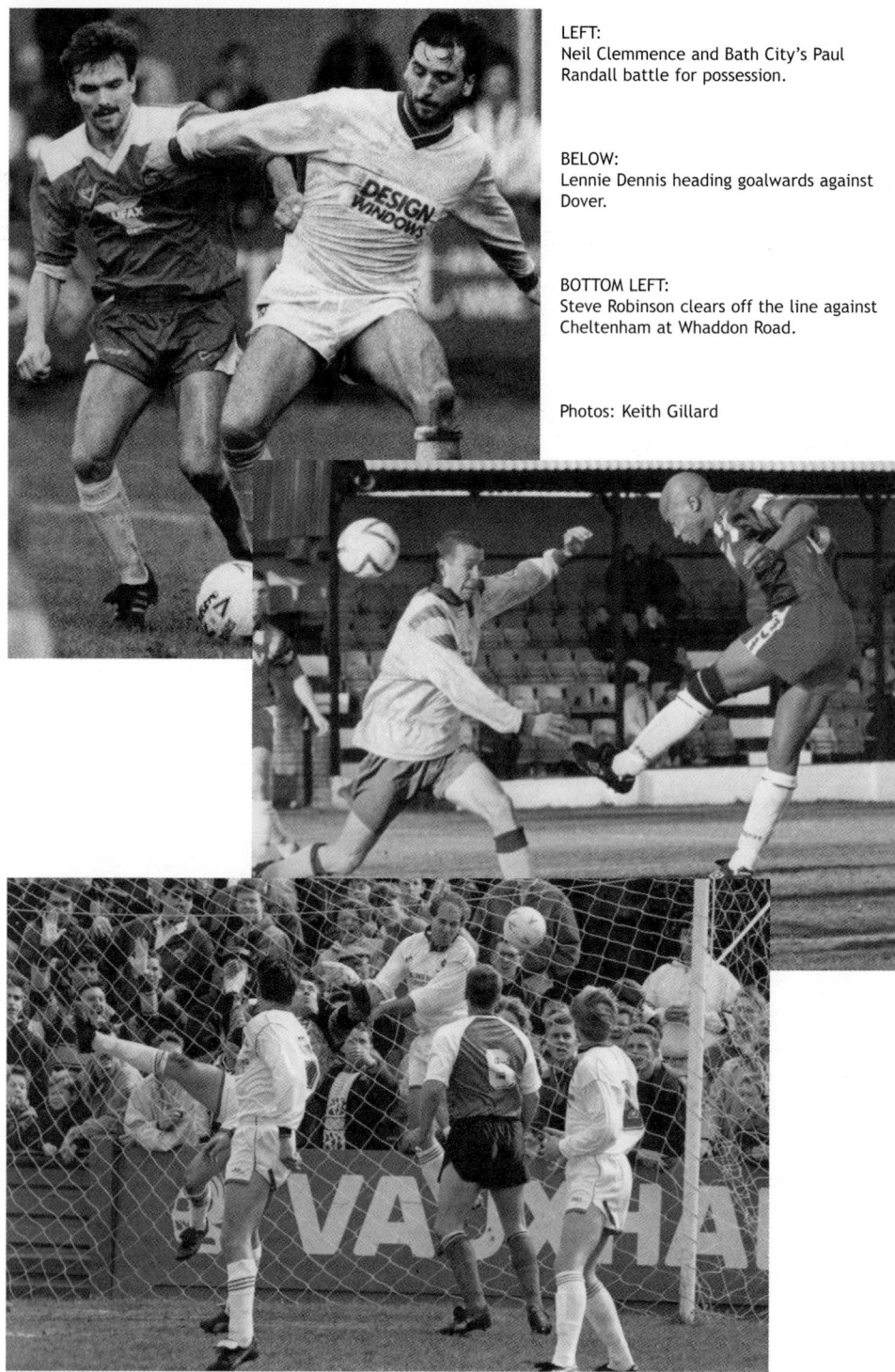

LEFT:
Neil Clemmence and Bath City's Paul Randall battle for possession.

BELOW:
Lennie Dennis heading goalwards against Dover.

BOTTOM LEFT:
Steve Robinson clears off the line against Cheltenham at Whaddon Road.

Photos: Keith Gillard

WEYMOUTH

FOUNDER MEMBERS elected from The Southern League
RELEGATED TO: The Southern League 1989
2004-2005 SEASON: Conference South

1987-88 Squad - Back Row (L-R): Bob Lucas (Physio), Willie Gibson, Richard Bourne, Anniello Iannone, Paul Compton, Peter Guthrie, Andy Rowland, Peter Turrell, Dean Roberts, Ashley Doidge, John Clarke (Trainer).
Front Row: Simon Burman, Michael Greeno, Steve Claridge, Paul Arnold, Stuart Morgan (Manager), Peter Conning, Everton Carr, Nickey Preston, Morgan Lewis. Photo: Vivien Bailey.

SEASONS
10

TOTAL POINTS
314 + 210 = 524

HIGHEST POSITION
2   (79/80)

LOWEST POSITION
21   (88/89)

HIGHEST ATTENDANCE
3500 Lincoln (26-8-87)

LOWEST ATTENDANCE
343 Worcester (17-2-82)

SEASON GOALSCORER
Tommy Patterson 25 (79/80)
Mick Doherty 25 (85/86)

CAREER GOALSCORER
Aniello Iannone 79(2p)

CAREER APPEARANCES
Aniello Iannone 309+10

| | HOME | | | | | | AWAY | | | | | | |
	P	W	D	L	F	A	Pts	P	W	D	L	F	A	Pts	Position
79-80	19	13	3	3	40	14	29	19	9	7	3	33	23	25	2
80-81	19	11	4	4	30	18	26	19	8	2	9	24	22	18	5
81-82	21	11	4	6	33	21	37	21	7	5	9	23	26	26	9
82-83	21	13	6	2	37	14	45	21	7	4	10	26	34	25	7
83-84	21	5	4	12	28	33	14	21	8	4	9	26	32	28	15
84-85	21	13	1	7	41	32	27	21	2	12	7	29	34	18	16
85-86	21	11	8	2	43	24	30	21	8	7	6	32	36	31	5
86-87	21	10	5	6	43	33	35	21	3	7	11	25	44	16	14
87-88	21	13	7	1	33	13	46	21	5	2	14	20	30	17	10
88-89	20	6	7	7	27	30	25	20	1	3	16	10	40	6	21
Total	205	106	49	50	355	232	314	205	58	53	94	248	321	210	

WEYMOUTH

	Altrincham		A P Leamington		Aylesbury United		Bangor		Barnet		Barrow		Bath City		Boston United		Cheltenham Town	
	H	A	H	A	H	A	H	A	H	A	H	A	H	A	H	A	H	A
79-80	0-0	2-3	2-1	2-0			4-2	2-1	1-1	2-0	1-0	1-0	1-2	2-4	3-0	2-2		
80-81	0-0	2-1	3-2	1-0			4-0	0-2	3-0	3-0	2-1	1-0	1-1	3-2	2-1	1-2		
81-82	1-0	0-0	1-2	2-2					0-2	3-0	3-0	0-2	2-0	1-2	2-1	2-0		
82-83	2-0	0-1					2-1	3-4	1-3	2-1	1-1	0-3	1-0	1-0	4-2	2-3		
83-84	0-1	1-2					5-0	3-1	2-2	1-1			0-1	0-1	0-2	3-4		
84-85	2-1	0-2							3-0	0-0	3-1	3-3	2-2	1-2	2-1	2-2		
85-86	0-0	1-3							4-2	2-2	3-2	4-3	0-0	2-2	0-0	0-5	0-0	1-0
86-87	2-2	1-2							3-3	2-2			1-2	1-2	3-4	1-1	4-3	0-2
87-88	1-0	0-3							2-0	2-3			3-1	1-3	3-1	0-1	1-1	1-2
88-89	1-3	1-2			0-0	1-4			1-1	1-4					2-2	0-2	3-2	1-1

	Chorley		Dagenham		Dartford		Enfield		Fisher Athletic		Frickley Athletic		Gateshead		Garvesend & N'fleet		Kettering Town	
	H	A	H	A	H	A	H	A	H	A	H	A	H	A	H	A	H	A
79-80															1-0	3-2	3-1	1-3
80-81											1-2	2-1			0-1	0-1	1-2	0-1
81-82			1-1	1-2	2-1	0-0	2-2	0-3			5-0	1-0			1-2	1-2	2-3	2-1
82-83			0-1	2-1			1-0	1-2			0-0	2-1					4-1	1-1
83-84			3-1	2-1			1-3	1-0			0-2	2-1	2-0	0-3			1-1	2-0
84-85			1-0	2-2	1-2	1-1	4-2	1-2			2-1	0-2	5-4	2-2			3-0	1-1
85-86			2-1	2-2	2-1	1-1	2-2	4-4			2-3	0-1					1-0	2-0
86-87			3-0	0-2			0-1	0-4			3-2	2-2	0-1	4-1			2-0	0-3
87-88			1-0	3-0			1-3	2-3	1-1	0-1							2-1	0-3
88-89	2-3	0-0					2-3	0-3	1-0	2-3							3-0	0-1

	Kidderminster H.		Lincoln City		Macclesfield Town		Maidstone United		Northwich Victoria		Nuneaton Borough		Redditch United		Runcorn		Scarborough	
	H	A	H	A	H	A	H	A	H	A	H	A	H	A	H	A	H	A
79-80							1-1	1-1	2-0	0-0	2-0	2-1	6-0	2-0			0-1	0-0
80-81							1-1	0-3	4-3	0-0	1-0	4-1					1-1	0-2
81-82							1-0	1-0	1-0	2-0					0-1	1-3	3-1	1-2
82-83							0-0	0-3	3-0	1-1	3-0	0-2			1-1	0-1	2-0	0-2
83-84	0-0	1-0					1-3	2-2	1-1	0-1	0-1	0-3			3-1	1-1	6-1	1-1
84-85	0-2	3-3					0-1	4-1	1-0	3-0	1-3	2-4			0-2	1-3	1-2	0-0
85-86	1-2	2-1					2-0	0-0	2-2	1-0	2-0	0-3			5-2	2-1	4-1	1-1
86-87	2-1	1-1					4-1	1-3	2-2	1-1	1-0	4-0			1-1	1-1	0-1	1-2
87-88	1-1	0-1	3-0	0-0	1-1	2-1	2-1	1-2	0-0	1-2					0-0	1-2		
88-89	3-1	0-1			1-2	0-2	1-3	0-3	2-2	0-2					1-1	0-1		

1984-85 Squad

1986-87 Squad - Back Row (L-R): R. Lucas (Physio), M. Rogers, G. Dine, A. Coombes, T. Agana, R. Bourne, A. Iannone, L. Bond, A. Doidge, M. Greeno, P. Rogers.
Front: M. Hirst, S. Claridge, P. Arnold (Captain), M. Doherty, G. Borthwick, G. Ayles, D. Steadman (Mascot).

Tony Agana.   Mick Doherty.

Paul Arnold, Anniello Iannone, Pete Rogers and Bobby Shinton with the Dorest Senior Cup (1984-85).

WEYMOUTH

	Stafford Rangers		Sutton United		Telford United		Trowbridge Town		Wealdstone		Welling United		Worcester City		Wycombe Wanderers		Yeovil Town	
	H	A	H	A	H	A	H	A	H	A	H	A	H	A	H	A	H	A
79-80	2-1	5-1			3-2	3-3			4-0	1-1			1-2	1-1			3-0	1-0
80-81	2-1	0-2			1-0	0-1			2-1	1-1			1-0	1-2			0-1	5-0
81-82	1-1	0-3			0-1	0-2	1-0	1-1					3-2	0-0			1-1	4-1
82-83	0-0	2-1			0-0	0-2	2-1	0-0	4-1	4-2			4-2	3-3			2-0	2-0
83-84					2-3	1-0	0-1	2-1	0-4	0-2			0-2	0-1			1-3	3-6
84-85					3-2	0-0			0-3	2-3			3-1	1-1			4-2	0-0
85-86	1-1	3-2			5-2	1-4			4-2	0-1					1-1	3-0		
86-87	1-3	0-0	2-2	3-2	3-0	1-5			3-2	1-3	3-2	0-5						
87-88	2-0	0-0	2-1	1-0	1-0	0-1			2-1	2-0	4-0	2-0			0-0	1-2		
88-89	1-0	0-1	2-2	1-3	0-0	0-1					1-0	0-4			0-3	0-0	0-2	3-2

	Home						Away					
	P	W	D	L	F	A	P	W	D	L	F	A
ALTRINCHAM	10	4	4	2	9	7	10	1	1	8	8	19
A P LEAMINGTON	3	2	0	1	6	5	3	2	1	0	5	2
AYLESBURY U	1	0	1	0	0	0	1	0	0	1	1	4
BANGOR C	4	4	0	0	15	3	4	2	0	2	8	8
BARNET	10	4	4	2	20	14	10	4	4	2	18	13
BARROW	6	5	1	0	13	5	6	3	1	2	9	11
BATH C	9	3	3	3	11	9	9	2	1	6	12	18
BOSTON U	10	6	2	2	21	14	10	1	3	6	13	22
CHELTENHAM T	4	2	2	0	8	6	4	1	1	2	3	5
CHORLEY	1	0	0	1	2	3	1	0	1	0	0	0
DAGENHAM	7	5	1	1	11	4	7	3	2	2	12	10
DARTFORD	3	2	0	1	5	4	3	0	3	0	2	2
ENFIELD	8	2	2	4	13	16	8	1	1	6	9	21
FISHER A	2	1	1	0	2	1	2	0	0	2	2	4
FRICKLEY A	7	3	1	3	13	10	7	4	1	2	9	8
GATESHEAD	3	2	0	1	7	5	3	1	1	1	6	6
GRAVESEND & N	3	1	0	2	2	3	3	1	0	2	4	5
KETTERING T	10	7	1	2	22	9	10	3	2	5	9	14
KIDDERMINSTER H	6	2	2	2	7	7	6	2	2	2	7	7
LINCOLN C	1	1	0	0	3	0	1	0	1	0	0	0
MACCLESFIELD T	2	0	1	1	2	3	2	1	0	1	2	3
MAIDSTONE U	10	4	3	3	13	11	10	2	3	5	10	18
NORTHWICH V	10	5	5	0	18	10	10	3	4	3	9	7
NUNEATON B	7	5	0	2	10	4	7	3	0	4	12	14
REDDITCH U	1	1	0	0	6	0	1	1	0	0	2	0
RUNCORN	8	2	4	2	11	9	8	1	2	5	7	13
SCARBOROUGH	8	4	1	3	17	8	8	0	4	4	4	10
STAFFORD R	8	4	3	1	10	7	8	3	2	3	10	10
SUTTON U	3	1	2	0	6	5	3	2	0	1	5	5
TELFORD U	10	6	2	2	18	10	10	1	2	7	6	19
TROWBRIDGE T	3	2	0	1	3	2	3	1	2	0	3	2
WEALDSTONE	8	6	0	2	19	14	8	2	2	4	11	13
WELLING U	3	3	0	0	8	2	3	1	0	2	2	9
WORCESTER C	6	4	0	2	12	9	6	0	4	2	6	8
WYCOMBE W	3	0	2	1	1	4	3	1	1	1	4	2
YEOVIL T	7	3	1	3	11	9	7	5	1	1	18	9
TOTALS	205	106	49	50	355	232	205	58	53	94	248	321

Peter Guthrie. Photo: Paul Lewis.　　　　Annie Iannone.

Mel Gwinnett pulls off a fine save to deny this Barnet attack during their 1-1 draw in the 1988-89 season. Photo: M Close.

WEYMOUTH   APPEARANCES

	79-80	80-81	81-82	82-83	83-84	84-85	85-86	86-87	87-88	88-89	TOTAL
AGANA Tony					11	37	42	36			126
ALFORD Danny				0+1	10+2						10+3
ARNOLD Paul	31+2	29	32	37	42	32+1	41	36+1	16+1		296+5
AYLES Greg							0+1				0+1
BABER Mark				39+1							39+1
BAIRD Sandy									9+2		9+2
BAKER Keiron			39	36							75
BELL Andy					7+1						7+1
BENJAFIELD Brian			31	15	2+2						48+2
BLOXHAM Ken									1		1
BOND Len						33	35	36			104
BORTHWICK Gary		7	33+2	37		39+1	39				155+3
BOURNE Richard			19	14+3	35	35	27+1	16+2	4		150+6
BRAY Wayne					13+4						13+4
BROWN Jeremy						9+1					9+1
BROWN Roger								3			3
BUNCE Paul									8+2		8+2
BURMAN Simon									23	23+3	46+3
BYRNE Gerry	29	34									63
CARR Everton									3+1		3+1
CARROLL John								22			22
CHALK Steve	37										37
CHESTERS Colin							5	3			8
CHURCHILL Reagan										2	2
CLARIDGE Steve							37	26+6	38+3		101+9
CLARKE John	1										1
CLARKE Richard									1		1
COMPTON Paul									32	35	67
CONNING Peter									39+1	19+2	58+3
COOMBES Ashley						12	21+5				33+5
COOPER Richard										10	10
COSLETT Micky	7										7
COURTNEY Derek	9+6	22+2	1								32+8
CRABB Steve					18+2						18+2
DAWKINS Derek					18						18
DAWSON Tony									30+3	18+2	48+5
DIAZ Tony								0+1			0+1
DOHERTY Mick						24	42	36			102
DOHERTY Tony								5			5
DOIDGE Ashley					1+1	6	8+7	4+4	1		20+12
DONEGAL Glen										3+1	3+1
DOVE Kevin	37	22+1	20+2								79+3

733

Tony Oliver fists clear under pressure from Sutton United.

Goalscorer Steve Pugh (centre) is congratulated by his team mates.

Shaun Teale's challenge isn't enough to stop Gary Stewart putting Altrincham 1-0 up during the 1988-89 season. Photo: John Rooney.

WEYMOUTH   APPEARANCES

	79-80	80-81	81-82	82-83	83-84	84-85	85-86	86-87	87-88	88-89	TOTAL
DULLESTON Alan					3						3
DYER Steve	35+1	28	3								66+1
ELLIOTT Billy			26	39							65
FALCUS Steve				2	3						5
FINNIGAN Trevor		33+1	34+2	30+1							97+4
GEORGE Pat						1	6	6			13
GIBSON Willie									40	30	70
GILES Paul					1						1
GOW Gerry									1		1
GREAVES Danny					2						2
GREENO Micky							0+1	10+9			10+10
GRIMSHAW Martyn									12		12
GUTHRIE Pete									20		20
GWINNETT Mel									14		14
HANNIGAN Tony						1		0+1			1+1
HARRIS Billy									1		1
HAWKINS Peter	0+2	2									2+2
HIRST Martin							17+1	6+1			23+2
HOLMES Matty									4		4
HOLTHAM Dean					4	4					8
IANNONE Aniello	32+1	25	38	38	39	36	41	34+4	26+5		309+10
IMPEY John									6		6
JOHNSON Ian									18		18
JOHNSON Pete	38	29+2	18+4	16+7							101+13
JONES Tom								32			32
JOSEPH Antone		14+2									14+2
JOY Geoff					3+2						3+2
JUDD Jeremy						7					7
LAWRENCE Bryan	38	34	40	22	3	13+3					150+3
LEITCH Andy	4										4
LEWIS John									2+4		2+4
LEWIS Morgan									30+1	17+5	47+6
LINNEY Dave										12	12
MALCOLM Paul									5		5
MATTHEWS Phil					3						3
McBRIDE Darren										4+1	4+1
McCAFFERTY Jimmy	30+2	35	32								97+2
McCARTHY Paddy										2+2	2+2
McMANUS Dave					10+1	9+7	0+3				19+11
MEACHAM Jeff										12+2	12+2
MERRICK Neil	29+2	34	23+1	13+1							99+4
MITCHELL B					1						1

WEYMOUTH   APPEARANCES

	79-80	80-81	81-82	82-83	83-84	84-85	85-86	86-87	87-88	88-89	TOTAL
MOGG Dave									1		1
MORRELL Paul			38	36							74
MORRELL Peter				32+2	38+1						70+3
MUNDEE Brian								4+1		3	7+1
MYERS Chris									6+1		6+1
NARDIELLO Gerry									7+2	4+4	11+6
OLIVER Tony										18	18
PATTERSON Tommy	32+4	18+3	29+2								79+9
PEARSON Gerry			21+6	34+1	38	16					109+7
PENNY Shaun					15	16					31
PLATT David					24+4						24+4
POUNDER Tony										30+5	30+5
PREECE Andy										11	11
PRESTON Nicky						1		2+1	3+1		6+2
PUGH Steve									29+1	34+4	63+5
ROBERTS Dean									10+13	1+5	11+18
ROBERTS Graham	29										29
ROBERTS Kevin		38	3	6	7		1			3	58
ROBERTS Phil					3						3
ROGERS Martyn						26	29	33+1			88+1
ROGERS Peter						41	37	41			119
ROWLAND Andy									31+4		31+4
RUSSELL Pat							5+2				5+2
SANDERCOCK Phil					23						23
SANDERSON Paul									4		4
SHAW Chris					4+1						4+1
SHINTON Bobby						13+3					13+3
SIMPSON Gary							14				14
SINGLETON Dave		14+1	13+2								27+3
SLOUGH Alan					6+2						6+2
SMEULDERS John					23				15	5	43
SOUTHERN Clive							3+1				3+1
STEELE Hedley					11	21+3	26+2	42			100+5
STONE Micky					2						2
TANNER Micky										11	11
TAYLOR Robby										23+5	23+5
TEALE Shaun									33+1	19	52+1
THYNNE Chris					10+4						10+4
TOWNSEND Andy					10	22					32
TURNER John					9						9
TURRELL Peter							15+3		11+4	19+3	45+10
WILLIAMS Peter						3+1					3+1

WEYMOUTH GOALSCORERS

	79-80	80-81	81-82	82-83	83-84	84-85	85-86	86-87	87-88	88-89	TOTAL
AGANA Tony					3	9	13	12			37
ALFORD Danny					1						1
ARNOLD Paul	1	1	1			1		1			5
BABER Mark				10							10
BAIRD Sandy									1		1
BELL Andy					1						1
BENJAFIELD Brian				4	1						5
BORTHWICK Gary			2	2		5	1				10
BOURNE Richard			2		1	3	4	4			14
BRAY Wayne					1						1
BROWN Jeremy						3(1p)					3(1p)
BUNCE Paul									1		1
BYRNE Gerry	1										1
CARROLL John								1			1
CHESTERS Colin							4	1			5
CLARIDGE Steve							10	6	12		28
COMPTON Paul									1(1p)	2(2p)	3(3p)
CONNING Peter									10	4(1p)	14(1p)
COOMBES Ashley						2	2				4
COOPER Richard									1		1
COURTNEY Derek		8									8
CRABB Steve					3						3
DAWKINS Derek					1						1
DAWSON Tony									1	2	3
DOHERTY Mick						13(1p)	25	16			54(1p)
DOIDGE Ashley							2	1			3
DONEGAL Glen									1		1
DOVE Kevin	8	4(1p)	1								13(1p)
ELLIOTT Billy			3								3
FINNIGAN Trevor		6	7	12							25
GIBSON Willie									1	1	2
GREENO Micky								2			2
GRIMSHAW Martyn									1		1
HIRST Martin							3	1			4
HOLMES Matty									1		1
IANNONE Anniello	18	10(1p)	19(1p)	13	6	5	7	1			79(2p)
IMPEY John									1		1

WEYMOUTH GOALSCORERS

	79-80	80-81	81-82	82-83	83-84	84-85	85-86	86-87	87-88	88-89	TOTAL
JOHNSON Peter	8	3		2							13
JONES Tom								12(6p)			12(6p)
JOSEPH Antone		3									3
LAWRENCE Bryan			1								1
LEWIS Morgan									3		3
McBRIDE Darren									1		1
McCAFFERTY Jimmy	2	5	3								10
McMANUS Dave					1						1
MEACHAM Jeff									2		2
MERRICK Neil	3	1	1								5
MORRELL Paul				2							2
MORRELL Peter				2	1						3
NARDIELLO Gerry									4	1	5
PATTERSON Tommy	25	6	11								42
PEARSON Gerry			2	11(1p)	17(4p)	8(3p)					38(8p)
PENNY Shaun					5	5					10
PLATT David					6						6
POUNDER Tony									2		2
PREECE Andy									3		3
PUGH Steve								1	3		4
ROBERTS Dean								2(1p)	1		3(1p)
ROBERTS Graham	6										6
ROGERS Martyn						1					1
ROGERS Peter						1		1			2
ROWLAND Andy									12		12
SANDERSON Paul									1		1
SHAW Chris					1						1
SHINTON Bobby						2					2
SIMPSON Gary								3			3
SINGLETON Dave		5	4								9
SOUTHERN Clive							3				3
STEELE Hedley					1	1	1	1			4
TAYLOR Robby										1	1
TEALE Shaun										1	1
TOWNSEND Andy					3	10(2p)					13(2p)
TURRELL Pete								5	2	5	12

WITTON ALBION

PROMOTED FROM: The Northern Premier League 1991
RELEGATED TO: The Northern Premier League 1994
2004-2005 SEASON: The Northern Premier League

SEASONS	
3	

TOTAL POINTS	
142	

HIGHEST POSITION	
10th (91/92)	

LOWEST POSITION	
22nd (93/94)	

HIGHEST ATTENDANCE
2442 Northwich (28-12-92)

LOWEST ATTENDANCE
454 Woking (30-4-94)

SEASON GOALSCORER
Karl Thomas 21(2p) (91/92)

CAREER GOALSCORER
Karl Thomas 40(6p)

CAREER APPEARANCES
Keith Mason 90

1991-92 Squad.
Back Row (L-R): Darren Heesom, Lee Coathup, Joe Connor, Mike Lutkevitch, Keith Mason, Jim Connor, Jim McCluskie, Carl Alford, Mark Hughes, Keith Higgins (Physio).
Front Row: Billy robb (Kit man), Gary Stewart, Steve McNeilis, Andy Grimshaw, Peter O'Brien (Manager), Stewart Anderson (Captain), Karl Thomas, Mike Halliday, W.Dodd (Chief Scout).
Trophies (L-R):
HFS Loans Premier Division Championship Trophy.
HFS Loans League Challenge Shield.
HFS Loans League Presidents Cup.

	HOME						AWAY						
	P	W	D	L	F	A	Pts	P	W	D	L	F	A	Pts	Position
91-92	21	11	6	4	41	26	39	21	5	4	12	22	34	19	10
92-93	21	5	9	7	30	34	24	21	6	8	7	32	31	26	17
93-94	21	4	8	9	18	30	20	21	3	5	13	19	33	14	22

Carl Alford and Colin Rose. Photo: Keith Clayton.

Stuart Anderson. Photo: M Brooker.

Brendan Burke. Photo: Colin Stevens.

Joe Connor. Photo: Paul Dennis.

Steve Ellis. Photo: Duncan Cook.

	Altrincham		Barrow		Bath City		Boston United		Bromsgrove Rovers		Cheltenham Town		Colchester United		Dagenham & Rebridge * as Redbridge Forest		Dover Athletic	
	H	A	H	A	H	A	H	A	H	A	H	A	H	A	H	A	H	A
91-92	2-0	3-2	0-1	1-0	2-2	2-0	1-0	2-3			4-2	1-0	2-2	2-3	*2-0	1-3		
92-93	1-1	1-2			0-0	0-0	2-0	2-2	1-1	2-3					2-2	1-1		
93-94	0-1	3-1			0-3	1-1			4-1	3-3					1-1	1-2	1-2	0-1

	Farnborough Town		Gateshead		Halifax Town		Kettering Town		Kidderminster H.		Macclesfield Town		Merthyr Tydfil		Northwich Victoria		Runcorn	
	H	A	H	A	H	A	H	A	H	A	H	A	H	A	H	A	H	A
91-92	4-1	1-1	0-3	1-2			1-0	1-1	2-1	1-0	1-1	0-1	3-2	0-1	1-1	0-3	1-3	1-0
92-93	1-1	1-1	1-3	1-1			4-2	1-2	2-2	0-0	1-1	0-1	3-2	2-0	1-3	3-1	0-3	4-4
93-94			1-0	0-3	2-2	0-0	0-1	0-1	2-0	0-0	0-2	0-2	2-2	3-4	1-1	1-0	1-1	0-1

	Slough Town		Southport		Stafford Rangers		Stalybridge Celtic		Telford United		Welling United		Woking		Wycombe Wanderers		Yeovil Town	
	H	A	H	A	H	A	H	A	H	A	H	A	H	A	H	A	H	A
91-92	2-1	1-2			6-0	2-3			1-1	1-2	2-2	1-1			1-2	0-4	3-1	1-2
92-93	1-1	3-2			2-5	1-1	2-0	2-1	2-1	3-0	0-1	2-2	1-2	2-1	2-2	1-2	1-2	0-2
93-94	1-0	1-0	0-2	1-2	1-1	0-1	0-3	1-2	0-0	2-2	0-5	1-2	0-0	1-3			1-2	0-2

	HOME						AWAY					
	P	W	D	L	F	A	P	W	D	L	F	A
ALTRINCHAM	3	1	1	1	3	2	3	1	1	1	6	5
BARROW	1	0	0	1	0	1	1	1	0	0	1	0
BATH C	3	0	2	1	2	5	3	1	2	0	3	1
BOSTON U	2	2	0	0	3	0	2	0	1	1	4	5
BROMSGROVE R	2	1	1	0	5	2	2	0	1	1	5	6
CHELTENHAM T	1	1	0	0	4	2	1	1	0	0	1	0
COLCHESTER U	1	0	1	0	2	2	1	0	0	1	2	3
DAGENHAM & R	3	1	2	0	5	3	3	0	1	2	3	6
DOVER A	1	0	0	1	1	2	1	0	0	1	0	1
FARNBOROUGH T	2	1	1	0	5	2	2	0	2	0	2	2
GATESHEAD	3	1	0	2	2	6	3	0	0	3	2	8
HALIFAX T	1	0	1	0	2	2	1	0	1	0	0	0
KETTERING T	3	2	0	1	5	3	3	0	1	2	2	4
KIDDERMINSTER H	3	2	1	0	6	3	3	1	2	0	1	0
MACCLESFIELD T	3	0	2	1	2	4	3	0	0	3	0	4
MERTHYR T	3	2	1	0	8	5	3	1	0	2	5	5
NORTHWICH V	3	0	2	1	3	5	3	2	0	1	4	4
RUNCORN	3	0	1	2	2	7	3	1	1	1	5	5
SLOUGH T	3	2	1	0	4	2	3	2	0	1	5	4
SOUTHPORT	1	0	0	1	0	2	1	0	0	1	1	2
STAFFORD R	3	1	1	1	9	6	3	0	1	2	3	5
STALYBRIDGE C	2	1	0	1	2	3	2	1	0	1	3	3
TELFORD U	3	1	2	0	3	2	3	1	1	1	6	4
WELLING U	3	0	1	2	2	8	3	0	2	1	4	5
WOKING	2	0	1	1	1	2	2	1	0	1	3	4
WYCOMBE W	2	0	1	1	3	4	2	0	0	2	1	6
YEOVIL T	3	1	0	2	5	5	3	0	0	3	1	6
TOTALS	63	20	23	20	89	90	63	14	17	32	73	98

Jason Gallagher. Photo: Keith Clayton.

Billy Garton. Photo: Keith Clayton.

Andy Grimshaw. Photo: Mark Brooker.

Mike Lutkevitch. Photo: Mark Brooker.

Keith Mason. Photo: Mark Brooker.

Karl Thomas.

WITTON ALBION	APPEARANCES				GOALS			
	91/92	92/93	93/94	TOTAL	91/92	92/93	93/94	TOTAL
ADAMS Steve		23+1		23+1				
ALFORD Carl	15+5	23+12		38+17	4	12		16
ALLISON Mike			13	13				
ANDERSON Stewart	30+1	1+2		31+3	5			5
ASTLEY Jason			0+5	0+5				
BANCROFT Dave		5+10	0+2	5+12				
BENNETT Mike			1	1				
BLACKWOOD Bevan			7+10	7+10			2	2
BONDSWELL Andy		3	1+2	4+2		1		1
BULLOCK Steve		1		1				
BURKE Brendan		32+1	39	71+1		12	11	23
BURNDRED John	3			3				
BYRNE Ged			0+1	0+1				
COATHUP Lee	26+4	39		65+4				
CONNOR Jim	26+2	37		63+2	1	3		4
CONNOR Joe	31+10	8+5		39+15	6			6
CUDDY Paul	12+1			12+1				
CUNNINGHAM Harvey		8		8			2	2
DIXON Ben			3+1	3+1				
DOWELL Wayne			6	6				
DYSON Carl	1+3			1+3				
EDEY Cec			42	42			2	2
EDWARDS Mark	2+6			2+6				
ELLIS Steve	4+1			4+1	1			1
ESDAILE David			5	5				
FULLER Steve	3			3				
GALLAGHER Jason		26+6	39+1	65+7			1	1
GARDNER Steve		5+1		5+1				
GARTON Billy			22+1	22+1				
GODFREY Warren			2	2				
GRANT Brendan		5+5		5+5				
GRAYSON Simon			9+2	9+2			1	1
GRIMSHAW Andy	34			34				
HADDON Graham			3+3	3+3				
HALL Neil			9+5	9+5			2	2
HALLIDAY Mi8ke	17			17				
HEALEY John		1+1		1+1				
HEESOM Darren	12+2			12+2				
HENRY Tony			18+1	18+1				
HILL Jonathan	9			9	1			1
HOLMES Chris			2	2				
HOLT Matthew		6+5	1+1	7+6				
HOOTON Russ	8+2			8+2				
HUGHES Mark	11+1	7		18+1	1	3		4

WITTON ALBION

	APPEARANCES				GOALS			
	91/92	92/93	93/94	TOTAL	91/92	92/93	93/94	TOTAL
HUGHES Tony	1			1				
JACKSON Michael	1			1				
JARVIS Tony	0+1			0+1				
KELLY Paul		3		3				
KILNER Andy		4+1		4+1		1		1
LAMBERT Matthew		4		4				
LILLIS Mark		33+3		33+3		2		2
LODGE Paul	4			4				
LUTKEVITCH Mike	20+11	1+2		21+13	3			3
MASON Keith	35	29	26	90				
MAYNARD Dave			15+3	15+3			2	2
McCARTY Darrell		5	6+3	11+3				
McCLUSKIE Jim	20+11	0+2		20+13	9			9
McDONALD Alan	3			3				
McGARVEY Scott			0+1	0+1				
McNAB Neil			11+1	11+1				
McNEILIS Steve	39	32	8+1	79+1	2		1	3
MORGAN Dave	7			7				
MURPHY Aiden		2+2		2+2				
NEWALL Andy	1			1				
PALADINO Joe	3	13		16				
PARKINSON Steve			2	2				
PRITCHARD Dean			19+3	19+3			2	2
REDMAN Ian		9+1		9+1				
RICHARDSON Dave			5+2	5+2				
ROSE Colin	13	23+3	27+6	63+9	1	2	2	5
SAVAGE Mark			3	3				
SENIOR Steve		39	23	62		3		3
SHAW Chris			11+1	11+1			3	3
SMART Jason		1		1				
STEWART Gary	29+5	5+2		34+7	5(2p)	2		7(2p)
THOMAS Gary			29+4	29+4				
THOMAS Karl	34+1	37+2		71+3	21(2p)	19(4p)		40(6p)
THORPE Andy			11	11				
TIMMONS John			7+2	7+2			1	1
TOAL Kieran			5+1	5+1				
TOBIN Steve			13+5	13+5			2	2
TOMLINSON David		0+3		0+3				
WALKER Glen			5+3	5+3			1	1
WILLIAMS Lee			1	1				
WILLIAMS Oshor			5+3	5+3				
WILSON Paul	5+3			5+3				
ZELEM Ian	3			3				

WOKING

PROMOTED FROM: The Isthmian League 1992
2004-2005 SEASON: The Conference

1994-95 Squad. Back row, left to right:Darren Hay, Laurence Batty, Clive Walker, Gwtnne Berrt, Scott Steele, Kevan Brown and Dereck Brown. Front row: Colin Fielder, Kevin Rattray, Scott Steele,Barry Lakin, David Puckett and Mark Tucker.

SEASONS		HOME						AWAY						
12		P	W	D	L	F	A	Pts	P	W	D	L	F	A	Pts	Position

	P	**W**	**D**	**L**	**F**	**A**	**Pts**	**P**	**W**	**D**	**L**	**F**	**A**	**Pts**	**Position**
92-93	21	9	2	10	30	33	29	21	8	6	7	28	29	30	8
93-94	21	12	5	4	35	25	41	21	6	8	7	23	33	26	3
94-95	21	11	8	2	46	23	41	21	10	4	7	30	31	34	2
95-96	21	16	5	0	47	13	53	21	9	3	9	36	41	30	2
96-97	21	10	5	6	41	29	35	21	8	5	8	30	34	29	5
97-98	21	14	3	4	47	22	45	21	8	5	8	25	24	29	3
98-99	21	9	5	7	27	20	32	21	9	4	8	24	25	31	9
99-00	21	5	6	10	17	27	21	21	8	7	6	28	26	31	14
00-01	21	5	10	6	30	30	25	21	8	5	8	22	27	29	14
01-02	21	7	5	9	28	29	26	21	6	4	11	31	41	22	19
02-03	21	8	7	6	30	35	31	21	3	7	11	22	46	16	19
03-04	21	10	9	2	40	23	39	21	5	7	9	25	29	22	9
Total	252	116	70	66	418	309	418	252	88	65	99	324	386	329	

TOTAL POINTS
747

HIGHEST POSITION
2nd 1994-95, 95-96

LOWEST POSITION
19th 2001-02, 02-03

HIGHEST ATTENDANCE
4911 Wycombe W. 26.12.92

LOWEST ATTENDANCE
692 v Northwich V. 6.5.94

SEASON GOALSCORER
Clive Walker 19(8p) (94/95)

CAREER GOALSCORER
Darran Hay 85(3p)

CAREER APPEARANCES
Scott Steele 295+51

	Accrington Stanley		Aldershot Town		Altrincham		Barnet		Barrow		Bath City		Boston United		Bromsgrove Rovers		Burton Albion		Cheltenham Town	
	H	A	H	A	H	A	H	A	H	A	H	A	H	A	H	A	H	A	H	A
92-93					0-2	0-1					0-1	0-2	3-0	2-1	0-2	0-1				
93-94					1-1	2-0					4-1	1-0			0-0	0-0				
94-95					4-0	2-1					2-2	0-2			4-0	5-5				
95-96					2-0	0-2					2-0	3-0			1-1	1-2				
96-97					7-1	1-1					2-2	1-1			1-3	3-0				
97-98					0-1	1-1													2-0	2-3
98-99									2-3	2-1									1-0	1-1
99-00																				
00-01													1-1	0-0						
01-02							1-3	0-3					0-2	0-4						
02-03							0-0	0-0									2-2	2-0		
03-04	2-2	3-3	2-2	1-2			2-2	0-0									1-0	0-2		

	Chester City		Dagenham & Redbridge		Doncaster Rovers		Dover Athletic		Exeter City		Farnborough Town		Forest Green Rovers		Gateshead		Gravesend & N'fleet		Halifax Town	
	H	A	H	A	H	A	H	A	H	A	H	A	H	A	H	A	H	A	H	A
92-93			1-1	1-5							4-1	3-0			1-4	1-1				
93-94			1-8	4-3			3-0	0-5							1-0	1-1			2-6	3-2
94-95			3-5	2-0			0-0	3-2			3-2	2-0			1-1	0-2			1-3	0-4
95-96			2-2	0-0			1-0	3-4			2-1	2-0			2-0	1-0			2-0	2-2
96-97							1-1	1-5			0-2	2-1			1-1	2-3			2-2	4-0
97-98							4-0	2-0			3-0	0-3			3-1	2-1			2-2	0-1
98-99					2-0	1-0	1-2	2-3			4-0	1-2	1-1	2-0						
99-00					1-3	0-0	2-0	2-2							2-1	0-0				
00-01	1-0	3-3	4-4	2-1	1-1	1-0	4-1	0-0							2-0	0-0				
01-02	2-1	2-0	0-2	1-3	3-1	1-1	4-0	2-2			3-2	1-0	3-4	1-2						
02-03	1-0	2-2	0-0	1-1	2-2	1-3					1-1	0-5	1-0	2-3			2-3	2-4	2-1	1-1
03-04	1-2	1-2	0-0	0-1					1-0	2-1	3-2	0-1	1-1	2-2			3-2	2-2	2-2	2-2

WOKING

	Hayes		Hednesford Town		Hereford United		Kettering Town		Kidderminster H.		Kingstonian		Leek Town		Leigh RMI		Macclesfield Town		Margate	
	H	A	H	A	H	A	H	A	H	A	H	A	H	A	H	A	H	A	H	A
92-93							3-2	1-0	1-5	3-1							4-0	1-1		
93-94							0-0	0-3	1-0	1-3							3-0	1-1		
94-95							3-1	1-0	0-0	3-1							1-0	0-2		
95-96			3-0	1-2			1-1	0-3	0-0	0-2							3-2	2-3		
96-97	1-2	2-3	2-0	0-2			2-1	0-0	2-1	0-1							2-3	0-5		
97-98	3-0	0-3	4-2	1-1	3-1	1-2	0-1	1-0	0-1	1-1			5-2	0-2						
98-99	2-0	2-2	2-1	1-2	0-1	1-0	0-0	0-3	2-1	2-3	0-1	0-0	1-0	3-0						
99-00	0-3	0-0	0-1	0-3	0-2	4-2	1-1	0-0	1-0	2-3	1-1	2-0								
00-01	1-2	2-1	1-1	2-1	0-3	1-0	1-1	0-2			0-0	3-0			1-1	0-2				
01-02	0-1	1-4			1-0	2-2									1-1	1-3			0-1	3-4
02-03					1-2	0-5	2-1	3-0							3-0	0-1			1-5	1-2
03-04					0-1	1-0									2-0	1-0			0-0	2-1

	Merthyr Tydfil		Morecambe		Northwich Victoria		Nuneaton Borough		Runcorn		Rushden & Diamonds		Scarborough		Shrewsbury Town		Slough Town		Southport	
	H	A	H	A	H	A	H	A	H	A	H	A	H	A	H	A	H	A	H	A
92-93	0-2	5-1			1-0	0-1			4-0	3-2							1-2	1-0		
93-94	2-1	3-2			2-1	0-0			1-1	1-2							2-1	0-0	1-0	1-2
94-95	4-1	1-1			1-1	2-2			2-0	0-1									3-0	0-2
95-96			3-0	5-4	0-0	0-3			2-1	3-2							3-0	3-2	4-0	2-2
96-97			1-2	2-1	3-1	2-1					4-2	1-1					2-0	0-3	0-1	1-4
97-98			0-2	2-1	1-0	2-0					0-2	1-2					2-1	3-1	1-1	0-0
98-99			0-3	1-0	2-1	3-0					1-1	0-2							2-3	0-0
99-00			0-0	0-1	1-1	1-3	1-1	1-0			1-3	3-1	0-2	2-3					0-0	1-4
00-01			3-1	0-3	1-1	0-4	0-2	1-1			1-4	0-2	1-1	2-3					1-2	1-0
01-02			1-3	1-3	3-1	3-0	0-0	0-2					1-2	0-1					2-0	0-2
02-03			0-6	0-5	2-3	3-1	2-1	1-1					2-1	1-1					1-1	1-5
03-04			4-1	1-2	3-0	4-1							2-1	2-2	3-3	0-1				

WOKING

	Stafford Rangers		Stalybridge Celtic		Stevenage Borough		Sutton United		Tamworth		Telford United		Welling United		Witton Albion		Wycombe Wanderers		Yeovil Town	
	H	A	H	A	H	A	H	A	H	A	H	A	H	A	H	A	H	A	H	A
92-93	0-3	0-0	2-1	0-3							3-2	3-3	1-0	1-1	1-2	2-1	0-3	0-0	0-0	1-4
93-94	4-0	0-3	3-0	2-2							0-0	0-2	0-2	2-2	3-1	0-0			1-2	1-0
94-95	2-2	3-2	4-1	1-2	3-0	1-0					2-1	0-0	1-1	2-1					2-2	2-1
95-96			2-1	4-2	4-1	0-4					5-1	2-1	3-2	2-1						
96-97			3-2	2-0	3-1	3-0					0-0	2-1	2-1	1-1						
97-98			3-1	3-0	5-3	0-0					1-1	3-0	3-1	1-1					2-0	0-2
98-99					1-2	0-5					3-0	0-1	0-0	1-0					0-0	1-0
99-00					0-2	1-0	1-2	1-1			1-0	2-1	2-3	2-1					2-0	3-0
00-01					1-1	3-0					3-0	1-3							2-3	0-1
01-02			1-1	2-0	1-1	4-1					1-1	3-3							0-2	3-1
02-03					1-5	1-1					3-0	0-1							1-1	0-4
03-04					1-1	1-1			4-0	0-2	3-1	0-1								

1997-98 Squad. Back Row: Robin Taylor, Dave Timothy, Junior Hunter, Clive Walker. **Middle:** Malcolm Hague (Kit), Steve Foster, Terry Howard, Steve Wood, John Gregory, Lawrence Batty, Aiden Kilner, Justin Jackson, Tom Jones, Colin Lippiatt, Barry Kimber (Physio). **Front:** Shane Wye, Steve Thompson, Darren Hay, Kevan Brown, Geoff Chapple, Scot Steele, Andy Ellis, Lloyd Wye. Mascot.

		Home						Away			
	P	W	D	L	F	A	P	W	D	L	F	A
ACCRINGTON S	1	0	1	0	2	2	1	0	1	0	3	3
ALDERSHOT T	1	0	1	0	2	2	1	0	0	1	1	2
ALTRINCHAM	6	3	1	2	14	5	6	2	2	2	6	6
BARNET	3	0	2	1	3	5	3	0	2	1	0	3
BARROW	1	0	0	1	2	3	1	1	0	0	2	1
BATH C	5	2	2	1	10	6	5	2	1	2	5	5
BOSTON U	3	1	1	1	4	3	3	1	1	1	2	5
BROMSGROVE R	5	1	2	2	6	6	5	1	2	2	9	8
BURTON A	2	1	1	0	3	2	2	1	0	1	2	2
CHELTENHAM T	2	2	0	0	3	0	2	0	1	1	3	4
CHESTER C	4	3	0	1	5	3	4	1	2	1	8	7
DAGENHAM & R	8	0	5	3	11	22	8	3	2	3	11	14
DONCASTER R	5	2	2	1	9	7	5	2	2	1	4	4
DOVER A	9	6	2	1	20	4	9	2	3	4	15	23
EXETER C	1	1	0	0	1	0	1	1	0	0	2	1
FARNBOROUGH T	9	7	1	1	23	11	9	5	0	4	11	12
FOREST GREEN R	6	3	2	1	10	7	6	1	3	2	7	7
GATESHEAD	6	3	2	1	9	7	6	2	2	2	7	8
GRAVESEND & N	2	1	0	1	5	5	2	0	1	1	4	6
HALIFAX T	7	2	3	2	13	16	7	2	3	2	12	12
HAYES	6	2	0	4	7	8	6	1	2	3	7	13
HEDNESFORD T	6	4	1	1	12	5	6	1	1	4	5	11
HEREFORD U	7	2	0	5	5	10	7	4	1	2	10	11
KETTERING T	10	4	5	1	13	9	10	4	2	4	6	11
KIDDERMINSTER H	8	4	2	2	7	8	8	2	1	5	12	15
KINGSTONIAN	3	0	2	1	1	2	3	2	1	0	5	0
LEEK T	2	2	0	0	6	2	2	1	0	1	3	2
LEIGH RMI	4	2	2	0	7	2	4	1	0	3	2	6
MACCLESFIELD T	5	4	0	1	13	5	5	0	2	3	4	12
MARGATE	3	0	1	2	1	6	3	1	0	2	6	7
MERTHYR T	3	2	0	1	6	4	3	2	1	0	9	4
MORECAMBE	9	3	1	5	12	18	9	4	0	5	12	20
NORTHWICH V	12	7	4	1	20	10	12	6	2	4	20	16
NUNEATON B	4	1	2	1	3	4	4	1	2	1	3	4
RUNCORN	4	3	1	0	9	2	4	2	0	2	7	7
RUSHDEN & D	5	1	1	3	7	12	5	1	1	3	5	8
SCARBOROUGH	5	2	1	2	6	7	5	0	2	3	7	10
SHREWSBURY T	1	0	1	0	3	3	1	0	0	1	0	1
SLOUGH T	5	4	0	1	10	4	5	3	1	1	7	6
SOUTHPORT	10	4	3	3	15	8	10	1	3	6	7	21
STAFFORD R	3	1	1	1	6	5	3	1	1	1	3	5
STALYBRIDGE C	7	6	1	0	18	7	7	4	1	2	14	9
STEVENAGE B	10	4	3	3	20	17	10	5	3	2	14	12
SUTTON U	1	0	0	1	1	2	1	0	1	0	1	1
TAMWORTH	1	1	0	0	4	0	1	0	0	1	0	2
TELFORD U	12	8	4	0	25	7	12	4	3	5	16	17
WELLING U	8	4	2	2	12	10	8	4	4	0	12	8
WITTON A	2	1	0	1	4	3	2	1	1	0	2	1
WYCOMBE W	1	0	0	1	0	3	1	0	1	0	0	0
YEOVIL T	9	2	4	3	10	10	9	5	0	4	11	13
TOTAL	252	116	70	66	418	309	252	88	65	99	324	386

WOKING — LEADING APPEARANCES

	92-93	93-94	94-95	95-96	96-97	97-98	98-99	99-00	00-01	01-02	02-03	03-04	TOTAL
STEELE Scott	22+7	31+4	37+2	36+2	28+5	30+6	25+7	31+4	36+4	16+5	3+5		295+51
BATTY Laurence	39	38	38	40	32	38	29	17					271
BROWN Kevan	38	41	37	40	39	26		12+1	9+3				242+4
HAY Darran		8	25	30+10	18+9	28+4	25+10	29+9					163+42
SMITH Scott						21+9	39	39	33	28+1	11+6		171+16
ELLIS Andy			26+1	42	26+7	31+2	29+6						154+16
WEST Steve						16+5	25+7	36+1	38+2	22+2			137+17
FIELDER Colin	29+2	23+4	41	42	9+2								144+8
WALKER Clive		36+1	39	35+1	36+1								146+3
WYE Lloyd	17	25	39	27	21+5								129+5
PERKINS Steve							20+3	30+3	35+5	24+5			109+16
HOLLINGDALE Rob							28	35	35+1	15			113+1
PAYNE Grant			6+1		3	33+4	31+4	8+4			2+11		83+24
TUCKER Mark		28	42	33									103

WOKING — APPEARANCES

	92-93	93-94	94-95	95-96	96-97	97-98	98-99	99-00	00-01	01-02	02-03	03-04	TOTAL
ABBEY Ben										16+10			16+10
ABBEY Nathaniel						4							4
ADAMS Danny			4+3										4+3
AGBOOLA Reuben		6											6
AJOGE Nixon											7+1		7+1
AKROUR Nassim							38+4						38+4
ALEXANDER Tim	24		8+2	2+3									34+5
ALIGHIERI Dante							6+2	1+5					7+7
ALLMAN Anthony										15+4			15+4
ALLMAN Jon									0+2				0+2
ALLUM Lee											0+1		0+1
AUSTIN Dean										17			17
BANGER Nicky										11+9			11+9
BARON Trevor	11			8+2									19+2
BASFORD Luke								3					3
BASSO Adriano											3		3
BATTY Laurence	39	38	38	40	32	38	29	17					271
BAVERSTOCK Stuart								1					1
BAYES Ashley										5	35		40
BENNETT Gary		3											3
BENTON James			2										2
BERNARD Narada											8		8

WOKING APPEARANCES

	92-93	93-94	94-95	95-96	96-97	97-98	98-99	99-00	00-01	01-02	02-03	03-04	TOTAL
BERRY Gwynne		39+1	4+2										43+3
BETSY Kevin				1+1	39+2	7							47+3
BEVAN Scott										7		4	11
BIGGINS Mark	26	9+6											35+6
BOARDMAN Jonathan								9	12+1	38+1	37		96+2
BOLT Danny						31+6	6+14						37+20
BRADY Jon											12		12
BRODRICK Darren	3												3
BROOKS Simon			0+1		1								1+1
BROWN Delroy		2+3											2+3
BROWN Dereck	29+6	41	13+3										83+9
BROWN Kevan	38	41	37	40	39	26		12+1	9+3				242+4
BULLEN Michael								0+1					0+1
BURCH Robert											6		6
BURNETT Wayne											3		3
BUSHAY Ansil	12												12
BUZAGLO Richard	3+1												3+1
BUZAGLO Tim	7+8												7+8
CAMPBELL Jamie											13	3+1	16+1
CANHAM Scott											10	33+4	43+4
CARROLL Robbie	11+5												11+5
CHANDLER Dean										14			14
CHARLES Julian								4+8					4+8
CLARK Dean											2+4		2+4
CLEMENT Andy	23+1	32											55+1
COATES Jonathan											14+2		14+2
COCKERILL Glenn											1		1
COCKERILL Liam												20+3	20+3
CODNER Robert				2+1									2+1
COLEMAN David	6												6
COLLINS Chris											18+1		18+1
CORNWALL Luke												5+2	5+2
COWARD Ronell						1							1
CRADDOCK Jody		7											7
CRUMPLIN John			11+1	36									47+1
DA COSTA Jamal											0+2		0+2
DA COSTA Paulinho								0+3					0+3
DANZEY Michael					24+1	34	21						79+1
DAVIES Clint											2		2
DAVIES Matt									1				1
DE CARIS Paul			1										1
DENNIS Lenny		17+1	9+8										26+9
DOWE Julian				1+2									1+2
DREWETT Gary									0+1				0+1
DRUCE Mark									4+4				4+4
D'SANE Roscoe										11+6			11+6
EDGHILL Luke									1+1				1+1
ELLIS Andy			26+1	42	26+7	31+2	29+6						154+16
EVERS Sean											5+1		5+1
FARRELLY Steve											11+1		11+1

Nassim Akrour. Photo: Peter Barnes.

Kevin Betsy. Photo: M. Sandum.

Mark Biggins. Photo: Francis Short.

Dereck Brown. Photo: Graham cotterill.

Tim Buzaglo.

John Crumplin. Photo: Eric Marsh.

WOKING APPEARANCES

	92-93	93-94	94-95	95-96	96-97	97-98	98-99	99-00	00-01	01-02	02-03	03-04	TOTAL
FERGUSON Steve												32+7	32+7
FIELDER Colin	29+2	23+4	41	42	9+2								144+8
FINCH John	1												1
FLAHAVAN Darryl							13	25+1	6				44+1
FLEMING David		0+2											0+2
FLEMING Mark	28+1												28+1
FOSTER Steve					28								28
FOWLER Matthew									0+2				0+2
FOWLER Michael										8			8
FOYEWA Amos											3+4	20+14	23+18
FRENCH Steve							3+5	1					4+5
GARNER Simon					0+5								0+5
GILES Chris												6	6
GIRDLER Stuart			1+1	3+8		1+1	24+3	10+5					39+18
GODDARD Richard						7	14	7+6					28+6
GORDON Neville				1+1									1+1
GRAHAM Gareth										3+3			3+3
GRAY Andy		7											7
GRAZIOLI Guiliano					5								5
GREENE Dave	4+1		4										8+1
GREENE Dennis		2+1											2+1
GREGORY John				2	9+1								11+1
GRIDELET Phil							17	14					31
GRIFFIN Charlie									25+3	21+9			46+12
HAMILTON Ian										18+1			18+1
HARLISHA Izedin											0+1		0+1
HARRIS Richard											7		7
HAUGHTON Warren										8+21			8+21
HAULE Davis												5+19	5+19
HAY Darran		8	25	30+10	18+9	28+4	25+10	29+9					163+42
HAYFIELD Matt								13+1	27+4				40+5
HAYLOCK Paul		0+1											0+1
HAYWARD Andy						6							6
HENRY Liburd				2+1									2+1
HERITAGE Peter		3											3
HISLOP Connor		0+2											0+2
HODDLE Carl				4									4
HOLLINGDALE Rob							28	35	35+1	15			113+1
HONEY Daniel	1												1
HORNE Brian	1												1
HOWARD Terry					28+1	15+1							43+2
HUCKERBY Scott										5+6			5+6
HUNTER Junior				10+2	13+10	1							24+12
HUTCHINSON Grant		0+1											0+1
HYDE Paul					1								1
JACKSON Justin					14+2	9							23+2
JALAL Shwan											16		16
JOHNSON Michael												9+8	9+8
JONES Tom					30+3	9+3							39+6
JOYCE Tony	7												7

(L-R): Andy Clement, Colin Fielder and Dave Puckett. Photo: Dennis Nicholson.

Michael Danzey. Photo: Keith Clayton.

Steve Foster shoots for goal. Photo: Garry Letts.

Rob Hollingdale. Photo: Alan Watson.

Warren Patmore. Photo: A. Chitty.

WOKING   APPEARANCES

	92-93	93-94	94-95	95-96	96-97	97-98	98-99	99-00	00-01	01-02	02-03	03-04	TOTAL
KADI Junior									9+11	5+5			14+16
KAMARA Ben				2+3	3+2	3+2							8+7
KAMARA-TAYLOR Caleb									0+3				0+3
KELLY Paul	1												1
KEMBER Robert											25+2		25+2
KILNER Aiden			0+2	2+3	0+3								2+8
LAKIN Barry		7+6											7+6
LOUIS Jefferson												8	8
MARTIN Jae									5				5
MATASSA Vince									26				26
McAREE Rodney					9+1	0+1							9+2
McDONALD Gary												32	32
McFLYNN Terry										5+5			5+5
McGORRY Brian										2			2
McNAB Joe												0+1	0+1
METCALFE Christian									5+2				5+2
MILLER Barry								17					17
MILTON Steve	4+3												4+3
MOORE Barry										36+1	12+1		48+2
MORAH Ollie		1											1
MURPHY Aidan	2												2
MURRAY Karl												13	13
NADE Raphael											24	34+3	58+3
NEWBERY Richard			3+5										3+5
NOBLE Stuart												5	5
NUGENT Richard	32												32
O'DONNELL Lee									1				1
OLIVER Luke												1+1	1+1
OMIGIE Joe				3+3									3+3
ORMEROD Mark									9				9
PALMER Lee					7								7
PANTER Damian								4+4	0+3				4+7
PAPE Andy	1												1
PARMENTER Steve			1										1
PARSONS Phil											0+3		0+3
PATMORE Warren										20+5	31+7		51+12
PAYNE Grant			6+1		3	33+4	31+4	8+4			2+11		83+24
PERKINS Steve							20+3	30+3	35+5	24+5			109+16
PETERS Rob	7			2+5									9+5
PIPER David										42	13+4		55+4
PITCHER Geoff										13		3	16
PITMAN Jamie									27+2	21+3			48+5
PUCKETT David	25+10	17+8											42+18
RANDALL Martin									22+7	0+3			22+10
RATTRAY Kevin		24+3	21+10										45+13
RAVENSCROFT Craig			0+2										0+2
READ Tim		4	3+2										7+2
REECE Dominic										13			13
REEKS Stuart									5+3	11+6	9+2		25+11

Nick Roddis.

Scott Steele. Photo: Paul Dennis.

Steve Thompson. Photo: Ian Morsman.

Steve West.

Shane and Lloyd Wye. Photo: Eric Marsh.

WOKING

APPEARANCES

	92-93	93-94	94-95	95-96	96-97	97-98	98-99	99-00	00-01	01-02	02-03	03-04	TOTAL
REID Nicky				11+3									11+3
RODDIS Nick									36+1	10+1			46+2
RODGER Simon											1		1
ROFFE Greg	2												2
ROWE Zeke	1												1
RUGGLES Phil									0+2				0+2
SAILSMAN Steve						1							1
SANDFORD Lee											12		12
SAUNDERS Eddie						23	32+1	5		17+3			77+4
SELLEY Ian												30	30
SENIOR Trevor	26+5												26+5
SHARP Neil											23+1		23+1
SHARPLING Chris								14	26+4	23+8	11+11		74+23
SIMPEMBA Ian											14	5	19
SIMPSON Robert							1						1
SMITH Neil											19+1	30+4	49+5
SMITH Peter							16+1						16+1
SMITH Rob							7+1						7+1
SMITH Scott					21+9	39	39	33	28+1	11+6			171+16
STATHAM Brian							6						6
STEELE Paul								6	9+1	2+1			17+2
STEELE Scott	22+7	31+4	37+2	36+2	28+5	30+6	25+7	31+4	36+4	16+5	3+5		295+51
STEWART Simon						7							7
STOTT Steve								8+1					8+1
SUTTON Wayne						17+1	6						23+1
SWIFT Kieran		2+2											2+2
TAYLOR Richard									4				4
TAYLOR Robin				27+10	31	17+1							75+11
TEAGUE Simon									1+13				1+13
THOMPSON Steve			24+1	36	26								86+1
TIERLING Lee		22+5	3+3										25+8
TIMOTHY David			1+1	14+6	13+3	7+2	3+1						38+13
TOWNSEND Ben											16	33+5	49+5
TUCKER Anthony									35	2			37
TUCKER Mark		28	42	33									103
WALKER Clive		36+1	39	35+1	36+1								146+3
WANLESS Paul				5									5
WATSON Mark									8+5				8+5
WEBBER Lloyd										3+1			3+1
WEST Steve						16+5	25+7	36+1	38+2	22+2			137+17
WHITE Tom											2		2
WILKINSON Darron								22+10	2+1				24+11
WILLIAMS Martin											5+6		5+6
WOOD Steve					7	1							8
WOODCOCK Chris									0+1				0+1
WRIGHT Ben									3				3
WYE Lloyd	17	25	39	27	21+5								129+5
WYE Shane	19	9	28		25				15				96

757

LEADING GOALSCORERS

	92-93	93-94	94-95	95-96	96-97	97-98	98-99	99-00	00-01	01-02	02-03	03-04	TOTAL
HAY Darran		4	17	14	10	18(1p)	13(2p)	9					85(3p)
WALKER Clive		16(5p)	19(8p)	18(4p)	15(5p)								68(22p)
STEELE Scott	5	2	6	12	12	4	2(1p)	6(4p)	9(5p)	3			61(10p)
WEST Steve						8(1p)	12	7	3	4			34(1p)
PAYNE Grant			4		1	15(1p)	7	3			2		32(1p)
PATMORE Warren										11(3p)	14(4p)		25(7p)
SHARPLING Chris									9	5	5	5	24
GRIFFIN Charlie									13(1p)	10(1p)			23(2p)

Darren Hay. Photo: Peter Barnes.

Grant Payne. Photo: Eric Marsh.

Clive Walker celebrates Woking's 1995 Trophy win with manager Geoff Chapple and Kevan Browne.

WOKING GOALSCORERS

	92-93	93-94	94-95	95-96	96-97	97-98	98-99	99-00	00-01	01-02	02-03	03-04	TOTAL
ABBEY Ben											7(2p)		7(2p)
ADAMS Danny			3										3
AKROUR Nassim								12					12
AUSTIN Dean											2(2p)		2(2p)
BANGER Nicky											4		4
BARON Trevor	1			1									2
BATTY Laurence					1(1p)								1(1p)
BENNETT Gary		1											1
BETSY Kevin						6	2						8
BIGGINS Mark	5	1											6
BOARDMAN Jon										1	1	1	3
BOLT Danny							4(2p)	2(1p)					6(3p)
BRADY Jon										1			1
BROWN Derek	2	3											5
BROWN Kevan		1		2									3
BUSHAY Ansil	2												2
BUZAGLO Richard	1												1
BUZAGLO Tim	2												2
CANHAM Scott											2	2	4
CARROLL Robbie	2												2
CLEMENT Andy	2	3											5
COATES Jonathan										1			1
COLEMAN David	1												1
COLLINS Chris										1			1
CORNWALL Luke												3	3
CRADDOCK Jody		2											2
CRUMPLIN John			1	2									3
DANZEY Michael						3	2	1					6
DENNIS Lennie		6(1p)	8										14(1p)
D'SANE Roscoe										3			3
ELLIS Andy			3	7	1								11
FERGUSON Steve												9	9
FIELDER Colin	1		3	3(1p)									7(1p)
FLEMING Mark	5(4p)												5(4p)
FOSTER Steve					3								3
FOYEWA Amos											3	10	13
GIRDLER Stuart			1			1							2
GODDARD Richard						2							2
GRAY Andy		2											2
GRAZIOLI Guiliano					6								6
GREENE David	1		3										4
GRIDELET Phil						1							1
GRIFFIN Charlie									13(1p)	10(1p)			23(2p)
HARRIS Richard											2		2
HAUGHTON Warren										3			3
HAULE Davis												4	4
HAY Darran		4	17	14	10	18(1p)	13(2p)	9					85(3p)
HAYFIELD Matt									2	2(1p)			4(1p)
HAYWARD Andy					4								4
HOLLINGDALE Rob							1						1
HOWARD Terry					1	1							2

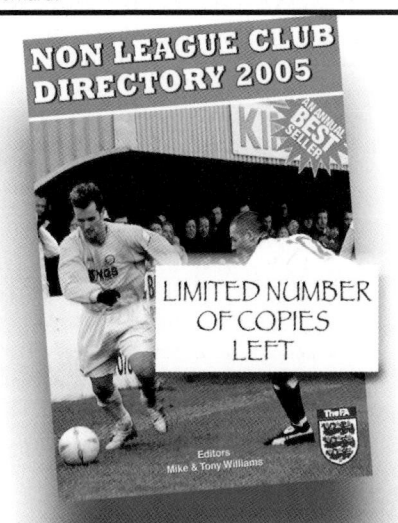

2003-2004 Back row, left to right: Nixon Ajoge, RaphaelNade, Jefferson Louis and Davis Haule.
Middle row: Ron Rawlings (Kit Manager), Joe McNab, Jamie Campbell, Chris Sharpling, Liam Cockeril, Ben Townsend, Ashley Bayes, Jon Boardman, Ryan Northmore, Dean Clark, Gary McDonald, Phil Parsons, Neil Sharp, Steve Snelling (Physio). Front row: Amos Foyewa, Ian Proctor, Ian Selley, Matt Crossley (Assistant Manager), Glenn Cockerill(Manager), Peter Johnson (Reserve and Youth Manager), Neil Smith (Captain) Scott Canham and Narada Bernard.

WORCESTER CITY

FOUNDER MEMBER elected from the Southern League
RELEGATED TO: The Southern League 1985
2004-2005 SEASON: Conference North

1981-82 Back row, left to right: Eric Brown, Brian Forsbrook (Res. Team Manager), Paul Morris, Malcolm Phelps, Graham Selby, Jimmy Cumbes, Tony Billingham, Barry Williams, Barry Lowe (Capt.), Andy Reeve, John Gillard (Physio).
Middle Row: Graham Oakey, Kevin Tudor, Graham Newton (Coach), Nobby Clark (Manager), Dave Roberts (Coach), Steve Crompton, Mick Tuohy.
Front Row: Gary Wright, Gerry O'Hara, Chris Fleming, Gary Stevens.

SEASONS
6

TOTAL POINTS
288

HIGHEST POSITION
3rd   1979-80

LOWEST POSITION
20th   1984-85

HIGHEST ATTENDANCE
2405 v Weymouth 20-8-79

LOWEST ATTENDANCE
736 v Boston U. 4-4-81

SEASON GOALSCORER
Micky Tuohy 18 (81/82)

CAREER GOALSCORER
Micky Tuohy 48

CAREER APPEARANCES
Steve Crompton 191+5

	HOME							**AWAY**							
	P	W	D	L	F	A	Pts	P	W	D	L	F	A	Pts	Position
79-80	19	12	6	1	29	15	30	19	7	5	7	24	21	19	3
80-81	19	10	4	5	33	25	24	19	4	3	12	14	29	11	12
81-82	21	12	4	5	38	23	40	21	9	4	8	32	37	31	4
82-83	21	10	7	4	43	33	37	21	2	3	16	15	54	9	17
83-84	21	9	7	5	36	22	25	21	6	6	9	28	33	24	8
84-85	21	7	4	10	29	36	18	21	5	5	11	26	48	20	20

WORCESTER CITY

	Altrincham		A P Leamington		Bangor City		Barnet		Barrow		Bath City		Boston United		Dagenham		Dartford	
	H	A	H	A	H	A	H	A	H	A	H	A	H	A	H	A	H	A
79-80	3-2	1-3	1-1	0-1	0-0	2-0	2-1	0-0	2-0	2-1	2-1	4-0	0-0	1-1				
80-81	0-0	0-1	3-3	1-2	1-1	1-1	4-0	2-0	2-4	0-1	0-2	0-3	1-4	1-3				
81-82	4-3	3-6	2-1	1-0			3-1	2-1	4-0	0-0	2-0	3-2	0-0	2-3	2-1	2-1	2-0	2-0
82-83	1-0	0-2			1-1	2-0	4-2	1-3	2-1	0-2	1-4	0-0	1-1	1-4	1-4	3-3		
83-84	0-1	4-3			0-0	4-2	2-0	0-2			2-4	0-0	2-2	1-0	2-2	1-0		
84-85	1-1	1-1					1-2	0-2	3-2	0-1	1-2	1-3	2-1	1-4	1-3	3-1	2-5	3-2
85-86																		

	Enfield		Frickley Athletic		Gateshead		Gravesend & N'fleet		Kettering Town		Kidderminster H.		Maidstone United		Northwich Victoria		Nuneaton Borough	
	H	A	H	A	H	A	H	A	H	A	H	A	H	A	H	A	H	A
79-80							1-0	2-3	1-4	0-0			3-1	1-2	2-1	0-1	1-1	0-1
80-81			3-0	1-1			3-1	1-2	2-1	0-1			2-1	0-2	2-1	0-3	1-0	3-2
81-82	1-2	2-1	3-2	2-1			2-1	1-1	1-1	1-0			4-1	2-2	0-1	0-3		
82-83	1-1	0-4	4-4	0-2					6-2	1-4			1-1	0-5	3-0	0-3	1-1	0-2
83-84	1-3	2-2	0-0	1-3	3-1	1-1			0-3	1-0	1-1	1-2	3-0	1-1	2-0	0-1	1-1	0-1
84-85	1-0	0-6	2-1	1-2	4-1	2-2			1-2	0-1	1-2	1-4	1-1	0-4	0-1	2-2	1-4	0-3
85-86																		

	Redditch United		Runcorn		Scarborough		Stafford Rangers		Telford United		Trowbridge Town		Wealdstone		Weymouth		Yeovil Town	
	H	A	H	A	H	A	H	A	H	A	H	A	H	A	H	A	H	A
79-80	3-0	1-1			0-0	1-4	1-0	0-0	2-1	1-0			2-1	4-2	1-1	2-1	2-0	2-0
80-81					2-0	0-0	1-1	0-1	0-3	2-1			4-1	2-1	2-1	0-1	0-1	0-3
81-82			0-1	2-5	2-4	0-1	1-1	2-0	2-1	2-3	3-1	1-1			0-0	2-3	0-1	0-3
82-83			1-0	1-3	1-3	1-4	3-0	0-0	1-0	0-2	4-1	3-2	1-3	0-2	3-3	2-4	2-1	0-3
83-84			3-0	1-2	3-0	4-4			0-1	0-2	5-2	1-2	1-1	1-3	1-0	2-0	4-0	2-2
84-85			2-0	2-1	4-1	2-1			0-0	1-1			0-4	3-3	1-1	1-3	0-2	2-1
85-86																		

WORCESTER CITY

	Home						Away					
	P	W	D	L	F	A	P	W	D	L	F	A
ALTRINCHAM	6	3	2	1	9	7	6	1	1	4	9	16
A P LEAMINGTON	3	1	2	0	6	5	3	1	0	2	2	3
BANGOR C	4	0	4	0	2	2	4	3	1	0	9	3
BARNET	6	5	0	1	16	6	6	2	1	3	5	8
BARROW	5	4	0	1	13	7	5	1	1	3	2	5
BATH C	6	2	0	4	8	13	6	2	2	2	8	8
BOSTON U	6	1	4	1	6	8	6	1	1	4	7	15
DAGENHAM	4	1	1	2	6	10	4	3	1	0	9	5
DARTFORD	2	1	0	1	4	5	2	2	0	0	5	2
ENFIELD	4	1	1	2	4	6	4	1	1	2	4	13
FRICKLEY A	5	3	2	0	12	7	5	1	1	3	5	9
GATESHEAD	2	2	0	0	7	2	2	0	2	0	3	3
GRAVESEND & N	3	3	0	0	6	2	3	0	1	2	4	6
KETTERING T	6	2	1	3	11	13	6	2	1	3	3	6
KIDDERMINSTER H	2	0	1	1	2	3	2	0	0	2	2	6
MAIDSTONE U	6	4	2	0	14	5	6	0	2	4	4	16
NORTHWICH V	6	4	0	2	9	4	6	0	1	5	2	13
NUNEATON B	5	1	3	1	5	7	5	1	0	4	3	9
REDDITCH U	1	1	0	0	3	0	1	0	1	0	1	1
RUNCORN	4	3	0	1	6	1	4	1	0	3	6	11
SCARBOROUGH	6	3	1	2	12	8	6	1	2	3	8	14
STAFFORD R	4	2	2	0	6	2	4	1	2	1	2	1
TELFORD U	6	3	1	2	5	6	6	2	1	3	6	9
TROWBRIDGE T	3	3	0	0	12	4	3	1	1	1	5	5
WEALDSTONE	5	2	1	2	8	10	5	2	1	2	10	11
WEYMOUTH	6	2	4	0	8	6	6	2	0	4	9	12
YEOVIL T	6	3	0	3	8	5	6	2	1	3	6	12
TOTALS	122	60	32	30	208	154	122	33	26	63	139	222

Des Lyttle transfered to Swansea City from Worcester for £12,500.
Photo: Gary Cave.

WORCESTER CITY — APPEARANCES

	79/80	80/81	81/82	82/83	83/84	84/85	TOTAL
ALLNER Graham	10+3						10+3
BAILEY John	5+1						5+1
BERESFORD Brian		4+2					4+2
BEVAN Paul	11	18	6				35
BILLINGHAM Tony	18	22+1	1				41+1
BOWATER Steve	14+1						14+1
BOWEN Eric		3+3	0+2				3+5
BRENNAN Mick					6+1		6+1
BROOKES Mick				6			6
BROWN Jimmy			37+2	17+4			54+6
CADDICK Colin					25+4	19+2	44+6
CARR Willie				15			15
CARTER Paul			13	16			29
CHAMBERS Mark		2+1					2+1
CHANEY Joe			5				5
CONNEALLY Martin			4				4
CROMPTON Steve	21	30+1	35	39	40+1	26+3	191+5
CUMBES Jim	25	32	24				81
DAINTY Jimmy	9						9
DALE Gary						9+1	9+1
DEEHAN Kevin	14+1						14+1
DEY Geoff						9	9
DRAYFORD Kenny		4					4
EDWARDS Dean				4			4
EVANS Bobby					5+2	8+2	13+4
FISH Nigel		1					1
FLANNAGAN John			3+1				3+1
FLEMING Chris		14+1	14+1				28+2
FRANCIS Trevor		4+4					4+4
GARDNER Duncan					10+7		10+7
GORDON Colin			5+2				5+2
GREEN Alan	11						11
GREEN Steve				0+3			0+3
GUNNELL Dave						8+1	8+1
HAMILTON Peter	1						1
HARTLAND Nick			0+2				0+2
HAYWARD Paul					39	42	81
HUGHES David				23	34	36+1	93+1
HUNT Paul			17+2	18+4			35+6
JAMES Adrian	1+1						1+1
JENNINGS Kirk	0+3						0+3
JONES Graham					4+1		4+1
JONES Roger	2						2
KNOX Paul						10+1	10+1
LANE John						9	9
LAWRANCE Ken	26						26
LAWRENCE Mick		1					1

WORCESTER CITY   APPEARANCES

	79/80	80/81	81/82	82/83	83/84	84/85	TOTAL
LAYTON John						16+1	16+1
LLOYD Kevin			34+1				34+1
LOMONACO Frank		0+1					0+1
LOWE Barry	30	34			24+2		88+2
MARSHALL Julian					4		4
MARTIN Lionel	2+3						2+3
McGRATH John				28	38	28	94
MOGFORD Bryan						22+9	22+9
MORRIS Paul		15					15
MOSS Craig			14+6				14+6
MOSS Paul			38	38+2	33		109+2
MOVERLEY Simon						20+2	20+2
MUMFORD Wayne						8+1	8+1
MURCOTT Steve			1				1
NARDIELLO Phil		1					1
NICHOLLS Phil				23+1			23+1
OAKEY Graham		21					21
O'HARA Gerry	28+1	7+1	4				39+2
PARKES Phil				20	3		23
PEACOCK John				3			3
PEMBERTON Norman	30						30
PHELPS Malcolm	35+2	33	39	40	22	14+1	183+3
PREECE Andy						0+1	0+1
PRESCOTT Mark						25+2	25+2
REECE Andy		8+1	12+4	5+1			25+6
RICHARDSON Kevin						5+3	5+3
SELBY Graham	26+1	21	39	27+1	36	31+1	180+3
SHINTON Bobby					35+3	26	61+3
SMITH Bobby		1+1					1+1
SMITH John						4	4
SPITTLE Paul						1	1
STANTON J				0+1			0+1
STEVENS Garry	29+1	16					45+1
STOKES Wayne					12		12
TELFORD Billy	2	25+3					27+3
THOMAS Valmore			1+1				1+1
TUDOR Kevin	34	33	37	18	24		146
TUOHY Micky		18	41	42	34		135
WADDINGTON Paul			3+2				3+2
WADE Don						10+2	10+2
WARD Chris	13						13
WEBSTER Ian						11	11
WILLIAMS Barry	13+1	27	28	20+1			88+2
WILLIAMS Jimmy			29	28+1	10+5		67+6
WILLS Alan		4					4
WRIGHT Bernie						14+2	14+2
WRIGHT Gary	8+4	19+4	30+3	18+2	19+7	18+5	112+25

WORCESTER CITY GOALSCORERS

	79/80	80/81	81/82	82/83	83/84	84/85	TOTAL
ALLNER Graham	3						3
BERESFORD Brian		1					1
BOWEN Eric		1					1
BRENNAN Mick					1		1
BROWN Jimmy			8(4p)	3			11(4p)
CADDICK Colin					3		3
CARR Willie				1			1
CROMPTON Steve	6	3	7	6	10	6	38
DALE Gary						1	1
EVANS Bobby					1	1	2
FLEMING Chris			1				1
GARDNER Duncan					3		3
GORDON Colin			1				1
GREEN Alan	4						4
HUGHES David				4	1(1p)	2(1p)	7(2p)
HUNT Paul			1				1
KNOX Paul						3	3
LANE John						1	1
LAWRANCE Ken	1						1
LAYTON John						1	1
LLOYD Kevin			3				3
LOWE Barry	3	5			2		10
MOGFORD Bryan						1	1
MORRIS Paul		8					8
MOSS Craig			1				1
MOSS Paul				11	17(3p)	17(2p)	45(5p)
MOVERLEY Simon						1	1
MUMFORD Wayne						1	1
O'HARA Gerry	10(1p)	1					11(1p)
PEMBERTON Norman	2						2
PHELPS Malcolm	11	3	7	6	4	3	34
PRESCOTT Mark						1	1
SELBY Graham			1			1	2
SHINTON Bobby					5	9	14
SPITTLE Paul						1	1
STEVENS Gary	5	1					6
STOKES Wayne					1		1
TELFORD Billy	1	2					3
TUDOR Kevin	1	4	3				8
TUOHY Micky		7	18	15	8		48
WILLIAMS Barry	2(1p)	4	2	1			9(1p)
WILLIAMS Jimmy			10	2	1		13
WRIGHT Bernie						2	2
WRIGHT Gary	2	5	8	8	7	3	33

WYCOMBE WANDERERS

PROMOTED FROM: Isthmian League 1985, 1987
RELEGATED TO: Isthmian League 1986 PROMOTED TO: The Football League 1993
2004-2005 SEASON: The Football League Division 2

SEASONS
7

TOTAL POINTS
269 + 196 = 465

HIGHEST POSITION
1   (92/93)

LOWEST POSITION
20   (85/86)

HIGHEST ATTENDANCE
7230 Slough (23-3-93)

LOWEST ATTENDANCE
540 Bath (25-3-86)

SEASON GOALSCORER
Mark West 24(3p) (90/91)

CAREER GOALSCORER
Mark West 99(10p)

CAREER APPEARANCES
Mark West 205 + 20

1990-91 Squad.
Back Row (L-R): John Reardon (Asst. Manager), Nicky Evans, Glyn Creaser, Keith Ryan, Martin Lambert, Dave Carroll, Simon Stapleton, John Granvil, Andy Kerr, Paul Franklyn, Matt Crossley (Yth. Team Manager), Martin O'Neill (Manager), dave Jones (Physio).
Front Row: Andy Robinson, Martin Blackler, Gary Smith, Steve Whitby, Chuck Moussadik, Robert Thorpe, Kevin Durham, Steve Guppy, Mark West.

	HOME						AWAY						Position
	P	W	D	L	F	A	Pts	P	W	D	L	F	A	Pts	
85-86	21	7	6	8	30	35	20	21	3	7	11	25	49	16	20
86-87														
87-88	21	8	5	8	32	43	29	21	3	8	10	18	33	17	18
88-89	20	9	7	4	34	25	34	20	11	4	5	34	27	37	4
89-90	21	11	6	4	42	24	39	21	6	4	11	22	32	22	10
90-91	21	15	3	3	46	17	48	21	6	8	7	29	29	26	5
91-92	21	18	1	2	49	13	55	21	12	3	6	35	22	39	2
92-93	21	13	5	3	46	16	44	21	11	6	4	38	21	39	1
Total	146	81	33	32	279	173	269	146	52	40	54	201	213	196	

Wycombe celebrate after beating Barnet 1-0 at Adams Park for the J.C. Thompson Championship Shield.
Back Row (L-R): Simon Hutchinson, Paul Hyde, Jason Cousins, Keith Ryan, Gary Smith, Steve Guppy.
Front Row: Mickey Nuttell, Andy Kerr, Glyn Creaser, Ty Gooden, Mark West, Dave Carroll. Photo: Steve Peart.

Mark Boyland scores Wycombe's goal during their 1-1 draw at Macclesfield Town. Photo: Paul Lewis.

WYCOMBE WANDERERS

	Altrincham		Aylesbury United		Barnet		Barrow		Bath City		Boston United		Bromsgrove Rovers		Cheltenham Town		Chorley		Colchester United	
	H	A	H	A	H	A	H	A	H	A	H	A	H	A	H	A	H	A	H	A
85-86	0-1	3-4			2-0	1-0	1-1	1-1	1-4	1-3	4-1	1-1			3-3	2-4				
86-87																				
87-88	1-0	2-4			0-7	1-1			2-2	1-2	1-2	0-4			5-3	2-2				
88-89	2-1	2-2	1-0	2-0	2-3	0-1					2-1	1-0			1-0	1-0	1-1	2-3		
89-90	1-1	2-1			1-0	0-2	4-0	3-0			1-0	0-2			0-4	1-1	4-0	0-1		
90-91	3-0	0-1			1-3	2-3	2-1	2-2	0-0	2-1	3-0	1-0			0-2	0-1			1-0	2-2
91-92	4-2	4-0					3-2	1-0	1-0	1-1	2-1	2-2			2-2	1-2			1-2	0-3
92-93	0-2	2-0							2-0	0-2	3-3	3-0	4-0	0-1						

	Dagenham		Dagenham & Redbridge		Darlington		Dartford		Enfield		Farnborough Town		Fisher Athletic		Frickley Athletic		Gateshead		Kettering Town	
	H	A	H	A	H	A	H	A	H	A	H	A	H	A	H	A	H	A	H	A
85-86	1-1	1-1					3-2	0-1	1-0	3-2					1-3	2-2			0-0	1-4
86-87																				
87-88	2-1	1-2							1-5	2-3			1-1	0-0					0-3	0-3
88-89									3-2	4-3			3-0	3-3					0-1	1-2
89-90					0-1	1-0			1-0	5-3	1-0	1-1	6-1	1-3					2-2	0-1
90-91													2-0	3-2			4-0	1-2	5-1	1-0
91-92			1-0	5-0							2-1	3-1					2-1	3-2	1-0	1-1
92-93			1-0	2-1							1-1	2-0					2-1	1-0	1-2	4-0

	Kidderminster Harriers		Lincoln City		Macclesfield Town		Maidstone United		Merthyr Tydfil		Northwich Victoria		Nuneaton Borough		Runcorn		Scarborough		Slough Town	
	H	A	H	A	H	A	H	A	H	A	H	A	H	A	H	A	H	A	H	A
85-86	2-5	2-8					2-2	1-1			1-1	0-4	2-0	0-3	0-1	1-2	2-1	2-1		
86-87																				
87-88	0-1	2-0	1-2	0-2	5-0	1-1	1-5	1-0			1-1	1-2			2-2	2-1				
88-89	1-0	0-2			1-1	1-0	2-3	3-1			1-4	3-2			3-3	3-2				
89-90	3-3	2-0			1-1	0-1			1-2	1-1	3-3	0-3			5-0	0-2				
90-91	2-3	2-1			0-0	0-0			2-1	4-2	3-0	1-1			1-1	1-1			2-1	3-3
91-92	2-0	0-1			0-1	1-3			4-0	2-1	2-0	1-0			1-0	2-1			3-0	1-0
92-93	1-1	4-1			0-1	1-1			4-0	4-1	1-0	0-0			5-1	1-2			1-0	1-1

Keith Barrett. Photo: Paul Lewis.

Glyn Creaser. Photo: Mick Cheney.

Matt Crossley. Photo: V.J. Robertson.

Nicky Evans.

WYCOMBE WANDERERS

	Stafford Rangers		Stalybridge Celtic		Sutton United		Telford United		Wealdstone		Welling United		Weymouth		Witton Albion		Woking		Yeovil Town	
	H	A	H	A	H	A	H	A	H	A	H	A	H	A	H	A	H	A	H	A
85-86	2-4	1-1					1-2	1-3	1-0	0-2			0-3	1-1						
86-87																				
87-88	0-4	0-3			1-1	2-2	2-1	0-0	1-0	0-0	3-1	0-1	2-1	0-0						
88-89	6-1	1-1			2-2	0-3	1-0	2-1			1-1	1-0	0-0	3-0					1-1	1-1
89-90	2-1	0-1			3-2	2-1	1-1	1-4			1-0	0-0							1-2	2-4
90-91	2-0	1-2			4-1	0-1	3-2	0-1			4-1	1-1							2-0	2-2
91-92	3-0	2-0					6-1	0-1			4-0	3-1			4-0	2-1			1-0	0-1
92-93	2-2	1-0	4-0	2-2			4-0	3-2			3-0	2-2			2-1	2-2	0-0	3-0	5-1	0-3

	Home						Away					
	P	W	D	L	F	A	P	W	D	L	F	A
ALTRINCHAM	7	4	1	2	11	7	7	3	1	3	15	12
AYLESBURY U	1	1	0	0	1	0	1	1	0	0	2	0
BARNET	5	2	0	3	6	13	5	1	1	3	4	7
BARROW	4	3	1	0	10	4	4	2	2	0	7	3
BATH C	5	2	2	1	6	6	5	1	1	3	5	9
BOSTON U	7	5	1	1	16	8	7	3	2	2	8	9
BROMSGROVE R	1	1	0	0	4	0	1	0	0	1	0	1
CHELTENHAM T	6	2	2	2	11	14	6	1	2	3	7	10
CHORLEY	2	1	1	0	5	1	2	0	0	2	2	4
COLCHESTER U	2	1	0	1	2	2	2	0	1	1	2	5
DAGENHAM	2	1	1	0	3	2	2	0	1	1	2	3
DAGENHAM & R	2	2	0	0	2	0	2	2	0	0	7	1
DARLINGTON	1	0	0	1	0	1	1	1	0	0	1	0
DARTFORD	1	1	0	0	3	2	1	0	0	1	0	1
ENFIELD	4	3	0	1	6	7	4	3	0	1	14	11
FARNBOROUGH T	3	2	1	0	4	2	3	2	1	0	6	2
FISHER A	4	3	1	0	12	2	4	1	2	1	7	8
FRICKLEY A	1	0	0	1	1	3	1	0	1	0	2	2
GATESHEAD	3	3	0	0	8	2	3	2	0	1	5	4
KETTERING T	7	2	2	3	9	9	7	2	1	4	8	11
KIDDERMINSTER H	7	2	2	3	11	13	7	4	0	3	12	13
LINCOLN C	1	0	0	1	1	2	1	0	0	1	0	2
MACCLESFIELD T	6	1	3	2	7	4	6	1	3	2	4	6
MAIDSTONE U	3	0	1	2	5	10	3	2	1	0	5	2
MERTHYR T	4	3	0	1	11	3	4	3	1	0	11	5
NORTHWICH V	7	3	3	1	12	9	7	2	2	3	6	12
NUNEATON B	1	1	0	0	2	0	1	0	0	1	0	3
RUNCORN	7	3	3	1	17	8	7	3	1	3	10	11
SCARBOROUGH	1	1	0	0	2	1	1	1	0	0	2	1
SLOUGH T	3	3	0	0	6	1	3	1	2	0	5	4
STAFFORD R	7	4	1	2	17	12	7	2	2	3	6	8
STALYBRIDGE C	1	1	0	0	4	0	1	0	1	0	2	2
SUTTON U	4	2	2	0	10	6	4	1	1	2	4	7
TELFORD U	7	5	1	1	18	7	7	2	1	4	7	12
WEALDSTONE	2	2	0	0	2	0	2	0	1	1	0	2
WELLING U	6	5	1	0	16	3	6	2	3	1	7	5
WEYMOUTH	3	1	1	1	2	4	3	1	2	0	4	1
WITTON A	2	2	0	0	6	1	2	1	1	0	4	3
WOKING	1	0	1	0	0	0	1	1	0	0	3	0
YEOVIL T	5	3	1	1	10	4	5	0	2	3	5	11
TOTALS	146	81	33	32	279	173	146	52	40	54	201	213

Steve Guppy. Photo: Dave West.

Hakan Hayrettin. Photo: Eric Marsh.

Paul Hyde. Photo: Dave West.

Andy Kerr.

WYCOMBE WANDERERS   LEADING APPEARANCES

	85/86	86/87	87/88	88/89	89/90	90/91	91/92	92/93	TOTAL
Mark WEST	34+2		38+2	37+3	35+2	36	20+3	5+8	205+20
Dave CARROLL				26+1	41+1	28+2	37	34+1	166+5
Andy KERR				18	42	34	34	37	165
Glyn CREASER				31	29	40	42	20	162
Simon STAPLETON					41+1	34+2	39	33	147+3
Matt CROSSLEY			8	15+2	33+2	32	22+1	35	145+5
Steve GUPPY					22+8	26+4	38+1	38	124+13
John GRANVILLE			11	34	42	33			120
Kevin DURHAM			34+2	38+1	34+4	0+2			106+9
Andy ROBINSON				39	31+1	19+11			89+12

WYCOMBE WANDERERS   APPEARANCES

	85/86	86/87	87/88	88/89	89/90	90/91	91/92	92/93	TOTAL
ABBLEY Steve				37+2	23				60+2
ASHFORD Noel			3						3
AYLOTT Trevor								3	3
BARNES Michael			1						1
BARRETT Keith			38	26+1					64+1
BARROWCLIFF Paul							1+1		1+1
BARRY Tim			3						3
BLACKLER Martin				23+4	4+3	12+2			39+9
BLOCHEL Jozef	22+1								22+1
BOYLAND Mark			19	1					20
BOYLE Gary	1+3								1+3
BRADLEY Dave	1								1
BRESSINGTON Graham	8+4		12						20+4
BUCKLE Paul							1+1		1+1
BURGESS Dave	37		5+1						42+1
BUTLER Mark				1+4	0+1				1+5
CARMICHAEL Matthew			8+2						8+2
CARROLL Dave				26+1	41+1	28+2	37	34+1	166+5
CASEY Kim							9+5	20+5	29+10
CASH Stuart						11+1			11+1
COLLINS Kevin	37+2								37+2
COLLINS Paul			3						3
CONNOLLY Kevin	6								6
COOK Mike						1+1			1+1
COOPER Geoff							4+3	5	9+3
CORBIN Kirk			31+2						31+2
COUSINS Jason							40	39	79
COVINGTON Gavin							3	1	4
COX Steve			3						3
CREASER Glyn				31	29	40	42	20	162
CROMPTON Steve				6					6
CROSSLEY Matt			8	15+2	33+2	32	22+1	35	145+5
DAY Kevin			29+1	10					39+1

Andy Robinson.

Keith Ryan.

Simon Stapleton. Photo: Colin Stevens.

Steve Thompson. Photo: Paul Dennis.

774

WYCOMBE WANDERERS   APPEARANCES

	85/86	86/87	87/88	88/89	89/90	90/91	91/92	92/93	TOTAL
DEAKIN John							8+5		8+5
DELL Bob	32+1								32+1
DEWHURST Robert								2	2
DODDS Rowan			8+3						8+3
DUBLIN Dion				1					1
DURHAM Kevin			34+2	38+1	34+4	0+2			106+9
EVANS Nicky				6	10	13			29
FAIRCHILD Roy	7+8								7+8
FERGUSON Ian			3						3
FRANKLIN Paul					17+3				17+3
GIPP David					2+3				2+3
GOODEN Ty							1+6	3+1	4+7
GRAHAM Andy			23+2						23+2
GRANVILLE John			11	34	42	33			120
GRAY Nigel			17+4						17+4
GREENAWAY Brian			8+5	1+4					9+9
GREENE Dennis							11+5	9+15	20+20
GUMBS David					1				1
GUPPY Steve					22+8	26+4	38+1	38	124+13
HANLAN Matthew						2			2
HARMAN Andy	8+6								8+6
HAYRETTIN Hakan								5	5
HUBBICK Billy	1+1								1+1
HUTCINSON Simon						22+9	12+12	21+5	55+26
HYDE Paul							42	40	82
JOHNSON Peter							8		8
KERR Andy				18	42	34	34	37	165
KERR John				28	5				33
LAMBERT Martin					19+1	0+4			19+5
LANGFORD Tim								11+1	11+1
LESTER Gary	42		31						73
LINK Declan	19								19
LINK George			5						5
LITTLE Barry			5						5
LONGSTAFF Andy	0+2								0+2
LOVELL Phil			6						6
MANN Adrian			8						8
MAYES Alan			4+6						4+6
McMAHON Des	18+2								18+2
MOUSSADIK Chuck						9		2	11
MYERS Alan			9+2						9+2
NORMAN Alecx								0+1	0+1
NORMAN Sean			26	35+3					61+3
NUTTELL Micky						8+5	9+1		17+6
OSBORNE Lawrence			3	11+4					14+4
PEARCE Graham	26								26
PEARSON Ricky					10+1				10+1
PIPER Chris					0+1				0+1
PRICE Jonathan						3			3
PRICE Neil	5		9						14
PRICE Sean	6								6

WYCOMBE WANDERERS   APPEARANCES

	85/86	86/87	87/88	88/89	89/90	90/91	91/92	92/93	TOTAL
RAY John			1						1
READ Simon	38								38
REGAN John				2+1					2+1
RICHARDSON John	2+1								2+1
RILEY Anthony	25+3								25+3
ROBINSON Andy				39	31+1	19+11			89+12
RODERICK Martin			1+1	0+1					1+2
RUSSELL Andy				1+2					1+2
RYAN Keith						24+6	10+3	14+9	48+18
SANDERSON Paul					5				5
SCOPE Dave						1+2			1+2
SCOTT Keith						11+1	32+1	36	79+2
SEACOLE Jason			7+6						7+6
SMITH Gary					9+5	19+5	24+3		52+13
SNOW Martin	2								2
SORRELL Tony								0+1	0+1
STANLEY Neil	37+2								37+2
STAPLETON Simon					41+1	34+2	39	33	147+3
TAYLOR Nigel			13	7					20
THOMPSON Les								7	7
THOMPSON Steve							11	30+2	41+2
THORPE Robert					0+10				0+10
TOLL Steve	7								7
VIRCAVS Anton	41							10	51
WALFORD Steve						20	6		26
WEST Mark	34+2		38+2	37+3	35+2	36	20+3	5+8	205+20
WESTLEY Graham			15+5						15+5
WHITBY Steve						24+2			24+2
WICKS Steve					7				7
WOODALL Martin			9						9
YOUNG Scott			5+4	6+5					11+9

WYCOMBE WANDERERS   GOALSCORERS

	85/86	86/87	87/88	88/89	89/90	90/91	91/92	92/93	TOTAL
ABBLEY Steve				1					1
BARRETT Keith			2						2
BLACKLER Martin				2		1			3
BLOCHEL Jozef	4								4
BOYLAND Mark			8						8
BURGESS Dave	1								1
CARMICHAEL Matthew			2						2
CARROLL Dave				6	10	8	4	7	35
CASEY Kim							5	10	15
COLLINS Kevin	2								2
CONNOLLY Kevin	1								1
COUSINS Jason							1		1
CREASER Glyn				1	2	4	4	1	12
CROSSLEY Matt					1		1		2

Dave Carroll. Photo: V.J. Robertson.

Kevin Durham.

Keith Scott. Photo: Eric Marsh.

Mark West. Photo: Dave West.

WYCOMBE WANDERERS — LEADING GOALSCORERS

	85/86	86/87	87/88	88/89	89/90	90/91	91/92	92/93	TOTAL
Mark WEST	13		14	20	15(3p)	24(3p)	9(3p)	4(1p)	99(10p)
Keith SCOTT						6	18(4p)	20(2p)	44(6p)
Dave CARROLL				6	10	8	4	7	35
Kevin DURHAM			3	12	7				22
Simon STAPLETON					5	2	5	7	19

WYCOMBE WANDERERS — GOALSCORERS

	85/86	86/87	87/88	88/89	89/90	90/91	91/92	92/93	TOTAL
DAY Kevin			1	1					2
DELL Bob	4(2p)								4(2p)
DEWHURST Robert								1	1
DODDS Rowan			3						3
DURHAM Kevin			3	12	7				22
EVANS Nicky				3	4	7			14
FRANKLIN Paul					1(1p)				1(1p)
GIPP David					3				3
GRAHAM Andy			2						2
GRAY Nigel			1						1
GREENAWAY Brian			2						2
GREENE Dennis							10	1	11
GUPPY Steve					3	1	7	6	17
HUTCHINSON Simon						2	4	5	11
KERR Andy				2	1	4	4	6	17
KERR John				12	1				13
LAMBERT Martin					5				5
LANGFORD Tim								5	5
LINK Declan	11(3p)								11(3p)
LOVELL Phil			1						1
MANN Adrian			3						3
NORMAN Sean			3	2					5
NUTTELL Micky						4	6		10
OSBORNE Lawrence				1					1
PEARCE Dave	1								1
PRICE Neil			1						1
READ Simon	12								12
ROBINSON Andy				1	3	2			6
RUSSELL Andy				1					1
RYAN Keith						6	1	2	9
SCOPE Dave						1			1
SCOTT Keith						6	18(4p)	20(2p)	44(6p)
SMITH Gary					1	1	2		4
STANLEY Neil	4								4
STAPLETON Simon					5	2	5	7	19
THOMPSON Steve							1	6	7
THORPE Robert					2				2
WEST Mark	13		14	20	15(3p)	24(3p)	9(3p)	4(1p)	99(10p)
WESTLEY Graham			4						4

YEOVIL TOWN

FOUNDER MEMBERS elected from The Southern League
RELEGATED TO: The Isthmian League 1985, 1995
PROMOTED FROM: The Isthmian League 1988, 1997
PROMOTED TO: The Football League 2003
2004-2005 SEASON: The Football League 2

2002-03 Squad - Back Row (L-R): Tom White, Abdoulai Demba, Steve Collis, Chris Weale, Jon Sheffield, Roy O'Brien, Chris Giles.
Middle Row: Stuart Housley (Youth Team Coach), Tony Farmer (Physio), Colin Pluck, Carl Alford, Anthony Tonkin, Gavin Williams, Adam Lockwood, Adam Stansfield, Stephen Reed, Ian Linney, Maurice O'Donnell (Reserve Team Manager), Tony Trott (Kit Manager), Steve Thompson (Assisant Manager). Front Row: Kim grant, Andy Lindegaard, Michael McINdoe, Nick Crittenden, Gary Johnson (Manager), Terry Skiverton, Darren Way, Lee Johnson, Olivier Brassart.

		HOME							AWAY							
SEASONS		**P**	**W**	**D**	**L**	**F**	**A**	**Pts**	**P**	**W**	**D**	**L**	**F**	**A**	**Pts**	**Position**
19	79-80	19	8	6	5	26	17	22	19	5	4	10	20	32	14	12
	80-81	19	9	2	8	37	30	20	19	5	4	10	23	34	14	14
TOTAL POINTS	81-82	21	10	4	7	33	27	34	21	4	7	10	23	41	19	13
599 434 1033	82-83	21	10	4	7	37	36	34	21	1	3	17	26	63	6	20
	83-84	21	9	5	7	34	28	23	21	3	3	15	21	49	12	20
HIGHEST POSITION	84-85	21	4	7	10	26	36	15	21	2	4	15	18	51	10	22
1 (02/03)	85-88															
	88-89	20	8	5	7	34	30	29	20	7	6	7	34	37	27	9
LOWEST POSITION	89-90	21	9	8	4	32	25	35	21	8	4	9	30	29	28	7
22 (84/85) (94/95)	90-91	21	9	5	7	38	29	32	21	4	6	11	20	29	18	14
	91-92	21	8	6	7	22	21	30	21	3	8	10	18	28	17	15
HIGHEST ATTENDANCE	92-93	21	13	5	3	42	21	44	21	5	7	9	17	28	22	4
8868 Rushden & D (21-4-01)	93-94	21	7	4	10	23	26	25	21	7	5	9	26	36	26	19
	94-95	21	5	8	8	29	31	23	21	3	6	12	21	40	15	22
LOWEST ATTENDANCE	95-97															
716 Barnet (28-3-84)	97-98	21	14	3	4	45	24	45	21	3	5	13	28	39	14	11
	98-99	21	8	4	9	35	32	28	21	12	7	2	33	22	43	5
SEASON GOALSCORER	99-00	21	11	4	6	37	28	37	21	7	6	8	23	35	27	7
Andy Bell 22(6p) (82/83)	00-01	21	14	3	4	41	17	45	21	10	5	6	32	33	35	2
	01-02	21	6	7	8	27	30	25	21	13	6	2	39	23	45	3
CAREER GOALSCORER	02-03	21	16	5	0	54	13	53	21	12	6	3	46	24	42	1
Micky Spencer 74	**Total**	394	178	95	121	652	501	599	394	114	102	178	498	673	434	
CAREER APPEARANCES																
Micky Spencer 199+15																

	Home						Away					
	P	W	D	L	F	A	P	W	D	L	F	A
ALTRINCHAM	14	6	3	5	21	19	14	2	4	8	18	31
A P LEAMINGTON	3	3	0	0	7	2	3	2	0	1	9	3
AYLESBURY U	1	1	0	0	1	0	1	0	0	1	2	3
BANGOR C	4	2	1	1	6	5	4	1	1	2	4	6
BARNET	11	6	1	4	25	19	11	2	3	6	18	24
BARROW	9	3	3	3	10	11	9	0	2	7	6	17
BATH C	11	6	1	4	16	14	11	0	2	9	5	22
BOSTON U	13	5	4	4	17	19	13	2	2	9	12	33
BROMSGROVE R	3	1	1	1	6	5	3	1	0	2	2	7
BURTON A	1	1	0	0	6	1	1	0	1	0	1	1
CHELTENHAM T	6	2	3	1	12	8	6	0	2	4	5	10
CHESTER CITY	3	1	1	1	3	3	3	0	2	1	4	5
CHORLEY	2	2	0	0	4	2	2	1	0	1	5	5
COLCHESTER U	2	1	0	1	2	1	2	1	0	1	1	4
DAGENHAM	4	2	0	2	5	7	4	0	0	4	0	9
DAGENHAM & R	7	1	3	3	10	15	7	1	4	2	7	6
DARLINGTON	1	0	0	1	0	2	1	0	0	1	0	1
DARTFORD	2	0	2	0	3	3	2	0	1	1	1	6
DONCASTER R	5	1	3	1	7	7	5	4	0	1	11	3
DOVER A	7	3	2	2	14	9	7	3	2	2	8	8
ENFIELD	6	2	1	3	9	10	6	0	2	4	3	14
FARNBOROUGH T	8	3	2	3	15	10	8	4	3	1	17	9
FISHER A	3	0	1	2	3	5	3	1	0	2	5	7
FOREST GREEN R	5	3	1	1	6	6	5	2	1	2	5	7
FRICKLEY A	5	3	0	2	12	8	5	0	0	5	3	13
GATESHEAD	8	3	2	3	13	14	8	2	2	4	12	13
GRAVESEND & N	4	1	2	1	6	7	4	1	2	1	7	7
HALIFAX T	4	2	1	1	6	2	4	1	1	2	6	8
HAYES	5	3	1	1	12	9	5	3	1	1	15	11
HEDNESFORD T	4	3	0	1	9	4	4	2	0	2	5	5
HEREFORD U	6	5	0	1	14	4	6	3	3	0	7	3
KETTERING T	18	9	5	4	26	15	18	4	3	11	19	37
KIDDERMINSTER H	12	5	5	2	16	11	12	3	4	5	13	23
KINGSTONIAN	3	2	0	1	7	6	3	2	1	0	5	3
LEEK T	2	2	0	0	5	1	2	1	0	1	4	4
LEIGH RMI	3	3	0	0	11	3	3	3	0	0	8	4
MACCLESFIELD T	7	3	2	2	10	5	7	4	1	2	11	9
MAIDSTONE U	7	4	1	2	11	6	7	2	1	4	8	18
MARGATE	2	1	0	1	3	3	2	2	0	0	3	1
MERTHYR T	6	1	3	2	11	10	6	0	6	0	7	7
MORECAMBE	6	3	1	2	10	7	6	2	3	1	9	5
NORTHWICH V	19	7	5	7	32	32	19	9	4	6	24	26
NUNEATON B	9	6	1	2	21	12	9	2	2	5	8	19
REDDITCH U	1	1	0	0	2	0	1	0	1	0	2	2
RUNCORN	11	4	3	4	17	17	11	1	3	7	14	25
RUSHDEN & D	4	1	1	2	6	4	4	2	2	0	7	5
SCARBOROUGH	10	2	5	3	10	11	10	0	5	5	9	20
SLOUGH T	5	4	0	1	15	6	5	1	1	3	7	12
SOUTHPORT	8	3	3	2	13	6	8	2	3	3	7	12
STAFFORD R	11	5	3	3	13	8	11	4	3	4	18	18
STALYBRIDGE C	5	2	2	1	6	3	5	1	2	2	7	9
STEVENAGE B	7	3	3	1	10	9	7	1	4	2	7	12
SUTTON U	4	2	1	1	6	4	4	1	0	3	4	9
TELFORD U	19	10	3	6	35	26	19	7	5	7	31	25
TROWBRIDGE T	3	2	0	1	5	2	3	1	0	2	5	5
WEALDSTONE	5	1	2	2	6	8	5	1	1	3	4	9
WELLING U	10	3	3	4	14	14	10	7	0	3	20	9
WEYMOUTH	7	1	1	5	9	18	7	3	1	3	9	11
WITTON A	3	3	0	0	6	1	3	2	0	1	5	5
WOKING	9	4	0	5	13	11	9	3	4	2	10	10
WORCESTER C	6	3	1	2	12	6	6	3	0	3	5	8
WYCOMBE W	5	3	2	0	11	5	5	1	1	3	4	10
TOTALS	394	178	95	121	652	501	394	114	102	178	498	673

1992-93 Squad - Back Row (L-R): Neil Coates, Richard Cooper, Paul Nevin, David Coles, Andy Wallace, Phil Ferns, Jeff Sherwood, Mark Shail. Middle Row: Tommy Taylor, Mike McEvoy, Steve Sivell, Hung Dang, Wayne Dobbins, Paul Batty, Steve Harrower. Seated: Chris Whalley (Community), Paul Wilson (Player/YTS officer), Steve Rutter (Player/Manager), Paul Rodgers (Coach), Tony Farmer (Physio), John Flatters (Youth Team). Front Row: Paul Dowding, Mark Rolls, Nathan Bush, Matthew Francis, Malcolm McPherson.

	Altrincham		A P Leamington		Aylesbury United		Bangor City		Barnet		Barrow		Bath City		Boston United		Bromsgrove Rovers	
	H	A	H	A	H	A	H	A	H	A	H	A	H	A	H	A	H	A
79-80	3-2	1-1	1-0	4-0			1-2	0-1	5-0	3-0	0-1	0-2	1-0	1-1	0-0	0-3		
80-81	1-1	1-2	3-0	0-1			1-0	2-0	1-2	4-4	2-1	1-2	1-2	1-2	2-1	1-3		
81-82	2-1	1-7	3-1	5-2					4-1	0-0	0-0	1-3	2-0	0-2	0-1	0-0		
82-83	2-1	1-4					3-2	2-2	4-2	4-4	2-2	1-3	1-0	0-2	0-4	3-6		
83-84	1-2	1-2					1-1	0-3	2-4	0-2			0-2	1-3	4-2	2-3		
84-85	1-2	0-2							2-1	1-4	1-2	2-2	3-2	0-1	2-4	0-3		
85-86																		
86-87																		
87-88																		
88-89	2-3	2-2			1-0	2-3			2-1	0-2					1-1	1-1		
89-90	0-0	1-2							3-2	0-1	2-2	1-2			2-1	1-0		
90-91	2-3	2-2							1-4	2-3	0-3	0-1	3-2	1-2	1-1	0-4		
91-92	2-1	1-2									2-0	0-0	1-1	1-3	1-1	3-1		
92-93	1-0	2-1											2-1	0-0	2-1	0-1	2-2	0-1
93-94	0-0	0-1											1-2	0-3			2-3	2-1
94-95	1-3	3-1											1-2	0-3			2-0	0-5
95-96																		
96-97																		
97-98																		
98-99																		
99-00	3-0	2-2											1-0	0-2				
00-01															2-1	1-4		
01-02									1-2	3-2					0-1	0-4		
02-03									0-0	1-2								

	Burton Albion		Cheltenham Town		Chester City		Chorley		Colchester United		Dagenham		Dagenham & Redbridge		Darlington		Dartford	
	H	A	H	A	H	A	H	A	H	A	H	A	H	A	H	A	H	A
79-80																		
80-81																		
81-82											1-4	0-3					1-1	0-5
82-83											2-0	0-3						
83-84											0-2	0-1						
84-85											2-1	0-2					2-2	1-1
85-86																		
86-87																		
87-88																		
88-89			1-3	1-1			2-1	3-2										
89-90			1-1	1-2			2-1	2-3							0-2	0-1		
90-91			4-0	0-1					2-0	1-0								
91-92			1-1	1-1					0-1	0-4			0-1	0-0				
92-93													0-3	1-1				
93-94													2-1	1-2				
94-95													2-2	0-0				
95-96																		
96-97																		
97-98			3-1	0-2														
98-99			2-2	2-3														
99-00																		
00-01					2-1	1-2									1-3	0-2		
01-02					0-1	1-1									3-3	1-1		
02-03	6-1	1-1			1-1	2-2									2-2	4-0		

Murray Fishlock, Warren Patmore and Steve Stott. Photo: Andrew Chitty.

	Doncaster Rovers		Dover Athletic		Enfield		Farnborough Town		Fisher Athletic		Forest Green Rovers		Frickley Athletic		Gateshead		Gravesend & Northfleet	
	H	A	H	A	H	A	H	A	H	A	H	A	H	A	H	A	H	A
79-80																	1-1	0-2
80-81													5-3	1-2			1-3	2-2
81-82					1-2	0-2							1-2	1-2			2-1	1-1
82-83					1-3	1-3							2-1	0-3				
83-84					3-2	0-3							3-0	0-3	0-0	2-4		
84-85					0-0	0-4							1-2	1-3	0-4	1-1		
85-86																		
86-87																		
87-88																		
88-89					1-2	1-1			1-2	2-4								
89-90					3-1	1-1	0-0	4-2	2-2	2-1								
90-91									0-1	1-2					4-1	1-1		
91-92							2-2	0-0							1-0	0-1		
92-93							5-2	1-2							1-3	1-4		
93-94			1-3	2-0											0-2	1-2		
94-95			1-3	1-1			0-1	3-0							1-1	3-0		
95-96																		
96-97																		
97-98			4-1	0-1			0-1	2-2							6-3	3-0		
98-99	2-2	2-0	1-1	2-1			6-3	0-0			0-4	2-1						
99-00	1-3	3-0	1-1	0-3							1-0	0-3						
00-01	2-0	0-2	4-0	1-1							2-0	1-0						
01-02	1-1	2-1	2-0	2-1					0-1	3-1	2-2	1-1						
02-03	1-1	4-0					2-0	4-2			1-0	1-2					2-2	4-2

	Halifax Town		Hayes		Hednesford Town		Hereford United		Kettering Town		Kidderminster Harriers		Kingstonian		Leek Town		Leigh RMI	
	H	A	H	A	H	A	H	A	H	A	H	A	H	A	H	A	H	A
79-80									1-1	3-5								
80-81									1-2	0-4								
81-82									1-1	1-1								
82-83									2-1	2-5								
83-84									2-0	3-2	1-1	2-1						
84-85									1-1	0-3	0-0	0-3						
85-86																		
86-87																		
87-88																		
88-89									2-2	0-1	1-3	2-2						
89-90									0-2	0-1	3-1	2-3						
90-91									0-1	1-1	2-0	0-0						
91-92									0-1	0-2	1-1	1-1						
92-93									2-1	0-3	2-2	1-1						
93-94	0-0	1-1							1-0	0-1	0-1	3-2						
94-95	3-1	1-2							1-1	2-3	1-1	0-3						
95-96																		
96-97																		
97-98	0-1	1-3	4-3	4-6	1-0	0-1	2-0	1-1	2-0	1-1	1-0	1-3			3-1	0-2		
98-99			1-1	1-1	1-2	3-2	3-0	1-0	2-1	2-1	3-1	1-0	1-3	0-0	2-0	4-2		
99-00			2-4	3-2	3-0	0-1	1-0	1-0	2-0	2-1	1-0	0-4	3-2	1-0				
00-01			3-0	3-2	4-2	2-1	2-3	2-2	2-0	1-2			3-1	4-3			6-1	3-2
01-02			2-1	4-0			2-1	2-0									2-1	1-0
02-03	3-0	3-2					4-0	0-0	4-0	1-0							3-1	4-2

Table 1

	Macclesfield Town		Maidstone United		Margate		Merthyr Tydfil		Morecambe		Northwich Victoria		Nuneaton Borough		Redditch United		Runcorn	
	H	A	H	A	H	A	H	A	H	A	H	A	H	A	H	A	H	A
79-80			3-0	1-0							1-1	1-0	2-1	0-3	2-0	2-2		
80-81			2-1	2-4							1-2	2-1	5-1	0-3				
81-82			1-0	1-0							4-1	1-1						
82-83			0-0	1-2							2-4	0-5	6-2	1-3			1-3	1-2
83-84			1-3	0-4							2-0	0-0	1-0	1-2			1-1	1-4
84-85			3-0	3-3							0-1	0-2	1-2	0-5			0-1	4-4
85-86																		
86-87																		
87-88																		
88-89	2-0	3-2	1-2	0-5							2-1	2-1					2-2	1-2
89-90	0-0	2-1					4-0	2-2			1-2	4-1					1-1	1-1
90-91	2-1	1-2					3-3	1-1			1-1	0-2					1-0	3-0
91-92	0-1	2-1					1-1	2-2			2-1	0-1					1-4	2-2
92-93	1-1	1-1					0-1	1-1			1-1	1-0					4-0	0-1
93-94	4-0	2-1					2-2	1-1			0-3	1-1					4-2	0-4
94-95	1-2	0-1					1-3	0-0			4-4	2-2					1-0	1-2
95-96																		
96-97																		
97-98									2-3	0-1	2-2	1-2						
98-99									0-1	1-1	1-2	2-1						
99-00									2-0	1-1	3-2	0-3	1-3	1-1				
00-01									3-2	0-0	1-0	2-1	0-0	2-0				
01-02					1-2	1-0			1-1	5-1	2-3	3-1	2-1	2-1				
02-03					2-1	2-1			2-0	2-1	2-1	2-1	3-2	1-1				

Table 2

	Rushden & Diamonds		Scarborough		Slough Town		Southport		Stafford Rangers		Stalybridge Celtic		Stevenage Borough		Sutton United		Telford United	
	H	A	H	A	H	A	H	A	H	A	H	A	H	A	H	A	H	A
79-80			1-1	0-0					3-1	1-2							0-2	3-0
80-81			0-0	1-2					3-4	1-1							1-2	1-0
81-82			0-0	2-2					2-1	1-3							1-2	1-2
82-83			2-1	2-2					0-0	3-1							3-4	2-3
83-84			1-2	0-3													1-0	2-2
84-85			2-2	1-2													3-3	1-3
85-86																		
86-87																		
87-88																		
88-89									2-0	6-2					0-0	2-5	4-3	1-0
89-90									0-0	1-0					3-1	1-3	1-0	1-1
90-91					7-2	0-2			0-0	1-1					2-1	0-1	1-2	2-1
91-92					1-0	4-1			0-1	0-0							0-2	0-1
92-93					5-1	0-3			2-0	1-0	1-1	1-1					1-0	0-1
93-94					0-2	2-5	3-2	1-1	0-1	2-4	0-0	2-1					1-0	1-1
94-95							0-1	0-0	1-0	1-4	3-0	1-3	0-0	0-5			1-1	0-1
95-96																		
96-97																		
97-98	1-2	2-2			2-1	1-1	0-0	1-2			2-0	2-3	2-1	1-2			5-3	4-1
98-99	0-1	2-1					3-1	3-2					1-3	1-1			4-0	2-2
99-00	5-1	1-1	1-2	0-5			1-1	1-1					2-2	0-0	1-2	1-0	2-1	1-3
00-01	0-0	2-1	0-1	2-2			0-1	0-3					1-1	0-0			2-0	2-1
01-02			2-2	0-0			0-0	0-3			0-2	1-1	2-1	3-2			1-1	2-2
02-03			1-0	1-2			6-0	1-0					2-1	2-2			3-0	5-0

	Trowbridge Town		Wealdstone		Welling United		Weymouth		Witton Albion		Woking		Worcester City		Wycombe Wanderers	
	H	A	H	A	H	A	H	A	H	A	H	A	H	A	H	A
79-80			1-1	0-5			0-1	0-3					0-2	0-2		
80-81			4-0	1-1			0-5	1-0					3-0	1-0		
81-82	2-0	4-2					1-4	1-1					3-0	1-0		
82-83	0-1	1-2	1-5	0-2			0-2	0-2					3-0	1-2		
83-84	3-1	0-1	0-0	0-1			6-3	3-1					2-2	0-4		
84-85			0-2	3-0			0-0	2-4					1-2	2-0		
85-86																
86-87																
87-88																
88-89					4-0	2-0	2-3	2-0							1-1	1-1
89-90					0-4	1-0									4-2	2-1
90-91					0-1	3-0									2-2	0-2
91-92					3-0	0-1			2-1	1-3					1-0	0-1
92-93					1-0	3-0			2-0	2-1	4-1	0-0			3-0	1-5
93-94					0-1	0-2			2-0	2-1	0-1	2-1				
94-95					3-3	1-2					1-2	2-2				
95-96																
96-97																
97-98					1-1	3-1					2-0	0-2				
98-99					1-3	2-1					0-1	0-0				
99-00					1-1	5-2					0-3	0-2				
00-01											1-0	3-2				
01-02											1-3	2-0				
02-03											4-0	1-1				

LEADING APPEARANCES

SPENCER Mickey	199+15	(214)
SHERWOOD Jeff	173	(173)
WALLACE Andy	160+8	(168)
WILSON Paul	159+8	(167)
BROWN Jeremy	147+15	(162)
PENNOCK Tony	161	(161)
GOLD Malcolm	156+3	(159)
SHAIL Mark	157+1	(158)
CONNING Peter	140+11	(151)
PATMORE Warren	146+3	(149)
RUTTER Steve	138+8	(146)
PAYNE Jess	137	(137)
SKIVERTON Terry	128+6	(134)
CORDICE Neil	120+10	(130)
HARROWER Steve	123+6	(129)
JAMES Phil	112+13	(125)
COOPER Richard	110+14	(124)
BELL Andy	116+6	(122)
FERNS Phil	116+5	(121)
PIPER Dave	111+9	(120)
CRITTENDEN Nick	111+6	(117)
COUSINS Rob	112+4	(116)
SMITH Ben	94+19	(113)
RITCHIE Steve	112	(112)
WAY Darren	102+6	(108)
PLATT David	99+7	(106)
CARROLL Robbie	93+12	(105)

Yeovil Town Appearances	79-80	80-81	81-82	82-83	83-84	84-85	85-88	88-89	89-90	90-91	91-92	92-93	93-94	94-95	95-97	97-98	98-99	99-00	00-01	01-02	02-03	TOTAL
AGGREY Jimmy																					2+6	2+6
ALFORD Carl																				27+11	3+11	30+22
ALLEN Kenny					2																	2
ANDREWS Bobby			9	32																		41
APPLETON Arthur																	0+3					0+3
ARCHER Lee																20+10		4+1				24+11
ASHTON Brian		7+3																				7+4
BAIRD Bob	1																					1
BAKER Keiron					15																	15
BARBER Chris						0+1																0+1
BARLOW Martin																			0+1			0+1
BARNES Colin						26																26
BARTLETT Marc					2+2	12+2																14+4
BATTAMS Geoff	21																					21
BATTY Paul										11	29+8	33+2										73+10
BECK Malcolm			33	24+1																		57+1
BELGRAVE Barrington																		7	36+3	4+4		47+7
BELL Andy		30	37+4	37+2	12																	116+6
BENBOW Ian														13+7								13+7
BENJAFIELD Tim				14+10	2+2																	16+12
BENT James																		3+4	15+11	0+1		18+16
BETTS Simon																			14+3			14+3
BIRKBY Dean																7+8	0+1					7+9
BLACK Simon														12+1								12+1
BLACKMAN Barry									19+7													19+7
BLUNT Jason																					0+1	0+1
BOND Len								17	12	8												37
BOOK Kim		7																				7
BORTHWICK Gary		25		37+1																		62+1
BOTHAM Ian					10																	10
BOULTON Mark										1+1	2+6											3+7
BRASSART Olivier																				12+2		12+2
BRAYBROOK Kevin																1+2						1+2
BROAD Joseph																				4		4

YEOVIL TOWN

Yeovil Town Appearances	79-80	80-81	81-82	82-83	83-84	84-85	85-88	88-89	89-90	90-91	91-92	92-93	93-94	94-95	95-97	97-98	98-99	99-00	00-01	01-02	02-03	TOTAL
BROCK Kevin														14+1								14+1
BROOM Glyn	32	12	0+2																			44+2
BROWN Jeremy		30+3	36+3	32+5	32+2	17+2																147+15
BROWN Kevan																11	38	18+4				67+4
BROWNE Stafford																		0+4				0+4
BROWNE Steve																19+4						19+4
BURKE Raphael													0+1									0+1
BURWOOD Danny														0+2								0+2
BUTLER Joe						3																3
BYE Andy													23									23
CALDERHEAD Rob																2+8						2+8
CARD Chris						0+2																0+2
CARROLL Robbie									36+1	29+6	28+5											93+12
CARVILLE Eric	2																					2
CHANDLER Dean																9	15+4	16+2				40+6
CHAPPELL Lou						0+1																0+1
CHARLES Paul					27+4	14+2																41+6
CHEESELY Paul						5+13																5+13
CLANCY John	8																					8
CLEEVELY Les														1								1
COATES Marc													12	21+12								33+12
COATES Neil												28+5	24+4									52+9
COLES David											23	42	31									96
COLL Owen														2								2
COLLIS Stephen																				1	1	2
CONNING Peter								12	33+4	33+3	37+2			25+2								140+11
CONNOR Terry													6+9									6+9
COOPER Michael																				0+1		0+1
COOPER Richard										21+1	22+6	29+2	20+2	18+3								110+14
COPELAND Peter								1	0+2													1+2
CORDICE Neil								39	26+7	7+1			17	31+2								120+10
COTTLE Tony	16+1	6+2																				22+3
COTTON Terry	2+2																					2+2
COUSINS Rob																41	39+1	32+3				112+4

787

Carl Alford. Photo: Roger Turner.

Paul Batty. Photo: Victor Robinson.

Nick Crittenden. Photo: Peter Barnes.

Phil Ferns.

Yeovil Town Appearances

	79-80	80-81	81-82	82-83	83-84	84-85	85-88	88-89	89-90	90-91	91-92	92-93	93-94	94-95	95-97	97-98	98-99	99-00	00-01	01-02	02-03	TOTAL
CREASER Glyn													4									4
CRITTENDEN Nick																			42	39+1	30+5	111+6
DALE Carl																	4+15					4+15
DAVIES Ian						4+1																4+1
DAWKINS Derek									25+5	8+1												33+6
DE SOUZA Miguel										22												22
DEMBA Abdoulai																					11+6	11+6
DENT Nicky									6+13	7+4												13+17
DENYS Ryan																2+3						2+3
DILLON Kevin														13								13
DIXON Liam											0+3											0+3
DOBBINS Wayne												17	13+6	8+5								38+11
DOHERTY Mick					24	12		18														54
DONNELLAN Gary								24+3	19+1													43+4
DURBIN Brian		22+3																				22+3
EATON Jason																		11+14				11+14
ECONOMOU Jon						23+1																23+1
EL KHOLTI Abdelhalim																					15+12	15+12
ELLIOTT Billy					32+2																	32+2
ENGWELL Micky																17+2						17+2
EVANS Richard														22+9								22+9
FERNS Phil								1+1	3+2		25+1	34+1	31	22								116+5
FIELDER Colin																28+7						28+7
FINNIGAN Trevor	36				40+1																	76+1
FISHLOCK Murray																	37	9+1				46+1
FLORY Andy														4+2								4+2
FLORY Nick											1	2+1	3+1									6+2
FORD Richard										1												1
FORINTON Howard																			1+1			1+1
FORINTON Howard																					11+3	11+3
FOSTER Adrian																		20+6	0+2			20+8
FRANCIS Terry			1	11																		12
FRANKLIN Damien																	2+3					2+3
FREEMAN Andy																2						2

789

Howard Forinton. Photo: Garry Letts.

Jerry Gill.

Rob Cousins.

Lee Johnson. Photo: Roger Turner.

Yeovil Town Appearances	79-80	80-81	81-82	82-83	83-84	84-85	85-88	88-89	89-90	90-91	91-92	92-93	93-94	94-95	95-97	97-98	98-99	99-00	00-01	01-02	02-03	TOTAL
FRY David									30	34	13											77
GALL Kevin																					11+2	11+2
GARDNER Martin										0+1												0+1
GIBSON Stuart					12	20																32
GILES Chris																		0+1	0+1	8+27	0+7	8+36
GILES Jimmy		15	39	17+1																		71+1
GILL Craig									8+6													8+6
GOLD Malcolm	15	26	20	36	25+3	34																156+3
GORMAN Andy													1+2									1+2
GOW Gerry						18																18
GOWANS Simon									16+1	9+6												25+7
GRANT Kim																				14+6	6+7	20+13
GREEN Andrew						6																6
GREEN Clive	37+1	30	16+1																			83+2
GRIFFIN Charlie																		3				3
GRIFFITHS Ashley			24																			24
GRIMSHAW Martyn								11+7														11+7
GRITTON Martin																			3+1			3+1
GROVES Lee														5+4			0+1					5+5
GWINNETT Mel								6														6
HALE Matt																		11+1				11+1
HANNIGAN Al-James																36+1	38					74+1
HARMISON Jimmy	31																					31
HARROWER Steve										26+1	37	39	21+5									123+6
HARVEY Lee																8+3						8+3
HAVERON Gary																				2+2		2+2
HAWKINS Peter																						23+9
HAYFIELD Matt																5	15+1	19+4				39+5
HAYWARD Steve		9																				9
HENDERSON Damian											2+2											2+2
HERVIN Mark											6											6
HIRONS Paul										8+9												8+9
HOLTHAM Dean						3																3
HORNBY Les														12								12

Yeovil Town Appearances	79-80	80-81	81-82	82-83	83-84	84-85	85-88	88-89	89-90	90-91	91-92	92-93	93-94	94-95	95-97	97-98	98-99	99-00	00-01	01-02	02-03	TOTAL
HORTON Ritchie																						40+6
HOUSELY Neil										1+1												1+1
HOUSELY Stuart	14+3																					14+3
HOWARD Terry																6+1						6+1
HUGHES Mark												1+2										1+2
HUGHES Wayne						22																22
HUNG DANG												1+6										1+6
ILES Bob								17														17
IRELAND Roy			11																			11
JACKSON Joe										17+1												17+1
JACKSON Kirk																					23	23
JAMES Phil			12	37+2	31+3	32+8																112+13
JARVIS Nigel				23+2		4+1																27+3
JOHNSON Lee																				36	41	77
JONES Bryn	17																					17
JONES Glyn			4																			4
JONES Marcus																			10+2			10+2
KEELING Darren																	10+9					10+9
KEMP Graham																11+10						11+10
KNIGHT Keith													3+1									3+1
KNOTT Barry	1																					1
KUMBAR Francis																				5		5
LANGLEY Steve			37	31																		68
LAUGHLIN Tony						0+1																0+1
LE BIHAN Neil														6								6
LEIGH Kevin	5																					5
LEITCH Andy		1+2																				1+2
LEONARD Dave												2	30+2									32+2
LEONARD Matthew														0+1								0+1
LEVY Tony		6																				6
LILLYGREEN Chris						4																4
LINDEGAARD Andy																		9	13+13	3+4	13+14	38+31
LINNEY Dave					37	37+1																74+1
LLEWELLYN Andy														13								13

Yeovil Town Appearances	79-80	80-81	81-82	82-83	83-84	84-85	85-88	88-89	89-90	90-91	91-92	92-93	93-94	94-95	95-97	97-98	98-99	99-00	00-01	01-02	02-03	TOTAL
LOCKWOOD Adam																				26+4	37+4	63+8
LOWE Trv								27+4	41	14+2				1								83+6
MASON Peter													11	41+1								52+1
McCARTHY Paddy								5+1														5+1
McCLELLAND John													8	20+1								28+1
McDERMOTT Brian										27+1	29+5											56+6
McEVOY Mike										1+1	8+5											9+6
McGINLAY John						7																7
McGRATH Steve																	2					2
McINDOE Michael																			13+3	34+1	41	88+4
McLAUGHLIN Paul					6+3																	6+3
McPHERSON Malcolm												1+3	8+6									9+9
MEACOCK Kevin					1+1																	1+1
MEARE Paul								0+2														0+2
MEECHAN Alex																			0+1			0+1
MERRICK Geoff			1																			1
MITCHELL Brian					0+1																	0+1
MORRALL Steve	26+1	20+1																				46+2
MORRIS Adie					1																	1
MORRIS Dave														16+3								16+3
MUIR Paul								0+1														0+1
MUNDEE Denny								10+1														10+1
MUSTOE Neil																					2+1	2+1
NEVIN Paul												12+15	3+5									15+20
NORTHOVER Grant					17	14																31
NORTON David																		7+4				7+4
O'BRIEN Brian																			15+11	7+4	20+13	42+28
O'DONNELL Brian				13																		13
OMEGBEHIN Colin																1						1
PAPARELLA Angelo					2+1																	2+1
PARKER Brian	36	31																				67
PARMENTER Steve																14+5	0+1					14+6
PATMORE Warren																36+1	38	37+1	35+1			146+3
PAYNE Jess	33	17	38	36	13																	137

Adam Lockwood. Photo: Peter Barnes.

Ray O'Brien. Photo: Graham Brown.

Brian Parker.

Tony Pennock. Photo: Keith Clayton.

Yeovil Town Appearances	79-80	80-81	81-82	82-83	83-84	84-85	85-88	88-89	89-90	90-91	91-92	92-93	93-94	94-95	95-97	97-98	98-99	99-00	00-01	01-02	02-03	TOTAL
PEARSON Gerry								17	6+4													23+4
PENNOCK Tony																42	37	42	40			161
PETERS Bradley																			4+3			4+3
PICKARD Owen																37+2	21+3					58+5
PIPER Dave																14	32+4	30+4	35+1			111+9
PITMAN Jamie																	5+2	34+1				39+3
PITMAN Steve				8+1																		8+1
PLATT David	8+2	20+2	34+1	29		8+2																99+7
PLUCK Colin																				24+2	32+5	56+7
PLUMLEY Gary					6																	6
POOLE Glenn																		8+3	2+4	1+1		11+8
POUNDER Tony						1+3										3+12	14+13	7+10				25+38
POWELL Lee														3+7								3+7
PRITCHARD Howard										12+5	8+5											20+10
PROSSER Neil					11+2																	11+2
QUINN Jimmy								24+1	15+1													39+2
RAMSAY Scott																				14+3		14+3
RANDALL Paul								18+11														18+11
REED Stephen									0+1													0+1
RICE Craig																					0+1	0+1
RICKETTS Tony								10+2														10+2
RIGBY Malcolm																	5					5
RISBRIDGER Gareth																			0+1			0+1
RITCHIE Steve	38	40		34																		112
RITCHIE Tom						19																19
ROBERTS Dave						5																5
ROBERTS Graham																5+1						5+1
ROBERTS Kevin					2																	2
ROBERTS Phil				20																		20
ROBINSON David											14											14
RODGERS Paul				4+5																		4+5
ROWBOTHAM Jason											5											5
ROWLAND Andy											4											4
RUTTER Steve								33	17+1	30+4	36+1	17+2	5									138+8
RYAN Nigel	17	35																				52

795

Tony Ricketts.

Steve Rutter. Photo: Bob Thomas.

Mark Shail. Photo: Dave West.

Terry Skiverton. Photo: Garry Letts.

Yeovil Town Appearances	79-80	80-81	81-82	82-83	83-84	84-85	85-88	88-89	89-90	90-91	91-92	92-93	93-94	94-95	95-97	97-98	98-99	99-00	00-01	01-02	02-03	TOTAL
SALE Mark										2+1												2+1
SANDERSON Paul												37+4	21+3									58+7
SCHRAM Tommy																				3+1		3+1
SCOTT Jimmy			30																			30
SCOTT Joey	11																					11
SHACKELL Jon				0+1																		0+1
SHAIL Mark								10	42	33+1	39	33										157+1
SHEFFIELD Jon																				14	7+1	21+1
SHEPHERD Darren								0+2														0+2
SHERWOOD Jeff								36	24	14		41	42	16								173
SIMPSON Phil																	10+4	0+2				10+6
SIVELL Steve											2	0+1										2+1
SKIVERTON Terry																		32+2	39	23+1	34+3	128+6
SLOUGH Alan						4																4
SMITH Ben																14	21+10	30+6	29+3			94+19
SMITH Dave				21																		21
SMITH Rob																	6+3					6+3
SMITH Steve						28																28
SPARKS Chris																		15				15
SPENCER Mickey								12	39	18+2	39+1	39+1	32+6	20+5								199+15
SPENCER Simon																0+1						0+1
STANSFIELD Adam																				22+1	1	23+1
STEELE Paul																	3	10+1	9+6			22+7
STEPHENS Archie								6														6
STEVENSON Nigel										19												19
STONE Andy						1+1																1+1
STOTT Steve																35	34+1	16				85+1
STOWELL Matt																		7				7
TAPLEY Steve								17+4														17+4
TAYLOR Tommy												2	3+1									5+1
THOMPSON Brian	10																					10
THOMPSON Dave																4						4
THOMPSON Richard								6+2	5+2													11+4
THOMPSON Steve																12	35	1+3	0+2	11+5		59+10
THORPE Paul						32		7+9	6+1													45+10
THWAITES Nigel													3+2									3+2

Yeovil Town Appearances	79-80	80-81	81-82	82-83	83-84	84-85	85-88	88-89	89-90	90-91	91-92	92-93	93-94	94-95	95-97	97-98	98-99	99-00	00-01	01-02	02-03	TOTAL
TINDAL Peter	7																					7
TISDALE Paul																		11+4				11+4
TONGE Keith								1+1														1+1
TONKIN Anthony																	1+1	12	37	39+1	7	96+2
TOOZE Martin						7																7
TOWNSEND Chris								1+2														1+2
TURNER Andy																				14+7		14+7
TURNER Garry	9																					9
WALLACE Andy								33	24+1	9	32	10+6	31+1	21								160+8
WARD Jamie		16+2	9+6		28+3	12+2																65+13
WAY Darren																			40+1	22+5	40	102+6
WEALE Chris																			2+2	27	34	63+2
WEST Mark													10+1									10+1
WESTLAKE Clive	1																					4
WHALE Leroy														10+1								10+1
WHITE Chris													10	30		12						52
WHITE Simon					1+4																	1+4
WHITE Tom																			28+2	26+9	2	56+11
WHITEHEAD Clive										1												1
WHITTINGHAM Guy								21														21
WILLIAMS Gavin																					38	38
WILLIAMS Ian						1																1
WILLIAMS John												7										7
WILLIAMS Mark	22+2	15+13		9+2																		46+17
WILLIAMS Nick														8								8
WILLMOTT Ian										8			7+1									15+1
WILMOT Ellis																		1+3				1+3
WILSON Paul									10+3	31+1	21+1	35+1	29+1	33+1								159+8
WIMBLE Shaun																1+2						1+2
WINSTON Sam																5+9						5+9
WINSTONE Simon																	0+2					0+2
WINTER Steve																2+5						2+5
WOLFF Shaun						2																2
WOODWARD Terry			8+1	5																		13+1
WOOLLARD Wayne			5+2																			5+2
WRAITTON Andy														1								1

798

LEADING GOALSCORERS

Yeovil Town Goalscorers	79-80	80-81	81-82	82-83	83-84	84-85	85-88	88-89	89-90	90-91	91-92	92-93	93-94	94-95	95-97	97-98	98-99	99-00	00-01	01-02	02-03	TOTAL
SPENCER Micky								6	12	5	16	15	16	4								74
PATMORE Warren																16(1p)	20(1p)	13(2p)	19			68(4p)
WILSON Paul									3	8	1	13	9	15								49
BELL Andy		8	4	22(6p)	2(1p)																	36(7p)
GREEN Clive	11	16	8(1p)																			35(1p)
WALLACE Andy								8(4p)	10(3p)	3	3	2	5(2p)	2								33(9p)
JAMES Phil		3	10	5		11																29
PICKARD Owen																17	11					28
PLATT David	3	5	17	3																		28
BROWN Jeremy	5	6	4(1p)	9(1p)		2(1p)																26(3p)
ALFORD Carl																				8	2	10
APPLETON Arthur																						1
ARCHER Lee																8						8
ASHTON Brian		1																				1
BARNES Colin						6(1p)																6(1p)
BATTY Paul										3		6(1p)										9(1p)
BECK Malcolm			3	3																		6
BELGRAVE Barrington																		1	9	2		12
BELL Andy		8	4	22(6p)	2(1p)																	36(7p)
BENJAFIELD Tim			2																			2
BENT James																		2	6			8
BETTS Simon																			1(1p)			1(1p)
BLACK Simon														4								4
BLACKMAN Barry									4													4
BORTHWICK Gary		2			1																	3
BOTHAM Ian						1																1
BOULTON Mark											2											2
BRASSART Olivier																				1		1
BROAD Joseph																				1		1
BROCK Kevin														2								2
BROOM Glyn		1																				1
BROWN Jeremy	5	6	4(1p)	9(1p)		2(1p)																26(3p)

799

Steve Stott. Photo: Keith Clayton.

Darren Way. Photo: Peter Barnes.

Chris Weale. Photo: Peter Barnes.

Guy Whittingham.

Yeovil Town Goalscorers	79-80	80-81	81-82	82-83	83-84	84-85	85-88	88-89	89-90	90-91	91-92	92-93	93-94	94-95	95-97	97-98	98-99	99-00	00-01	01-02	02-03	TOTAL
CARROLL Robbie									11	9	6											26
CHANDLER Dean																1	1					2
CHARLES Paul					1																	1
CHEESELY Paul						2																2
CLANCY John	1																					1
COATES Marc													2	5								7
COATES Neil												1										1
CONNING Peter								1	6	6	1			1								15
COOPER Richard												3	1	2								6
CORDICE Neil								3	2				1									6
COTTLE Tony	1(1p)																					1(1p)
COUSINS Rob																	1	1				2
CRITTENDEN Nick																			6	4	9(4p)	19(4p)
DALE Carl																	4(2p)					4(2p)
DEMBA Abdoulai																					6	6
DENT Nicky									4	6												10
DENYS Ryan																1						1
DILLON Kevin														2(1p)								2(1p)
DOBBINS Wayne														1								1
DOHERTY Mick					14	3		7(2p)														24(2p)
DONNELLAN Gary								4	1													5
DURBIN Brian		1																				1
EATON Jason																		2				2
EL KHOLTI Abdelhalim																					3	3
ELLIOTT Billy					1																	1
ENGWELL Micky																1						1
EVANS Richard														4								4
FERNS Phil													2									2
FIELDER Colin																2(2p)						2(2p)
FINNIGAN Trevor	9				7																	16
FISHLOCK Murray																	2					2
FORINTON Howard																			1		4	5
FOSTER Adrian																		9				9
FRANKLIN Damien																	2					2
FRY David										1												1

801

Gavin Williams. Photo: Peter Barnes.

Peter Conning.

Paul Wilson challenges Barrow's Glen Skivington.
Photo: Nigel Andrews.

Mickey Spencer.

Andy Wallace.

Yeovil Town Goalscorers	79-80	80-81	81-82	82-83	83-84	84-85	85-88	88-89	89-90	90-91	91-92	92-93	93-94	94-95	95-97	97-98	98-99	99-00	00-01	01-02	02-03	TOTAL
GALL Kevin																					13	13
GIBSON Stuart					1	1																2
GILES Chris																				7		8
GILES Jimmy		1	1																			2
GILL Gary									2													2
GOLD Malcolm						2																2
GRANT Kim																				5	1	6
GREEN Clive	11	16	8(1p)																			35(1p)
GRIFFIN Charlie																		1				1
GRIFFITHS Ashley			2																			2
GRIMSHAW Martyn								3														3
HALE Matt																		2				2
HANNIGAN Al-James																1	4					5
HARROWER Steve												3										3
HAWKINS Peter			3													1	1					5
HAYFIELD Matt																		8				10
HAYWARD Steve		1																				1
HIRONS Paul										4												4
HORTON Richie						1																1
HOUSLEY Stuart	1																					1
HUNG DANG												1										1
JACKSON Kirk																					19	19
JAMES Phil			3	10	5	11																29
JOHNSON Lee																				5	4	9
KEELING Darren																	5					5
KUMBAR Francis																				3		3
LEIGH Keith	2																					2
LEONARD Dave													2									2
LEVY Tony		1																				1
LILYGREEN Chris																						1
LINDEGAARD Andy																		1		1	6	8
LINNEY Dave						1																1
LOCKWOOD Adam																					3	3
LOWE Tiv								1	2													3
McCARTHY Paddy								1														1

Yeovil Town Goalscorers	79-80	80-81	81-82	82-83	83-84	84-85	85-88	88-89	89-90	90-91	91-92	92-93	93-94	94-95	95-97	97-98	98-99	99-00	00-01	01-02	02-03	TOTAL
McCLELLAND John														1								1
McDERMOTT Brian										8(1p)	4											12(1p)
McGINLAY John						3																3
McINDOE Michael																			3	7	12(3p)	22(3p)
McPHERSON Malcolm													2									2
MORRALL Steve	3	5																				8
MORRIS Dave														2								2
NEVIN Paul												3										3
NORTON David																		1				1
O'BRIEN Roy																			1			1
PAPARELLA Angelo					2																	2
PARMENTER Steve																3(1p)						3(1p)
PATMORE Warren																16(1p)	20(1p)	13(2p)	19			68(4p)
PAYNE Jess	3		3	6	3																	15
PEARSON Gerry								2														2
PICKARD Owen																17	11					28
PIPER Dave																	1	1	1			3
PITMAN Jamie																		2				2
PLATT David	3	5	17	3																		28
PLUCK Colin						3										1						4
POUNDER Tony																	2			2	2	6
PRITCHARD Howard											2											2
PROSSER Neil					3																	3
QUINN Jimmy								3(1p)														3(1p)
RAMSAY Scott																				4		4
RANDALL Paul								8(2p)														8(2p)
RITCHIE Steve		2		5												1						8
ROBERTS Graham																1						1
ROBINSON David											3											3
RUTTER Steve										1	1		1									3
SANDERSON Paul												4	5									9
SCOTT Jimmy		1																				1
SCOTT Joey	4																					4
SHAIL Mark								1	2		1	4										8
SHERWOOD Jeff								1	1	1		2	1									6

YEOVIL TOWN

GOALSCORERS

Yeovil Town Goalscorers	79-80	80-81	81-82	82-83	83-84	84-85	85-88	88-89	89-90	90-91	91-92	92-93	93-94	94-95	95-97	97-98	98-99	99-00	00-01	01-02	02-03	TOTAL
SKIVERTON Terry																		6	3	1	7	17
SMITH Ben																5	2	4	3			14
SMITH Dave				1																		1
SPENCER Micky								6	12	5	16	15	16	4								74
STANSFIELD Adam																				8		8
STEELE Paul																		3	4			7
STEVENSON Nigel										1												1
STONE A						1																1
STOTT Steve																7(1p)	5					12(1p)
THOMPSON Dave																1						1
THOMPSON Steve																1	4	1		1		7
THORPE Paul						4																4
TINDAL Peter	1																					1
TISDALE Paul																		1				1
TONGE Keith								2														2
TONKIN Anthony																			2			2
TOOZE Martin						1																1
TURNER Andy																				1		1
WALLACE Andy								8(4p)	10(3p)	3	3	2	5(2p)	2								33(9p)
WARD Jamie		8	2		4	1																15
WAY Darren																			9(5p)	3(1p)	1	13(6p)
WEST Mark													2									2
WHALE Leroy														2								2
WHITE Chris														1								1
WHITE Simon					1																	1
WHITE Tom																			1			1
WHITTINGHAM Guy								16														16
WILLIAMS Gavin																					6	6
WILLIAMS Mark	6	3		5																		14
WILSON Paul									3	8	1	13	9	15								49
WINSTON Sam																6						6
WOOLLARD Wayne			2																			2

ALL-TIME APPEARANCES - TOP 50 (AS AT END OF 03/04)

PLAYER	TOTAL	CLUBS
Paul Davies (pictured right)	467+21	Trowbridge Kidderminster Hednesford
Dave Mogg	446	Bath Weymouth Cheltenham
Elfyn Edwards	442+2	Runcorn Altrincham Macclesfield Southport Halifax
Chris Brindley	439+2	Telford Kidderminster Hednesford
Dave Ryan	432	Northwich
Kevin Charlton	422+1	Bangor Telford
John Glover	397+7	Nuneaton Maidstone Welling
Rob Cousins	392+16	Bath Yeovil Forest Green
Micky Tuohy	389+15	Worcester Kidderminster Cheltenham Stafford
Martin Weir	385+11	Kidderminster
Ryan Price	371	Stafford Macclesfield Telford Tamworth
Jeff Sherwood	366+6	Bath Yeovil Merthyr
Paul Wilson	363+16	Frickley Boston Yeovil
Gary Anderson	361+11	Altrincham Runcorn
John McKenna	357+1	Nuneaton Boston Dagenham & Redbridge Southport
Kevin Willetts	356+13	Cheltenham Kidderminster
Edwin Stein	349+17	Dagenham Barnet
Duncan Horton	348+6	Maidstone Welling Barnet
Antone Joseph	346+43	Weymouth Telford Kidderminster
Fraser Wood	345+27	Stafford Kidderminster
Nicky Evans	342+9	Kettering Barnet Wycombe
Mark Smith	338+7	Stevenage Dagenham&R
Richard Crowley	337+10	Bath Cheltenham
Mark Carter	335+14	Bangor Runcorn Barnet Gateshead
Wayne Simpson	334+4	Stafford Hednesford Nuneaton
Gary Abbott	333+30	Welling Barnet Enfield Slough Gravesend
Nigel Ransom	327+4	Welling
Terry Robbins	326+9	Maidstone Welling
Carl Alford	323+60	Witton Macclesfield Kettering Rushden&D Dover Stevenage Doncaster Yeovil Nuneaton Leigh
Mark West	320+39	Wycombe Kidderminster Yeovil Slough Farnborough
Phil Brown	312+27	Lincoln Kettering
Stuart White	311+12	Welling
Aniello Iannone	310+11	Weymouth Barnet
Glyn Creaser	310+2	Kettering Barnet Wycombe Yeovil Dagenham & Redbridge
Kevan Brown	309+8	Woking Yeovil
Kevin Blackwell	309	Barnet Boston Scarborough Telford Kettering
Kim Casey	304+42	AP Leamington Kidderminster Cheltenham Wycombe
John Askey	303+6	Macclesfield
Frank Murphy	302+40	Kettering Nuneaton Barnet Slough
Gary Mallender	301+5	Boston Frickley
Neil Cordice	298+37	Wealdstone Yeovil
Ronnie Ellis	297+33	Runcorn Altrincham Macclesfield Northwich
Mark Jones	296+10	Northwich
Gary Simpson	296+7	Boston Stafford Weymouth
Paul Arnold	296+5	Weymouth
Scott Steele	295+51	Woking
Mike Roberts	295+9	Bangor Runcorn Macclesfield
Jamie Bates	293+17	Runcorn Stalybridge Northwich
Keith Brown	292+15	Bath Cheltenham
Eddie Hogan	292+5	Telford Nuneaton

PLAYER	GOALS	CLUBS
Paul Davies	176	Kidderminster
Mark Carter	173	Bangor Runcorn Barnet Gateshead
Kim Casey	173	AP Leamington Kidderminster Cheltenham Wycombe
Nicky Evans	163	Kettering Barnet Wycombe
Carl Alford	159	Witton Macclesfield Kettering Stevenage Rushden & D Dover Yeovil Nuneaton
Frank Murphy	150	Kettering Nuneaton Barnet Slough
Mark West	144	Wycombe Yeovil Farnborough Slough
David Leworthy	140	Colchester Farnborough Dover Rushden & D Kingstonian
Terry Robbins (pictured right)	139	Welling
Gary Abbott	137	Enfield Welling Barnet Slough
Paul Wilson	136	Frickley Boston Yeovil
Ken McKenna	132	Telford Stafford Runcorn Altrincham
Mick Doherty	124	Weymouth Yeovil Maidstone Altrincham Runcorn Macclesfield Farnborough
Paul Cavell	118	Stafford Boston Dagenham & R Gateshead Macclesfield
Colin Cowperthwaite	116	Barrow
Steve Burr	110	Stafford Macclesfield Hednesford
Mick Tuohy	110	Worcester Kiddeerminster Stafford
Darran Hay	106	Woking Stevenage
Lenny Dennis	103	Sutton Welling Woking
Dave Mather	98	Bangor Telford Runcorn
Malcolm O'Connor	97	Northwich
Colin Williams	97	Northwich Scarborough Telford
Paul Culpin	94	Nuneaton Barnet Telford
Warren Patmore	94	Yeovil Woking Margate
Phil Power	94	Northwich Chorley Barrow Stalybridge Macclesfield Altrincham
Chris Cook	93	Boston
Paul McKinnon	93	Sutton Slough
Ian Arnold	89	Stalybridge Kettering Kidderminster Southport Morecambe
Mark Graves	89	Wealdstone
Graham Bennett	86	Altrincham Northwich Stafford
John Bartley	84	Maidstone Welling
Steve Butler	84	Maidstone Stevenage
Gary Hooley	83	Frickley Scarborough Altrincham
Noel Ashford	82	Enfield Maidstone Barnet
Paul Reid	82	Northwich Altrincham
Phil Brown	81	Lincoln Kettering
Aniello Iannone	79	Weymouth
Justin Jackson	79	Morecambe Woking Rushden & D Doncaster
Darren Collins	76	Rushden & D Kettering
Keith Scott	76	Wycombe Dover Gateshead Boston Scarborough Leigh
Clive Walker	76	Woking Cheltenham
John Askey	75	Macclesfield
Mickey Spencer	75	Yeovil
Karl Thomas	75	Witton Runcorn
John Norman	74	Morecambe Hednesford
Graham Withey	74	Bath Cheltenham
Ken Charlery	73	Maidstone Fisher Boston Dagenham & R Farnborough
Ronnie Ellis	73	Runcorn Altrincham Macclesfield
Daryl Clare	70	Boston Chester
Brendan Burke	67	Witton Stalybridge Altrincham
Phil Derbyshire	67	Stafford Macclesfield Altrincham

Keith Gillard has covered Welling United for many seasons and has produced some wonderful action photos. The three on this page act as a tribute to him and the devastating heading ability of Welling United and England's diminutive striker Terry Robbins who is seen here scoring against Runcorn (top), Gateshead (above) and Stafford Rangers (left).

There are many excellent photos featured in the club pages but we found a few more that we really couldn't leave out.

Goalkeepers are usually popular with photographers and these goalmouth action shots show Stafford Rangers' Ryan Price saving brilliantly at Slough (left), Welling United's Darren Williams showing a safe pair of hands against Bromsgrove Rovers (above) and in a memorable match, a save by Kidderminster Harriers' Stuart Brock at Altrincham where, after a goalless draw in 2000, Alty left the Conference for the Unibond Premier Division and Kidderminster Harriers achieved their ambition of Football League status (below). Photo by Bill Wheatcroft.

Concentration, balance and power are all shown in abundance in these photos with Keith Gillard again providing excellent action as Welling United's Nigel Ransome clears his lines in his last game for the club (above) and Roy Hales scores against Barnet despite a desperate defensive lunge (below).

You don't often see good individual action photos of non-league players, so here's one of top quality featuring Woking's Michael Danzey and taken by Peter Barnes.

Two very different goalmouth action photos were provided by John Vass, a great Enfield supporter before moving home to Scotland and James Wood of Northwich. John catches the most amazing example of Telford United defending in depth (top) and James records a goal for his local team and some wonderful expressions on the Maidstone United defenders faces as the realise Steve McNelis's effort is going in (above).

PLAYER INDEX

INDEX of Individual Players featured in action or portrait photographs.
The clubs listed are those for whom the player was playing in the photo.
If a player is featured in more than one club those teams are listed in alphabetical order
not in the order he played for them.
The Club Index is on Page 829

A

Abbott, Gary (Slough Town and Welling United)
Acton, Darren (Telford United)
Adamson, David (Boston United)
Adcock, Paul (Bath City)
Adebola, Dele (Northwich Victoria)
Agana, Tony (Leek Town)
Agorinde, Sammy (Stalybridge Celtic)
Akrour, Nassim (Woking)
Akuamoah, Eddie (Kingstonian)
Alexander, Keith (Barnet)
Alford, Carl (Kettering Town, Stevenage B, Witton A & YeovilT)
Allen, Shaun (Chorley)
Anderson, Dale (Burton Albion)
Anderson, Gary (Altrincham)
Anderson, Stuart (Witton Albion)
Angel, Brett (Cheltenham Town)
Angel, Mark (Boston United)
Arnold, Ian (Kidderminster Harriers)
Ashby, Nick (Kettering Town and Rushden & Diamonds)
Ashford, Noel (Barnet and Enfield)
Askey, John (Macclesfield Town)

B

Bailey, Dennis (Forest Green Rovers & Wealdstone)
Bancroft, Paul (Kettering Town & Kidderminster Harriers)
Banks, Chris (Cheltenham Town)
Barnes, Colin (Barnet)
Barnett, Aaron (Gravesend & Northfleet)
Barrett, Keith (Enfield & Wycombe Wanderers)
Barrett, Mike (Cheltenham Town)
Bartley, John (Maidstone United)
Barry, Paul (Bath City)
Bastock, Paul (Boston United)
Bates, Jamie (Runcorn)
Batty, Paul (Yeovil Town)
Bauress, Gary (Stalybridge Celtic)
Beattie, Andy (Merthyr Tydfil)
Beesley, Paul (Chester City)
Bell, Derek (Gateshead)
Benbow, Ian (Telford United)
Bennett, Gary (Altrincham)
Bennett, Graham (Northwich Victoria)
Benstead, Graham (Kettering Town)
Berry, Gwynne (Sutton United)

Carroll, John (Runcorn)
Carter, Mark (Barnet and Runcorn)
Carter, Recky (Bromsgrove Rovers)
Cartwright, Neil (Kidderminster Harriers)
Casey, Kim (Cheltenham Town)
Casey, Paul (Boston United)
Cavell, Paul (Boston United & Dag & Red)
Chapple, Geoff (Kingstonian & Woking)
Charles, Lee (Aldershot Town, Hayes and Nuneaton B)
Charlton, Kevin (Telford United)
Chenoweth, Paul (Bath City)
Chettle, Steve (Burton Albion)
Chilton, Tony (Barrow)
Christie, Trevor (Kettering Town)
Clare, Daryl (Boston United)
Clark, Billy (Forest Green Rovers)
Clark, Dean (Hayes)
Clark, Martin (Southport)
Clarke, Andy (Barnet)
Clemance, Neil (Welling United)
Clement, Andy (Woking)
Clough, Nigel (Burton Albion)
Coates, Marc (Macclesfield Town)
Coathup, Lee (Stalbridge Celtic)
Coleman, David (Farnborough Town)
Colkin, Lee (Morecambe)
Collins, Darren (Rushden & Diamonds)
Collins, Eamonn (Colchester United)
Collins, Kevin (Hednesford Town)
Collins, Paul (Fisher Athletic)
Collins, Phil (Margate)
Collymore, Stan (Stafford Rangers)
Comyn, Andy (Hednesford Town)
Coney, Dean (Farnborough Town)
Conning, Peter (Yeovil Town)
Connor, Joe (Runcorn& Witton Albion)
Connor, Steve (Dagenham & Redbridge)
Constable, Shaun (Altrincham)
Cook, Chris (Boston United)
Cook, Rob (Forest Green Rovers)
Cooke, Ian (Northwich Victoria)
Cooke, Robbie (Kettering Town)
Cooksey, Scott (Bromsgrove Rovers& Hednesford T)
Coombes, Paul (Farnborough Town)
Cooper, John (Enfield)
Cordice, Alan (Wealdstone)
Corner, David (Gateshead)
Cornwall, Mike (Sutton United)
Cotterill, Steve (Cheltenham Town)
Cousins, Rob (Bath City, Forest Green R & Yeovil T)
Cowperthwaite, Colin (Barrow)
Cox, Paul (Kettering Town)
Crawley, Ian (Telford United)
Creane, Ged (Boston United)
Creaser, Glyn (Wycombe Wanderers)
Crisp, Mark (Bromsgrove Rovers)

PLAYER INDEX

F

Farrell, Peter (Barrow)
Farrelly, Steve (Kingstonian)
Ferris, Paul (Barrow)
Fisher, Matt (Kettering Town)
Flack, Steve (Exeter City)
Forsyth, Richard (Kidderminster Harriers)
Foster, Adrian (Forest Green Rovers)
Foster, Ian (Kidderminster Harriers)
France, Paul (Altrincham)
Francis, Nicky (Enfield)
Freegard, John (Bath City)
Freeman, Clive (Altrincham)
Friel,George (Slough Town)
Fry Barry (Barnet)
Furlong, Paul (Enfield)

G

Gall, Mark (Maidstone United)
Gallagher, Jason (Altrincham)
Gardiner, Mark (Northwich Victoria& Macclesfield T)
Garner, Tim (Aylesbury United)
Gilmour, Billy (Barrow)
Glover, John (Maidstone United)
Gower, Mark (Barnet)
Graham, Andy (Northwich Victoria)
Graham, Jon (Kettering Town)
Gray, Andy (Cheltenham Town)
Grayson, Neil (Hereford United, Forest Green R & Cheltenham T)
Green, Ron (Kidderminster Harriers)
Gridelet, Phil (Barnet)
Goodliffe, Jason (Hayes)
Goodwin, Mark (Kettering Town)
Gordon, Ken (Barrow)
Gothard, Paul (Hayes)
Gould, James (Boston United)
Guppy, Steve (Wycombe Wanderes)

H

Haarhoff, Jimmy (Chester City)
Hallam, Mark (Forest Green Rovers)
Halliday, Bruce (Gateshead)
Hanlon, Steve (Macclesfield Town)
Hayrettin, Hakan (Wycombe Wanderers)
Hanson, Dave (Nuneaton Borough)
Harding, Paul (Barnet)
Hardy, Martin (Boston United
Hardy, Niell (Northwich Victoria)
Hargreaves, Chris (Hereford United)
Harlow, David (Farnborough Town)
Harris, Mark (Kingstonian)
Harvey, Jim (Morecambe)
Hatch, Liam (Gravesend & Northfleet)
Heald, Greg (Barnet)
Heathcote, Graham (Altrincham)
Hedges, Ian (Forest Green Rovers)

Hemmings, Tony (Hednesford Town, Macclesfield T & Northwich V)
Hendy, Martin (Boston United)
Hercules, Cliff (Aylesbury United)
Heyes, Darren (Halifax Town)
Hill, Gordon (Northwich Victoria)
Hill, Kenny (Maidstone United)
Hodson, Simeon (Kidderminster Harriers)
Holden, Steve (Kettering Town)
Horsfield, Geoff (Halifax Town)
Horton, Jamie (Farnborough Town)
How, Trevor(Slough Town)
Howard, Barry (Altrincham)
Howarth, Neil (Macclesfield Town)
Howat, Ian (Bangor City)
Howell, David (Enfield)
Howell, Peter (Kidderminster Harriers)
Howells, Lee (Cheltenham Town)
Hughes, Gareth (Bangor City)
Hughes, Lee (Kidderminster Harriers)
Hughes, Russ (Stalybridge Celtic)
Hull, Kenny (Maidstone United)
Hulme, Kevin (Halifax Town)
Humphreys, Delwyn (Kidderminster Harriers)
Humphreys, Steve (Barnet)
Hunt, Andy (Kettering Town)
Hunt, Paul (Forest Green Rovers)
Huxford, Richard (Kettering Town)
Hyde, Paul (Wycombe Wanderers)

I
Ironton, Nicky (Enfield)

J
Jackson, Jimmy (Gravesend & Northfleet)
Jackson, Justin (Morecambe)
James, Chris (Leek Town)
James, Tony (Hereford United)
Johnson, Jeff (Altrincham)
Jones, Alex (Halifax Town)
Jones, Gary (Kettering Town)
Jones, Paul (Kidderminster Harriers)
Jones, Steve (Leigh RMI)
Jordan, Nick (Cheltenham Town)
Joseph, Antone (Kidderminster Harriers)

K
Keast, Dougie (Kettering Town)
Kerr, Andy (Wycombe Wanderers)
Kerr, David (Chester City)
Kilcline, Brian (Haliax Town)
Kilgour, Mike (Forest Green Rovers)
Kimble, Gary (Dagenha & Redbridge)
Kimmins, Ged (Hednesford Town)
King, Steve (Enfield)
Kinsella, Mark (Colchester United)
Knight, Keith (Cheltenham Town)
Knowles, Michael (Morecambe)

L

Lake, Stuart (Hednesford Town)
Lambert, Colin (Hednesford Town& Macclesfield T)
Lane, Chris (Hereford United)
Langford, Tim (Kidderminster Harriers)
Latiff, Paul (Slough Town)
Lawley, Frank (Frickley Athletic)
Lee, Matt (Gravesend & Northfleet)
Lewis, Robin (Oxford)
Leworthy, David (Kingstonian& Farnborough Town)
Lodge, Paul (Northwich Victoria)
Lowe, Kenny (Barrow & Gateshead)
Luckett, Colin (Kingstonian)
Lyons, Darren (Macclesfield Town)

M

McDonnell, Peter (Barrow)
McDonough, Roy (Colchester United and Dag & Red)
McDougald, Junior (Dagenham & Redbridge)
McGavin, Steve (Colchester United)
McGinlay, John (Boston United)
McGoldrick, Eddie (Nuneaton Borough)
McGregor, Marc (Nuneaton Borough & Forest Green R)
McKenna, John (Boston United)
McKenzie, Chris (Nuneaton Borough)
McKinnon, Paul (Slough Town)
Mahon, Gavin (Hereford United)
Malkin, Chris (Northwich Victoria)
Mallinson, Pat (Boston United)
Marsh, Mike (Kidderminster Harriers)
Martin, Lee (Halifax Town)
Masters, Mike (Colchester United)
Matthews, Lee (Dagenham & Redbridge)
Mendoca, Bruno (Farnborough Town)
Messenger, Gary (Barrow)
Midgley, Neil (Barrow)
Milton, Russell (Cheltenham Town)
Monk, Ian (Leigh RMI)
Moss, Ernie (Kettering Town)
Murphy, Frank (Barrow & Kettering Town)
Mustafa, Tarkan (Kingstonian)

N

Neal, Dean (Fisher Athletic)
Nicol, Paul (Kettering Town)
Newson, Mark (Maidstone United)
Norbury, Mickey (Hednesford Town)
Norman, Craig (Kettering Town)
Nugent, Richard (Barnet)

O

O'Connor, Joe (Hednesford Town)
O'Meara, Shaun (Bromsgrove Rovers)
O'Regan, Kieran (Halifax Town)
Osborne, Paul (Morecambe)
Owen, Robert (Gravesend & Northfleet)

Owen, Val (Northwich Victoria)
Owens, John (Altrincham)

P

Page, Steve (Kidderminster Harriers)
Pape, Andy (Enfield)
Parker, Derek (Northwich Victoria)
Paterson, Jamie (Halifax Town)
Patterson, Gary (Kingstonian)
Payne, Steve (Macclesfield Town)
Peake, Trevor (Nuneaton Borough)
Pearce, Chris (Bromsgrove Rovers)
Peyton, Warren (Nuneaton Borough)
Phillips, Ian (Kettering Town)
Phillips, Gary (Barnet)
Pitcher, Geoff (Kingstonian)
Poole, Gary (Barnet)
Power, Paul (Macclesfield Town)
Price, Ryan (Macclesfield Town)
Procter, Kevin (Barrow)
Proudlock, Paul (Gateshead)
Purdie, Jon (Cheltenham Town& Kidderminster H)
Purser, Wayne (Barnet)
Putnam, Mick (Slough Town)

Q

Quamina, Mark (Slough Town)
Quayle, Mark (Nuneaton Borough)

R

Radburn, Colin (Bromsgrove Rovers)
Randall, Martin (Hayes)
Read, Simon (Farnborough Town)
Regis, Dave (Barnet)
Reid, Andy (Altrincham)
Reid, Paul (Northwich Victoria)
Reilly, George (Barnet)
Richards, Carl (Enfield)
Richardson, Derek (Maidstone United)
Richardson, Kevin (Bromsgrove Rovers)
Richardson, Paul (Dagenham & Redbridge)
Ricketts, Tony (Bath City)
Roberts, Micky (Macclesfield Town)
Robinson, Andy (Wycombe Wanderers)
Robinson, Liam (Northwich Victoria)
Robinson, Phil (Hereford United)
Roderick, Martin (Kettering Town)
Roddis,Niick (Aldershot Town)
Rodwell, Jim (Boston United)
Rogers, John (Altrincham)
Rose, Kevin (Kidderminster Harriers)
Ross, Brian (Chorley)
Rowlands, Paul (Altrincham& Barrow)
Ryan, Dave (Northwich Victoria)
Ryan, Keith (Wycombe Wanderers)

S

Sanderson, Dave (Merthyr Tydfil)
Sayer, Andy (Slough Town)
Scott, Keith (Wycombe Wanderers)
Shutt, Carl (Kettering Town)
Shail, Mark (Yeovil Town)
Shaw, Nigel (Altrincham)
Sheldon, Gareth (Exeter City)
Shipp, Danny (Dagenham & Redbridge)
Shoemake, Kevin (Kettering Town)
Showler, Paul (Altrincham)
Simmonite, Gordon (Boston United)
Simpson, Wayne (Hednesford Town)
Singleton, Dave (Bath City)
Sissons, Jon (Slough Town)
Skelding, Jimmy (Bromsgrove Rovers)
Skinner, Justin (Gravesend & Northfleet)
Skiverton, Terry (Yeovil Town)
Skivington, Glen (Barrow)
Slack, Trevor (Kettering Town)
Smart, Gary (Bath City)
Smith, Adie (Bromsgrove Rovers)
Smith, Adie (Kidderminster Harriers)
Smith, Chris (Bath City)
Smith, Darren (Gravesend & Northfleet)
Smith, John (Northwich Victoria)
Smith, Nicky (Colchester United)
Smith, Simon (Gateshead)
Snape, John (Hereford United)
Sorvel, Neil (Macclesfield Town)
Spencer, Mickey (Yeovil Town)
Stanley, Neal (Slough Town)
Stanmore, Andrew (Boston United)
Stapleton, Simon (Wycombe Wanderers)
Steele, Lee (Northwich Victoria)
Stein, Eddie (Barnet)
Stevens, David (Hayes)
Stott, Steve (Bromsgrove Rovers&Yeovil Town)
Strouts, Jimmy (Gravesend & Northfleet)
Straw, Rob (Nuneaton Borough)
Strevens, Ben (Barnet)
Stride, Darren (Burton Albion)
Sugden, Ryan (Morecambe)
Sykes, Alex (Forest Green Rovers)

T

Tait, Paul (Northwich Victoria)
Terry, Paul (Dagenham & Redbridge)
Thompson, Brian (Maidstone United)
Thompson, Steve (Slough Town,Wycombe W & Yeovil Town)
Timmons, John (Altrincham& Macclesfield T)
Todhunter, Stuart (Barrow)
Tucker, Mark (Merthyr Tydfil)
Tuohy, Mick (Kidderminster Harriers)
Turner, Lee (Margate)

U

V

Victory, Jamie (Cheltenham Town)
Vowden, Colin (Kettering Town)

W

Wager, Gary (Merthyr Tydfil)
Walker, Clive (Cheltenham Town)
Wallace, Andy (Yeovil Town)
Walters, Steve (Northwich Victoria)
Ward, Mark (Northwich Victoria)
Watkins, Dale (Cheltenham Town)
Watson, John (Barnet)
Watts, Alvin (Hayes)
Wealands, Jeff (Altrincham)
Webb, Paul (Bromsgrove Rovers)
Webb. Paul (Kidderminster Harriers)
Webley, Dave (Merthyr Tydfil)
Webster, Aaron (Burton Albion)
Weir, Martin (Kidderminster Harriers)
West, Mark (Slough Town, Wycombe W)
Wheatley, Danny (Barrow)
Whitbread, Barry (Altrincham)
Whitehall, Steve (Chester City)
Whitehouse, Mark (Kidderminster Harriers)
Whittingham, Guy (Yeovil Town)
Wickerson, Paul (Slough Town)
Wigg, Nathan (Forest Green Rovers
Wigmore, Jim (Farnborough Town)
Willis, Roger (Barnet)
Wilson, Paul (Frickley Athletic & Yeovil Town)
Wilcox, Russ (Frickley Athletic)
Wilkins, Craig (Gravesend & Northfleet)
Wilkerson, Paul (Gravesend & Northfleet)
Williams, Barry (Nuneaton Borough)
Williams, Carwyn (Northwich Victoria)
Williams, Gavin (Hereford United & Yeovil Town)
Williams, Ceri (Merthyr Tydfil)
Wingfield, Phil (Kingstonian)
Withey, Graham (Bath City)
Wooding, Tim (Boston United)
Wragg, Peter (Macclesfield Town)
Wright, Andy (Kettering Town)
Wright, Mally (Frickey Athletic)

X

Y

Yates, Mark (Kidderminster Harriers)

Z

Zelem, Alan (Macclesfield Town)

Team photos featuring many more players are also included in club sections.

THE PHOTOGRAPHERS

John Harman's wonderful statistics have been balanced in this book by an equally impressive collection of photographs taken by a dedicated team of amateur photographers whose hobby is touring English Non-League Football grounds.

We have been able to allocate credits for most of the photographs used in this book as they were originally supplied for Team Talk magazine and the Non-League Club Directory but some are missing and we apologise for this.

Hopefully all the photographers names will be listed in our acknowledgments listed below and books will have been sent to all those for whom we have an address.

Special congratulations and thanks go to Peter Barnes who has supplied nearly 100 photographs in this book and of course we would also point out the wonderful services given to their special clubs by Keith Gillard for Welling United, the late Mick Cheney for Kettering Town (ref pages 360), Ged Rule at Barrow and John Rooney at Altrincham.

To all these wonderful enthusiasts who have toured the country in all weathers, our thanks and congratulations on their excellent photographs. We have been able to trace captions to most photos but our apologies to those featured in the pictures that defeated our investigating team

We have also included a selection of our very special Conference photographs that we feel present the excitement and quality of a great competition. We hope you enjoy them all.   T.W.

Paul Barber	Steve Holloway	R Scott
Peter Barnes	T Hough	Elaine Sergeant
Mark Brooker	Simon Jacobs	S E Sports Extra
Neil Brookman	N Jackson	P J Shepperd
Graham Brown	Kapper Sports Pictures	Francis Short
Pat Campion	W Leigh	R Sims
Alan Case	Gary Letts	Southport Visitor
Gary Cave	Paul Lewis	Sportsfile
Miick Cheney	Peter Lirettoc	Colin Stevens
Andrew Chittty	Paul Maher	Paul Tasca
Keith Clayton	A & K Markham	Neil Thaler
M Close	Eric Marsh	Bob Thomas Sports
Keith Collard	A Miller	Photography
John Collings	Jeff Mimwood	Darren Thomas
Duncan Cook	Ian Morsman	Malc Thompkins
Alan Coomes	N. G. Photography	A R Turner
Jo Corkett	John Newton	Roger Turner
Graham Cotterill	Dennis Nicholson	John Vass
Malcolm Couzens	Northwich Chronicle	Alan Watson
David Dales	Ray Pepper	David Watson
Martin Dalton	Roger Price	David Webb
Paul Dennis	Steve Read	Dave West
P Ellis-Neville	C Roberts	Bill Wheatcroft
Mike Floate	Vic Roberts	Bob Whittaker
Keith Gillard	Victor Robertson	Alec White
Gloucester Echo	Mr & Mrs C Rogers	Graham Whiting
D H Gregory	*John Rooney	Les Williams
Joy Griffiths	Rob Ruddock	John Womach
John Griffiths	Ged Rule	Dave Wood
Halifax Evening Courier	Runcorn Weekly News	Martin Wray
M M Hoff	Mark Sandon	

CLUB INDEX

All statistics in this book refer to league matches only and are correct up to and including the 2003-04 season.

Total Seating Solutions

Arena Sports Stand and Tiered Spectator Seating

A classic design, with a cantilevered roof cover providing an unimpeded view

Arena LT Grandstand

Each grandstand is fabricated in painted box section steel and clad in box profile steel

Bespoke Seating Solutions

Our in-house team of design engineers can solve any of your seating requirements

NEW BOOKS
FOR 2005 - 2006

John Harman's statistics will once again be providing some exciting new titles and as in this publication they will be liberally illustrated by photographs spanning the complete history of the Conference including the 2004 - 2005 campaign.

So if you would like details of the following publications please tick in the box(es) and we will send you all the information you need when a publishing date has been settled.

1) A complete list of players who have *played* in the Conference in alphabetical order, including F.A. Cup and F.A. Trophy games. Illustrated with over 500 photos.

Please send me details on the above book. ☐

2) The complete list of players have *scored* in the Conference in alphabetical order, plus goals scored in the F.A. Cup and F.A. Trophy. Illustrated with over 300 photos.

Please send me details on the above book. ☐

3) A two page spread for every season (giving lineups, scores, attendances, goalscorers and substitutions) for every club. Over 600 pages with over 100 team photos.

Please send me details on the above book. ☐

Please send your information requests to:

Tony Williams Publications
FREEPOST
Taunton
TA3 6BR

or fax to: 01823 491 481

TONY WILLIAMS PUBLICATIONS
Helland, North Curry, Taunton
Somerset TA3 6DU

Tel: 01823 490080/490684
Fax: 01823 491281